BASIC MATERIALS ON CRIMINAL EVIDENCE

By

JOHN KAPLAN
Jackson Eli Reynolds Professor of Law,
Stanford University

JON R. WALTZ
Edna B. and Ednyfed H. Williams Professor of Law
and Lecturer in Medical Jurisprudence,
Northwestern University

Mineola, New York
THE FOUNDATION PRESS, INC.
1980

COPYRIGHT © 1980
By
THE FOUNDATION PRESS, INC.
All rights reserved

Library of Congress Catalog Card Number: 79–55351

ISBN 0-88277-468-9

Kaplan & Waltz–Crim.Evid. MCB
1st Reprint—1992

To David Louisell

PREFACE

In one sense, this work is a successor to PRINCIPLES OF EVIDENCE AND PROOF, authored by the late David Louisell and the two authors of this volume. In another sense, however, it is quite a different book, justifying a new title rather than merely the sobriquet of a new edition.

First of all, BASIC MATERIALS ON CRIMINAL EVIDENCE is much shorter. Cutting out a great deal of material on civil matters has allowed us to produce a book of about half the length of PRINCIPLES.

Secondly, the book has been redesigned, as it were, from the bottom up. We have added chapters on the Exclusionary Rule and Eye-Witness Identification and changed the organization to reflect better the needs of police science students.

In addition, since students using this book need not be concerned with the depth of conceptual analysis necessary for budding trial lawyers, we have used different kinds of cases concentrating on the more basic rules of evidence, with analytic problems only where their exceptional importance makes understanding vital. And we have supplemented the cases with a considerable amount of text, designed to make the job of both teachers and students much easier, while at the same time keeping the course interesting.

We have also attempted to highlight an issue which we did not begin to address in PRINCIPLES OF EVIDENCE AND PROOF. We have tried to show non-lawyers the inner morality of the criminal trial process and the reasons for what most non-lawyers consider the sacrifices of truth and justice made on the altar of the adversary system.

Despite the fact that BASIC MATERIALS IN CRIMINAL EVIDENCE is designed for the education of non-lawyers, it is intended that the course be taught by an attorney—either one on the staff of the teaching institution or a lawyer from the community. Our law of evidence is replete with so many technicalities, which must be understood by the teacher, that we would not feel confident of the book's value if it were to be taught by the most able teachers if they lacked some experience as trial lawyers.

In the hands of those who will teach from it, we commend this book in the hope that it will help in the interesting and effective teaching of a basic course in Criminal Evidence.

JOHN KAPLAN
JON R. WALTZ

November, 1979

SUMMARY OF CONTENTS

	Page
PREFACE	V
TABLE OF CASES	XXI
TABLE OF FEDERAL RULES OF EVIDENCE	XXIII
TABLE OF CALIFORNIA EVIDENCE CODE SECTIONS	XXV

CHAPTER I. EVIDENCE IN CRIMINAL TRIALS

Part
- A. Evidence and the Adversary System — 1
  1. Sources of the Law of Evidence — 1
  2. The Adversary Trial System — 2
  3. Two Fundamental Questions About Evidence — 4
  4. The Problem of Admissibility — 5
- B. The Vocabulary of Evidence — 5
  1. Types of Evidence — 5
  2. Forms of Evidence — 7
  3. More on Admissibility — 8
  4. The Weight of Admitted Evidence — 9

CHAPTER II. PROOF IN CRIMINAL CASES

- A. Judicial Notice and the Need for Evidence — 11
- B. Burden of Proof and Presumptions — 15
  1. Proof Beyond a Reasonable Doubt — 15
  2. Presumptions — 20

CHAPTER III. RELEVANCE

- A. The Concept of Relevant Evidence — 28
  1. In General — 28
  2. "Mathematical" Relevance — 37
- B. Balancing the Probative Value Against the Prejudicial Effect — 52
- C. Character Evidence — 57
  1. The Inadmissibility of the Defendant's — 57
  2. The Defendant's Right to Use Evidence of Character — 61
     a. His Own Good Character — 61
     b. Cross-Examination of Defendant's — 73
     c. The Character of the Victim — 77

SUMMARY OF CONTENTS

Part		Page
D.	Otherwise Relevant Acts—Which May Also Show Character—Other Crimes	87
E.	Extrinsic Policies, Compromise and Withdrawn Pleas of Guilty	100
	1. Compromise	100
	2. Withdrawn Pleas of Guilty	105

CHAPTER IV. THE HEARSAY RULE AND ITS EXCEPTIONS

A.	The Rationale and Meaning of Hearsay	109
	1. In General	109
	2. Out-of-Court Statements That Are Not Hearsay	121
	3. What Is a Statement	129
	a. Non-Human Evidence	129
	b. Non-Assertive Conduct	137
B.	Exceptions to the Hearsay Rule	146
	1. Admissions	146
	a. In General	146
	b. Admissions by Silence	149
	c. Admissions by Conduct	152
	d. Admissions by Co-Conspirators	154
	2. Former Testimony	157
	3. Dying Declarations	163
	4. Spontaneous and Contemporaneous Declarations	166
	5. Declarations Against Interest	172
	6. State of Mind	176
	7. Prior Identification	188
	8. Past Recollection Recorded	197
	9. Business and Public Records	202
	10. Miscellaneous Hearsay Exceptions	212
C.	The Future of Hearsay	215
	1. Lessening the Restrictions on the Admissibility of Hearsay Evidence	215
	2. Confrontation	221
	3. The Defendant's Right to Present Evidence	223

CHAPTER V. IMPEACHMENT AND CROSS-EXAMINATION

A.	Direct Examination	235
B.	Cross-Examination	239
	1. In General	239
	2. Scope of Cross-Examination	246

SUMMARY OF CONTENTS

Part		Page
C.	Cross-Examination and Impeachment	249
	1. Credibility of the Witness	249
	a. In General	249
	b. Prior Bad Acts	252
	c. Conviction of a Felony	258
	d. Bad Reputation for Truth and Veracity	268
	e. Psychiatric Condition	270
	2. Prior Inconsistent Statements	278
	3. Bias	284
	4. Rehabilitation of the Impeached Witness	291

CHAPTER VI. PRIVILEGE AND CONFIDENTIALITY

A.	The Attorney-Client Relationship	294
	1. Introduction	294
	2. The Attorney-Client Privilege	300
	a. The Statutory Framework	300
	b. Confidentiality in Action	307
	3. The Attorney's Duty of Loyalty to the Client	316
B.	Miscellaneous Privileges	328
	1. The Marital Privileges	328
	a. The "Spousal Incapacity"	328
	b. The Privilege for Confidential Marital Communications	333
	2. Physician-Patient Privilege; Psychotherapist-Patient Privilege	343

CHAPTER VII. THE PRIVILEGE AGAINST COMPULSORY SELF–INCRIMINATION

A.	Introduction	345
B.	In the Courts	350
C.	In the Stationhouse	359
D.	Non-Testimonial Evidence	375

CHAPTER VIII. GOVERNMENTAL PRIVILEGES

A.	State Secrets	382
B.	The Informer Privilege	388

SUMMARY OF CONTENTS

CHAPTER IX. REAL EVIDENCE

Part		Page
A.	Authentication of Real Evidence	407
	1. Documents	407
	2. Other Real Evidence	410
B.	The Best Evidence Rule	418

CHAPTER X. OPINION, EXPERTS AND EXPERTISE; SCIENTIFIC AND DEMONSTRATIVE EVIDENCE

			Page
A.	Opinion Testimony		428
	1. Lay Witnesses		428
	2. Expert Witnesses		435
B.	Scientific and Demonstrative Evidence		450
	1. Selected Issues in Scientific Evidence		450
		a. The "Lie Detector"	450
		b. "Voice Prints"	463
		c. Tests for Intoxication and Drugs	468
	2. Demonstrative Evidence		483

CHAPTER XI. THE EXCLUSIONARY RULE (Page 491)

CHAPTER XII. EYEWITNESS IDENTIFICATION (Page 503)

Index ___ 527

TABLE OF CONTENTS

	Page
Preface	V
Table of Cases	XXI
Table of Federal Rules of Evidence	XXIII
Table of California Evidence Code Sections	XXV

CHAPTER I. EVIDENCE IN CRIMINAL TRIALS

Part
A. Evidence and the Adversary System ---- 1
   1. Sources of the Law of Evidence ---- 1
   2. The Adversary Trial System ---- 2
   3. Two Fundamental Questions About Evidence ---- 4
   4. The Problem of Admissibility ---- 5

B. The Vocabulary of Evidence ---- 5
   1. Types of Evidence ---- 5
   2. Forms of Evidence ---- 7
   3. More on Admissibility ---- 8
   4. The Weight of Admitted Evidence ---- 9

CHAPTER II. PROOF IN CRIMINAL CASES

A. Judicial Notice and the Need for Evidence ---- 11
   Lilly, An Introduction to the Law of Evidence ---- 11
   State v. Lawrence ---- 12
   Rules of Evidence for United States Courts and Magistrates ---- 15

B. Burden of Proof and Presumptions ---- 15
   1. Proof Beyond a Reasonable Doubt ---- 15
      In Re Winship ---- 15
      Kaplan, Decision Theory and the Fact-Finding Process ---- 18
      Pattern Jury Instructions (Criminal Cases) ---- 19
   2. Presumptions ---- 20
      Lilly, An Introduction to the Law of Evidence ---- 20
      Proposed Rules of Evidence for United States Courts and Magistrates ---- 22
      Commonwealth v. Pauley ---- 23
      Collateral Readings ---- 26

TABLE OF CONTENTS

CHAPTER III. RELEVANCE

Part		Page
A.	The Concept of Relevant Evidence	28
	1. In General	28
	Harlot v. Harlot	28
	Waltz, Criminal Evidence	29
	Rules of Evidence for United States Courts and Magistrates	31
	Knapp v. State	31
	Regina v. Onufrejczyk	33
	2. "Mathematical" Relevance	37
	Closing Argument, People v. T. & W.	37
	Houts, From Evidence to Proof	41
	People v. Collins	43
	Racing Odds as Criminal Evidence	49
	Collateral Readings	51
B.	Balancing the Probative Value Against the Prejudicial Effect	52
	Lilly, An Introduction to the Law of Evidence	52
	Rules of Evidence for United States Courts and Magistrates	53
	People v. Burns	53
	United States v. Jackson	54
C.	Character Evidence	57
	1. The Inadmissibility of the Defendant's	57
	Bad Character	57
	Camus, The Stranger	57
	People v. Zackowitz	58
	2. The Defendant's Right to Use Evidence of Character	61
	a. His Own Good Character	61
	Lilly, An Introduction to the Law of Evidence	61
	Sample Examination of a Character Witness	64
	California Jury Instructions Criminal	64
	Theodore Roosevelt as Character Witness	64
	Ladd, Techniques and Theory of Character, Testimony	69
	Rules of Evidence for United States Courts and Magistrates	72
	b. Cross-Examination of Defendant's	73
	Character Witness	73
	Michelson v. United States	73
	c. The Character of the Victim	77
	Commonwealth v. Castellana	77
	Cardozo, The Nature of the Judicial Process	80
	Rules of Evidence for United States Courts and Magistrates	81
	Berger, Man's Trial, Woman's Tribulation: Rape Cases in the Courtroom	83

TABLE OF CONTENTS

Part		Page
D.	Otherwise Relevant Acts—Which May Also Show Character—Other Crimes	87
	Trautman, Logical or Legal Relevancy—A Conflict in Theory	87
	McCormick's Handbook of the Law of Evidence	89
	People v. Massey	97
E.	Extrinsic Policies, Compromise and Withdrawn Pleas of Guilty	100
	1. Compromise	100
	Rules of Evidence for United States Courts and Magistrates	100
	United States v. Herman	100
	2. Withdrawn Pleas of Guilty	105
	State v. Thomson	105
	Note on the Nolo Contendere Plea	107

CHAPTER IV. THE HEARSAY RULE AND ITS EXCEPTIONS

		Page
A.	The Rationale and Meaning of Hearsay	109
	1. In General	109
	State v. English	110
	Waltz, Criminal Evidence	113
	Tribe, Triangulating Hearsay	117
	Rules of Evidence for United States Courts and Magistrates	120
	2. Out-of-Court Statements That Are Not Hearsay	121
	Lilly, An Introduction to the Law of Evidence	121
	Subramaniam v. Public Prosecutor	125
	Draper v. United States	126
	3. What is a Statement	129
	Rules of Evidence for United States Courts and Magistrates	129
	a. Non-Human Evidence	129
	Waltz, Criminal Evidence	129
	Morgan, Hearsay and Non-Hearsay	130
	Buck v. State	131
	b. Non-Assertive Conduct	137
	Waltz, Criminal Evidence	137
	Commonwealth v. Knapp	138
	People v. Barnhart	140
	Morton, the Rothschilds	141
	Morgan, Evidence Exam, Summer Term, 1946, Harvard Law School	142
	Collateral Readings	145

TABLE OF CONTENTS

Part		Page
B.	Exceptions to the Hearsay Rule	146
	1. Admissions	146
	a. In General	146
	Waltz, Criminal Evidence	146
	Rules of Evidence for United States Courts and Magistrates	148
	b. Admissions by Silence	149
	United States v. Alker	149
	Note, Tacit Criminal Admissions	150
	LaBuy, Jury Instructions in Federal Criminal Cases	152
	c. Admissions by Conduct	152
	Coke, Third Institute, 1747	152
	McCormick's Handbook on the Law of Evidence	153
	LaBuy, Jury Instructions in Federal Criminal Cases	154
	d. Admissions by Co-Conspirators	154
	United States v. Petrozziello	154
	Collateral Readings	156
	2. Former Testimony	157
	Rules of Evidence for United States Courts and Magistrates	157
	United States v. Lynch	157
	People v. Moran	161
	3. Dying Declarations	163
	Rules of Evidence for United States Courts and Magistrates	163
	William Shakespeare, King John	163
	People v. Sarzano	164
	4. Spontaneous and Contemporaneous Declarations	166
	United States v. Napier	166
	People v. Damen	168
	Rules of Evidence for United States Courts and Magistrates	171
	5. Declarations Against Interest	172
	Rules of Evidence for United States Courts and Magistrates	172
	United States v. Alvarez	172
	6. State of Mind	176
	Rules of Evidence for United States Courts and Magistrates	176
	Mutual Life Ins. Co. of N. Y. v. Hillmon	176
	People v. Talle	179
	United States v. Pheaster	181
	7. Prior Identification	188
	Rules of Evidence for United States Courts and Magistrates	188
	Weinstein and Berger, Weinstein's Evidence	188

TABLE OF CONTENTS

Part

B. Exceptions to the Hearsay Rule—Continued Page
    United States v. Marchand 190
    Comment, The Use of Prior Identification Evidence in Criminal Trials Under the Federal Rules of Evidence .. 194

  8. Past Recollection Recorded 197
    Kinsey v. State 197
    Lilly, An Introduction to the Law of Evidence 200
    Rules of Evidence for United States Courts and Magistrates 201

  9. Business and Public Records 202
    Maryland—District of Columbia—Virginia Criminal Practice Institute Trial Manual 202
    Johnson v. Lutz 203
    Rules of Evidence for United States Courts and Magistrates 206
    United States v. Smith 206
    United States v. Grady 210
    Rules of Evidence for United States Courts and Magistrates 211

  10. Miscellaneous Hearsay Exceptions 212
    Waltz, Criminal Evidence 212
    Rules of Evidence for United States Courts and Magistrates 214

C. The Future of Hearsay 215
  1. Lessening the Restrictions on the Admissibility of Hearsay Evidence 215
    Saturday Review, Cartoon 215
    Rules of Evidence for United States Courts and Magistrates 216
    United States v. Medico 217
  2. Confrontation 221
    Lilly, An Introduction to the Law of Evidence 221
  3. The Defendant's Right to Present Evidence 223
    Chambers v. Mississippi 223
    Collateral Readings 231
    McNaughton, Evidence Exam, Harvard Law School, First Semester, 1960–1961 232

CHAPTER V. IMPEACHMENT AND CROSS-EXAMINATION

A. Direct Examination 235
    Kaplan and Waltz, The Trial of Jack Ruby 235
    Amsterdam, Segal & Miller, Trial Manual 3 for the Defense of Criminal Cases 236

TABLE OF CONTENTS

Part		Page
A.	Direct Examination—Continued	
	Mathew, Forensic Fables by O	238
	Rules of Evidence for United States Courts and Magistrates	238
B.	Cross-Examination	239
	1. In General	239
	Susanna and the Elders	239
	Mathew, Forensic Fables by O	241
	Amsterdam, Segal & Miller Trial Manual 3 for the Defense of Criminal Cases	241
	Keeton, Trial Tactics and Methods	243
	Collateral Readings	245
	2. Scope of Cross-Examination	246
	Carlson, Cross-Examination of the Accused	246
	Rules of Evidence for United States Courts and Magistrates	247
	Collateral Readings	248
C.	Cross-Examination and Impeachment	249
	1. The Credibility of the Witness	249
	a. In General	249
	Rules of Evidence for United States Courts and Magistrates	249
	Lilly, An Introduction to the Law of Evidence	249
	McCormick's Handbook on the Law of Evidence	250
	b. Prior Bad Acts	252
	People v. Sorge	252
	Wellman, The Art of Cross-Examination	254
	Rules of Evidence for United States Courts and Magistrates	257
	Collateral Readings	258
	c. Conviction of a Felony	258
	United States v. Jackson	258
	United States v. Boyer	263
	Lilly, An Introduction to the Law of Evidence	264
	Rules of Evidence for United States Courts and Magistrates	266
	Collateral Readings	267
	d. Bad Reputation for Truth and Veracity	268
	Lilly, An Introduction to the Law of Evidence	268
	e. Psychiatric Condition	270
	People v. Bastian	270
	United States v. Pugliese	272
	Falknor, Evidence, 1950 Annual Survey of American Law	273
	State v. Renneberg	276
	Collateral Readings	278

TABLE OF CONTENTS

Part		Page
C.	Cross-Examination and Impeachment—Continued	
	2. Prior Inconsistent Statements	278
	United States v. Long Soldier	278
	Goldstein, Trial Technique	282
	Rules of Evidence for United States Courts and Magistrates	283
	Collateral Readings	284
	3. Bias	284
	People v. Taylor	284
	People v. Torres	287
	Waltz, Criminal Evidence	289
	Rules of Evidence for United States Courts and Magistrates	290
	Collateral Readings	290
	4. Rehabilitation of the Impeached Witness	291
	People v. Singer	291

CHAPTER VI. PRIVILEGE AND CONFIDENTIALITY

A.	The Attorney-Client Relationship	294
	1. Introduction	294
	Hazard, Ethics in the Practice of Law	294
	Mitchell, The Ethics of Defending the Guilty and Dangerous—New Answers to Old Questions 3–5	298
	2. The Attorney-Client Privilege	300
	a. The Statutory Framework	300
	Rules of Evidence for United States Courts and Magistrates	300
	California Evidence Code, §§ 911–913, 915–919, 950–952, 954–956	301
	California Penal Code, § 636	307
	b. Confidentiality in Action	307
	Amsterdam, Segal & Miller, Trial Manual 3 for the Defense of Criminal Cases	307
	People v. Belge	309
	Clark v. State	311
	3. The Attorney's Duty of Loyalty to the Client	316
	In re Ryder	316
	An Exchange of Letters	324
B.	Miscellaneous Privileges	328
	1. The Marital Privileges	328
	a. The "Spousal Incapacity"	328
	California Evidence Code, §§ 970–973	328
	Wyatt v. United States	330

TABLE OF CONTENTS

Part

B. Miscellaneous Privileges—Continued   **Page**
- b. The Privilege for Confidential Marital Communications _____ 333
  - California Evidence Code, §§ 980–981, 985–987 _____ 333
  - Lilly, An Introduction to the Law of Evidence [§ 87] 335
  - People v. Melski _____ 338
- 2. Physician-Patient Privilege; Psychotherapist-Patient Privilege _____ 343
  - Lilly, An Introduction to the Law of Evidence _____ 343

CHAPTER VII. THE PRIVILEGE AGAINST COMPULSORY SELF–INCRIMINATION

A. Introduction _____ 345
- Constitution of the United States, Fifth Amendment _____ 345
- Malloy v. Hogan _____ 347

B. In the Courts _____ 350
- Griffin v. California _____ 350
- Traver, Anatomy of a Murder _____ 354
- Waltz, Criminal Evidence _____ 356

C. In the Stationhouse _____ 359
- Kamisar, Equal Justice in the Gatehouses and Mansions of American Criminal Procedure _____ 359
- Sutherland, Crime and Confession _____ 363
- Miranda v. Arizona _____ 364
- Hall and Kamisar, Modern Criminal Procedure _____ 370
- Harris v. New York _____ 372

D. Non-Testimonial Evidence _____ 375
- Schmerber v. California _____ 375
- Collateral Readings _____ 379

CHAPTER VIII. GOVERNMENTAL PRIVILEGES

A. State Secrets _____ 382
- California Evidence Code, § 1040 _____ 382
- United States v. Nixon _____ 382

B. The Informer Privilege _____ 388
- Roviaro v. United States _____ 388
- California Evidence Code, §§ 1041–1042 _____ 392
- McCray v. Illinois _____ 394
- Waltz, Criminal Evidence _____ 399
- Jefferson, California Evidence Benchbook and Supplement _____ 401
- Collateral Readings _____ 405

TABLE OF CONTENTS

CHAPTER IX. REAL EVIDENCE

Part | Page
A. Authentication of Real Evidence — 407
  1. Documents — 407
     McCormick, Evidence — 407
     Rules of Evidence for United States Courts and Magistrates — 408
  2. Other Real Evidence — 410
     Lilly, An Introduction to the Law of Evidence — 410
     Gallego v. United States — 415
     Waltz, Criminal Evidence — 417
     Collateral Readings — 418

B. The Best Evidence Rule — 418
   McCormick, Evidence — 418
   Lilly, An Introduction to the Law of Evidence — 419
   Chandler v. United States — 422
   People v. Enskat — 423
   Rules of Evidence for United States Courts and Magistrates — 425

CHAPTER X. OPINION, EXPERTS AND EXPERTISE; SCIENTIFIC AND DEMONSTRATIVE EVIDENCE

A. Opinion Testimony — 428
  1. Lay Witnesses — 428
     State v. Garver — 428
     Commonwealth v. Holden — 429
     Lilly, An Introduction to the Law of Evidence — 432
     Rules of Evidence for United States Courts and Magistrates — 435
  2. Expert Witnesses — 435
     Waltz, Criminal Evidence — 435
     People v. Crooks — 443
     Rules of Evidence for United States Courts and Magistrates — 447
     Waltz, The New Federal Rules of Evidence: An Analysis — 449
     Collateral Readings — 449

B. Scientific and Demonstrative Evidence — 450
  1. Selected Issues in Scientific Evidence — 450
     a. The "Lie Detector" — 450
        State v. Valdez — 450
        Waltz, Criminal Evidence — 456
        Note, The Psychological Stress Evaluator: Yesterday's Dream—Tomorrow's Nightmare — 459

TABLE OF CONTENTS

Part
B. Scientific and Demonstrative Evidence—Continued Page
    b. "Voice Prints" 463
        Waltz, Criminal Evidence 463
        United States v. Franks 465
        Lisko, Are the Courts Listening to Voiceprints? ... 467
    c. Tests for Intoxication and Drugs 468
        Waltz, Criminal Evidence 468
        State v. Baker 474
        People v. Williams 480
  2. Demonstrative Evidence 483
    Waltz, Criminal Evidence 483
    Collateral Readings 490

CHAPTER XI. THE EXCLUSIONARY RULE

Mapp v. Ohio 491
Stone v. Powell 494
Silberman, Criminal Violence, Criminal Justice 498
Kaplan, The Limits of the Exclusionary Rule 500

CHAPTER XII. EYEWITNESS IDENTIFICATION

People v. Horodecki 503
Amsterdam, Segal and Miller, Trial Manual 3 for the Defense of Criminal Cases 506
Fishman and Loftus, Expert Psychological Testimony on Eyewitness Identification 508
Manson v. Braithwaite 517
Oakland Police Department, Departmental General Order 521

Index 527

TABLE OF CASES

Principal cases are in italic. Nonprincipal cases are in roman.
References are to Pages.

Alker, United States v., 149
Alvarez, United States v., 172

Baker, State v., 474
Barbara, People v., 456
Barnhart, People v., 140
Bastian, People v., 270, 272
Belge, People v., 309
Boyer, United States v., 263
Buck v. State, 131
Burns, People v., 53

Castellana, Commonwealth v., 77
Chambers v. Mississippi, 223
Chandler v. United States, 422
Clark v. State, 311
Collins, People v., 43
Commonwealth v. _____ (see opposing party)
Crooks, People v., 443

Damen, People v., 168
Draper v. United States, 126

Ellis, People v., 379
English, State v., 110
Enskat, People v., 423

Franks, United States v., 465

Gallego v. United States, 415
Garver, State v., 428
Grady, United States v., 210
Griffin v. California, 350

Harlot v. Harlot, 28
Harris v. New York, 372
Herman, United States v., 100
Holden, Commonwealth v., 429
Horodecki, People v., 503

In re (see name of party)

Jackson, United States v., 54, 153, 258
Johnson v. Lutz, 203

Kinsey v. State, 197
Knapp v. State, 31
Knapp, Commonwealth v., 138

Lawrence, State v., 12
Long Soldier, United States v., 278
Lynch, United States v., 157

McCray v. Illinois, 394
Malloy v. Hogan, 347
Manson v. Braithwaite, 517
Mapp v. Ohio, 491
Marchand, United States v., 190
Massey, People v., 97
Medico, United States v., 217
Melski, People v., 338
Michelson v. United States, 73
Miranda v. Arizona, 364
Moran, People v., 161
Morrell v. State, 327
Mutual Life Ins. Co. of New York v. Hillmon, 176

Napier, United States v., 166
Nixon, United States v., 382

People v. _____ (see opposing party)

Onufrejczyk, Regina v., 33
Onzufrejeck, Regina v., 153

Pauley, Commonwealth v., 23
Petrozziello, United States v., 154
Pheaster, United States v., 181
Pugliese, United States v., 272

Regina v. _____ (see opposing party)
Renneberg, State v., 276
Roviaro v. United States, 388
Ryder, In re, 316

Sarzano, People v., 164, 166
Schmerber v. California, 375, 379
Singer, People v., 291
Smith, United States v., 206

TABLE OF CASES

Sorge, People v., 252
State v. _____ (see opposing party)
Stone v. Powell, 494
Subramaniam v. Public Prosecutor, 125
Sudduth, People v., 379

Talle, People v., 179
Taylor, People v., 284
Thomson, State v., 105
Torres, People v., 287

United States v. _____ (see opposing party)

Valdez, State v., 450

Williams, People v., 480
Winship, In re, 15
Wyatt v. United States, 330

Zackowitz, People v., 58

TABLE OF FEDERAL RULES OF EVIDENCE

Fed.Evid. Rule	This Work Page
105	53
201	15
201(e)	12
303	22
401	31
402	31
403	31
	53
404	81
405	72
410	100
412	82
501	300
602	447
607	249
608	257
609	266
611	238
	247
612	201
613	283
701	435
702	447
703	447
704	447
705	448
706	448
801	120
	129
	148
	188
	283

Fed.Evid. Rule	This Work Page
801(d)(2)	290
801(d)(2)(C)	290
801(d)(2)(D)	290
801(d)(2)(E)	290
802	121
803	171
	176
	201
	211
	214
	216
804	157
	163
	172
	216
805	206
806	290
901	408
902	409
903	410
1001	425
1002	426
1003	426
1004	426
1005	426
1006	427
1007	427

TABLE OF CALIFORNIA EVIDENCE CODE SECTIONS

West's Ann. Evid. Code Sec.	This Work Page	West's Ann Evid. Code Sec.	This Work Page
911	301	956	307
912	301	970	328
913	302	971	328
915	302	972	329
916	303	973	329
917	303	980	333
918	303	981	334
919	303	985	334
950	304	986	335
951	304	987	335
952	304	1040	382
954	305	1041	392
955	306	1042	393

BASIC MATERIALS ON
CRIMINAL EVIDENCE

Chapter I

EVIDENCE IN CRIMINAL TRIALS *

A. EVIDENCE AND THE ADVERSARY SYSTEM

1. SOURCES OF THE LAW OF EVIDENCE

Case Law and Codes. Until recently it would have been fairly accurate to say that nearly all evidentiary rules are judge-made; that is, that they are a product of the common law, which is law that has been announced by judges functioning in areas not governed by statutes, ordinances, and governmental regulations. The common law can be extracted from judicial opinions found in law libraries in books called *reports* or *reporters*. There had been a few attempts to consolidate all the different rules of evidence and codify them in statutes or codes but they met with little success. The Uniform Rules of Evidence, drafted by the Commissioners on Uniform State Laws and issued in 1954, exerted some influence on courts but was formally adopted in only a small number of states. A prior effort to codify the rules of evidence, the American Law Institutes's 1942 Model Code of Evidence, was not adopted anywhere.

Now, however, the Congress has enacted the Federal Rules of Evidence, applicable in federal courts. Organized into eleven articles, this code covers most of the traditional evidentiary rules and makes some innovations. Earlier, California, after years of research and discussion by its Law Revision Commission, adopted in statutory form an Evidence Code that was quite complete. A few other states have already adopted evidence codes modeled on the lines of the federal and the California codes; in the years to come many more states will do so.

* Prepared by Professor Jon R. Waltz.

These efforts to develop codes of evidence are, for the most part, just that and not much more: they are attempts to describe in one place the evidentiary principles which have been firmly settled for a long while. Only occasionally do the evidence codes break new ground.

This means that the law enforcement agent and others involved in the criminal justice process must now understand not only the emerging evidence codes but also the case law, the prior judicial opinions. An understanding of these opinions will carry with it an understanding of the governing evidentiary principles in those jurisdictions which have not yet adopted codifications of the rules of evidence.

Accordingly, the book you hold in your hands will draw its content from both the case law and the codes as well as from explanatory secondary materials such as legal treatises and law review articles.

First, however, it should be worthwhile to present an overview of the trial process and the classifications of evidence.

2. THE ADVERSARY TRIAL SYSTEM

An Unscientific Approach. Many experienced law enforcement agents—especially those who regularly appear in court—would agree that the Anglo-American adversary trial system is enough to make one wonder—to wonder if it is properly constructed to reach its announced goal, the ascertainment of truth, to wonder, beyond that, how the system ever works at all.

There is nothing remotely scientific about the litigation (trial) process. Professor Robert E. Keeton of the Harvard Law School has said that "A trial is a competition of inconsistent versions of facts and theories of law." Defying all the accepted precepts of scientific fact-finding, the trial system often works surprisingly well. To paraphrase a famous remark of Winston Churchill (who was speaking of democracy), our system of adjudication is the most imperfect one in the world, except for all the others. "Adversariness"—which one prominent trial lawyer described simply as "setting the parties fighting"—seems to be the best method yet devised for forcing the truth into the open.

Distinctive Characteristics. Our adversary trial system has some distinctive characteristics, a few of which will be mentioned now and others of which will become evident from a reading of subsequent materials in this book.

In the main, court cases are conducted by the parties, acting through their legal representatives—their lawyers. Specifically, criminal cases are prepared and prosecuted by an elected or appointed representative of the people (a United States Attorney or a State's Attorney, for example). They are defended by lawyers hired (lawyers prefer the term "retained") by the accused or, if the accused is without funds (indigent), by counsel—often a member of a Public Defender Office—who has been appointed by the trial court. These lawyers, supervised by a judge, control the content and flow of the evidence in a criminal trial.

Another characteristic of our litigation process is that it is at least theoretically two-sided, not one-sided, in the sense that each side has a more or less equal opportunity to investigate the case and present his side of it at trial by means of evidence and argument. (Although each party has an equal *opportunity* to do this, the criminal defendant may not always possess equal *means* of doing so. Ordinarily, the prosecution has a genuine advantage in the investigation and preparation of cases because it is backed by the skills of trained law enforcement agents and related personnel.)

The Trial Judge's Role. In an American jury case the judge acts only as a sort of umpire or referee. He/she applies the procedural rules to the lawyers and explains the substantive propositions of law to the jurors but ordinarily the jurors, and they alone, decide what facts have been established (proved) beyond a reasonable doubt by the evidence produced in court.

To put it another way, the trial judge is the arbiter of the law; the jury members are the arbiters of the facts. In reaching their verdict, the jurors apply to the facts, as found by them, the law as it has been explained to them by the judge in his instructions (often called the judge's "charge" to the jury). Of course, if neither side wants a trial by jury (jury trial has been "waived"), then the trial judge himself will determine the facts and apply the substantive law to them in what is referred to as a *bench trial*.

The Lawyers' Role. The parties to a criminal case, through their lawyers, produce the evidence which the jury is to consider in arriving at its verdict of Guilty or Not Guilty. In a way, trial lawyers are like theatrical producers and stage managers. Except in rare instances, the trial judge lacks any power to tell the parties what evidence to produce or to produce any himself, and the jurors never have any such power. (Occasionally the trial judge may himself select and summon to the witness stand one or more supposedly impartial experts; for example, a psychiatrist in a case involving an insanity defense. By and large, however, it is the lawyers who set the stage, locate the props, and generate the cast of characters for a criminal trial.)

Although it might at first blush seem odd that the parties, acting through their legal counsel, are free to decide what evidence the factfinder will hear and see—free, in other words, to decide how the trial will be staged—the workings of the adversary trial system usually guarantee that what one side suppresses the other will triumphantly produce, with the result that the first side will very likely introduce it initially rather than be charged with hiding relevant information.

This process of smoking out the evidence would prove ineffective if one side were ignorant of favorable evidence held by the opposite side. In past times, criminal accused were frequently at a distinct disadvantage in this regard because there were not many procedures by which they could discover the prosecution's evidence in advance of trial. This disadvantage is gradually being eliminated by new rules of criminal procedure which give the defendant freer access to the evidence which law enforcement agents have assembled for the prosecution.

Propositions of Law and Questions of Fact. The outcome of criminal trials is determined by propositions and questions that inevitably come up during the course of them: (1) There are *propositions of law* (What are the statutory elements of first-degree murder?); and (2) there are *questions of fact* (Did the accused, with premeditation, kill someone?).

In most criminal cases it will be fact-questions, rather than law-propositions, which have the most powerful impact on the trial's outcome. The rules of evidence serve to control the materials that can be used by a factfinder (jury or judge) in resolving these fact-questions.

3. TWO FUNDAMENTAL QUESTIONS ABOUT EVIDENCE

And so we are going to be talking about evidence. At the outset there are two crucial questions about evidence that have to be examined. First, what matters and what materials should be *admitted* into evidence (received) for the factfinder to consider? Then, what *use* can properly be made by the factfinder of those matters and materials which are ruled admissible into evidence?

Most evidence rules relate to the first of these two questions. That is, most evidence rules relate to the problem of what ought to be received in evidence—the problem of *admissibility.*

The second question—What *use* can properly be made of received evidence?—is an important one but no entirely satisfactory means exist to control the way a factfinder, particularly a jury, deals with items of admitted evidence. By way of example, in a criminal prosecution a judge may instruct the jury that certain evidence, perhaps a witness's prior inconsistent statement, is admissible only for the purpose of casting doubt on (impeaching) the witness's credibility and is not to be used as substantive evidence affirmatively establishing any element of the alleged offense. Here is matter, admitted into evidence, which has one permissible use and one impermissible use. Consciously or unconsciously, however, the jurors may nonetheless make both the permissible and the impermissible use of the evidence; they may use the evidence as proof of *guilt.*

Because most of the rules of evidence apply to the admissibility of evidence, and not to the ways in which it can thereafter be used, we turn now to admissibility.

4. THE PROBLEM OF ADMISSIBILITY

Admissibility; Its Meaning. "Admissibility" is a term which identifies the decision as to what matters and materials the factfinder will be allowed to hear, see, read, and perhaps even touch or smell. Two large concerns influence the admissibility problem.

Wasting of Time. There is concern about wasteful time-consumption. A limiting of the matters to be brought out during a trial is essential; were it otherwise, litigations would drag on forever. The rules of evidence, as someone once said, are a concession to the mortality of man. A criminal case would go on for an unconscionable length of time if there were no reasonably restrictive evidentiary principles putting outer limits on the sheer bulk of evidence to be admitted. And so we have rules of relevance, and rules against repetitious (cumulative) evidence.

Jury-Protection. Secondly, and some think more importantly, there is the supposed need to protect lay jurors from all manner of assertedly improper influences. Most of the complexities of our evidentiary rules are a direct product of a system that uses non-experts —the jurors—as factfinders. The assumption is that inexperienced factfinders must be carefully shielded from misleading or prejudicial influences that might induce them to arrive at an incorrect verdict. The fundamental inquiry is, What can we safely let lay jurors see, hear, and read? The importance of this question is borne out by the circumstance that many evidence problems are the result of efforts by flamboyant trial lawyers to score points with the lay jury by using methods of advocacy that would probably have little impact on an experienced judge who was serving as the trier of the facts in a bench trial.

B. THE VOCABULARY OF EVIDENCE

1. TYPES OF EVIDENCE

Two Basic Types. There are two fundamental types of evidence: (1) *direct* evidence, and (2) *indirect* or *circumstantial* evidence.

Direct Evidence. As its identifying label more than suggests, direct evidence is the type that proves a fact-proposition directly rather than by a process of inference. It goes directly, in a single step, to a material issue in the case. Here, for example, is some testimony that constitutes direct evidence:

> Q: [BY THE PROSECUTING ATTORNEY] What happened next, if anything?

A: I saw the defendant pull a knife out of his inside jacket pocket and shove it into the chest of the man standing in front of him.

Direct evidence is frequently called "eye-witness" evidence. (The example above was of eye-witness testimony.) This is a simplistic approach, however. Direct evidence is the product of a person's sensory perception and most people, but not all of them, have five senses: sight, hearing, touch, taste, and smell. As we have said, the person who observed the accused draw a knife from his pocket and stab his victim was giving eye-witness testimony. Had he also testified, "I heard the defendant shout, 'That's for messing around with my girl!,'" he would have supplied an example of what could accurately be termed direct "ear-witness" testimony. The person who testifies, "It smelled like whiskey" is a "nose-witness"; the person who testifies, "I felt his wrist and couldn't detect any pulse," is a "touch-witness." "It tasted like hard liquor" is, of course, direct evidence based on the witness's sense of taste. These are all examples of direct evidence, since nothing is left to inference. The issue, we may assume, is whether the accused stabbed a man; the quoted testimony goes directly to that question. The same can be said of the subsequent examples of ear, nose, touch, and taste testimony.

Indirect or Circumstantial Evidence. In sharp contrast to direct evidence, and frequently encountered in criminal cases, is indirect or circumstantial evidence. This type of evidence depends on *inference* for its relationship to the fact-proposition to be proved. It does not establish that proposition directly; it is indirect evidence. It is evidence of a subsidiary or underlying fact, even a collateral fact, from which—alone or in combination with a group of additional facts—the existence of an ultimate fact-proposition can be inferred by the factfinder. This is the long way of saying that one fact, or a group of them, may logically imply the existence of yet another fact.

The classic shot-in-a-locked-room case exemplifies circumstantial evidence and conveys a sense of its occasionally potent force. Bushmat and Lishniss are seen entering a room that has only one entrance and exit, a door. That door is locked behind them. A loud "bang," coming from inside the room, is heard by persons outside the door. The door is immediately broken down. Bushmat is observed by all of the witnesses standing over the prostrate body of Lishniss, who has a bleeding circular wound in his forehead. Bushmat is gripping a revolver in his right hand. There is one spent cartridge in the chamber; it is still warm to the touch. All of this is circumstantial (indirect) evidence that Bushmat shot Lishniss in the head. It is not direct evidence that he did so because no one actually saw Bushmat shoot Lishniss. Of course, Bushmat's own declaration that "nothing unusual has happened in here," or, more to the print, "I didn't shoot Lishniss," *would* be direct evidence, since Bushmat was plainly an eye-witness to what went on in the locked room. Neither type of evidence is conclusive. The circumstantial evidence gives rise to a legitimate (*i. e.*, permissible) inference that Bushmat shot Lishniss but it does not conclusively foreclose the possibility that Lishniss shot himself, after which Bushmat picked up the suicide weapon. And the factfinder might, for a variety of reasons, choose to disbelieve Bushmat's direct testimonial evidence.

Most of the evidence rules concerning relevance and most of the exclusionary rules of evidence to be encountered in this book relate to circumstantial evidence, because this type of evidence generates more problems of reliability. Direct evidence, such as eye-witness accounts, is almost invariably admissible so long as it is relevant to the issues in the case.

2. FORMS OF EVIDENCE

Four Basic Forms. The two fundamental types of evidence (direct and circumstantial) come in four basic forms: (1) testimonial; (2) tangible; (3) tangible-testimonial; and (4) judicially noticed evidence.

Testimonial Evidence. This is oral (spoken) testimony given by a courtroom witness from the witness stand, under oath or solemn affirmation.

Tangible Evidence. This refers to the physical exhibits in a case. Exhibits—various tangible things—can be offered into evidence for the factfinder's consideration if they bear upon the issues in the case.

There are two basic types of tangible evidence. First there is what Dean Wigmore, the great evidence scholar, called *real evidence*. This is the "real thing" in the case: the actual murder weapon, the heroin allegedly sold to an undercover agent, the counterfeit twenty dollar bill.

Second, there is *demonstrative evidence*. This is not the real thing. It is a visual and sometimes an audio-visual aid for the factfinder. It may be a model or mock-up of the crime scene, a chart showing the defendant's annual expenditures in a net worth tax evasion prosecution, a diagram, an anatomical model, and so on.

Tangible-Testimonial. This is a hybrid, the best examples being a deposition or the transcript of a witness's testimony in an earlier trial.

Judicially Noticed Evidence. Some matters, because they are subject to common knowledge in the community or to verification by recourse to some highly reliable source, do not have to be proved in the usual manner. Instead of requiring formal proof, a court will take judicial notice of the fact in question and instruct the jurors that they are to take it as conclusively established in the case without formal proof. (It is not correct to say that judicial notice is a substitute for *evidence;* any fact judicially noticed constitutes evidence. But it is accurate to say that judicial notice is a substitute for formal *proof.*)

3. MORE ON ADMISSIBILITY

For years now the airwaves have been heavily freighted with lawyer series, the great grandfather of them all being *Perry Mason.* The truth of the matter is that some of these television dramas present a fairly accurate picture of the rules of evidence in operation. (And some of them give a wildly inaccurate picture of how trial lawyers actually function, just as many television depictions of police work are fanciful in the extreme.)

On television one hears Mr. Mason intone, "Object, your Honor. Irrelevant, immaterial, and incompetent!" Mason has invoked the classic objection, known to trial lawyers since time out of memory as "The Three I's." And those three I's fairly accurately summarize the entire body of evidence rules.

At the core of evidence law lies this proposition: To be properly receivable for the factfinder's consideration, evidence must be *probative* of a *material* issue in the case and otherwise *competent* under the rules of evidence. Every item of evidence that is to be offered in a criminal case must pass the tests of *materiality, probativeness,* and *competency.*

Materiality, the First Ingredient of Relevance. The first question to ask when assessing the admissibility of evidence is this: Toward what issue is the offered evidence directed? What is the issue? is a fundamentally important question in connection with the receipt of any evidence. Is that issue, whatever it may be, a material one in the case, made so by the wording of the charge against the defendant, the rulings of the trial judge, and the stipulations of the prosecuting attorney and the defense counsel? If the issue to which the offered evidence goes is not a material one in the case, the evidence will be excluded on objection by opposing counsel. Thus evidence pertaining to the way the defendant treats his mother-in-law probably pertains to no material issue in an arson prosecution—unless, of course, she was a resident of the torched building.

Probativeness, the Second Ingredient of Relevance. If the issue to which the offered evidence is directed is a material one in the case, it next is necessary to inquire, Is the offered evidence probative of that issue? That is, does the evidence tend to establish the material fact-proposition? Putting it yet another way, Does the offered evidence tend to make the fact-proposition more probably true, or untrue, than it would be without that evidence? If the answer to the question of probativeness is in the affirmative, the *relevance* question has been answered, since materiality and probativeness, taken in combination, add up to relevance. Relevance, in other words, can be defined as a tendency to prove a fact-proposition that is properly provable in the particular case.

An example: The fact that the defendant stole three packages of chewing gum from a corner candy store when he was a schoolboy is not probative of his guilt in a grand larceny prosecution arising twenty years later.

Competency. Even if both branches of the relevance question (materiality; probativeness) can be answered in the affirmative, there still remains a large additional question: Is the offered evidence nonetheless incompetent (inadmissible) because of some special exclusionary rule of law? To answer this third and last question, one must have a working knowledge of the entire body of evidence rules.

Evidence can be probative of a material issue, even sometimes powerfully probative of it, and still be excluded by some special rule because the particular type of evidence is thought to be generally unreliable (for example, much hearsay evidence); too disruptive of trial procedure (for example, surprise testimony as to which advance notice must be given under some applicable rule—alibi evidence, for instance); misleadingly but overwhelmingly probative, that is, evidence whose potential for unfair prejudice far outweighs its substantive value (for example, relevant but inflammatory evidence, ranging from a gruesome photograph of a dead body to the testimony of a qualified mathematician that the odds are a trillion to one against the police having arrested the wrong man); contrary to policies favoring confidentiality in order to protect and encourage certain relationships (for example, attorney-client, physician-patient, husband-wife, clergyman-penitent); or violative of some constitutional doctrine (for example, principles applying to self-incrimination or unlawful search and seizure).

From the foregoing thumbnail sketch it will be evident that the exclusionary rules, leading to the incompetency of evidence, are often closely bound up with the work of law enforcement agents, and thereby often dictate the appropriate scope of that work.

4. THE WEIGHT OF ADMITTED EVIDENCE

Full Weight, Little Weight, No Weight At All. The fact that an item of evidence has been ruled admissible does not mean that it is conclusive or binding on the factfinder. It means only that the item of evidence has been deemed worthy of the factfinder's consideration. After its receipt the factfinder can decide to give the item full weight, little weight, or no weight at all; it is for the factfinder to determine what if any weight to accord it. Thus jurors, being the finders of the facts, are entitled to assess the persuasiveness or believability of evidence. They can give it no weight at all if its believability is suspect; they can give it full weight where it is persuasive and uncontradicted by other evidence.

Instructive examples can be found in alibi defenses. The defendant's girlfriend takes the witness stand on his behalf and testifies that the defendant was with her during the entire night on which he is charged with having committed a liquor store robbery. However, on cross-examination and through other witnesses the prosecutor develops the distinct probability that on the night in question the defendant's girlfriend had been in another city. Under these somewhat dramatic circumstances the jurors would undoubtedly give no weight, or very little weight, to the direct testimony of the defendant's girlfriend, having it also in mind that she may be more than slightly interested in the outcome of the trial. The jurors might have given the witness's testimony full weight had it not been so thoroughly impeached.

Chapter II

PROOF IN CRIMINAL CASES

A. JUDICIAL NOTICE AND THE NEED FOR EVIDENCE

LILLY, AN INTRODUCTION TO THE LAW OF EVIDENCE *

10–13 (1978).

An interesting accommodation of the roles of judge, counsel, and jury occurs when an adjudicative fact has the degree of certainty that justifies the invocation of judicial notice. The device of judicial notice allows certain, specified facts to be established without the introduction into the record of supportive evidence. Modern authority holds that a "judicially noticed fact must be one not subject to reasonable dispute in that it is either (1) generally known within the territorial jurisdiction of the trial court or (2) capable of accurate and ready determination by resort to sources whose accuracy cannot reasonably be questioned." The fact that Mission Street is a place of business activity is generally known to those in San Francisco, California; the time of sunrise or sunset can be ascertained by reference to reliable sources, as can many historical, geographical, or scientific facts.

The judge may take judicial notice on his own motion. Under the preferable view, he must do so (assuming it is appropriate) if requested by counsel and provided with such information as may be necessary to facilitate the process. There is vigorous debate, however, over whether the noticed fact must be accepted by the jury as conclusively established or whether the opponent may attempt to secure a contrary finding. If judicial notice of adjudicative fact is limited to indisputable facts, it is incongruous to permit a contrary finding by the jury. Thus, most jurisdictions hold that, at least in civil cases, judicial notice is conclusive, and disproof by contrary evidence and argument is impermissible. In criminal cases, however, there is a decided tendency to let the jury refuse to find any fact alleged against the accused; the rationale is that the accused's right to jury trial, which prevents the judge from directing a verdict against him, makes it similarly inappropriate to bind the jury by judicial notice.

* * *

Considerations of judicial control and trial expedition should influence a judge to take the initiative and declare as settled all of

---

* Reprinted with permission from Lilly's "An Introduction to the Law of Evidence," West Publishing Co. (1978).

those facts that he finds are indisputable. But the adversary system has not always contained procedures that secure the rights of the parties to participate in this process. Counsel at least should have the opportunity to present argument as to why a particular fact does not meet the criteria of judicial notice. This opportunity to be heard had not gained wide recognition until recently, when it was adopted as part of the rule governing judicial notice in federal courts: Rule 201(e) of the Federal Rules of Evidence entitles a party, upon request, to the opportunity of showing the impropriety of taking judicial notice.

STATE v. LAWRENCE

Supreme Court of Utah, 1951.
120 Utah 323, 234 P.2d 600.

CROCKETT, Justice.

This case comes to us on an appeal from a conviction of grand larceny, arising out of the theft of an automobile. Two questions are presented: First, where there is no evidence of value except a description of the property involved, is it prejudicial error for the court to instruct the jury that the value of the property is greater than $50 and that if defendant is guilty at all he is guilty of grand larceny. The necessity of answering the first question in the affirmative gives rise to the second: Where such error has been committed, can the cause be remanded for retrial without violating the constitutional guarantee of the accused not to be placed twice in jeopardy for the same offense. After a consideration of the problems involved touching upon those questions we answer both in the affirmative.

At the conclusion of the evidence, the defendant's counsel moved the court for a directed verdict on the ground that there had been no evidence of value of the stolen car. The State's attorney might properly and with little difficulty have moved to reopen and supply the missing evidence. He did not do so but instead argued that judicial notice could be taken of the value of the car. The court denied defendant's motion and included in its instructions to the jury the following:

"Grand Larceny so far as it might be material in this case is committed when the property taken is of a value exceeding $50.00.

"In this case you will take the value of this property as being in excess of $50.00 and therefore the defendant, if he is guilty at all, is guilty of grand larceny."

It is conceded by the State that there was no direct evidence of value and that the only testimony in the record upon which a finding of value could be based was that of the owner of the automobile describing it saying it was in excellent condition.

This is not a case where the defendant either expressly or impliedly admitted the value, nor by conduct or statements of himself or counsel, allowed it to be assumed that the matter was not disputed. His plea of not guilty cast upon the State the burden of proving every essential element of the offense by evidence sufficient to convince the jury beyond a reasonable doubt. In a charge of grand larceny, one of those essentials is that the value be greater than $50. A conviction for that offense cannot stand unless there is satisfactory evidence of the value of the property. * * * Ordinarily, judicial notice will not be taken of the value of personal property, * * * and as will later appear herein, this is unquestionably so in connection with the instruction given in this case.

We direct our attention to the argument of the prosecution that the court could take judicial notice of the value of the car and so instruct the jury: Judicial notice is the taking cognizance by the court of certain facts without the necessity of proof, * * * One class of factual material which is the subject of judicial notice is that dealt with by statute. Section 104–46–1, U.C.A.1943, provides: "Courts take judicial notice of the following facts:" and proceeds to list in eight separate categories, such things as English words, whatever is established by law, acts of departments of government, seals of courts, states and the United States, etc. It would be of no value to list them all here because the value of the car in question could not be thought to come under any subdivision of that statute by any stretch of the imagination.

* * *

Beyond the scope of the statue providing that certain matters will be taken judicial notice of, there is another class of facts which are so well known and accepted that they are judicially noticed without taking the time, trouble and expense necessary to prove them. Under this doctrine the court will consider, without proof of such generally known facts, its knowledge of what is known to all persons of ordinary intelligence. * * * The taking of judicial notice of this latter class of commonly known evidentiary facts does not establish them so conclusively as to prevent the presentation of contrary evidence or the making of a finding to the contrary. * * * Wigmore on Evidence states * * *: "(a) That a matter is judicially noticed means merely that it is taken as true without the offering proof by the party who should ordinarily have done so. This is because the court assumes that the matter is so notorious that it will not be disputed. But the opponent is not prevented from disputing the matter by evidence, if he believes it disputable."

In discussing this further, Wigmore refers to statutes which expressly provide that the judicial notice is the final determination and binding on the jury; he * * * continues: " * * * Does it signify that the settlement of the matter rests with the judge and not with the jury, that the jury are to accept the facts from the judge, and that so far as any further investigation is concerned, it is for the judge alone? Such is the view sometimes found, in decisions as well as statutes [citing statutes including Utah]. *Yet it seems rather that the jury are not concluded;* that the process of notice is intended chiefly for expedition of proof; *and remains possible for the jury to negative it."* (Emphasis added.)

Accordingly, if we assume that the value of the car is of that class of facts which is so well known that judicial notice should be taken thereof, that would not necessarily be conclusive upon the jury. It would merely take place of evidence. Upon that basis the court could have instructed the jury to this effect: If you believe from the evidence beyond a reasonable doubt that the defendant stole the automobile in question and that it was a 1947 Ford Sedan in good condition, then you may take into consideration your knowledge acquired in the every day affairs of life in determining what value you will place upon said automobile.

* * *

It is to be admitted that upon the surface there doesn't appear to be much logic to the thought that a jury would not be bound to find that the car involved here (1947 Ford 2-Door Sedan) is worth more than $50. However, under our jury system, it is traditional that in criminal cases juries can, and sometimes do, make findings which are not based on logic, nor even common sense. No matter how positive the evidence of a man's guilt may be, the jury may find him not guilty and no court has any power to do anything about it. Notwithstanding the occasional incongruous result, this system of submitting all of the facts in criminal cases to the jury and letting them be the exclusive judges thereof has lasted for some little time now and with a fair degree of success. If the result in individual cases at times seems illogical, we can be consoled by the words of Mr. Justice Holmes, that in some areas of the law, "a page of history is worth a volume of logic." We, who live with it, have a fervent devotion to the jury system, in spite of its faults. We would not like to see it destroyed nor whittled away. If a court can take one important element of an offense from the jury and determine the facts for them because such fact seems plain enough to him, then which element cannot be similarly taken away, and where would the process stop?

* * *

Judgment of the lower court is reversed and the cause remanded for a new trial.

WADE, McDONOUGH, and HENRIOD, JJ., concur.

[Dissent omitted.]

RULES OF EVIDENCE FOR UNITED STATES COURTS AND MAGISTRATES

Rule 201

JUDICIAL NOTICE OF ADJUDICATIVE FACTS

(a) Scope of rule. This rule governs only judicial notice of adjudicative facts.

(b) Kinds of facts. A judicially noticed fact must be one not subject to reasonable dispute in that it is either (1) generally known within the territorial jurisdiction of the trial court or (2) capable of accurate and ready determination by resort to sources whose accuracy cannot reasonably be questioned.

(c) When discretionary. A court may take judicial notice, whether requested or not.

(d) When mandatory. A court shall take judicial notice if requested by a party and supplied with the necessary information.

(e) Opportunity to be heard. A party is entitled upon timely request to an opportunity to be heard as to the propriety of taking judicial notice and the tenor of the matter noticed. In the absence of prior notification, the request may be made after judicial notice has been taken.

(f) Time of taking notice. Judicial notice may be taken at any stage of the proceeding.

(g) Instructing jury. In a civil action or proceeding, the court shall instruct the jury to accept as conclusive any fact judicially noticed. In a criminal case, the court shall instruct the jury that it may, but is not required to, accept as conclusive any fact judicially noticed.

B. BURDEN OF PROOF AND PRESUMPTIONS

1. PROOF BEYOND A REASONABLE DOUBT

IN RE WINSHIP

Supreme Court of the United States, 1970.
397 U.S. 358, 90 S.Ct. 1068, 25 L.Ed.2d 368.

[A twelve-year-old boy was accused of entering a locker and stealing $112 from a woman's pocketbook. The New York Family Court declared the boy "delinquent"—defined as a juvenile who commits an act that would be a crime if committed by an adult. The judge made it clear that he relied on a preponderance of the evidence standard, i. e., the evidence made it more likely than not that the boy had committed the offense, rather than applying the usual criminal burden—beyond a reasonable doubt. The judge then sentenced Winship to 18 months to 6 years in training school. On appeal, Winship's lawyers argued that the Constitution requires proof beyond a reasonable doubt in any "criminal-like" proceeding.]

Mr. Justice BRENNAN delivered the opinion of the Court.

* * * This case presents the single, narrow question whether proof beyond a reasonable doubt is among the "essentials of due process and fair treatment" required during the adjudicatory stage when a juvenile is charged with an act which would constitute a crime if committed by an adult.

* * *

The reasonable-doubt standard plays a vital role in the American scheme of criminal procedure. It is a prime instrument for reducing the risk of convictions resting on factual error. The standard provides concrete substance for the presumption of innocence—* * *.

The requirement of proof beyond a reasonable doubt has this vital role in our criminal procedure for cogent reasons. The accused during a criminal prosecution has at stake interest of immense importance, both because of the possibility that he may lose his liberty upon conviction and because of the certainty that he would be stigmatized by the conviction. * * *

Moreover, use of the reasonable-doubt standard is indispensable to command the respect and confidence of the community in applications of the criminal law. It is critical that the moral force of the criminal law not be diluted by a standard of proof that leaves people in doubt whether innocent men are being condemned. It is also important in our free society that every individual going about his ordinary affairs have confidence that his government cannot adjudge him guilty of a criminal offense without convincing a proper factfinder of his guilt with utmost certainty.

* * *

Reversed

Mr. Justice HARLAN, concurring.

* * *

* * * [w]e have before us a case where the choice of the standard of proof has made a difference: the juvenile court judge below forthrightly acknowledged that he believed by a preponderance of the evidence, but was not convinced beyond a reasonable doubt, that appellant stole $112 from the complainant's pocketbook. Moreover, even though the labels used for alternative standards of proof are vague and not a very sure guide to decisionmaking, the choice of the standard for a particular variety of adjudication does, I think, reflect a very fundamental assessment of the comparative social costs of erroneous factual determinations.

To explain why I think this so, I begin by stating two propositions, neither of which I believe can be fairly disputed. First, in a judicial proceeding in which there is a dispute about the facts of some earlier event, the factfinder cannot acquire unassailably accurate knowledge of what happened. Instead, all the factfinder can acquire is a belief of what *probably* happened. The intensity of this belief—the degree to which a factfinder is convinced that a given act actually occurred—can, of course, vary. In this regard, a standard of proof represents an attempt to instruct the factfinder concerning the degree of confidence our society thinks he should have in the correctness of factual conclusions for a particular type of adjudication. Although the phrases "preponderance of the evidence" and "proof beyond a reasonable doubt" are quantitatively imprecise, they do communicate to the finder of fact different notions concerning the degree of confidence he is expected to have in the correctness of his factual conclusions.

A second proposition, which is really nothing more than a corollary of the first, is that the trier of fact will sometimes, despite his best efforts, be wrong in his factual conclusions. In a lawsuit between two parties, a factual error can make a difference in one of two ways. First, it can result in a judgment in favor of the plaintiff when the true facts warrant a judgment for the defendant. The analogue in a criminal case would be the conviction of an innocent man. On the other hand, an erroneous factual determination can result in a judgment for the defendant when the true facts justify a judgment in plaintiff's favor. The criminal analogue would be the acquittal of a guilty man.

The standard of proof influences the relative frequency of these two types of erroneous outcomes. If, for example, the standard of proof for a criminal trial were a preponderance of the evidence rather than proof beyond a reasonable doubt, there would be a smaller risk of factual errors that result in freeing guilty persons, but a far greater risk of factual errors that result in convicting the innocent. Because the standard of proof affects the comparative frequency of these two types of erroneous outcomes, the choice of the standard to be applied in a particular kind of litigation should, in a rational world, reflect an assessment of the comparative social disutility of each.

* * *

In a criminal case, * * * we do not view the social disutility of convicting an innocent man as equivalent to the disutility of acquitting someone who is guilty. As Mr. Justice Brennan wrote for the Court in Speiser v. Randall, 357 U.S. 513, 525–526, * * * (1958):

> "There is always in litigation a margin of error, representing error in factfinding, which both parties must take into account. Where one party has at stake an interest of tran-

scending value—as a criminal defendant his liberty—this margin of error is reduced as to him by the process of placing on the other party the burden * * * of persuading the fact-finder at the conclusion of the trial of his guilt beyond a reasonable doubt."

In this context, I view the requirement of proof beyond a reasonable doubt in a criminal case as bottomed on a fundamental value determination of our society that it is far worse to convict an innocent man than to let a guilty man go free. It is only because of the nearly complete and long-standing acceptance of the reasonable-doubt standard by the States in criminal trials that the Court has not before today had to hold explicitly that due process, as an expression of fundamental procedural fairness, requires a more stringent standard for criminal trials than for ordinary civil litigation.

* * *

Mr. Chief Justice BURGER, with whom Mr. Justice STEWART joins, dissenting.

[The dissenting opinion of Mr. Chief Justice BURGER is omitted.]

KAPLAN, DECISION THEORY AND THE FACT-FINDING PROCESS
20 Stan.L.Rev. 1065, 1073–74 (1968).*

* * * One of the fundamental feelings of our society is that it is far more serious to convict an innocent man than to let a guilty man go free. * * * This attitude explains the criminal law's insistence that in order to convict, the jury must be convinced of the defendant's guilt "beyond a reasonable doubt."

We are here assuming that the defendant, if he is not guilty, is not guilty because he did not commit the act in question or because even though he did do so he did have the requisite state of mind. In both these situations the disutility of convicting him is clear (although more so in the former case). What, however, if the defendant is not guilty because he committed the crime in another state or because the statute of limitations has run? * * * Here, interestingly enough, we do not require proof beyond a reasonable doubt, but are satisfied with proof by the preponderance-of-the-evidence standard.

The very indefiniteness of the term "reasonable doubt" raises a number of issues. In civil cases where the preponderance test is used, the finder of fact is often instructed in some detail on the burden of proof; yet in criminal cases there is no such specification, even though "reasonable doubt" is a far more indefinite term. Nor do judges appear at all interested in the likelihood that reasonable

* Copyright, 1968 by Stanford Law Review.

doubt might be much more comprehensible if expressed in quantitative terms. After all, we can understand much better "a 2-out-of-3 chance" than we can "pretty probable." Similarly, we can understand 999 out of 1,000 more precisely and even intuitively than we can understand the concept of overwhelming probability.

Several reasons explain this policy. First and most obvious, if we tell the jury that they must be 99.5-percent certain of the guilt of the accused before they convict him, we are telling them that they will and indeed are expected to convict 1 innocent man in each 200 guilty verdicts. We recoil from admitting that the imperfection of knowledge and of human beings makes it inevitable that we convict some defendants who are innocent, though of course this is the case.

Probably the most important reason why we do not attempt to express reasonable doubt in terms of quantitative odds, however, is that in any rational system the utilities* (or disutilities) that determine the necessary probability of guilt will vary with the crime for which the defendant is being tried, and indeed with the particular defendant. In a criminal trial, as in any decision process, we must consider the utilities associated with differing decisions of the particular case at issue—not just the average utilities over many disparate types of criminal cases. Thus, the rational fact-finder should consider the disadvantages of convicting *this* defendant of *this* crime if he is innocent as compared with those of acquitting him if he is guilty. It is obviously far less serious to society, for instance, to acquit an embezzler, who, in any event, may find it very difficult to be placed again in a position of trust, than it would be to acquit a child molester, since the latter crime is one that tends to be repeated. The utilities, * * * will vary then, not only with the seriousness of the offense, but with the danger of its repetition.

PATTERN JURY INSTRUCTIONS (CRIMINAL CASES)

3B (West 1979).

The indictment or formal charge against a Defendant is not evidence of guilt. Indeed, the Defendant is presumed by the law to be innocent. The law does not require a Defendant to prove his innocence or produce any evidence at all, and no inference whatever may be drawn from the election of a Defendant not to testify. The Government has the burden of proving him guilty beyond a reasonable doubt, and if it fails to do so you must acquit him.

Thus, while the Government's burden of proof is a strict or heavy burden, it is not necessary that the Defendant's guilt be proved beyond all possible doubt. It is only required that the Government's

---

* By "utilities" the author means the excess of advantages over the disadvantages of a course of conduct.—Ed.

proof exclude any "reasonable doubt" concerning the Defendant's guilt. A "reasonable doubt" is a real doubt, based upon reason and common sense after careful and impartial consideration of all the evidence in the case.

Proof beyond a reasonable doubt, therefore, is proof of such a convincing character that you would be willing to rely and act upon it without hesitation in the most important of your own affairs. If you are convinced that the accused has been proved guilty beyond reasonable doubt, say so. If you are not convinced, say so.

2. PRESUMPTIONS

LILLY, AN INTRODUCTION TO THE LAW OF EVIDENCE *
47–51 (1978).

A trial involves many instances in which the trier of fact makes a factual determination by a process of inference. The factfinder first accepts the existence of a certain fact or set of facts and then infers the existence of a related fact or facts. Human experience yields countless situations in which a fact or group of facts, if believed to exist, can by the process of inferential reasoning lead to a related factual conclusion. For example, if there is evidence that a letter was addressed properly and thereafter posted, it may be inferred that the addressee received the letter. As further examples: if a vehicle is labeled with the name of a person or company, it may be inferred that the name is that of the owner; if a person can not be found and neither family nor acquaintances have heard from him for a long period of years, it may be inferred that he is dead. In each of these situations certain *basic* facts (proper mailing, name on vehicle, absence without word) support a finding of the *inferred* facts (receipt, ownership, death).

Although the number and variety of basic facts that can lead to an inferential conclusion are countless, certain patterns, such as those found in the foregoing illustrations, frequently recur. The courts and legislatures have singled out many sets of basic and inferred facts such as mailing-receipt, absence-death, labeling-ownership, and have given to them the status of presumptions. In many of these recurring instances, there appears to be a strong likelihood of the existence of the inferred or, more accurately, *presumed* conclusion. In other instances, the probative force of the basic facts may not be so convincing, yet some policy rationale or procedural convenience may make the presumed conclusion desirable. Thus, when an article is found to be damaged after having been transported by more than one carrier, a presumption is raised that the last carrier caused the damage. Here, as among several carriers, the probative value of the presumption that the damage occurred while the property was in the custody of the last carrier may appear weak. Absent any evidence

* Reprinted with permission from Lilly's "An Introduction to the Law of Evidence," West Publishing Co. (1978).

that pinpoints the cause of damage, it could be argued that it is no more probable that damage occurred while the goods were on the terminal carrier than it is that the damage occurred on one of the prior carriers. On the other hand, if the goods already were damaged at the time the last carrier took custody, it perhaps is probable that the last carrier would have noted or recorded the damaged condition. More important, the presumption here serves as a procedural device that gives to the plaintiff (who in the setting just described is disadvantaged in ascertaining the facts) a fair chance to recover by tentatively placing the damage with the last carrier.

At this point, a presumption must be distinguished from an inference. Although the language used with reference to presumptions is exasperatingly indiscriminate, a genuine presumption is raised by a basic fact or facts that, when accepted as true by the trier, give rise to a *mandatory* inference, properly called a presumed fact. Once the basic facts are believed, the resulting presumed fact must be accepted by the trier *unless* it is rebutted by contravening evidence. An inference never has such a compulsory effect. The trier always is at liberty either to accept or reject an inferred fact. Note further that because a presumption creates a compulsory finding that remains obligatory until the presumed fact is rebutted, the raising of a presumption always shifts to the opposing party the *burden of producing evidence*. This is not true of an inference, which results only in creating a jury question whether the inferred fact exists.

Although the terms "presumption" and "inference" as defined above have gained general usage, terminology in this area is not uniform. For example, judges and lawyers sometimes speak of "permissive presumptions" or "presumptions of facts," by which terms they usually mean an inference. The cases also contain the term "presumption of law," which usually means a rebuttable presumption of the kind herein denominated simply a presumption. Finally, a "conclusive presumption," often encountered in statutes, is not really a presumption at all, but rather is a rule of substantive law. This "presumption" declares that certain basic facts, once established, give rise to an *irrebuttable* conclusion. For example, it may be presumed conclusively that a child under the age of seven years cannot commit a felony. This rule, although stated in presumptive language, is merely a substantive principle that serious criminal responsibility may not be imposed upon one under the age of seven.

In criminal cases, special considerations limit the effect of presumptions. To begin with, a directed verdict against the accused is never permitted in a criminal case; in a jury trial, a conviction must rest upon a jury finding that each element of the offense was present. Accordingly, despite the common use of the term "presumption" in criminal cases, the establishment of basic facts in a criminal case only creates an inference. In criminal cases, a "presumption" still leaves the trier at all times free to reject the presumed fact.

This comports with the basic principle that the trier has the sole and unfettered responsibility of determining guilt, which must be established beyond a reasonable doubt. Consequently, the judge does not instruct the jury that upon finding certain basic facts, they must accept as true the related presumed fact. Rather, the judge instructs the jury that they *may* find the existence of the presumed fact from the basic facts.

It is probable that in a criminal case the United States Constitution forbids the use against the accused of a presumption that has a mandatory effect until sufficient rebuttal evidence is presented. Furthermore, the Constitution has been interpreted to require in criminal cases, a strong probative connection between the basic facts and the "presumed" fact. This connection must be supported by human experience such that it is *at least* more likely than not that the basic fact will be accompanied by the presumed fact. Moreover, recent cases strongly indicate that if a presumed fact is an element of an offense or operates to negate a defense, the basic facts must render the existence of the presumed fact certain beyond a reasonable doubt.

RULES OF EVIDENCE FOR UNITED STATES COURTS AND MAGISTRATES

Rule 303. Presumptions in Criminal Cases

(a) **Scope.** Except as otherwise provided by Act of Congress, in criminal cases, presumptions against an accused, recognized at common law or created by statute, including statutory provisions that certain facts are prima facie evidence of other facts or of guilt, are governed by this rule.

(b) **Submission to Jury.** The judge is not authorized to direct the jury to find a presumed fact against the accused. When the presumed fact establishes guilt or is an element of the offense or negatives a defense, the judge may submit the question of guilt or of the existence of the presumed fact to the jury, if, but only if, a reasonable juror on the evidence as a whole, including the evidence of the basic facts, could find guilt or the presumed fact beyond a reasonable doubt. When the presumed fact has a lesser effect, its existence may be submitted to the jury if the basic facts are supported by substantial evidence, or are otherwise established, unless the evidence as a whole negatives the existence of the presumed fact.

(c) **Instructing the Jury.** Whenever the existence of a presumed fact against the accused is submitted to the jury, the judge shall give an instruction that the law declares that the jury may regard the basic facts as sufficient evidence of the presumed fact but does not require it to do so. In addition, if the presumed fact establishes guilt or is an element of the offense or negatives a defense, the judge shall instruct the jury that its existence must, on all the evidence, be proved beyond a reasonable doubt.

COMMONWEALTH v. PAULEY

Supreme Judicial Court of Massachusetts, 1975.
331 N.E.2d 901, appeal dismissed sub nom. Pauley v. Massachusetts,
423 U.S. 887, 96 S.Ct. 181, 46 L.Ed.2d 119.

KAPLAN, Justice. On March 19, 1974, Alfred W. Blago, a State police officer on duty at the East Boston exit from the Callahan Tunnel, heard one of the automatic toll collection machines signal that a vehicle had passed through on its way out of the tunnel without a deposit by the operator of the proper twenty-five cent toll. Blago noted the license plate number of the car, but having no more than a side and back view of the operator, who was alone in the vehicle, he could only observe that the operator had long shoulder length hair and wore glasses. Blago did not stop the car and apprehend the operator. It may be surmised he was not in a position to do so.

Blago retrieved a copper slug from the machine, further assuring himself that the operator had violated * * * [the law] which provides that "[n]o person shall do * * * any act with intent to evade payment of toll * * *."

From the license plate number it was learned that the car was registered to the defendant, Joseph C. Pauley. Blago accordingly swore out a complaint in the East Boston District Court charging that Pauley, "being the driver of a motor vehicle which had used the Callahan Tunnel * * * did * * * deposit a copper slug * * * in a meter at the end of the tunnel with intent to evade payment of toll." After trial, Pauley was found guilty and fined the maximum $50, with costs of $12.50. Pauley appealed to the Jury of Twelve Session of the Municipal Court of the City of Boston. He then duly waived a jury. At the trial in the Municipal Court, Blago was the only witness. He testified to the incident at the tunnel as recounted above. The defendant, who was present in court, had short hair and was not wearing glasses. Blago said he could not, "under oath," make positive identification of the defendant as the operator. It was, however, stipulated that the defendant was the registered owner, and that the operator at the time and place testified to had attempted to evade payment of the toll in violation of the tunnel regulation. The Commonwealth finally offered the tunnel rules and regulations in evidence, directing the court's attention to Part Five, Section 2, which provides that "[i]f a vehicle is operated within tunnel property in violation of any provision of these rules and regulations and the identity of the operator of such vehicle cannot be determined, the person in whose name such vehicle is registered shall be deemed prima facie responsible for such violation." The regulation was received over the defendant's objection and exception. The defendant offered no evidence. The judge found him guilty and fined him $25, with costs of $6.25. No findings were made. The case is before us on a substitute bill of exceptions, and the issue is the validity as a matter of due process of the last quoted regulation, particularly the use made of it to furnish an evidential link to prove that the defendant was the person who committed the act with intent to evade the toll.

1. We turn to a closer reading of the regulation to ascertain the meaning of the expression *"prima facie* responsible." * * * To avert this result, the opponent must assume the burden of production (the burden of persuasion remains with the proponent). It is only when the opponent has introduced sufficient evidence, which, cast against the natural inferential value of the basic fact, creates an issue of fact for the trier, that the opponent has satisfied his burden and the mandatory effect disappears. In a case tried by jury where the opponent does not assume his burden, the judge should charge that if the jury find the basic fact, they are required to find the inferred fact; if the basic fact is admitted or otherwise undisputed, the judge should charge that the jury must find the inferred fact, and if the inferred fact encompasses the substance of the case, the judge should direct a verdict.

* * *

* * * The handling of unrebutted *"prima facie* evidence" in a criminal case in the Commonwealth is illustrated by the judge's charge to the jury in Commonwealth v. Anselvich, 186 Mass. 376, 71 N.E. 790 (1904). In that case a junk dealer was tried for violating a statute, R.L. c. 72, § 17, forbidding the trafficking in so called registered bottles; the statute provided that "possession by any junk dealer * * * of any such vessels, without the written consent of, or purchase from, the owner thereof, shall be *prima facie* evidence of unlawful * * * traffic in the same." The judge instructed the jury that "if this party was a junk dealer * * * the possession of these articles without the written consent of the owner, or without their having been purchased from the owner, is sufficient, and nothing else appearing, to warrant the jury in finding that he has done the things that the law prohibits him from doing. The words '*prima facie*' mean practically this: That on that evidence alone, nothing else appearing, you would be warranted in finding * * * in the words of the statute, that there was an unlawful * * * traffic in them." * * * Thus, in the absence of competing evidence, the jury were permitted, but not required, to find that the inferred or presumed fact was true beyond a reasonable doubt.

As the present case is criminal * * * it is to be assumed that the judge understood and applied the term *"prima facie* responsible" in the sense just mentioned: "nothing else appearing," the regulation permitted, but did not oblige him, to draw from the basic agreed fact that the defendant was the registered owner of the car, the inferred or presumed fact that the defendant was "responsible" for the undisputed intentional evasion of the toll by the operator of the car.

2. A line of cases in the Supreme Court of the United States has discussed the constitutional validity of the use in criminal trials of permissive inferences or presumptions structurally the same as the Massachusetts *prima facie* inference at bar. The court has upheld such inferences as applied to certain situations, and struck them down as applied to others. It has had trouble developing a rationale for its decisions. But the problems encountered are clear. If too loosely allowed, permissive inferences would tend to compromise the constitutional canon in criminal cases that "the Due Process Clause protects the accused against conviction except upon proof beyond a reasonable doubt of every fact necessary to constitute the crime with which he is charged." In re Winship, 397 U.S. 358 * * *; (1970). On the other hand, suppose the natural probability underlying the inference is strong, yet the defendant may easily produce evidence to rebut it, if false, without infringing his privilege against self-incrimination. Much can then be said for permitting the fact finder to draw the inference if persuaded that the combination of natural chance and absence from the evidence of an explanation consistent with innocence shows the defendant to be guilty beyond a reasonable doubt. * * * It should be emphasized that the permissive inference or presumption involves no shift in the burden of persuasion, which remains on the State throughout, and that the weight to be accorded the inference in all the circumstances of a particular case is for the trier in the last analysis. The trier may decline to make the inference even when the basic fact is undisputed and no rebuttal has been attempted; the trier may do so the more readily when the evidence is not altogether one-sided.

* * *

In the present case, taking what common sense suggests about the relationship of registration to operation together with the failure to produce, we think * * * that the judge as trier could justly find the defendant guilty beyond a reasonable doubt, although he was not obliged to do so. * * * As to the matter of production, in the normal course of events a defendant who was not using his car at the time of the alleged infraction should be able to demonstrate that fact with minimum effort without himself testifying, or, with no more effort, indicate why he was not in a position to make the demonstration and so should be accounted innocent. The present decision does not open the way to the unrestricted creation of statutory inferences resting on feeble foundations, for the constitutional questions would appear in a different light if the connection between basic and inferred facts were not intimate, or rebuttal evidence were less available to a defendant, or direct evidence were more readily available to the Commonwealth.

Exceptions overruled.

So ordered.

COLLATERAL READINGS

Judicial Notice

Wigmore, Evidence (3rd ed. 1940) Vol. 9, §§ 2565–2583

McCormick's Handbook of the Law of Evidence §§ 328–335 (2d ed. 1975)

Comment, The Presently Expanding Concept of Judicial Notice, 13 Vill.L.Rev. 528 (1968)

Note, Binding Effect of Judicial Notice Under the Common Knowledge Test, 21 Baylor L.Rev. 208 (1969)

Note, Judicial Notice in the Proposed Federal Rules of Evidence, 1969 Wash.U.L.Q. 453.

Roberts, Judicial Notice: An Exercise in Exorcism, 19 N.Y.L.F. 745 (1974)

The Burden of Proof and Presumptions

Wigmore, Evidence (3rd ed. 1940) Vol. 9, §§ 2490–2493, 2498a, 2499–2540

McCormick's Handbook of the Law of Evidence §§ 336–347 (2d ed. 1972)

Falknor, Notes on Presumptions, 15 Wash.L.Rev. 71 (1940)

Morgan, Further Observations on Presumptions, 16 So.Calif.L.Rev. 245 (1943)

McBaine, Burden of Proof: Degrees of Belief, 32 Calif.L.Rev. 242 (1944)

Degnan, The Law of Federal Evidence Reform, 76 Harv.L.Rev. 275 (1962)

Waters, Blood Tests and the Presumption of Legitimacy, 118 New L.J. 79 (1968)

Comment, California's Tangled Web: Blood Tests and the Conclusive Presumption of Legitimacy, 20 Stan.L.Rev. 754 (1968)

Note, Abrogation of Criminal Statutory Presumptions, 5 Suffolk U.L.Rev. 161 (1970)

Fornoff, Presumptions—The Proposed Federal Rules of Evidence, 24 Ark.L.Rev. 401 (1971)

Hayes, Use of Blood Tests in the Pursuit of Truth, 87 L.Q.Rev. 86 (1971)

Note, Criminal Presumption and Inference Instructions, 6 Willamette L.J. 497 (1971)

Dworkin, Easy Cases, Bad Law, and Burdens of Proof, 25 Vand.L. Rev. 1151 (1972)

Hug, Presumptions and Inferences in Criminal Law, 56 Mil.L.Rev. 81 (1972)

Murray and Aitken, Constitutionality of California's Under-the-Influence-of-Alcohol Presumption, 45 S.Cal.L.Rev. 955 (1972)

Note, Presumptions and Burden of Proof, 21 Loyola L.Rev. 377 (1975)

Note, Statutory Presumptions: A Permissible Instruction, 29 Ark. L.Rev. 247 (1975)

Chapter III

RELEVANCE

A. THE CONCEPT OF RELEVANT EVIDENCE

1. IN GENERAL

HARLOT v. HARLOT

1 Kings 3:16–28 (King James) (c. 650 B.C.)

Then came there two women, that were harlots, unto the king, and stood before him. And the one woman said, "O my lord, I and this woman dwell in one house; and I was delivered of a child with her in the house. And it came to pass the third day after that I was delivered, that this woman was delivered also: and we were together; there was no stranger with us in the house, save we two in the house. And this woman's child died in the night; because she overlaid it. And she arose at midnight, and took my son from beside me, while thine handmaid slept, and laid it in her bosom, and laid her dead child in my bosom. And when I rose in the morning to give my child suck, behold, it was dead: but when I had considered it in the morning, behold, it was not my son, which I did bear." And the other woman said, "Nay; but the living is my son, and the dead is thy son." And this said, "No; but the dead is thy son, and the living is my son." Thus they spoke before the king. Then said the king, "The one saith, 'This is my son that liveth, and thy son is the dead': and the other saith, 'Nay; but they son is the dead, and my son is the living.'" And the kind said, "Bring me a sword." And they brought a sword before the king. And the king said, "Divide the living child in two, and give half to the one, and half to the other." Then spoke the woman whose the living child was unto the king, for her bowels yearned upon her son, and she said, "O my lord, give her the living child, and in no wise slay it." But the other said, "Let it be neither mine nor thine, but divide it." Then the king answered and said, "Give her the living child, and in no wise slay it: she is the mother thereof." And all Israel heard of the judgment which the king had judged; and they feared the king: for they saw that the wisdom of God was in him, to do judgment.

WALTZ, CRIMINAL EVIDENCE
49–52 (1975).*

RELEVANCE

* * * Relevance is a combination of (1) materiality and (2) probativeness. If the offered item of evidence is probative of (tends to establish) a material issue in the case, it is relevant. Now we can delve more deeply into the notion of relevance.

Despite the seeming simplicity of our two-step definition, relevance is a concept that is difficult to define in a really helpful way. Relevance is easier to recognize that it is to describe. It is reminiscent of U. S. Supreme Court Justice Potter Stewart's remark about obscenity: "I can't define it but I know it when I see it."

Definitions and Tests of Relevance

Impact on the Probabilities. Relevance, in the sense of probativeness, has to do with the ability of evidence to prove or disprove a material issue. Relevance has to do with the probabilities of a situation. If we say that relevance has to do with the tendency of evidence to render a fact-issue more probably true, or untrue, than it would have been without the particular evidence, we are talking about probabilities. Will the offered evidence make the existence of a proposition (material fact-issue) probable (or *not* probable)? If it will, it has probative force and is therefore relevant.

To put it another way, the question is, Will the offered evidence *help* the fact finder?

Relevance and Circumstantial Evidence. Relevance problems, as was suggested in chapter 2 when the basic types of evidence—direct and circumstantial—were being examined, arise in connection with circumstantial evidence, since direct evidence of a material fact-issue is invariably relevant (probative) and will be ruled admissible unless it runs afoul of some special exclusionary rule such as a testimonial privilege.

Relevance Involves Content, Not Form. Relevance relates to the *content* or *substance* of evidence, not the *form* or *manner* in which the evidence is offered. Relevance, in other words, is concerned with the *subject matter* of evidence, not with how it is offered. For example, an objection based on the rule against hearsay goes to the *form* of the evidence; the evidence is being offered in the form of hearsay.

It can be said, as a general principle, that all relevant evidence is admissible if it is offered in an unobjectionable form and manner and does not violate some special exclusionary rule such as privilege.

* Copyright, 1975 by Jon R. Waltz.

Tests of Relevance. Are there any tests that can be used to detect relevance? In chapter 2 the key questions were given:

(1) What is the offered evidence being used to prove?

(2) Is this a material issue in the case?

(3) Is the offered evidence probative of (does it tend to establish) that issue?

Courts probably decide most relevance questions on the basis of (1) a "feeling" about the offered evidence, and (2) settled judicial precedent, if there is any. Judges sometimes have a feeling about evidence, an intuitive reaction to it, that is based on their experience, common sense, and knowledge of the way the world turns. Their problem with relevance questions is greatly eased, of course, if they can find a decided case by another court in which similar or identical evidence was ruled either relevant or irrelevant. Recourse to prior judicial precedent is always reassuring to judges.

Although there are few real tests for relevance, there are some significant warning signals.

Whenever in a trial one becomes aware that testimony is being brought out, or exhibits are being offered, that relate to a *time*, a *person*, or an *event* other than the time, the persons, or the events directly involved in the case that is being tried, one becomes acutely sensitive to the relevance problem.

Remoteness in time can be particularly important. A circumstance that would be relevant if it happened in close time-proximity to the event in question is irrelevant if instead it was greatly removed in time from the event in question.

Example:

To establish value of personal property, proof that similar items sold on the open market for $1,000 during the year in which the alleged larceny took place would be *relevant*. Proof that similar items sold for $1,000 twenty years earlier would be *irrelevant*.

Relevance and the State of Mankind's Knowledge. Relevance is sometimes dependent upon mankind's increasing knowledge and expertise in specialized fields. There was a day when firearms identification evidence—so-called ballistics evidence—was considered irrelevant, even preposterous. Nowadays judicial notice of its general validity will be taken. Mankind's knowledge has expanded enough to give us faith in such evidence. We have similar faith in the reliability of radar equipment, blood-alcohol testing equipment and, in some jurisdictions, so-called voiceprints. So far, no court has had sufficient faith in the reliability of polygraph tests (the "lie detector").

RULES OF EVIDENCE FOR UNITED STATES COURTS AND MAGISTRATES

Rule 401

DEFINITION OF "RELEVANT EVIDENCE"

"Relevant evidence" means evidence having any tendency to make the existence of any fact that is of consequence to the determination of the action more probable or less probable than it would be without the evidence.

Rule 402

RELEVANT EVIDENCE GENERALLY ADMISSIBLE; IRRELEVANT EVIDENCE INADMISSIBLE

All relevant evidence is admissible, except as otherwise provided by the Constitution of the United States, by Act of Congress, by these rules, or by other rules prescribed by the Supreme Court pursuant to statutory authority. Evidence which is not relevant is not admissible.

Rule 403

EXCLUSION OF RELEVANT EVIDENCE ON GROUNDS OF PREJUDICE, CONFUSION, OR WASTE OF TIME

Although relevant, evidence may be excluded if its probative value is substantially outweighed by the danger of unfair prejudice, confusion of the issues, or misleading the jury, or by considerations of undue delay, waste of time, or needless presentation of cumulative evidence.

KNAPP v. STATE

Supreme Court of Indiana, 1907.
168 Ind. 153, 79 N.E. 1076.

GILLETT, J. Appellant appeals from a judgment in the above-entitled cause, under which he stands convicted of murder in the first degree. Error is assigned on the overruling of a motion for new trial.

Appellant, as a witness in his own behalf, offered testimony tending to show a killing in self-defense. He afterwards testified, presumably for the purpose of showing that he had reason to fear the deceased, that before the killing he had heard that the deceased, who was the marshal of Hagerstown, had clubbed and seriously injured an old man in arresting him, and that he died a short time afterwards.

On appellant being asked, on cross-examination, who told him this, he answered: "Some people around Hagerstown there. I can't say as to who it was now." The state was permitted, on rebuttal, to prove by a physician, over the objection and exception of the defense, that the old man died of senility and alcoholism, and that there were no bruises or marks on his person. Counsel for appellant contend that it was error to admit this testimony; that the question was as to whether he had, in fact, heard the story, and not as to its truth or falsity. While it is laid down in the books that there must be an open and visible connection between the fact under inquiry and the evidence by which it is sought to be established, yet the connection thus required is in the logical processes only, for to require an actual connection between the two facts would be to exclude all presumptive evidence. * * * Within settled rules, the competency of testimony depends largely upon its tendency to persuade the judgment. * * * As said by Wharton: "Relevancy is that which conduces to the proof of a pertinent hypothesis." 1 Wharton, Ev. § 20. In Stevenson v. Stuart, 11 Pa. 307, it was said: "The competency of a collateral fact to be used as the basis of legitimate argument is not to be determined by the conclusiveness of the inferences it may afford in reference to the litigated fact. It is enough if these may tend in a slight degree to elucidate the inquiry, or to assist, though remotely, to a determination probably founded in truth." * * *

We are of opinion that the testimony referred to was competent. While appellant's counsel are correct in their assertion that the question was whether appellant had heard a story to the effect that the deceased had offered serious violence to the old man, yet it does not follow that the testimony complained of did not tend to negative the claim of appellant as to what he had heard. One of the first principles of human nature is the impulse to speak the truth. "This principle," says Dr. Reid, whom Professor Greenleaf quotes at length in his work on Evidence (volume 1, § 7n), "has a powerful operation, even in the greatest liars; for where they lie once they speak truth 100 times." Truth speaking preponderating, it follows that to show that there was no basis in fact for the statement appellant claims to have heard had a tendency to make it less probable that his testimony on this point was true. Indeed, since this court has not, in cases where self-defense is asserted as a justification for homicide, confined the evidence concerning the deceased to character evidence, we do not perceive how, without the possibility of a gross perversion of right, the state could be denied the opportunity to meet in the manner indicated the evidence of the defendant as to what he had heard, where he, cunningly perhaps, denies that he can remember who gave him the information. The fact proved by the state tended to discredit appellant, since it showed that somewhere between the fact and the testimony there was a person who was not a truth speaker, and, appellant being unable to point to his informant, it must at least be said that the testimony complained of had a tendency to render his claim as to what he had heard less probable.

Judgment affirmed.

REGINA v. ONUFREJCZYK

Court of Criminal Appeals of England.
I.Q.B. 388, 1 All E.R. 247 (CCA), (1955).

LORD GODDARD, C. J. The appellant, a Pole who has been in this country since 1947, was convicted before Oliver, J. at the last assizes for Swansea of the murder of his partner, another Pole, named Sykut. The trial lasted for some 12 days and was summed up with meticulous care by the judge, who analysed the evidence in what I think I might describe as a masterly fashion, and the principal question argued on this appeal is whether there was proof of what the law calls a corpus delicti. For the remarkable fact about this case—and it has remained remarkable and unexplained—is that the body of Sykut who was last seen, so far as anybody knows, on December 14, 1953, has completely disappeared, and there is no trace whatever either of him or his clothes or his ashes.

It has been submitted to us that unless the body can be found or an account given of the death, the law is that there is no proof of a corpus delicti. Corpus delicti means, first, that a crime has been committed, that is to say, that the man is dead, and that his death has been caused by a crime. * * *

Now it is perfectly clear that there is apparently no reported case in English law where a man has been convicted of murder when there has been no trace of the body at all. But it is equally clear that the fact of death, like any other fact, can be proved by circumstantial evidence, that is to say, evidence of facts which lead to one conclusion, provided that the jury are satisfied and are warned that it must lead to one conclusion only. * * *

The case against the prisoner was this: He and Sykut had a farm. The farm was a failure, and the appellant had come to the end of his resources. He was in dire need of money; of that there cannot be any doubt, for his own letters show it. He was trying to borrow money from this person and that, that relation and near friend; and he failed every time. He had actually got to the point when he was obviously considering fraud, for he was hoping to find a valuer who would overvalue the farm so that he might be able to raise more money on mortgage from his bank. Meanwhile, Sykut wanted to break off his association with the appellant. There was a suggestion that he should be paid out. Sykut had invested his money in the farm and was willing to sell his share in it for £700 if he could get it from the appellant; otherwise, Sykut had said, the farm must be put up for sale. They had been to Mr. Roberts, a solicitor of Llandilo, and their difficulties had been discussed before him. There was evidence—though for myself I do not think that it was anything like so strong or convincing, as was much of the other evidence, as to point towards murder—that the men had quarrelled; but by December 14 nothing had happened for any conclusion to be reached between the two men about the sale of the farm. Whether or not the appellant had at that time any money beyond perhaps a few shillings or a few pounds it seems clear that he had nothing at all to enable him to buy out his partner. He, the appellant, was very anxious to avoid the sale by auction and wanted to get the whole farm, because presumably he thought that if he had the whole of it he could make a satisfactory business out of it.

On December 14 Sykut disappeared, not only from Carmarthenshire, not only from England but, so far as is known, from the face of the earth. Letters came from Poland from his wife after his complete disappearance when there would have been ample time for him to have got back to Poland and to have got into touch with his friends, which would seem to show that he had not gone back to Poland; and the last person who is known to have seen Sykut is the appellant.

The appellant's activities after December 14 were certainly very remarkable. There was evidence, and very strong evidence, that the appellant must have posted a letter to a Polish woman living not very far away not later than a quarter to five, or possibly five o'clock, on December 18. In that letter he said: "My case is already completed, but I must if only for a few hours pop in to London to take from my acquaintances money. I gave my partner the gross of the money"—I suppose that means the larger part of the money—"because I borrowed for a few weeks, only I must sell what is possible. So beg you very much to help me in this matter and I will be very grateful, at the moment this is all for now, the rest we talk over when Mrs. comes over. Beg you to inquire whether it is possible to sell the poultry alive before the holidays, as I must have at least part of the money to begin something and may be some of the cattle. Hand kisses, expecting as soon as possible to see you because my partner is leaving for 14 days and might change his mind. Please don't wait a moment because it might be too late." There he is saying that he has fixed up matters with his partner, that he has paid him most of the money and that he is expecting him to go away for a few days. What we know is that the appellant went to London and that he was trying by every means in his power to borrow money from relatives there to enable him to pay off his partner. He was getting a woman, who gave evidence and who evidently impressed the judge, to forge—there is no other word for it, though she may not have known that she was forging—documents purporting to be agreements, and then adding a signature to them which purported to be the signature of Sykut, and he was giving all sorts of contradictory accounts. When he was required to give an account of how his partner disappeared, he told the sort of story that might well be found in a magazine or a detective story, or a story by the late Phillips Oppenheim, as to how a large, dark car, sometimes described as black and sometimes as green, had arrived at this lonely farm at 7:30 at night, finding its way up a dreadful rocky path; that there were three men, one of whom had had a revolver; and that the unfortunate Sykut was put into the car at the point of the revolver and driven away. That was the kind of story that was told; and yet, remarkably enough, on December 18, when a sheriff's officer had gone to the farm before 7 p.m. to levy an execution against the appellant alone, and in order to ensure that he was not levying on partnership property the officer had asked: "Where is Mr. Sykut?" he was told: "Oh, Sykut has gone to a doctor at Llandilo." According to the evidence that was given he never went to a doctor at Llandilo, but at 7:30 that night he was supposed to have been kidnapped and taken to London. ==The appellant said in his evidence that he was expecting his partner back at the farm, and yet all the letters which he wrote at that time seem to say that his partner had gone to Poland and that he would not see him back; his letters can only be explained on the footing that he knew perfectly well that his partner could never appear again.==

It seems to me that one of the matters of the greatest possible importance is that when the appellant was in London, telling all sorts of contradictory stories to the people from whom he was trying to borrow money, he made two remarkable proposals. First, he asked Mrs. Pokora, with whom he was evidently on terms of close friendship, to send him sham registered letters, that is to say, to get registered envelopes, put sheets of paper in them, and send them to him, purporting to send him a couple of hundred pounds. Another more remarkable proposal was that he actually asked that Mrs. Pokora's husband should go with him to see a solicitor at Llandilo and impersonate his partner. Could he have done that—would he have dared to do that, if he had thought that there was the smallest chance of this man appearing again? Yet he said in his evidence that he did expect Sykut to come back again. Sykut had new clothes and other property, and yet, if the appellant's story is true, he went off with these people, whether to Poland or somewhere else, leaving his clothes and everything behind and never came back or made any attempt to come back. Indeed, the appellant said that he knew one of the men, Jablonski— which I daresay is as good as any other name if one is using a Polish name—and that Mr. Jablonski had arranged to meet his partner at Paddington Station at 3 o'clock, on which day does not matter; that he went there and waited till 3 o'clock and that nobody came. Later, he said that he met Jablonski and Sykut at a Polish club and that there a document was signed; and that the signature said by the prosecution to be a forgery was affixed by Sykut in the presence of

Jablonski and another gentleman; but nobody was called from the Polish club to say that these people ever existed at all.

I do not propose to go all through the evidence called, but one very remarkable piece of evidence cannot possibly be accounted for in any way other than that the appellant was deliberately trying to manufacture evidence with regard to the life of Sykut. That was the evidence of the local blacksmith. On December 14, the last day on which anyone saw Sykut alive, the appellant had taken a horse from the farm to the blacksmith for shoeing; the horse had been fetched away from the forge by Sykut, and the blacksmith had charged 17s. 6d. for shoeing the horse. The blacksmith's evidence was perfectly clear about that. He said that there was no doubt in his mind at all about it. Whether he referred to his books or not I do not know, but I think that he did; and it was on December 14 that Sykut came and took away the horse. Later in the month, at the end of December, when the police were beginning to make inquiries, the appellant visited the blacksmith and paid him the money, and he then tried to persuade the blacksmith to say that it was on December 17 that Sykut had gone there to take the horse away. The case for the prosecution was that Sykut was dead by the 17th, having been killed either on or immediately after the 14th. December 14 was the last day on which anybody had seen that unhappy man alive. Yet here was the appellant, at the end of December, when the police had begun to make inquiries, trying to get a man whose evidence on one point was vital, to give untrue evidence as to the date on which Sykut had fetched the horse. There can be no doubt about it; the blacksmith's evidence was either true or untrue. If it was true, the appellant was trying to get him to say something untrue.

Those are all matters which were pointed out to the jury by the judge, matters on which they had the advantage of hearing counsel on both sides. It is true that the judge did not point out to the jury all the matters. A judge does very often say to a jury: "It is very remarkable that such a point has not been proved, and if it could be, it ought to have been proved." The case for the prosecution was: this man has disappeared: he has completely gone from the ken of mankind; it is impossible to believe that he is alive now. I suppose that it would have been possible for him to have got out of the country and become immured behind what is sometimes called the "iron curtain"; but here there are facts which point inevitably, as it is said irresistibly, towards the appellant being the person who knows what happened to the missing man and who disposed of that man in one way or another. It may be that it would have been desirable to emphasize to the jury that the first thing to which they must apply their minds was whether a murder had been committed; but, speaking for myself, I think that the way the judge put it in the two passages which I have read did sufficiently direct the attention of the jury to the fact that they had to be satisfied of that, and that if they

Ch. 3 RELEVANCE 37

were satisfied of the death, the violent death, of this man, they need not go any further. It is no doubt true that the prosecution relied considerably on certain minute spots in the kitchen—a minute quantity on the wall and a minute quantity on the ceiling—which were found to be blood when scientifically examined; spots so small that they might easily have escaped the attention of somebody who was trying to wash or wipe up blood. The appellant did not deny that the blood which was found was that of his partner. He said that it was due to the fact that his partner had cut his hand in the field, on one of the tractors, and that on coming in he must have shaken his hand and shaken off some blood. That, of course, was a possibility, and it was put to the jury. It was also a possibility that Sykut was disposed of in the kitchen; but there is no evidence that he was; indeed, as Mr. Elwyn Jones has very properly stressed, there is no evidence at all as to how the man met his death. But this court is of opinion that there was evidence on which the jury could infer that he did meet his death, and that he was dead; and if he was dead, the circumstances of the case point to the fact that his death was not a natural one. If that establishes, as it would, a corpus delicti, the evidence was such that the jury were entitled to find that the appellant murdered his partner.

For these reasons, we have been unable to find any misdirection by the judge, or anything in the summing up which would justify us in saying that the case was not properly presented to the jury. We have come to the conclusion that there was evidence on which the jury were entitled to find that the appellant's partner was murdered and that the appellant was the murderer, and accordingly this appeal is dismissed.

So ordered.

2. "MATHEMATICAL" RELEVANCE

CLOSING ARGUMENT, PEOPLE v. T AND W

IN THE SUPERIOR COURT OF THE STATE OF CALIFORNIA, IN AND FOR THE CITY AND COUNTY OF SAN FRANCISCO.

DEPARTMENT—EXTRA SESSION NO. 3
HONORABLE MILTON D. S_____, Judge

THE PEOPLE OF THE STATE OF CALIFORNIA, Plaintiff,
v.
JOSEPH T_____ and ERNEST W_____, Defendants

No. 39,863

A FELONY, to wit: MURDER

REPORTER'S TRANSCRIPT

September 2, 19—

APPEARANCES:

For the PEOPLE: Hon. EDMUND G. B_____,
                  District Attorney, BY:
                  NORMAN E_____, Assistant
For Defendant ERNEST W_____: District Attorney
For Defendant JOSEPH T_____: JOSEPH G_____, Esq.
                  WILLIAM L. F_____, Assistant Public Defender

(On September 10, 19—, Police Officer Charles O_____ was found dead in Dan's Creamery. He had been beaten around the face but the cause of death was a bullet wound through the body.)

People's Exhibit No. 3—A Gun.
No. 17—A bullet.

THE COURT: You may proceed with your closing argument, Mr. E_____.

Mr. E_____: Your Honor, and ladies and gentlemen of the jury:

Page 891 et seq. of transcript:

Now, did this gun, People's Exhibit No. 3, fire the shot that killed Officer O_____?

Now, Tommy F_____ says that it was; this is the gun that Joseph T_____ had with him that night. But we have additional evidence.

We have the testimony of Francis L_____. Francis L_____ says that while sometimes it is possible to tell with scientific exactness that a given bullet was fired from a given gun, because when a bullet is fired through the gun the barrel of the gun leaves on the side of the bullet microscopic markings from the barrel. He said that in this case the barrel is very badly worn. It is worn much more than the barrel of a new gun. So that any bullet which is fired through this gun fits very loosely, and I think that is evidenced too from the killing of Officer O_____. The bullet had no more force than to go through his body; it couldn't even penetrate his outside clothing. And the fact that it wasn't a tight fit leads us to the conclusion there wasn't too much force. Anyway, this gun is too badly worn. In order for him to say with scientific exactitude that this is the gun which fired the bullet which killed Officer Charles O_____, Francis L_____ does say this: He was asked, "What is the caliber of the bullet which killed Officer O_____?" Mr. L_____ says, "It is a .38 caliber." "What is the caliber of this gun?" "This is a .38 caliber gun."—So far exactly the same, except there are a number of different calibers, .22, .25, .30, .32, .38, but they happen to be the same caliber.

Now, he was asked, "What about the rifling? Is it right hand or left hand?"

He says, "The gun had a right hand rifling, right hand lands, and grooves."

"What about the rifling on the bullet?"

"That also was right hand,—was fired by a gun that had right hand lands and grooves."

Then he was asked: "How many lands and grooves?"

Remember, the lands are the high spots inside the barrel and the grooves the low spots.

"How many lands and how many grooves do you find in this gun?"

He says: "There are five lands and five grooves."

Then he was asked: "How many lands and grooves were there in the gun which fired the murder bullet?"

And he said: "There were five lands and five grooves."—Again exactly as this gun.

Then he was asked about whether he found in this gun any misalignment between the revolving cylinder of the gun and the barrel of the gun, and he said: "Yes, the gun is so badly worn that when it is fired the chamber of the cylinder comes to rest not exactly in line, but a little off center, so that when the bullet leaves the chamber of the cylinder, and enters the barrel of the revolver, a portion of the side was shaved off."

Then he was asked: "How about the bullet which killed Officer O_____?"

He says exactly the same thing, that the side of the bullet was shaved off.

Then it is clear to us that the bullet that killed Officer O_____ was fired from a revolver and not from an automatic, an automatic being a gun without the revolving cylinder, one of those black-looking affairs, quite different from this.

We know that that was the case because of the shaving off of the side of the bullet. So the bullet that killed Officer O_____ was fired from a revolver, and this is a revolver.

Now, let's consider the probabilities that are involved in a matter like this. The mathematicians can reduce probabilities to a mathematical formula, I think it is called the law of chance. It is a formula that where you can figure with mathematical precision the probabilities of a given thing happening.

Now, the murder bullet was a .38 caliber, and the gun was a .38 caliber. There are a half dozen different kinds of calibers, starting from .22, .25, .30, .32; there might be a .35, I know there is a .38, .42, .45; that is seven at least.

Let's make it one and five, the chances are one and five that a given gun against a coincidence like this happening that the caliber happens to be exactly the same as the gun, as the gun from which the bullet was fired. Then there is the question of the right and left hand rifling. The chances are one in two that a gun would be right hand or that it would be left hand. So that would be one in two. Then the matter of the five lands and five grooves; Mr. L_____ told us that there were eight lands and eight grooves, there were seven lands and seven grooves, there were six lands and six grooves, there were five, there were four; there are a great many different kinds of numbers of lands and grooves. Let's make it four to one, to make it conservative. It just happens by chance that this bullet happened to have the same number of lands and grooves as the murder revolver. Then there is the fact that the bullet was fired by a revolver with the chamber out of line with the barrel. That is a very unusual thing, but I think it would be safe to say it couldn't happen more than one time in five. I think you will probably agree that it doesn't happen more than one time in fifty, but let's say that one in five would be the probability there. Then the fact that the bullet and the gun happened—the bullet happened to be fired from the revolver, and this gun is a revolver, again one and two, because it might have been an automatic.

Now, Dr. K_____ told us about the law of chance. In the first place, it is one to five; but when you have another one to two probability it becomes one to ten; when you have another one to four probability superimposed on that, it becomes one to forty; when you have another one to five probability on that, it would be—it is one to two hundred, five times forty; when you have another one to two probability it is four hundred. So you have in this case quite a part in the testimony of Tommy F_____, who said "This is the gun we used there that night." And those figures, I think are conservative, one to four hundred, that this is the gun that was used in the killing of Officer Charles O_____ that night.

Those things just don't happen by coincidence. They didn't happen by coincidence; it doesn't happen by coincidence that the bullet was the same caliber as the gun; it doesn't happen that the barrel is out of line with the chambers of the magazine; any one of those things could happen, but it just doesn't happen in the manner that it would have to happen in this case in order that it would be just a coincidence that the bullet happens to fit the gun.

HOUTS, FROM EVIDENCE TO PROOF

132–134 (1956).*

AND IT PROBABLY DIDN'T

My dictionary defines probability as "The state or quality of being probable." Probable is then defined as "1. Having more evidence than the contrary but not proof; likely to be true or to happen, but leaving room for doubt. 2. That which renders something worthy of belief, but falling short of demonstration; as probable evidence."

Unfortunately, it has become the vogue in recent years to bolster sagging cases by applying the law of probability in an attempt to strengthen weak or nonexistent evidence.

I have discussed the matter with several mathematicians and they are unanimous in their opinions that the law of probability has absolutely no application to the forensic field. Its mathematical utility is founded on exact statistical research; and in no field of proof has this research progressed to a point sufficient to warrant the use of precise mathematical equations. I am further advised that the type of research required is not likely to come within the foreseeable future.

It is a relatively simple matter to toss a coin 10,000 times and record the number of times it lands heads and the number tails. It is a totally different matter to compile statistical data on the scale counts of human hair, the lands and grooves of bullets, striations made by crowbars or the refractive indexes of certain types of plate glass. To achieve statistical accuracy, all possible combinations and variations must be considered—a problem too staggering in magnitude to warrant the expenditures of time and money required to master it.

The proponents of this substitute for proof readily admit that they must assume or assign a probability when they prepare to launch their journeys off into mathematical space. They admit that the assumptions are arbitrary and not founded on research—or if they do claim to have research data, it turns out to be so limited and unreliable that it is actually misleading. They do not realize that to be on sound mathematical ground, the independence or dependence of the numbers or factors used must be firmly established. They then offer to cure this deficiency by meekly pledging conservatism in the assignment.

This may be well and good, except that when you multiply 10 times 10 times 10 for 15 times, the result is far from conservative.

* Copyright, 1956 by Charles C. Thomas. Publisher.

The advocates of the law of probability immediately point to fingerprints and say that this science is founded on probability. I take energetic issue with them. The value of fingerprint evidence rests on our experience in examining millions of sets of prints and in finding no two identical. As a safety factor, twelve points of identity have been established as a minimum standard before two prints are declared exactly alike. If the examiner finds these points, he makes his comparison and declares that he has a match.

He would be scorned by his professional associates if he found only five points of identity to which he assigned a probability of one in twenty and ended up with an assertion that the probabilities are one in 3,200,000 that the two prints are identical—even though only five matching points can be found.

The quickest way to discredit the conclusive probative weight accorded fingerprint evidence is to have some pseudo-expert—and some are now doing it—testify that he has counted the pores in one friction ridge and finds that there are fifteen, to which he assigns a "conservative" probability of one in ten. Thus, on the basis of one friction ridge alone, the probabilities become one in 1,000,000,000,000,000 that the two prints are identical. When it subsequently develops that the two prints were not identical, fingerprint evidence will lose much of its wallop.

A ballistics expert identifies two bullets because their markings are such that he can look at them through a comparison microscope and say that they match positively. He doesn't start counting striations and assigning a probability of one in ten to each line. If he did, he could soon reach an astronomical figure of probability that two bullets were from the same gun—even though his integrity and past experience will permit no such honest conclusion.

The handwriting expert can assume a conservative probability of one in two that the Spencerian characteristics of the questioned writing are the same as those of the known specimen. By the time he has discovered 500 letters in a note, he has a probability of a positive identification of the two writings that would stagger the expert who keeps track of the national debt. Yet, any self-respecting handwriting expert would laugh out loud at this infantile method of establishing handwriting identity.

Two tire impressions are identified because they have a sufficient number of observable, individual characteristics—not because someone reaches into a hat and assigns a probability of one to five to each of fifty or sixty lines and grooves.

I have never seen the law of probability attempted in any case where convincing proof existed. It is only applied where no solid proof exists—where something must be fabricated from nothing before one side can prevail.

As this manuscript is being prepared, Smith Edward Jordan and Robert Otis Pierce await execution in San Quentin for the murder of an Oakland cab driver. The only evidence connecting them with the scene of the crime is the testimony of an expert witness that on the basis of seven matching fiber transfers between the clothing of the victim and the defendants, the probabilities are one in 1,280,000,000 that the defendants contacted the victim and his cab.* This is the same expert who advocated the conservative probability of one in 100 billion in the Trujillo-Woodmansee case.

I have discussed this testimony with a number of leading forensic experts in the United States and they only describe it as "incredible," "unbelievable," and "utterly fantastic."

PEOPLE v. COLLINS

Supreme Court of California, 1968.
68 Cal.2d 319, 66 Cal.Rptr. 497, 438 P.2d 33.

SULLIVAN, Justice. We deal here with the novel question whether evidence of mathematical probability has been properly introduced and used by the prosecution in a criminal case. While we discern no inherent incompatibility between the disciplines of law and mathematics and intend no general disapproval or disparagement of the latter as an auxiliary in the fact-finding processes of the former, we cannot uphold the technique employed in the instant case. As we explain in detail infra, the testimony as to mathematical probability infected the case with fatal error and distorted the jury's traditional role of determining guilt or innocence according to long-settled rules. Mathematics, a veritable sorcerer in our computerized society, while assisting the trier of fact in the search for truth, must not cast a spell over him. We conclude that on the record before us defendant should not have had his guilt determined by the odds and that he is entitled to a new trial. We reverse the judgment.

A jury found defendant Malcolm Ricardo Collins and his wife defendant Janet Louise Collins guilty of second degree robbery (Pen. Code, §§ 211, 211a, 1157). Malcolm appeals from the judgment of conviction. Janet has not appealed.[1] * * *

At the seven-day trial the prosecution experienced some difficulty in establishing the identities of the perpetrators of the crime. The victim could not identify Janet and had never seen defendant. The identification by the witness Bass, who observed the girl run out of

---

* *Compare* People v. Jordan, 45 Cal.2d 697, 290 P.2d 484 (1955).

[1]. Hereafter, the term "defendant" is intended to apply only to Malcolm, but the term "defendants" to Malcolm and Janet.

the alley and get into the automobile, was incomplete as to Janet and may have been weakened as to defendant. There was also evidence, introduced by the defense, that Janet had worn light-colored clothing on the day in question, but both the victim and Bass testified that the girl they observed had worn dark clothing.

In an apparent attempt to bolster the identifications, the prosecutor called an instructor of mathematics at a state college. Through this witness he sought to establish that, assuming the robbery was committed by a Caucasian woman with a blond ponytail who left the scene accompanied by a Negro with a beard and mustache, there was an overwhelming probability that the crime was committed by any couple answering such distinctive characteristics. The witness testified in substance, to the "product rule," which states that the probability of the joint occurrence of a number of *mutually independent* events is equal to the product of the individual probabilities that each of the events will occur. *Without presenting any statistical evidence whatsoever in support of the probabilities for the factors selected*, the prosecutor then proceeded to have the witness *assume* probability factors for the various characteristics which he deemed to be shared by the guilty couple and all other couples answering to such distinctive characteristics.[10]

Applying the product rule to his own factors the prosecutor arrived at a probability that there was but one chance in 12 million that any couple possessed the distinctive characteristics of the defendants. Accordingly, under this theory, it was to be inferred that there could

---

10. Although the prosecutor insisted that the factors he used were only for illustrative purposes—to demonstrate how the probability of the occurrence of mutually independent factors affected the probability that they would occur together—he nevertheless attempted to use factors which he personally related to the distinctive characteristics of defendants. In his argument to the jury he invited the jurors to apply their own factors, and asked defense counsel to suggest what the latter would deem as reasonable. The prosecutor himself proposed the individual probabilities set out in the table below. Although the transcript of the examination of the mathematics instructor and the information volunteered by the prosecutor at that time create some uncertainty as to precisely which of the characteristics the prosecutor assigned to the individual probabilities, he restated in his argument to the jury that they should be as follows:

Characteristic	Individual Probability
A. Partly yellow automobile	1/10
B. Man with mustache	1/4
C. Girl with ponytail	1/10
D. Girl with blond hair	1/3
E. Negro man with beard	1/10
F. Interracial couple in car	1/1000

In his brief on appeal defendant agrees that the foregoing appeared on a table presented in the trial court.

be but one chance in 12 million that defendants were innocent and that another equally distinctive couple actually committed the robbery. Expanding on what he had thus purported to suggest as a hypothesis, the prosecutor offered the completely unfounded and improper testimonial assertion that, in his opinion, the factors he had assigned were "conservative estimates" and that, in reality "the chances of anyone else besides these defendants being there, * * * having every similarity, * * * is somewhat like one in a billion."

Objections were timely made to the mathematician's testimony on the grounds that it was immaterial, that it invaded the province of the jury, and that it was based on unfounded assumptions. The objections were "temporarily overruled" and the evidence admitted subject to a motion to strike. When that motion was made at the conclusion of the direct examination, the court denied it, stating that the testimony had been received only for the "purpose of illustrating the mathematical probabilities of various matters, the possibilities for them occurring or re-occurring." * * *

As we shall explain, the prosecution's introduction and use of mathematical probability statistics injected two fundamental prejudicial errors into the case: (1) The testimony itself lacked an adequate foundation both in evidence and in statistical theory; and (2) the testimony and the manner in which the prosecution used it distracted the jury from its proper and requisite function of weighing the evidence on the issue of guilt, encouraged the jurors to rely upon an engaging but logically irrelevant expert demonstration, foreclosed the possibility of an effective defense by an attorney apparently unschooled in mathematical refinements, and placed the jurors and defense counsel at a disadvantage in sifting relevant fact from inapplicable theory.

We initially consider the defects in the testimony itself. As we have indicated, the specific technique presented through the mathematician's testimony and advanced by the prosecutor to measure the probabilities in question suffered from two basic and pervasive defects—an inadequate evidentiary foundation and an inadequate proof of statistical independence. First, as to the foundation requirement, we find the record devoid of any evidence relating to any of the six individual probability factors used by the prosecutor and ascribed by him to the six characteristics as we have set them out in footnote 10, *ante*. To put it another way, the prosecution produced no evidence whatsoever showing, or from which it could be in any way inferred, that only one out of every ten cars which might have been at the scene of the robbery was partly yellow, that only one out of every four men who might have been there wore a mustache, that only one out of every ten girls who might have been there wore a ponytail, or that any of the other individual probability factors listed were even roughly accurate.[12]

The bare, inescapable fact is that the prosecution made no attempt to offer any such evidence. Instead, through leading questions having perfunctorily elicited from the witness the response that the latter could not assign a probability factor for the characteristics involved,[13] the prosecutor himself suggested what the various probabilities should be and these became the basis of the witness' testimony (see fn. 10, ante). It is a curious circumstance of this adventure in proof that the prosecutor not only made his own assertions of these factors in the hope that they were "conservative" but also in later argument to the jury invited the jurors to substitute their "estimates" should they wish to do so. We can hardly conceive of a more fatal gap in the prosecution's scheme of proof. A foundation for the admissibility of the witness' testimony was never even attempted to be laid, let alone established. His testimony was neither made to rest on his own testimonial knowledge nor presented by proper hypothetical questions based upon valid data in the record. * * *

But, as we have indicated, there was another glaring defect in the prosecution's technique, namely an inadequate proof of the statistical independence of the six factors. No proof was presented that the characteristics selected were mutually independent, even though the witness himself acknowledged that such condition was essential to the proper application of the "product rule" or "multiplication rule." [14] To the extent that the traits or characteristics were not mutually independent (e. g. Negroes with beards and men with mustaches obviously represent overlapping categories [15]), the "product rule" would

---

12. We seriously doubt that such evidence could ever be compiled since no statistician could possibly determine after the fact which cars, or which individuals "might" have been present at the scene of the robbery; certainly there is no reason to suppose that the human and automotive populations of San Pedro, California, include all potential culprits—or, conversely, that all members of these populations are proper candidates for inclusion. Thus the sample from which the relevant probabilities would have to be derived is itself undeterminable.

13. The prosecutor asked the mathematics instructor: "Now, let me see if you can be of some help to us with some independent factors, and you have some paper you may use. Your specialty does not equip you, I suppose, to give us some probability of such things as a yellow car as contrasted with any other kind of car, does it? * * * I appreciate the fact that you can't assign a probability for a car being yellow as contrasted to some other car, can you? A. No, I couldn't."

14. It is there stated that: "A trait is said to be independent of a second trait when the occurrence or non-occurrence of one does not affect the probability of the occurrence of the other trait. The multiplication rule cannot be used without some degree of error where the traits are not independent."

15. Assuming *arguendo* that factors B and E (see fn. 10, ante), were correctly estimated, nevertheless it is still arguable that most Negro men with beards *also* have mustaches (exhibit 3 herein, for instance, shows defendant

inevitably yield a wholly erroneous and exaggerated result even if all of the individual components had been determined with precision.
* * *

In the instant case, therefore, because of the aforementioned two defects—the inadequate evidentiary foundation and the inadequate proof of statistical independence—the technique employed by the prosecutor could only lead to wild conjecture without demonstrated relevancy to the issues presented. It acquired no redeeming quality from the prosecutor's statement that it was being used only "for illustrative purposes" since, as we shall point out, the prosecutor's subsequent utilization of the mathematical testimony was not confined within such limits.

We now turn to the second fundamental error caused by the probability testimony. Quite apart from our foregoing objections to the specific technique employed by the prosecution to estimate the probability in question, we think that the entire enterprise upon which the prosecution embarked, and which was directed to the objective of measuring the likelihood of a random couple possessing the characteristics allegedly distinguishing the robbers, was gravely misguided. At best, it might yield an estimate as to how infrequently bearded Negroes drive yellow cars in the company of blonde females with ponytails.

The prosecution's approach, however, could furnish the jury with absolutely no guidance on the crucial issue: *Of the admittedly few such couples, which one, if any, was guilty of committing this robbery?* Probability theory necessarily remains silent on that question, since no mathematical equation can prove beyond a reasonable doubt (1) that the guilty couple *in fact* possessed the characteristics described by the People's witnesses, or even (2) that only *one* couple possessing those distinctive characteristics could be found in the entire Los Angeles area.

As to the first inherent failing we observe that the prosecution's theory of probability rested on the assumption that the witnesses called by the People had conclusively established that the guilty couple possessed the precise characteristics relied upon by the prosecution. But no mathematical formula could ever establish beyond a reasonable doubt that the prosecution's witnesses correctly observed and accurately described the distinctive features which were employed to link defendants to the crime. * * * Conceivably, for ex-

with both a mustache and a beard, indeed in a hirsute continuum); if so, there is no basis for multiplying ¼ by ¹⁄₁₀ to estimate the proportion of Negroes who wear beards *and* mustaches. Again, the prosecution's technique could *never* be meaningfully applied, since its accurate use would call for information as to the degree of interdependence among the six individual factors.

Such information cannot be compiled, however, since the relevant sample necessarily remains unknown.

ample, the guilty couple might have included a light-skinned Negress with bleached hair rather than a Caucasian blonde; or the driver of the car might have been wearing a false beard as a disguise; or the prosecution's witnesses might simply have been unreliable.[16]

The foregoing risks of error permeate the prosecution's circumstantial case. Traditionally, the jury weighs such risks in evaluating the credibility and probative value of trial testimony, but the likelihood of human error or of falsification obviously cannot be quantified; that likelihood must therefore be excluded from any effort to assign a *number* to the probability of guilt or innocence. Confronted with an equation which purports to yield a numerical index of probable guilt, few juries could resist the temptation to accord disproportionate weight to that index; only an exceptional juror, and indeed only a defense attorney schooled in mathematics, could successfully keep in mind the fact that the probability computed by the prosecution can represent, *at best*, the likelihood that a random couple would share the characteristics testified to by the People's witnesses —*not necessarily the characteristics of the actually guilty couple.*

As to the second inherent failing in the prosecution's approach, even assuming that the first failing could be discounted, the most a mathematical computation could *ever* yield would be a measure of the probability that a random couple would possess the distinctive features in question. In the present case, for example, the prosecution attempted to compute the probability that a random couple would include a bearded Negro, a blond girl with a ponytail, and a partly yellow car; the prosecution urged that this probability was no more than one in 12 million. Even accepting this conclusion as arithmetically accurate, however, one still could not conclude that the Collinses were probably *the* guilty couple. On the contrary, as we explain in the Appendix, the prosecution's figures actually implied a likelihood of over 40 percent that the Collinses could be "duplicated" by at least *one other couple who might equally have committed the San Pedro robbery*. Urging that the Collinses be convicted on the basis of evidence which logically establishes no more than this seems as indefensible as arguing for the conviction of X on the ground that a witness saw either X or X's twin commit the crime.

Again, few defense attorneys, and certainly few jurors, could be expected to comprehend this basic flaw in the prosecution's analysis. Conceivably even the prosecutor erroneously believed that his equation established a high probability that *no* other bearded Negro in the

---

16. In the instant case, for instance, the victim could not state whether the girl had a ponytail, although the victim observed the girl as she ran away. The witness Bass, on the other hand, was sure that the girl whom he saw had a ponytail. The demonstration engaged in by the prosecutor also leaves no room for the possibility, although perhaps a small one, that the girl whom the victim and the witness observed was, in fact, the same girl.

Los Angeles area drove a yellow car accompanied by a ponytailed blonde. In any event, although his technique could demonstrate no such thing, he solemnly told the jury that he had supplied mathematical proof of guilt.

Sensing the novelty of that notion, the prosecutor told the jurors that the traditional idea of proof beyond a reasonable doubt represented "the most hackneyed, stereotyped, trite, misunderstood concept in criminal law." He sought to reconcile the jury to the risk that, under his "new math" approach to criminal jurisprudence, "on some rare occasion * * * an innocent person may be convicted." "Without taking that risk," the prosecution continued, "life would be intolerable * * * because * * * there would be immunity for the Collinses, for people who chose not to be employed to go down and push old ladies down and take their money and be immune because how could we ever be sure they are the ones who did it?"

In essence this argument of the prosecutor was calculated to persuade the jury to convict defendants whether or not they were convinced of their guilt to a moral certainty and beyond a reasonable doubt. * * * Undoubtedly the jurors were unduly impressed by the mystique of the mathematical demonstration but were unable to assess its relevancy or value. Although we make no appraisal of the proper applications of mathematical techniques in the proof of facts * * * we have strong feelings that such applications, particularly in a criminal case, must be critically examined in view of the substantial unfairness to a defendant which may result from ill conceived techniques with which the trier of fact is not technically equipped to cope. * * * We feel that the technique employed in the case before us falls into the latter category.

We conclude that the court erred in admitting over defendant's objection the evidence pertaining to the mathematical theory of probability and in denying defendant's motion to strike such evidence. * * *

The judgment is reversed.

TRAYNOR, C. J., and PETERS, TOBRINER, MOSK and BURKE, JJ., concur.

McCOMB, Justice. I dissent. I would affirm the judgment in its entirety.

[Appendix omitted.]

1,000,000,000,000,000,000,000,000,000,000 TO 1

Odds Trip Up Pair in New York Race Bet Case *

MINEOLA, L.I. A Queens woman and a Baldwin, L.I., man have been convicted in an unusual case over disputed claims to a winning parimutuel ticket worth $5,050.

* Copyright, 1976 by Newsday.

Key elements in the Nassau County Court trial were a Belmont Park racetrack computer printout of more than 350 bets made at a particular betting window on the day in question, and a Hofstra University mathematics professor's testimony that the odds against two different people independently choosing the same combination of nine $2 bets in nine races on the same day were a decillion to one.

The jury trial stemmed from a complaint to racetrack security personnel and later to the Nassau County Police and district attorney's office by a Brooklyn nurse, Rose Grant. She said she had been cheated out of her winning ticket on the track's ninth-race triple bet for May 21, 1974.

The triple is a high-return betting arrangement in which the bettor must pick the first, second and third-place finishers in exact order. At other tracks it is known as the trifecta.

According to Grant's complaint, she went to the track that day but had to leave early. She said she wrote down her picks in each of the nine races on a piece of lavatory paper before leaving. She said she gave the paper and an old, wrinkled $20 bill to a track lavatory matron, Evelyn Jones, with a request that Jones place the $2 bets as listed for her. She said Jones consented.

The next day or so she learned that her triple bet had paid off and was worth $5,050, Grant said. So she went to the track to get her winning ticket from the matron. But she said that Jones told her she had not been able to place the bets after all and that Jones handed her back her paper with the choices and a $20 bill. The bill, Grant said, was a new one and not the one she had had originally. Grant filed a complaint with the track.

Within about a week, Howard R. Graham, a retired restaurateur, tried to cash a winning ticket on that triple, Graham said he had placed his own bet. That ticket was the only winning triple ticket sold at Window 18.

Jones and Graham were indicted in January on charges of second-degree grand larceny and first-degree criminal possession of stolen property.

A computer printout of bets placed at Window 18 on May 21, 1974, showed that the precise series of 27 betting choices noted on Grant's paper had indeed been made that day. Track personnel also testified that the ticket produced by Graham came from Window 18. Assistant Dist. Atty. James Boland produced an expert witness, Hofstra mathematics Professor Sylvia Pines, who said the chances of two strangers deciding on their own to bet the same 27 choices in sequence at the same window the same day were 1,000,000,000,000,000,000,000,000,000,000 to 1.

The jury found Jones guilty of grand larceny and Graham guilty of criminal possession.

COLLATERAL READINGS

The Concept of Relevance

McCormick's Handbook of The Law of Evidence §§ 184–185, 204 (2d ed. 1972)

Weinstein and Berger, Weinstein's Evidence 401–10 to 401–37, 403–4 to 403–42 (1975)

Wigmore, Evidence §§ 27–28 (3rd ed. 1940)

James, Relevancy, Probability and the Law, 29 Calif.L.Rev. 689 (1941)

Trautman, Logical or Legal Relevancy—a Conflict in Theory, 5 Vand.L.Rev. 385 (1952)

Morgan and Maguire, Looking Backward and Forward At Evidence, 1886–1936, 50 Harv.L.Rev. 909 (1937)

Slough, Relevancy Unraveled, 5 Kans.L.Rev. 1 (1956)

Ball, The Moment of Truth: Probability Theory and the Standards of Proof, 14 Vand.L.Rev. 807 (1961)

Stoebuck, Relevancy and the Theory of Probability, 51 Iowa L.Rev. 849 (1966)

Kingston, Probability and Legal Proceedings, 57 J.Crim.L. 93 (1966)

Comment, Criminal Law: Mathematical Probabilities Misapplied to Circumstantial Evidence, 50 Minn.L.Rev. 745 (1966)

Liddle, Mathematical and Statistical Probability as a Test of Circumstantial Evidence, 19 Case Western Reserve L.Rev. 254 (1968)

Weinstein and Berger, Basic Rules of Relevancy in the Proposed Federal Rules of Evidence, 4 Ga.L.Rev. 43 (1969)

Tribe, Trial by Mathematics: Precision and Ritual in the Legal Process, 84 Harv.L.Rev. 1329 (1971)

Finkelstein and Fairley, A Comment on "Trial by Mathematics," 84 Harv.L.Rev. 1801 (1971)

Tribe, A Further Critique of Mathematical Proof, 84 Harv.L.Rev. 1810 (1971)

Comment, Evidence—Rule of Admissibility and the Law of Probability, 8 Land and Water L.Rev. 285 (1973)

Coleman and Walls, The Evaluation of Scientific Evidence, 1974 Crim.L.Rev. 276

Schmertz, Relevancy and Its Policy Counterweights: A Brief Excursion Through Article IV of the Proposed Rules of Evidence, 33 Fed.B.J. 1 (1974)

B. BALANCING THE PROBATIVE VALUE AGAINST THE PREJUDICIAL EFFECT

LILLY, AN INTRODUCTION TO THE LAW OF EVIDENCE *

29–34 (1978).

Every item of relevant evidence must be measured against several practical bases of exclusion. Thus, relevant evidence which assumptively is admissible will be rejected by the trial judge if he determines that the probative value of the evidence is outweighed by considerations of prejudice, confusion of the issues, misleading the jury, undue consumption of time, or, possibly, unfair surprise. These considerations of policy are counterweights to relevance, justifying exclusion in instances where the probative benefit of the evidence fails to outweigh the practical burdens of its admission.

The decision whether the probative value of the evidence outweighs one or more of the counterweights is made by the trial judge, usually after objection by counsel. Appellate courts wisely have reposed in the trial court considerable discretion in applying this balancing test. Unless there is a clear abuse of this discretion, no error is committed.

* * * some specific situations [recur] in which appellate courts, after an assessment of relevance and the applicable counterweights, have directed the trial court either to admit or to exclude particular items or types of evidence. These appellate pronouncements, which have hardened into absolute rules, govern the trial judge's action in resolving certain recurring evidentiary issues. Nonetheless, many issues of relevance are not governed by the foregoing rules. These issues often arise in circumstances peculiar to the case being tried. Hence, questions involving evidence claimed by the proponent to be relevant and admissible are often resolved by the trial judge on an ad hoc basis. He first determines if the proffered evidence is relevant, and he then measures the probative value of the evidence against the practical reasons for exclusion.

* * *

Federal Rule of Evidence 403, * * * generally accords with the common-law rule as developed in most federal and state cases. Two points, however, should be noted. If the balance is close between probative force and one or more counterweights, the federal rule favors admissibility. That is, it provides for exclusion only if one or more practical reasons for rejection "substantially" outweigh probative value. Further, the rule does not include, as some cases have, unfair surprise as a basis for rejecting relevant evidence. This omission represents a judgment that in cases where surprise occurs, a continuance, rather than exclusion of the evidence, is the preferred remedy.

---
* Reprinted with permission from Lilly's "An Introduction to the Law of Evidence," West Publishing Co. (1978).

RULES OF EVIDENCE FOR UNITED STATES COURTS AND MAGISTRATES

Rule 105

LIMITED ADMISSIBILITY

When evidence which is admissible as to one party or for one purpose but not admissible as to another party or for another purpose is admitted, the judge, upon request, shall restrict the evidence to its proper scope and instruct the jury accordingly.

Rule 403

EXCLUSION OF RELEVANT EVIDENCE ON GROUNDS OF PREJUDICE, CONFUSION, OR WASTE OF TIME

Although relevant, evidence may be excluded if its probative value is substantially outweighed by the danger of unfair prejudice, confusion of the issues, or misleading the jury, or by considerations of undue delay, waste of time, or needless presentation of cumulative evidence.

PEOPLE v. BURNS

District Court of Appeal of California, 1952.
109 Cal.App. 524, 241 P.2d 308.

BRAY, Justice. Defendant appeals * * * from a conviction by a jury of murder in the second degree * * *.

It is the theory of the prosecution that deceased died from being beaten about the head by defendant. The defendant contends that her death was due to injuries from falls. * * *

Over defendant's objection three photographs of deceased were admitted in evidence. They were pictures of the face, neck, and torso, taken after the autopsy. They were particularly horrible because the head was completely shaved. The head shows large incisions which had been made for the autopsy and were thereafter sewn together. In two pictures the lips were practically turned inside out and held with instruments to show the cuts. Both arms showed marks or punctures made by the surgeon, one being particularly ugly. Bruises and abrasions appear on the face, neck and arms. Most of them are quite faint. No one disputed that the deceased received them. Defendant contended that they came from the falls and striking the objects on the beach. The prosecution claimed that they came from defendant's fists and hands. How looking at the pictures would help the jury understand what caused them or how they could cause death, it is difficult to understand. The completely bald head, the surgical cuts and sutures, the ugly punctures, the inverted lips with the instruments attached, make the body so grotesque and horrible that it is doubtful if the average juror could be persuaded to look at the pictures while the witness pointed out the bruises and abrasions. In view of the fact that no question was raised as to these bruises and abrasions, and the fact that a view of them was of no particular value to the jury, it is obvious that the only purpose of exhibiting them was to inflame the jury's emotions against defendant. In Pennsylvania these photographs would be inadmissible for that reason. * * * In California it has been held that photographs of this kind are admissible even though they show marks of the incisions for the autopsy, * * * and even though they might inflame the minds of the jurors against the defendant. * * * However, in every case in which they were admitted, with the possible exception of the Burkhart case, supra, where the "evidence points positively and unmistakably to the defendant as the perpetrator of the homicide", * * * there was some necessity for exhibiting the wound or wounds to the jury. In People v. Elmore, 167 Cal. 205, 212, 138 P. 989, the court pointed out that photographs should not be offered or admitted for any purpose other than to help the jury. The admission of photographs of this type is within the sound discretion of the trial court. Surely, there is a line between admitting a photograph which is of some help to the jury in solving the facts of the case and one which is of no value other than to inflame the minds of the jurors. That line was crossed in this case. The error was not waived by the fact that after the court had admitted the photographs and the district attorney asked the doctor to point out on them the injuries shown thereon, defendant objected on the ground that the photographs speak for themselves. There was an abuse of discretion here. * * *

The judgment and order denying a new trial are reversed.

UNITED STATES v. JACKSON

United States District Court, E.D. New York, 1975.
405 F.Supp. 938.

MEMORANDUM AND ORDER

WEINSTEIN, District Judge.

Defendant, accused of robbing a bank at gunpoint, has made pretrial motions for advance rulings * * * that evidence that he used a false name on being arrested in Georgia shortly after the robbery is inadmissible because its probative value is outweighed by the risk of unfair prejudice. The motions are granted on conditions designed to prevent the defendant from gaining any unfair advantage from exclusion.

Rule 403 of the Federal Rules of Evidence grants discretion to exclude relevant evidence in the interest of preventing unfair prejudice to a party. It states: . . .

> Although relevant, evidence may be excluded if its probative value is substantially outweighed by the danger of unfair prejudice, confusion of the issues, or misleading the jury, or by considerations of undue delay, waste of time, or needless presentation of cumulative evidence."

Relevance, for purposes of the Rule, is defined by Rule 401 as a tendency to affect the trier's assessment of the probability that a factual proposition material to the outcome of the litigation is true. It reads: . . .

> "Relevant evidence" means evidence having any tendency to make the existence of any fact that is of consequence to the determination of the action more probable or less probable than it would be without the evidence."

Defendant's motion raises a complex Rule 403 question, rich in factual nuances. The bank robbery took place on August 23, 1971. Defendant was arrested in Georgia on November 7, 1971 when a local policeman thought defendant and his passengers were acting suspiciously in an area where an armed robbery had just taken place. Stopped for a traffic check, defendant had no license but did have false identification. The defendant was arrested for driving without a license. * * * Guns were found in the car. Subsequently, defendant escaped from the local jail.

Presence in another jurisdiction is arguably proof of flight resulting from consciousness of guilt. * * * Use of a false name increases the probative force of this circumstantial line of proof.

Because a person may leave a jurisdiction for any number of innocent reasons, courts are often reluctant to admit evidence of flight. See, e. g., Wong Sun v. United States, 371 U.S. 471, * * * ("[W]e have consistently doubted the probative value in criminal trials of evidence that the accused fled the scene of an actual or supposed crime."); * * *.

The probability that defendant left New York to escape arrest for the bank robbery is somewhat reduced by the fact that at the time of his departure he had been indicted by the state for * * * [another crime, an assault]. It seems improbable, however, that if he were fleeing it was from the earlier assault since the indictment had been handed up in July, 1971, and the evidence will apparently show that the defendant remained in New York until just after the bank robbery in August.

The probative value of defendant's conduct is heightened by the posture of the government's proof. It is apparent that the surveillance photographs and the eye-witness testimony are not likely to make out a completely positive identification of defendant. The government, therefore, has legitimate need for corrobative evidence. On balance, then, the Georgia events have significant probative value.

The other side of the coin under Rule 403 is the possibility that defendant will be unfairly prejudiced. The Georgia patrolman's testimony will acquaint the jury with the fact of defendant's unrelated arrest and surrounding uncomplimentary circumstances. This revelation will necessarily impinge on the protective policy of Rule 404(b) of the Federal Rules of Evidence which excludes other crimes when their primary use is to show generalized propensity to violate the law.* Even if the fact that defendant and his companions were heavily armed and subsequently escaped from the local Georgia jail were concealed, the jury might well infer from the Georgia events that defendant was engaged in a nation-wide crime spree. Beyond all this, the government's argument—flight, therefore guilty mind respecting the bank robbery, therefore guilt of that robbery—cannot be fairly evaluated without revelation of the state court indictment. This would acquaint the jury with the assault incident that resulted in a conviction the court has held inadmissible to impeach.

* * *

With the evidentiary and pertinent policy considerations in such an ambiguous posture, it is apparent that a ruling that the government's proof is either wholly admissible or wholly inadmissible would not be completely satisfactory. Accordingly, we hold that the evidence relating to defendant's arrest in Georgia will be inadmissible at trial, provided that defendant enter into a stipulation to the effect that he was in Goergia shortly after the robbery and that while there he used a false name.

* * *

CONCLUSION

At earlier pretrial proceedings in this case the court ruled that neither side may make any reference to defendant's membership in the Black Liberation Army, a militant organization of Black nationalists, even though some of its members admittedly participated in the robbery. This ruling was designed to protect the jury from prejudicial influences, to eliminate unnecessary collateral issues, and to guarantee that the trial proceeds expeditiously. The present rulings are intended to further these same objectives.

There are, of course, dangers when a trial is so hedged with restrictions and somewhat misleading presentations to the jury. Wit-

---

* "Rule 404(b): *Other crimes, wrongs, or acts.* Evidence of other crimes, wrongs, or acts is not admissible to prove the character of the person in order to show that he acted in conformity therewith. It may, however, be admissible for other purposes, such as motive, opportunity, intent, preparation, plan, knowledge, identity, or absence of mistake or accident."

Note: This rule and the reasons for it are discussed at pp. 57–100.

nesses, counsel and the court have to be wary lest some forbidden fact slip out. The jurors, who tend to be extremely sensitive to courtroom nuances, may get the impression—wholly accurate in most cases—that they are not getting the entire story and they may let their imaginations fill in the gaps to the prejudice of one side or another. Moreover, it is disquieting to be trying a carefully constructed and sanitized version of life—a kind of two dimensional cartoon rendition of the three dimensional world. But trials are not designed to get at the total truth in all its mystery; they only allow decision of narrow issues of fact and law within the limitations of a moderately effective litigation system. Given those limits, the conditions imposed in this case are justifiable.

The motions to exclude * * * are granted, subject to the conditions described.

So ordered.

C. CHARACTER EVIDENCE

1. THE INADMISSIBILITY OF THE DEFENDANT'S BAD CHARACTER

CAMUS, THE STRANGER
79–81 (1946).*

[The protagonist is awaiting trial before an Algerian Court on a charge of murdering an Arab in a brawl. The defense is self-defense. His lawyer visits him in jail] * * * [H]e said that they'd been making investigations into my private life. They had learned that my mother died recently in a home. Inquiries had been conducted at Marengo and the police informed that I'd shown "great callousness" at my mother's funeral.

"You must understand," the lawyer said, "that I don't relish having to question you about such a matter. But it has much importance, and, unless I find some way of answering the charge of 'callousness,' I shall be handicapped in conducting your defense. And that is where you, and only you can help me."

He went on to ask if I had felt grief on that "sad occasion." The question struck me as an odd one; I'd have been much embarrassed it I'd had to ask anyone a thing like that.

I answered that, of recent years, I'd rather lost the habit of noting my feelings, and hardly knew what to answer. I could truthfully say I'd been quite fond of Mother—but really that didn't mean much.

---

* Copyright, 1946 by Alfred A. Knopf, Inc. Vintage Books (A division of Random House).

All normal people, I added as an afterthought, had more or less desired the death of those they loved, at some time or another.

Here the lawyer interrupted me, looking greatly perturbed.

"You must promise me not to say anything of that sort at the trial, or to the examining magistrate."

I promised, to satisfy him, but I explained that my physical condition at any given moment often influenced my feelings. For instance, on the day I attended Mother's funeral, I was fagged out and only half awake. So, really, I hardly took stock of what was happening. Anyhow, I could assure him of one thing: that I'd rather Mother hadn't died.

The lawyer, however, looked displeased. "That's not enough," he said curtly.

After considering for a bit he asked me if he could say that on that day I had kept my feelings under control.

"No," I said. "That wouldn't be true."

He gave me a queer look, as if I slightly revolted him; then informed me, in an almost hostile tone, that in any case the head of the Home and some of the staff would be cited as witnesses.

"And that might do you a very nasty turn," he concluded.

When I suggested that Mother's death had no connection with the charge against me, he merely replied that this remark showed I'd never had any dealings with the law.

PEOPLE v. ZACKOWITZ

Court of Appeals of New York, 1939.
172 N.E. 466, 254 N.Y. 192.

[Appeal from a judgment of the Kings County Court, rendered March 25, 1930, upon a verdict convicting the defendant of the crime of murder in the first degree.]

CARDOZO, Ch. J. On November 10, 1929, shortly after midnight, the defendant in Kings county shot Frank Coppola and killed him without justification or excuse. A crime is admitted. What is doubtful is the degree only.

Four young men, of whom Coppola was one, were at work repairing an automobile in a Brooklyn street. A woman, the defendant's wife, walked by on the opposite side. One of the men spoke to her insultingly, or so at least she understood him. The defendant, who had dropped behind to buy a newspaper, came up to find his wife in tears. He was told she had been insulted, though she did not then repeat the words. Enraged, he stepped across the street and upbraided the offenders with words of coarse profanity. He informed them, so the survivors testify, that "if they did not get out of there in five minutes, he would come back and bump them all off." Rejoining his wife, he walked with her to their apartment house located close at hand. He was heated with liquor which he had been drinking at a dance. Within the apartment he induced her to tell him what the insulting words had been. A youth had asked her to lie with him, and had offered her two dollars. With rage aroused again, the defendant went back to the scene of the insult and found the four young men still working at the car. In a statement to the police, he said that he had armed himself at the apartment with a twenty-five calibre automatic pistol. In his testimony at the trial he said that this pistol had been in his pocket all the evening. Words and blows followed, and then a shot. The defendant kicked Coppola in the stomach. There is evidence that Coppola went for him with a wrench. The pistol came from the pocket, and from the pistol a single shot, which did its deadly work. The defendant walked away and at the corner met his wife who had followed him from the home. The two took a taxicab to Manhattan where they spent the rest of the night at the dwelling of a friend. On the way the defendant threw his pistol into the river. He was arrested on January 7, 1930, about two months following the crime.

At the trial the vital question was the defendant's state of mind at the moment of the homicide. Did he shoot with a deliberate and premeditated design to kill? Was he so inflamed by drink or by anger or by both combined that, though he knew the nature of his act, he was the prey to sudden impulse, the fury of the fleeting moment? * * * If he went forth from his apartment with a preconceived design to kill, how is it that he failed to shoot at once? How reconcile such a design with the drawing of the pistol later in the heat and rage of an affray? These and like questions the jurors were to ask themselves and answer before measuring the defendant's guilt. * * * Delicate enough and subtle is the inquiry, even in the most favorable conditions, with every warping influence excluded. There must be no blurring of the issues by evidence illegally admitted and carrying with it in its admission an appeal to prejudice and passion.

Evidence charged with that appeal was, we think, admitted here. Not only was it admitted, and this under objection and exception, but the changes were rung upon it by prosecutor and judge. Almost at the opening of the trial the People began the endeavor to load the defendant down with the burden of an evil character. He was to be put before the jury as a man of murderous disposition. To that end they were allowed to prove that at the time of the encounter and at that of his arrest he had in his apartment, kept there in a radio box, three pistols and a tear-gas gun. There was no claim that he had brought these weapons out at the time of the affray, no claim that with any of them he had discharged the fatal shot. He could not have done so, for they were all of different calibre. The end to be served by laying the weapons before the jury was something very different. The end was to bring persuasion that here was a man of vicious and dangerous propensities, who because of those propensities was more likely to kill with deliberate and premeditated design than a man of irreproachable life and amiable manners. Indeed, this is the very ground on which the introduction of the evidence is now explained and defended. The District Attorney tells us in his brief that the possession of the weapons characterized the defendant as "a desperate type of criminal," a "person criminally inclined." The dissenting opinion, if it puts the argument less bluntly, leaves the substance of the thought unchanged. "Defendant was presented to the jury as a man having dangerous weapons in his possession, making a selection therefrom and going forth to put into execution his threats to kill." The weapons were not brought by the defendant to the scene of the encounter. They were left in his apartment where they were incapable of harm. In such circumstances, ownership of the weapons, if it has any relevance at all, has relevance only as indicating a general disposition to make use of them thereafter, and a general disposition to make use of them thereafter is without relevance except as indicating a "desperate type of criminal," a criminal affected with a murderous propensity. * * *

If a murderous propensity may be proved against a defendant as one of the tokens of his guilt, a rule of criminal evidence, long believed to be of fundamental importance for the protection of the innocent, must be first declared away. Fundamental hitherto has been the rule that character is never an issue in a criminal prosecution unless the defendant chooses to make it one * * *. In a very real sense a defendant starts his life afresh when he stands before a jury, a prisoner at the bar. There has been a homicide in a public place. The killer admits the killing, but urges self-defense and sudden impulse. Inflexibly the law has set its face against the endeavor to fasten guilt upon him by proof of character or experience predisposing to an act of crime * * *. The endeavor has been often made, but always it has failed. At times, when the issue has been self-defense, testimony has been admitted as to the murderous propensity of the deceased, the victim of the homicide * * *, but never of such a propensity on the part of the killer. The principle back of the exclusion is one, not of logic, but of policy * * *. There may be cogency in the argument that a quarrelsome defendant is more likely to start a quarrel than one of milder type, a man of dangerous mode of life more likely than a shy recluse. The law is not blind to this, but equally it is not blind to the peril to the innocent if character is accepted as probative of crime. "The natural and inevitable tendency of the tribunal—whether judge or jury—is to give excessive weight to the vicious record of crime thus exhibited, and either to allow it to bear too strongly on the present charge, or to take the proof of it as justifying a condemnation irrespective of guilt of the present charge" * * *.

A different question would be here if the pistols had been bought in expectation of this particular encounter. They would then have been admissible as evidence of preparation and design * * *. A different question would be here if they were so connected with the crime as to identify the perpetrator, if he had dropped them, for example, at the scene of the affray * * *. They would then have been admissible as tending to implicate the possessor (if identity was disputed), no matter what the opprobrium attached to his possession. Different, also, would be the question if the defendant had been shown to have gone forth from the apartment with all the weapons on his person. To be armed from head to foot at the very moment of an encounter may be a circumstance worthy to be considered, like acts of preparation generally, as a proof of preconceived design. There can be no such implication from the ownership of weapons which one leaves behind at home.

The endeavor was to generate an atmosphere of professional criminality. It was an endeavor the more unfair in that, apart from the suspicion attaching to the possession of these weapons, there is nothing to mark the defendant as a man of evil life. He was not in crime as a business. He did not shoot as a bandit shoots in the hope of wrongful gain. He was engaged in decent calling, an optician regularly employed, without criminal record, or criminal associates. If his own testimony be true, he had gathered these weapons together as curios, a collection that interested and amused him. Perhaps his explanation of their ownership is false. There is nothing stronger than mere suspicion to guide us to an answer. Whether the explanation be false or true, he should not have been driven by the People to the necessity of offering it. Brought to answer a specific charge, and to defend himself against it, he was placed in a position where he had to defend himself against another, more general and sweeping. He was made to answer to the charge, pervasive and poisonous even if insidious and covert, that he was a man of murderous heart, of criminal disposition. * * *

The judgment of conviction should be reversed, and a new trial ordered.

[Dissent omitted.]

2. THE DEFENDANT'S RIGHT TO USE EVIDENCE OF CHARACTER

a. HIS OWN GOOD CHARACTER

LILLY, AN INTRODUCTION TO THE LAW OF EVIDENCE *
108–112 (1978).

Because most criminal acts involve deliberate conduct, it is plausible that the trier would be especially aided by knowledge of the ac-

* Reprinted with permission from Lilly's "An Introduction to the Law of Evidence," West Publishing Co. (1978).

cused's character. If the accused is generally disposed towards criminal acts, this disposition increases the likelihood that he committed the act with which he is charged. Further, the probative link between character and conduct is strengthened in cases where a *specific* character trait directly relates to particular alleged conduct. For example, the character trait of dishonesty relates directly to a criminal act involving fraud, cheating, or deception. Again, however, the probative value of character evidence must be weighed against the policies of exclusion. At least two related risks of serious prejudice to the accused attend the use of character evidence. First, the trier might accord undue probative force to evidence of the accused's bad character, using it as the major determinant of guilt in the crime charged. Secondly, the trier might deemphasize the risk of an incorrect determination of the crime charged because evidence of the accused's unfavorable character provokes the belief that he should be confined or otherwise penalized. These dangers of prejudicial effect, when combined with the counterweights of time consumption, distraction, and confusion of the issues have caused the courts to unite in a general principle: the prosecution may not initially show the defendant's bad character trait(s) for the inference that he is more likely to have committed the crime charged.

The accused, on the other hand, is entitled to use character evidence in presenting his defense. The gravity of a criminal conviction, involving the possible loss of life or liberty, has influenced all courts to give special dispensation to an accused: he is permitted to show character traits (e. g., honesty, peacefulness) inconsistent with the crime charged. The dangers of prejudice to the accused do not exist with respect to evidence of a relevant trait of "good" character offered by the accused, although the potential costs to the trial process of increased time consumption and distraction are present. The courts, however, consider paramount the accused's interest in protecting his freedom and hence they subordinate the countervailing practical considerations.

The principle that the accused may "place his character in issue," as the cases often express it, does not answer the question of what kind of evidence is admissible for this purpose. In addressing this problem, it first should be recalled that the basic requirement of all evidence is that of relevance. In the present context, the principle of relevance demands a showing that the character trait portrayed by the defendant is inconsistent with the crime charged. We have noted that this requirement would not be satisfied, for example, where an accused charged with criminal fraud offered evidence that he was a nonviolent person. Assuming, however, relevance is satisfied, there are several types of character evidence which have probative value to establish the accused's desirable character traits. These are, as we have already observed: (1) previous acts relevant to the character trait in question; (2) opinion testimony given by one or more witnesses who know the accused and who testify as to his (relevant) good character; and (3) testimony of witnesses familiar with his (relevant) good reputation.

The traditional view, which emphasizes judicial expedition, still prevails in most jurisdictions and limits the accused to evidence of his community reputation. His "character witnesses" are subjected to a comparatively brief period of interrogation during which they state their familiarity with his reputation. Increasingly, however, courts have come to doubt the existence of a community reputation for many persons, especially those who reside in large metropolitan areas. A partial escape from the restrictions of the orthodox rule is found in those jurisdictions that allow evidence of reputation within the employment community where the accused works. A more direct approach, endorsed by the Federal Rules and a minority of jurisdictions, is to permit proof of character by receiving the opinion of persons who are sufficiently familiar with the accused to be able to testify concerning the trait in question. The probative force of opinion evidence surpasses that of reputation evidence: the former is the product of direct observation and conclusion; the latter is merely the recital of an opinion or conclusion that is based on the more remote source of community hearsay.

Proof by opinion evidence may, however, involve a greater expenditure of time than proof by reputation because the cross-examiner can (within reasonable limits set by the trial judge) probe the specific occurrences and observations that underlie the opinion. Surely, however, this expenditure of time is a small price for the increased probative force of personal opinion. Additional reasons supporting the admissibility of opinion by a knowledgeable witness are, first, the practical difficulty of finding a qualified "reputation witness" willing to testify and, second, the superiority of opinion in providing the trier with a basis for making an intelligent evaluation of the subject's character.

Note, however, that most courts do not permit the accused to establish his character by introducing evidence of specific instances of past conduct. Evidence of specific occurrences is potentially the most time consuming and distracting of the three possible means of showing character. The consequence of admitting this evidence is that the principal focus of both direct and cross-examination of the character witness is upon selected past acts of the accused. These inquiries can raise collateral issues concerning the existence, number, or nature of past acts, thus exacting additional costs in time consumption, distraction, and possibly, confusion and surprise.

SAMPLE EXAMINATION OF A CHARACTER WITNESS FOR THE DEFENDANT IN A LARCENY CASE

1. What is your name, please?
2. Where do you live, Mr./Ms. (name)?
3. Where do you work now?
4. How long have you been employed there?
5. What have your job duties and responsibilities been?
6. Do you know the defendant, (name)?
7. How long have you known him/her?
8. During the period of your acquaintance with the defendant, how often have you seen him/her?
9. What is the nature of your relationship with the defendant?
10. Do you know other people who knew him/her?
11. Did you discuss with these people, or did you ever hear discussed, the defendant's reputation for honesty and integrity?
12. What generally is his/her reputation for honesty and integrity among those people?

CALIFORNIA JURY INSTRUCTIONS CRIMINAL

(4th rev. ed. West 1979.)

Evidence has been received which may tend to show the good character of the defendant for those traits ordinarily involved in the commission of a crime, such as that charged in this case.

Good character for the traits involved in the commission of the crime[s] charged may be sufficient by itself to raise a reasonable doubt as to the guilt of a defendant. It may be reasoned that a person of good character as to such traits would not be likely to commit the crime[s] of which the defendant is charged.

THEODORE ROOSEVELT AS CHARACTER WITNESS

10 Journal of the Cleveland Bar Assoc. 36 (Dec. 1938).

(Note—In this installment of the address which was delivered by President Frank J. Hogan, of the American Bar Association, before our members at the October meeting, we start with the entrance of the late President Theodore Roosevelt into the courtroom at Washington to testify as a character witness for Charles G. Glover, president of the largest national bank in the capital city.)

As Teddy Roosevelt stepped up into the room it appeared as though he had stepped on a button that would set off the applause, and first the applause started with hand clapping, and then everybody in the courtroom stood up. * * *

When quiet was restored and a few minutes passed and Roosevelt had waved to everybody whether he knew them or not, the Judge ascended the bench and we put Teddy on as the first witness.

Now, all of you, I don't know whether your rule is as strict with respect to reputation witnesses here, but in most states, of course, the witness is allowed to identify himself and then say he knows the defendant, and then he is asked whether the defendant's character or reputation for the trait involved is good or bad, and in some states they tie it down to good, bad or excellent, or very good, or something of that kind. In our jurisdiction we are allowed a little greater latitude, our Court of Appeals having held that one might have a good reputation or a superlatively good reputation, and that also we have a right to show who the character witness is so that the jury can give greater or less weight to the man who thus testifies.

But whether we had those rules of "good" or "bad" or monosyllabic responses would have made no difference to Roosevelt. Rules of evidence might be worshipped by a Wigmore, but if Roosevelt ever heard of them he heard of them only to laugh at them. (Laughter).

He was asked his name, and then many in the audience noticed what the older of this audience must know, that Theodore Roosevelt had a perpetually boy's changing voice—got a great reputation for over-emphasis which he could not help. He had a slight St. Vitus's dance which made him go as though he were going to spit something out and he could not help it any more than I can help winking one eye every now and then—one of those ties that the psychoanalyst says shows something's wrong up here. When one's voice was changing as a boy, when he was going through that period that makes mother angry when she calls up and says, "Johnny, it's dinner time," and he says, "All right (bass voice). I will be down in a minute (high-pitched voice)," and she says, "Don't both answer at once," and scolds the daughter for joining in—he had almost that kind of a voice, and, as I say, it gave a sort of an added, not practiced, unintentional emphasis to what he had to say.

And when we asked him his name, he said, "Theodore Roosevelt." (Voice breaking from bass to high-pitched). We asked what his profession was, and he said "Write." (High-pitched voice). We asked where he lived; he said, "Used to be New York." (High-pitched voice). And then without imitating him any more I will tell you he went on that way, getting that up and down. It was fascinating when you realized that the man was intensely interested in what he was saying.

He was asked whether or not he had ever lived in Washington and he twisted around to the jury, and he said, "May I state what happened without any further question?"

And I said, "Yes, go ahead."

He said, "I came to Washington as Civil Service Commissioner when conditions were very bad. Politics, politics alone, governed whether—are any of you in the government service? Oh, no. I forgot jurymen can't be in the government service. Well, those of your neighbors would be shoved in and out of office all the time, and we were trying to make something permanent in the tenure of government officials, and we did it. But it was very routine: it wasn't exciting at all; and I was called back to New York—Judge, you will remember this; you are old enough to remember it—called back to New York, and when I got there I became Police Commissioner. Oh, gentlemen of the jury, I know I can't tell you stories about it today, but it was bully fun—it was bully fun. And I was interested in that. It's fine work where the policemen are generally honest policemen, and we made them honest in New York. We did, gentlemen of the jury, and the citizens of New York would be proud of our work. Oh, but I am getting off. I am coming back, Judge. I am coming back.

"Then I came to Washington as Assistant Secretary of the Navy. That got my interest. When this country gets a great big strong navy it won't have any reason to fear anybody, and people won't be going around saying, 'I didn't raise my son to be a soldier.' You won't hear that any more because the navy will take care of it. We need a strong navy.

"I know, Judge, you are just about to tell me, but I am coming now to it. That's when I was in Washington, though." (Laughter). "And at that time I opened—I know you want me, Mr. Hogan, to say this—I opened an account at the Riggs National Bank. You know, I had a deposit at the Riggs National Bank ever since, and I had it because my faith in Mr. Glover was so great, I wouldn't take it out no matter where I lived."

There was still no stopping him. The district attorney had sense enough to know that if you stopped him you would be bowled over in some way.

He said, "Then came the Spanish-American War. That was terrible, but it was interesting, it was fine, and I had a real life for a while. Then I became governor of New York, so I was back there again for quite a while. Then, gentlemen of the jury, they made me Vice-President. It was the most terrible experience, a perfectly terrible experience. I don't think I would have lived through it if I had to take four years, but I had my account here at the Riggs National Bank as Vice-President just as I had it when I was President; and as you know, I was President for about seven and a half years, living here all the time, keeping my account at the Riggs National Bank.

"And by the way, Judge, I knew I had met you somewhere. I appointed you because of your civic righteousness, because of your interest in the poor of this city, on my committee to clean out the slums. That's what I did, and you were one of the best men on the committee I ever had. I know, gentlemen of the jury, you are glad to hear that about your Judge. I knew I recognized him. And you did splendid work." And the Judge, who was just on the soft and kindly side, was agreeing with my man, particularly when he said "You did that splendid work." He went on for some time. Then he said, "Now have I covered it?"

And I said, "Well, you have covered the fact that you had an account at the Riggs National Bank."

"And didn't I tell you why I put it there? Because of my confidence in Mr. Glover, because of his integrity, because of the splendid man he was and the fine bank he ran and what a fine credit it had all over the United States."

I said, "Yes, Colonel, you have told us that." Well; we were getting away with it. Now, we weren't doing anything wrong; we were simply presenting a man as nature had made him, and we could no more control him, parenthesis, if we wanted to, and parenthesis, (laughter) than could the judge or the jury, or the district attorney, had he attempted it.

Well, we went a little further—I won't go into all the details—and finally he was asked, "Do you know the reputation of Mr. Glover for honesty, probity, and integrity and veracity?" Getting them all in, you know.

He said, "Do I know it? Why, everybody in the city of Washington knows it. Of course. Nobody could live here, nobody could at any time have had any dealings that amounted to anything, and not know what his reputation is. It was"—

I said, "Just a moment, Colonel. You know that reputation, do you not? I am speaking now of his reputation in the community among people who knew him as you knew him."

"Well," he said "even everybody knew him, so everybody must have known the reputation as I knew it."

"All right. Now, Colonel, will you tell us what that reputation was?"

He pulled his chair forward almost to the edge of the jury platform, leaned over to the jury—he had very heavy hands, put them down on his knees, and he said "I knew Mr. Glover as a civic minded citizen who did more to make the national capitol the perfectly beautiful, outstanding capitol of the world that it is today than any other man that ever lived in America. I knew Mr. Glover as one who in all philanthropic and charitable enterprises—like the Judge; like you, Judge—would always come forward and respond, whether a neighbor or the President of the United States called him.

"I knew Mr. Glover in his home. We visited. My daughter was out there staying with his daughter. We visited out there. We visited as good old chums, because we have been very friendly, and I knew him as a family man loved by all of his own relatives and reverenced by all of his neighbors, and I knew Mr. Glover as a banker whose credit was so high, whose reputation was so fine, whose word was so good, that nobody ever questioned for a moment the safety of his deposit, whether it be large or small. That is the way I knew Mr. Glover."

And then the district attorney couldn't stand it any longer. He arose with a solemnity that I recall vividly to this day. He said, "If your Honor please, I move to strike out the entire answer of the witness. Colonel Roosevelt has said that he knew Mr. Glover in these various capacities, these various ways. He has not said a word about what his reputation was, and I move"—

The Court said, "I am with you, Mr. District Attorney; I will grant your motion," turned apologetically to Colonel Roosevelt and said, "Colonel, you have testified to your own knowledge of Mr. Glover. The rule is that you can testify only to general reputation, general repute. That's what you can do, and nothing more. So I'll have to strike out your answer. Now, please keep that in mind."

I said, "Go ahead, Colonel. Please give us your answer again, keeping the Judge's admonition in mind."

Again he turned to the Judge, again the thick finger went out. He said, "You are right. I should have known that. Thanks ever so much.

"Gentlemen of the jury, I knew Mr. Glover by general reputation and general repute—I'm right now, Judge, am I not? I am right now." (Laughter). And he went all over the whole thing again, with elaborations.

The district attorney whispered to me, "Oh, hell."

And I said, "I should have known better."

But there was no cross-examination. And then, as though that were not enough, Colonel Roosevelt, whom we had promised to let get the 11:00 o'clock train back to New York if he got through with his testimony as we thought he would, came over, and he was wearing his great big sombrero that all of you who ever saw him or pictures of him would recognize, that he always wore in campaign years, and he grabbed it and swished it in to the ladies. One of my associates was to take him to the train, and he had to pass right in front of the jury on his way out. Getting right in the middle in front of the jury, clenching his hand, using that terrific thick finger, he squatted himself as though for a football rush, and he said, "Judge or no Judge,"— * * * "Goodbye, gentlemen of the jury. I always like to appear before a jury of my fellow citizens, for you are rendering a public service. You are rendering a really great public service, just as much as the Judge there. You are here to do justice. That's why you are here—and I know you are going to do it, I know you are going to do it." (Laughter and applause).

With that he went out leaving the courtroom in a perfect storm of disorder. * * * Of course, may I add, again in parenthesis, that justice was done. (Laughter). * * *

LADD, TECHNIQUES AND THEORY OF CHARACTER TESTIMONY *

24 Iowa L.Rev. 498, 507–10, 513–15 (1938).

METHODS OF PROVING CHARACTER

The courts have readily accepted the place of character as it relates * * * to probability in criminal cases, but they have critically scrutinized the means by which character is to be proved. Many facts which might throw light upon a person's true character have been discarded by the courts, either because of dangers involved in their misuse or because of their questionable reliability as evidence of character. The problem of the time required to present collateral facts also becomes a significant element to be considered. Should particular acts of misconduct or good conduct be used by the courts in determining character? Is the personal opinion of a qualified witness an effective means of discovering what the character of a person is? Should proof of character by reputation constitute the sole means of character analysis in the court room?

Particular Acts of Misconduct. * * * Nor can the commission of similar crimes be used to show the propensity of an accused person to commit the particular acts of which he is charged. For some other purposes specific acts are admissible (for example, in criminal cases where they may be shown to prove guilty knowledge, identity, intent, and the like) but upon the issue of character this direct method is excluded. The rule precluding specific acts to prove character has but few exceptions, the most common of which is the admission of the conviction of a single crime for the purpose of impeachment of the credibility of a witness.

The objection to the use of specific acts to prove the character of a person is based largely on the time it would take and the confusion which would result from going into the many collateral issues which would arise. If the law were to permit proof of the bad acts of each witness, to allow those to be counteracted by showing the good deeds which each had done, then to endeavor to solve the truth of the existence of the good or bad deeds, and finally to permit the results to be considered as they disclose the character of the witness which in turn may have a bearing upon the truth of testimony as to other facts in the actual controversy in the litigation, all trials would become bur-

---

* Copyright, 1939 by the State University of Iowa.

dened with confusion and be endlessly prolonged. Furthermore, if the details of the past life of all witnesses were to be generally opened to investigation it would make the task of being a witness an unpopular one. There is also the question of the relation of particular acts to general tendencies. It may be reasonably contended that in most cases the general quality of the individual as an abstract observation is a more accurate basis of predicting human conduct than his occasional misdoings or good deeds. As regards the character of the accused in criminal cases there is the additional policy consideration against requiring the defendant to be prepared to defend all the events of his life rather than the particular charge against him, of which he has notice. Furthermore, if particular acts of misconduct were admitted generally as being an indication of his character there is danger that prejudice resulting from their proof might overbalance the probative value of their character-testing qualities. For these many reasons, perhaps the principal of which is the inadaptability to court procedure, particular acts of misconduct have generally been held inadmissible as proof of character except as indirectly raised in cross-examination of character witnesses to test knowledge of reputation.

Personal Opinion of Character.—Personal opinion of a witness as to the character of another witness or of one accused of crime is excluded in most jurisdictions as a means of proof. This has been severely criticised by Dean Wigmore as being historically unsound and an unfortunate rule practically. He points out that by the orthodox and original practice character witnesses regularly gave their personal opinon of the character of the person in question, and that the remarks in the earlier cases limiting proof to "general character" or "reputation" were directed against proof of particular facts and specific qualities of the witness in question but not against giving proof of character by the expression of the personal opinion of the witness testifying. The remark of Lord Ellenborough that "It is reputation; it is not what a person knows", which may be used to prove character was undoubtedly used in the above sense. Although misunderstood, it became the source of the new doctrine which appeared in Regina v. Rowton, where the court excluded personal opinion to prove character and required inquiry to be directed exclusively to reputation for character. The indirect method of proving character by general reputation rather than the direct method of proving it by personal opinion became almost universally accepted, few courts even questioning the right to ask the witness who has testified as to *X's* reputation, whether from his knowledge of that reputation he would believe *X* upon oath.

Once a rule is established it often grows because its exists. The fact that it has gained life seems to be regarded as a reason for nourishing it, although an intentional infanticide or mercy killing might have been the better course. The exclusion of the personal opinion of a qualified witness on the issue of character is a rule that has lived to the point of becoming venerable because of its age. Here and there a court escapes from its bondage, but generally a rule once made, good or bad, is hard to change. Indeed, diligent search often produces what appear to be good reasons for bad rules. * * *

Reputation as the Means of Proof of Character.—The object of the law in making reputation the test of character is to get the aggregate judgment of a community rather than the personal opinion of the witness which might be considered to be warped by his own feeling or prejudice. Even reputation must, to be admitted, be general in a community rather than based upon a limited class. While it is not necessary that a character witness know what the majority of the people of the neighborhood think of a person, he must know of the general regard with which the party is commonly held.

It is the general concurrence of a great number of people reflecting the sentiment towards the party whose character is subject to inquiry that is necessary to establish a reputation and to warrant its use as evidence. In this, the theory of the law is that trustworthiness is gained from the expressions of many people in their estimation of a person which would not be obtained by the individual opinion of a single witness, however well acquainted he might be with the party's character. The requirement that the reputation be broadly general rather than that of a particular group, such as members of a church, lodge, or the police, again emphasizes the effort to get away from a secularized and consequently biased estimate of character. Reputation testimony is based upon the hearsay of a community and although hearsay is held inadmissible to prove other facts it becomes the very source of reliability for this type of proof. If differs from rumor which is not a fixed conviction and may relate only to some particular fact rather than the general character of a person. While bad reputation is dependent upon consensus of expressed adverse opinion, good reputation may rest upon the absence of any expression or comment. The reputed character of a person is created from the slow-spreading influence of community opinion growing out of his behavior in the society in which he moves and is known, and upon this basis is accepted as proof of what his character actually is.

The confidence which the law places in reputation as the only admissible evidence of character may be seriously doubted. Surely it is more adaptable to small rural communities than to the complex organization of urban society. In the modern social life of cities with apartment house living, with limited associations in community life, with people living in one place and engaged in business in another, the language universally found in the cases about reputation in a neighborhood represents the obsolete terminology of an earlier type of living. People are not today known by their neighbors as they were a hundred years ago when the doctrine was in its development. Yet the idea of neighborhood communications is basic to the concept of reputation as distinguished from opinion. Reference to the community at large or to the vicinity makes possible a reputation in a city, but the larger the center the more scattered the sources of comment and the less possible reputation testimony becomes. The Florida court, in Hamilton v. State, recently solved the problem by permitting character witnesses to testify to the reputation of the accused in the place in the city in which she was best known. The defendant was charged with possession of stolen property, and offered to prove her reputation for honesty by persons who knew her and came into daily contact with her at the place where she had worked for several years. She was employed in a downtown hotel in Miami but lived some distance from the city. The trial court excluded the character testimony because the witnesses, although fellow employees with whom or under whose direction she worked day after day, had not visited her in her home and could not testify that they knew her reputation in the community or neighborhood where she resided. On appeal the court held the ruling erroneous, and expanded the meaning of community or neighborhood to include the place in the city where the accused was best known through her daily contact with many people. The opinion approved the admission of a reputation among a specific class of co-employees in as much as that was the only reputation that the accused had. This case shows what may be a necessary alteration of the rules relating to reputation testimony, particularly in urban society. It may show the need for returning to the admissibility of opinion rather than reputation testimony because the evidence available in this case was little more than the opinion of fellow workers that the accused was an honest person. * * *

RULES OF EVIDENCE FOR UNITED STATES COURTS AND MAGISTRATES

Rule 405

METHODS OF PROVING CHARACTER

(a) **Reputation or opinion.** In all cases in which evidence of character or a trait of character of a person is admissible, proof may be made by testimony as to reputation or by testimony in the form of an opinion. On cross-examination, inquiry is allowable into relevant specific instances of conduct.

* * *

b. CROSS–EXAMINATION OF DEFENDANT'S CHARACTER WITNESS

MICHELSON v. UNITED STATES

Supreme Court of the United States, 1948.
335 U.S. 469, 69 S.Ct. 213, 93 L.Ed. 168.

Mr. Justice JACKSON delivered the opinion of the Court.

In 1947 petitioner Michelson was convicted of bribing a federal revenue agent. The Government proved a large payment by accused to the agent for the purpose of influencing his official action. The defendant, as a witness on his own behalf, admitted passing the money but claimed it was done in response to the agent's demands, threats, solicitations, and inducements that amounted to entrapment. It is enough for our purposes to say that determination of the issue turned on whether the jury should believe the agent or the accused.

On direct examination of defendant, his own counsel brought out that, in 1927, he had been convicted of a misdemeanor having to do with trading in counterfeit watch dials. On cross-examination it appeared that in 1930, in executing an application for a license to deal in second-hand jewelry, he answered "No" to the question whether he had theretofore been arrested or summoned for any offense.

Defendant called five witnesses to prove that he enjoyed a good reputation. Two of them testified that their acquaintance with him extended over a period of about thirty years and the others said they had known him at least half that long. A typical examination in chief was as follows:

"Q. Do you know the defendant Michelson? A. Yes.

"Q. How long do you know Mr. Michelson? A. About 30 years.

"Q. Do you know other people who know him? A. Yes.

"Q. Have you had occasion to discuss his reputation for honesty and truthfulness and for being a law-abiding citizen? A. It is very good.

"Q. You have talked to others? A. Yes.

"Q. And what is his reputation? A. Very good."

These are representative of answers by three witnesses; two others replied, in substance, that they never had heard anything against Michelson.

On cross-examination, four of the witnesses were asked, in substance, this question: "Did you ever hear that Mr. Michelson on March 4, 1927, was convicted of a violation of the trademark law in New York City in regard to watches?" This referred to the twenty-year-old conviction about which defendant himself had testified on direct examination. Two of them had heard of it and two had not.

To four of these witnesses the prosecution also addressed the question the allowance of which, over defendant's objection, is claimed to be reversible error:

"Did you ever hear that on October 11th, 1920, the defendant, Solomon Michelson, was arrested for receiving stolen goods?"

None of the witnesses appears to have heard of this.

The trial court asked counsel for the prosecution, out of presence of the jury, "Is it a fact according to the best information in your possession that Michelson was arrested for receiving stolen goods?" Counsel replied that it was, and to support his good faith exhibited a paper record which defendant's counsel did not challenge.

The judge also on three occasions warned the jury, in terms that are not criticized, of the limited purpose for which this evidence was received.

Defendant-petitioner challenges the right of the prosecution so to cross-examine his character witnesses. The Court of Appeals held that it was permissible. The opinion, however, points out that the practice has been severely criticized and invites us, in one respect, to change the rule. Serious and responsible criticism has been aimed, however, not alone at the detail now questioned by the Court of Appeals but at common-law doctrine on the whole subject of proof of reputation or character. It would not be possible to appraise the usefulness and propriety of this cross-examination without consideration of the unique practice concerning character testimony, of which such cross-examination is a minor part.

Courts that follow the common-law tradition almost unanimously have come to disallow resort by the prosecution to any kind of evidence of a defendant's evil character to establish a probability of his guilt. Not that the law invests the defendant with a presumption of good character, * * * but it simply closes the whole matter of character, disposition and reputation on the prosecution's case-in-chief. The State may not show defendant's prior trouble with the law, specific criminal acts, or ill name among his neighbors, even though such facts might logically be persuasive that he is by propensity a probable perpetrator of the crime. The inquiry is not rejected because character is irrelevant; on the contrary, it is said to weigh too much with the jury and to so overpersuade them as to prejudge one with a bad general record and deny him a fair opportunity to defend against a particular charge. The overriding policy of excluding such evidence, despite its admitted probative value, is the practical experience that its disallowance tends to prevent confusion of issues, unfair surprise and undue prejudice.

But this line of inquiry firmly denied to the State is opened to the defendant because character is relevant in resolving probabilities of guilt. He may introduce affirmative testimony that the general estimate of his character is so favorable that the jury may infer that he would not be likely to commit the offense charged. This privilege is sometimes valuable to a defendant for this Court has held that such testimony alone, in some circumstances, may be enough to raise a reasonable doubt of guilt and that in the federal courts a jury in a proper case should be so instructed.

When the defendant elects to initiate a character inquiry, another anomalous rule comes into play. Not only is he permitted to call witnesses to testify from hearsay, but indeed such a witness is not allowed to base his testimony on anything but hearsay. What commonly is called "character evidence" is only such when "character" is employed as a synonym for "reputation." The witness may not testify about defendant's specific acts or courses of conduct or his possession of a particular disposition or of benign mental and moral traits; nor can he testify that his own acquaintance, observation, and knowledge of defendant leads to his own independent opinion that defendant possesses a good general or specific character, inconsistent with commission of acts charged. The witness is, however, allowed to summarize what he has heard in the community, although much of it may have been said by persons less qualified to judge than himself. The evidence which the law permits is not as to the personality of defendant but only as to the shadow his daily life has cast in his neighborhood.

* * *

While courts have recognized logical grounds for criticism of this type of opinion-based-on-hearsay testimony, it is said to be justified by "overwhelming considerations of practical convenience" in avoiding innumerable collateral issues which, if it were attempted to prove character by direct testimony, would complicate and confuse the trial, distract the minds of jurymen and befog the chief issues in the litigation.

* * *

Thus the law extends helpful but illogical options to a defendant. Experience taught a necessity that they be counterweighted with equally illogical conditions to keep the advantage from becoming an unfair and unreasonable one. The price a defendant must pay for attempting to prove his good name is to throw open the entire subject which the law has kept closed for his benefit and to make himself vulnerable where the law otherwise shields him. The prosecution may pursue the inquiry with contradictory witnesses to show that damaging rumors, whether or not well-grounded, were afloat—for it is not the man that he is, but the name that he has which is put in issue. Another hazard is that his own witness is subject to cross-examination as to the contents and extent of the hearsay on which he bases his conclusions, and he may be required to disclose rumors and reports that are current even if they do not affect his own conclusion. It may test the sufficiency of his knowledge by asking what stories were circulating concerning events, such as one's arrest, about which people normally comment and speculate. Thus, while the law gives defendant the option to show as a fact that his reputation reflects a life and habit incompatible with commission of the offense charged, it subjects his proof to tests of credibility designed to prevent him from profiting by a mere parade of partisans.

* * *

Wide discretion is accompanied by heavy responsibility on trial courts to protect the practice from any misuse. The trial judge was scrupulous to so guard it in the case before us. He took pains to ascertain, out of presence of the jury, that the target of the question was an actual event, which would probably result in some comment among acquaintances if not injury to defendant's reputation. He satisfied himself that counsel was not merely taking a random shot at a reputation imprudently exposed or asking a groundless question to waft an unwarranted innuendo into the jury box.

The question permitted by the trial court, however, involves several features that may be worthy of comment. Its form invited hearsay; it asked about an arrest, not a conviction, and for an offense not closely similar to the one on trial; and it concerned an occurrence many years past.

* * *

Arrest without more does not, in law any more than in reason, impeach the integrity or impair the credibility of a witness. It happens to the innocent as well as the guilty. Only a conviction, therefore, may be inquired about to undermine the trustworthiness of a witness.

Arrest without more may nevertheless impair or cloud one's reputation. False arrest may do that. Even to be acquitted may damage one's good name if the community receives the verdict with a wink and chooses to remember defendant as one who ought to have been convicted. A conviction, on the other hand, may be accepted as a misfortune or an injustice, and even enhance the standing of one who mends his ways and lives it down. Reputation is the net balance of so many debits and credits that the law does not attach the finality to a conviction when the issue is reputation, that is given to it when the issue is the credibility of the convict.

The inquiry as to an arrest is permissible also because the prosecution has a right to test the qualifications of the witness to bespeak the community opinion. If one never heard the speculations and rumors in which even one's friends indulge upon his arrest, the jury may doubt whether he is capable of giving any very reliable conclusions as to his reputation.

* * *

The inquiry here concerned an arrest twenty-seven years before the trial. Events a generation old are likely to be lived down and dropped from the present thought and talk of the community and to be absent from the knowledge of younger or more recent acquaintances. The court in its discretion may well exclude inquiry about rumors of an event so remote, unless recent misconduct revived them. But two of these witnesses dated their acquaintance with defendant as commencing thirty years before the trial. Defendant, on direct examination, voluntarily called attention to his conviction twenty years before. While the jury might conclude that a matter so old and indecisive as a 1920 arrest would shed little light on the present reputation and hence propensities of the defendant, we cannot say that, in the context of this evidence and in the absence of objection on this specific ground, its admission was an abuse of discretion.

* * *

The judgment is affirmed.

[A concurring opinion by Mr. Justice FRANKFURTER and a dissenting opinion by Mr. Justice RUTLEDGE are omitted]

c. THE CHARACTER OF THE VICTIM

COMMONWEALTH v. CASTELLANA

Supreme Court of Pennsylvania, 1923.
277 Pa. 117, 121 A. 50.

MOSCHZISKER, C. J. Defendant, Mike Castellana, appeals from a sentence on a conviction of murder of the first degree. The homicide occurred March 16, 1922. The fact that appellant killed the deceased, Paul Siena, was not contested at trial. The defense was as follows: Siena and Castellana had known each other in a friendly way for at least six years, Edith Rizzo, a sister of the latter, having lived at one time with the former; during a walk these two men were taking together on the day of the homicide, Siena insisted Edith should return to him, and Castellana, while not opposing his companion's desire, expressed the opinion it would not be complied with; after more of such talk, Siena drew a revolver, pressed it against Castellana and said, unless the sister resumed her former life with him, he would kill defendant and the "whole Castellana family" (a threat which he wished the jury to believe deceased had repeated to third parties on other occasions, though uncommunicated to Castellana); defendant, in fright, ran away, and, having first picked up a club, entered a barn, to which he was pursued by Siena, with the pistol in his hand; a struggle followed, wherein Castellana, after striking Siena with the club, wrested the revolver from him, and then, according to defendant's testimony (which the verdict shows was not accepted by the jury), he shot and killed deceased in order to defend himself from what he says was a murderous assault.

The commonwealth contended that Siena was not the aggressor; we find no testimony indicating that Castellana bore on his person any marks of violence; but the body of deceased showed a fracture about an inch long on the top of the head, a shot in the left breast, and the throat cut from ear to ear. This last-mentioned injury defendant made no attempt to explain. * * *

Defendant testified, in support of his plea of self-defense, that deceased had made a wicked and unprovoked attack on him, with a deadly weapon, as set forth more fully at the beginning of this opinion. In rebuttal, the commonwealth was permitted, over the objection of defendant, to introduce evidence of the reputation of deceased as a peaceable and law-abiding citizen, the trial judge stating, when he made his rulings in this regard, that he allowed the testimony because of the nature of the defense; these rulings are criticized in several specifications of error.

It is highly improbable the rulings in question affected the verdict, for the kind of evidence objected to was given by only two witnesses, one of whom admitted he really knew nothing of deceased's reputation, while, so far as the record indicates, little was made of the testimony of the other; nevertheless we shall give full consideration to the guiding principles which govern the matters of complaint, and which should control the question of the admissibility of the evidence here attacked.

One on trial for an offense against the criminal law is allowed to introduce evidence of his good reputation in any respect which has "proper relation to the subject-matter" of the charge at issue * * * ; this is permitted on the theory that general reputation reflects the character and a person with a good character for peaceableness, for example, would not in all reasonable probability commit an unlawful act of violence. Wigmore on Evidence, § 55, and cases there cited. Such evidence may of itself prove sufficient to acquit the accused * * *, or it may create a reasonable doubt of guilt and thus acquit * * * ; but to create or to clear up a doubt is "not the only office of evidence of good character; * * * it is substantive evidence to be weighed and considered in connection with all the other evidence in the case." * * *. This kind of proof is allowed to the defendant in a criminal court because, as said in Hanney v. Com., supra, one accused of crime may be able to produce no evidence except his own oath and proof of good character to exculpate himself from the charge against him. On the same theory, when a prisoner sets up a defense, like the one at bar, wherein he charges the deceased with an act of personal violence against him, and thereby becomes the accuser and makes deceased the accused, why should not the commonwealth, the only one that can answer for the accused deceased, in reply to this charge, have the same privilege as the defendant when a similar charge is made against him, and be allowed to put in evidence the good reputation of the deceased (who in this instance is the accused) as a peaceable citizen?

The question just asked is raised by the assignments now under consideration, and, so far as the decisions of this court are concerned, is one of first impression. The general rule seems to be that the state cannot, in the first instance, offer evidence of deceased's reputation as a peaceable citizen, for, until attacked by the defense, his reputation is presumed to be good * * * but when evidence sufficient to impeach the character of deceased and overcome this presumption is admitted on behalf of defendant, the state may, in rebuttal, offer proof of the peaceable character of deceased. The real difficulty, wherein the courts take widely different views, is met in determining just what constitutes such an attack on the character of deceased as to permit this rebuttal testimony.

Although seemingly it is not the view of the majority of jurisdictions * * *, yet in at least two states the plea of self-defense, accompanied by evidence tending to support it, has been treated as sufficient to open the door to rebuttal offers of deceased's reputation for peaceableness * * *; it is not necessary, however, to go that far in the present case.

Without regard to the rules which govern the admission of testimony to show the character of the deceased when such proofs are introduced to throw light on alleged apprehensions of a defendant caused by aggressions of the former, we are of opinion that evidence of the peaceable character of the deceased may be received, on an issue of self-defense, when the circumstances of a case so warrant, in order to show the improbability of his having made the aggressions attributed to him (and, where evidence is admitted on this theory, it is immaterial whether or not defendant had knowledge of deceased's good reputation. * * * just as in the numerous cases where testimony of deceased's bad reputation was admitted, in support of a plea of self-defense, for the purpose of corroborating defendant's allegations of violent acts on the part of the former. * * *

The argument usually made against the admission of testimony of the character under discussion is that it would tend to open the door to proof of collateral matters, and thus confuse the jury and unduly extend the trial. * * * A like argument might as well be made against permitting evidence of the good reputation of defendant; but it loses force in either case when we remember that such testimony is properly confined to the mere fact of general reputation, the courts refusing to permit proofs of particular acts.

To return to the case in hand, the prisoner's sole plea was the affirmative one of self-defense, and to prove this, which he was obliged to do in order to secure an acquittal, he became the accuser of the deceased, charging that the latter, without provocation, attacked him with a deadly weapon; to sustain this allegation, he produced a number of witnesses, who while not expressly called to establish the bad reputation of Siena, all gave testimony tending to show, and with the evident purpose of proving, that as a matter of fact deceased was a bad and dangerous man who would be likely to commit an assault such as that charged. Surely, on this state of the proofs, the fact that Siena was a peaceable, law-abiding citizen was a relevant circumstance, tending to prove the improbability of his having done the unlawful acts of violence alleged against him by defendant, and therefore it was proper to admit the evidence assigned as error. At least, this rule ought to prevail in a case like the one at bar, where, because defendant and deceased were the only persons present, no actual witness to the occurrence under investigation could be called by the commonwealth, which was obliged to depend for its entire proofs on the (somewhat self-serving) confessions of the prisoner, certain points made against him on cross-examination, and the physical facts in the case.

* * *

It must be admitted that reported instances are rare where evidence of the kind here received was admitted on the offer of the commonwealth; we are not prepared to hold, however, that, under the peculiar circumstances of this case, the admission of such testimony presents reversible error. It remains but to say we have read the evidence and think it fully warrants the verdict; for this reason, and those already given, the assignments of error are overruled.

The judgment is affirmed and the record remitted to the court below, for the purpose of execution.

CARDOZO, THE NATURE OF THE JUDICIAL PROCESS

156–157 (1921).*

* * * The considerations of policy that dictate adherence to existing rules where substantive rights are involved, apply with diminished force when it is a question of the law of remedies. Let me take an illustration from the law of evidence. A man is prosecuted for rape. His defense is that the woman consented. He may show that her *reputation* for chastity is bad. He may not show specific, even though repeated, acts of unchastity with another man or other men. The one thing that any sensible trier of the facts would wish to know above all others in estimating the truth of his defense, is held by an inflexible rule, to be something that must be excluded from the consideration of the jury. * * *

Undoubtedly a judge should exercise a certain discretion in the admission of such evidence, should exclude it if too remote, and should be prompt by granting a continuance or otherwise to obviate

---

*Copyright, 1921 by Yale University Press.

any hardship resulting from surprise. That is not the effect of the present rule. The evidence is excluded altogether and always. Some courts, indeed, have taken a different view, but their number unfortunately is small. Here, as in many other branches of the law of evidence we see on exaggerated reliance upon general reputation as a test for the ascertainment of the character of litigants or witnesses. Such a faith is a survival of more simple times. It was justified in days when men lived in small communities. Perhaps it has some justification even now in rural districts. In the life of great cities, it has made evidence of character a farce. * * *

NOTE

Where the defendant introduces evidence attacking the character of the victim does this open the door to the prosecution's similarly attacking the character of the defendant? See Roberson v. State, 91 Okla.Crim. 217, 218 P.2d 414 (1950).

RULES OF EVIDENCE FOR UNITED STATES COURTS AND MAGISTRATES

Rule 404

CHARACTER EVIDENCE NOT ADMISSIBLE TO PROVE CONDUCT; EXCEPTIONS; OTHER CRIMES

(a) **Character evidence generally.** Evidence of a person's character or a trait of his character is not admissible for the purpose of proving that he acted in conformity therewith on a particular occasion, except:

(1) *Character of accused.* Evidence of a pertinent trait of his character offered by an accused or by the prosecution to rebut the same;

(2) *Character of victim.* Evidence of a pertinent trait of character of the victim of the crime offered by an accused, or by the prosecution to rebut the same, or evidence of a character trait of peacefulness of the victim offered by the prosecution in a homicide case to rebut evidence that the victim was the first aggressor;

(3) *Character of witness.* * * * [See pp. 257, 266, 268].

(b) **Other crimes, wrongs, or acts.** Evidence of other crimes, wrongs, or acts is not admissible to prove the character of a person in order to show that he acted in conformity therewith. It may, however, be admissible for other purposes, such as proof of motive, opportunity, intent, preparation, plan, knowledge, identity, or absence of mistake or accident.

Rule 412

RAPE CASES; RELEVANCE OF VICTIM'S PAST BEHAVIOR

(a) Notwithstanding any other provision of law, in a criminal case in which a person is accused of rape or of assault with intent to commit rape, reputation or opinion evidence of the past sexual behavior of an alleged victim of such rape or assault is not admissible.

(b) Notwithstanding any other provision of law, in a criminal case in which a person is accused of rape or of assault with intent to commit rape, evidence of a victim's past sexual behavior other than reputation or opinion evidence is also not admissible, unless such evidence other than reputation or opinion evidence is—

(1) admitted in accordance with subdivisions (c)(1) and (c)(2) and is constitutionally required to be admitted; or

(2) admitted in accordance with subdivision (c) and is evidence of—

(A) past sexual behavior with persons other than the accused, offered by the accused upon the issue of whether the accused was or was not, with respect to the alleged victim, the source of semen or injury; or

(B) past sexual behavior with the accused and is offered by the accused upon the issue of whether the alleged victim consented to the sexual behavior with respect to which rape or assault is alleged.

(c)(1) If the person accused of committing rape or assault with intent to commit rape intends to offer under subdivision (b) evidence of specific instances of the alleged victim's past sexual behavior, the accused shall make a written motion to offer such evidence not later than fifteen days before the date on which the trial in which such evidence is to be offered is scheduled to begin, except that the court may allow the motion to be made at a later date, including during trial, if the court determines either that the evidence is newly discovered and could not have been obtained earlier through the exercise of due diligence or that the issue to which such evidence relates has newly arisen in the case. Any motion made under this paragraph shall be served on all other parties and on the alleged victim.

(2) The motion described in paragraph (1) shall be accompanied by a written offer of proof. If the court determines that the offer of proof contains evidence described in subdivision (b), the court shall order a hearing in chambers to determine if such evidence is admissible. At such hearing the parties may call witnesses, including the alleged victim, and offer relevant evidence. Notwithstanding subdivision (b) of rule 104, if the relevancy of the evidence which the

accused seeks to offer in the trial depends upon the fulfillment of a condition of fact, the court, at the hearing in chambers or at a subsequent hearing in chambers scheduled for such purpose, shall accept evidence on the issue of whether such condition of fact is fulfilled and shall determine such issue.

(3) If the court determines on the basis of the hearing described in paragraph (2) that the evidence which the accused seeks to offer is relevant and that the probative value of such evidence outweighs the danger of unfair prejudice, such evidence shall be admissible in the trial to the extent an order made by the court specifies evidence which may be offered and areas with respect to which the alleged victim may be examined or cross-examined.

(d) For purposes of this rule, the term "past sexual behavior" means sexual behavior other than the sexual behavior with respect to which rape or assault with intent to commit rape is alleged.

BERGER, MAN'S TRIAL, WOMAN'S TRIBULATION: RAPE CASES IN THE COURTROOM

77 Colum.L.Rev. 1 (1977).*

In the past few years over half the states have enacted "rape shield" laws designed to control or even prohibit the use of evidence respecting the rape complainant's chastity. In addition, bills on this subject are constantly being introduced in the legislatures of other states and in Congress as well. Meanwhile, several organizations and some of their members have issued calls for legal reform ranging from general exhortations to detailed, well thought-out proposals.

What different forms do the many recent statutes take? Virtually all explicitly scuttle the traditional (often unstated) assumption that the victim's history should come in, at least when garbed in the dull raiment of reputation. Iowa's law is typical in affirming a new exclusionary norm: "In prosecutions for the crime of rape, evidence of the prosecuting witness' previous sexual conduct shall not be admitted, nor reference made thereto in the presence of the jury, *except* as provided herein. Almost every new statute also makes some kind of special provision for proof of prior sexual relations with the defendant, allowing it either in every case or on a showing of materiality. Regarding other substantive standards, the laws present no unified picture. But one can at least discern patterns or orientations that indicate the range of solutions adopted or under consideration.

Broadly, individual laws might be classified by where they fall on a spectrum of views of admissibility: from highly restrictive to highly permissive. Louisiana furnishes one example of a type of statute favoring the victim. It bans all use of evidence of the woman's prior sexual conduct or reputation for chastity "except for inci-

* Copyright, 1977 by Columbia Law Review.

dents arising out of the victim's relationship with the accused." Michigan provides another, somewhat different version of a strict exclusionary preference. Its law admits only conduct with the defendant and "specific instances of sexual activity showing the source or origin of semen, pregnancy, or disease," if the proof "is material to a fact at issue" and "its inflammatory or prejudicial nature does not outweigh its probative value."

At the opposite pole are Texas and New Mexico, which admit sexual history evidence of any variety whatsoever if, and to the extent that, the judge believes probative value exceeds prejudice. Also in the defendant's corner is the scheme adopted by New York, which first states a rule of exclusion, then lists specific exemptions (such as, for instance, prior activity with the accused), and finally appends a catchall provision allowing in evidence "determined by the court * * * to be relevant and admissible in the interests of justice." One might ask why legislatures bothered to enact statutes such as these. Trial judges already possess broad discretion to exclude relevant items of proof that tend unduly to confuse, delay or unfairly prejudice the proceedings. Arguably, laws like New York's may admit certain evidence absolutely while automatically barring nothing, thus theoretically narrowing the court's inherent powers of exclusion and expanding the material's admissibility. In practice, however, such a result is most unlikely and seems contrary to the drafters' intent. At a minimum the laws fulfill the purpose of flagging attention to the problem: warning defendants not to count on using evidence of unchastity, spurring prosecutors to object to its introduction, and reminding judges that this kind of proof is presumptively inadmissible and merits extremely careful scrutiny. The hope is that a clear change in the spirit of the rules will lead to a change in their application.

The bulk of the statutes fall somewhere in between the extremes of victim or defendant orientation. Minnesota's law, for example, expresses a principle of exclusion but then provides for admission of certain classes of proof where probative value outweighs prejudice. Unlike the restrictive Michigan scheme, it allows in more than evidence of previous conduct with the accused or specific instances of sexual activity bearing on the source of certain listed physical conditions. Subject to the balancing test, the statute also states in somewhat intricate fashion: "When consent or fabrication by the complainant is the defense * * * evidence of [the complainant's previous sexual] conduct tending to establish a common scheme or plan of similar sexual conduct under circumstances similar to the case at issue * * * [shall be admitted]." But "[e]vidence of such conduct engaged in more than one year prior to the date of the alleged offense is inadmissible" under this heading. Finally, the statute permits introduction of sexual proof for the purpose of impeachment when the victim herself raises the subject of her chastity and accordingly opens the door to rebuttal. * * *

Up to this point the statutes have been grouped quite grossly, in terms of their relative receptivity to proof of the victim's sexual history. One could draw other, not unrelated, distinctions as well. For example, quite a few of the laws expressly differentiate between substantive use of the evidence and admission solely to impeach the complainant's credibility; others make no such discrimination. California, in a pattern followed by some other states, prohibits—with only two exceptions—the introduction of this proof in order to show that the woman consented. The Act, however, cautions that nothing within the law "shall be comstrued to make inadmissible any evidence offered to attack the credibility of the complaining witness * * *." Florida, by contrast, states a general rule of exclusion for proof of the victim's sexual conduct with third parties, but provides for admission under certain conditions when the victim's consent is placed in issue; impeachment is not referred to at all. Jurisdictions taking this approach do not indicate when, if ever, the defense may attack the complainant's story by means of sexual history evidence. As shall be seen, some kinds of impeachment (for instance, for bias) may be so crucial to the defendant that restriction of his right to offer evidence on the issue would amount to a constitutional infringement. Therefore, drafters of rape shield laws had best deal with this subject directly since statutory slippage here could imperil the whole attempt at change.

One can also distinguish the laws that differentiate types of evidence rather than, or in addition to, the questions on which the proof is relevant. Several statutes cover only specific acts, not evidence of reputation; the vast majority, however, embrace all methods of proof within the general exclusionary ban. Moreover, one could group some of the varied statutes according to their explicit exceptions. It has been mentioned that the new laws regard relations with the defendant as admissible, conditionally or absolutely. Two other common exemptions (again, qualified or complete) are evidence to counter the state's showing of prior chastity or to prove the source or origin of semen, pregnancy or disease. A few jurisdictions impose time limits (often, a year) in order to eliminate stale evidence of sexual character or expressly provide for impeachment by prior felony convictions—presumably referring to a record for serious sexual offenses. With respect to other specific exceptions, the laws present a hodge-podge of individual provisions. Some of the more important ones would admit evidence tending to show: that the victim had a motive to lie; that she engaged in voluntary sexual relations "with any person under particular and characteristic circumstances sufficiently similar to those of the encounter with the defendant * * * as to establish that she consented * * *"; or that the accused (reasonably) believed the woman was willing, even if she in fact was not.

In procedural as well as substantive ways the rape shield statutes attempt to alter prior practice respecting proof of sexual history. California's scheme is typical: In order to use such evidence as the law does not entirely bar, the accused must first make a written motion accompanied by an affidavit stating his offer of proof of relevance. If the court finds the offer sufficient, it orders a hearing away from the jury to determine whether the proposed material meets applicable legal standards. On ruling in the defendant's favor, the judge "may make an order stating what evidence may be introduced * * * and the nature of the questions to be permitted. The defendant may then offer evidence pursuant to the order of the court."

Unlike California, some jurisdictions do not specify a written motion or affidavit; indeed, a few set no pre-hearing requirements at all. States also differ on whether a hearing is mandatory, or, as in the statute described above, conditioned upon an adequate offer. With respect to the hearing, further points of distinction include: necessity for a court order, with or without findings of fact; provision for questioning the victim or other potential witnesses; and mandates governing time and place and who may attend. Most of the laws do not discuss the form of the hearing but do ultimately call for an order. A majority also expressly demand that proceedings regarding admissibility occur in camera or otherwise out of the jury's hearing. On matters of timing the laws vary as to whether they posit a hearing before or during trial or simply prior to the proof's admission. A few statutes fail to provide for any kind of preliminary procedure: hearing, motion or offer of proof. In these jurisdictions substantive standards are very restrictive, and therefore there is little need to anticipate evidentiary battles.

Some of the foregoing seemingly minor variations present practical or even constitutional problems. Unhappily, many reform efforts, well-meant but ill-conceived, pose more dilemmas than they resolve. Drafters of future rape shield statutes should take care that, in lightening the heavy burden of victims, they do not merely shift the weight of oppression onto the backs of hapless defendants.

D. OTHERWISE RELEVANT ACTS—WHICH MAY ALSO SHOW CHARACTER—OTHER CRIMES

TRAUTMAN, LOGICAL OR LEGAL RELEVANCY— A CONFLICT IN THEORY

5 Vand.L.Rev. 385, 403–05 (1952).*

(a) *The Rule of Absolute Exclusion*

At the outset it is important to define and distinguish the rule of absolute exclusion from the rule of discretionary exclusion by the trial judge. It is generally agreed that there is a rule of absolute exclusion with respect to evidence of other crimes offered as substantive evidence. But unfortunately there is a basic conflict in the authorities as to what that rule is. A rational approach to the problem would seek to identify the basis of exclusion, and if it is one of judicial policy, to define precisely its scope so as to avoid future uncertainty.

The great majority of American jurisdictions state the rule in the form of a broad rule excluding all evidence of other crimes committed by the accused:

> "The general rule of evidence applicable to criminal trials is that the state cannot prove against a defendant any crime not alleged in the indictment, either as a foundation for a separate punishment, or as aiding the proofs that he is guilty of the crime charged."

To this broad rule of exclusion the courts applying it then provide a long list of exceptions admitting evidence of other crimes by the accused when it is logically relevant to prove the identity, motive, intent, guilty knowledge, design plan or common scheme; when the other crime is an inseparable part of the crime in question (*"res gestae"*); to contradict claims of accident or mistake; and sometimes to contradict sweeping assertions of virtue and good conduct by the accused. The scope of these exceptions is so broad as to have prompted the remark that "it is difficult to determine which is the more extensive, the doctrine or the acknowledged exceptions."

The excellent research of Professor Julius Stone on the history and development of the rule of absolute exclusion has persuasively demonstrated that originally this rule was a very narrow one,—that if the offered evidence is relevant solely by a series of inferences which proceed from the other crimes to the disposition of the accused to commit such crimes, and thence to the probability of his having committed the crime charged, it is not admissible. Under this narrow rule evidence of other crimes (which does not depend upon evil

---

* Copyright, 1952 by the Vanderbilt University Press.

dispositions as a basis of logical inference) may be freely admitted in the discretion of the trial judge whenever it is logically relevant to either an ultimate or intermediate probandum before the court; not just in case it can be fitted into the pigeonhole of an exception to the broad rule of exclusion, but rather because it is completely outside the scope of the rule of absolute exclusion. "As so easily occurs in the common law, however, the tendency to crystallize particular determinations of relevance into categories of admissibility appeared. Toward the middle of the century the notion appears that the register of types of relevant similar facts is closed. From that position to the position that the register of types of admissible similar facts is closed is but a short step."

The rule of narrow exclusion originally announced by the early English and American decisions has been given new life in recent years by the American Law Institute's Model Code of Evidence. Rule 9(f) provides that "all relevant evidence is admissible"; Rule 303 provides for the area of discretionary exclusion; and Rule 311 makes explicit the policy of absolute exclusion in the following words:

> "* * * evidence that a person committed a crime or civil wrong on a specified occasion is inadmissible as tending to prove that he committed a crime or civil wrong on another occasion if, but only if, the evidence is relevant solely as tending to prove his disposition to commit such a crime or civil wrong or to commit crimes or civil wrongs generally."

The precission and simplicity of the rule of narrow exclusion is also attracting the attention of the courts. It was excellently stated in affirmative style in a recent opinion by Chief Justice Gibson of the California Supreme Court:

> "It is settled in this state that except when it shows merely criminal disposition, evidence which tends logically and by reasonable inference to establish any fact material for the prosecution, or to overcome any material fact sought to be proved by the defense, is admissible although it may connect the accused with an offense not included in the charge."

There are several important advantages to the narrow rule of absolute exclusion and its statement in affirmative form. It makes clear the basis of exclusion and directs the attention of the trial courts to the question of logical relevancy. But even more important to the thesis of this paper is the fact that the particular policy of exclusion so identified can now be evaluated in terms of efficient judicial administration. * * *

McCORMICK'S HANDBOOK OF THE LAW OF EVIDENCE
447–454 (2d ed. 1972).*

Character to Evidence Conduct—(c) Application of Rule of Exclusion to Forbid the Prosecution to Introduce Evidence Initially of Bad Character of Accused: Other Crimes.

The disfavor for receiving proof of the character of a person as evidence that on a particular occasion he acted in keeping with his disposition is strongly felt when the state seeks to show that the accused is a bad man and thus more likely to have committed the crime. The long-established rule, accordingly, forbids the prosecution, unless and until the accused gives evidence of his good character, to introduce initially evidence of the bad character of the accused. It is not irrelevant, but in the setting of jury trial the danger of prejudice outweighs the probative value.

This danger is at its highest when character is shown by other criminal acts, and the rule about the proof of other crimes is but an application of the wider prohibition against the initial introduction by the prosecution of evidence of bad character. The rule is that the prosecution may not introduce evidence of other criminal acts of the accused unless the evidence is substantially relevant for some other purpose than to show a probability that he committed the crime on trial because he is a man of criminal character.[32] There are numer-

---

* Copyright, 1972 by West Pub. Co.

32. For a similar formulation see Model Code of Evidence Rule 311: "* * * evidence that a person committed a crime or civil wrong on a specified occasion is inadmissible as tending to prove that he committed a crime or civil wrong on another occasion if, but only if, the evidence is relevant solely as tending to prove his disposition to commit such a crime or civil wrong or to commit crimes or civil wrongs generally." * * *

See also Uniform Rule 55: * * * evidence that a person committed a crime or civil wrong on a specified occasion, is inadmissible to prove his disposition to commit crime or civil wrong as the basis for an inference that he committed another crime or civil wrong on another specified occasion but, * * * such evidence is admissible when relevant to prove some other material fact including absence of mistake or accident, motive, opportunity, intent, preparation, plan, knowledge or identity." To similar effect is F.R.Ev. 404(b) [see pp. —].

A frequent form of statement is a general rule that evidence of other crimes is inadmissible except when offered for certain particular named purposes. See, e. g., People v. Molineux, 168 N. Y. 264, 61 N.E. 286, 293, 294 (1901): "The general rule of evidence applicable to criminal trials is that the state cannot prove against a defendant any crime not alleged in the indictment, either as a foundation for a separate punishment, or as aiding the proofs that he is guilty of the crime charged. * * * The exceptions to the rule cannot be stated with categorical precision. Generally speaking, evidence of other crimes is competent to prove the specific crime charged when it tends to establish (1) motive; (2) intent; (3) the absence of mistake or accident; (4) a common scheme or plan embracing the commission of two or more crimes so related to each other that proof of one tends to establish the others; (5) the identity of the person charged with the commission of the crime on trial." In that case, a prosecution for murder by poisoning, the evidence was held not to fit any of these exceptions.

ous other purposes for which evidence of other criminal acts may be offered, and when so offered the rule of exclusion is simply inapplicable. Some of these purposes are listed below but warning must be given that the list is not complete, for the range of relevancy outside the ban is almost infinite; and further that the purposes are not mutually exclusive, for a particular line of proof may fall within several of them. Neither are they strictly coordinate. Some are phrased in terms of the immediate inferences sought to be drawn, such as plan or motive, others in terms of the ultimate fact, such as knowledge, intent, or identity which the prosecution seeks to establish.[33] The list follows.

(1) To complete the story of the crime on trial by proving its immediate context of happenings near in time and place.[34] This is often characterized as proving a part of the "same transaction" or the "res gestae."

(2) To prove the existence of a larger continuing plan, scheme, or conspiracy, of which the present crime on trial is a part.[35] This

---

A similar statement of the rule has sometimes been embodied in statutes.

The spirit of the rule condemns not only evidence of other crimes not independently relevant, but also questions which, though negatively answered, carry with them the insinuation that the accused committed the other crimes. * * *

[33]. "Motive, intent, absence of mistake, plan and identity are not really all on the same plane. Intent, absence of mistake, and identity are facts in issue—*facta probanda*. Motive, plan, or scheme are *facta probantia*, and may tend to show any *facta probanda*." Stone, op. cit., 51 Harv.L.Rev. 988, 1026n.

[34]. State v. Villavicencio, 95 Ariz. 199, 388 P.2d 245 (1964) (sales of narcotics to A and B at same time and place; evidence of sale to A admissible in prosecution for the sale to B; "This principle that the complete story of the crime may be shown even though it reveals other crimes has often been termed 'res gestae.' * * * [W]e choose to refer to this as the 'complete story' principle, rather than 'res gestae.'"); State v. Klotter, 274 Minn. 58, 142 N.W.2d 568 (1968) (burglary of sporting goods store; evidence of burglary of home of friend of defendant's family, 5 miles away on same night admissible, where guns from both burglaries found in defendant's possession; "connected closely enough in time, place and manner"); State v. Hendrix, 310 S.W.2d 852 (Mo.1958) (prosecution of convict for damaging penitentiary building by sawing bars on window; evidence of attempted escape of defendant and others, which was the purpose of the sawing, admissible as "circumstantial evidence of guilt") * * *

[35]. Makin v. Attorney General of New South Wales, [1894] App.C. 57 (Privy Council) (murder of an infant left with defendants for their care, with an inadequate premium; evidence that the bodies of ten other babies were found buried in the gardens of three houses formerly occupied by the accused, property received, on question whether adoption bona fide and deaths accidental); Leonard v. United States, 324 F.2d 911 (9th Cir. 1963) (defendant obtained Treasury checks payable to others, induced A to forge payees' endorsements, then induced B to obtain false credentials, cash checks and split proceeds with defendant; all admissible to show scheme); State v. Toshishige Yoshimo, 45 Hawaii 206, 364 P.2d 638 (1961) (defendant and others robbed A and obtained from him name and address of B as holder of another sum of money, proceeded to B's house and assaulted and robbed B; evidence of first robbery admissible in prosecution for second); State v. Long, 195 Ore. 81, 244 P.2d 1033 (1952) (that defendant after kill-

will be relevant as showing motive, and hence the doing of the criminal act, the identity of the actor, and his intention, where any of these is in dispute.

(3) To prove other like crimes by the accused so nearly identical in method as to earmark them as the handiwork of the accused.[36] Here much more is demanded than the mere repeated commission of crimes of the same class, such as repeated burglaries or thefts. The device used must be so unusual and distinctive as to be like a signature.[37]

(4) To show a passion or propensity for illicit sexual relations with the particular person concerned in the crime on trial.[38] Other like sexual crimes with other persons do not qualify for this purpose.[39]

ing owner of truck, for which he is now on trial, in use of truck next day for robbery shot F.B.I. man while leaving scene of robbery properly proved as part of planned course of action); Haley v. State, 84 Tex.Cr. 629, 209 S.W. 675 (1919) (murder: that defendant desiring to continue illicit relations with wife of deceased, formed a plan to kill his own wife and deceased, provable but state's evidence here of his poisoning his wife not sufficiently cogent to be received).

36. R. v. George Joseph Smith (1915), reported in Notable British Trials (1922), and described in Marjoribanks, For the Defence: The Life of Edward Marshall Hall 321 (1937) (the famous "brides of the bath" case; defendant accused of murdering his wife, who left her property to him by will, by drowning her in the bathtub: defendant leaves their boardinghouse on a pretended errand, and then on his return purports to discover his wife drowning in the tub and so reports to the landlady; held proper to show that he had previously married several wives, who left him their property and were discovered by him drowned in the bath); People v. Peete, 28 Cal. 2d 306, 169 P.2d 924 (1946) (where defendant had been previously convicted of killing another who was killed by means of a bullet from behind, severing the spinal cord at the neck, and deceased in present prosecution was shot from behind at close range in an attempt to sever the spinal cord, evidence of the prior homicide was admissible as tending to identify defendant as the murderer.); and see Note,

35 Colum.L.Rev. 131 (1935) which at p. 136 examines the distinction between this and purpose (2) above; Whiteman v. State, 119 Ohio St. 285, 164 N.E. 51, 63 A.L.R. 595 (1928) (robbery; evidence of other robberies committed by defendants according to same peculiar plan, as used in the robbery now on trial, that is, by using uniforms, impersonating officers, and stopping cars, thus "earmarking" the crimes as committed by the same persons).

37. See, e. g., State v. Sauter, 125 Mont. 109, 232 P.2d 731, 732 (1951) (forcible rape by defendant and S in automobile after picking victim up in barroom; held, error to admit evidence of rapes accomplished after similar pickups of other victims; "too common * * * to have much evidentiary value in showing a systematic scheme of plan"; two judges dissenting). * * *

38. Woods v. State, 250 Ind. 132, 235 N.E.2d 479 (1968) (rape and incest; other like acts on victim admissible to show "depraved sexual instinct"); State v. Schut, 71 Wash.2d 400, 429 P.2d 126 (1967) (incest; prior acts with victim admissible to show a lustful inclination toward the offended female). * * *

39. Landon v. State, 77 Okl.Cr. 190, 140 P.2d 242 (1943) (statutory rape on daughter: other offenses with another daughter on other occasions excluded); * * *. But though not receivable to show propensity the evidence may come in on other theories. * * *

It has been argued that certain unnatural sex crimes are in themselves so unusual and distinctive that previous such acts by the accused with anyone are strongly probative of like acts upon the occasion involved in the charge,[40] but the danger of prejudice is likewise enhanced here, and most courts have in the past excluded such acts with other persons for this purpose. More recent cases show signs of lowering this particular barrier to admission.[41]

(5) To show, by similar acts or incidents, that the act on trial was not inadvertent, accidental, unintentional,[42] or without guilty knowledge.[43]

40. A few decisions have admitted the evidence seemingly on the theory, in part at least, of showing a special propensity. * * * See also Comm. v. Kline, 361 Pa. 434, 65 A.2d 348 (1949) (statutory rape on daughter: State allowed to prove that defendant indecently exposed himself to a neighbor woman, as showing he was an exhibitionist and thus had a moral trait consistent with the crime on trial).

41. Commentators assert that recently the limitations on proof of other offenses are being reduced in prosecutions for sex crimes, either directly, on the basis of the argument described in the text, or by forcing the evidence into the exceptions relating to design or intention. * * *

42. United States v. Ross, 321 F.2d 61 (2d Cir. 1963) cert. denied 375 U.S. 894 (securities fraud; where defendant claimed he was an unwitting tool of his employer, proper for prosecution to show on cross-examination that he had long drifted among firms engaged in selli g worthless securities by similar methods); People v. Williams, 6 Cal.2d 500, 58 P.2d 917 (1936) (larceny of coin-purse; state's theory and evidence were that defendant posing as customer standing near owner of bag, took purse from bag while owner was shopping; defendant claimed to have picked the purse from the floor, thinking it lost; held evidence of detectives that they had seen defendant take another purse from another woman's bag in same manner, admissible); State v. Lapage, 57 N.H. 245, 294 (1876) (Cushing, C. J.; "Another class of cases consists of those in which it becomes necessary to show that the act for which the prisoner was indicted was not accidental,—e. g., where the prisoner had shot the same person twice within a short time, or where the same person had fired a rick of grain twice, or where several deaths by poison had taken place in the same family, or where the children of the same mother had mysteriously died. In such cases it might well happen that a man should shoot another accidentally, but that he should do it twice within a short time would be very unlikely. So, it might easily happen that a man using a gun might fire a rick of barley once by accident, but that he should do it several times in succession would be very improbable. So, a person might die of accidental poisoning, but that several persons should so die in the same family at different times would be very unlikely."); 2 Wigmore, Evidence § 302. The similarity of the other acts need not be as great as under purpose (3) in the text above, nor is a connection by common plan as in purpose (2) demanded. The trial judge has a range of discretion in determining whether the probative value justifies admission. * * * Subsequent as well as prior acts have been held admissible for this purpose. * * * However, when the act charged is not equivocal, but the criminal intent is a necessary conclusion from the act, this theory of other acts as showing intent may not be availed of. People v. Lonsdale, 122 Mich. 388, 81 N.W. 277 (1899) (abortion where there was no room for inference of accident or that operation was performed to save life); * * *.

43. United States v. Brand, 79 F.2d 605 (2d Cir. 1935), cert. denied 296 U.S. 655 (knowingly transporting stolen car in interstate commerce; evidence of

Ch. 3 RELEVANCE 93

(6) To establish motive.[44] This in turn may serve as evidence of the identity of the doer of the crime on charge, or of deliberateness, malice, or a specific intent constituting an element of the crime.

(7) To show, by immediate inference, malice, deliberation, ill will or the specific intent required for a particular crime.[45]

(8) To prove identity. This is accepted as one of the ultimate purposes for which evidence of other criminal conduct will be received.[46] It is believed, however, that a need for proving identity is

previous sale of a stolen car). * * *

44. State v. Simborski, 120 Conn. 624, 182 Atl. 221 (1936) (murder of officer who was seeking to arrest defendant; fact that defendant had committed two burglaries a short time before, admissible to show motive and as res gestae); People v. Odum, 27 Ill.2d 237, 188 N.E.2d 720 (1963) (murder; evidence that victim's name had been indorsed as witness on indictment against defendant for another crime, admissible to show motive, although conviction here reversed for other error); Gibbs v. State, 201 Tenn. 491, 300 S.W.2d 890 (1957) (defendant killed A, then killed Mrs. A when she discovered this, then killed A's daughter when she discovered Mrs. A's body; in trial for murder of Mrs. A, evidence as to the other killings admissible to show motive and as "inseparable components of a completed crime;" the killing of A's daughter, however, clearly belongs under (9) infra, as an admission of guilt by conduct, where the prosecution is for the killing of Mrs. A); State v. Simborski, 120 Conn. 624, 182 Atl. 221 (1936) (murder of an officer who was seeking to arrest defendant; fact that defendant had committed two burglaries a short time previously on the same morning admissible to show motive, and as res gestae); State v. Long, 195 Ore. 81, 244 P.2d 1033 (1952) (murder of owner of truck: that defendant a short time afterward used the truck to commit robbery admitted); Comm. v. Heller, 269 Pa. 467, 87 A.2d 287 (1952) (murder of wife: evidence of illicit relations with sister-in-law and attempt to procure her to get divorce admissible); State v. Gaines, 144 Wash. 446, 258 Pac. 508 (1927) (murder of daughter; evidence of incestuous relations between defendant and deceased and that daughter was threatening to end the relation). * * *

45. Copeland v. United States, 152 F.2d 769 (D.C.Cir. 1945) (murder in first degree; that defendant after shooting deceased pursued and shot sister of deceased, proper to show first act done, not accidentally or in self-defense but with deliberate intent to kill); * * * Clark v. State, 151 Tex.Cr.R. 383, 208 S.W.2d 637 (1948) (murder, by beating, of five year old stepson: previous whippings, to show malice); * * *.

46. People v. McMonigle, 29 Cal.2d 730, 177 P.2d 745 (1947) (murder of girl enticed by accused into his automobile; evidence that a naval T shirt, similar to that worn by murderer, was stolen by accused some weeks before, properly received to show plan to entice, and identity); * * *. State v. King, 111 Kan. 140, 206 Pac. 883, 22 A.L.R. 1006 (1922) (murder; victim, an employee of defendant, disappeared, after which accused was in possession of his effects; ten years later victim's body found burned in defendant's premises; held, finding of other bodies on same premises of persons who had disappeared and whose effects were in defendant's possession, admissible to identify accused as murderer); Helton v. Comm., 244 S.W.2d 762 (Ky.1951) (assault committed as member of mob of miners; accused denied being present; "other incidents" on same morning presumably involving accused, admissible to show larger plan, motive and identity); State v. Bock, 229 Minn. 449, 39 N.W.2d 887 (1949) (attempt to pass forged check, by making small purchase and getting cash for balance; evidence of similar subsequent passing of other checks at other stores, under similar plan, ad-

not ordinarily of itself a ticket of admission, but that the evidence will usually follow, as an intermediate channel, some one or more of the other theories here listed. Probably the second (larger plan), the third (distinctive device) and the sixth (motive) are most often resorted to for this purpose.[47]

(9) Evidence of criminal acts of accused, constituting admissions by conduct, intended to obstruct justice or avoid punishment for the present crime.[48]

(10) To impeach the accused when he takes the stand as a witness, by proof of his convictions of crime.

Some general observations may be added. In the first place, it is clear that the other crime, when it is found to be independently relevant and admissible, need not be established beyond a reasonable doubt, either as to its commission or as to defendant's connection therewith, but for the jury to be entitled to consider it there must of course be substantial evidence of these facts, and some courts have used the formula that it must be "clear and convincing." And it is believed that before the evidence is admitted at all, this factor of the substantial or unconvincing quality of the proof should be weighed in the balance.

Two considerations, one substantive and the other procedural, affect the ease or difficulty of securing admission of proof of other crimes. The first is that the courts are stricter in applying their standards of relevancy when the ultimate purpose of the state is to prove identity, or the doing by the accused of the criminal act charged than they are when the evidence is offered on the ultimate issue of knowledge, intent or other state of mind.[53] The second is

missible in discretion to identify person who attempted to pass check in question here; but error to exclude evidence of accused that some other person passed these other checks) * * *

47. See decisions cited under these headings, above and cases in next preceding note.

48. People v. Gambino, 12 Ill.2d 29, 145 N.E.2d 42 (1957) cert. denied 356 U.S. 904 (escape and attempted escape while awaiting trial); People v. Spaulding, 309 Ill. 292, 141 N.E. 196 (1923) (killing of only eyewitness to crime); State v. Brown, 231 Ore. 297, 372 P.2d 779 (1962) (stealing cars to escape) * * *.

53. United States v. Fierson, 419 F.2d 1020 (7th Cir. 1970) (mere formal issue is not sufficient); Jones v. Com., 303 Ky. 666, 198 S.W.2d 969, 970, 971 (1947) ("The application of the rule of admissibility is more liberal in the matter of establishing guilty knowledge or intent where intent is a material ingredient of the offense charged, for a series of similar offenses tends to show the party knew or intended to do what he was doing on the particular occasion. Where the purpose is to identify the defendant, the circumstances may govern the degree of liberality or strictness. * * * where it is a question of the particular individual committing the particular offense, as it was here, the latitude is much smaller."); and see People v. Molineux, 168 N.Y. 264, 313, 61 N.E. 286, 302 (1901) ("As to identity: Another exception to the general rule is that, when the evidence of an extraneous crime tends to identify the person who committed it as the same person

that when the crime charged involves the element of knowledge, intent, or the like, the state will often be permitted to show other crimes in rebuttal, after the issue has been sharpened by the defendant's giving evidence of accident or mistake, more readily than it would as part of its case in chief at a time when the court may be in doubt that any real dispute will appear on the issue.[54]

There is an important consideration in the practice as to the admission of evidence of other crimes which is little discussed in the opinions. This is the question of rule versus discretion. Most of the opinions ignore the problem and proceed on the assumption that the decision turns solely upon the ascertainment and application of a rule. If the situation fits one of the classes wherein the evidence has been recognized as having independent relevancy, then the evidence is received, otherwise not. This mechanical way of handling these questions has the advantage of calling on the judge for a minimum of personal judgment. But problems of lessening the dangers of prejudice without too much sacrifice of relevant evidence can seldom if ever be satisfactorily solved by mechanical rules. And so here there is danger that if the judges, trial and appellate, content themselves with merely determining whether the particular evidence of other crimes does or does not fit in one of the approved classes, they may lose sight of the underlying policy of protecting the accused against unfair prejudice. The policy may evaporate through the interstices of the classification.

Accordingly, some of the wiser opinions (especially recent ones) recognize that the problem is not merely one of pigeonholing, but one

---

who committed the crime charged in the indictment, it is admissible. There are not many reported cases in which this exception seems to have been affirmatively applied. A far larger number of cases, while distinctly recognizing its existence, have held it inapplicable to the particular facts then before the court.").

54. See, e. g., People v. Knight, 92 Cal. App. 143, 216 Pac. 96 (1923) (lewd acts with children; defendant testifies that he committed the acts but with no lewd intent; held no error to receive evidence of similar acts with other children: "defendant opened the door"); State v. Gilligan, 92 Conn. 526, 103 Atl. 649 (1918) (murder by keeper of old folks' home of one of the inmates: receiving evidence of other poisonings where state's evidence did not suggest possibility of accident, held error, "without prejudice to its possible admission in rebuttal").

The remarks of Lord Sumner in Thompson v. The King, [1918] App.C. 221, 232 are pertinent: "Before an issue can be said to be raised, which would permit the introduction of such evidence so obviously prejudicial to the accused, it must have been raised in substance if not in so many words, and the issue so raised must be one to which the prejudicial evidence is relevant. The mere theory that a plea of not guilty puts everything material in issue is not enough for this purpose. The prosecution cannot credit the accused with fancy defences in order to rebut them at the outset with some damning piece of prejudice."

Compare the situation where the defendant or his lawyer for him imprudently makes claim to an unblemished character or record. Holding that this opens the door to evidence of other crimes: People v. Westek, 31 Cal.2d 469, 190 P.2d 9, 13, 18 (1948); * * *.

of balancing,[55] on the one side, the actual need for the other-crimes evidence in the light of the issues and the other evidence available to the prosecution,[56] the convincingness of the evidence that the other crimes were committed and that the accused was the actor, and the strength or weakness of the other-crimes evidence in supporting the issue, and on the other, the degree to which the jury will probably be roused by the evidence to overmastering hostility.

Such a balancing calls for a large measure of individual judgment about the relative gravity of imponderables. Accordingly, some opinions stress the element of discretion. It should be recognized, however, that this is not a discretion to depart from the principle that evidence of other crimes, having no substantial relevancy except to ground the inference that accused is a bad man and hence probably committed this crime, must be excluded. The leeway of discretion lies rather in the opposite direction, empowering the judge to exclude the other-crimes evidence, even when it has substantial independent relevancy, if in his judgment its probative value for this purpose is outweighed by the danger that it will stir such passion in the jury as to sweep them beyond a rational consideration of guilt or innocence of the crime on trial.[58] Discretion implies not only leeway but responsibility. A decision clearly wrong on this question of balancing probative value against danger of prejudice will be corrected on appeal as an abuse of discretion.

55. Quarles v. Com., 245 S.W.2d 947, 948 (Ky.1951) (" * * * evidence of an independent offense is inadmissible even though it may have some tendency to prove the commission of the crime charged, because the probative value of the evidence is greatly outweighed by its prejudicial effect. This is especially so where the evidence is of an isolated, wholly disconnected offense. But the balance of scales is believed to be the other way where there is a close relationship to the offense charged.").

56. The importance of this is clearly pointed out by Beach, J., in State v. Gilligan, 92 Conn. 526, 103 Atl. 649, 652, 653 (1918). * * * In discussing a question of the admission of a declaration, competent for one purpose, incompetent for another, he said: "The matter is largely one of discretion on the part of the trial judge. If the point to prove which the evidence is competent can just as well be proven by other evidence, or if it is of but slight weight or importance upon that point, the trial judge might well be justified in excluding it entirely, because of its prejudicial and dangerous character as to other points." * * *

Another factor mentioned as entitled to consideration is surprise. * * * The remedy here would seem to be notice, as required in State v. Spreigl, 272 Minn. 488, 139 N.W.2d 167 (1965); * * *.

* * *

58. State v. Goebel, 36 Wash.2d 367, 218 P.2d 300, 306 (1950) (Hill, J.: " * * * this class of evidence, where not essential to the establishment of the state's case, should not be admitted, even though falling within the generally recognized exceptions of the rule of exclusion, when the trial court is convinced that its effect would be to generate heat instead of diffusing light, or, as is said in one of the law review articles above referred to, where the minute peg of relevancy will be entirely obscured by the dirty linen hung upon it. This is a situation where the policy of protecting a defendant from undue prejudice conflicts with the rule of logical relevance, and a proper determination as to which should prevail rests in the sound discretion of the trial court, and not merely on whether the evidence comes within certain categories which constitute exceptions to the rule of exclusion."); * * *.

PEOPLE v. MASSEY

District Court of Appeal of California, 1961.
196 Cal.App.2d 230, 16 Cal.Rptr. 402.

KAUFMAN, P. J. By an information dated August 9, 1960, the appellant, Richard L. Massey, was charged with the burglary (Pen. Code, § 459) of an apartment at 620 Jones Street, San Francisco, on May 2, 1960; and with two prior felony convictions in Iowa. He admitted the prior convictions and entered a plea of not guilty. A jury found him guilty of burglary in the first degree and the court sentenced him for the term prescribed by law, and decreeing that the sentence was to run concurrently with any prior incompleted sentence. On this appeal from the judgment of conviction entered on the verdict and the order denying his motion for a new trial, appellant argues that: * * * the evidence relating to another burglary of which he was acquitted was erroneously admitted * * *

The record reveals the following facts: About 4:30 a. m. on the morning of May 2, 1960, Mrs. Sarah Finley, who lived alone in a one-room apartment, was awakened when she felt "a terrific jerk." She saw a Negro man hovering over her face and screamed. The intruder hurried to the open window, leaped out and ran off. Mrs. Finley took a pill for her heart condition and telephoned for help. The police arrived and discovered that $13 was missing from her purse, as well as a few other small items from the apartment. A large rectangular piece had been cut out of the sheet on Mrs. Finley's bed, probably with the scissors on the nearby table. Later the same day, Mrs. Finley's apartment was dusted for latent fingerprints by an officer from the crime laboratory. A fingerprint was found on the inside of the window in Mrs. Finley's room and a knife outside the window.

Mrs. Finley had lived for several years in the apartment on the first floor of the Gaylord Hotel at 620 Jones Street in San Francisco. Her apartment had only two windows which overlooked the porch and the hotel next door. On the prior evening, May 1, 1960, she retired about 10 p. m.; as the night was very warm, she opened both windows, locked them with the chain, and covered herself only with a sheet.

The above occurrence remained unsolved for several weeks. About 3 a. m. on the morning of May 26, 1960, Elsie Cox, who lived alone in a two-room apartment at 757 Sutter Street, awoke and in the large mirror facing her bed, saw the reflection of a man entering the living room where she slept. She could see him very clearly as the living-room window extended almost the entire wall and overlooked the brightly lit Trader Vic's parking area next door. The venetian blinds on the window were down but open. She watched the prowler creep around her bed, and noticed that he kept a white cloth over his hand as he flashed a light into the closet and took a leisurely survey. He then turned and lifted up the pillow next to hers and pushed his hand under it. Then he straightened up, proceeded to the end of the bed, and the other side of the room. After he climbed out the kitchen window, she called the police. Later, she discovered that only a dish towel was missing, although several things were awry. Miss Cox's apartment was on the second floor; there were a fire escape and some pipes near the kitchen window. Shortly thereafter, a police officer saw the appellant walking down Post Street near Mason Street, and returned with him to Miss Cox's apartment. Miss Cox positively identified the appellant as the prowler at that time and at the later trial.

On June 9, 1960, while in custody on the Cox matter, the appellant was questioned about the Finley burglary. He denied being at Mrs. Finley's apartment on the morning in question and indicated he did not wish to make any further statements. On July 26, 1960, the preliminary hearing was held in Mrs. Finley's room because of her heart condition. At this time, Mrs. Finley testified that the prowler who was in her room on the morning of May 2 did not look like the appellant but was huskier, fatter and older. At the trial, she testified that the prowler looked very much like the appellant but admitted that she had observed the prowler for only about half a second and that it was so dark that she couldn't tell. She explained that the inconsistency in her identification was due to her nervousness at the preliminary.

The prosecution's expert witness testified that in his opinion, the latent fingerprint found on the window of Mrs. Finley's apartment was appellant's. The appellant took the stand, admitted the two prior felony convictions and being on parole from the Iowa Men's Reformatory for one of them. He testified that on May 1, he had gone to bed around 10 o'clock at the home of his sister and brother-in-law at 184 Hoff Street. The appellant's sister and her husband also testified that the appellant was in his bed on the night of May 1 at their home in the Ingleside district. It was also brought out at the trial that one week earlier, the appellant had been tried and acquitted of the Cox burglary. * * *

Appellant next argues that the evidence relating to the subsequent burglary of Miss Cox's apartment was not admissible because of his acquittal and because of its prejudicial effect. It is well established, however, that an acquittal does not prevent the admissibility of evidence concerning another wrongful act (People v. Huston,[59] 156

---

59. [In People v. Huston the defendant was charged with three counts of sex offenses with one girl and a fourth count with another girl. He was acquitted on the fourth count and argued on appeal that "The defense could not object to the testimony when given because the witness was the prosecutrix of count IV of the complaint. However, defendant was acquitted of count IV. Thus the admission of the evidence became improper and prejudicial error." The court rejected this argument.]

Cal.App.2d 670, 671, 320 P.2d 175); * * * as conviction of the offense is not a prerequisite to the introduction of such evidence.

As stated in People v. Brown, [168 Cal.App.2d 549 at] 552–553: "The ultimate fact to be proved is the defendant's guilt of the crime with which he is charged and not the other offense. The evidence of the other offense is admissible even though the defendant was not convicted of it, provided such evidence is relevant. Therefore, the rule concerning the admissibility of other offenses expressed in the *Raleigh* case must be limited to those circumstances where the proof is relevant and material to the crime for which the defendant is being tried."

Appellant here argues that the Cox burglary is not relevant to the Finley burglary; the attorney general argues that the evidence was relevant and admissible as the Cox burglary was committed in the same neighborhood (about 2 blocks from the Gaylord Hotel where Mrs. Finley lived), was committed within the same month in the early hours of the morning, and both involved the use of a white cloth, Miss Cox's dish cloth, and by inference, the piece cut from Mrs. Finley's sheet.

The general rule of the admissibility of other criminal acts is stated in People v. Sanders, 114 Cal. 216, at page 230, 46 P. 153:

"If the evidence of another crime is necessary or pertinent to the proof of the one charged, the law will not thwart justice by excluding that evidence, simply because it involves the commission of another crime. The general tests of the admissibility of evidence in a criminal case are: 1. Is it a part of the *res gestae*? 2. If not, does it tend logically, naturally, and by reasonable inference, to establish any fact material for the people, or to overcome any material matter sought to be proved by the defense? If it does, then it is admissible, whether it embraces the commission of another crime or does not, whether the other crime be similar in kind or not, whether it be part of a single design or not * * *." * * * We think the evidence of the Cox burglary was pertinent to the issue of intent. * * *

[Affirmed.]

E. EXTRINSIC POLICIES, COMPROMISE AND WITHDRAWN PLEAS OF GUILTY

1. COMPROMISE

RULES OF EVIDENCE FOR UNITED STATES COURTS AND MAGISTRATES

Rule 410

INADMISSIBILITY OF PLEAS, PLEA DISCUSSIONS, AND RELATED STATEMENTS

Except as otherwise provided in this rule, evidence of the following is not, in any civil or criminal proceeding, admissible against the defendant who made the plea or was a participant in the plea discussions:

(1) A plea of guilty which was later withdrawn; (2) a plea of Nolo Contendere; (3) any statement made in the course of any proceedings under Rule 11 of the Federal Rules of Criminal Procedure or comparable state procedure regarding either of the foregoing pleas; or (4) any statements made in the course of plea discussions with an attorney for the prosecuting authority which do not result in a plea of guilty or which result in a plea of guilty later withdrawn.

However, such a statement is admissible (i) in any proceeding wherein another statement made in the course of the same plea or plea discussions has been introduced and statement ought in fairness be considered contemporaneously with it, or (ii) in a criminal proceeding for perjury or false statement if the statement was made by the defendant under oath, on the record and in the presence of counsel.

UNITED STATES v. HERMAN

United States Court of Appeals, Fifth Circuit, 1977.
544 F.2d 791.

GOLDBERG, Circuit Judge:

Glen Herman stands accused of robbing a United States Post Office and killing a postal employee. On the basis of recent changes in the governing Federal Rules of Criminal Procedure and Evidence, the district court granted Herman's pretrial motion to suppress certain incriminating statements he made to two postal inspectors during what Herman claims were plea negotiations. The government appeals, arguing that the statements were not made "in connection with" any plea discussions and therefore are admissible. We disagree and therefore affirm.

I. FACTS

The crime occurred in Orange County, Florida on July 21, 1975. Postal inspectors advised the Columbus, Georgia police department that a warrant had been issued charging Herman with the killing, and Columbus police arrested him. On August 11, 1975 two postal inspectors, O. J. Broadwater and L. S. Crawford, transported Herman from the county jail to the Columbus federal courthouse for a removal hearing. The inspectors advised him of his constitutional rights.

At the hearing Herman requested that an attorney be appointed to represent him. The magistrate promptly recessed the hearing and left to obtain an attorney. Herman remained in the hearing room with the two postal inspectors. Herman initiated a conversation during which he stated, sometimes in response to Inspector Broadwater's questions, that he was not guilty of and should not be charged with murder, that his alleged partner Brunson had fired the fatal shot, and that only one shot had been fired. Herman also asked who had brought his name into the case, whether Brunson had talked and whether authorities had recovered Brunson's gun.

At some point during the conversation Herman made the offer that is of crucial importance to this case: he said he would plead guilty to robbery charges and produce the gun if authorities would agree to drop the murder charges. Inspector Crawford testified that the plea offer came near the beginning of the discussion, following only Herman's statement that he should not be charged with murder and his inquiry as to who implicated him. Inspector Broadwater, on the other hand, testified that Herman's plea offer occurred at the end of the discussion. Both inspectors agreed that in response to Herman's plea offer Broadwater said that they were not "in position" to make any deals. Crawford testified that the discussion ended when Herman said he did not want to disclose his gun's location before speaking to an attorney.

On August, 27, 1975 a two-count indictment in the United States District Court for the Middle District of Florida charged Herman with killing the postal employee * * * and robbing the post office * * *. Herman moved to suppress the statements made to Inspectors Broadwater and Crawford at the August 11 removal hearing, claiming that they were made involuntarily and in violation of Miranda v. Arizona, 384 U.S. 436 86 S.Ct. 1602, 16 L.Ed.2d 694 (1966), and that they were made in connection with an offer to plead guilty. * * * The district court held that the statements were voluntary and did not contravene *Miranda,* but excluded the statements as plea-related. The government immediately filed this appeal.

* * *

III. MERITS

Fed.R.Crim.P. 11(e)(6) * makes inadmissible any statement made "in connection with" any offer to plead guilty or nolo contendere to the charged crime or to any other crime. Fed.R.Ev. 410 contains exactly the same provision. During the course of Herman's discussion with the postal inspectors, he offered to plead guilty to robbery. The question before us is whether Herman's other statements were made "in connection with" the plea offer.

To construe rule 11(e)(6) correctly we must set it in proper perspective. Plea bargaining is a practice many have criticized and few have enthusiastically endorsed. Nevertheless, plea bargaining has become an accepted fact of life. By 1971 the Supreme Court was able to encourage the practice, albeit on grounds of necessity rather than right:

> The disposition of criminal charges by agreement between the prosecutor and the accused, sometimes loosely called "plea bargaining," is an essential component of the administration of justice. Properly administered, it is to be encouraged. If every criminal charge were subjected to a full-scale trial, the States and the Federal Government would need to multiply by many times the number of judges and court facilities.

Santobello v. New York, 404 U.S. 257, 260, * * * (1971).

The legal battleground has thus shifted from the propriety of plea bargaining to how best to implement and oversee the process. Plea bargaining is a tool of conciliation. It must not be a chisel of deceit or a hammered purchase and sale. The end result must come as an open covenant, openly arrived at with judicial oversight. A legal plea bargain is made in the sunshine before the penal bars darken. Accordingly, we must examine plea bargains under the doctrine of caveat prosecutor.

Even before the enactment of rule 11(e)(6), we held that plea-related statements are inadmissible, recognizing the inescapable truth

---

* Federal Rules of Criminal Procedure 11(e)(6):

(6) **Inadmissibility of Pleas, Offers of Pleas, and Related Statements.** Except as otherwise provided in this paragraph, evidence of a plea of guilty, later withdrawn, or a plea of nolo contendere, or of an offer to plead guilty or nolo contendere to the crime charged or any other crime, or of statements made in connection with, and relevant to, any of the foregoing pleas or offers, is not admissible in any civil or criminal proceeding against the person who made the plea or offer. However, evidence of a statement made in connection with, and relevant to, a plea of guilty, later withdrawn, a plea of nolo contendere, or an offer to plead guilty or nolo contendere to the crime charged or any other crime, is admissible in a criminal proceeding for perjury or false statement if the statement was made by the defendant under oath, on the record, and in the presence of counsel.

that for plea bargaining to work effectively and fairly, a defendant must be free to negotiate without fear that his statements will later be used against him. In excluding a defendant's plea-related statements, Judge Coleman wrote:

> If, as the Supreme Court said in *Santobello,* plea bargaining is an essential component of justice and, properly administered, is to be encouraged, it is immediately apparent that no defendant or his counsel will pursue such an effort if the remarks uttered during the course of it are to be admitted in evidence as proof of guilt. Moreover, it is inherently unfair for the government to engage in such an activity, only to use it as a weapon against the defendant when negotiations fail.

United States v. Ross, 493 F.2d 771, 775 (5th Cir. 1974). * * * The *Ross* holding was codified in rule 11(e)(6).

Against this backdrop the inappropriateness of giving the rule an inhospitable reading becomes clear. Excluded statements must be made "in connection with" plea offers, but if we are overly exacting in deciding which statements come within this standard, we will deter the unrestrained candor that often produces effective plea negotiations. Defendants must be free to participate in open and uninhibited plea discussions, and their decisions to do so must not later be subjected to microscopic judicial examination to determine whether the statements were closely enough related to the plea offers. Statements are inadmissible if made at any point during a discussion in which the defendant seeks to obtain concessions from the government in return for a plea.

Indeed, even settlement negotiations in civil cases have been curtained by evidentiary impenetrability. See, e. g., Fed.R.Ev. 408. The necessity for sanctuaries in plea bargaining in criminal cases is no less compelling. If plea bargaining is pragmatically justified despite its potential for abuse, we should encourage candor by the accused, eschewing an interpretation of the rules that would make the accused less amenable to forthright plea discussions. The accused in the pretrial bargaining should be encouraged by knowledge that the discussions will have a sanctity. Hypertechnical considerations should not determine whether pretrial bargaining may come into the testimony at the trial. Having embarked on the road that permits plea bargaining, the government should be most careful lest it be accused of bad faith in throwing open to the trial matters that the accused thought were not to be used against him or her. To hold otherwise would greatly diminish, if not nullify, the use of plea bargaining.

The government argues, however, that if all such statements are excluded, clever defendants will append plea offers to their incriminating statements and thereby render the statements inadmissible.

The government does not explain why clever defendants would not simply refrain from making incriminating statements altogether, nor how the offering of an inadmissible statement will impede the prosecutor's ability independently to assemble a case as he or she always must. The government's speculative concern gives us no cause to subordinate the policy of encouraging open plea discussions or to ignore the rule's plain language. In the long run prosecutors will benefit from the more effective plea negotiating process that today's result will foster. We need not fear that sophisticated defendants will abuse the rule we announce today, but if we were to construe the "in connection with" standard more narrowly sophisticated prosecutors might sometimes use the rule as a trap for the unwary. To allow prosecutors to use plea-related incriminating statements to prove a defendant's guilt would be inherently unfair, as we noted in *Ross*.

Moreover, the government's inability to introduce the statements made in a bargaining session does not place it in a worse position than it would occupy if an accused chose not to engage in plea bargaining at all. If we permit the facts concerning a plea bargain to be brought out in evidence, we will have silence on the part of every knowledgeable accused. Discussion will not be worth the price of the potential bargain. An unexpansive reading of relatedness would go to the heart of the rule, which is the protection of plea discussions. The rule's central feature is that the accused is encouraged candidly to discuss his or her situation in order to explore the possibility of disposing of the case through a consensual arrangement. Such candid discussion will often include incriminating admissions. If we were to follow the government's argument, however, such admissions would be admissible if not accompanied by a preamble explicitly demarcating the beginning of plea discussions. To allow the government to introduce statements uttered in reliance on the rule would be to use the rule as a sword rather than a shield. This we cannot allow; the rule was designed only as a shield.

If Congress had wanted plea bargaining to be formalized, ritualized or structured, the rules could have so provided. But Congress, believing that plea bargaining is a necessary ingredient in criminal prosecutions of the magnitude we face, wanted an accused freely to discuss his or her plight, the probability of punishment and the possible range thereof. Having embarked on the plea bargaining route, Congress did not intend the accused to be convicted by the bargaining words Congress had encouraged him or her to utter. We cannot ascribe to Congress any intention to sandbag an accused in his or her plea bargaining sessions. The government, as one of the dancing partners, should not be able to lead its partner to a trap door on the dance floor

Rule 11(e)(6) recognizes the existence and practice of plea bargaining and is a rule of encouragement. It should not be construed as a tempting rule with built-in deception. It should not be used to seduce confession or admission. It is a rule of evidentiary exclusion, and it should exclude lest it be destructive of the very predicate upon which it was evolved.

What remains is only to measure Herman's statements against the standard we have announced. Herman made the statements during the course of a conversation in which he sought concessions from the government in return for a guilty plea. In particular, Herman sought to have the government drop the murder charges in return for his guilty plea to robbery charges. The rule requires no more; all Herman's statements are inadmissible.

The government argues, however, that Herman's statements could not have been plea-related because the postal inspectors had no authority to negotiate a plea. We reject the government's position. The relevant factor is a defendant's perception of the government official's negotiating authority, not the official's actual authority. The twin goals of encouraging unrestrained plea negotiations and assuring fairness to defendants dictate that any statements made by a defendant as part of an effort to reach a plea agreement must be excluded; it makes no difference that the defendant's efforts are misguided because the official cannot or will not accept the offer.

* * *

The district court held Herman's statements plea-related, and only in an egregious case would we overturn such a district court finding. The order suppressing Herman's statements is affirmed.

[Concurring opinion omitted.]

2. WITHDRAWN PLEAS OF GUILTY

STATE v. THOMSON

Supreme Court of Oregon, 1954.
203 Or. 1, 278 P.2d 142.

LUSK, Justice. The defendant has appealed from a judgment of conviction of the crime of assault with intent to kill.

The indictment alleged that the defendant, on the tenth day of September, 1953, in Lincoln County "did then and there unlawfully and feloniously assault one James Meuler, by then and there striking, beating, bruising, and wounding him, the said James Meuler, with a certain iron pipe, and by then and there at said time and place wilfully and intentionally driving and projecting the automobile in which the said James Meuler was riding as a passenger, off of the travelled portion of the roadway and over and off a precipice approximately 400 feet high, while the said James Meuler was still in said automobile, all with the intent on the part of him, the said Richard E. Thomson, to then and there kill the said James Meuler".

Error is assigned to the admission in evidence, over the defendant's objection, of a record of the Circuit Court for Lincoln County establishing that on September 15, 1953, the defendant waived indictment and pleaded guilty to an information charging the same offense. The evidence shows that the defendant, through his counsel, on September 21, 1953, filed a motion for permission to withdraw his plea of guilty and to substitute for it a plea of not guilty. The motion was supported by defendant's affidavit in which he swore in substance that, while under great mental strain and shock and after long questioning by peace officers, he signed a written statement relating to the charge against him, the contents of which he did not remember but in which, as he was advised by his attorneys, appeared a statement that he struck Jim Meuler with intent to kill him, and that he had planned to kill him for several months; that he did not strike Meuler with intent to kill him and never planned to kill him, and had made no statement to that effect; that at the time he entered his plea of guilty he was not represented by counsel and was not advised of the elements necessary to constitute the crime of assault with intent to kill as charged, and that he was not guilty of that crime.

On September 21, 1953, the court entered an order allowing the motion. Thereafter the case was submitted to the grand jury, which on November 20, 1953, returned the indictment, the charging part of which we have quoted, and to which the defendant duly entered a plea of not guilty.

The question presented by the assignment of error is whether evidence of a plea of guilty entered to an information or indictment and later withdrawn by permission of the court, with leave to enter a plea of not guilty, is admissible in evidence against the defendant on his subsequent trial. * * *

* * *

It is generally held that a plea of guilty entered at a preliminary hearing is admissible in evidence on the trial of the accused. * * * Some of the cases cited in the state's brief are of that kind and are to be distinguished from cases involving a withdrawn plea of guilty. In United States v. Adelman, 2 Cir., 107 F.2d 497, 499, it was contended by the defendant, on the authority of the Kercheval case, that the trial judge committed error in admitting in evidence defendant's plea of guilty upon arraignment before a United States commissioner. The court distinguished the Kercheval case, saying:

> " * * * There a defendant who had pleaded 'guilty' to an indictment was allowed to withdraw his plea and go to trial on the substituted plea of 'not guilty.' Upon the trial his withdrawn plea was received in evidence as an admission. This was held error. *When a court allows a defendant to withdraw a plea of 'guilty' it is because the court finds that circumstances exist which make it unfair to hold him to it. Such circumstances make it equally unfair to use it against him as an admission.* * * * " (Emphasis added.)

While we recognize that the argument supporting the state's position is not without merit, we think that it must yield to the paramount considerations of fairness and justice to the accused. As Mr. Justice Rutledge said when he was a justice of the United States Court of Appeals for the District of Columbia, "receiving the plea would conclude the case against the defendant and destroy the effect of the plea of not guilty and the evidence supporting it." Wood v. United States, 75 U.S.App.D.C. 274, 128 F.2d 265, 273, * * *. The reasons for excluding the evidence have been stated with such clarity and convincing force by the eminent judges from whose opinions we have quoted that it would serve no purpose for us to attempt to add anything to what they have written. We hold that admission in evidence of the withdrawn plea of guilty was reversible error.

The state urges that even though the ruling was erroneous it was, in view of the record, not prejudicial. In State v. Folkes, 174 Or. 568, 150 P.2d 17, we examined with much care the question of this court's authority in a criminal case to affirm a judgment of conviction notwithstanding error committed on the trial. Because the defendant in that case "was conclusively proven guilty by his own confession corroborated by other unimpeached and uncontradicted evidence", we held that the receipt of incompetent evidence (unsigned transcripts of confessions, which were otherwise established by the testimony of witnesses) "which would have warranted a reversal under other circumstances, did not constitute reversible error". * * * Regardless of what might be contended here as to the strength of the prosecution's case, still the evidence was conflicting, and the question of defendant's guilt, whether of the crime as charged or of some lesser degree thereof, was for the jury to determine, uninfluenced by incompetent evidence. The error was not technical, but one the gravity of which is sufficiently indicated by the authorities which we have cited. In criminal cases, we have said, "unless the record conclusively shows that the error in the admission of incompetent evidence was not prejudicial to the party objecting, the judgment should be reversed." State v. Hatcher, 29 Or. 309, 313, 44 P. 584, 586. We cannot say that that is the state of the record before us.

For the error in admitting in evidence of the defendant's withdrawn plea of guilty the judgment is reversed and the cause remanded for a new trial.

[Concurring opinion omitted.]

NOTE ON THE NOLO CONTENDERE PLEA

Most states and the federal courts recognize the nolo contendere (Latin for "I do not wish to contend") plea, although its grant is usually discretionary with the court. A nolo contendere plea has consequences identical to those of a plea of guilty with one crucial difference: No legal admission of guilt arises from the nolo plea, except in that same case. Therefore the plea cannot be introduced as evidence in a later civil trial arising from the same circumstances as the criminal prosecution. Defendants who do not wish to expend the time and money to defend a minor violation and those accused of infractions with possibly devastating repercussions (such as prospective defendants in treble damage antitrust suits or lawyers worried about disbarment after conviction) often request permission to plead nolo contendere.

Chapter IV

THE HEARSAY RULE AND ITS EXCEPTIONS

A. THE RATIONALE AND MEANING OF HEARSAY

1. IN GENERAL

The general rule excluding hearsay statements did not become firmly fixed in England until the latter part of the 17th Century. Thus Sir Walter Raleigh had his problems with hearsay earlier in that century.

Sir Walter Raleigh's Case (J. G. Phillimore, "History and Principles of the Law of Evidence," 1850, p. 157). (1603. Raleigh was tried for a conspiracy of treason to dethrone Elizabeth and to put Arabella Stuart in her place, by the aid of Spanish money and intrigue. Sir Edward Coke, attorney-general, conducted the prosecution. The principal evidence against him was the assertion of Lord Cobham, a supposed fellow-conspirator, who had betrayed Raleigh in a sworn statement made before trial. Cobham himself was in prison, and was not produced on the trial.) * * *

Raleigh. "But it is strange to see how you press me still with my Lord Cobham, and yet will not produce him; it is not for gaining of time or prolonging my life that I urge this; he is in the house hard by, and may soon be brought hither; let him be produced, and if he will yet accuse me or avow this confession of his, it shall convict me and ease you of further proof."

Lord Cecil. "Sir Walter Raleigh presseth often that my Lord Cobham should be brought face to face; if he ask a thing of grace and favour, they must come from him only who can give them; but if he ask a matter of law, then, in order that we, who sit here as commissioners, may be satisfied, I desire to hear the opinions of my Lords, the judges, whether it may be done by law."

The Judges all answered, "that in respect it might be a mean to cover many with treasons, and might be prejudicial to the King, therefore, by the law, it was not sufferable."

Popham, C. J. "There must not such a gap be opened for the destruction of the King as would be if we should grant this; you plead hard for yourself, but the laws plead as hard for the King. Where no circumstances do concur to make a matter probable, then an accuser may be heard; but so many circumstances agreeing and confirming the accusation in this case, the accuser is not to be produced; for, having first confessed against himself voluntarily, and so charged another person, if we shall now hear him again in person, he may, for favour or fear, retract what formerly he hath said, and the jury may, by that means, be inveigled." * * *

Raleigh.—"I never had intelligence with Cobham since I came to the Tower."

Lord Cecil.—"Sir Walter Raleigh, if my Lord Cobham will now affirm, that you were acquainted with his dealings with Count Aremberg, that you knew of the letter he received, that you were the chief instigator of him, will you then be concluded by it?"

Raleigh.—"Let my Lord Cobham speak before God and the King, and deny God and the King if he speak not truly, and will then say that ever I knew of Arabella's matter, or the money out of Spain, or the Surprising Treason, I will put myself upon it."

Lord Henry Howard.—"But what if my Lord Cobham affirm anything equivalent to this; what then?"

Raleigh.—"My Lord, I put myself upon it."

Attorney-General.—"I shall now produce a witness viva voce:"

He then produced one *Dyer*, a pilot, who, being sworn, said, "Being at Lisbon, there came to me a Portuguese gentleman, who asked me how the King of England did, and whether he was crowned? I answered him, that I hoped our noble king was well, and crowned by this; but the time was not come when I came from the coast of Spain. 'Nay,' said he 'your king shall never be crowned, for Don Cobham and Don Raleigh will cut his throat before he come to be crowned.' And this, in time, was found to be spoken in mid July."

Raleigh.—"This is the saying of some wild Jesuit or beggarly priest; but what proof is it against me?"

Attorney-General.—"It must perforce arise out of some preceding intelligence, and shews that your treason had wings." * * *

Thus on the single evidence of Cobham, never confronted with Raleigh, who retracted his confession, and then (according to the advocates of the Crown) recalled his retraction, did an English jury, to the amazement and horror of the bystanders, and the perpetual disgrace of the English name, find the most illustrious of their fellow subjects guilty of high treason.

STATE v. ENGLISH

Supreme Court of North Carolina, 1931.
201 N.C. 295, 159 S.E. 318.

* * * The defendant offered evidence tending to show that on Sunday, the day after the murder, a Negro by the name of Dave Locke, was arrested in Wilmington, and this Negro, in the presence of three Wilmington officers, admitted that he killed Berta English "and described the house, the conditions of the body and the entire conditon of the woman" as she was afterwards found. This Negro

also stated that he killed Mrs. English with a fire poker and tore her bloomers off, and stated that the fire poker was bent at one end, and that in the struggle with Mrs. English he lost two buttons from his overalls, and that he produced these buttons and showed them to the officers at the time of the confession. The statement of the suspect gave "a pretty good description of the house and of the roads about the premises."

Thereafter on January 19, 1930, a warrant was issued for Locke, charging him with the murder of Mrs. English. This warrant was returnable before a magistrate. The record is not clear, but apparently the Negro was discharged and has since not been seen about that part of the country. All of the foregoing evidence was excluded by the court.

Thereafter, another Negro by the name of Dave Brockington was arrested and charged with the murder of Mrs. English.

Subsequently, on March 5, 1930, the defendant, Stephen English, husband of the deceased woman, was arrested and charged with the murder of his wife. The star witness for the state was Raeford Albertson, who testified in substance that on January 18, about 10 o'clock in the morning, he went to the home of the defendant; that he went into the house and talked to the defendant and his wife until about 12 o'clock and ate dinner there. Witness testified that he then went out on the porch and the defendant came out behind him and said, "Let's go to the stables." The state's witness then continued: "I went out there with him and he approached the subject about Bertie Brinson. He told me about meeting her at the show and what a good time he had, and that she was the sweetest thing to him he ever laid eyes on. Said he never loved anybody but her—that he would love her the longest day he lived. * * * I don't love my wife except as a friend. I will give you my Ford if you will kill her. I will give you $50.00 in money. I haven't got the money, but I have got the stuff that I can get it out of.

* * * This same state's witness testified that about a week after the death of Mrs. English he went by the defendant's house about night and the defendant went in the house and built a fire and made a fire in the stove and then went in the kitchen loft and got a pair of pants down with blood on them and pushed them under the wood in the fire, and went to the stable and got the stick and cut that up and put it in the stove and looked at me and said, "Thank God, I have not got to worry about anybody ever seeing them," and as we came on that morning from his father's, he got against the graveyard and said, "Walk to the graveyard with me," and we went up to the grave where she was buried and the flowers were fresh on the grave, and he said, "Look at it," and tears came in his eyes and he said: "If I had it to do over again what I have done, I would kill myself before I'd do it."

* * * The jury convicted the defendant of murder in the second degree, "asking the mercy of the court." Upon the verdict the court pronounced judgment that the defendant be confined in the state's prison for a term of not less than twenty years nor more than thirty years.

From the foregoing judgment defendant appealed.

BROGDEN, J. Is the voluntary confession of a third party made to officers of the law, that he killed the deceased, detailing the circumstances, competent evidence in behalf of the defendant charged with the murder?

The admissibility of confessions of a third party in criminal actions has been bitterly assailed and warmly defended by courts and text-writers. The numerical weight of authority excludes such testimony. About one hundred years ago it appears in State v. May, 15 N.C. 328, that a defendant was charged with stealing a slave. At that time this was a capital felony in North Carolina, and the defendant having been convicted, the judgment of death was pronounced against him. In that case the defendant offered testimony that another man had confessed to stealing the slave and had made compensations therefor. The testimony was rejected. The court said: "Except the facts of the respective residences of the parties, which of themselves, do not tend to establish guilt in either of the parties, it is obvious, that all the evidence, as well that received as that rejected, consists of the acts and declarations of other persons to which neither the State nor the prisoner is privy. I think the whole of it was inadmissible. The confession is plainly so. It is mere hearsay. It may seem absurd to one not accustomed to compare proofs, and estimate the weight of testimony according to the tests of veracity within our power, that an unbiased confession of one man that he is guilty of an offense with which another is charged, should not establish the guilt of him who confesses it, and by consequence, the innocence of the other, but the law must proceed on general principles; and it excludes such a confession upon the ground, that it is hearsay evidence—the words of a stranger to the parties, and not spoken on oath. Indeed, all hearsay might have more or less effect, and from some persons of good character, well known to the jury, it might avail much. Yet it is all rejected, with very few exceptions; which do not in terms or principle extend to this case. Even a judgment upon the plea of guilty could not be offered in evidence for or against another; much less a bare confession. As a declaration of another establishing his own guilt, the confession of a slave might be used upon the same principle."

* * *

The great jurist who wrote the May Case, confesses that the holding might seem absurd to a layman, "but the law must proceed on general principles," and hence if proffered testimony is technically and legalistically hearsay, then the technical interpretation must prevail. Furthermore, the suggested possibility that some man accused of crime would procure a confession of guilt by a slave and thus escape punishment, might have been a consequence which law-writers of a hundred years ago were seeking to avoid.

The writer of this opinion, speaking for himself, strings with the minority, but it was the duty of the trial judge to apply the law as written, and the exceptions of the defendant are not sustained. * * *

No error.

NOTE

In the first significant English treatise on the law of evidence, probably written early in the 18th Century, the author huffed that "a mere *hearsay* is no evidence" Gilbert, Evidence 135 (6th ed. Sedgwick 1801) (author's emphasis). But what is "a mere hearsay"? And why do we have a rule, riddled with exceptions, against the receipt in evidence of "hearsay"? Is "a mere hearsay" invariably as contemptible an item of evidence as Gilbert implied? Many definitions of hearsay, or of the hearsay rule, have been attempted. The extract from Professor Waltz's text, *Criminal Evidence*, which follows, outlines current approaches to the subject.

WALTZ, CRIMINAL EVIDENCE

61–72 (1975).*

THE RULE AGAINST HEARSAY

A.

Definitions of Hearsay

Common Law Definition. The broadest common law (judge-made, as distinguished from statutory) definition of hearsay evidence is: An oral or written assertion, or verbal or nonverbal conduct that carries with it a conscious or unconscious assertion, made or carried on by someone other than a witness while testifying at a trial or hearing, which is offered in evidence to establish the truth of the matter asserted.

The Evidence Codes. Some recent evidence codes, most notably the Federal Rules of Evidence and the California Evidence Code, define hearsay evidence more narrowly. For example, Rule 801 of the Federal Rules excludes from the operation of the hearsay rule (1) nonassertive conduct, (2) certain types of prior statements by a witness, and (3) admissions made by an opposing party.

For the time being, our discussion will be based on the broad common law defintion of hearsay rather than upon the recent codes.

---

* Copyright, 1975 by Jon R. Waltz.

Types of Hearsay. Under the common law definition given above, hearsay can be (1) oral, (2) written, or (3) by conduct; that is, actions.

A Three-Part Process. Hearsay evidence unfolds in a three-part process: (1) An assertion (or action—conduct—that *translates* into an assertion, such as pointing at someone to identify him), that assertion (or action) having been (2) made or done by someone other than a testifying witness on the stand (in other words, by an *out-of-court declarant* or *actor*), which is (3) offered in evidence to prove the *truth* of the matter asserted.

In view of the third step in this process—the evidence is being offered to establish the *truth* of the matter asserted—a crucial question by which to test an out-of-court declaration is, To what *issue* is the evidence directed?

Example:

The witness on the stand testifies, in response to counsel's questioning, "On April 2, 1973, the accused said to me, 'Yesterday I was in New Orleans.'" If the *issue* is whether the accused was in New Orleans on April 1, 1973 (that is, if the accused's out-of-court declaration is being offered to prove the *truth* of the assertion contained in it), the testimony is classic hearsay.

On the other hand, it is not hearsay if the issue is whether on April 2, 1973, the accused was capable of *talking*.

Hearsay as Belief. It may be helpful to think of hearsay as being *belief* translated into either *words* (spoken or written) or *actions*. Testimony as to these words or actions by an out-of-court declarant or actor is offered in evidence at trial, through some other witness, to prove the *truth* of the underlying belief.

Thus the hearsay process works this way: A witness on the stand testifies, "Bushmat told me the automobile was going 90 miles an hour." In other words, Bushmat—the out-of-court declarant—*said* the car was going 90 miles an hour, which indicates that he really *believed* that it was going 90 miles an hour. And, so the hearsay process goes, if Bushmat believed that the car was going 90 miles an hour, it is probably *true* that it was going 90 miles an hour. Bushmat's *belief* about something he thought he perceived in the outside world (a speeding automobile) was translated by him into *words* ("The automobile was going 90 miles an hour."). A witness in court is asked to repeat Bushmat's words as evidence that the car was in fact going 90 miles an hour (Bushmat's out-of-court words are being offered to prove the *truth* of what they asserted).

Now we come to the risks involved in receiving hearsay evidence. The difficulty is that, in the example given above, the validity of Bushmat's belief, and thus of his verbalization of it, depends on a number of unknown factors.

Ch. 4 THE HEARSAY RULE & ITS EXCEPTIONS

(1) The validity of Bushmat's belief depends on how good his eyesight was, on how close he was to the car, on whether visibility was in any way obstructed, on how good Bushmat was at estimating the speed of rapidly moving objects. In short, the validity of the out-of-court declarant's belief depends on the level of his *perception*.

(2) The validity of Bushmat's stated belief was dependent on how good his *memory* of the event was at the time he spoke about it.

(3) It also depends on whether Bushmat had any motivation to lie about the speed of the automobile. That is to say, the validity of his out-of-court declaration depends on Bushmat's *veracity* or *sincerity*.

(4) Finally, the worth of Bushmat's belief depends on how effective he was at communicating to others precisely what he meant. This can be termed the problem of *articulateness*.

To put it another way, underlying the general rule against admission of hearsay evidence are serious concerns about the *reliability* of this type of evidence.

Putting it yet another way, the law is concerned about opposing counsel's inability to *test* the reliability of hearsay evidence, since the declarant or actor is not on the witness stand in court at the time of his declaration or act. The person on the witness stand, reporting what he heard Bushmat say, is a mere conduit for the out-of-court declarant's words or acts. And, in effect, the person on the stand is insulating the out-of-court declarant from cross-examination by opposing counsel.

An Absurd Example: The Toadlike Witness. An absurd but helpful example of classic hearsay involves an overly innovative trial lawyer's method of dealing with a crucial eyewitness who presents a poor appearance and probably would make a bad impression on the jury. (The witness is absolutely toadlike in appearance, nervous, and inarticulate.) Let us suppose that the prosecution has such a witness. The prosecuting attorney could solve his problem by telling the toadlike witness, "When you come to the courthouse don't go anywhere near the courtroom. Go directly to the basement and wait there. Let no one see you." On the witness stand the prosecutor would place the most attractive and articulate person he can find, despite the fact that this person knows nothing about the facts of the case. The prosecutor, in examining this attractive witness, will say, "Down in the basement you will find a man who was an eyewitness to the events involved in this matter. I'm going to give you some questions to ask him. Go to the basement, ask my questions of the eyewitness, and then come back up here and tell the jury what the eyewitness's answers were."

This approach would be an effective way to keep the jurors from seeing the repulsive eyewitness. It would also be an effective way to prevent defense counsel from using cosss-examination to test the perception, memory, veracity, and articulateness of the only witness whose perception, memory, veracity, and articulateness really count —the eyewitness in the cellar. Needless to say, it is abundantly clear that this imaginative maneuver would run afoul of the rule against hearsay evidence. The unsworn words (assertions) of the out-of-court declarant (the toadlike witness in the basement) are being offered in court to prove their truth.

Summary. To summarize, underlying the rule against hearsay evidence are serious worries about the worth of such evidence, since (1) it was not under oath or solemn affirmation, and (2) it was not subject to cross-examination to test for the presence of hearsay risks or dangers. Opposing counsel was deprived of the opportunity to test the perception, memory, veracity, and articulateness of the out-of-court declarant, or actor, upon whose reliability the worth of the in-court testimony depends.

Some Examples Drawn from the Reported Cases. The most important example of classic hearsay to be found in the report of an actual case is that of Sir Walter Raleigh. It was Raleigh's case that led to the formulation of the rule against hearsay evidence. On the basis of two out-of-court statements, Raleigh was charged with treason. The first statement was by Lord Cobham. It was to the effect that Raleigh had joined with Cobham in a conspiracy to overthrow Queen Elizabeth I. The second statement was by a Portuguese gentleman as reported to the tribunal by a British ship's pilot. It was to the effect that Raleigh had expressed an intention of cutting King James's throat. The prosecution used both of these out-of-court declarations to prove the truth of the assertions contained in them. Thus both statements were hearsay. Raleigh asked for, but was not given, an opportunity to confront and cross-examine Lord Cobham. Disgust with the result in Raleigh's case resulted, in the latter part of the seventeenth century, in the rule against hearsay.

* * *

E.

"Straight from the Horse's Mouth"

Everyone has heard the phrase that supposedly originated with a bookie who was supremely confident of his tips on the races because he got his information "straight from the horse's mouth." The bookie did not realize it, but the readers of this volume comprehend that he was also giving a pretty good description of the hearsay rule's demands. Criminal cases cannot be made on gossip and secondhand accounts of what happened. The law of evidence has a strong preference for witnesses who can testify from personal knowledge based on direct observation, not "I was told it happened this way," but "I saw the whole thing and this is the way it happened."

In view of the hearsay rule, the competent criminal investigator will always endeavor to get his information "straight from the

Ch. 4 THE HEARSAY RULE & ITS EXCEPTIONS

horse's mouth." If the investigator turns up someone who says, "I heard it from Clyde Bushmat, who tells me he was present at the time and that Lishniss shot Stitz last Saturday night," he is on his way to some usable evidence, but he is only on the way. He has not gotten to the right witness yet. The witness he needs is Bushmat, who apparently has some direct knowledge. Bushmat's account will not be secondhand; if he really was present at the shooting of Stitz he can testify from personal knowledge. Armed with a comprehension of the rule against hearsay evidence, the criminal investigator will search for Bushmat.

Any time a knowledgeable law enforcement agent hears someone say to him, "I was told * * *," he knows that the hearsay rule is probably involved and that he should locate the person who did the telling. The agent will know that courtroom testimony beginning with "I was told * * *" will be excluded from evidence—unless, of course, one of the numerous *exceptions* to the hearsay rule comes into play.

TRIBE, TRIANGULATING HEARSAY

87 Harvard Law Review 957, 958–61 (1974).*

I. THE TESTIMONIAL TRIANGLE

The basic hearsay problem is that of forging a reliable chain of inferences, from an act or utterance of a person not subject to contemporaneous in-court cross-examination about that act or utterance, to an event that the act or utterance is supposed to reflect. Typically, the first link in the required chain of inferences is the link from the act or utterance to the belief it is thought to express or indicate. It is helpful to think of this link as involving a "trip" into the head of the person responsible for the act or utterance (the declarant) to see what he or she was really thinking when the act occurred. The second link is the one from the declarant's assumed belief to a conclusion about some external event that is supposed to have triggered the belief, or that is linked to the belief in some other way. This link involves a trip out of the head of the declarant, in order to match the declarant's assumed belief with the external reality sought to be demonstrated.

The trier must obviously employ such a chain of inferences whenever a witness testifies in court. But the process has long been regarded as particularly suspect when the act or utterance is not one made in court, under oath, by a person whose demeanor at the time is witnessed by the trier, and under circumstances permitting immediate cross-examination by counsel in order to probe possible inaccu-

---

* Copyright © 1974 by the Harvard Law Review Association.

racies in the inferential chain. These inaccuracies are usually attributed to the four testimonial infirmities of ambiguity, insincerity, faulty perception, and erroneous memory. In the absence of special reasons, the perceived untrustworthiness of such an out-of-court act or utterance has led the Anglo-Saxon legal system to exclude it as hearsay despite its potentially probative value.

There exists a rather simple way of schematizing all of this in terms of an elementary geometric construct that serves to structure its several related elements. The construct might be called the Testimonial Triangle. By making graphic the path of inferences, and by functionally grouping the problems encountered along the path, the triangle makes it easier both to identify when a hearsay problem exists and to structure consideration of the appropriateness of exceptions to the rule that bars hearsay inferences.

The diagram is as follows:

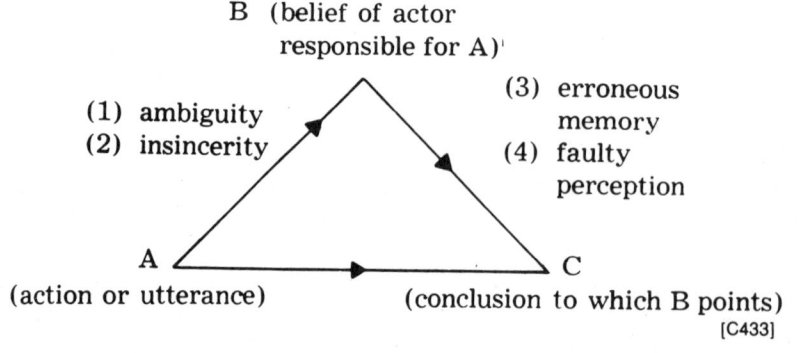

```
              B (belief of actor
                 responsible for A)

                    /\                (3) erroneous
   (1) ambiguity   /  \                   memory
   (2) insincerity/    \               (4) faulty
                 /      \                  perception
                /        \
               A----------C
         (action or utterance)    (conclusion to which B points)
```
[C433]

If we use the diagram to trace the inferential path the trier must follow, we begin at the lower left vertex of the triangle (A), which represents the declarant's (X's) act or assertion. The path first takes us to the upper vertex (B), representing X's belief in what his or her act or assertion suggests, and then takes us to the lower right vertex (C), representing the external reality suggested by X's belief. When "A" is used to prove "C" along the path through "B," a traditional hearsay problem exists and the use of the act or assertion as evidence is disallowed upon proper objection in the absence of some special reason to permit it.

It is of course a simple matter to locate the four testimonial infirmities on the triangle to show where and how they might impede the process of inference. To go from "A" to "B," the declarant's belief, one must remove the obstacles of (1) ambiguity and (2) insincerity. To go from "B" to "C," the external fact, one must further remove the obstacles of (3) erroneous memory and (4) faulty perception.

When it is possible to go directly from "A" to "C" with no detour through "B," there is no hearsay problem unless the validity of the trier's conclusion depends upon an implicit path through "B."[1] Suppose, for example, that the issue in a lawsuit is whether the Government took adequate safety precautions in connection with the nuclear test at Amchitka in 1971. James Schlesinger, then Chairman of the Atomic Energy Commission, "told reporters at Elmendorf Air Force Base outside Anchorage that he was taking his wife * * * and daughters * * * with him [to the site of the Amchitka blast] in response to Alaska Gov. William E. Egan's invitation. Egan strongly disapprove[d] of the test."[2] In these circumstances, the trip from "A," the Chairman's proposed travel with his family to the site of the blast, to "C," the conclusion that the blast was reasonably safe, may appear at first to be purely "circumstantial," but in fact that trip requires a journey into the Chairman's head and out again—a journey through the belief "B" suggested by his willingness to be near the blast with his family. The journey from "A" to "B" involves problems of possible ambiguity and of insincerity in that the Chairman was apparently seeking to dispel fears of danger, so that his act may not bespeak an actual belief in the test's safety. And the journey from "B" to "C" involves problems of memory and perception in that he may not have recalled all the relevant data and may have misperceived such data in the first instance, so that his belief in the test's safety, even if we assume the journey from "A" to "B" safely completed, may not correspond to the facts sought to be demonstrated. On both legs of the triangle, therefore, there are testimonial infirmities that cross-examination contemporaneous with the act "A" could help to expose.

By contrast, when the trier's inference can proceed from "A" directly to "C," the infirmities of hearsay do not arise. For example, the out-of-court statement "I can speak" would be admissible as nonhearsay to prove that the declarant was capable of speech, for it is the fact of his speaking rather than the content of the statement

1. An uncompromising behaviorist might insist that no detour through mental states is ever necessary because every trip from an act or utterance "A" to a conclusion "C" is reducible to a circumstantial inference about the statistical frequency with which "C" is present when "A" is present. There are difficulties with accepting the behaviorist perspective as a coherent one. * * * But even if one does adopt such a perspective, it does not follow that the trier's way of using the evidence "A" will in fact mirror that perspective, for the trier is likely to reason about states of mind even if it is in some sense incorrect or unnecessary to do so. Moreover, the connection between "A" and "C" may well be such that the frequency with which the latter accompanies the former depends upon the actor's testimonial capacities so that, even from a behaviorist perspective, information about a declarant's use of language, tendency to lie, eyesight, and so forth, may increase or decrease the statistical correlation between the utterance and the fact reported.

2. Boston Globe, Nov. 5, 1971, at 16. The fact pattern of the Amchitka example is remarkably similar to a hypothetical presented by Baron Parke in his opinion in Wright v. Doe dem. Tatham, 7 Ad. & E. 313, 388, 112 Eng. Rep. 488, 516 (K.B.1837) (experienced ship captain inspecting and setting sail on a ship).

which permits the inference, and that involves no problems of the statement's ambiguity, or of sincerity, memory, or perception.

Though anything but revolutionary, the Testimonial Triangle may constitute an analytic aid of considerable clarifying and simplifying power. It has been presented to a large number of students at Harvard Law School, and their reactions seem to indicate that it has been a helpful guide to the intricacies of hearsay law. In particular, the triangle seems most useful in indicating when an utterance which appears to be used circumstantially actually involves the infirmities of hearsay. Thus, its use can meet one of the longstanding complaints about the application of the hearsay rule in American courts, which Morgan expressed in these terms:

> [T]he serious objection is that * * * the courts do not ordinarily get down to fundamentals * * * [by going] through the series of inferences which must be made in the mental journey from the item of evidence to the fact which it is offered to prove.

The triangle allows one to structure this "mental journey" quickly and efficiently and to check it for testimonial hazards. The diagrammatic approach also helps to organize the exceptions to the hearsay rule and to highlight the policies which various groups of exceptions might express or implement. And with problems of multiple hearsay, it is normally an easy matter to dissect the various hearsay layers and to pinpoint the difficulties involved by constructing a separate triangle for each critical act or utterance.

RULES OF EVIDENCE FOR UNITED STATES COURTS AND MAGISTRATES

Rule 801

DEFINITIONS

The following definitions apply under this article:

(a) **Statement.** [See pp. 129–141].

(b) **Declarant.** A "declarant" is a person who makes a statement.

(c) **Hearsay.** "Hearsay" is a statement, other than one made by the declarant while testifying at the trial or hearing, offered in evidence to prove the truth of the matter asserted.

Ch. 4   THE HEARSAY RULE & ITS EXCEPTIONS   121

Rule 802

HEARSAY RULE

Hearsay is not admissible except as provided by these rules or by other rules prescribed by the Supreme Court pursuant to statutory authority or by Act of Congress.

2. OUT–OF–COURT STATEMENTS THAT ARE NOT HEARSAY

LILLY, AN INTRODUCTION TO THE LAW OF EVIDENCE *
160–169 (1978).

§ 50. Application of the General Principle

* * *

We have seen that the hearsay stigma attaches when, and only when, the proponent offers the declarant's assertion for a purpose which requires that the trier accept as true the facts it embodies. If the proponent's probative purpose can be achieved without the factfinder's reliance upon the truth of the declarant's statement, the hearsay rule is inapplicable.

There are several situations in which a serial repetition serves a recognized evidentiary purpose without requiring that the factfinder rely upon the declarant's credibility. One circumstance is where the proponent offers the declarant's statement because of its *legal significance independent* of its truth, or otherwise stated, independent of the declarant's subjective intent. For example, when the issue is whether B accepted A's offer for certain painting services, a witness W may testify that he overheard B say to A: "I accept your offer to paint my porch." Under the objective view of contract formation, the statement by B resulted in the formation of the agreement—assuming a reasonable offeror would have construed B's statement as an acceptance. The proponent only need establish that the operative words which formed the contract were spoken, not that these words were, in any sense, true. It is of no consequence that the cross-examiner is deprived of an opportunity to test the defects in B's perception, memory, sincerity or transcription. What matters is that B spoke the words of acceptance, not (for example) that he may have been insincere because he secretly intended to reject A's offer. Note there is no proper hearsay objection as to whether B spoke the words of acceptance, because W, who asserts he overheard B, is in court and available for cross-examination. The cross-examiner can interrogate W concerning what B said—that is, he can probe fully the issue of what (if any) words were spoken. Hence, W, who was, so to speak, the *auditor of* B's statement can be cross-examined regarding what B

---
* Reprinted with permission from Lilly's "An Introduction to the Law of Evidence," West Publishing Co. (1978).

said. *B*, the declarant, need not be examined because his statement is not offered for its truth.

The foregoing discussion reveals that there are two inquiries regarding the use of a declarant's out-of-court statement. The first question is whether there is admissible evidence that the declaration was made. If the statement is oral, it usually is necessary to call as a witness the auditor, who can give testimony concerning what the declarant said. If the statement is in writing, it usually is required that the writing be produced and identified as having been authored by the declarant. The proponent of the evidence must be able to prove the statement was made without violating any rule of evidence, *including the hearsay rule*. Assuming there is admissible evidence that the statement was made, the second inquiry is whether the declarant's statement is offered for its truth. In the illustration involving the formation of an oral contract, there was proper (admissible) evidence that the declarant-offeree spoke the words of acceptance. And since his declaration was not offered for its truth, it falls outside the exclusionary reach of the hearsay rule.

Consider Mr. Justice Holmes's classic example of the man who falsely shouts fire in a crowded theater. Suppose that in the accused's prosecution for the resulting offense of disturbing the peace, a witness offers to testify that he heard the defendant shout "fire," and the defense objects on the grounds of hearsay. Because the statement is offered only to show that the declarant spoke the warning (and not to show that there was a fire in the theater), the objection fails. Note that the witness called to testify was an auditor-witness, in that he claims to have actually overheard the defendant shout the warning. What if the witness testified that another person, *B*, told him that the defendant shouted fire but the witness himself had not heard the shout? The proffered testimony would be hearsay. The prosecution would be introducing the witness's testimony for a purpose (viz, to show that the defendant shouted the warning) requiring the trier to accept the *truth of B's statement*. The defect in this latter instance is that the proponent offers hearsay evidence that the statement ("fire") was uttered: instead of calling an auditor, he calls a witness who did not hear the defendant's shout, and hence who can testify only that the auditor *B* stated that the defendant shouted "fire." The cross-examiner is denied the opportunity to test the *auditor's* assertion that the defendant gave the warning.

* * *

Another instance in which a statement is not offered for its truth is when the purpose of offering the statement is to *show its probable effect upon another person*. Suppose, for example, a patron sues a grocery store for injuries sustained from slipping on the contents of a broken ketchup bottle. The defendant store calls to the stand a checkout clerk (the auditor) who will testify that he heard the manager cry out to the patron: "Lady, please don't step on the bottle of ketchup." The evidence is consequential (material) because the patron's conduct, which may involve contributory negligence, should be evaluated in light of the warning. The purpose for which the evidence is offered is satisfied if the trier decides that words of warning were spoken. It is unnecessary to use the declarant's statement for proof that there was a bottle of ketchup on the floor. Without reliance upon the truth of the declarant's statement, the trier can evaluate the plaintiff's conduct in light of whether she was reasonably warned of the hazardous condition. The question is what effect the warning had or should have had upon her, a question that can be addressed without accepting the clerk's declaration for its truth. Indeed if the plaintiff maintains that she thought the manager was joking, she may so testify. Since it is the reasonableness of the *plaintiff*'s conduct that is the issue on which the evidence is offered, it is immaterial whether or not the *declarant* actually thought there was a broken bottle of ketchup on the floor.

* * *

In such cases as the foregoing, the fact that the statement was made is itself consequential because the utterance gives notice of a hazard or threatening circumstance which reasonably might affect the hearer's conduct. If the trier believes that the statement was made and that the actor heard it, it will weigh this evidence in deciding whether his actions were reasonable or justified. Compare the related but distinct case in which the substantive law makes it consequential that a declarant had an awareness or knowledge of a certain event or circumstance, and he makes a statement disclosing that knowledge. Here again the hearsay rule can be avoided. If, for example, it is consequential that the declarant knew that his brakes were defective, testimony that he stated that his brakes were bad would be admitted if the evidence were limited to showing that he had knowledge. A similar rationale would admit evidence that a declarant stated that his company's manufacturing process was poisoning nearby aquatic life. These statements would be hearsay if offered to show defective brakes or that the declarant's firm was contaminating the water. However, if the evidence is *limited to the issue of the declarant's knowledge*, which under the substantive law (we have assumed) is a determinant of liability, there is no hearsay violation. Note that the proponent would have to supply additional evidence if he sought to prove that the brakes in fact were defective or that discharged pollutants in fact were killing fish. But the words spoken demonstrate a knowledge or awareness, making it unnecessary to rely upon the declarant's credibility when awareness is the proposition at which the evidence is directed. Even though the statement of knowledge is couched in terms of the fact to be proved ("*I know* my brakes are bad") the statement "can still rest on the nonhearsay ground that (bad brakes having been otherwise shown)

* * * [the declarant's] remark tends to show that if the brakes were bad he was aware of it."

* * *

We now have encountered three general classes of statements that fall outside the hearsay rule. In the first, the act of speaking certain words has an *independent legal effect* quite aside from the truth or falsity of the assertion. The acceptance of a contract is a classic example; the same rationale classifies as nonhearsay a statement made by a depositor to his bank, directing that his deposit be held in trust for his daughter—assuming that under the substantive law the very utterance of the words creates a trust. In the second class of cases, the words spoken are offered for their probable *effect upon the listener*, for example, the statement made by the declarant to A that A should be careful of the broken bottle in the aisle. A similar rationale supports the admission of a threat to kill made by declarant against the accused if the purpose of the evidence is to show that the accused was reasonable in taking steps to defend himself when he encountered the declarant. A third class of nonhearsay statements consists of those assertions by a declarant which exhibit his *knowledge of a fact or condition* in a case where this knowledge is material to the outcome. For example, a declarant states that his vehicle has defective brakes and this statement is offered to show his knowledge or awareness. A similar rationale might admit a statement by the declarant that he was forbidden by court order from visiting his child: this statement exhibits an awareness of that provision of the order, and would not be hearsay if offered in a contempt proceeding for the limited purpose of showing that the declarant knew of the restriction.

* * *

None of the examples thus far discussed involves a written declaration, but it should be clear that assertive documentary evidence can be hearsay. If a declarant's writing is offered for the truth of the assertion it contains, the hearsay rule is applicable: the cross-examiner cannot test the reliability of the written assertion—unless, of course, the author testifies, in which case the writing may be superfluous. As with verbal declarations, however, a writing may serve a nonhearsay purpose and, if properly offered, it escapes objection. Suppose, for example, A sues B for the fraudulent sale of a rare book. The complaint alleges that B, in connection with the sale, fraudulently stated that the volume bore the signature of Thomas Jefferson. Could B introduce into evidence a written warranty from his supplier (the declarant) authenticating Jefferson's signature as genuine? If B offers the warranty to support the proposition that the signature is genuine the written evidence (an out-of-court assertion by the supplier) is hearsay. But if B offers the evidence only to show that he had no intent to deceive A (thus attempting to negate the element of deceit), there is no violation of the hearsay rule. Of-

Ch. 4   THE HEARSAY RULE & ITS EXCEPTIONS   125

fering the statement contained in the warranty for the limited purpose of showing its probable effect upon *B*'s mind enables the trier to consider the book supplier's assertion without relying upon his credibility.

SUBRAMANIAM v. PUBLIC PROSECUTOR

Judicial Committee of the Privy Council, 1956.
100 Solicitor's Journal 566.

This was an appeal, by special leave, by Subramaniam, a rubber tapper, from an order of the Supreme Court of the Federation of Malaya (Court of Appeal at Kuala Lumpur), dated 12th September, 1955, dismissing his appeal against a judgment and order of the High Court of Johore Bahru, whereby he was found guilty on a charge of being in possession of twenty rounds of ammunition without lawful authority, contrary to reg. 4(1)(*b*) of the Emergency Regulations, 1951, and sentenced to death. It was common ground that on 29th April, 1955, at a place in the Rengam District in the State of Johore, the appellant was found in a wounded condition by certain members of the security forces; that when he was searched there was found around his waist a leather belt with three pouches containing twenty live rounds of ammunition. The defence put forward was that he had been captured by terrorists, that at all material times he was acting under duress, and that at the time of his capture by the security forces he had formed the intention to surrender, with which intention he had come to the place where he was found. He gave evidence describing his capture and sought to give evidence of what the terrorists said to him, but the trial judge ruled that evidence of the conversation with the terrorists was not admissible unless they were called. The judge said that he could find no evidence of duress, and in the result the appellant, as stated, was convicted.

Mr. L. M. D. De Silva, giving the judgment, said that the trial judge was in error in ruling out peremptorily the evidence of conversation between the terrorists and the appellant. Evidence of a statement made to a witness by a person who was not himself called as a witness might or might not be hearsay. It was hearsay and inadmissible when the object of the evidence was to establish the truth of what was contained in the statement. It was not hearsay and was admissible when it was proposed to establish by the evidence, not the truth of the statement, but the fact that it was made. Statements could have been made to the appellant by the terrorists which, whether true or not, if they had been believed by the appellant, might, within the meaning of s. 94 of the Penal Code of the Federated Malay States, reasonably have induced in him an apprehension of instant death if he failed to conform to their wishes. Thus a complete, or substantially complete, version according to the appellant of what was said to him by the terrorists and by him to them had been shut out, and their lordships had to consider whether, in the circumstances of this case, that exclusion of admissible evidence afforded sufficient reason for allowing the appeal. In Muhammad Nawaz v. King-Emperor (1941), L.R. 68 I.A. 126, at p. 128, it was said: "Broadly speaking, the Judicial Committee will only interfere where there has been an infringement of the essential principles of justice. An obvious example would be * * * where [the accused] was not allowed to call relevant witnesses." In the present case the appellant had not been allowed to give relevant and admissible evidence, which was a circumstance very similar in its consequence to not being allowed "to call relevant witnesses." The appellant's version, if believed, could and might have afforded cogent evidence of duress brought to bear on him. He had not been allowed to give relevant and admissible evidence, and it could not be held with any confidence that had the excluded evidence, which went to the very root of the defence of duress, been admitted, the result of the trial would probably have been the same. Their lordships, for those reasons, had humbly advised Her Majesty that the appeal should be allowed.

[Reversed.]

DRAPER v. UNITED STATES

Supreme Court of the United States, 1959.
358 U.S. 307, 79 S.Ct. 329, 3 L.Ed.2d 327.

Mr. Justice WHITTAKER delivered the opinion of the Court.

Petitioner was convicted of knowingly concealing and transporting narcotic drugs * * *. His conviction was based in part on the use in evidence against him of two "envelopes containing [865 grains of] heroin" and a hypodermic syringe that had been taken from his person, following his arrest, by the arresting officer.

[Defendant claimed that his constitutional rights had been violated, and that the evidence seized should be excluded at trial.]

* * *

The evidence offered at the hearing on the motion to suppress was not substantially disputed. It established that one Marsh, a federal narcotic agent with 29 years' experience, was stationed at Denver; that one Hereford had been engaged as a "special employee" of the Bureau of Narcotics at Denver for about six months, and from time to time gave information to Marsh regarding violations of the narcotic laws, for which Hereford was paid small sums of money, and that Marsh had always found the information given by Hereford to be accurate and reliable. On September 3, 1956, Hereford told Marsh that James Draper (petitioner) recently had taken up abode at a stated address in Denver and "was peddling narcotics to several addicts" in that city. Four days later, on September 7, Hereford told Marsh "that Draper had gone to Chicago the day before [September 6] by train [and] that he was going to bring back three ounces of heroin [and] that he would return to Denver either on the morning of the 8th of September or the morning of the 9th of September also by train." Hereford also gave Marsh a detailed physical description of Draper and of the clothing he was wearing, and said that he would be carrying "a tan zipper bag," and that he habitually "walked real fast."

On the morning of September 8, Marsh and a Denver police officer went to the Denver Union Station and kept watch over all incoming trains from Chicago, but they did not see anyone fitting the description that Hereford had given. Repeating the process on the morning of September 9, they saw a person, having the exact physical attributes and wearing the precise clothing described by Hereford, alight from an incoming Chicago train and start walking "fast" toward the exit. He was carrying a tan zipper bag in his right hand and the left was thrust in his raincoat pocket. Marsh, accompanied by the police officer, overtook, stopped and arrested him. They then searched him and found the two "envelopes containing heroin" clutched in his left hand in his raincoat pocket, and found the syringe in the tan zipper bag. Marsh then took him (petitioner) into custody. Hereford died four days after the arrest and therefore did not testify at the hearing on the motion.

* * *

The crucial question for us then is whether knowledge of the related facts and circumstances gave Marsh "probable cause" within the meaning of the Fourth Amendment, and "reasonable grounds" * * * to believe that petitioner had committed or was committing a violation of the narcotic laws. If it did, the arrest, though without a warrant, was lawful and the subsequent search of petitioner's person and the seizure of the found heroin were validly made incident to a lawful arrest, and therefore the motion to suppress was properly overruled and the heroin was competently received in evidence at the trial. * * *

Petitioner does not dispute this analysis of the question for decision. Rather, he contends (1) that the information given by Hereford to Marsh was "hearsay" and, because hearsay is not legally competent evidence in a criminal trial, could not legally have been considered, but should have been put out of mind, by Marsh in assessing whether he had "probable cause" and "reasonable grounds" to arrest petitioner without a warrant, and (2) that, even if hearsay could lawfully have been considered, Marsh's information should be held insufficient to show "probable cause" and "reasonable grounds" to believe that petitioner had violated or was violating the narcotic laws and to justify his arrest without a warrant.

Considering the first contention, we find petitioner entirely in error. * * * [In a similar case,] the convict contended "that the factors relating to inadmissibility of the evidence [for] *purposes of proving guilt at the trial,* deprive[d] the evidence as a whole of sufficiency to show probable cause for the search * * *." (Emphasis added.) But this Court, rejecting that contention, said: "[T]he so-called distinction places a wholly unwarranted emphasis upon the criterion of admissibility in evidence, to prove the accused's guilt, of the facts relied upon to show probable cause. That emphasis, we think, goes much too far in confusing and disregarding the difference between what is required to prove guilt in a criminal case and what is required to show probable cause for arrest or search. It approaches requiring (if it does not in practical effect require) proof sufficient to establish guilt in order to substantiate the existence of probable cause. There is a large difference between the two things to be proved [guilt and probable cause], as well as between the tribunals which determine them, and therefore a like difference in the *quanta* and modes of proof required to establish them." 4   338 U.S. at pages 172–173   *   *   *.

Nor can we agree with petitioner's second contention that Marsh's information was insufficient to show probable cause and reasonable grounds to believe that petitioner had violated or was violating the narcotic laws and to justify his arrest without a warrant. The information given to narcotic agent Marsh by "special employee" Hereford may have been hearsay to Marsh, but coming from one employed for that purpose and whose information had always been found accurate and reliable, it is clear that Marsh would have been derelict in his duties had he not pursued it. And when, in pursuing that information, he saw a man, having the exact physical attributes and wearing the precise clothing and carrying the tan zipper bag that Hereford had described, alight from one of the very trains from the very place stated by Hereford and start to walk at a "fast" pace toward the station exit, Marsh had personally verified every facet of the information given him by Hereford except whether petitioner had accomplished his mission and had the three ounces of heroin on his person or in his bag. And surely, with every other bit of Hereford's information being thus personally verified, Marsh had "reasonable grounds" to believe that the remaining unverified bit of Hereford's information—that Draper would have the heroin with him—was likewise true.

4. In United States v. Heitner, 2 Cir., 149 F.2d 105, 106, Judge Learned Hand said: "It is well settled that an arrest may be made upon hearsay evidence; and indeed, the 'reasonable cause' necessary to support an arrest cannot demand the same strictness of proof as the accused's guilt upon a trial, unless the powers of peace officers are to be so cut down that they cannot possibly perform their duties." Grau v. United States, 287 U.S. 124, 128, * * * contains a *dictum* that "A search warrant may issue only upon evidence which would be competent in the trial of the offense before a jury * * *." But the principles underlying that proposition were thoroughly discredited and rejected [by the Supreme Court].

"In dealing with probable cause, * * * as the very name implies, we deal with probabilities. These are not technical; they are the factual and practical considerations of everyday life on which reasonable and prudent men, not legal technicians, act." Brinegar v. United States, * * * Probable cause exists where "the facts and circumstances within their [the arresting officers'] knowledge and of which they had reasonably trustworthy information [are] sufficient in themselves to warrant a man of reasonable caution in the belief that" an offense has been or is being committed. * * *

We believe that, under the facts and circumstances here, Marsh had probable cause and reasonable grounds to believe that petitioner was committing a violation of the laws of the United States relating to narcotic drugs at the time he arrested him. The arrest was therefore lawful, and the subsequent search and seizure, having been made incident to that lawful arrest, were likewise valid. It follows that petitioner's motion to suppress was properly denied and that the seized heroin was competent evidence lawfully received at the trial.

Affirmed.

The Chief Justice and Mr. Justice FRANKFURTER took no part in the consideration or decision of this case.

[A dissenting opinion by Mr. Justice DOUGLAS is omitted.]

3. WHAT IS A STATEMENT?

RULES OF EVIDENCE FOR UNITED STATES COURTS AND MAGISTRATES

Rule 801

DEFINITIONS

The following definitions apply under this article:

(a) **Statement.** A "statement" is (1) an oral or written assertion or (2) nonverbal conduct of a person, if it is intended by him as an assertion.

a. NON–HUMAN EVIDENCE

WALTZ, CRIMINAL EVIDENCE

70 (1975).

Nonhuman Evidence

Is It Hearsay? Does it violate the rule against hearsay when a police witness on the stand testifies that radar equipment "said" that the defendant was driving his automobile at 90 miles an hour? Is violence done to the rule when a meter maid testifies that the parking meter "said" the defendant's allotted time had expired? * * *

Are these machines all out-of-court declarants within the meaning of the common law hearsay rule?

On the theory that machines, unlike some humans, lack a conscious motivation to tell lies, and because the operation (including the accuracy and reliability) of machines can be explained by human witnesses who are then subject to probing cross-examination by opposing counsel, the law permits so-called nonhuman hearsay.

MORGAN, HEARSAY AND NON-HEARSAY

48 Harv.L.Rev. 1138, 1145-6 (1935).*

* * * The courts constantly and correctly receive as reliable evidence what careful analysis discloses to be hearsay. They sometimes obscure the question by a resort to the doctrine of judicial notice. Where a court receives an almanac as evidence of an astronomical fact, it is not taking judicial notice of the fact: it is admitting anonymous hearsay and taking judicial notice of the reliability of the almanac as a source of authentic information. Again, nothing is more common than to allow a witness to rely upon a timepiece in stating the time of day when an event happened. If he should testify that he looked at a Western Union clock and noted the time, he would be considered as giving particularly accurate testimony, but would it not be anonymous hearsay upon anonymous hearsay? Certainly the person in charge of the master mechanism which regulated the clock consulted by the witness did not make the astronomical observations in accordance with which that clock was made to indicate the hour and minute of the day. Yet just as certainly an objection upon the ground of hearsay would receive scant attention. Only a little less easy is a demonstration of the hearsay element in the indication of time upon a sundial unless preceded by the testimony of a witness who checked it against his own astronomical observations. Much the same may be said of the automatic weighing machines which in return for a coin furnish a printed assertion of a person's weight, and of nonautomatic scales where the position of the marker which produces a balance of the beam announces the weight of the object upon the platform. In each of these cases, the anonymous maker or regulator of the machine intended that the reaction of the machine should operate as an assertion. In each of them he may have fixed the instrument so as to produce a false declaration, as where the faker who gambles upon his pretended ability to guess his victim's weight controls the balance by a hidden mechanism, or a practical joker sets a series of timepieces so as to cause another to miss an appointment. Generally speaking, however, the court regards these mechanisms as sufficiently accurate to justify a trier of fact in relying upon their

---

* Copyright, 1934, 1935 by the Harvard Law Review Association.

reactions for most purposes, at least after a preliminary showing of reasonable accuracy. In other words, it takes judicial notice of the reliability of these sources of information under ordinary circumstances, notwithstanding their hearsay character.

Somewhat the same process is used when expert witnesses are permitted to base their opinions upon data as to which they have not the slightest personal knowledge. Though no witness gives firsthand evidence of the truth expressed or implied in these data, the expert is permitted to draw deductions therefrom which the jury may hear and consider.

BUCK v. STATE

Criminal Court of Appeals of Oklahoma, 1943.
77 Okl.Cr. 17, 138 P.2d 115.

BAREFOOT, Judge. Defendant, G. R. Buck, was charged in the District Court of Okmulgee County with the crime or arson, was tried, convicted and sentenced to serve a term of two years in the State Penitentiary, and has appealed.

The only contention presented in the brief of defendant is that the evidence is insufficient to sustain the judgment and sentence, and that the court erred in refusing to direct a verdict of not guilty.

This case may be said to rest almost wholly upon circumstantial evidence. It presents to this Court for the first time the question of the admissibility in evidence of the trailing of one by bloodhounds. We find that this question has heretofore been presented to the highest appellate courts of many states, and that some consideration has been given thereto by textbook writers. However, this Court has never been called upon to consider the question, although the use of bloodhounds at the State Penitentiary has been in vogue for many years.

An investigation of the authorities has been most interesting and profitable. The earliest case in this country in which consideration was given to the question was that of Hodge v. State, 98 Ala. 10, 13 So. 385, 39 Am.St.Rep. 17. In that case the death penalty was upheld, and the evidence of tracking by the dog to defendant's home was sustained as competent evidence. Since this case in 1893, many courts have passed upon the question, and by the great weight of authority it has been held that the evidence is admissible under certain rules and conditions, as will be hereinafter stated.

Among the states upholding the rule are Alabama, Florida, Iowa, Kansas, Kentucky, North Carolina, South Carolina, New York, Missouri, Ohio, Texas, Mississippi, Georgia, Tennessee, Arkansas and Louisiana * * *.

The states, some of which recognize that in some cases the evidence might be admissible, yet refuse to follow the rule are Nebraska, Illinois and Indiana, and one case from Iowa. * * *

In the early case of State v. Thomas Hall, 4 Ohio Dec. 147, a history of the bloodhound is given as follows:

"It is a matter of common knowledge, and therefore a matter of which courts will take notice, that the breed of dogs known as bloodhounds is possessed of a high degree of intelligence, and acuteness of scent, and may be trained to follow human tracks with considerable certainty and success, if put upon a recent trail. In Chambers' Encyc., under the title 'Bloodhound,' it is said of this dog, that 'it is remarkable for its exquisite scent and for its great sagacity and perseverance in tracking any object to the pursuit of which it has been trained;' that 'it has been frequently used for the pursuit of felons and deerslayers, and, in America, for the capture of fugitive slaves;' and the writer refers to the use of these dogs in border warfare, and to their importation 'into Jamaica in 1796 to be used in suppressing the Maroon insurrection, but the terror occasioned by their arrival produced the effect without their actual employment.' The Encyc. Britannica (9th Ed.) under the title 'Dog,' bears this testimony to the well known traits of this animal: 'The bloodhound is remarkable for its acuteness of scent, its discrimination in keeping to the particular scent on which it is first laid, and the intelligence and pertinacity with which it pursues its object to a successful issue. These qualities have been taken advantage of not only in the chase, but also in the pursuit of felons and fugitives of every kind. According to Strabo, these dogs were used in an attack upon the Gauls. In the clan feuds of the Scottish Highlands, and in the frequent wars between England and Scotland, they were regularly employed in tracking fugitive warriors, and were thus employed, according to early chroniclers, in pursuit of Wallace and Bruce. The former is said to have put the hound off the scent by killing a suspected follower, on whose corpse the hound stood. For a similar purpose captives were often killed. Bruce is said to have baffled his dogged pursuer as effectually, though less cruelly, by wading some distance down stream, and then ascending a tree by a branch which overhung the water and thus breaking the scent. In the histories of border feuds these dogs constantly appear as employed in the pursuit of enemies, and the renown of the warrier was great, who,

> "'By wily turns and desperate bounds, Had baffled Percy's best bloodhounds.'

"In suppressing the Irish rebellion in the time of Queen Elizabeth, the Earl of Essex had, it is said, 800 of these animals accompanying the army. * * *

"Both history, therefore, and natural history testify to the exceptional keenness of scent and capacity for training of this variety of hound. Whatever may be said of the wisdom or humanity of resorting to this means of detecting and securing the apprehension of criminals, there can be no doubt, that, where a well trained dog is set

Ch. 4   THE HEARSAY RULE & ITS EXCEPTIONS   133

upon a recent track and follows it, in the usual manner of such dogs in following a trail, up to the person or home of the accused, these facts may, on the plain principles governing circumstantial evidence, be shown as tending to connect him with the crime charged. It was so held in the case of Hodge v. State, 98 Ala. 10 [13 So. 385], 39 Am. St.Rep. 17, which is the only case I have found directly in point.

"Of course in such cases full opportunity should be given to inquire into the breeding, training and testing of the dog, and to all the circumstances attending the trailing in the case on trial, and to the manner in which the dog then acted and was handled by the person having it in charge. The weight to be given to the tracking as evidence against the accused will depend largely upon these matters."

Also in the case of Blair v. Commonwealth, 181 Ky. 218, 204 S.W. 67, 68, in which a beautiful tribute is paid to the dog, where it is said:

"It is next insisted that the court should have sustained appellant's objection to the testimony relating to the trailing of Blair and Crump by two bloodhounds immediately after the offense was committed. The former opinion reiterated the rule upon that subject first announced in this state in 1898, in Pedigo v. Commonwealth, 103 Ky. 41, 44 S.W. 143, * * * holding such testimony to be competent when properly guarded. The rule may now be said to be thoroughly established in this jurisdiction. * * * And it cannot be said that the doctrine is wholly a novel one.

"If we may credit Sir Walter Scott, such evidence was looked upon with favor as early as the twelfth century. In the Talisman it is related that in the joint crusade of Richard I of England and Phillip II of France, Roswell, the hound, pulled from the saddle Conrade, Marquis of Montserrat, thus mutely accusing him of the theft of the banner of England. Phillip defended the Marquis with the remark:

" 'Surely the word of a knight and a prince should bear him out against the barking of a cur.'

"To which Richard replied:

" 'Royal brother, recollect that the Almighty who gave the dog to be companion of our pleasures and our toils, both invested him with a nature noble and incapable of deceit. He forgets neither friend nor foe; remembers, and with accuracy, both benefit and injury. He hath a share of man's intelligence, but no share of man's falsehood. You may bribe a soldier to slay a man with his sword, or a witness to take life by false accusation; but you cannot make a hound tear his benefactor; he is the friend of man save when man justly incurs his enmity. Dress yonder Marquis in what peacock robes you will, disguise his appearance, alter his complexion with drugs and washes, hide himself amidst a hundred men; I will yet pawn my scepter that the hound detects him, and expresses his resentment, as you have this day beheld.'

"The doctrine of the admissibility of bloodhound evidence in criminal prosecutions has been slowly gaining ground during the past 20 years.

* * * "The general rules deductible from these decisions are as follows:

"(1) The bloodhound in question must be shown to have been trained to follow human beings by their tracks and to have been tested as to its accuracy in trailing upon one or more occasions; and,

"(2) The evidence of the acts of bloodhounds in following a trail may be received merely as circumstantial or corroborative evidence against a person towards whom other circumstances point as being guilty of the commission of the crime charged.

"The admission of this class of evidence is therefore hedged about with abundant safeguards in the way of other and human testimony; and as long as these rules are adhered to bloodhound evidence is no more dangerous than any other class of circumstantial evidence.

"In Kentucky it is settled that testimony as to trailing by bloodhounds of one charged with crime may be permitted to go to the jury for what it is worth, as one of the circumstances which may tend to connect the defendant with the crime only after it has been shown by some one having personal knowledge of the facts: (a) That the dog in question is of pure blood and of a stock characterized by acuteness of scent and power of discrimination; (b) is itself possessed of these qualities and has been trained or tested in the tracking of human beings; and (c) that the dog so trained and tested was laid on the trail, whether visible or not, concerning which testimony has been admitted, at the point where the circumstances tend clearly to show that the guilty party had been, or upon a track which such circumstances indicated had been made by him."

* * * The evidence with reference to the history, qualification and experience of the dogs was given by the witness M. I. Stokes. He testified that he was employed by the State of Oklahoma at the State Penitentiary at McAlester. That he had charge of the dogs, about fifteen or twenty in number. That the witness Hubert Wilson was a trusty at the penitentiary who had been appointed to assist him in handling the dogs. That the witness had had fifteen or twenty years' experience in the handling of dogs. That he had been at the State Penitentiary at McAlester in this capacity for about three years, and that the two dogs which he brought to Okmulgee on the 22nd of August, 1938, were "Old Boston," and "Diana." That he selected them as his two best dogs from a pack of fifteen or twenty. "Old Boston" was nine years old and "Diana" a younger dog. He testified at length as to the experience and training which these dogs had received, and especially "Old Boston" and gave individual instances of performances by him in the trailing of human beings. He testified:

"Q. And they can distinguish between the smells of human beings? A. I will answer that question like this, it has been my experience with bloodhounds, with a trained bloodhound, they have an instinct, we call it, I call it a sense to trail a man better than any other dog would trail anything else, and apparently they have an instinct that will enable them to carry a trail through places that apparently other dogs couldn't carry it at all, and they always know one track from the other. It is impossible for you to cause them to change tracks, they won't do that.

"Q. You mean, if he is a well trained and experienced bloodhound, if he starts on the track of one human being, he will stay with that particular track? A. He will trail no other track than that. It is impossible to get him to change tracks." * * *

"Q. Does it make a difference whether the trail is fresh or cold? A. Those two dogs I had there would trail a twenty-four hour track. I have known them to do that. They wouldn't trail as fast as one we call warmer, fresher track, you understand, but those dogs would trail a ten or twelve hour track and move right along with it; but a four or five hour track is nothing at all for them.

"Q. Would that be considered a comparatively fresh trail? A. It certainly would.

"Q. Now then, you used Old Boston as the lead dog, did you? A. Yes sir. However, we had this Diana there, one of the greatest dogs I ever knew and one of the most accurate dogs.

"Q. Did you select those two dogs out of a kennel of how many dogs? A. We had fifteen or twenty dogs, but on all special occasions I used those two dogs because they were the best I had and the best I ever saw.

"Q. Let's take, for instance, Old Boston, I understand he has since died, since the trailing of this track up there? A. Yes, sir.

"Q. When did she die? A. Boston died, I think, about a month after I left down there.

"Q. To refresh your memory, was it sometime in March, 1939? A. Right along then, yes sir.

"Q. And what age dog was she? A. Boston was about nine years of age.

"Q. Was that dog owned by the state of Oklahoma? A. Yes sir. Yes, she was owned by the State.

"Q. How long were you its keeper or trainer? A. Boston individually?

"Q. Yes. A. I only ran Boston about two and a half years. I used him some several years before that when they first got him from Texas. That was before I went to Granite.

"Q. What age dog was he, if you know, when he was brought to Oklahoma? A. He was said to be about three years of age.

"Q. Have you ever seen him on a man's trail? A. Yes, several hundred."

* * *

"Q. Did you ever know Old Boston to lie on any trail? A. I never knew him to make a mistake."

* * *

"A. I would have to answer that question like this, that this Master Mind dog of Pennsylvania has a greater reputation than Boston. Boston was considered the second dog in the United States at that time."

He then testified to the individual work of these dogs in many cases that came under his personal observation, and where they had successfully tracked human beings, and then testified as to the instant case as above related. On cross examination he was asked:

"Q. There hasn't been any monument or any money or anything appropriated to build a monument to Boston since he died? A. I don't know. There ought to be."

In view of this testimony, we have decided that the tribute to the hound by Richard I of England, as above quoted, shall be a monument or tribute to "Old Boston," and for this reason we perpetuate his name in the law books of this State. Though the State has not erected a monument to his memory, his services will ever be remembered, not only in the instant case but others.

As above stated, the evidence in this case is almost wholly based upon circumstantial evidence, and while we recognize the rule announced in the decisions which have been cited, that a conviction will not be upheld upon the evidence alone of trailing by bloodhounds, yet that evidence being competent as a circumstance, together with the other evidence in the case, where competent proof has been given as to the qualifications, training and experience of the bloodhounds used, as in the instant case, this testimony together with the other evidence in the case presented a question of fact for the jury to pass upon as to the guilt or innocence of the defendant.

There can be no question but that the evidence as to the training and experience of the two dogs, and especially "Old Boston," was such that it entitled the court to submit it to the jury for their consideration, together with the other facts and circumstances and under the law we can not say that the verdict of the jury should be set aside.

We have, therefore, reached the conclusion that the judgment and sentence of the District Court of Okmulgee County should be affirmed.

JONES, P. J., and DOYLE, J., concur.

b. NON-ASSERTIVE CONDUCT

WALTZ, CRIMINAL EVIDENCE
65–67 (1975).

* * *

Assertive and Nonassertive Conduct as Hearsay. The common law definition of hearsay is broad enough to embrace *conduct* as well as spoken or written words. In fact, the common law rule against hearsay covers two types of out-of-court conduct: assertive and nonassertive.

(1) *Assertive conduct* is conduct which is consciously *intended* as an assertion; for example, pointing at someone or something for identifying purposes, or nodding one's head to indicate "yes" or "no." Here, action is simply substitued for words. The conduct is hearsay, just as would be the words.

Example:

BY THE PROSECUTING ATTORNEY: Officer Krupke, what did you do next?

A: We arranged for a lineup and I told the little girl to point out the person who molested her if she saw him in the line-up.

Q: What did she do, if anything?

A: She pointed to the third man from the left, the defendant in this case.

BY DEFENSE COUNSEL: Object, your Honor. Hearsay by conduct.

THE COURT: The objection is sustained. The jury will disregard the witness's last answer in its entirety.

(2) *Nonassertive conduct* is conduct which was *not* consciously intended as a direct assertion concerning an issue in the case but which nonetheless can be translated into such an assertion by a process of inference. That is, the out-of-court conduct carries with it an implied assertion concerning a material issue.

At common law, but not under some of the new evidence codes, nonassertive conduct violates the rule against hearsay, just as does assertive conduct (finger-pointing).

The landmark example of nonassertive conduct as hearsay is an old English case in which the issue was whether the maker of a will, one Marsden, was mentally competent. The person (a stableboy) to whom Marsden's will left everything sought to introduce three letters which had been addressed to Marsden and which requested him to perform acts that only a sane person could do. The letter-writers, in other words, had treated Marsden as a mentally competent person.

The English court refused to admit the letters on the ground that they were hearsay. The letters did not directly and consciously *assert* the matter in issue, Marsden's mental condition. Nevertheless, by implication they did show that the letter-writers *believed* Marsden to be mentally competent. The writing of the letters was nonassertive conduct and, under the common law, this is hearsay.

Another example of nonassertive conduct as hearsay can be found in a famous closing argument for the prosecution made by Daniel Webster. The accused in the case was tied to the alleged murder through one Crowninshield, who had recently killed himself. If Crowninshield's involvement in the murder could not be established, there would be no independent evidence linking the accused to the homicide. Webster skillfully tried to demonstrate that Crowninshield's suicide was nonassertive conduct attesting a guilty conscience. His suicide was asserted to be a natural consequence of his having been the killer. However, at common law this would be considered hearsay. (And of course prosecutor Webster did not take into account other possible explanations for Crowninshield's suicide —he was a terminal cancer patient, or had had a tragic love affair— Webster neatly sidestepped the relevance problem.)

Nonassertive Conduct Under the Evidence Codes. Section 1200(a) of the influential California Evidence Code states that " 'hearsay evidence' is evidence of a *statement* * * * " (italics added). Section 225 of that code states that " 'statement' means (a) oral or written verbal expression or (b) nonverbal conduct of a person *intended by him as a substitute for oral or written verbal expression*" (italics added). Thus nonassertive conduct is not hearsay under California's Evidence Code. Rule 801 of the Federal Rules of Evidence is to the same effect. Clearly, the modern trend is to treat only deliberately assertive words or actions as hearsay.

COMMONWEALTH v. KNAPP

Supreme Judicial Court of Massachusetts, 1830.
VII American State Trials 395, 515–516.

[John Francis Knapp was tried in 1830 for the murder of one Joseph White. The prosecution, headed by Daniel Webster, claimed that Knapp aided and abetted one Crowninshield, who actually struck the fatal blows. It was therefore crucial to the prosecution to show Crowninshield's guilt—even though Crowninshield himself had committed suicide before the trial. In his closing argument, Daniel Webster discussed the probative value of the suicide on the issue of Crowninshield's guilt—Ed.]

The fatal blow is given! and the victim passes, without a struggle or a motion, from the repose of sleep to the repose of death! It is the assassin's purpose to make sure work, and he yet plies the dagger, though it was obvious that life had been destroyed by the blow of the bludgeon. He even raises the aged arm, that he may not fail in his aim at the heart, and replaces it again over the wounds of the poignard! To finish the picture, he explores the wrist for the pulse! he feels it, and ascertains that it beats no longer! It is accomplished. The deed is done. He retreats, retraces his steps to the window, passes out through it, as he came in, and escapes. He has done the murder—no eye has seen him, no hear has heard him. The secret is his own, and it is safe!

Ah! gentlemen, that was a dreadful mistake. Such a secret can be safe nowhere. The whole creation of God has neither nook nor corner, where the guilty can bestow it, and say it is safe. Not to speak of that eye which glances through all disguises, and beholds everything, as in the splendor of noon, such secrets of guilt are never safe from detection, even by men. True it is, generally speaking, that "murder will out." True it is, that Providence hath so ordained, and doth so govern things, that those who break the great law of heaven, by shedding man's blood, seldom succeed in avoiding discovery. Especially, in a case exciting so much attention as this, discovery must come, and will come, sooner or later. A thousand eyes turn at once to explore every man, every thing, every circumstance, connected with the time and place; a thousand ears catch every whisper; a thousand excited minds intensely dwell on the scene, shedding all their light, and ready to kindle the slightest circumstance into a blaze of discovery. Meantime the guilty soul cannot keep its own secret. It is false to itself; or rather it feels an irresistible impulse of conscience to be true to itself. It labors under its guilty possession, and knows not what to do with it. The human heart was not made for the residence of such an inhabitant. It finds itself preyed on by a torment which it does not acknowledge to God nor man. A vulture is devouring it, and it can ask no sympathy or assistance, either from heaven or earth. The secret which the murderer possesses soon comes to possess him; and, like the evil spirits of which we read, it overcomes him, and leads him whithersoever it will. He feels it beating at his heart, rising to his throat, and demanding disclosure. He thinks the whole world sees it in his face, reads it in his eyes, and almost hears its workings in the very silence of his thoughts. It has become his master. It betrays his discretion, it breaks down his courage, it conquers his prudence. When suspicions, from without, begin to embarrass him, and the net of circumstance to entangle him, the fatal secret struggles with still greater violence to burst forth. It must be confessed, it will be confessed; there is no refuge from confession but suicide, and suicide is confession.

PEOPLE v. BARNHART

District Court of Appeal of California, 1944.
66 Cal.App.2d 714, 153 P.2d 214.

[Defendant was convicted of keeping a house for the purpose of taking bets on horse races. One of the grounds for the defendant's appeal was that the arresting officers were allowed to testify as to telephone calls received by them on defendant's telephone during the arrest. These calls were received from anonymous callers who stated over the telephone that they wished to place bets—Ed.]

* * *

Under the authority of [past case law] * * * evidence of telephonic conversations between arresting officers and persons calling the establishment are properly admitted as tending to establish the fact that the premises were occupied for the purpose of bookmaking.

* * *

For the reasons stated, the judgment is affirmed.

DORAN, J. I concur in the judgment.—But I know of no rule or principle of law that authorizes or justifies a relaxation of the hearsay rule for expediency. The evidence of the telephone conversations was pure hearsay. Evidence of the fact that a conversation was received would be admissible for the purpose of proving that the telephone was in order and functioning, but for no other purpose; the substance of the conversation is unnecessary for this purpose. The argument in People v. Joffe, 45 Cal.App.2d 233, 235, 113 P.2d 901, namely, that such evidence is admissible because "it tended to establish the fact that the premises were occupied for the purpose of recording wagers on horse races," clearly permits a consideration of hearsay for the purpose of proving the very offense charged. And the same inaccurate reasoning appears in People v. Reifenstuhl, 37 Cal.App.2d 402, 405, 99 P.2d 564, where the court declared, referring to such evidence that "It was not subject to the hearsay rule. The conversation was not admitted for the purpose of proving its own contents * * * but to prove the use to which the telephone was subjected by the public and to demonstrate the reaction of the defendant at the time. The use of the room occupied by defendant was in issue and the nature of the telephonic call was a circumstance to establish the truth. The uses to which a telephone is put reveal more truthfully the character of the establishment that houses the instrument than do the words of description attached to the listing."

It is futile to argue that such evidence is not hearsay. In my judgment the preservation of the hearsay rule is not only important but vital in the administration of justice. To relax the rule just to uphold the conviction of a bookmaker, or for any other purpose, is nothing short of judicial stupidity.

WHITE, J., concurred.

Hearing denied; CARTER and SCHAUER, JJ., dissenting.

MORTON, THE ROTHSCHILDS *

49–50 (1962).

And there was no news more precious than the outcome of Waterloo. For days the London 'Change[1] had strained its ears. If Napoleon won, English consols[2] were bound to drop. If he lost, the enemy empire would shatter and consols rise.

For thirty hours the fate of Europe hung veiled in cannon smoke. On June 19, 1815, late in the afternoon a Rothschild agent named Rothworth jumped into a boat at Ostend. In his hand he held a Dutch gazette still damp from the printer. By the dawn light of June 20 Nathan Rothschild stood at Folkstone harbor and let his eye fly over the lead paragraphs. A moment later he was on his way to London (beating Wellington's envoy by many hours) to tell the government that Napoleon had been crushed. Then he proceeded to the stock exchange.

Another man in his position would have sunk his worth into consols. But this was Nathan Rothschild. He leaned against "his" pillar. He did not invest. He sold. He dumped consols.

His name was already such that a single substantial move on his part sufficed to bear or bull an issue. Consols fell. Nathan leaned and leaned, and sold and sold. Consols dropped still more. "Rothschild knows," the whisper rippled through the 'Change. "Waterloo is lost."

Nathan kept on selling, his round face motionless and stern, his pudgy fingers depressing the market by tens of thousands of pounds with each sell signal. Consols dived, consols plummeted—until, a split second before it was too late, Nathan suddenly bought a giant parcel for a song. Moments afterwards the great news broke, to send consols soaring.

We cannot guess the number of hopes and savings wiped out by this engineered panic. We cannot estimate how many liveried servants, how many Watteaus and Rembrandts, how many thoroughbreds in his descendants' stables, the man by the pillar won that single day.

* Copyright 1962 by The Curtis Publishing Co.

1. The international currency exchange —Ed.

2. Pounds—Ed.

THE HEARSAY RULE & ITS EXCEPTIONS

TEST ON HEARSAY *

Which of the following items is hearsay?

Y.... 1. On the issue whether X and D were engaged to be married, D's statement to X, "I promise to marry you on June 1, 1931."

N.... 2. On the issue of the sanity of D, a woman, D's public statement, "I am the Pope."

N.... 3. On the issue of X's provocation for assaulting Y, D's statement to X, her husband, "Y ravished me."

N.... 4. On the issue of D's consciousness after the attack, D's statement, "X shot me, as he often threatened to do."

Y.... 5. On the issue of identity of the shooter, D's statement in 4.

Y.... 6. On the issue whether X made threats to shoot D, D's statement in 4.

N.... 7. On the issue of X's knowledge of speedily impending death, D's statement to X, "You have only a few minutes to live."

Y.... 8. In 7, X's statement, "I realize that I am dying."

Y.... 9. On the issue of reasonableness of X's conduct, in the shooting of Y by X, D's statement to X, "Y has threatened to kill you on sight."

N.... 10. On the issue in 9, Y's reputation, known to X, as a violent, quarrelsome man.

...... 11. Action for malicious prosecution of P by X on the charge of murdering Y. On the issue of probable cause, P's reputation as a gangster, known to X.

...... 12. In 11, Y's reputation, known to X, as a quiet, peace-loving citizen.

...... 13. As tending to prove that X was suffering from tuberculosis, the fact that D, a physician, ordered X to a tuberculosis sanitarium for six months, concealing from X and X's relatives the character of the hospital.

N.... 14. As tending to prove X's honesty, the mere fact that D, X's employer, promoted him from the position of order clerk to cashier.

Y.... 15. As tending to prove D's guilt of the crime of killing X, the fact that D fled under suspicious circumstances

---

* Morgan, Evidence Exam, Summer Term, 1946, Harvard Law School.

Ch. 4 THE HEARSAY RULE & ITS EXCEPTIONS 143

immediately after X's murder, in order to draw suspicion upon himself.

..N.. 16. As tending to prove X's insanity, the fact that he was confined in an insane asylum.

...... 17. As tending to prove forgery of a will by X, D's angry statement to X, "Well, I never forged a will, anyway!"

..N.. 18. As tending to prove D's guilt of a particular criminal act, the fact that D fled under suspicious circumstances immediately after the criminal act was committed, solely in order to escape.

..Y.. 19. As tending to show that D had a revolver at an affray, W offers to testify that as D passed W's house, W called his wife's attention to a revolver sticking out of D's pocket.

* * *

...... 20. W testified that he saw D do act X, and offers to testify: "I told M within one hour after the event that I had seen D do act X." Offered to show D's conduct.

* * *

...... 21. W testified that he saw D do act X, could not remember the date, but within an hour thereafter reported to M. M offers to testify that at 3:30 p. m. of June 1, 1944, W told M that he had just seen D do act X. M's testimony is offered to fix the time.

..N.. 22. To prove that the defendant committed the crime, the prosecution offers a confession made to police officers.

...... 23. To prove that the defendant committed a crime, the prosecution offers evidence that the defendant remained silent after being arrested for the crime.

...... 24. To prove that the defendant committed the crime, the prosecution offers into evidence a certified copy of a prior judgment of conviction for the same offense.

...... 25. To prove that the defendant committed the crime, the prosecution offers a witness to testify that he was present and observed the jury return a verdict of guilty in a prosecution of the defendant for a similar prior offense.

...... 26. To prove that her husband was insane, a wife offers evidence that he lived in a nest in the top of a tree for the last five years.

...... 27. To prove that the defendant committed a crime, the prosecution offers evidence that the F.B.I. offered a reward for his capture.

...... 28. In an heirship proceeding, the claimant testifies that the deceased was his father.

144 THE HEARSAY RULE & ITS EXCEPTIONS Ch. 4

...... 29. To prove paternity, the plaintiff offers evidence that the defendant referred to the child as "my son."

...... 30. To fix the time of a murder, the prosecution offers a witness who testifies that minutes after he heard the shot, he heard a clock chime three times.

...... 31. To prove adultery, the husband offers proof that a house guest after a visit had described to one of his cronies a birthmark that the accused wife has on an intimate part of her anatomy. The existence of the mark has previously been testified to by the husband while the wife has testified that only her parents and her husband knew of the mark.

...... 32. To prove that a couple is married, a witness is offered to testify that he heard the exchange of nuptial vows.

...... 33. In a common disaster case, in order to establish survivorship, evidence is offered that after the accident one of the victims was heard to cry: "I'm alive."

...... 34. In a prosecution for the theft of valuable homing pigeons, evidence is offered that when the defendant's pigeon coop was opened, all of the birds flew to the home of the victim.

...... 35. In a prosecution for sale of pornography, the prosecution offers one hundred letters sent to the defendant's post office box, each of which says, in substance: "Send me some of those dirty books."

...... 36. Personal injury case. To show pain and suffering, plaintiff calls a nurse who testifies that the plaintiff was screaming when he was brought to the hospital.

...... 37. In a divorce case, after the husband has testified that his wife was always nagging him at the top of her voice, the wife calls a neighbor to testify that she never heard any nagging.

...... 38. In a paternity suit, the mother takes the stand and when asked to identify the father of her child, she points to the defendant.

...... 39. To prove that defendant is the father of her child, the mother offers a letter in evidence from defendant's attorney in which the attorney states that his client has admitted he is the father of the child.

...... 40. Personal injury litigation. Plaintiff testifies that there was a sign facing the intersection toward the direction that the defendant had come from without stopping and that the sign said: "STOP".

...... 41. To prove that the insured under a life policy is dead, his wife offers a death certificate.

Ch. 4 THE HEARSAY RULE & ITS EXCEPTIONS 145

...... 42. In a plagiarism suit, the plaintiff testifies that he caught the defendant in his apartment copying portions of the plaintiff's typed manuscript in longhand on a sheet of paper.

...... 43. Murder prosecution. To support a self-defense claim, defendant introduces witnesses who testify that before the killing defendant told them he was afraid of the victim.

...... 44. To show that defendant was home and thus could have killed his wife the prosecution calls her paramour who testifies that when hubby was gone and the coast was clear, the wife always pulled down a shade on a particular window but when he was home the shade was always open. Then prosecution calls a neighbor who testifies that on the night of the murder the shade was open.

COLLATERAL READINGS

The Hearsay Rule

McCormick's Handbook of the Law of Evidence §§ 244–52, 254 (2d ed. 1972)

Weinstein and Berger, Weinstein's Evidence 801–51 to 801–87 (1975)

Wigmore, Evidence §§ 1361–1365 (3rd ed. 1940)

Morgan, Hearsay, 25 Miss.L.J. 1 (1953)

Morgan, Hearsay Dangers and The Application of the Hearsay Concept, 62 Harv.L.Rev. 177 (1948)

Falknor, The Hearsay Rule and its Exceptions, 2 U.C.L.A.L.Rev. 43 (1954)

McCormick, The Borderland of Hearsay, 39 Yale L.J. 489 (1930)

Cross, The Scope of the Rule Against Hearsay, 72 L.Q.Rev. 91 (1956)

Finman, Implied Assertions as Hearsay, 14 Stan.L.Rev. 682 (1962)

Ladd, The Hearsay We Admit, 5 Okl.L.Rev. 271 (1952)

Davis, Hearsay in Administrative Hearings, 32 Geo.L.Rev. 689 (1964)

Falknor, Hearsay, [1969] Law & Soc. Order 591

Comment, Animal Behavior Evidence, 31 Mont.L.Rev. 257 (1970)

Comment, Constitutional Law—The Confrontation Test for Hearsay Exceptions: An Uncertain Standard, 59 Cal.L.Rev. 580 (1971)

Note, Hearsay, 27 Ark.L.Rev. 229 (1973)

Evans, Article Eight of the Federal Rules of Evidence, 8 Val.U.L. Rev. 1 (1974)

Prince, Policy Considerations and Changes in the Hearsay Rule: A Comment, 19 N.Y.L.F. 761 (1974)

Tribe, Triangulating Hearsay, 87 Harv.L.Rev. 957 (1974)

Comment, Abolish the Rule Against Hearsay, 35 U.Pitt.L.Rev. 609 (1974)

B. EXCEPTIONS TO THE HEARSAY RULE

1. ADMISSIONS

a. IN GENERAL

WALTZ, CRIMINAL EVIDENCE
77–80 (1975).*

Admissions

An Important Exception. The exception to the hearsay rule that permits the receipt in evidence of a party's admissions is an important one because it is encountered in both civil and criminal litigation with great frequency. On the civil side, personal injury lawsuits (to name only one type of case) are often based in large part on the defendant's pretrial admissions of negligent conduct.

Example:

BY PLAINTIFF'S COUNSEL [examining an occurrence witness]: What happened next?

A: The driver of the truck jumped down out of the cab, ran over to plaintiff, and said to him, "I'm sorry about this. I was looking for a lighted cigarette I'd dropped and I wasn't watching where I was going."

And many a criminal case involves admissions made by the accused prior to trial. They may have been made in casual conversation or in response to interrogation by the police or by a member of the prosecutor's staff. (A confession achieved by means of a properly conducted interrogation is simply a special type of evidentiary admission for purposes of the present hearsay exception.)

Example a.:

BY THE PROSECUTING ATTORNEY [examining an alleged accomplice of the accused who has turned State's evidence]: When the defendant Bushmat came back to the car where you say you were waiting, did he say anything?

A: Yes, he did.

Q: What did he say to you?

A: He said, "Sam was in the garage. I shot him twice. I got him good. Sam won't be talking to any grand jury."

Example b.:

BY THE PROSECUTING ATTORNEY [examining a police interrogator]: Officer, during the course of this interrogation session did the accused make any kind of statement to you?

A: Yes, sir, he did.

* Copyright, 1975 by Jon R. Waltz.

Ch. 4 THE HEARSAY RULE & ITS EXCEPTIONS 147

BY DEFENSE COUNSEL: Your Honor, we object to anything further at this time. We'll ask for the usual hearing, out of the presence of the jury.

THE COURT: We will be in recess for half an hour. [Trial judge holds a hearing on admissibility. Was the accused's statement voluntary? Was he given the *Miranda* warnings? Court will resume after the judge makes a preliminary ruling that the statement is admissible.]

Q: Was the accused's statement reduced to writing?

A: It was.

Q: [The prosecuting attorney poses additional foundation questions, leading to the eventual receipt in evidence of the accused's signed incriminating statement.]

It may seem odd that an accused's own statements are considered to be hearsay. Certainly it would be a strange spectacle to see defense counsel object, on hearsay grounds, to receipt in evidence of an admission made by the accused himself. How can the accused object to his own statement? Can he complain that he was not under oath at the time he spoke? Can he argue that he had no opportunity to cross-examine himself? The fact is that the accused's admission or confession is usually categorized as hearsay for no more weighty reason than that it was an out-of-court declaration. It is therefore not surprising that the Federal Rules of Evidence do not treat admissions as hearsay at all and that state jurisdictions have a clear-cut hearsay exception for such statements.

* * *

Elements of the Admissions Exception. The present exception involves any statement or conduct made or carried on by the accused prior to trial which, at the time of trial, is against his interests. (Note that this exception is applicable to statements by a party, the accused, in contrast to the hearsay exception for so-called declarations against interest by nonparties. See pp. 172–176.)

(1) The accused's statement need not have been against interest (that is, inculpatory) at the time it was *made;* it need only be incriminating as of the time of trial.

(2) Lack of *personal knowledge* does not necessarily exclude a party's admissions. For example, the president of the defendant corporation said, "My company has carefully investigated the matter and all of the reports indicate that we have been polluting the river."

(3) A statement in the form of an *opinion,* as distinguished from a hard fact, is not necessarily excludable under this exception. For example, the president of the defendant corporation said, "Our dumping of all that oil into the river was negligent."

RULES OF EVIDENCE FOR UNITED STATES COURTS AND MAGISTRATES

Rule 801

DEFINITIONS

The following definitions apply under this article:

* * *

(d) **Statements which are not hearsay.** A statement is not hearsay if—

* * *

(2) Admission by party-opponent. The statement is offered against a party and is (A) his own statement, in either his individual or a representative capacity or (B) a statement of which he has manifested his adoption or belief in its truth, or (C) a statement by a person authorized by him to make a statement concerning the subject, or (D) a statement by his agent or servant concerning a matter within the scope of his agency or employment, made during the existence of the relationship, or (E) a statement by a coconspirator of a party during the course and in furtherance of the conspiracy.

NOTE

Instead of regarding the admision as an exception to the hearsay rule as was the case at common law and in virtually all previous evidence codes, the Federal Rules of Evidence defined admissions as not hearsay. In effect this did not change any rules and most lawyers still speak of admissions as an exception to the hearsay rule.

NOTE

The following quotation is from William Shakespeare's Othello, Act III, Sc. iii. The speaker is Iago.

* * * I lay with Cassio lately,
And being troubled with a raging tooth,
I could not sleep.
There are a kind of men so loose of soul,
That in their sleeps will mutter their affairs:
One of this kind is Cassio:
In sleep I heard him say 'Sweet Desdemona,
Let us be wary, let us hide our loves;'
An then, sir, would he gripe and wring my hand,
Cry 'O sweet creature!' and then kiss me hard,
As if he pluk'd up kisses by the roots,
That grew upon my lips: then laid his leg
Over my thigh, and sigh'd and kiss'd, and then
Cried 'Cursed fate that gave thee to the Moor!'

Is this "testimony" of Iago hearsay? Would it on any ground be admissible against Cassio? Or Desdemona? Is it relevant? This type of statement is sometimes referred to as a "nocturnal admission."

b. ADMISSIONS BY SILENCE

UNITED STATES v. ALKER

United States Court of Appeals, Third Circuit, 1958.
255 F.2d 851.

HASTIE, Circuit Judge. The appellant was tried on two indictments. The first charged him * * * [with] willfully attempting to evade part of the estate tax due on the estate of Winfred S. Hurst, deceased. The second and third counts of this indictment charged violations * * * in the submitting of false and fraudulent documents to the Secretary of the Treasury. The second indictment charged that the appellant and two others conspired to commit the substantive offenses of the first indictment. After the prosecution had presented its case, the district court granted a motion to dismiss the conspiracy charges. The jury subsequently found the appellant guilty of the substantive offenses on all three counts of the first indictment. He was sentenced to six months imprisonment on each count, the terms to run concurrently, and was fined $8,000 on the first count and $1,000 on each of the others. Various errors are alleged on this appeal.

The government sought to prove that the day after Winfred Hurst died, the defendant, who was his executor, removed $35,000 belonging to Hurst from Hurst's safe, and thereafter did not report this money in the estate tax return as part of the assets of the estate. Government witnesses testified that the day after Hurst's death, appellant met in the decedent's office with four beneficiaries under the will; that the defendant then opened Hurst's safe, and took out seven packages of money. The testimony as to what occurred next is exemplified by the following excerpt from the examination of Jane Roth, a prosecution witness who was one of those present at the opening of the safe:

"Q. Did anything come out of the safe? A. There was money * * *.

"Q. If you know, how much money? A. When Mr. Alker was taking it out of the safe, he said something about —there were bundles of money, and he said something about it being $500 in each bundle, and Mr. Carpenter corrected him, and said 'No. $5,000.00'.

"Defense Counsel: I object and move that that be stricken, sir.

"The Court: Overruled".

It appeared that appellant made no reply when he was thus corrected.

The appellant now asks us to find the testimony of what Carpenter said about the amount of money in each bundle inadmissible and prejudicial hearsay. However, we think this is a very clear and striking example of evidence receivable as an admission by adoption.

* * *

Here an occasion had been arranged for an executor to take possession of the contents of his decedent's safe in the presence of legatees. One of the most obvious and important purposes of such an assemblage is to obviate any future dispute or suspicion about the nature and amount of the property which the executor is taking into his hands. And in any event, it is important to the executor as a responsible fiduciary that there be independent witnesses to corroborate him as to the amount of property for which he is accountable. In these circumstances there is normally a very clear and strong inference of the executor's assent to be drawn from his failure to challenge a substantial verbal correction voiced on such an occasion as this in response to the executor's own statement of the amount being taken into his possession. There is no suggestion here that the appellant did not understand what was said to him or that he was prevented from replying, or that the circumstances were in any way extraordinary. It was entirely proper that the jury should be permitted to draw the normal inference of assent from the appellant's silence.

The judgment and commitment will be affirmed as to count one of the indictment and reversed as to counts two and three.

NOTE, TACIT CRIMINAL ADMISSIONS

112 U.Pa.L.Rev. 210 (1963).*

The doctrine of tacit admissions is firmly entrenched in state and federal criminal prosecutions. Courts have assumed that a reasonable juror could find a person more likely to deny an accusation he knows to be false than one he knows to be true. According to one theory, a failure to deny an accusation shows that the accused intended to communicate agreement, and thus adopted the accusation. A second theory holds that whether or not the accused desired to admit the statement, his failure to deny was behavior manifesting a consciousness that he was guilty of the particular crime. These theories apparently have not been empirically tested, but rest solely upon intuitive concepts of normal human conduct. Doubt has been cast upon their validity by trained psychoanalysts who suggest that an accused may manifest guilt feelings from a general sense of guilt, or from guilt of another crime.

---

* Copyright, 1963–1964 by the University of Pennsylvania.

Because of the uncertainty in any given case that an accused's silence is an implied admission of the statement made, many courts have indicated that this evidence is "dangerous, and should always be received with caution." Some courts have accordingly held that evidence of a tacit admission alone will not sustain a verdict of guilty. On balance, however, courts have universally upheld the relevancy of evidence that an accused failed to deny inculpatory statements made in his presence.

Hearsay objections to tacit admissions are more troublesome than the relevancy issue. Statements uttered out of court are inadmissible to prove the facts asserted in the statement unless they comply with one of the exceptions to the hearsay rule. Evidence of a tacit admission consists not only of the defendant's response or lack thereof, but also of the out-of-court assertion by another person inculpating the defendant. Although the hearsay rule would exclude the inculpatory statement were it offered to prove the truth of the matter asserted, under the tacit admissions doctrine the truth of the statement is immaterial, and the only issue is whether it occurred. Therefore, the reaction of the accused is the only substantive evidence, and the inculpatory statement is admitted only to explain the significance of the defendant's response.

* * *

* * * courts generally have imposed seven conditions for the introduction of evidence that an alleged admission by silence occurred. If silence is the only response by the defendant, the accusation must have occurred (1) in the defendant's presence and (2) within his hearing; (3) he must have understood it; (4) it ordinarily must have embraced facts within his personal knowledge; (5) he must have been physically able to speak and (6) psychologically at liberty to speak; and (7) the statement and surrounding circumstances must have naturally called for a reply. If, however, the defendant made an ambiguous statement indicating that these conditions existed, the inquiry is only whether the response affords a permissible inference of guilt. Many courts have recognized that no such inference can be drawn from silence unless each of the seven elements is present. Agreement on generalities, however, conceals a wide divergence in judicial application of these principles.

When tacit admissions allegedly occur in the presence of the police, additional evidentiary considerations are introduced, and there is a risk that the constitutional rights of the accused will be undermined. Evidence of an admission by silence forces the defendant tactically to elect between his right not to testify at trial and the obvious need to explain his reaction to the accusation, thus indirectly affecting his privilege against self-incrimination. This type of evidence also raises a more direct self-incrimination issue to the extent that one purpose of that privilege is to prevent the silence of an accused in

the presence of authorities from being used against him at trial. Many state and federal courts, therefore, hold that the arrest of an accused per se excludes evidence of a subsequent admission by silence.
* * *

LA BUY, JURY INSTRUCTIONS IN FEDERAL CRIMINAL CASES

63–65 (1963).**

Section 6.15 Accusatory Statements

Evidence has been presented that statements accusing the defendant of the crime charged in the indictment were made in his presence, and that such statements were neither denied, nor objected to by him. If the jury finds that defendant actually heard and understood the accusatory statements, and that they were made under such circumstances that defendant would have denied them if they were not true, then the jury should consider whether defendant's silence was an admission of the truth of the statements. However, where defendant is under arrest, his silence in the face of accusatory statements does not in any way constitute an admission of the truth of the statements, nor create any inference of guilt.

c. ADMISSIONS BY CONDUCT

COKE, THIRD INSTITUTE, 1747

In the county of Warwick there were two brethren, the one having issue a daughter, and being seized of lands in fee devised the government of his daughter and his lands, until she came to her age of sixteen years, to his brother and died. The uncle brought up his niece very well both at her book and needle, etc., and she was about eight or nine years of age; her uncle for some offence correcting her, she was heard to say, Oh good uncle kill me not. After which time the child after much inquiry, could not be heard of: whereupon the uncle being suspected of the murder of her, the rather for that he was her next heir, was upon examination committed to the gaol for suspicion of murder, and was admonished by the justices of assise to find out the child, and thereupon bailed him until the next assises. Against which time, for that he could not find her, and fearing what would fall out against him, took another child as like unto her both in person and years as he could find, and apparelled her like unto the true child, and brought her to the next assises, but upon view and examination, she was found not to be the true child; and upon these presumptions he was indicted and found guilty, had judgment, and was hanged. But the truth of the case was, that the child being beat-

---

** 7th Cr. Judicial Conference West Pub. Co., 1963.

en over night, the next morning when she should go to school, ran away into the next county; and being well educated was received and entertained of a stranger: and when she was sixteen years old, at what time she should come to her land, she came to demand it, and was directly proved to be the true child. Which case we have reported for a double caveat: first to judges, that they in case of life judge not too hastily upon bare presumption: and secondly, to the innocent and true man, that he never seek to excuse himself by false or undue means, lest thereby he offending God (the author of truth) overthrow himself, as the uncle did.

McCORMICK'S HANDBOOK ON THE LAW OF EVIDENCE
655–656 (2d ed. 1972).**

Admissions by Conduct—(c) Flight and Similar Acts

"The wicked flee when no man pursueth." Many acts of a defendant after the crime seeking to escape the toils of the law are uncritically received as admissions by conduct, constituting circumstantial evidence of consciousness of guilt and hence of the fact of guilt itself. In this class are flight from the scene or from one's usual haunts after the crime, assuming a false name, shaving off a beard, resisting arrest, attempting to bribe arresting officers, forfeiture of bond by failure to appear, escapes or attempted escapes from confinement, and attempts of the accused to take his own life.

If the flight is from the scene of the crime, evidence of it seems to be wholly acceptable as a means of locating the accused at the critical time and place. However, in many situations, the inference of consciousness of guilt of the particular crime is so uncertain and ambiguous and the evidence so prejudicial that one is forced to wonder whether the evidence is not directed to punishing the "wicked" generally rather than resolving the issue of guilt of the offense charged. Particularly troublesome are the cases where defendant flees when sought to be arrested for another crime, or is wanted for another crime, or is not shown to know that he is suspected of the particular crime. Is a general sense of guilt to be accepted? Perhaps the chief offenders are the cases of attempted suicide.

* * *

The entire area calls for closer scrutiny of the validity of the suggested inference under the facts and circumstances of each particular case.

NOTE

Notice that two cases we read earlier, Regina v. Onzufrejeck and United States v. Jackson (see pp. 33–37 and 54–57), also involve admissions by conduct.

* Copyright, 1972 by West Pub. Co.

LA BUY, JURY INSTRUCTIONS IN FEDERAL CRIMINAL CASES

63–65 (1963).*

Section 6.14 Exculpatory Statements

Evidence has been introduced that defendant made certain exculpatory statements outside of the courtroom explaining his actions to show that he was innocent of the crime charged in the indictment. Evidence contradicting such statements has also been introduced. If the jury finds that the exculpatory statements were untrue, and that the defendant made them voluntarily with knowledge of their falsity, the jury may consider the statements as circumstantial evidence of defendant's consciousness of guilt.

d. ADMISSIONS BY CO–CONSPIRATORS

UNITED STATES v. PETROZZIELLO

United States Court of Appeals, First Circuit, 1977.
548 F.2d 20.

COFFIN, Chief Judge.

In early October, 1975, appellant was tried and convicted of conspiring to distribute heroin, of possessing heroin with intent to distribute it, and of carrying a firearm while committing these crimes. All three convictions grew out of a drug transaction that took place on February 13, 1975. On that day, federal agents arranged to purchase heroin from a drug dealer. The transaction was to take place at a Chinese restaurant later in the day. The agents drove the dealer to his "connection's" house. A few minutes later, appellant and the dealer left the house in appellant's car; they drove to the Chinese restaurant but left before the agent who arranged the deal could arrive. The agent later talked to the dealer by phone and persuaded him to return.** Again the dealer and appellant showed up in ap-

---

* 7th Cir. Judicial Conference, West Pub. Co., 1963.

** Let us assume that the dealer's statement which the prosecution introduced, and to which the defendant objects, was made during this phone call. The conversation, then, went something like this:
  Agent: Well, why did you leave before I got there?
  Dealer: That place bugs me. Why don't you meet us at . . .
  Agent: No, man, I'm in a hurry. Why don't you bring your connection back over here and we'll sew up the deal?
  Dealer: (after short muffled conversation with someone else) Okay. We'll meet you at the restaurant in ten minutes.

The prosecution introduced this statement against the "connection" for two purposes: (1) to prove that a conspiracy existed between the dealer and the connection, and (2) as an admission by a co-conspirator during the course of and in furtherance of a conspiracy. Consider the above conversation for yourself in light of the hearsay dangers discussed earlier: the declarant's (here the dealer's) *perception*, *memory* (not so important here since the statement was immediate), *veracity* (could the dealer in fact have been lying?), and *articulateness*.

pellant's car. The dealer entered the doorway of the restaurant and showed a package of heroin to the federal agent, who arrested him. Other agents moved in on appellant, who made a brief effort to drive away but found himself blocked by the agents' car.

* * *

Appellant's last claim is that the evidence against him was insufficient. In particular, he focuses on the dearth of independent, non-hearsay evidence that a conspiracy existed between appellant and the dealer. Evidence of this sort, he argues, is a necessary foundation for the hearsay statements of the dealer, which were admitted under the co-conspirator exception. Because appellant was tried a few months after the new federal rules of evidence took effect, we must consider their impact. The new rules recognize the co-conspirator exception; statements are "not hearsay" if they are offered against a party who conspired with the declarant, and if they are made during and in furtherance of the conspiracy. Fed.R.Evid. 801(d)(2)(E). However, the rules make a change in the way the co-conspirator exception is applied. In this circuit, the jury has had a prominent role in deciding whether the co-conspirator exception can be invoked. Trial courts instruct the jury that a co-conspirator's hearsay may be used against a defendant only if the defendant's membership in the conspiracy has been established by independent, non-hearsay evidence. * * * The new rules, however, give the jury only a narrow responsibility for deciding questions of admissibility. Most issues are resolved finally by the judge. Contrary to this division of responsibility, the trial judge below allowed the jury to weigh the admissibility of the dealer's statements to the agents. Appellant, however does not argue that this was error, and we will not disturb the verdict on this ground. * * *

That, however, is not the end of the matter. The new rules, by eliminating the jury's role, place a greater burden on the judge, for his decision is now conclusive. In years past, this circuit has followed the general rule that the judge should admit hearsay against a defendant if the judge finds enough independent, non-hearsay evidence to make a prima facie case of conspiracy. * * * This standard makes sense when the jury has the last word; the judge should refuse to admit a co-conspirator's hearsay only when no reasonable jury could find that there was a conspiracy. But rule 104(a) requires that questions of admissibility be "determined" by the judge, and finding a prima facie case is not the same as "determining" that a conspiracy existed. A higher standard is implicit in the judge's new role.

Other changes in the rules also suggest a higher standard. The new rules permit a trial judge to base his "determination" on hearsay and other inadmissible evidence. Fed.R.Evid. 104(a). Continued reliance on a prima facie standard will either broaden the co-conspirator exception unconscionably or plunge the courts into metaphysical speculation about how a prima facie case can be built on inadmissible evidence.[2]

Although the prima facie standard is no longer appropriate, we see no reason to require that conspiracy be proved beyond a reasonable doubt. That is the standard the jury will apply to the evidence as a whole. The judge is ruling on admissibility, not guilt or innocence; the government's burden need not be so great. * * * The ordinary civil standard is sufficient: if it is more likely than not that the declarant and the defendant were members of a conspiracy when the hearsay statement was made, and that the statement was in furtherance of the conspiracy, the hearsay is admissible.

Here, the judge applied a prima facie standard rather than the one we find appropriate. But appellant never objected to the standard applied, nor did he make the arguments we now find persuasive. Without the benefit of an appellate decision on the issue, the judge's use of the traditional standard was not plain error. * * * Moreover, the non-hearsay evidence of conspiracy was strong. It showed that appellant and the dealer arrived at the restaurant in appellant's car. Appellant watched over his shoulder as the dealer entered the doorway to complete the sale. When agents approached the car, showing their badges but not their weapons, appellant nearly ran one down in an attempt to escape. At the time of his arrest, appellant was carrying heroin, and he had a loaded gun on the front seat of his car. We think this evidence makes it more likely than not that appellant and the dealer had conspired to sell heroin to the federal agents.

Affirmed.

COLLATERAL READINGS

Admissions

McCormick's Handbook of the Law of Evidence §§ 262–275 (2d ed. 1972)

Weinstein and Berger, Weinstein's Evidence 801–110 to 801–159 (1975)

Wigmore, Evidence §§ 1048–1059 (3rd ed. 1940)

2. The use of inadmissible evidence to determine the existence of a conspiracy seems to contradict the traditional doctrine that conspiracy must be proved by independent, non-hearsay evidence. It suggests that a conspiracy may be proved by the very statement seeking admittance. While the logic of the new rule may permit bootstrapping of this sort, earlier case law rejects it. Glasser v. United States, 315 U.S. 60, 74–75, * * * (1942). At the least, the *Glasser* teaching survives as an admonition that trial judges should give little weight to bootstrap evidence in deciding whether to admit hearsay under the coconspirator exception. We do not chart this terra incognita in detail, for we conclude below that the admissible evidence was enough by itself to meet the standard we apply.

Ch. 4   THE HEARSAY RULE & ITS EXCEPTIONS   157

Falknor, Vicarious Admissions and the Uniform Rules, 14 Vand.L. Rev. 855 (1961)

Morgan, Admissions as an Exception to the Hearsay Rule, 30 Yale L.J. 355 (1921)

Morgan, Admissions, 1 U.C.L.A.L.Rev. 18 (1953)

Note, The Miranda Decision and Its Effects on the Tacit Admissions Rule in Pennsylvania, 28 U.Pa.L.Rev. 77 (1967)

Garland, The Co-Conspirator's Exception to the Hearsay Rule, 63 J.Crim.L.C. & P.S. 1 (1972)

Dow, Criminal Hearsay Rules: Constitutional Issues, 53 Neb.L.Rev. 425 (1974)

2. FORMER TESTIMONY

RULES OF EVIDENCE FOR UNITED STATES COURTS AND MAGISTRATES

Rule 804

HEARSAY EXCEPTIONS: DECLARANT UNAVAILABLE

* * *

(b) **Hearsay exceptions.** The following are not excluded by the hearsay rule if the declarant is unavailable as a witness:

(1) Former testimony. Testimony given as a witness at another hearing of the same or a different proceeding, or in a deposition taken in compliance with law in the course of the same or another proceeding, if the party against whom the testimony is now offered, or, in a civil action or proceeding, a predecessor in interest, had an opportunity and similar motive to develop the testimony by direct, cross, or redirect examination.

UNITED STATES v. LYNCH

United States Court of Appeals, District of Columbia Circuit, 1974.
499 F.2d 1011.

McCREE, Circuit Judge. On August 29, 1968, at approximately two a. m., Robert Mitchell was shot and killed on the corner of 7th and N Streets, N.W. The appellant, Perry Lynch, was arrested on October 4, 1968, and was tried by jury, beginning on April 28, 1971, in the United States District Court for the District of Columbia upon a two-count indictment charging first degree murder and carrying a dangerous weapon. After all the evidence had been presented, the court granted appellant's motion for a judgment of acquittal on the first degree murder charge but denied the motion for acquittal on the lesser included offenses. The case was submitted to the jury, which returned a verdict of guilty of both second degree murder and the dangerous weapons offense. The court imposed concurrent sentences of from five to twenty years for murder and of one year for carrying a dangerous weapon.

On appeal the appellant raises nine issues, the most significant of which are, in our view, * * * (2) whether the district court erred in admitting in evidence at trial the preliminary hearing testimony of the only eyewitness who identified appellant, when this witness, although apparently still within the jurisdiction of the court, failed to appear at the trial. * * * We agree, however, that the government should not have been permitted to introduce the preliminary hearing testimony of the absent witness because it did not adequately demonstrate that this critical witness was "unavailable" at the time of trial. Accordingly, we hold that the admission of the preliminary hearing testimony at trial was erroneous as a matter of federal evidentiary law. Appellant's conviction is vacated and because of our decision on this issue, we find it unnecessary to consider the other issues raised on appeal.

* * *

II

We turn now to appellant's contention that the district court erred in permitting the government in its case in chief to introduce into evidence the preliminary hearing testimony of Laverne Brown. Because Miss Brown's status as a "crucial" government witness is significant, it is necessary to describe at some length the other evidence offered against appellant in connection with the death of Robert Mitchell.

There was substantial and undisputed evidence offered by the government at trial showing that the appellant was in close physical proximity to the deceased at the time of the fatal shooting. Shortly before the shooting, Mitchell, the deceased, who was a known seller of narcotics and an addict himself, was seen by several witnesses in the vicinity of 7th and N Streets. Priscilla Thompson testified that about ten or fifteen minutes prior to the shooting the deceased sold her some stockings in the carryout restaurant where she worked at the corner of 7th and N Streets. Decedent also attempted to sell some stockings to a woman in the company of Melvin Davis near the corner of 8th and N Streets before walking up toward the corner of 7th and N. About five minutes later Davis observed appellant and a companion, James Wade, both known addicts, walking past him and proceeding in the direction of 7th Street. Five or ten minutes later, Davis heard several shots, and several minutes thereafter he saw a man running out of a nearby alley. Upon hearing a shot, Miss Thompson looked through the window in the carry-out shop and saw a man lying on the sidewalk. She then ran out into the street where she saw Wade taking money from the deceased's pockets.

* * *

Another witness, Ronald Crowder, who was walking with his girlfriend Laverne Brown and others to the carryout shop, testified that he saw Wade and another man, whom he could not identify, come down the street with a third man whom they had "against the wall." Crowder also testified that he heard two shots, that he did not see the gun, but that Wade did not fire the shots.

* * *

Laverne Brown who had been walking with Ronald Crowder, did not testify at trial, but because it was determined that she was "unavailable", her testimony from appellant's preliminary hearing was read into evidence over the objection of the defense. This testimony reveals, and the government concedes, that Miss Brown was a "crucial" witness because she was the only eyewitness to the murder who identified appellant as the slayer. In contrast, the testimony of Davis and Thompson appears to implicate Wade as much as, if not more than, it implicates appellant.

Laverne Brown had testified at the preliminary hearing that she knew both Wade and appellant previously, and that she observed them walking together and approach a man who had been attempting to sell stockings. Appellant, she testified, asked the man "Do you have the stuff," and after the man replied "no", she heard appellant say something like " 'You're going to get yours' ". Appellant and Wade then walked away but came back in about five minutes. Then, according to Miss Brown, appellant shot the deceased while Wade stood a few feet away.

* * *

Appellant supports both claims [of constitutional error] by his contention that Miss Brown was not "unavailable." In addition, appellant bolsters his constitutional claim with the alternative theory that even if the witness were unavailable, the requirements of the confrontation clause were not met in this case because there was an inadequate opportunity for cross-examination at the preliminary hearing where appellant was represented by a different attorney. The government responds, first, that the evidence clearly established that Miss Brown was unavailable at the time of trial; and, second, that the requirements of the confrontation clause are clearly met where the defendant had an opportunity to cross-examine and did in fact cross-examine the witness at the preliminary hearing.

Preliminary hearing testimony is hearsay, * * * and hearsay evidence is generally inadmissible because it is less reliable than nonhearsay testimony: it may not have been offered under oath; there may have been no opportunity for cross-examination; and the jury is given no opportunity to observe the demeanor of the witness. * * * However, under certain circumstances, exigencies permit the use of hearsay even in criminal trials, despite its dangers, and a number of exceptions to the general prohibition have been recognized by the courts.

The requirement that "unavailability" must be demonstrated as a predicate to the introduction of the prior-recorded testimony of a witness makes even more sense when, as here, it is prior testimony from a preliminary hearing, instead of that from a previous trial, which is sought to be introduced.

* * *

We conclude that the district court's determination that Miss Brown was "unavailable" was erroneous. At least where the evidence indicates that a crucial government witness, who is physically and mentally capable of testifying, is within the jurisdiction of the court, the prosecution must demonstrate that it has been unable to obtain the witness' presence through a search exercised both in good faith and with reasonable diligence and care. In the ordinary case, this will require a search equally as vigorous as that which the government would undertake to find a critical witness if it has no preliminary hearing testimony to rely upon in the event of "unavailability."

In attempting to prove that it met the requirements for unavailability, the prosecution made much of its efforts to locate Miss Brown. Miss Brown was personally served with a subpoena, and the prosecutor, who had observed Miss Brown in court during the trial, told her at the conclusion of the court day preceding the one on which her testimony was desired, to appear in court, ready to testify on Monday, May 3, 1971. When she failed to appear on Monday morning, the government called another witness and took steps to locate Miss Brown. After that witness testified, the trial was recessed early and the case continued so the government could continue its efforts to locate the missing witness. A detective was sent to locate Miss Brown. The detective went to the home of her grandmother, interrogated her about Miss Brown's whereabouts, and ascertained that the grandmother thought she was across the street at an apartment with another girl. He then went to this apartment, knocked at the door and "kicked at the door * * * to make sure whoever was in would have heard me." He then went back to the grandmother's house and asked one of Laverne's younger brothers to try to arouse the occupants. He was unable to do so. The detective and his colleague then cruised the general area seeking to find her on the streets. That evening at 7 p. m., the detective again went to the home of the grandmother, who stated that she had not seen Miss Brown, but if she did she would call the homicide office to contact the detective. Subsequently, this detective left instructions for the detective who relieved him to have two men go to the grandmother's house in the morning to attempt to locate the witness and "if she was not there, to cross the street [to the friend's apartment]." These efforts did not result in any personal contact with Miss Brown. Subsequently, it was learned that Miss Brown was in the apartment when the detective first knocked, that she spent the night in the apartment, and left about 6 a. m. before the detectives arrived. The two detectives then stayed on the scene at the apartment and were still there waiting to locate the witness when the court convened.

Although appellant has not suggested, and we do not hold, that the prosecution acted in bad faith in attempting to locate Miss Brown, we conclude that the government's efforts were insufficient. The prosecution does not claim to have inquired at the local hospitals, area police departments, the morgue, or of Miss Brown's employer. Indeed, the government itself asserted that its efforts to locate Miss Brown were limited on May 3 because policemen were needed elsewhere to work on "disturbance matters" arising from the May Day peace demonstrations on the previous weekend and because many detectives were "sleeping after having worked 24 hours straight."

* * *

We are not prepared to equate "unavailability" with "evasiveness." The government failed to establish that Miss Brown could not have been located and brought to trial by a reasonably diligent search. Accordingly, we hold that the witness was not "unavailable" and therefore the predicate for the introduction of Miss Brown's preliminary hearing testimony at trial was not established. Moreover, the error was not harmless because the evidence improperly admitted was critical to the government's case.

* * *

[Conviction vacated.]

[Dissent omitted.]

PEOPLE v. MORAN

District Court of Appeal of California, 1974.
39 Cal.App.3d 398, 114 Cal.Rptr. 413.

[Prosecution for murder. The key prosecution witness, William "Whispering Bill" Pifer, was dying of throat cancer at the time of the preliminary examination. As a precaution, therefore the prosecution videotaped his testimony.]

TAYLOR, Presiding Judge

* * *

The major contention on appeal concerns the admission into evidence of the eight-hour video tape of Pifer's preliminary hearing testimony. The question is one of first impression in this state.

The record indicates that immediately after the prosecution indicated that it planned to introduce the video tape, defendant objected on several grounds, discussed below. Defendant clearly indicated that if the court determined that the video tape was admissible, the entire tape should be admitted into evidence without the excision of any portions contrary to the suggestion of the prosecution.

When defendant raised the threshold question of Pifer's availability for the trial, his physician, Dr. Cohen, indicated that Pifer had just been admitted to the hospital and was near death. In fact, Pifer died during the first days of the jury trial. Pifer's condition was known at the time of the preliminary. Accordingly, it "was assumed by all concerned that Pifer would be dead by the time of trial." Defendant's counsel at the preliminary, Mr. Russell, indicated that his cross-examination of Pifer would be "considerably more lengthy" than that of the other attorneys. Mr. Russell was true to his word and made extensive efforts to impeach Pifer on the basis of his prior acts of misconduct, his consumption, sale and transportation of narcotics, the grant of transactional immunity for all state and federal offenses, his prior statements, his physical condition and motive for testifying, and his bias against defendant.

The record indicates that the entire eight hours of the video tape was carefully previewed by the court and all counsel. Almost the entire week of pretrial proceedings was spent on the viewing, and dicussion of the issues relating to the video tape. The trial court then ruled that the entire video tape would be admitted. Thereafter, the parties stipulated that no additional reporter's transcript of the video tape was to be made at the trial since there was a correct transcript already in existence. Prior to the playing of the video tape before the jury, an extensive foundation was laid as to qualifications and exact procedures (including placement of the microphones) followed by J. P. Ruisinger, the special agent who recorded the video tape. Reisinger explained that Mr. Corson, an experienced and qualified lip reading interpreter, was used on the sound portion to clarify some of Pifer's whispered words on the tape. At all times, the court and counsel took extreme care to assure that everyone had a good view. Defendant expressly consented to the showing of the cross-examination of Pifer by all counsel. During the showing, Reisinger identified every reel.

Defendant * * * first contends that the use of the tape improperly deprived him of his Sixth Amendment right of confrontation. There is no merit to this contention. It is well established that * * * the testimony of an unavailable witness at the preliminary hearing is "former testimony" and may be admitted at the trial. * * * The requirements of the confrontation clause are satisfied if at the prior hearing the accused was afforded a complete and adequate opportunity to cross-examine * * * In the instant case, there is no question as to Pifer's unavailability at the trial. Nor, in view of the knowledge of Pifer's condition at the time of the preliminary, the announced expectation that the testimony would be used at the trial, and the unusually extensive cross-examination, was there any denial of confrontation rights.

* * *

The judgment is affirmed.

KANE and ROUSE, JJ., concur.

[Dissent omitted.]

3. DYING DECLARATIONS

RULES OF EVIDENCE FOR UNITED STATES COURTS AND MAGISTRATES

Rule 804

HEARSAY EXCEPTIONS: DECLARANT UNAVAILABLE

* * *

(b) **Hearsay exceptions.** The following are not excluded by the hearsay rule if the declarant is unavailable as a witness:

* * *

(2) Statement under belief of impending death. In a prosecution for homicide or in a civil action, a statement by the declarant while believing that his death was imminent, concerning the cause or circumstances of what he believed to be his impending death.

WILLIAM SHAKESPEARE KING JOHN

Act V, iv, 10–61

SALISBURY

May this be possible? may this be true?

MELUN

Have I not hideous death within my view,
Retaining but a quantity of life,
Which bleeds away, even as a form of wax
Resolveth from his figure 'gainst the fire?
What in the world should make me now deceive,
Since I must lose the use of all deceit?
Why should I then be false, since it is true
That I must die here and live hence by truth?
I say again, * * *

PEOPLE v. SARZANO

Court of Appeals of New York, 1914.
212 N.Y. 231, 106 N.E. 87.

Per Curiam. The appellant was convicted of the crime of murder in the first degree in Erie county, on February 28, 1913. He shot Saverio Gragnanello November 17, 1912, at Buffalo. Gragnanello died January 22, 1913, as the result of the shooting, as the jury found.

The trial court erred in receiving in evidence as a dying declaration the statement made by the deceased on November 17, 1912, after he had been taken to the hospital. The statement was made to Dr. George B. Stocker, who was the deputy medical examiner for Erie county. Dr. Stocker told the deceased "that his condition was critical and we expected he would die from the way he was and we wanted his statement for use later." "I talked to him and told him the condition he was in and that he was going to die, and I wanted an antemortem statement for purposes that might arise later." The deceased said "all right," he would give it, and made statements which were written down and read to him by Dr. Stocker. The written statement was:

"Dying declaration of Salvita Greniera made on the 17th day of November, 1912, at Emergency Hospital in the City of Buffalo, County of Erie, to Geo. B. Stocker, Deputy Medical Examiner of said County.

"He says: I consider my condition critical, and am under the influence of an impression that I am about to die, and have no hopes of my recovery from the effects of my wound. I make this statement under that impression.

"I live at 164–8 Erie Street and am a saloonkeeper by occupation. My wife was in back room of saloon and this man Mike by name and I do not know his last name went back to this room and I went back there and asked him what he wanted and told him to go out. He drew a gun and said he would shoot me. I asked him what he wanted to shoot for and again told him to go out. He immediately shot me five times. Then he ran out of the back door. I never had any trouble with him before. He was not drunk. This was between seven and eight o'clock to-night.

"SALVITAS (X) GRENIERA."
his   mark

The objection to its admission "on the ground there is nothing in evidence except the statement which the doctor wrote that showed he thought he was going to die and that his death was to be speedy" was overruled with an exception.

Ch. 4   THE HEARSAY RULE & ITS EXCEPTIONS   165

The learned district attorney seems confident that the statement was admissible. He points out the existence of the three wounds, that the deceased was about to undergo an operation, that a doctor told him he was in a critical condition and they did not expect him to live, and that he stated he was under the influence of an impression or under an impression that he was about to die. The statements of the district attorney must, however, be modified in these particulars: There is no proof that the deceased knew that he was about to undergo an operation, or that the person talking to him was a doctor, or that he stated that he was under the impression that he was about to die. The statement was upon a printed blank and the only affirmative statements of the deceased it contains are those including and following the words "I live at 164–8 Erie Street." Above those the blanks of the printed form were properly filled and the entire statement read to him, and he said it was true.

The principle upon which dying declarations are received in evidence is that the mind, impressed with the awful idea of approaching dissolution, acts under a sanction equally powerful with that which it is presumed to feel by a solemn appeal to God upon an oath. The declarations, therefore, of a person dying under such circumstances are considered as equivalent to the evidence of the living witness upon oath. * * * Safety in receiving such declarations lies only in the fact that the declarant is so controlled by a belief that his death is certain and imminent that malice, hatred, passion and other feelings of like nature are overwhelmed and banished by it. The evidence should be clear that the declarations were made under a sense of impending death without any hope of recovery. * * * Statements made by a doctor to and accepted by a declarant that there was no chance of his recovering are admissible. * * * If the declarant thinks there is a slight chance of living the declarations are inadmissible. * * * The mere fact that the doctor told declarant that recovery was impossible is insufficient. There must be proof that the declarant believed it and had no hope of recovery. * * * Declarant's certainty that he is about to die and lack of all hope of recovery may be proven by his express language or conduct, or inferred from his physical condition and obvious danger, or evidence of his acquiescence in the opinions of doctors or others stated to him, or other adequate circumstances. * * *

In the present case the preliminary proof was too slight and indefinite to justify the admission of the statement. The transaction, apart from the wounds, was this: A strange man said to the deceased when received at the hospital that his condition was critical and he was going to die and they wanted an ante-mortem statement for purposes that might arise later, and the deceased said "all right, he would give it;" and the statement that he made the statement under "the influence of an impression that I am about to die, and have no hopes of my recovery from the effects of my wound, I make this statement under that impression," was read over to him with the other parts of the statement and said by him to be true. The declarant did not ask for wife, children, friends or priest or by word or act indicate that he believed his death certain and imminent. He did not say or show that he believed he would not recover and was without any hope whatsoever of living. It would be extending the rule beyond the decision in any case we have read or found and we think beyond safety to approve the reception in evidence of the statement. But we do not think we should reverse the judgment because of its reception. The guilt of the defendant was fully proven without it. It, in fact, added nothing to the case. The facts stated in it were proven *aliunde* and with great fullness and detail. It is inconceivable that the verdict of the jury would have been different had it been rejected.

The judgment of conviction should be affirmed.

WILLARD BARTLETT, Ch. J., WERNER, CHASE and COLLIN, JJ., concur; HOGAN and CARDOZO, JJ., concur in result; CUDDEBACK, J., not voting.

Judgment of conviction affirmed.

NOTE

Do you agree with the court in *Sarzano*? Do you think the facts surrounding the victim's death could support the trial court's inference that his statements were made under a sense of impending death?

Why did the appellate court disagree?

4. SPONTANEOUS AND CONTEMPORANEOUS DECLARATIONS

UNITED STATES v. NAPIER

United States Court of Appeals, Ninth Circuit, 1975.
518 F.2d 316.

SNEED, Circuit Judge:

Defendant Jimmy Lee Napier was indicated on four counts of interstate transportation of a stolen motor vehicle * * * and one count of interstate kidnapping * * *. Following a five-day jury trial, defendant was convicted by a jury on all counts.

Counts IV and V of the indictment alleged that defendant kidnapped Mrs. Caruso in Oregon, transported her to Washington, and then drove her stolen car back to Oregon. There was very strong circumstantial evidence of defendant's involvement in the incident. Mrs. Caruso, a resident of Portland, Oregon, was found unconscious, with severe head injuries, near Vancouver, Washington. A broken rifle lay by her body. Blood and hair on the hammer of the weapon matched those of Mrs. Caruso; the barrel of the gun bore the fingerprints of the defendant. Tire tracks nearby corresponded to those of the Caruso car, which was later recovered in Oregon. Defendant's fingerprints were found on the car (including the steering wheel) and his personal papers and effects were discovered therein with Mrs. Caruso's purse. * * *

* * *

I.

[Mrs.] Caruso was hospitalized for seven weeks following the assault, during which time she underwent two brain operations. There was testimony that she suffered brain damage which rendered her unable to comprehend the significance of an oath and therefore incapable of testifying at trial. It was also testified, although her memory was intact, that her communication with others was restricted to isolated words and simple phrases, often precipitated by situations of stress and strain. Approximately one week after Caruso returned home from the hospital, her sister, Eileen Moore, showed her a newspaper article containing a photograph of the defendant. Moore testified that Caruso looked at the photograph (but did not read the accompanying article), and her "immediate reaction was one of great distress and horror and upset," and that Caruso "pointed to it and she said very clearly, 'He killed me, he killed me.'" Moore also testified that no member of the family had attempted to discuss the incident with Caruso prior to the display of the photograph. The court admitted the statement, over defendant's objection that it was inadmissible hearsay, as a "spontaneous exclamation." We hold that the statement was properly admitted.

Although the government insists that the statement is a "verbal act" and thus not hearsay at all, we do not pass on this contention because it is our view that even if the statement is hearsay it falls within the exception for "spontaneous exclamation" or "excited utterances." Fed.R.Evid. 803(2) provides: "A statement relating to a startling event or condition made while the declarant was under the stress of excitement caused by the event or condition [is not excluded by the hearsay rule]." Appellant disputes the applicability of the "spontaneous exclamation" exception. He argues that, since the statement "he killed me" refers to the assault, that event constitutes the "startling" event. Because the statement was not made under the stress of excitement caused by the assault, appellant insists that the statement is not within the exception. We reject appellant's analysis. The display of the photograph, on the facts of this case, qualifies as a sufficiently "startling" event to render the statement made in response thereto admissible.

Although in most cases the "startling" events which prompt "spontaneous exclamations" are accidents, assaults, and the like, * * * there is no reason to restrict the exception to those situations. Wigmore, in the classic statement of the admissibility of spontaneous exclamations, writes:

> This general principle is based on the experience that, under certain external circumstances of physical shock, a stress of nervous excitement may be produced which stills the reflective faculties and removes their control, so that the utterance which then occurs is a spontaneous and sincere response to the actual sensations and perceptions already produced by the external shock. Since this utterance is made under the immediate and uncontrolled domination of the senses, and during the brief period when considerations of self-interest could not have been brought fully to bear by reasoned reflection, the utterance may be taken as particularly trustworthy (or, at least, as lacking the usual grounds of untrustworthiness), and thus as expressing the real tenor of the speaker's belief as to the facts just observed by him; and may therefore be received as testimony to those facts. The ordinary situation presenting these conditions is an affray or a railroad accident. But the principle itself is a broad one.

6 Wigmore, Evidence § 1747, at 135 (3d ed. 1940) * * * And McCormick writes of the nature of the event which underlies the exception: "The courts seem to look primarily to the effect upon the declarant and, if satisfied that the event was such as to cause adequate excitement, the inquiry is ended." McCormick, Evidence § 297, at 705 (2d ed. 1972). In the instant case where Caruso, having never discussed the assault with her family, was suddenly and unexpectedly confronted with a photograph of her alleged assailant, there can be no doubt that the event was sufficiently "startling" to provide adequate safeguards against reflection and fabrication.

* * *

We find defendant's other contentions which we have discussed in an unpublished memorandum devoid of merit and affirm the conviction.

PEOPLE v. DAMEN

Supreme Court of Illinois, 1963.
28 Ill.2d 464, 193 N.E.2d 25.

UNDERWOOD, Justice. Following a jury trial in the criminal court of Cook County, George Damen was convicted of the forcible rape of his wife. The jury fixed the punishment at 30 years imprisonment. The proceedings are before us on a writ of error, defendant contending that the complainant consented to the intercourse, and that prejudicial errors occurred in the evidentiary rulings.

Ch. 4   THE HEARSAY RULE & ITS EXCEPTIONS   169

The accusation that defendant raped his wife, while a legal possibility, is unusual and must be predicated upon actual sexual intercourse between a third party and the non-consenting wife to which the husband is an accessory and prosecuted under our statute as a principal, since consent by the wife to sexual relationships with her husband is implicit in the marital contract. * * *

The factual situation here is bizarre and thoroughly revolting, and will not be detailed in this opinion except where necessary to an understanding of the alleged errors in the trial proceedings. * * *

Complaint is made of the action of the trial court in permitting proof of complainant's statements to officer Corbett following defendant's arrest. The officer testified that complainant told him that "her husband had stabbed her in the breast with his meat fork, and that he had hit her with the broken telephone there on the floor in pieces, and also, I think, his shoe", and "that he had forced her to have intercourse with two men". Defendant argues that no portion of this statement should have been admitted because it was inadmissible hearsay, and that prejudicial error was committed by the court in overruling defendant's objections thereto. The State argues that all of the testimony was admissible either as a spontaneous declaration or as a corroborative complaint, and asks that we clarify the rules relating thereto. While defendant argues that the statements occurred at the hospital in the process of a question and answer statement being taken from prosecutrix by the officer, we do not so interpret the record. Officer Corbett testified that part of his conversation with complainant occurred at the apartment when the officers arrived there, and part at the hospital later, and that the quoted statements were the first things she told him. He further testified that he asked complainant "what happened", prior to her declaration. The language used by the witness referring to the telephone as being "there on the floor" makes it clear to us that this conversation occurred at the apartment, particularly in view of the officer's testimony that the foregoing quotations were the first things the complainant told him.

With these facts in mind we proceed to a consideration of the rules of evidence applicable thereto. We agree with the People that some confusion exists in this area as to the limitations upon admissibility. Text writers and courts generally have recognized the existence of an exception to the hearsay rule in what are known as spontaneous declarations or exclamations. One of the more cogent explanations of the basis upon which this exception exists is to be found in the following excerpt from the opinion of Justice Lockwood in Keefe v. State, 50 Ariz. 293, 72 P.2d 425: "A spontaneous exclamation may be defined as a statement or exclamation made immediately after some exciting occasion by a participant or spectator and asserting the circumstances of that occasion as it is observed by him. The admissibility of such exclamation is based on our experience that, under certain external circumstances of physical or mental shock, a stress of nervous excitement may be produced in a spectator which stills the reflective faculties and removes their control, so that the utterance which then occurs is a spontaneous and sincere response to the actual sensations and perceptions already produced by the external shock. Since this utterance is made under the immediate and uncontrolled domination of the senses, rather than reason and reflection, and during the brief period when consideration of self-interest could not have been fully brought to bear, the utterance may be taken as expressing the real belief of the speaker as to the facts just observed by him." * * * In People v. Poland, 22 Ill.2d 175, at page 181, 174 N.E.2d 804, at page 807, we stated: "Three factors are necessary to bring a statement within this exception to the hearsay rule: (1) an occurrence sufficiently startling to produce a spontaneous and unreflecting statement; (2) absence of time to fabricate; and (3) the statement must relate to the circumstances of the occurrence." If a statement is a true spontaneous declaration or exclamation, it is admissible, for testimonial purposes, to prove the truth of what was said, in all types of action and not just in rape or related cases. * * * Nor does the rule necessarily require the utterance in question to have been made by a participant in the event. It applies with equal force to the exclamations or declarations by excited observers.

In our opinion, the statement made by complainant immediately following the occurrence qualified, under the requirements of Poland, as a spontaneous declaration admissible in full. The fact that the officer asked complainant "what happened" is, we believe, insufficient to destroy its spontaneity. * * *

A second class of cases exists in which the complaints of rape victims have been admitted as corroborative statements. While statements qualifying under this rule may also be admissible as spontaneous declarations, statements by the prosecutrix as to what occurred, which are made at a time too remote to qualify as spontaneous declarations, a sufficient opportunity for "reflection and invention" having intervened, may gain admission hereunder. (People v. Poland, 22 Ill.2d 175, 174 N.E.2d 804.) The basis of their admission is that it is entirely natural that the victim of forcible rape would have spoken out regarding it, and the fact that she did not do so would in effect be evidence of the fact that nothing violent had occurred. If proof of such complaints were not permitted, the judge or jury might naturally assume that no complaint was made, and it is for that reason the prosecution is allowed to forestall this assumption by showing that the woman was not silent and that a complaint was in fact made. Under the early rule of hue-and-cry, it was necessary that the complaint should have been freshly made, and many courts, in enunciating the modern rule, state that the complaint must have been recent in order that the fact of its making may be admitted.

* * * Our decisions have generally required that the complaint be promptly made * * * but we have also admitted proof of complaints made some two months following the occurrence where the interval of delay was satisfactorily explained. * * * It is clear from our decisions that there is no fixed or definite limit of time within which the complaint must be made * * * but that a complaint made without inconsistent or unexplained delay may properly be shown. * * * It must have been spontaneous and not made as a result of a series of questions to which answers were given. * * * Under this rule, as recognized by our prior decisions, only the fact of the complaint, and not the details thereof, may be admitted into evidence, and it is necessary, before such statement is admissible at all, that the complainant be a witness in the proceeding in which the statement is introduced. * * * The reason for this is simply that since admissibility is for the purpose of rebutting the presumption arising from the silence of the complainant, it is unnecessary to show the details of the declaration, but only the fact of its making in order to negative the presumption arising from silence. * * * While the contents of a spontaneous declaration may be shown *in toto,* proof of complainant's corroborative statement, which fails to qualify as a spontaneous declaration because of the lapse of time, is, we believe, best restricted to the fact that a complaint was made with only such additions, if any, as may be necessary to identify the event as the one before the court. * * *

It is our opinion that the defendant received a fair trial, and the judgment of the criminal court of Cook County is hereby affirmed.

Judgment affirmed.

RULES OF EVIDENCE FOR UNITED STATES COURTS AND MAGISTRATES

Rule 803

HEARSAY EXCEPTIONS; AVAILABILITY OF DECLARANT IMMATERIAL

The following are not excluded by the hearsay rule, even though the declarant is available as a witness:

(1) **Present sense impression.** A statement describing or explaining an event or condition made while the declarant was perceiving the event or condition, or immediately thereafter.

(2) **Excited utterance.** A statement relating to a startling event or condition made while the declarant was under the stress of excitement caused by the event or condition.

5. DECLARATIONS AGAINST INTEREST

RULES OF EVIDENCE FOR UNITED STATES COURTS AND MAGISTRATES

Rule 804

HEARSAY EXCEPTIONS: DECLARANT UNAVAILABLE

* * *

(b) **Hearsay exceptions.** The following are not excluded by the hearsay rule if the declarant is unavailable as a witness:

* * *

(3) *Statement against interest.* A statement which was at the time of its making so far contrary to the declarant's pecuniary or proprietary interest, or so far tended to subject him to civil or criminal liability, or to render invalid a claim by him against another, that a reasonable man in his position would not have made the statement unless he believed it to be true. A statement tending to expose the declarant to criminal liability and offered to exculpate the accused is not admissible unless corroborating circumstances clearly indicate the trustworthiness of the statement.

UNITED STATES v. ALVAREZ

United States Court of Appeals, Fifth Circuit, 1978.
584 F.2d 694.

LEWIS R. MORGAN, Circuit Judge:

The appellant, Gilberto Alvarez, was convicted of heroin trafficking charges by the words of a dead man. The decedent's statements allegedly implicating Alvarez were heard only by Lopez, the prosecution's principal witness, who had earlier pled guilty to narcotics charges and received probation. In addition to other alleged trial errors, the appellant urges that Lopez' in-court testimony of the out-of-court statements by the decedent constituted inadmissible hearsay and violated his constitutional right of confrontation. We agree, and therefore reverse the judgment of the court below.

Alvarez' arrest and conviction followed a government investigation of heroin dealing in Rio Grande, Texas during the fall of 1975. An agent working undercover made contact with Jose "Chema" Lopez, the alleged "out front" man for the operation. The agent succeeded in purchasing almost 20 ounces of heroin from Lopez. Lopez would later testify that he in turn, had obtained the heroin from Lucio Mejorado, the middleman, who supposedly told Lopez that the heroin was supplied by the appellant Alvarez. At no time, however, did Lopez or any government agent communicate directly with Alvarez. Nor was Alvarez ever seen meeting with Mejorado or any other alleged members of the conspiracy. In January, 1976, indictments issued charging Lopez, Mejorado, Alvarez, and several others with violating narcotics laws. Within a few days, Alvarez left for Mexico where he remained for most of a year until extradition was effected. Meanwhile, Lopez pled guilty, received probation, and became the government's most communicative witness. Mejorado was convicted but died in a car accident prior to Alvarez' return to this country. When Alvarez finally came to trial, the critical evidence connecting him to the conspiracy was Lopez' report that Mejorado had identified Alvarez as the supplier. Thus, the government's case depends mightily upon the admission of the decedent's out-of-court statements. Such evidence is rank hearsay, which, prior to 1975, would have been patently inadmissible. * * * With the adoption of the new Federal Rules of Evidence, however, the realm of admissibility has been significantly expanded. These rules infuse the government's claim for admission with much more serious merit than would previously have existed. Applying these new rules of evidence, and recent decisions construing them, we turn to the government's arguments that the deceased witness' words were properly used to convict the appellant.

* * *

Rule 804(b)(3): Declaration Against Penal Interest

Rejecting the government's contention that Lopez' testimony was admissible under the coconspirator's exception, we consider the claim that the hearsay fell within the exemption of Federal Rule 804(b)(3). The revised rules permit the admission of an out-of-court declaration against the declarant's penal interest when three tests are met: (1) the declarant must be unavailable, (2) the statement must so far tend to subject the declarant to criminal liability " 'that a reasonable man in his position would not have made the statement unless he believed it to be true'; and [(3)] if offered to exculpate the accused, [the statement] must be corroborated by circumstances clearly indicating its trustworthiness." * * * In the present case, the unavailability of the declarant, the deceased Lucio Mejorado, is manifest.

Turning to the second test, we conclude that Mejorado's statement was sufficiently contrary to his penal interest for Rule 804(b)(3) purposes. The incriminating declarations by Mejorado include his statement that "the heroin was Gilberto Alvarez' " and assertions that he was calling Alvarez to set up the transaction. The appellant urges that these declarations did not really contravene the interest of Mejorado, but instead served primarily to incriminate Alvarez. This court, however, has not limited the "against interest" exception to the declarant's direct confession of guilt. * * * "Rather, by referring to statements that 'tend' to subject the declarant to criminal liability, the Rule encompasses disserving statements by a declarant that would have probative value in a trial against the declarant." * * * In the present case Mejorado's remarks "strongly implied his personal participation in the * * * crimes and hence would tend to subject him to criminal liability." * * * Examined in context, Mejorado's statements clearly indicated his participation "since (they) strengthened the impression that he had an insider's knowledge of the crimes." United States v. Barrett, 539 F.2d at 252. Accordingly, we hold that Mejorado's out-of-court statements readily meet the expansive test this circuit has adopted for determining whether remarks contravene the declarant's interest.

Rule 804(b)(3) explicitly adds a third requisite to admissibility for statements offered to exculpate the accused. In such cases, there must be corroborating circumstances that "clearly indicate the trustworthiness of the statement." Fed.R.Evid. 804(b)(3). In this case, however, we consider a statement offered to *inculpate* the accused. No express provision safeguards declarations against a defendant; the reasoning behind this omission is reflected in legislative history:

> The House amended this exception to add a sentence making inadmissible a statement or confession offered against the accused in a criminal case, made by a codefendant or other person implicating both himself and the accused. The sentence was added to codify the constitutional principle announced in Bruton v. United States, 391 U.S. 123, 88 S.Ct. 1620, 20 L.Ed.2d 476 (1968). Bruton held that the admission of the extrajudicial hearsay statement of one codefendant inculpating a second codefendant violated the confrontation clause of the sixth amendment.
>
> The committee decided to delete this provision because the basic approach of the rules is to avoid codifying, or attempting to codify, constitutional evidentiary principles, such as the fifth amendment's right against self-incrimination and, here, the sixth amendment's right of confrontation. Codification of a constitutional principle is unnecessary and, where the principle is under development, often unwise.

S.Rep. No. 93–1277, 93d Cong., 2d Sess., *reprinted in* 1974 U.S.Code Cong. and Admin.News pp. 7051, 7068.

Thus, while specifically addressing exculpatory statements, the draftsmen of the new rules left to the courts the task of delineating prerequisites to the admissibility of inculpatory against-interest hearsay.

* * *

To bring Rule 804(b)(3) within [the constitutional] mandate for reliability, we hold that the admissibility of *inculpatory* declarations against interest requires corroborating circumstances that "clearly indicate the trustworthiness of the statement." We believe that this construction * * * will thus avoid the constitutional difficulties that Congress acknowledged but deferred to judicial resolution. Further, by transplanting the language governing exculpatory statements onto the analysis for admitting inculpatory hearsay, a unitary standard is derived which offers the most workable basis for applying Rule 804(b)(3).

Moreover, attaching a requirement of trustworthy circumstances to the declaration against interest exception is necessary to a logical interrelation between that rule and the earlier discussed exemption for a coconspirator's "hearsay" under Rule 801(d)(2)(E). The great majority of statements traditionally evaluated under the coconspirator's exception may now fall within the markedly reduced threshold for against-interest hearsay. Most of the things conspirator "A" might say that could incriminate conspirator "B" could also *tend* to incriminate "A" because such a remark could "strengthened the impression that he (A) had an insider's knowledge of the crimes." * * * "A's" hearsay could not be admitted against "B" under the coconspirator's exception absent proof *aliunde* of "B's" complicity in the conspiracy. * * * By its terms, however, the against-interest exception would generally authorize admission irrespective of *Glasser* so long as the declarant is unavailable. Thus, there is a serious danger that the declaration against interest exception will swallow the coconspirator's exception with its attendant *Glasser* safeguard. The danger of this incongruity fortifies our conviction that the availability of Rule 804(b)(3) is predicated upon establishing circumstances of trustworthiness.

Accordingly, we hold that Lopez' hearsay testimony is admissible under Rule 804(b)(3) only if "corroborating circumstances clearly indicate the trustworthiness of the statement." * * * While the against-interest component of this exception poses a legal issue, the consideration of the statement's trustworthiness raises a question of fact ordinarily to be reviewed according to a clearly erroneous standard. * * * However, "(b)ecause the trial judge never reached this final question under Rule 804(b)(3), we are not bound to the 'clearly erroneous' standard * * * (r)ather, we look to the record to adduce the corroboration" for Lopez' testimony. * * *

Examining the record, we conclude that the trustworthiness of Lopez' testimony has not been sufficiently established. Under Rule 804(b)(3), trustworthiness is determined primarily by analysis of two elements: the probable veracity of the in-court witness, and the reliability of the out-of-court declarant. * * * Applying the first standard, we note that Lopez presumably testified in the hope of receiving preferential treatment and thus could have been motivated by a desire to "curry favor with the authorities." * * * Turning to the second facet of trustworthiness, we observe that the traditional surety of reliability for this hearsay exception, the statement's contravention of the declarant's interest, is extremely weak in this case. * * *

Moreover, both aspects of trustworthiness are seriously undermined by the virtual dearth of circumstances corroborating the hearsay accusation against Alvarez. "This requirement goes beyond minimal corroboration." * * * Indeed, the standard mandates "clear" corroboration. * * * For largely the same reasons that we earlier found the independent evidence in this case insufficient to invoke the coconspirator's exemption, we also rule that the circumstances do not clearly corroborate and indicate the trustworthiness of the hearsay within the meaning of Rule 804(b)(3). Therefore, we hold that Lopez' hearsay testimony may not be admitted into evidence under the exemption for declarations against interest.

* * *

Reversed.

6. STATE OF MIND

RULES OF EVIDENCE FOR UNITED STATES COURTS AND MAGISTRATES

Rule 803

HEARSAY EXCEPTIONS; AVAILABILITY OF DECLARANT IMMATERIAL

The following are not excluded by the hearsay rule, even though the declarant is available as a witness:

* * *

(3) **Then existing mental, emotional, or physical condition.** A statement of the declarant's then existing state of mind, emotion, sensation, or physical condition (such as intent, plan, motive, design, mental feeling, pain, and bodily health), but not including a statement of memory or belief to prove the fact remembered or believed unless it relates to the execution, revocation, identification, or terms of declarant's will.

MUTUAL LIFE INS. CO. OF NEW YORK v. HILLMON

Supreme Court of the United States, 1892.
145 U.S. 285, 12 S.Ct. 909, 36 L.Ed. 706.

[Actions by Sallie E. Hillmon against two insurance companies to recover on policies on the life of her husband, John W. Hillmon. The chief issue was whether a body found at Crooked Creek was that of the insured Hillmon or, as contended by defendants, that of one Walters. To show that the body was that of Walters, defendants offered in evidence letters from Walters to his sister and fiance which expressed his intention to leave Wichita and go with Hillmon to Colorado, where Crooked Creek is located. The trial court rejected these

Ch. 4 THE HEARSAY RULE & ITS EXCEPTIONS 177

letters. (For an interesting account of the history of this protracted litigation, involving the ouster during the Populist movement of three insurance companies from Kansas, see Wigmore, Problems of Judicial Proof, pp. 856–896 (1913)—Ed.]

Mr. Justice GRAY, after holding for the court that there had been a procedural error, continued:

There is, however, one question of evidence so important, so fully argued at the bar, and so likely to arise upon another trial, that it is proper to express an opinion upon it.

This question is of the admissibility of the letters written by Walters on the first days of March, 1879, which were offered in evidence by the defendants, and excluded by the court. In order to determine the competency of these letters, it is important to consider the state of the case when they were offered to be read.

The matter chiefly contested at the trial was the death of John W. Hillmon, the insured; and that depended upon the question whether the body found at Crooked Creek on the night of March 18, 1879, was his body, or the body of one Walters.

Much conflicting evidence had been introduced as to the identity of the body. The plaintiff had also introduced evidence that Hillmon and one Brown left Wichita in Kansas on or about March 5, 1879, and travelled together through Southern Kansas in search of a site for a cattle ranch, and that on the night of March 18, while they were in camp at Crooked Creek, Hillmon was accidentally killed, and that his body was taken thence and buried. The defendants had introduced evidence, without objection, that Walters left his home and his betrothed in Iowa in March, 1878, and was afterwards in Kansas until March, 1879; that during that time he corresponded regularly with his family and his betrothed; that the last letters received from him were one received by his betrothed on March 3 and postmarked at Wichita March 2, and one received by his sister about March 4 or 5, and dated at Wichita a day or two before; and that he had not been heard from since.

The evidence that Walters was at Wichita on or before March 5, and had not been heard from since, together with the evidence to identify as his the body found at Crooked Creek on March 18, tended to show that he went from Wichita to Crooked Creek between those dates. Evidence that just before March 5 he had the intention of leaving Wichita with Hillmon would tend to corroborate the evidence already admitted, and to show that he went from Wichita to Crooked Creek with Hillmon. Letters from him to his family and his betrothed were the natural, if not the only attainable, evidence of his intention.

The position taken at the bar, that the letters were competent evidence, * * * as memoranda made in the ordinary course of business, cannot be maintained, for they were clearly not such.

But upon another ground suggested they should have been admitted. A man's state of mind or feeling can only be manifested to others by countenance, attitude or gesture, or by sounds or words, spoken or written. The nature of the fact to be proved is the same, and evidence of its proper tokens is equally competent to prove it, whether expressed by aspect or conduct, by voice or pen. When the intention to be proved is important only as qualifying an act, its connection with that act must be shown, in order to warrant the admission of declarations of the intention. But whenever the intention is of itself a distinct and material fact in a chain of circumstances, it may be proved by contemporaneous oral or written declarations of the party.

The existence of a particular intention in a certain person at a certain time being a material fact to be proved, evidence that he expressed that intention at that time is as direct evidence of the fact, as his own testimony that he then had that intention would be. After his death there can hardly be any other way of proving it; and while he is still alive, his own memory of his state of mind at a former time is no more likely to be clear and true than a bystander's recollection of what he then said, and is less trustworthy than letters written by him at the very time and under circumstances precluding a suspicion of misrepresentation.

The letters in question were competent, not as narratives of facts communicated to the writer by others, nor yet as proof that he actually went away from Wichita, but as evidence that, shortly before the time when other evidence tended to show that he went away, he had the intention of going, and of going with Hillmon, which made it more probable both that he did go and that he went with Hillmon, than if there had been no proof of such intention. In view of the mass of conflicting testimony introduced upon the question whether it was the body of Walters that was found in Hillmon's camp, this evidence might properly influence the jury in determining that question.

The rule applicable to this case has been thus stated by this court: "Wherever the bodily or mental feelings of an individual are material to be proved, the usual expressions of such feelings are original and competent evidence. Those expressions are the natural reflexes of what it might be impossible to show by other testimony. If there be such other testimony, this may be necessary to set the facts thus developed in their true light, and to give them their proper effect. As independent explanatory or corroborative evidence, it is often indispensable to the due administration of justice. Such declarations are regarded as verbal acts, and are as competent as any other testimony, when relevant to the issue. Their truth or falsity is an inquiry for the jury." Insurance Co. v. Mosley, 8 Wall. 397, 404, 405.

* * *

Upon principle and authority, therefore, we are of opinion that the two letters were competent evidence of the intention of Walters at the time of writing them, which was a material fact bearing upon the question in controversy; and that for the exclusion of these letters, as well as for the undue restriction of the defendants' challenges, the verdicts must be set aside, and a new trial had.

As the verdicts and judgments were several, the writ of error sued out by the defendants jointly was superfluous, and may be dismissed without costs; and upon each of the writs of error sued out by the defendants severally the order will be

Judgment reversed, and case remanded to the Circuit Court, with directions to set aside the verdict and to order a new trial.

PEOPLE v. TALLE

District Court of Appeal of California, 1952.
111 Cal.App.2d 650, 245 P.2d 633.

PETERS, P. J. * * * This error *alone* would require a reversal. However, there were other serious and prejudicial errors committed. One of these involved a typewritten statement prepared by the deceased four months prior to her death which was offered by the prosecution as part of its case in chief, and which was admitted, over the objections of the defense. This got into the record through the testimony of an attorney, Elmer Jensen. Sometime in 1948 Marge consulted Jensen in reference to one of her actions for separate maintenance. In 1949 Jensen asked her to prepare "a statement giving me her story of her life with Tom Talle" to aid him in the preparation of the case. Marge prepared and delivered this statement to Jensen in August, 1949. This statement is typed, is unsigned, consists of seven single-spaced pages, of varying length, and was handed to Jensen in an envelope. According to Jensen, when this statement was delivered to him, Marge directed "In case anything happens to me turn this envelope over to the District Attorney."

This statement was admitted into evidence as part of the prosecution's case in chief. The statement purports to give a history, from Marge's standpoint, of her life with appellant. There are references to several occasions when Marge states that appellant used physical force against her. She charges that he pointed a gun at her; once put her out of their automobile in the rain; offered her $10,000 to give him a divorce. The letter refers to Marge's belief that Talle was in contact with his first wife, Mary, and charges that he asked her, Marge, for a divorce. It charges that Talle accused her of marrying him for his money. It also states that Mrs. Shoemaker had told Marge that Talle had threatened that he was going to kill her. It charges that Talle had told several people that he wanted to divorce Marge so that he could remarry his first wife, Mary. It charges that Talle was tight with his money, etc., etc.

The statement is obviously hearsay, and, in some respects, hearsay on hearsay. No contention is or can be made that it was admissible as a dying declaration, or as evidence of any of the past acts therein referred to. It was the theory of the prosecution that it was admissible for the purpose of showing the state of mind of the deceased. The trial judge admitted it for this limited purpose, and, before it was read to the jury, instructed that it was to be considered for this limited purpose, and repeated this limitation in his final instructions. Thereafter, it was read to the jury, and, in whole or in part, reread to the jury several times. It was repeatedly referred to in the arguments to the jury. Time and time again the district attorney, in spite of the limitations placed on this evidence by the trial court, used the statement as if it were evidence of the facts recited, and used it as if it were evidence of motive, intent and premeditation.

It is too clear to require extended discussion that the statement was hearsay, and not admissible to show state of mind of the deceased, or for any other purpose. It was, of course, a self-serving document prepared by the deceased purporting to recount past events, and giving her side of the story in reference to her marital difficulties, for the purpose of aiding her in the separate maintenance action then pending. The state of mind of the deceased was never an issue in the case. The defense was that appellant did not commit the crime, and that he was so drunk that he could not remember anything that happened the day his wife was killed. At the time the evidence was introduced, there was no claim of self-defense or that deceased had quarreled with or provoked Talle. There was no claim of suicide. Respondent points out that some mention of such possible defenses was made on the *voir dire* examination of the jury, but it is obvious that what was then said did not put into issue the state of mind of the deceased four months before she was killed. There is not one word in the transcript that during the trial appellant relied upon self-defense or suicide or provocation. * * *

* * * Here was a voice from the grave charging appellant with past acts of brutality and cruelty, and charging that he had made threats against his wife's life. How could the jury possibly disentangle the charges in that letter and treat the letter only as evidence of state of mind, and forget about the substance of the charges? How could the defendant meet such a situation? He could not cross-examine the deceased. Her lips were sealed. Here was a self-serving statement prepared for a partisan purpose against which the accused was powerless to defend. It will not do to say that it was admitted for the limited purpose of showing state of mind of the deceased, and, even if erroneously admitted could not be prejudicial. To be admissible, even when state of mind is in issue (which it was not), the statement must be made under circumstances so as to make it reasonably certain it was not the result of a partisan premeditated plan to accuse. That did not exist here.

The district attorney referred to this letter of the deceased in his opening statement. He read and reread the letter to the jury, in whole or in part, several times during the trial. During the arguments to the jury it was read and reread, in whole or in part, time and time again. Although the district attorney would occasionally state, or the court would state, that the letter was admitted solely on the issue of the state of mind of the deceased, time and again it was argued that the letter corroborated Mrs. Shoemaker, or was evidence of motive, premeditation or intent. If the district attorney could not limit the letter to the limited purpose fixed by the court, how was the jury to accomplish that almost impossible feat? * * *

The judgement and order appealed from are reversed, and a new trial ordered.

UNITED STATES v. PHEASTER

United States Court of Appeals, Ninth Circuit, 1976.
544 F.2d 353.

RENFREW, District Judge:

I. FACTS

This case arises from the disappearance of Larry Adell, the 16-year-old son of Palm Springs multi-millionaire Robert Adell. At approximately 9:30 P.M. on June 1, 1974, Larry Adell left a group of his high school friends in a Palm Springs restaurant known as Sambo's North. He walked into the parking lot of the restaurant with the expressed intention of meeting a man named Angelo who was supposed to deliver a pound of free marijuana. Larry never returned to his friends in the restaurant that evening, and his family never saw him thereafter.

The long, agonizing, and ultimately unsuccessful effort to find Larry began shortly after his disappearance. At about 2:30 A.M. on June 2, 1974, Larry's father was telephoned by a male caller who told him that his son was being held and that further instructions would be left in Larry's car in the parking lot of Sambo's North. Those instructions included a demand for a ransom of $400,000 for the release of Larry. Further instructions regarding the delivery of the ransom were promised within a week. Although the caller had warned Mr. Adell that he would never see Larry again if the police or the F.B.I. were notified, Mr. Adell immediately called the F.B.I., and that agency was actively involved in the investigation of the case from the beginning.

Numerous difficulties were encountered in attempting to deliver the ransom, necessitating a number of communications between the kidnappers and Mr. Adell. The communications from the kidnappers included a mixture of instructions and threats, as well as messages from Larry. Before the kidnappers finally broke off communications on June 30, 1974, Mr. Adell had received a total of ten letters from the kidnappers, nine of which were typed in a "script" style and one of which was handwritten. In addition, Mr. Adell had received two telephone calls from the kidnappers, one of which was tape-recorded by the F.B.I. In these communications, the kidnappers gave instructions for a total of four attempts to deliver the ransom, but it was never delivered for a number of reasons, and Larry was never released.

The instructions for the first delivery, set for June 8th, were nullified by the late delivery of the letter containing them on June 9th. The second delivery failed when, on June 12th, Mr. Adell balked at turning over the money without more adequate assurances that his son would be released. The third delivery on June 23d was aborted, apparently because of the kidnappers' awareness that the pick-up site was being monitored. A duffel bag containing the ransom money was thrown into the designated spot, but it was never retrieved by the kidnappers. The fourth and final attempt never really began. On June 30th, pursuant to instructions, Mr. Adell went to a designated hotel pay telephone to await further instructions but was never contacted. No further communications were received from the kidnappers, despite Mr. Adell's attempt to renew contact by messages published in the Los Angeles Times.

When it appeared that further efforts to communicate with the kidnappers would be futile, the F.B.I. arrested appellants, who had been under surveillance for some time, in a coordinated operation on July 14, 1974.

* * *

Admissibility of Hearsay Testimony Concerning Statements of Larry Adell

Appellant Inciso argues that the district court erred in admitting hearsay testimony by two teenaged friends of Larry Adell concerning statements made by Larry on June 1, 1974, the day that he disappeared. Timely objections were made to the questions which elicited the testimony on the ground that the questions called for hearsay. In response, the Government attorney stated that the testimony was offered for the limited purpose of showing the "state of mind of Larry". After instructing the jury that it could only consider the testimony for that limited purpose and not for "the truth or falsity of what [Larry] said", the district court allowed the witnesses to answer the questions. Francine Gomes, Larry's date on the evening that he disappeared, testified that when Larry picked her up that evening, he told her that he was going to meet Angelo at Sambo's North at 9:30 P.M. to "pick up a pound of marijuana which Angelo had promised him for free". * * * She also testified that she had been with Larry on another occasion when he met a man named Angelo, and she identified the defendant as that man. Miss Gomes stated that it was approximately 9:15 P.M. when Larry went into the parking lot. Doug Sendejas, one of Larry's friends who was with him at Sambo's North just prior to his disappearance, testified that Larry had made similar statements to him in the afternoon and early evening of June 1st regarding a meeting that evening with Angelo. Mr. Sendejas also testified that when Larry left the table at Sambo's North to go into the parking lot, Larry stated that "he was going to meet Angelo and he'd be right back." * * *

Inciso's contention that the district court erred in admitting the hearsay testimony of Larry's friends is premised on the view that the statements could not properly be used by the jury to conclude that Larry did in fact meet Inciso in the parking lot of Sambo's North at approximately 9:30 P.M. on June 1, 1974. The correctness of that assumption is, in our view, the key to the analysis of this contention of error. The Government argues that Larry's statements were relevant to two issues in the case. First the statements are said to be relevant to an issue created by the defense when Inciso's attorney attempted to show that Larry had not been kidnapped but had disappeared voluntarily as part of a simulated kidnapping designed to extort money from his wealthy father from whom he was allegedly estranged. In his brief on appeal, Inciso concedes the relevance and, presumably, the admissibility of the statements to "show that Larry did not voluntarily disappear". However, Inciso argues that for this limited purpose, there was no need to name the person with whom Larry intended to meet, and that the district court's limiting instruction was insufficient to overcome the prejudice to which he was exposed by the testimony. Second, the Government argues that the statements are relevant and admissible to show that, as intended, Larry did meet Inciso in the parking lot at Sambo's North on the evening of June 1, 1974. If the government's second theory of admissibility is successful, Inciso's arguments regarding the excision of his name from the statements admitted under the first theory is obviously mooted.

In determining the admissibility of the disputed evidence, we apply the standard of Rule 26 of the Federal Rules of Criminal Procedure which governed at the time of the trial below. Under that standard, the District Court was required to decide issues concerning the "admissibility of evidence" according to the "the principles of the common law as they may be interpreted by the courts of the United States in the light of reason and experience."

The Government's position that Larry Adell's statements can be used to prove that the meeting with Inciso did occur raises a difficult and important question concerning the scope of the so-called "*Hillmon* doctrine", a particular species of the "state of mind" exception to the general rule that hearsay evidence is inadmissible. The doctrine takes its name from the famous Supreme Court decision in Mutual Life Insurance Co. v. Hillmon, 145 U.S. 285, 12 S.Ct. 909, 36 L. Ed. 706 (1892). That the *Hillmon* doctrine should create controversy and confusion is not surprising, for it is an extraordinary doctrine. Under the state of mind exception, hearsay evidence is admissible if it bears on the state of mind of the declarant and if that state of mind is an issue in the case. For example, statements by a testator which demonstrate that he had the necessary testamentary intent are admissible to show that intent when it is in issue. The exception embodied in the *Hillmon* doctrine is fundamentally different, because it does not require that the state of mind of the declarant be an actual issue in the case. Instead, under the *Hillmon* doctrine the state of mind of the declarant is used inferentially to prove other matters which are in issue. Stated simply, the doctrine provides that when the performance of a particular act by an individual is an issue in a case, his intention (state of mind) to perform that act may be shown. From that intention, the trier of fact may draw the inference that the person carried out his intention and performed the act. Within this conceptual framework, hearsay evidence of statements by the person which tend to show his intention is deemed admissible under the state of mind exception. Inciso's objection to the doctrine concerns its application in situations in which the declarant has stated his intention to do something *with another person*, and the issue is whether he did so. There can be no doubt that the theory of the *Hillmon* doctrine is different when the declarant's statement of intention necessarily requires the action of one or more others if it is to be fulfilled.

* * *

The *Hillmon* doctrine has been applied by the California Supreme Court in People v. Alcalde, 24 Cal.2d 177, 148 P.2d 627 (1944), * * * In *Alcalde* the defendant was tried and convicted of first degree murder for the brutal slaying of a woman whom he had been seeing socially. One of the issues before the California Supreme Court was the asserted error by the trial court in allowing the introduction of certain hearsay testimony concerning statements made by the victim on the day of her murder. As in the instant case, the testimony was highly incriminating, because the victim reportedly said that she was going out with Frank, the defendant, on the evening she was murdered. On appeal, a majority of the California Supreme Court affirmed the defendant's conviction, holding that *Hillmon* was "the leading case on the admissibility of declarations of intent to do an act as proof that the act thereafter was accomplished." 148 P.2d at 631.

* * *

* * * The court found no error in the trial court's admission of the disputed hearsay testimony. "Unquestionably the deceased's statement of her intent and the logical inference to be drawn therefrom, namely, that she was with the defendant that night, were relevant to the issue of the guilt of the defendant." Id. at 632.

* * *

In addition to the decisions in *Hillmon* and *Alcalde*, support for the Government's position can be found in the California Evidence Code and the new Federal Rules of Evidence, although in each instance resort must be made to the comments to the relevant provisions.

Section 1250 of the California Evidence Code carves out an exception to the general hearsay rule for statements of a declarant's "then existing mental or physical state". The *Hillmon* doctrine is codified in Section 1250(2) which allows the use of such hearsay evidence when it "is offered to prove or explain acts or conduct of the declarant." The comment to Section 1250(2) states that, "Thus, a statement of the declarant's intent to do certain acts is admissible to prove that he did those acts." Although neither the language of the statute nor that of the comment specifically addresses the particular issue now before us, the comment does cite the *Alcalde* decision and, therefore, indirectly rejects the limitation urged by Inciso.

* * * Rule 803(3) provides an exemption from the hearsay rule for the following evidence:

> "*Then existing mental, emotional, or physical condition.* A statement of the declarant's then existing state of mind, emotion, sensation, or physical condition (such as intent, plan, motive, design, mental feeling, pain, and bodily health), but not including a statement of memory or belief to prove the fact remembered or believed unless it relates to the execution, revocation, identification, or terms of declarant's will."

Although Rule 803(3) is silent regarding the *Hillmon* doctrine, both the Advisory Committee on the Proposed Rules and the House Committee on the Judiciary specifically addressed the doctrine. After noting that Rule 803(3) would not allow the admission of statements of memory, the Advisory Committee stated broadly that

> "The rule of Mutual Life Ins. Co. v. Hillmon [citation omitted] allowing evidence of intention as tending to prove the doing of the act intended, is, of course, left undisturbed." Note to Paragraph (3), 28 U.S.C.A. at 585.

Significantly, the Notes of the House Committee on the Judiciary regarding Rule 803(3) are far more specific and revealing:

> "However, the Committee intends that the Rule be construed to limit the doctrine of Mutual Life Insurance Co. v. Hillmon [citation omitted] so as to render statements of intent by a declarant admissible *only to prove his future conduct, not the future conduct of another person.*" House Report No. 93–650, Note to Paragraph (3), 28 U.S.C.A. at 579 (emphasis added).

Although the matter is certainly not free from doubt, we read the note of the Advisory Committee as presuming that the *Hillmon* doctrine would be incorporated in full force, including necessarily the application in *Hillmon* itself. The language suggests that the Advisory Committee presumed that such a broad interpretation was not the prevailing common law position. The notes of the House Committee on the Judiciary are significantly different. The language used there suggests a legislative intention to cut back on what that body also perceived to be the prevailing common law view, namely, that the *Hillmon* doctrine could be applied to facts such as those now before us.

Although we recognize the force of the objection to the application of the *Hillmon* doctrine in the instant case,[18] we cannot conclude

---

18. Criticism of the *Hillmon* doctrine has come from very distinguished quarters, both judicial and academic. However, the position of the judicial critics is definitely the minority position, stated primarily in dicta and dissent.

In his opinion for the Court in Shepard v. United States, 290 U.S. 96, 54 S.Ct. 22, 78 L.Ed.2d 196 (1933), Justice Cardozo indicated in dicta an apparent hostility to the *Hillmon* doctrine. *Shepard* involved hearsay testimony of a dramatically different character from that in the instant case. The Court reviewed the conviction of an army medical officer for the murder of his wife by poison. The asserted error by the trial court was its admission, over defense objection, of certain hearsay testimony by Mrs. Shepard's nurse concerning statements that Mrs. Shepard had made during her final illness. The nurse's testimony was that, after asking whether there was enough whiskey left in the bottle from which she had drunk just prior to her collapse to make a test for poison, Mrs. Shepard stated, "Dr. Shepard has poisoned me." One theory advanced by the Government on appeal was that the testimony was admissible to show that Mrs. Shepard did not have suicidal tendencies and, thus, to refute the defense argument that she took her own life. The Court rejected that theory, holding that the testimony had not been admitted for the limited purpose suggested by the Government and that, even if it had been admitted for that purpose, its relevance was far outweighed by the extreme prejudice it would create for the defendant. In rejecting the Government's theory, the Court refused to "extend the state of mind exception to statements of memory. In his survey of the state of mind exception, Justice Cardozo appeared to suggest the the *Hillmon* doctrine is limited to "suits upon insurance policies", id. at 105, 54 S.Ct. 22, although the cases cited by the Court in *Hillmon* refute that suggestion.

The decision in *Shepard* was relied upon by Justice Traynor of the California Supreme Court in his vigorous dissent from the decision reached by the majority in People v. Alcalde, supra, 148 P.2d 627. Justice Traynor argued that the victim's declarations regarding her meeting with Frank could not be used to "induce the belief that the defendant went out with the deceased, took her to the scene of the crime and there murdered her * * * without setting aside the rule against hearsay." Id. at 633. Any other legitimate use of the declaration, in his opinion, was so insignificant that it was outweighed by the enormous prejudice to the defendant in allowing the jury to hear it.

Finally, the exhaustive analysis of a different, but related, hearsay issue by the Court of Appeals for the District of Columbia in United States v. Brown, 160 U.S.App.D.C. 190, 490 F.2d 758 (1974), provides inferential support for the position urged by Inciso. The issue in that case was the admissibility of hearsay testimony concerning a victim's extrajudicial declarations that he was "[f]rightened that he may be killed" by the defendant. Id. at 762. After surveying the relevant cases, the court stated a "synthesis" of the governing principles.

Ch. 4   THE HEARSAY RULE & ITS EXCEPTIONS   187

that the district court erred in allowing the testimony concerning Larry Adell's statements to be introduced.

* * *

[Judgment affirmed.]

[Concurring and dissenting opinion omitted.]

Hypotheticals

Let us assume that the issue is, "Was the declarant with Angelo that night?" Examine the following hypothetical statements made by the declarant the previous evening:

a. "Angelo is going to the parking lot at Sambo's North tonight." (Other evidence shows that the declarant went there that night).

b. "I am going to the parking lot at Sambo's North tonight." (Other evidence shows that Angelo went there that night).

c. "I am going to meet Angelo at the parking lot at Sambo's North tonight."

d. "Angelo is coming to my apartment tonight."

e. "I am going to Angelo's apartment tonight."

f. "I will not go out with anyone other than Angelo tonight." (Other evidence showing that he went out with someone.)

g. "I am going to wait at home for Angelo until he picks me up and we will go out." (Other evidence shows that the declarant left his apartment that night).

h. "I am going out to meet Angelo tonight."

One of the cases which was criticized by the court was the decision of the California Supreme Court in People v. Merkouris, 52 Cal.2d 672, 344 P.2d 1 (1959), a case relied upon by the Government in the instant case. The court in *Merkouris* held that hearsay testimony showing the victim's fear of the defendant could properly be admitted to show the probable identity of the killer. The court in Brown expressed the following criticism of that holding, a criticism which might also apply to the application of the *Hillmon* doctrine in the instant case:

"Such an approach violates the fundamental safeguards necessary to the use of such testimony [citation omitted]. Through a circuitous series of inferences, the court reverses the effect of the statement so as to reflect on *defendant's* intent and actions rather than the state of mind of the declarant (victim). This is the very result that it is hoped the limiting instruction will prevent." 490 P.2d at 771 (emphasis in original).

For a frequently cited academic critique of the *Hillmon* doctrine, see Maguire, The Hillmon Case—Thirty-Three Years After, 38 Harv.L.Rev. 709 (1925).

7. PRIOR IDENTIFICATION

RULES OF EVIDENCE FOR UNITED STATES COURTS AND MAGISTRATES

Rule 801

DEFINITIONS

* * *

(d) *Statements which are not hearsay.* A statement is not hearsay if—

(1) *Prior statement of a witness.* The declarant testifies at the trial or hearing and is subject to cross-examination concerning the statement, and the statement is

* * *

(c) one of identification of a person made after perceiving him.

WEINSTEIN AND BERGER, WEINSTEIN'S EVIDENCE

801–803 (1975).*

* Copyright, 1975 by Matthew Bender.

1975 AMENDMENT

Congress amended [Fed.Rule] 801(d)(1) by adding subparagraph (C) which excludes from the definition of hearsay a statement "of identification of a person made after perceiving him." This subparagraph had been contained in the rules as promulgated by the Supreme Court and as passed by the House of Representatives, but had been struck by the Senate. See *Congressional Changes,* infra. The House had acquiesced in the Senate version in order to ensure passage of the Rules of Evidence. Statement of Rep. Hungate, Cong. Rec.H. 9653 (daily ed. October 6, 1975). The amendment was signed into law on October 16, 1975 with an effective date of October 31, 1975, P.L. 94–113.

At the Congressional debate on the amendment, it was noted that enactment would return "this section of the hearsay rule to the status it had reached by process of natural judicial evolution," and that this provision had been deleted only because of strenuous objection by Senator Ervin which jeopardized passage of the Rules of Evidence. Cong.Rec. H9654 (daily ed. Oct. 6, 1975).

The Report of the Senate Committee on the Judiciary considering the amendment explained this opposition as stemming from concern "that a conviction could be based upon such unsworn, out-of-court testimony." However, the Report noted that this was a misconception since all constitutional protections were retained and in addition, the requirements of Rule 801(d)(1) that the identifier be available for cross examination at the trial is continued. The Report reads:

> The purpose of the provision was to make clear, in line with the recent law in the area, that nonsuggestive lineup, photographic and other identifications are not hearsay and therefore are admissible. In the lineup case of Gilbert v. California, 388 U.S. 263, 272 n. 3 (1967), the Supreme Court, noting the split of authority in admitting prior out-of-court identifications, stated, "The recent trend, however, is to admit the prior identification under the exception [to the hearsay rule] that admits as substantive evidence a prior communication by a witness who is available for cross-examination at the trial." And the Federal Courts of Appeals have generally admitted these identifications.

* * *

> In the course of processing the Rules of Evidence in the final weeks of the 93d Congress, the provision excluding such statements of identification from the hearsay category was deleted. Although there was no suggestion in the committee report that prior identifications are not probative, concern was there expressed that a conviction could be based upon such unsworn, out-of-court testimony. Upon further reflection, that concern appears misdirected. First, this exception is addressed to the "admissibility" of evidence and not to the "sufficiency" of evidence to prove guilt. Secondly, except for the former testimony exception to the hearsay exclusion, all hearsay exceptions allow into evidence statements which may not have been made under oath. Moreover, under this rule, unlike a significant majority of the hearsay exceptions, the prior identification is admissible only when the person who made it testifies at trial and is subject to cross-examination. This assures that if any discrepancy occurs between the witness' in-court and out-of-court testimony, the opportunity is available to probe, with the witness under oath, the reasons for that discrepancy so that the trier of fact might determine which statement is to be believed.

> Upon reflection, then, it appears the rule is desirable. Since these identifications take place reasonably soon after an offense has been committed, the witness' observations are still fresh in his mind. The identification occurs before his recollection has been dimmed by the passage of time. Equally as important, it also takes place before the defendant or some other party has had the opportunity, through bribe or threat, to influence the witness to change his mind.

* * *

UNITED STATES v. MARCHAND

United States Court of Appeals, Second Circuit, 1977.
564 F.2d 983.

FRIENDLY, Circuit Judge:

Robert P. Marchand, Jr. appeals from his conviction, * * * on one count of an indictment charging the possession and distribution of 180 pounds of marijuana.

* * *

The appeal has been presented as if this were a case where there is substantial doubt that defendant is the person who committed the crime charged in the indictment. Marchand relies on an array of cases, somewhat weakened as a result of recent Supreme Court decisions, which had laid down stringent requirements to prevent "the awful risks of misidentification" by persons with relatively scant opportunity to observe the defendant, * * *. But, as the trial judge and the jury seem to have been well aware, that is not this case at all. The case is rather one of accomplice witnesses, one of whom had known the marijuana supplier for years. The jury could well have inferred that any difficulty these witnesses expressed about identification was due to unwillingness rather than inability to identify. It was a similar case of seeming unwillingness that led us, in United States v. De Sisto, * * * to rule that previous identification or grand jury testimony of a trial witness could be used not simply for "impeachment" but as substantive evidence—a ruling which Congress has now translated into Federal Rule of Evidence 801(d)(1)(A) and (C). None of this means that Marchand did not have the right, accorded every criminal defendant, to a fair trial in accordance with governing rules of law. It does mean that statements in decisions involving dubious identifications by bystanders, law enforcement officers or victims should not be woodenly applied to the wholly different situation here and that the case offers ample occasion for recalling Judge Learned Hand's observation in Dyer v. MacDougall, 201 F.2d 265, 269 (2 Cir. 1952), that a jury is free, on the basis of a witness' demeanor, to "assume the truth of what he denies" although a court cannot allow a civil action, much less a criminal prosecution, to go to the jury on the basis of this alone.

* * *

Sometime before June 1971, Victor Roy, Jr. became acquainted with a man at bars in Amherst, Mass. When testifying before the grand jury, Roy identified this person as "Big Foot" or "Bob"; at trial he insisted on the appellation "Big Foot". In March or April, 1975, Roy met the same individual, again in a bar in Brattleboro, Vermont; he was with a girl whom Roy identified before the grand jury as Ann.[4] The man gave Roy a telephone number, which Roy called occasionally. In May 1975, Roy, accompanied by Richard Perkins, met the individual at a Howard Johnson's restaurant in Springfield, Mass., to discuss the purchase of marijuana. On two occasions within the following three weeks, Roy and Perkins made purchases of marijuana from Big Foot at the Springfield Howard Johnson's.

During the period June 9—July 16, 1975, there were four one minute phone calls from Perkins' number in Waitsfield, Vt., to the numbers listed in the name of Ann Curtis and Robert Marchand in Guilford, which is near Brattleboro, Vermont; there was proof that Bob Marchand was living with Ann Curtis at the time. On July 17 there was a four minute phone call from Perkins' number to Marchand's. The next day, July 18, Perkins and Roy drove to Brattleboro, waited for a while at the Howard Johnson's restaurant there, met Big Foot and another male, and then drove out into the country where 180 pounds of marijuana were transferred from Big Foot's car to Perkins'. On this date there were three phone calls to Ann Curtis' number in Guilford which were billed to Perkins' number n Waitsfield. The first, from Perkins' home phone, lasted three minutes. The other two—each lasting not over one minute—were from Brattleboro, where Perkins and Roy met Big Foot for the marijuana transaction. Perkins and Roy were arrested later in the day when they tried to sell the marijuana to an undercover agent.

Roy refused to make any statement to the arresting officer, Agent Handoga of the Drug Enforcement Administration (DEA). Within two weeks after the arrest, Perkins gave Agent Handoga a description of the seller as "a six foot one, 220 pound man with blond hair", aged between 25 and 30, and "big features", defined to include "a big nose, big hands, broad shoulders". About a month later, Perkins who had some ability as a portraitist, drew a sketch which was designed to be a picture of the marijuana supplier.

Agent Handoga testified at the suppression hearing later referred to that in August 1975 he had received information from an undisclosed source that Marchand was the supplier. Accordingly the Government sought an indictment of Marchand.

In September 1975 Perkins testified before a grand jury. He stated that "he found out [Big Foot's] name was Bob Marchand." Roy did not appear before this grand jury and it was discharged before the investigation was complete, without the filing of an indictment against Marchand.

---

4. Roy was quite positive about this when he testified before the grand jury in July, 1976. At trial he could not "really * * * recall" whether Marchand had a girl with him and said that his grand jury testimony was "not completely truthful." However, he repeated that the girl's name "could have been Ann." The jury was amply justified in inferring that it was.

On April 26, 1976 Perkins was shown fifteen photographs by Agent Handoga and was asked to pick two that most closely resembled the people he had seen at the time of the marijuana transaction. He first picked three and later narrowed his choices to two. One was a photo of Marchand. Perkins testified at the suppression hearing that he did not feel he was being encouraged or pressured to select the photograph that he did but was not certain that the individual depicted was the supplier. Roy, according to his testimony at the suppression hearing, was in Colorado during this period. On his return to Vermont he was served with a subpoena to appear before the grand jury. Immediately before his appearance on July 1, 1976, Roy arrived at the office of the United States Attorney in Burlington and went to a small interview room accompanied by Agent Handoga and Assistant United States Attorney O'Neill. Roy informed the agent that he had received the marijuana from someone named "Bob" or "Big Foot". Agent Handoga showed Roy a series of 14 photographs. On his first and second viewings he selected a photograph of someone he thought to be Jim Hathaway of Burlington; he was told he was in error. On a third viewing Roy selected a photograph of Marchand but added "this picture looks funny." The agent then produced a larger photograph of Marchand, interjecting, "Oh, here's a Bob, what about this one?" Roy responded that the larger photograph "looks similar". The agent then said "Ah, that's Marchand."

* * *

Marchand moved to suppress the photographic identification by Perkins and Roy * * * Chief Judge Holden conducted a hearing and made findings of fact, on which we have relied in the previous section, and conclusions of law.

The court denied the motion to suppress Perkins' photographic identification, overruling objections that the array included bearded individuals, some with long hair, whereas the person outlined in Perkins' sketch was clean-shaven with short hair, that the array included two photographs of Marchand, and that Marchand's was one of only two large photographs in the array.

With respect to Roy's identification, the judge found that Roy had made no positive identification of Marchand and also that his identification, "such as it was" was "infected by suggestion." Accordingly he granted the motion to suppress [that] evidence.

* * *

[Appellant's] first claim is that the array was impermissibly suggestive because "the neutral effect of multiple numbers was totally undercut by the fact that Marchand's picture was the only one which recurred and that of the two large photographs his was the only one of a light-haired man." (Brief, p. 52). The defense also criticizes the nine months delay in presenting the array, and the use of a photograph display rather than a lineup. We are not persuaded by any of these points. The small photograph of Marchand was somewhat marred by glare; also the larger photograph seems to depict him at a later age. Indeed, the photographs were sufficiently different to cause Perkins to select only one. Under such circumstances, over-representation of a defendant in the array does not make the procedure impermissibly suggestive, let alone give rise to "a very substantial likelihood of irreparable misidentification." * * *

* * *

The differences of hair and skin color noted by Marchand were not of great significance since all but three of the pictures were on black and white film. Nor did the differences in size of the pictures cause impermissible suggestiveness. As we have recently said:

> The due process clause does not require law enforcement officers to scour about for a selection of photographs so similar in their subject matter and composition as to make subconscious influences on witnesses an objective impossibility.

United States v. Bubar, 567 F.2d 192, (2 Cir. 1977).

Although the delay was regrettable, it is not decisive * * * moreover, Agent Handoga testified that he had no photographs of Marchand until late 1975 or early 1976. While it is preferable for law enforcement officers to use a line-up rather than photographic identification when the suspect is available, this is not a requirement.

* * *

The defense further contends that evidence of Perkins' pre-trial photographic identification and of the making of the sketch was not within Federal Rule of Evidence 801(d)(1)(C) which says that "A statement is not hearsay if * * * the declarant testifies at the trial or hearing and is subject to cross-examination concerning the statement, and the statement is * * * (C) one of identification of a person made after perceiving him" since that rule allegedly is limited to corporeal identifications. This argument rests on reading the final words "after perceiving him" as referring to the perception at the time of the identification rather than at the time of the crime and then confining "him" to the defendant's person rather than to representations of it. This is too confining. The purpose of the rule was to permit the introduction of identifications made by a witness when memory was fresher and there had been less opportunity for influence to be exerted upon him. We thus agree that "Rule 801 (d)(1)(C) should * * * be interpreted as allowing evidence of prior identification by the witness of a photograph of the person whom he had initially perceived," 4 Weinstein & Berger, Commentary on Rules of Evidence for the United States Courts and Magistrates 801–107 to 108 (1976), and also to descriptions and sketches.

The defendant further contends that the purpose of the Rule to allow introduction of more probative evidence than in-court identifications dictates exclusion of the uncertain and unreliable identifications by Perkins. We have already expressed our views with regard to the certainty of the photographic selection. * * * [We can] not hold that the Rule requires exclusion of this evidence. Protection against identifications of questionable certainty is afforded by the requirement that the declarant be available for cross-examination; questions of the probative value of the testimony are thus for the jury. * * * While the trial judge doubtless has discretion under Rules 102 and 403 to exclude an identification which he considers to have been too flimsy to warrant the jury's consideration, appellate courts should be wary of reversing where the judge has decided that the identification was sufficiently certain to be appropriate for submission.

* * *

The judgment of conviction is affirmed.

COMMENT, THE USE OF PRIOR IDENTIFICATION EVIDENCE IN CRIMINAL TRIALS UNDER THE FEDERAL RULES OF EVIDENCE

66 J.Crim.L. & C. 240 (1975).*

INTRODUCTION

The hearsay rule and its many exceptions have troubled legal scholars and practitioners since as early as the sixteenth century. One of the most controversial exceptions concerns the admission of prior identification evidence in criminal trials. Prior identifications are in essence a special sub-class of prior statements: the declarant at some time prior to the trial has identified the accused, and that statement is now being offered in court as evidence, generally to corroborate or impeach, either by the declarant himself or by a second person, often a police officer, who observed the declarant make the identification. The validity and accuracy of identifications in general has been seriously questioned by a number of scholars and strongly supported by almost as many other scholars. In addition, a number of works have appeared dealing with the problems of misidentification in actual cases. Misidentification may not only lead to the conviction of the wrong person, but to failure to convict the right person.

At common law, such an identification would have been admitted, if at all, under the prior statement exception to the hearsay rule. However, on January 3, 1975, President Ford signed into law the new Federal Rules of Evidence to take effect on July 1, 1975. It is this statutory code which now governs admission of evidence in *federal* courts.

* * *

---

* Copyright, 1975 by Northwestern University School of Law.

THE RELIABILITY OF A PRIOR IDENTIFICATION

There is no consensus as to whether a prior identification should be admitted as substantive evidence, or whether it should be admitted at all. A number of writers have taken the position that a prior out of court identification is more reliable than one made in court because it contains characteristics making it inherently trustworthy and thus there is some necessity for the admission of the hearsay evidence. The theory is that, unlike most hearsay evidence, the risks of lack of memory, misperception and the problem of misinterpretation are not present, especially where the witness and the declarant are the same. Such identifications are made nearer in time to the criminal event involved when the recollection of the witness is fresher and less likely to have been influenced by distracting external influences, not the least of which is that inherent in the courtroom environment. Such surroundings are quite suggestive of affirmative identification, increasing the danger that the courtroom identification is based on the impression made at the time of the prior identification rather than on an impression made at the time of the offense.

The principal objection to admitting prior identifications either collaterally (as corroboration or as rebuttal) or as substantive evidence is the lack of opportunity to cross-examine at the time the identification was made. However, proponents of admission counter that where the declarant is available as a witness, cross-examination is available at the trial and is an adequate safeguard of reliability. In addition, legal and psychological authority, coupled with experimental data, are often used to demonstrate that the statement made nearer in time to the offense is generally more reliable.

On the other hand, the more modern trend has been to criticize as erroneous the long-standing assumption about the reliability of human perception and memory upon which admission of prior identification testimony has been based. In addition, the situation in which such identifications are obtained, lineups and showups in general, have come under increasing attack as being prejudicial and suggestive. Considering that no evidence, other than an outright confession, probably carries this much weight, not only with lay jurors but with many law enforcement officials as well, such criticisms are by no means academic.

The principal thrust of the attack centers on the questionable reliability of human perceptions and memory necessary to making any identification, especially in the stress-filled environment in which the victim or witness of a crime finds himself or herself. Too often, critics charge, the law appears disproportionately concerned with deliberate falsification as compared with its concern over honest errors in perception and memory produced by the "normal" operation of our five senses. Until recently, the assumptions underlying testimonial reliability were based on little more than a subjective and unsystematic study of human testimony based upon a "highly rationalistic view of man." But, with more scientific studies it is urged that the observer is an active recorder rather than a passive or photographic recorder; the eye, the ear, and the other sense organs are "social" organs as well as physical organs. Perception and memory, in effect, are decision-making, not copying processes and are therefore subject to error. The observer, inundated with an overabundance of information, is influenced by a principle of economy into perceiving and remembering by formulating a general over-all impression. The result is that stereotypes exert an important influence, and people may in the end testify to the occurrence of events or the identity of a person that they have not in fact witnessed.

Robert Buckhart has written in *Scientific American* of the sources of unreliability. Some are implicit in the original situation, including, for example, the insignificance—at the time and to the observer—of the events, the length of time of observation, and the less than ideal observation conditions which generally apply (distance, poor lighting, fast movement, or crowds). The witness himself is a major source of unreliability, due to the effect of observing under stress (especially applicable in the case of observers who are the victims as well), or often to defects in physical condition such as age, sickness, or fatigue.

Finally, critics of the validity of prior identification evidence challenge the identification process itself. If the lineup, showup, or photographic array are conducted unfairly either because of suggestion, hints, or pressure by the law enforcement authorities, or because they are carelessly conducted or even rigged, the trustworthiness of the observer's identification correspondingly suffers.

The federal courts, like the commentators, are divided in the admission of this evidence, with varying positions being taken by the circuits. Most frequently, prior identification evidence has been admitted to rehabilitate a witness' in-court identification which has been impeached as the product of recent contrivance. Less frequently, it has been admitted to corroborate the witness' in-court identification prior to any impeachment of the witness. The Ninth Circuit, in a 1938 case, rejected as too prejudicial the use of prior identification evidence. The Second Circuit, however, has taken the lead in *allowing* the use of prior identification testimony in the prosecution's case in chief when the person making the prior identification is present and testifying. No circuit, though, has admitted as substantive evidence the testimony of a third person who observed an *unavailable* declarant's out-of-court identification.

8. PAST RECOLLECTION RECORDED

KINSEY v. STATE

Supreme Court of Arizona, 1937.
49 Ariz. 201, 65 P.2d 1141.

[Appeal from judgment on a conviction for second degree murder. The prosecution called as a witness at trial the court reporter who had taken down a statement made by defendant in the office of the county attorney. The trial court, over objection permitted this witness to read to the jury a transcript of his shorthand notes of defendant's statement—Ed.]

LOCKWOOD, Judge. * * * The fundamental question before us is the extent to which a written record of a statement made or act done, which was reduced to writing at the time by or under the direction of a person who actually heard the statement or saw the act, may be used in evidence. Whenever a proposition involving facts is at issue, there are two possible methods by which the tribunal which determines the ultimate fact may be persuaded. The first is by the production and presentation to the tribunal of the thing itself as to which persuasion is desired. Familiar instances of this method are the viewing of premises by the jury, the offering in evidence of blood-stained clothing, of the bullet which produced death, of a written contract, and many similar matters. The second method of persuasion falls into two classes, (a) the assertion of some human being that the thing in issue actually does exist, or (b) the assertion of a witness as to the existence of some fact from which the existence of the thing in issue may be reasonably and logically inferred. The first is commonly referred to by the text-writers as testimonial or direct evidence; the other is commonly called circumstantial or indirect evidence.
* * *

We consider next the various kinds of testimonial evidence, for it is in that class that the evidence under consideration in the present case falls; that is, the testimony of a witness who heard a statement is offered as proof that the statement was made. It is obvious that since such statements are always made at some time prior to the trial where the testimony of the witness is offered, the latter must be speaking as to his recollection or memory of what occurred at some previous time. In so doing, his memory of the previous transaction will be based upon one of three different conditions. First, he may say, "The fact impressed itself so vividly on my consciousness at the time that it is now clear and fresh in my memory, without the aid of any extrinsic matters." Second, he may say, "Lapse of time and the circumstances surrounding the occurrence of the fact are such that I have no unaided independent memory sufficient to enable me now to testify as to the exact thing which occurred, but if you will permit me to refresh or aid my memory by certain extraneous objects, such as a memorandum, it will revivify that memory to such an extent that I will then be able to testify to the thing from an independent recollection thereof." Third, the witness may say: "I have no present independent recollection of the thing. You offer me, to refresh that recollection, a memorandum of the thing which I made at that time. I regret that this is not sufficient to refresh my memory to such an extent that I now have an independent revived recollection of the details of the occurrence. I can, however, state positively from both my independent recollection and my present knowledge that I did make or cause to be made the memorandum offered me at the time of the occurrence of the event, and that it was, to my knowledge, a correct record of what actually happened." These three methods of recollection are commonly referred to as: (a) Recollection in general; (b) present recollection revived; and (c) past recollection recorded. * * * The first is universally accepted as a proper method of showing the recollection of a witness, and we need not discuss it. The second is also generally permitted, although obviously this method is subject to much abuse for, as was said by Bentham in his Rationale of Judicial Evidence: "If on the part of the witness the testimony be the product of the imagination, instead of the memory,—incorrectness is, in so far, the quality given to it. If, for want of such helps which on the particular occasion may happen to be necessary, recollection fail to bring to view any such real facts as with these helps might and would have been brought to view,—incompleteness in the mass of the evidence is the result. But, by the same suggestions by which, in case of veracity, memory alone would be assisted and fertilized, it may also happen that *invention* (which, where testimony is in question, is synonymous with mendacity) shall also be set to work, and rendered productive."

Notwithstanding this danger of abuse, it is generally accepted that any memorandum or object whatever, no matter when made nor under what circumstances, is eligible for use if it appears that it does revive the present recollection of the witness, but in such a case the witness must testify from his recollection, as *revived*, and not from it as *recorded in the memorandum*. It is the third class of recollection over which much controversy in the courts has arisen. In the early English cases, the distinction between the use of the memorandum as an aid to recollection and its use as evidence of past recollection was hardly appreciated, but by the middle of the eighteenth century, these courts generally permitted the use of the memorandum itself as a direct evidence of past recollection recorded.

* * *

* * * The American authorities are in hopeless conflict upon the question whether a past recorded recollection of events in general is admissible, but a majority, and we think the better considered, opinions, in civil cases at least, uphold the rule of the admissibility of such memoranda of past recollection recorded when the witness who made them or under whose direction they were made testifies (a) that he at one time had personal knowledge of the facts, (b) that the writing was, when made, an accurate record of the event, and (c) that after seeing the writing, he has not sufficient present independent recollection of the facts to testify accurately in regard thereto. This rule has been applied more sparingly in criminal cases, but even there, we think the better considered cases uphold it.

Regardless of the weight of the authority on the question, it seems to us that upon every principle of logic and common sense, evidence of this class should be admissible. It is an undisputed and undisputable fact that the human memory weakens with the passage of time, more with some individuals, less with others, but to some extent with all, and that a written record, unless changed by extrinsic forces, remains the same for all time. * * * The recorded memory of the witness is just as much the statement of that witness as to what he personally saw or heard as is his present independent recollection of the same fact. We think the confusion as to hearsay has arisen from cases where it was endeavored to prove the authenticity of the memorandum which was offered in evidence by some person other than the one who made it or under whose direction it was made. In such a case, of course, the memorandum would be hearsay just as much as if there were an attempt to prove by a third person an oral statement of the person who made the memorandum, in regard to the facts in issue. But when the person who witnessed the event testifies to the accuracy of the memorandum as made, that memorandum is just as much direct and not hearsay evidence as the language of the witness when he testifies to his independent recollection of what he saw. The objection in regard to cross-examination, on its face, might seem to have some weight, but we think a careful analysis of the question will show that it also is unfounded. What is the purpose of cross-examination? Obviously it is to convince the triers of fact, in some manner, that the testimony of the witness is untrue, for if the cross-examiner accepts it as true, there will be no need nor desire for cross-examination. How, then, may the truthfulness of the evidence of a witness be attacked through cross-examination? It seems to us that all attacks thereon must be reduced to one of three classes: (a) Upon the honesty and integrity of the witness; (b) upon his ability to observe accurately at the time the incident occurred; and (c) upon his accuracy of recollection of the past events. When a witness testifies as to his present recollection, independent or revived, he may, of course, be cross-examined fully on all three of these points. When he testifies as to his past recollection recorded, he can be examined to the same extent and in the same manner as to the first and second of these matters. He cannot well be cross-examined on the third point, but this is unnecessary, for he has already stated that he has *no* independent recollection of the event, which is all that could be brought out by the most rigid cross-examination on this point when the witness testifies from his present recollection, independent or revived.

* * *

[Affirmed.]

LILLY, AN INTRODUCTION TO THE LAW OF EVIDENCE *
231–232 (1978).

The present exception, past recorded recollection, should be considered in conjunction with the principles that govern refreshing a witness's present recollection. These principles, * * * may be summarized as follows: when a witness evinces an inability to remember, interrogating counsel may attempt to revive the witness's memory by producing a writing (or some other item) intended to induce recollection. If the interrogator succeeds in restoring the witness's memory so that the latter can testify from present recollection, the only evidence received by the court is the witness's testimony, not the writing. The writing serves the limited purpose of aiding memory; consequently, the counsel who used the writing for this narrow purpose has no right to introduce it into evidence. Under these circumstances, which are usually designated "present recollection refreshed," there is no hearsay difficulty because no "off-the-stand" assertion is offered for its truth. The witness testifies from present (revived) memory just as if he had not experienced a temporary inability to recall the event in question.

A different situation is encountered when the witness's memory cannot be revived satisfactorily and an earlier writing, authored or previously verified by the witness, if offered *in lieu of* his present testimony. If the proponent introduces the writing for a purpose which requires the trier to accept the truth of the assertions it contains, the writing is hearsay: the cross-examiner neither can cross-examine the writing, nor can he interrogate the witness about the details of the events described in it, since the witness is unable to recall these. Under these circumstances, admissibility must rest upon the use of some exception to the hearsay rule. If the witness can provide a foundation which attests to the accuracy of the writing by reason of its timely and accurate preparation, the present exception for recorded recollection will suffice.

* Reprinted with permission from Lilly's "An Introduction to the Law of Evidence," West Publishing Co. (1978).

RULES OF EVIDENCE FOR UNITED STATES COURTS AND MAGISTRATES

Rule 803

HEARSAY EXCEPTIONS; AVAILABILITY OF DECLARANT IMMATERIAL

The following are not excluded by the hearsay rule, even though the declarant is available as a witness:

* * *

(5) **Recorded recollection.** A memorandum or record concerning a matter about which a witness once had knowledge but now has insufficient recollection to enable him to testify fully and accurately, shown to have been made or adopted by the witness when the matter was fresh in his memory and to reflect that knowledge correctly. If admitted, the memorandum or record may be read into evidence but may not itself be received as an exhibit unless offered by an adverse party.

RULES OF EVIDENCE FOR UNITED STATES COURTS AND MAGISTRATES

Rule 612

WRITING USED TO REFRESH MEMORY

Except as otherwise provided in criminal proceedings by section 3500 of title 18, United States Code, if a witness uses a writing to refresh his memory for the purpose of testifying, either—

(1) while testifying, or

(2) before testifying, if the court in its discretion determines it is necessary in the interests of justice,

an adverse party is entitled to have the writing produced at the hearing, to inspect it, to cross-examine the witness thereon, and to introduce in evidence those portions which relate to the testimony of the witness. If it is claimed that the writing contains matters not related to the subject matter of the testimony the court shall examine the writing in camera, excise any portions not so related, and order delivery of the remainder to the party entitled thereto. Any portion withheld over objections shall be preserved and made available to the appellate court in the event of an appeal. If a writing is not produced or delivered pursuant to order under this rule, the court shall make any order justice requires, except that in criminal cases when the prosecution elects not to comply the order shall be one striking the testimony or, if the court in its discretion determines that the interest of justice so require, declaring a mistrial.

9. BUSINESS AND PUBLIC RECORDS

MARYLAND–DISTRICT OF COLUMBIA—VIRGINIA CRIMINAL PRACTICE INSTITUTE TRIAL MANUAL

2–5, 2–9 (1964).*

2.02 Introducing Business Records

1. Your Honor, I would like to have this instrument marked as defense exhibit # 1 for identification.

2. State your name.

3. Where do you reside, Mr. [witness]?

4. And what is your occupation?

5. Where are you employed?

6. What is the nature of your employer's business?

7. And what is the nature of your work there?

8. Were you so employed there on [date in question]?

9. Now, as the [position title], do you have responsibility of keeping the records concerning [subject matter]?

10. What is the method utilized for keeping these records?

11. Is this followed with respect to every [entry] [patient, etc.]?

12. I show you defendant's exhibit #1 for identification, purporting to be [document title], and ask you whether these are the original records which you have kept in your position?

13. Were these records in your custody on [date]?

14. And were they in your custody prior to your bringing them to court this morning?

15. Where were they kept?

16. Were the entries made herein made shortly after the transaction they record?

17. Who provided the information contained therein?

18. Was it his duty to collect this data and pass it on to you?

19. And were these entries made in the usual and ordinary course of business?

20. To the best of your knowledge, are they true and correct?

[Then move the admission of defense exhibit #1 for identification into evidence.]

---

* Copyright, 1964 by Lerner Law Book Company.

JOHNSON v. LUTZ

Court of Appeals of New York, 1930.
253 N.Y. 124, 170 N.E. 517.

HUBBS, J. This action is to recover damages for the wrongful death of the plaintiff's intestate, who was killed when his motorcycle came into collision with the defendants' truck at a street intersection. There was a sharp conflict in the testimony in regard to the circumstances under which the collision took place. A policeman's report of the accident filed by him in the station house was offered in evidence by the defendants under section 374–a of the Civil Practice Act, and was excluded. The sole ground for reversal urged by the appellants is that said report was erroneously excluded. That section reads: "Any writing or record, whether in the form of an entry in a book or otherwise, made as a memorandum or record of any act, transaction, occurrence or event, shall be admissible in evidence in proof of said act, transaction, occurrence or event, if the trial judge shall find that it was made in the regular course of any business, and that it was the regular course of such business to make such memorandum or record at the time of such act, transaction, occurrence or event, or within a reasonable time thereafter. All other circumstances of the making of such writing or record, including lack of personal knowledge by the entrant or maker, may be shown to affect its weight, but they shall not affect its admissibility. The term business shall include business, profession, occupation and calling of every kind."

Prior to the decision in the well-known case of Vosburgh v. Thayer, 12 Johns. 461, decided in 1815, shopbooks could not be introduced in evidence to prove an account. The decision in that case established that they were admissible where preliminary proof could be made that there were regular dealings between the parties; that the plaintiff kept honest and fair books; that some of the articles charged had been delivered; and that the plaintiff kept no clerk. At that time it might not have been a hardship to require a shopkeeper who sued to recover an account to furnish the preliminary proof required by that decision. Business was transacted in a comparatively small way, with few, if any, clerks. Since the decision in that case, it has remained the substantial basis of all decisions upon the question in this jurisdiction prior to the enactment in 1928 of section 374–a, Civil Practice Act.

Under modern conditions, the limitations upon the right to use books of account, memoranda, or records, made in the regular course of business, often resulted in a denial of justice, and usually in annoyance, expense, and waste of time and energy. A rule of evidence that was practical a century ago had become obsolete. * * *

The report of the Legal Research Committee of the Commonwealth Fund, published in 1927, by the Yale University Press, under the title, "The Law of Evidence—Some Proposals for Its Reform," dealt with the question in chapter 5, under the heading, "Proof of Business Transactions to Harmonize with Current Business Practice." That report, based upon extensive research, pointed out the confusion existing in decisions in different jurisdictions. It explained and illustrated the great need of a more practical, workable, and uniform rule, adapted to modern business conditions and practices. The chapter is devoted to a discussion of the pressing need of a rule of evidence which would "give evidential credit to the books upon which the mercantile and industrial world relies in the conduct of business." At the close of the chapter, the committee proposed a statute to be enacted in all jurisdictions. In compliance with such proposal, the Legislature enacted section 374–a of the Civil Practice Act in the very words used by the committee.

It is apparent that the Legislature enacted section 374–a to carry out the purpose announced in the report of the committee. That purpose was to secure the enactment of a statute which would afford a more workable rule of evidence in the proof of business transactions under existing business conditions.

In view of the history of section 374–a and the purpose for which it was enacted, it is apparent that it was never intended to apply to a situation like that in the case at bar. The memorandum in question was not made in the regular course of any business, profession, occupation, or calling. The policeman who made it was not present at the time of the accident. The memorandum was made from hearsay statements of third persons who happened to be present at the scene of the accident when he arrived. It does not appear whether they saw the accident and stated to him what they knew, or stated what some other persons had told them.

The purpose of the Legislature in enacting section 374–a was to permit a writing or record, made in the regular course of business, to be received in evidence, without the necessity of calling as witnesses all of the persons who had any part in making it, provided the record was made as a part of the duty of the person making it, or on information imparted by persons who were under a duty to impart such information. The amendment permits the introduction of shopbooks without the necessity of calling all clerks who may have sold different items of account. It was not intended to permit the receipt in evidence of entries based upon voluntary hearsay statements made by third parties not engaged in the business or under any duty in relation thereto. It was said, in Mayor, etc., of New York City v. Second Ave. R. Co., 102 N.Y. 572, at page 581, 7 N.E. 905, 909, "It is a proper qualification of the rule admitting such evidence that the account must have been made in the ordinary course of business, and that it should not be extended so as to admit a mere private memorandum, not made in pursuance of any duty owing by the person making it, or when made upon information derived from another who made the communication casually and voluntarily, and not under the sanction of duty or other obligation."

An important consideration leading to the amendment was the fact that in the business world credit is given to records made in the course of business by persons who are engaged in the business upon information given by others engaged in the same business as part of their duty.

"Such entries are dealt with in that way in the most important undertakings of mercantile and industrial life. They are the ultimate basis of calculation, investment, and general confidence in every business enterprise. Nor does the practical impossibility of obtaining constantly and permanently the verification of every employee affect the trust that is given to such books. It would seem that expedients which the entire commercial world recognizes as safe could be sanctioned, and not discredited, by courts of justice. When it is a mere question of whether provisional confidence can be placed in a certain class of statements, there cannot profitably and sensibly be one rule for the business world and another for the court-room. The merchant and the manufacturer must not be turned away remediless because the methods in which the entire community places a just confidence are a little difficult to reconcile with technical judicial scruples on the part of the same persons who as attorneys have already employed and relied upon the same methods. In short, courts must here cease to be pedantic and endeavor to be practical." 3 Wigmore on Evidence (1923) § 1530, p. 278.

The Legislature has sought by the amendment to make the courts practical. It would be unfortunate not to give the amendment a construction which will enable it to cure the evil complained of and accomplish the purpose for which it was enacted. In construing it, we should not, however, permit it to be applied in a case for which it was never intended.

The judgment should be affirmed, with costs.

CARDOZO, C. J., and POUND, CRANE, LEHMAN, KELLOGG, and O'BRIEN, JJ., concur.

Judgment affirmed.

Hypotheticals

Examine the following hypotheticals involving a suit by A against B arising out of an automobile accident.

The police report contains the following statement:

a. "I was standing at my beat and the red Chevrolet [which we now know to be the defendant's car] went through the red light and struck the green Ford [which other testimony shows is the plaintiff's car]."

b. "I arrived at one thirty [which other evidence indicates was twenty minutes after the accident] and noticed a skid mark, which I measured at 93 feet, leading directly to the rear wheels of the Chevrolet."

c. "I arrived within twenty seconds of the impact and heard a bystander scream, 'Did you see that crazy red car go through the red light?'"

d. "I arrived a few minutes after the accident and asked the man in the red Chevrolet what happened. He stated that he had fallen asleep at the wheel and did not rightly know."

e. "I arrived a few minutes after the accident and Officer Jones approached me and said that he had seen the accident and that the red Chevrolet had gone through the red light and hit the green Ford."

f. "I arrived a few minutes after the accident and Officer Jones had told me that he had gotten there just before I did and asked the Chevrolet driver what had happened and that he had said, 'I fell asleep at the wheel and I don't rightly know.'"

g. "I arrived a few minutes after the accident and I asked a bystander what had happened. He said that he had seen it all and the red Chevrolet was going too fast and couldn't stop for the red light and went right through the red light and hit the green Ford."

RULES OF EVIDENCE FOR UNITED STATES COURTS AND MAGISTRATES

Rule 805

HEARSAY WITHIN HEARSAY

Hearsay included within hearsay is not excluded under the hearsay rule if each part of the combined statements conforms with an exception to the hearsay rule provided in these rules.

UNITED STATES v. SMITH

United States Court of Appeals, District of Columbia Circuit, 1975.
521 F.2d 957.

J. SKELLY WRIGHT, Circuit Judge:

Appellant was convicted in the District Court of robbery in violation of 22 D.C.Code § 2901 (1973) and sentenced to eight years imprisonment pursuant to the Youth Corrections Act, 18 U.S.C. § 5010(c) (1970). In this court he charges the District Court with reversible error in refusing to admit into evidence Police Department Form 251, the official report of the police officer who received the initial complaint of the robbery, and the transcript of that officer's subsequent radio broadcasts. He further claims the court compounded its error by failing to admit the P.D. Form 251 following a specific request from the jury. We agree the District Court was in error, and we remand the case to the District Court for further proceedings.

I

Appellant was accused of robbing at gunpoint one James Williams, a taxi driver, in his cab shortly before 8:00 a. m. on March 18, 1971. Appellant was charged with armed robbery, robbery, and assault with a dangerous weapon. At trial Williams testified that he picked appellant up in the vicinity of 58th and East Capitol Streets and was told to take him to 529 51st Street, N. E., a boarded-up and deserted apartment in a two-building complex. Upon arriving at that address, appellant allegedly displayed a pistol and demanded Williams' money. Williams turned over $28.00 in bills and coins, whereupon his assailant left the cab demanding that Williams drive on and not look back. Disobeying this instruction, Williams waited until his assailant was out of sight and then backed his cab up in time to see the robber enter an apartment in the building in the complex facing that containing 529. Because of the angle at which he was watching, Williams could not be certain exactly which apartment was entered, but he testified that it had to be one of two possibilities. One of the two was 527 51st Street, where appellant lived with his mother and sisters.

After circling the block Williams was able to locate and stop a police car driven by Officer John T. Carr. He reported the robbery to Officer Carr and described the robber. Officer Carr recorded this information on his Form 251 and then broadcast the report to the police dispatcher. Thereupon Carr and Williams returned to the apartment complex where they were joined by other officers who had monitored the radio dispatch. Because the officers misunderstood Williams' directions as to which building the robber had entered, they were concentrating their attention on the building containing Apartment 529 when appellant emerged from Apartment 527. Officer Roy J. Miller, who was just leaving Apartment 521, observed appellant's exit and noted that he matched Williams' description. Simultaneously Williams, who was waiting in a police car, noticed appellant and immediately identified him as his assailant, whereupon appellant was arrested. The police never searched appellant's apartment, or sought a warrant to do so, and the money and the gun were never recovered.

At trial the crucial evidence against appellant was Williams' identification. Williams was absolutely certain that appellant was his assailant, testifying not only that he identified him at the second sighting immediately after the robbery, but that he had seen appellant around the neighborhood over a four- or five-year period. Williams testified that he visited with a friend approximately once a week over this period in an apartment in the same complex as appellant's, and that he had frequently seen appellant standing on the street. He testified that he recognized appellant as soon as he picked him up and thus was particularly surprised when the robbery took place, asking his assailant, "You don't know me?"

Since Williams' identification of appellant was so important to the Government's case—indeed, it was virtually the entire case—appellant's counsel strenuously tried to impeach Williams' credibility. He did so by attempting to develop inconsistencies between Williams' stated description of the crime and his assailant, and the report as recorded on Form 251 and as broadcast to the police dispatcher. Most of the discrepancies appeared in the Form 251.

* * *

When appellant sought to use the Form 251 to impeach Williams, the court refused to allow it into evidence, ruling that it was not his statement, but was hearsay and as such could not be used to impeach Williams. If it was to be admitted at all, it was to be through Officer Carr. At the conclusion of Officer Carr's testimony, however, the court refused to allow admission of either P.D. 251 or the broadcast transcript, ruling that their use was still for purposes of impeachment and as such, they were inadmissible hearsay.

* * *

Appellant alleges that the District Court erred in excluding the Form 251 and the broadcast transcript from introduction into evidence. He claims they are admissible as business records and may be used to impeach the credibility of the complaining witness, Williams. We agree.

The business record exception to the hearsay rule, unlike most other exceptions has been codified for some time, and is contained in the new Federal Rules of Evidence (FRE) in a form similar to that in which it appeared in the United States Code. FRE, Rule 803(6). The exception is intended to allow introduction of reliable and accurate records without the necessity of calling every person who made or contributed to the record. A business record is admissible whether or not the maker is available to take the stand. While no case in this circuit has yet so held, at least five other circuits have found that a police record constitutes a business record within the meaning of the Act. We adopt the approach of these circuits. While the record sought to be admitted must, of course, be shown to meet the standards of the Business Record Act, we see no reason to exclude a police record made in the regular course of business, it being the regular course of police work to make the record at issue. Thus Form 251 and the radio broadcast transcript were properly admissible as business records upon a showing of their trustworthiness.

* * *

* * * Williams' statements to Officer Carr, as recorded in the Form 251 and as broadcast over the police radio, are inadmissible to prove the truth of Williams' assertions, since Williams was not acting in the course of his business. But once the documents are established as business records, it is presumed that Officer Carr accurately transcribed and reported Williams' story. Thus the statements would be admissible to impeach Williams' present testimony, so long as the proper foundation for impeachment is laid, as it was here. The fact that Officer Carr testified does not preclude admission of the documents. A business record is admissible even if its maker testifies, for it is the record that is the most reliable evidence of what the maker heard, and of any contradiction that might impeach Williams' credibility. The jury deserved to see the records.

We hasten to specify the limits of our decision. We do not hold that a police record is admissible in a criminal proceeding as a business record, either as substantive evidence or for impeachment purposes, whenever the record meets the test of trustworthiness. We hold only that such a record is so admissible *when offered by a criminal defendant to support his defense.* We do not believe that such records may properly be so employed by the prosecution.

* * *

While we believe the District Court should have admitted the documents into evidence, our review of the record convinces us that their exclusion alone would not cause appellant sufficient prejudice to warrant reversal. Williams' identification was an extremely strong one, based not only on the robbery itself, but on observing appellant with some regularity over a four- or five-year period. Thus any inconsistency between the documents and Williams' testimony was far less important than the persuasiveness with which Williams described his past sightings of appellant and certainty with which he identified him in court. More importantly, the contents of the documents were fully aired and argued to the jury. Williams and Carr were both cross-examined closely about the inconsistencies contained in the documents. While admission of the documents was the proper action, ordinarily this full airing would make any resulting prejudice to appellant harmless.

* * *

* * * In our view that erroneous conclusion was harmless, and, without more, we would affirm. But it is the jury, and not this court, that is the trier of fact, and the jury thought the Form 251 was of sufficient importance to ask to see it. We cannot say that visual examination of Form 251 by the jury would not have affected its verdict. We note that the form was directly relevant to Williams' credibility. The jury was obviously concerned about that credibility because Williams was the only witness to the crime. It acquitted appellant on the armed robbery count, evidence of which depended solely upon Williams' testimony.

On the other hand, we cannot say it would have been an abuse of discretion had the trial court exercised discretion to deny the jury's request. * * * We do think, however, that the jury's request was of sufficient importance to the jury that the trial court should at least have the opportunity to rule upon it knowing the documents are admissible. Accordingly, we * * * remand the case to the District Court to consider the jury request anew. If the court concludes that it would have exercised its discretion to let the jury see the documents and that its failure to do so was not harmless, it must order a new trial for appellant. Otherwise, the conviction may stand.

So ordered.

UNITED STATES v. GRADY

United States Court of Appeals, Second District, 1976.
544 F.2d 598.

OAKES, Circuit Judge:

The waves of tragedy from the internecine conflict in Northern Ireland have their ripple effects in this country. Appellants here are Frank Grady, a sympathizer with the Catholic minority in Ulster, and John Jankowski, a licensed firearms dealer in Yonkers, New York. Each was convicted of conspiracy to violate the federal firearms law, * * * which require a licensed firearms dealer to make true entries in a federal firearms record, and of ten substantive counts of making or causing to be made false entries as to ten .30-caliber semiautomatic rifles in Jankowski's record or "logbook"; Grady was also convicted of one count of unlawful exportation without a permit of these same rifles, * * *.

* * *

IV. ADMISSION OF IRISH POLICE RECORDS

Much is made in the briefs of the admission into evidence of records of the formidable-sounding Department of Industrial and Forensic Science of the Ministry of Commerce and of the Royal Ulster Constabulary. These were entitled "Material Forwarded for Examination" and "Order for Disposal of Firearms/Ammunition." The ground of objection was that the documents constituted inadmissible hearsay. At most this admission would be harmless error, because the transfer of the weapons to Northern Ireland was relevant solely to Count 19, charging only Grady with unlawful export, and there was live testimony at trial (by Richard Anderson, officer in the Royal Ulster Constabulary) that four of the rifles had come into his official possession in Northern Ireland subsequent to their dates of purchase from Jankowski.

For the limited purpose of showing that the specified weapons were found in Northern Ireland on dates subsequent to the May,

1970, purchases, however, we think the records were admissible under the public records exception to the hearsay rule, codified in Fed. R.Evid. 803(8)(B). Rule 803(8)(B) allows admission of records and reports of public offices or agencies setting, forth "matters observed pursuant to duty imposed by law as to which matters there was a duty to report," but is subject to an exception for "matters observed by police officers and other law enforcement personnel." In adopting this exception, Congress was concerned about prosecutors attempting to prove their cases in chief simply by putting into evidence police officers' reports of their contemporaneous observations of crime. * * * The reports admitted here were not of this nature; they did not concern observations by the Ulster Constabulary of the appellants' commission of crimes. Rather, they simply related to the routine function of recording serial numbers and receipt of certain weapons found in Northern Ireland. They did not begin to prove the Government's entire case; they were strictly routine records.

* * *

Judgments affirmed.

RULES OF EVIDENCE FOR UNITED STATES COURTS AND MAGISTRATES

Rule 803

HEARSAY EXCEPTIONS; AVAILABILITY OF DECLARANT IMMATERIAL

The following are not excluded by the hearsay rule, even though the declarant is available as a witness:

* * *

(6) **Records of regularly conducted activity.** A memorandum, report, record, or data compilation, in any form, of acts, events, conditions, opinions, or diagnoses, made at or near the time by, or from information transmitted by, a person with knowledge, if kept in the course of a regularly conducted business activity, and if it was the regular practice of that business activity to make the memorandum, report, record, or data compilation, all as shown by the testimony of the custodian or other qualified witness, unless the source of information or the method or circumstances of preparation indicate lack of trustworthiness. The term "business" as used in this paragraph includes business, institution, association, profession, occupation, and calling of every kind, whether or not conducted for profit.

(7) **Absence of entry in records kept in accordance with the provisions of paragraph (6).** Evidence that a matter is not included in the memoranda reports, records, or data compilations, in any form, kept in accordance with the provisions of paragraph (6), to prove the

nonoccurrence or nonexistence of the matter, if the matter was of a kind of which a memorandum, report, record, or data compilation was regularly made and preserved, unless the sources of information or other circumstances indicate lack of trustworthiness.

(8) Public records and reports. Records, reports, statements, or data compilations, in any form, of public offices or agencies, setting forth (A) the activities of the office or agency, or (B) matters observed pursuant to duty imposed by law as to which matters there was a duty to report, excluding, however, in criminal cases matters observed by police officers and other law enforcement personnel, or (C) in civil actions and proceedings and against the Government in criminal cases, factual findings resulting from an investigation made pursuant to authority granted by law, unless the sources of information or other circumstances indicate lack of trustworthiness.

(9) Records of vital statistics. Records or data compilations, in any form, of births, fetal deaths, deaths, or marriages, if the report thereof was made to a public office pursuant to requirements of law.

(10) Absence of public record or entry. To prove the absence of a record, report, statement, or data compilation, in any form, or the nonoccurrence or nonexistence of a matter of which a record, report, statement, or data compilation, in any form, was regularly made and preserved by a public office or agency, evidence in the form of a certification in accordance with rule 902, or testimony, that diligent search failed to disclose the record, report, statement, or data compilation, or entry.

10. MISCELLANEOUS HEARSAY EXCEPTIONS

WALTZ, CRIMINAL EVIDENCE

103–104 (1975).

Judgment of Previous Conviction

American courts have taken three different approaches to the admissibility of a prior criminal conviction as evidence of facts the existence of which would have been essential to that conviction: (1) The majority rule has been that a prior criminal conviction cannot be introduced in a later case except to impeach credibility. (2) Some jurisdictions will admit prior convictions for whatever they may be worth. (3) And some courts will admit prior criminal convictions as *conclusive* proof of the facts on which they are based.

The trend of the cases and codes is toward the second approach. Evidence of a final judgment, entered after a trial or on a plea of guilty, adjudging a person guilty of a crime punishable by death or imprisonment in excess of one year (i. e., a felony), will be received to prove any fact which was essential to that judgment.

Convictions of minor offenses are excluded from this exception's operation because the motivation to defend at this low level—for example, traffic court—is often minimal or nonexistent, with the consequence that a plea of guilty may not be a true confession of culpability.

Judgments based on a plea of *nolo contendere* or "no contest" are also ordinarily excluded from this exception. The law prefers to encourage the making of such pleas.

Miscellaneous Exceptions to the Hearsay Rule

We have not discussed all of the recognized exceptions to the hearsay rule since a number of them are rarely encountered in criminal cases. For the sake of completeness, however, it should be mentioned that there are also exceptions to the rule against hearsay covering the following types of evidence: * * *

2. *Commercial and Scientific Publications.* Certain commercial and scientific publications are receivable in evidence under an exception to the hearsay rule. This exception's coverage differs from jurisdiction to jurisdiction, but in general it can be said to cover tabulations, lists, directories, and other published compilations generally relied upon by the public or by persons in particular occupations; scientific treatises; books of history; scholarly works on the arts; atlases; and market quotations.

3. *Vital Statistics.* There is an exception for records or data compilations of births, deaths, and marriages, where the report of them was made to some public office pursuant to the requirements of the law, such as a public health law.

4. *Family History.* A hearsay exception has been developed for statements relating to family history—births, deaths, marriages, ancestry, and the like—contained in the regularly kept records of a religious organization, such as a church.

5. *Marriage Certificates and the Like.* There is an exception for marriage, baptismal, and similar certificates, when made by a clergyman, public official, or other person authorized to perform the act certified and purporting to have been issued more or less contemporaneously with the act.

6. *Family Records.* There is a hearsay exception for statements in a family record such as a genealogy, family Bible, engravings on tombstones, and the like, when they are offered to prove birth, marriage, divorce, or other similar fact of family history.

7. *"Ancient" Documents.* "Ancient" documents are covered by a hearsay exception. An "ancient" document is usually defined as one that is more than thirty years old and whose authenticity is demonstrated in the evidence.

8. *Reputation Regarding Family History.* There is an exception permitting proof of reputation among members of a person's

family by blood or, sometimes, by marriage, concerning that person's birth, marriage, divorce, death, legitimacy, relationship by blood or marriage, ancestry, or other similar fact about the person's personal or family history.

9. *Reputation as to Character.* A long-settled exception to the hearsay rule provides for proof of a person's character, where relevant, by reputation testimony.

RULES OF EVIDENCE FOR UNITED STATES COURTS AND MAGISTRATES

Rule 803

HEARSAY EXCEPTIONS; AVAILABILITY OF DECLARANT IMMATERIAL

The following are not excluded by the hearsay rule, even though the declarant is available as a witness:

* * *

(22) Judgment of previous conviction. Evidence of a final judgment entered after a trial or upon a plea of guilty (but not upon a plea of nolo contendere), adjudging a person guilty of a crime punishable by death or imprisonment in excess of one year, to prove any fact essential to sustain the judgment, but not including, when offered by the Government in a criminal prosecution for purposes other than impeachment, judgments against persons other than the accused. The pendency of an appeal may be shown but does not affect admissibility.

Ch. 4   THE HEARSAY RULE & ITS EXCEPTIONS   215

C. THE FUTURE OF HEARSAY

1. LESSENING THE RESTRICTIONS ON THE ADMISSIBILITY OF HEARSAY EVIDENCE

"Sure, it's hearsay—but it's great hearsay!" *

[C434]

* Copyright, 1966 by Saturday Review, Inc. Saturday Review (June 4, 1966, p. 341).

RULES OF EVIDENCE FOR UNITED STATES COURTS AND MAGISTRATES

Rule 803

HEARSAY EXCEPTIONS; AVAILABILITY OF DECLARANT IMMATERIAL

The following are not excluded by the hearsay rule, even though the declarant is available as a witness:

* * *

(24) **Other exceptions.** A statement not specifically covered by any of the foregoing exceptions but having equivalent circumstantial guarantees of trustworthiness, if the court determines that (A) the statement is offered as evidence of a material fact; (B) the statement is more probative on the point for which it is offered than any other evidence which the proponent can procure through reasonable efforts; and (C) the general purposes of these rules and the interests of justice will best be served by admission of the statement into evidence. However, a statement may not be admitted under this exception unless the proponent of it makes known to the adverse party sufficiently in advance of the trial or hearing to provide the adverse party with a fair opportunity to prepare to meet it, his intention to offer the statement and the particulars of it, including the name and address of the declarant.

Rule 804

HEARSAY EXCEPTIONS: DECLARANT UNAVAILABLE

* * *

(b) **Hearsay exceptions.** The following are not excluded by the hearsay rule if the declarant is unavailable as a witness:

* * *

(5) *Other exceptions.* A statement not specifically covered by any of the foregoing exceptions but having equivalent circumstantial guarantees of trustworthiness, if the court determines that (A) the statement is offered as evidence of a material fact; (B) the statement is more probative on the point for which it is offered than any other evidence which the proponent can procure through reasonable efforts; and (C) the general purposes of these rules and the interests of justice will best be served by admission of the statement into evidence. However, a statement may not be admitted under this exception unless the proponent of it makes known to the adverse party sufficiently in advance of the trial or hearing to provide the adverse party with a fair opportunity to prepare to meet it, his intention to offer the statement and the particulars of it, including the name and address of the declarant.

UNITED STATES v. MEDICO

United States Court of Appeals, Second Circuit, 1977.
557 F.2d 309.

Before MANSFIELD and VAN GRAAFEILAND, Circuit Judges, and CARTER, District Judge.

ROBERT L. CARTER, District Judge:

On May 27, 1976, there was an armed robbery of the Chemical Bank at 23–98 Bell Boulevard, Queens, New York by two masked men. While one of the men held a shotgun to the assistant bank manager, the other came into the tellers' area, and took almost $23,000 in cash from the tellers' drawers. The two then left the bank. Rosario Frisina, the branch manager, and Barbara Balzarini, a teller, were in the tellers' area. Appellant was indicted and convicted for the crime. He appeals on the grounds that errors at a pre-trial suppression hearing and errors at trial warrant reversal.

On June 2, 1976, at separate interviews, F.B.I. agent David Carman showed Frisina, Balzarini and Louis Castabile, another bank employee, a group of eight photographs of white males, one of which was that of the appellant. Each selected appellant's photograph as that of one of the bank robbers.

Shortly thereafter, on June 2, appellant was apprehended, and on the same day, F.B.I. agents picked up Maria Medico, appellant's wife. They went with her to her apartment, searched the apartment and took from it unused cartridges, spent cartridges dug out of the furniture and walls of the apartment, and a pair of red pants riddled with bullet holes.

On June 24, 1976, Judge Weinstein held a pre-trial suppression hearing to determine whether the procedures employed by agent Carman in displaying the photographs to Frisina, Balzarini and Castabile were unduly suggestive and whether the Medico apartment had been entered and searched with Mrs. Medico's consent. He found no basis for invalidating the photographic display to the bank employees, nor for suppressing the evidence seized at the apartment. We agree with the trial court.

* * *

William Carmody, a bank employee, testified that about five minutes after the robbers had fled with the bank funds and while he was locking the entrance door, a bank customer knocked on the door. Carmody had seen this customer monthly at the bank for the past five years, but he did not know his name and had not seen him since the robbery. A young man about 20 years old whom Carmody did not know was sitting outside in a car giving the customer the make and license plate number of the getaway car. The customer relayed the information through the door to Carmody who took it down on his check book. Carmody could not hear what the young man was saying to the customer, although he could see the youth's lips move as the customer was telling him what was being said. Carmody took down the description of the getaway car as a "tan Dodge Valiant" with license plate number "700 CQA". Judge Weinstein allowed the testimony in under Rule 804(b)(5), Fed.R.Ev. The judge offered appellant a five day adjournment to meet the testimony or make his own investigation. Appellant declined the invitation asserting that the government had indicated that it had made serious attempts to locate the two witnesses without success. On admitting the testimony the district judge advised the jury that it was hearsay, that since the two witnesses were not present, the statement was not subject to cross examination; that the probative value of the statement was for the jury to determine, bearing in mind that the two missing witnesses were not subject to cross examination and their testimony was not under oath.

William Cariola testified that he used to work with Medico for a taxicab company and would see Medico driving an off-white Dodge with license plate number 700 CQA. He denied ownership of a car bearing license plate number 700 CQA. At the side bar the government advised the court that according to Cariola he had lost and then recovered his wallet. The wallet contained all his identification. When he regained possession of his wallet, it contained a registration certificate for a car with license plate number 700 CQA, registered in Cariola's name by a third party whom Cariola believed to be Medico. The government wanted to question Cariola about the matter before the jury. Appellant's counsel demurred saying "I think we ought to leave that out." The court agreed and the government rested. It is claimed that admission of this double hearsay testimony also constituted reversible error.

Determination

The admission of the hearsay statements of the bystanders concerning the getaway car raises at first blush serious problems.[1]

---

1. We would have little difficulty in upholding Judge Weinstein's ruling as a proper exercise of discretion had this been a civil case. We are faced here, however, with the Sixth Amendment's mandate that in "all criminal prosecutions, the accused shall enjoy the right * * * to be confronted with the witnesses against him." This has created some confusion as to whether the reach of the hearsay rules and the confrontation clause are coterminous. * * * The Supreme Court, however, has made clear that while the hearsay rule and the confrontation clause "stem from the same roots," Dutton v. Evans, 400 U.S. 74, 86, 91 S.Ct. 210, 27 L.Ed.2d 213 (1970) and "are generally designed to protect similar values," California v. Green, 399 U.S. 149, 155, 90 S.Ct. 1930, 1933, 26 L.Ed.2d 489 (1970), their reach is not coextensive. * * * The Sixth Amendment guarantee of confrontation, therefore, should not blind us to the reality that the question of the admission of the hearsay statements, whether in a criminal or civil case, turns on due process considerations of fairness, reliability and trustworthiness. Experience has taught that the stated exceptions now codified in the Federal Rules of Evidence meet these conditions.

Those difficulties become even more acute if the hearsay issue is not kept separate and apart from the refusal of the district court to allow the government to question Cariola more closely about the Dodge with license plate 700 CQA being registered in Cariola's name.

The testimony was admitted under the overall residual hearsay exception as provided in Rule 804(b)(5), Fed.R.Ev., which reads:

> "(b) Hearsay exceptions. The following are not excluded by the hearsay rule if the declarant is unavailable as a witness:
>
> * * *
>
> (5) Other exceptions. A statement not specifically covered by any of the foregoing exceptions but having equivalent circumstantial guarantees of trustworthiness, if the court determines that (A) the statement is offered as evidence of a material fact; (B) the statement is more probative on the point for which it is offered than any other evidence which the proponent can procure through reasonable efforts; and (C) the general purposes of these rules and the interests of justice will best be served by admission of the statement into evidence. However, a statement may not be admitted under this exception unless the proponent of it makes known to the adverse party sufficiently in advance of the trial or hearing to provide the adverse party with a fair opportunity to prepare to meet it, his intention to offer the statement and the particulars of it, including the name and address of the declarant."

This court has not yet had occasion to define the proper scope of Rule 804(b)(5) in a criminal trial. However, in United States v. Iaconetti, 540 F.2d 574 (2d Cir. 1976), in upholding the admission of hearsay statements in reliance on Rule 803(24), a residual hearsay exception identical to 804(b)(5), this court found the "statements in question possessed sufficient indicia of reliability, and were the best evidence to corroborate" the account of one of the government's witnesses as to what took place. It was also pointed out that "the statements were relevant to a material proposition of fact," id. at 578.

The proposed new Federal Rules of Evidence, as prescribed by the Supreme Court and transmitted to Congress contained identical provisions in Rules 803 and 804 authorizing federal courts to admit any hearsay statement not covered by stated exceptions. The Advisory Committee Note advises that these residual hearsay exceptions were included in the proposed rules because it would be "presumptuous to assume that all possible desirable exceptions to the hearsay rule have been catalogued; * * *" and that the unfettered exercise of judicial discretion was not contemplated, but the residual hearsay exception in Rules 803 and 804 would permit the courts to deal with new and presently unanticipated situations which demonstrate a trustworthiness within the spirit of the specifically stated exceptions. The residual exceptions as proposed, however, were rejected by the House Committee on the Judiciary because it was felt that the two provisions injected "too much uncertainty in the law of evidence and [might impair] the ability of practitioners to prepare for trial." H.Rep. No. 650, 93rd Cong., 1st Sess. 5–6, U.S. Code Cong. & Admin.News 1974, p. 7079.

Indeed the testimony meets all the specific requirements for admission as a present sense impression under Rule 803(1) under which a hearsay statement will not be excluded even though the declarant is available. As the Advisory Committee Note to Rule 803(1) indicates, the theory for this exception is that the "contemporaneity of event and statement negate the likelihood of deliberate or conscious misrepresentation." Precise contemporaneity is not required, thus a "slight lapse is allowable." Ibid. The Committee Advisory Note points out that the cases reveal a hesitancy to admit the statement without more when the bystander's identity is unknown. Ibid. This may well be the reason Judge Weinstein decided to rely on Rule 804(b)(5). That fact, however, that the statement meets all the specific standards for admissions under 803(1) but fails to meet all the criteria set forth in the supportive judicial rationale surely brings it within the grant of discretion which 804(b)(5) accords to a trial judge, consonant with the legislative purposes which the residual exception was designed to achieve.

Moreover, several factors contribute to the reliability of Carmody's testimony. The two unavailable witnesses were at the scene of the crime. One was in position to perceive and describe the car and license plate number the robbers used to effect their escape; and while the other did not claim to have himself observed the car or the license plate, he relayed to Carmody that information just told to him by the first bystander who personally had seen the robbers drive away in the getaway car. The time frame in which the information was passed from the eyewitness to the bank customer and then from the customer to Carmody was very brief and followed the actual getaway so closely, that the likelihood of inaccuracies is small and the possibility that truth was undercut by speculation or fabrication reduced. The probability that the information was accurate is enhanced by the fact that Carmody transcribed it onto his checkbook as it was being told to him.

Carmody's testimony was highly relevant, clearly material, and the need for that evidence was great. No other evidence providing the same information or being more probative of the fact for which the statement was offered was available to the government. It would have been preferable, certainly, to have had the youth and/or the bank customer testify. However, the government made serious efforts to locate these witnesses to no avail, and the defense was offered an adjournment to prepare to meet this evidence or make investigations of its own. The offer was declined. In light of these circumstances, the admission of Carmody's testimony was proper under Rule 804(b)(5). Clearly the trustworthiness and necessity for the admission of the statement and the specific facts and circumstances warranting allowing the testimony to come before the jury are on par with those which justify the enumerated exceptions.

* * *

[Affirmed.]

[Dissent omitted.]

2. CONFRONTATION

LILLY, AN INTRODUCTION TO THE LAW OF EVIDENCE *

273–278 (1978).

Any assessment of the future role of hearsay evidence, at least in criminal trials, must take account of the Constitution's Sixth Amendment guarantee to an accused of the right "to be confronted with the witnesses against him." Although "the confrontation cases are in disarray and the policies to be served by the constitutional protection are far from clear," certain conclusions may be drawn from the cases.

The confrontation clause never has been read so literally as to preclude generally the use of hearsay evidence in criminal trials. Indeed, the cases are replete with instances of hearsay statements admitted under the recognized exceptions. It is fairly certain that there is no constitutional prohibition against either the substantive use of a prior extrajudicial declaration of a witness present at trial (at least where it clearly is shown that the prior statements were made) or, in cases of unavailability, against the use of prior testimony in circumstances in which the accused had an earlier opportunity to conduct a fair and full cross-examination. Even admission against the accused of dying declarations apparently is permissible, and most courts have turned aside confrontation clause challenges to such hearsay exceptions as declarations against interest, business entries, and party admissions by coconspirators.

Nonetheless, the confrontation clause places limits, however uncertain, upon the freedom with which the prosecution may deny the accused adequate opportunity to cross-examine witnesses (including, in some circumstances, hearsay declarants) and the right to have adverse statements secured under oath and in the presence of the trier of fact. The Supreme Court apparently has rejected both of the most extreme readings of the confrontation clause. Under one of these constructions, every hearsay declarant would be viewed as a witness against the accused and his presence at trial would be compelled constitutionally, thus blocking substantially all hearsay evidence. Under

---

* Reprinted with permission from Lilly's "An Introduction to the Law of Evidence," West Publishing Co. (1978).

the opposite reading, the constitutional command would require merely a guarantee that evidence used to convict the accused be presented through trial witnesses. The source of the witness's information, while perhaps raising issues under an exclusionary rule of evidence such as the hearsay rule, would not present a constitutional problem.

In several cases, the Supreme Court has struck down under the confrontation clause evidence of inculpatory statements that the accused could not subject to meaningful cross-examination. Use of a transcript of prior testimony elicited from a witness during the accused's preliminary hearing at which the accused was not represented by counsel was found constitutionally objectionable. Similarly rejected was improper "evidence" (although not formally admitted) of a prosecutor's use of the confession of the accused's codefendant: after the codefendant-witness invoked the fifth amendment and refused to testify, the prosecutor used the guise of refreshing the witness's recollection to read aloud the codefendant's earlier confession which implicated the accused. In a third case, in which the accused did not take the stand, the use of a codefendant's confession which inculpated the accused was held to violate the latter's right of confrontation; an instruction to the jury that it consider the confession only with regard to the codefendant's guilt was deemed ineffective. The Supreme Court also has indicated that the confrontation clause limits when a witness can be considered "unavailable" for purposes of a hearsay exception. In one case, state authorities who knew that a prosecution witness was in a federal penitentiary in another state made no attempt to secure his presence at trial. The Court held that the state denied the accused's right of confrontation when it used the witness's out-of-state custody as a ground for invoking the exception for prior recorded testimony.

The Court has yet to clarify the reach of the confrontation clause, but reason suggests an analytical framework for future decisions. Like other constitutional provisions, the right of an accused "to be confronted with witnesses against him" should not be inflexible. Confrontation is a relative term to be given a functional meaning. Although the values to be protected by the confrontation clause are not altogether clear, the notion of confronting a witness implies a right to interrogate him effectively under oath and to bring him within the observation of the trier of fact. At a minimum, it guarantees that the accused may effectively confront and cross-examine those who testify against him at trial. Cross-examination may not be limited so as to significantly emasculate its effectiveness. In all probability, the right of confrontation also ensures that an accused will not be convicted on the basis of statements by absent declarants that fall within no recognized exception to the hearsay rule. Thus, prosecutorial use at trial of the ex parte affidavit of an absent declarant to supply significant proof against the accused probably would violate his sixth amendment right to confrontation.

Beyond these situations, application of the confrontation clause should depend upon whether considerations of trustworthiness and adversarial fairness are satisfied. In ascertaining whether the confrontation of a witness at trial who merely presents documents or who gives testimony which embodies the assertions of absent declarants satisfies the sixth amendment, at least three factors should be determinative: trustworthiness, the ease with which a declarant can be produced, and the importance of the evidence in question. If there is strong reason to distrust the reliability of the evidence, the preference for live testimony should be compelling. If the declarant reasonably can be produced, his courtroom presence should be demanded. In instances where the declarant is deceased or otherwise not available, the question whether the right of confrontation has been violated should depend on the degree of risk that the evidence will produce an erroneous finding. If the statements in question fall within a hearsay exception and thus have the imprimatur of judicial and legislative experience, this fact should weigh heavily in favor of a determination that the right to confrontation has been satisfied. Finally, the significance of an accused's right to confront a witness should bear a direct relation to the significance of the evidence supplied by the witness. When this evidence is comparatively inconsequential, cross-examination of the in-court witness should be sufficient confrontation even though the source of the witness's testimony may be traced to an absent declarant.

The foregoing analysis may fit as comfortably within a due process analysis as it does within the framework of the confrontation clause. Nonetheless, the Supreme Court already has embarked upon a course that accords the confrontation clause content beyond that found in the restrictive interpretation described earlier. A middle ground permitting ample flexibility to accommodate the growth of the hearsay rule seems consonant with the existing cases and highly desirable.

3. THE DEFENDANT'S RIGHT TO PRESENT EVIDENCE

CHAMBERS v. MISSISSIPPI

Supreme Court of the United States, 1973.
410 U.S. 284, 93 S.Ct. 1038, 35 L.Ed. 297.

Mr. Justice POWELL delivered the opinion of the Court.

Petitioner, Leon Chambers, was tried by a jury in a Mississippi trial court and convicted of murdering a policeman. The jury assessed punishment at life imprisonment, and the Mississippi Supreme Court affirmed, one justice dissenting. * * * Subsequently, the petition for certiorari was granted, * * * to consider whether petitioner's trial was conducted in accord with principles of due process under the Fourteenth Amendment. We conclude that it was not.

I

The events that led to petitioner's prosecution for murder occurred in the small town of Woodville in southern Mississippi. On Saturday evening, June 14, 1969, two Woodville policemen, James Forman and Aaron "Sonny" Liberty, entered a local bar and pool hall to execute a warrant for the arrest of a youth named C. C. Jackson. Jackson resisted and a hostile crowd of some 50 or 60 persons gathered. The officers' first attempt to handcuff Jackson was frustrated when 20 or 25 men in the crowd intervened and wrestled him free. Forman then radioed for assistance and Liberty removed his riot gun, a 12-gauge sawed-off shotgun, from the car. Three deputy sheriffs arrived shortly thereafter and the officers again attempted to make their arrest. Once more, the officers were attacked by the onlookers and during the commotion five or six pistol shots were fired. Forman was looking in a different direction when the shooting began, but immediately saw that Liberty had been shot several times in the back. Before Liberty died, he turned around and fired both barrels of his riot gun into an alley in the area from which the shots appeared to have come. The first shot was wild and high and scattered the crowd standing at the face of the alley. Liberty appeared, however, to take more deliberate aim before the second shot and hit one of the men in the crowd in the back of the head and neck as he ran down the alley. That man was Leon Chambers.

Officer Forman could not see from his vantage point who shot Liberty or whether Liberty's shots hit anyone. One of the deputy sheriffs testified at trial that he was standing several feet from Liberty and that he saw Chambers shoot him. Another deputy sheriff stated that, although he could not see whether Chambers had a gun in his hand, he did see Chambers "break his arm down" shortly before the shots were fired. The officers who saw Chambers fall testified that they thought he was dead but they made no effort at that time either to examine him or to search for the murder weapon. Instead, they attended to Liberty, who was placed in the police car and taken to a hospital where he was declared dead on arrival. A subsequent autopsy showed that he had been hit with four bullets from a .22-caliber revolver.

Shortly after the shooting, three of Chambers' friends discovered that he was not yet dead. James Williams, Berkley Turner, and Gable McDonald loaded him into a car and transported him to the same hospital. Later that night, when the county sheriff discovered that Chambers was still alive, a guard was placed outside his room. Chambers was subsequently charged with Liberty's murder. He pleaded not guilty and has asserted his innocence thoughout.

The story of Leon Chambers is intertwined with the story of another man, Gable McDonald. McDonald, a lifelong resident of Woodville, was in the crowd on the evening of Liberty's death. Sometime

Ch. 4   THE HEARSAY RULE & ITS EXCEPTIONS   225

shortly after that day, he left his wife in Woodville and moved to Louisiana and found a job at a sugar mill. In November of that same year, he returned to Woodville when his wife informed him that an acquaintance of his, known as Reverend Stokes, wanted to see him. Stokes owned a gas station in Natchez, Mississippi, several miles north of Woodville, and upon his return McDonald went to see him. After talking to Stokes, McDonald agreed to make a statement to Chambers' attorneys, who maintained offices in Natchez. Two days later, he appeared at the attorneys' offices and gave a sworn confession that he shot Officer Liberty. He also stated that he had already told a friend of his, James Williams, that he shot Liberty. He said that he used his own pistol, a nine-shot .22-caliber revolver, which he had discarded shortly after the shooting. In response to questions from Chambers' attorneys, McDonald affirmed that his confession was voluntary and that no one had compelled him to come to them. Once the confession had been transcribed, signed, and witnessed, McDonald was turned over to the local police authorities and was placed in jail.

One month later, at a preliminary hearing, McDonald repudiated his prior sworn confession. He testified that Stokes had persuaded him to confess that he shot Liberty. He claimed that Stokes had promised that he would not go to jail and that he would share in the proceeds of a lawsuit that Chambers would bring against the town of Woodville. On examination by his own attorney and on cross-examination by the State, McDonald swore that he had not been at the scene when Liberty was shot but had been down the street drinking beer in a cafe with a friend, Berkley Turner. When he and Turner heard the shooting, he testified, they walked up the street and found Chambers lying in the alley. He, Turner, and Williams took Chambers to the hospital. McDonald further testified at the preliminary hearing that he did not know what had happened, that there was no discussion about the shooting either going to or coming back from the hospital, and that it was not until the next day that he learned that Chambers had been felled by a blast from Liberty's riot gun. In addition, McDonald stated that while he once owned a .22-caliber pistol he had lost it many months before the shooting and did not own or possess a weapon at that time. The local justice of the peace accepted McDonald's repudiation and released him from custody. The local authorities undertook no further investigation of his possible involvement.

Chambers' case came on for trial in October of the next year. At trial, he endeavored to develop two grounds of defense. He first attempted to show that he did not shoot Liberty. Only one officer testified that he actually saw Chambers fire the shots. Although three officers saw Liberty shoot Chambers and testified that they assumed he was shooting his attacker, none of them examined Chambers to see whether he was still alive or whether he possessed a gun.

Indeed, no weapon was ever recovered from the scene and there was no proof that Chambers had ever owned a .22-caliber pistol. One witness testified that he was standing in the street near where Liberty was shot, that he was looking at Chambers when the shooting began, and that he was sure that Chambers did not fire the shots.

Petitioner's second defense was that Gable McDonald had shot Officer Liberty. He was only partially successful, however, in his efforts to bring before the jury the testimony supporting this defense. Sam Hardin, a lifelong friend of McDonald's, testified that he saw McDonald shoot Liberty. A second witness, one of Liberty's cousins, testified that he saw McDonald immediately after the shooting with a pistol in his hand. In addition to the testimony of these two witnesses, Chambers endeavored to show the jury that McDonald had repeatedly confessed to the crime. Chambers attempted to prove that McDonald had admitted responsibility for the murder on four separate occasions, once when he gave the sworn statement to Chambers' counsel and three other times prior to that occasion in private conversations with friends.

In large measure, he was thwarted in his attempt to present this portion of his defense by the strict application of certain Mississippi rules of evidence. Chambers asserts in this Court, as he did unsuccessfully in his motion for new trial and on appeal to the State Supreme Court, that the application of these evidentiary rules rendered his trial fundamentally unfair and deprived him of due process of law. It is necessary, therefore, to examine carefully the rulings made during the trial.

II

Chambers filed a pretrial motion requesting the court to order McDonald to appear. Chambers also sought a ruling at that time that, if the State itself chose not to call McDonald, he be allowed to call him as an adverse witness. Attached to the motion were copies of McDonald's sworn confession and of the transcript of his preliminary hearing at which he repudiated that confession. The trial court granted the motion requiring McDonald to appear but reserved ruling on the adverse-witness motion. At trial, after the State failed to put McDonald on the stand, Chambers called McDonald, laid a predicate for the introduction of his sworn out-of-court confession, had it admitted into evidence, and read it to the jury. The State, upon cross-examination, elicited from McDonald the fact that he had repudiated his prior confession. McDonald further testified, as he had at the preliminary hearing, that he did not shoot Liberty, and that he confessed to the crime only on the promise of Reverend Stokes that he would not go to jail and would share in a sizable tort recovery from the town. He also retold his own story of his actions on the evening of the shooting, including his visit to the cafe down the street, his absence from the scene during the critical period, and his subsequent trip to the hospital with Chambers.

At the conclusion of the State's cross-examination, Chambers renewed his motion to examine McDonald as an adverse witness. The trial court denied the motion, stating: "He may be hostile, but he is not adverse in the sense of the word, so your request will be overruled." On appeal, the State Supreme Court upheld the trial court's ruling, finding that "McDonald's testimony was not adverse to appellant" because "[n]owhere did he point the finger at Chambers." 252 So.2d, at 220.

Defeated in his attempt to challenge directly McDonald's renunciation of his prior confession, Chambers sought to introduce the testimony of the three witnesses to whom McDonald had admitted that he shot the officer. The first of these, Sam Hardin, would have testified that, on the night of the shooting, he spent the late evening hours with McDonald at a friend's house after their return from the hospital and that, while driving McDonald home later that night, McDonald stated that he shot Liberty. The State objected to the admission of this testimony on the ground that it was hearsay. The trial court sustained the objection.

Berkley Turner, the friend with whom McDonald said he was drinking beer when the shooting occurred, was then called to testify. In the jury's presence, and without objection, he testified that he had not been in the cafe that Saturday and had not had any beers with McDonald. The jury was then excused. In the absence of the jury, Turner recounted his conversations with McDonald while they were riding with James Williams to take Chambers to the hospital. When asked whether McDonald said anything regarding the shooting of Liberty, Turner testified that McDonald told him that he "shot him." Turner further stated that one week later, when he met McDonald at a friend's house, McDonald reminded him of their prior conversation and urged Turner not to "mess him up." Petitioner argued to the court that, especially where there was other proof in the case that was corroborative of these out-of-court statements, Turner's testimony as to McDonald's self-incriminating remarks should have been admitted as an exception to the hearsay rule. Again, the trial court sustained the State's objection.

The third witness, Albert Carter, was McDonald's neighbor. They had been friends for about 25 years. Although Carter had not been in Woodville on the evening of the shooting, he stated that he learned about it the next morning from McDonald. That same day, he and McDonald walked out to a well near McDonald's house and there McDonald told him that he was the one who shot Officer Liberty. Carter testified that McDonald also told him that he had disposed of the .22-caliber revolver later that night. He further testified that several weeks after the shooting, he accompanied McDonald to Natchez where McDonald purchased another .22 pistol to replace the one he had discarded. The jury was not allowed to hear Carter's testimony. Chambers urged that these statements were admissible, the State objected, and the court sustained the objection. On appeal, the State Supreme Court approved the lower court's exclusion of these witnesses' testimony on hearsay grounds. 252 So.2d, at 220.

In sum, then, this was Chambers' predicament. As a consequence of the combination of Mississippi's "party witness" or "voucher" rule and its hearsay rule, he was unable either to cross-examine McDonald or to present witnesses in his own behalf who would have discredited McDonald's repudiation and demonstrated his complicity. Chambers had, however, chipped away at the fringes of McDonald's story by introducing admissible testimony from other sources indicating that he had not been seen in the cafe where he said he was when the shooting started, that he had not been having beer with Turner, and that he possessed a .22 pistol at the time of the crime. But all that remained from McDonald's own testimony was a single written confession countered by an arguably acceptable renunciation. Chambers' defense was far less persuasive than it might have been had he been given an opportunity to subject McDonald's statements to cross-examination or had the other confessions been admitted.

III

The right of an accused in a criminal trial to due process is, in essence, the right to a fair opportunity to defend against the State's accusations. The rights to confront and cross-examine witnesses and to call witnesses in one's own behalf have long been recognized as essential to due process. Mr. Justice Black, writing for the Court in In re Oliver, 333 U.S. 257, 273, identified these rights as among the minimum essentials of a fair trial:

> "A person's right to reasonable notice of a charge against him, and an opportunity to be heard in his defense—a right to his day in court—are basic in our system of jurisprudence; and these rights include, as a minimum, a right to examine the witnesses against him, to offer testimony, and to be represented by counsel."

* * * Both of these elements of a fair trial are implicated in the present case.

A

Chambers was denied an opportunity to subject McDonald's damning repudiation and alibi to cross-examination. He was not allowed to test the witness' recollection, to probe into the details of his alibi, or to "sift" his conscience so that the jury might judge for itself whether McDonald's testimony was worthy of belief. * * * The right of cross-examination is more than a desirable rule of trial procedure. It is implicit in the constitutional right of confrontation, and helps assure the "accuracy of the truth-determining process." Dutton v. Evans, 400 U.S. 74, 89, (1970). * * * It is, indeed, "an essential and fundamental requirement for the kind of fair trial which is this country's constitutional goal." Pointer v. Texas, 380 U.S. 400, 405, (1965). Of course, the right to confront and to cross-examine is not absolute and may, in appropriate cases, bow to accommodate other legitimate interests in the criminal trial process. * * * But its denial or significant diminution calls into question the ultimate " 'integrity of the fact-finding process' " and requires that the competing interest be closely examined. * * *

In this case, petitioner's request to cross-examine McDonald was denied on the basis of a Mississippi common-law rule that a party may not impeach his own witness. The rule rests on the presumption —without regard to the circumstances of the particular case—that a party who calls a witness "vouches for his credibility." * * * Although the historical origins of the "voucher" rule are uncertain, it appears to be a remnant of primitive English trial practice in which "oathtakers" or "compurgators" were called to stand behind a particular party's position in any controversy. Their assertions were strictly partisan and, quite unlike witnesses in criminal trials today, their role bore little relation to the impartial ascertainment of the facts.

Whatever validity the "voucher" rule may have once enjoyed, and apart from whatever usefulness it retains today in the civil trial process, it bears little present relationship to the realities of the criminal process. It might have been logical for the early common law to require a party to vouch for the credibility of witnesses he brought before the jury to affirm his veracity. Having selected them especially for that purpose, the party might reasonably be expected to stand firmly behind their testimony. But in modern criminal trials, defendants are rarely able to select their witnesses: they must take them where they find them. Moreover, as applied in this case, the "voucher" rule's impact was doubly harmful to Chambers' efforts to develop his defense. Not only was he precluded from cross-examining McDonald, but, as the State conceded at oral argument, he was also restricted in the scope of his direct examination by the rule's corollary requirement that the party calling the witness is bound by anything he might say. He was, therefore, effectively prevented from exploring the circumstances of McDonald's three prior oral confessions and from challenging the renunciation of the written confession.

In this Court, Mississippi has not sought to defend the rule or explain its underlying rationale. Nor has it contended that its rule should override the accused's right of confrontation. Instead, it argues that there is no incompatability between the rule and Chambers' rights because no right of confrontation exists unless the testifying witness is "adverse" to the accused. The State's brief asserts that the "right of confrontation applies to witnesses *against* an accused." Relying on the trial court's determination that McDonald was not "adverse," and on the State Supreme Court's holding that McDonald did not "point the finger at Chambers," the State contends that Chambers' constitutional right was not involved.

The argument that McDonald's testimony was not "adverse" to, or "against," Chambers is not convincing. The State's proof at trial excluded the theory that more than one person participated in the shooting of Liberty. To the extent that McDonald's sworn confession tended to incriminate him, it tended also to exculpate Chambers. And, in the circumstances of this case, McDonald's retraction inculpated Chambers to the same extent that it exculpated McDonald. It can hardly be disputed that McDonald's testimony was in fact seriously adverse to Chambers. The availability of the right to confront and to cross-examine those who give damaging testimony against the accused has never been held to depend on whether the witness was initially put on the stand by the accused or by the State. We reject the notion that a right of such substance in the criminal process may be governed by that technicality or by any narrow and unrealistic definition of the word "against." The "voucher" rule, as applied in this case, plainly interfered with Chambers' right to defend against the State's charges.

* * *

The hearsay statements involved in this case were originally made and subsequently offered at trial under circumstances that provided considerable assurance of their reliability. First, each of McDonald's confessions was made spontaneously to a close acquaintance shortly after the murder had occurred. Second, each one was corroborated by some other evidence in the case—McDonald's sworn confession, the testimony of an eyewitness to the shooting, the testimony that McDonald was seen with a gun immediately after the shooting, and proof of his prior ownership of a .22-caliber revolver and subsequent purchase of a new weapon. The sheer number of independent confessions provided additional corroboration for each. Third, whatever may be the parameters of the penal-interest rationale, each confession here was in a very real sense self-incriminatory and unquestionably against interest.

* * *

* * * McDonald stood to benefit nothing by disclosing his role in the shooting to any of his three friends and he must have been aware of the possibility that disclosure would lead to criminal prosecution. Indeed, after telling Turner of his involvement, he subsequently urged Turner not to "mess him up." Finally, if there was any question about the truthfulness of the extrajudicial statements, McDonald was present in the courtroom and was under oath. He could have been cross-examined by the State, and his demeanor and responses weighed by the jury. * * * The availability of McDonald significantly distinguishes this case from the prior Mississippi precedent, Brown v. State, supra, and from the *Donnelly*-type situ-

ation, since in both cases the declarant was unavailable at the time of trial.

Few rights are more fundamental than that of an accused to present witnesses in his own defense. * * * In the exercise of this right, the accused, as is required of the State, must comply with established rules of procedure and evidence designed to assure both fairness and reliability in the ascertainment of guilt and innocence. Although perhaps no rule of evidence has been more respected or more frequently applied in jury trials than that applicable to the exclusion of hearsay, exceptions tailored to allow the introduction of evidence which in fact is likely to be trustworthy have long existed. The testimony rejected by the trial court here bore persuasive assurances of trustworthiness and thus was well within the basic rationale of the exception for declarations against interest. That testimony also was critical to Chambers' defense. In these circumstances, where constitutional rights directly affecting the ascertainment of guilt are implicated, the hearsay rule may not be applied mechanistically to defeat the ends of justice.

We conclude that the exclusion of this critical evidence, coupled with the State's refusal to permit Chambers to cross-examine McDonald, denied him a trial in accord with traditional and fundamental standards of due process. In reaching this judgment, we establish no new principles of constitutional law. Nor does our holding signal any diminution in the respect traditionally accorded to the States in the establishment and implementation of their own criminal trial rules and procedures. Rather, we hold quite simply that under the facts and circumstances of this case the rulings of the trial court deprived Chambers of a fair trial.

The judgment is reversed and the case is remanded to the Supreme Court of Mississippi for further proceedings not inconsistent with this opinion.

It is so ordered.

[The concurring opinion of Justice WHITE and the dissenting opinion of Justice REHNQUIST are omitted.]

COLLATERAL READINGS

The Future of Hearsay

McCormick's Handbook of the Law of Evidence §§ 325–327 (2d ed. 1972)

McCormick, Law and the Future: Evidence, 51 Nw.U.L.Rev. 218 (1956)

Chadbourn, Bentham and the Hearsay Rule—A Benthamic View of Rule 63(4)(c) of the Uniform Rules of Evidence, 75 Harv.L.Rev. 932 (1962)

Moore and Bendix, Congress, Evidence, and Rulemaking, 84 Yale L.J. 9 (1974)

James, The Role of Hearsay in a Rational Scheme of Evidence, 34 Ill.L.Rev. 788 (1940)

Weinstein, Probative Force of Hearsay, 46 Iowa L.Rev. 331 (1961)

Note, Preserving the Right to Confrontation—A New Approach to Hearsay Evidence in Criminal Trials, 113 U.Pa.L.Rev. 741 (1965)

Note, Admission of Printed Materials as an Exception to the Hearsay Rule, 19 Baylor L.Rev. 280 (1967)

English Evidence Act, 1968, Current Law Stat.Ann.1968 (Sweet & Maxwell)

Comment, Hearsay Under the Proposed Federal Rules: A Discretionary Approach, 15 Wayne L.Rev. 1077 (1969)

Griswold, The Due Process Revolution and Confrontation, 119 U.Pa. L.Rev. 711 (1971)

Comment, Constitutional Law—The Confrontation Test for Hearsay Exceptions: An Uncertain Standard, 59 Cal.L.Rev. 580 (1971)

McNAUGHTON, EVIDENCE EXAM, HARVARD LAW SCHOOL, FIRST SEMESTER, 1960–1961

B. 50 HEARSAY QUESTIONS

Each of the following questions has two parts. (a) Is the item hearsay? Answer "Yes" or "No." And (b), if hearsay, under what exception or exceptions might the item reasonably fall? In the blank following the question, write one of the following three things: (i) "Not applicable" (or "N/A") if the item is not hearsay; (ii) "None" if the hearsay link falls under no exception; (iii) the appropriate hearsay exception(s) under which the hearsay link might reasonably fall.

SPECIAL INFORMATION: (1) Even if the facts given are insufficient to supply all of the prerequisites of an exception, you should mention the exception if the facts given reasonably suggest and are not inconsistent with it. (2) Treat past recollection recorded, the business entry statute and "Houston Oxygen"—pg—as separate exceptions to the hearsay rule.

If the item is multiple, or "totem pole," hearsay, indicate in some appropriate way which exceptions (if any) apply to which hearsay link.

Hearsay?
(Yes or No) . . .

....Yes... 76. Prosecution of D for killing V. On the issue of D's fear of V, W1 testifies that he heard W2 say to D, "V has knifed three people in the last year."
(Exception(s) ....
....)

Ch. 4   THE HEARSAY RULE & ITS EXCEPTIONS   233

Yes .... 77. Same as 76 except the issue is whether V or D was the aggressor. (Exception(s) ....
....)

NO .... 84. As tending to show that D had a revolver in his possession, the state offers the testimony of W that, as D passed W's house, W called her husband's attention to a revolver sticking out of D's pocket. (Exception(s) *N/A* ....
....)

NO .... 85. On the issue whether plaintiff's decedent (V) was still alive after his car was struck by the first of two cars, W (who was in V's car with V) testifies that, before the second car struck, V said "My head hurts." (Exception(s) *Spontaneous*
utterances ....)

.... 86. On the issue of the existence of injuries to V's head caused by the first car, the testimony in 85. (Exception(s) ....
....)

Yes .... 87. On the issue of the sanity of D, a woman, W testifies that D on numerous occasions said publicly, "I am the Pope." (Exception(s) ....
....)

(Yes or No)
.... 88. On the issue of D's guilt of the crime of killing V, W testifies that D told him that he (D) fled the scene immediately after V's murder. (Exception(s) ....
....)

.... 89. On the issue of X's sanity, W testifies that X was confined to an insane asylum. (Exception(s) ...
....)

.... 102. On the issue of witness W1's hostility toward defendant (D), W2 testifies for D that W1 said to D in an angry tone, while D remained silent, "Well, at least I've never stolen money from my employer like you have!" (Exception(s) ....
....)

.... 103. On the issue of D's stealing money from his employer plaintiff (P) offers the evidence in 102. (Exception(s) ....
....)

.... 104. To prove the license number of the car involved in a hit-run accident, P offers a crumpled slip of paper on which appears the number EE2468 and

the testimony of a woman that, though she cannot now recall the number of the car, she did, while the number was fresh in her mind, write the number down on the piece of paper offered in evidence. (Exception(s) ....
......................................)

.... 105. To prove the license number of the car involved in a hit-run accident, P offers a photograph of a retreating automobile bearing the license plate EE2468 and the testimony of a woman that, though she cannot now remember the number of the car, she did know it at the time and that she took the photograph offered in evidence of the accident car as it left the scene. (Exception(s) ....)

. . .

.... 108. On the issue of the speed of a locomotive, P introduces the tape printed by an automatic speed-recording device in the train. (Exception(s) .....
......................................)

.... 109. On the issue of D's guilt of a crime, P offers a moving picture of D re-enacting the crime. (Exception(s) ....
......................................)

.... 110. On the issue of the voluntariness of D's confession, P offers the moving picture in 109. (Exception(s) ....
......................................)

.... 115. Action P v. D. W1 testifies for P that D's car was going "over 50 miles an hour." To impeach W1, D offers the testimony of W2 that W1 said a day after the accident that D was going "slow." (Exception(s) ....
......................................)

.... 116. The evidence in 115 offered by D to prove that he (D) was going slowly. (Exception(s) ....
......................................)

.... 117. In 115, W2 is a police officer with no present recollection of W1's statement, so D offers the officer's (W2's) accident report, made up the day after the accident, containing the alleged W1 statement. (Exception(s) ....
......................................)

.... 118. To prove that X was ill, W testifies that X, at the time, complained of a pain in his chest. (Exception(s) ....
......................................)

Chapter V

IMPEACHMENT AND CROSS–EXAMINATION

A. DIRECT EXAMINATION

KAPLAN AND WALTZ, THE TRIAL OF JACK RUBY

120–121 (1965).

* * * Unlike the practice in most European countries, where the witness merely stands up and delivers a long narrative concerning what he knows about the case, in Anglo-American law the witnesses relate their stories through the question-and-answer method. Although some lawyers argue that by focusing the witnesses' attention on specific details, our method actually is simpler and faster, most lawyers would agree that it is in fact slower and most cumbersome. The reason it is used is that the rules of evidence in our jurisprudence are vastly more detailed, complicated and strict than those of most other countries. Relying on a jury untrained in the law, we make every possible effort to keep from the jurors the sort of information which they might rely on but which experience teaches is either unfair to the defendant or for some reason dangerously misleading. We therefore require the witness to give his answers in response to relatively pointed questions so that the opposing attorney, forewarned by the question that the jury may be about to hear inadmissible material, can object in time to prevent receipt of the damaging answer.

In Anglo-American law not only must the parties proceed by question and answer, but they must adhere to certain forms of questions. And the restrictions are far more severe on the side calling the witness to the stand. The examination of one's own witness—direct examination as distinguished from cross-examination—must be made without the use of leading questions, that is, questions which suggest their own answer. A typical leading question is, "Was the defendant's black automobile going about fifty miles an hour when you first saw it on the right, bearing down on you?" The witness may answer "Yes," but it is the attorney's version of the story that the jury hears. Leading questions, although technically prohibited, are generally used to save time on unimportant and background matters. "Is your name Joe Smith?" However, as soon as important matters are reached, most trial lawyers automatically switch from leading question to avoid a barrage of objections which are properly sustained by the court.

A second major restriction encountered in direct examination is that the side calling the witness is, as lawyers say, "bound by his testimony." This means not that the lawyer must assume the truth of every fact testified to by his own witnesses but rather that he cannot argue with them or seek by further questioning to modify their testimony unless he can convince the judge that the witness is hostile or has taken him by surprise.

In cross-examination these restrictive rules do not apply. The cross-examiner can ask as many leading questions as he wishes and, if the answers prove unsatisfactory, he can go at the matter again and again in as many different ways as he can devise to press the witness into delivering the desired answers. * * *

AMSTERDAM, SEGAL & MILLER, TRIAL MANUAL 3 FOR THE DEFENSE OF CRIMINAL CASES
§ 393 (1977).*

Presenting direct testimony of the defendant. (A) Direct examination of the defendant should be concise and orderly, yet at the same time it should not telescope his testimony so that important details will be passed over rapidly. His testimony *is* a central event at his trial, and it ordinarily should not be rushed or made to seem less than full. Except as suggested in the following subparagraph, questions should call for explanatory answers rather than mere "yes" and "no" responses and should give the client freedom to do the testifying. It is important that the defendant appear to want to tell his story, and that it appear to be *his* story. He should not be tightly restricted so as to appear to be telling only what counsel wants to present. The more articulate, personable, and sympathetic he is, the more freedom he should have to project his image. On the other hand, the scope of direct examination must be limited to relevant matters lest areas be opened where damaging cross-examination can be pursued. Counsel should keep in mind likely points of prejudicial cross-examination and tell his client to keep away from matters that will open the door to them. In particular, the client should be warned that, both on direct and on cross-examination, he must avoid broad protestations of innocence—"I've never been in trouble in my life," "I don't even know what marijuana smells like," "I would never do anything like that"—since such protestations may be treated by the court as raising the issue of character and therefore as opening the door to prosecutorial proof of bad character.

(B) It is frequently desirable to begin the examination of the defendant with a short, well-rehearsed set piece, involving crisp, easy-to-remember answers that categorically and emphatically deny guilt and make clear the theory of the defense. Take, for example, a case in which the defendant is arrested while driving a car with one passenger in it; marijuana is found on the floor between the rider's

---

* Copyright 1978 by The American Law Institute. Reprinted with the permission of The American Law Institute–American Bar Association Committee on Continuing Professional Education.

and driver's seats; the defendant is charged with possession; and his defense is that the marijuana must have been the passenger's, since the defendant knew nothing of its presence until the police removed it from between the seats. The defendant's testimony might open in this fashion:

Q. Please state your name for the record.
A. Richard Silvers.
Q. Where do you live, Richard?
A. 341 Elm Street.
Q. Now, Richard, you have heard the testimony of the prosecution witnesses, and you know what you are charged with. Before I ask you anything else, I want you to tell His Honor and the ladies and gentlemen of the jury, are you guilty of this crime that you are charged with here today?
A. No.
Q. When you were arrested on April 14, did not know that there was marijuana in your car?
A. No.
Q. Did you put that marijuana in your car?
A. No.
Q. When did you first learn that there was marijuana in the car?
A. When the police showed it to me and said it was marijuana.
Q. All right, then, going back to that morning, before the police stopped your car, and directing your attention to approximately 10 a. m., would you please tell the jury where you were. * * *

This kind of an opening has several advantages. First, it comes on strong and clear. The jury will want to hear the defendant unequivocally and forcefully deny his guilt at some point in his testimony. His doing it at the outset makes a good impression. Second, testimony of this sort states the theory of the defense sharply and succinctly and permits the jurors to appreciate the significance of the defendant's factual story when he next proceeds to relate it in detail. Third, this sort of set piece gives the defendant confidence in himself and in his counsel. The answers that it requires are short and obvious; counsel's questions do not force the defendant to think and worry about what he is saying at the very beginning of his testimony when he is likely to be most nervous; and, unlike other short-answer questions, these do not appear to be cautiously leading the defendant to tell only so much of his story as the lawyer wants told. The answers are short because they tell the whole story; and in the examination that follows immediately afterwards, the defendant will be giving longer, more discursive answers as he freely tells all he knows about the facts in his own words. In the meantime, he has had the comfort of getting settled on the stand with no surprises. The knowledge that his examination is going exactly as it was rehearsed and as counsel told him it would go reassures him and puts him at his ease when he comes to the portions of his testimony that require him to think and to express himself more carefully.

MATHEW, FORENSIC FABLES BY O
267–68 (1961).

THE BEGINNER WHO THOUGHT HE WOULD DO IT HIMSELF

A Beginner, in the Temporary Absence of his Leader, Found himself Opposed to a Big Pot in the Commercial Court. Though Greatly Alarmed, the Beginner Bore himself Bravely. To his Surprise and Delight the Beginner Managed to Cross-Examine the Big Pot's Principal Witness with Such Effect that he Needed a Good Deal of Rehabilitation. Rising to Re-Examine, the Big Pot Airily Observed to the Principal Witness: "I Suppose What you Meant by Your Last Answer was This," and Proceeded to Tell the Principal Witness Quite Clearly what he Meant. When the Beginner made a Dignified Protest the Judge Smilingly Suggested that the Big Pot might Shape his Question rather Differently. The Next Day the Beginner was in a County Court. The Plaintiff (for whom the Beginner Appeared) having Made an Awkward Admission to his Learned Friend on the Other Side, the Beginner Thought he would Employ the Excellent Formula of the Big Pot. He Did so. The Scene that Followed Beggars Description. The County Court Judge in a Voice of Thunder Ordered the Beginner to Sit Down. He then Rebuked the Beginner for his Gross Misconduct and Discussed the Question whether he would Commit him for Contempt, or Merely Report him to the General Council of the Bar. Finally he Expressed the Hope that the Incident would be a Lesson to the Beginner and directed that the Case should be re-Heard on a Later Date before a Fresh Jury.

Moral.—*Wait till You're a Big Pot.*

RULES OF EVIDENCE FOR UNITED STATES COURTS AND MAGISTRATES

Rule 611

MODE AND ORDER OF INTERROGATION AND PRESENTATION

(a) **Control by court.** The court shall exercise reasonable control over the mode and order of interrogating witnesses and presenting evidence so as to (1) make the interrogation and presentation effective for the ascertainment of the truth, (2) avoid needless consumption of time, and (3) protect witnesses from harassment or undue embarrassment.

* * *

(c) Leading questions. Leading questions should not be used on the direct examination of a witness except as may be necessary to develop his testimony. Ordinarily leading questions should be permitted on cross-examination. When a party calls a hostile witness, an adverse party, or a witness identified with an adverse party, interrogation may be by leading questions.

B. CROSS–EXAMINATION

1. IN GENERAL

SUSANNA AND THE ELDERS

(C. 130 B.C.).

from

THE BIBLE

The Old and the New Testaments in the King James Version
Simon and Schuster, New York, 1936.

* * *

Then the two elders stood up in the midst of the people, and laid their hands upon her head. And she weeping looked up toward heaven: for her heart trusted in the Lord. And the elders said, "As we walked in the garden alone, this woman came in with two maids, and shut the garden doors, and sent the maids away. Then a young man, who there was hid, came unto her, and lay with her. Then we that stood in a corner of the garden, seeing this wickedness, ran unto them. And when we saw them together, the man we could not hold: for he was stronger than we, and opened the door, and leaped out. But having taken this woman, we asked who the young man was, but she would not tell us: these things so we testify."

Then the assembly believed them, as those that were the elders and judges of the people: so they condemned her to death.

Then Susanna cried out with a loud voice, and said, "O everlasting God, that knowest the secrets, and knowest all things before they be: thou knowest that they have borne false witness against me, and behold, I must die; whereas I never did such things as these men have maliciously invented against me."

The Lord heard her voice.

Therefore when she was led to be put to death, the Lord raised up the holy spirit of a young youth, whose name was Daniel: who cried with a loud voice, "I am clear from the blood of this woman."

Then all the people turned them toward him, and said, "What mean these words that thou hast spoken?"

So he standing in the midst of them said, "Are ye such fools, ye sons of Israel, that without examination or knowledge of the truth ye have condemned a daughter of Israel? Return again to the place of judgment: for they have borne false witness against her."

Wherefore all the people turned again in haste, and the elders said unto him, "Come, sit down among us, and show it us, seeing God hath given thee the honour of an elder."

Then said Daniel unto them, "Put these two aside one far from another, and I will examine them."

So when they were put asunder one from another, he called one of them, and said unto him, "O thou that art waxed old in wickedness, now thy sins which thou has committed aforetime are come to light: for thus hast pronounced false judgment, and hast condemned the innocent, and hast let the guilty go free; albeit the Lord saith, 'The innocent and righteous shalt thou not slay.' Now then, if thou hast seen her, tell me under what tree sawest thou them companying together?"

Who answered, "Under the mastic tree."

And Daniel said, "Very well; thou hast lied against thine own head; for even now the angel of God hath received the sentence of God to cut thee in two."

So he put him aside, and commanded to bring the other, and said unto him, "O thou seed of Chanaan, and not of Juda, beauty hath deceived thee, and lust hath perverted thine heart. Thus have ye dealt with the daughters of Israel, and they for fear companied with you: but the daughter of Juda would not abide your wickedness. Now therefore tell me under what tree didst thou take them companying together?"

Who answered, "Under a holm tree."

Then said Daniel unto him, "Well; thou hast also lied against thine own head: for the angel of God waiteth with the sword to cut thee in two, that he may destroy you."

With that all the assembly cried out with a loud voice, and praised God, who saveth them that trust in him. And they arose against the two elders, for Daniel had convicted them of false witness by their own mouth: and according to the law of Moses they did unto them in such sort as they maliciously intended to do their neighbour: and they put them to death. Thus the innocent blood was saved the same day.

Therefore Chelcias and his wife praised God for their daughter Susanna, with Joacim her husband, and all the kindred, because there was no dishonesty found in her.

Ch. 5   IMPEACHMENT AND CROSS–EXAMINATION   241

MATHEW, FORENSIC FABLES BY O
87–88 (1961).

MR. WHITEWIG AND THE RASH QUESTION

MR. WHITEWIG was Greatly Gratified when the Judge of Assize Invited him to Defend a Prisoner who was Charged with Having Stolen a Pair of Boots, a Mouse-Trap, and Fifteen Packets of Gold Flakes. It was his First Case and he Meant to Make a Good Show. Mr. Whitewig Studied the Depositions Carefully and Came to the Conclusion that a Skilful Cross-Examination of the Witnesses and a Tactful Speech would Secure the Acquittal of the Accused. When the Prisoner (an Ill-Looking Person) was Placed in the Dock, Mr. Whitewig Approached that Receptacle and Informed the Prisoner that he Might, if he Wished, Give Evidence on Oath. From the Prisoner's Reply (in which he Alluded to Grandmothers and Eggs) Mr. Whitewig Gathered that he did not Propose to Avail Himself of this Privilege. The Case Began. At First All Went Well. The Prosecutor Admitted to Mr. Whitewig that he Could not be Sure that the Man he had Seen Lurking in the Neighbourhood of his Emporium was the Prisoner; and the Prosecutor's Assistant Completely Failed to Identify the Boots, the Mouse-Trap, or the Gold Flakes by Pointing to any Distinctive Peculiarities which they Exhibited. By the Time the Police Inspector Entered the Witness-Box Mr. Whitewig Felt that the Case was Won. Mr. Whitewig Cunningly Extracted from the Inspector the Fact that the Prisoner had Joined Up in 1914, and that the Prisoner's Wife was Expecting an Addition to her Family. He was about to Sit Down when a Final Question Occurred to him. "Having Regard to this Man's Record," he Sternly Asked, "How Came You to Arrest him?" The Inspector Drew a Bundle of Blue Documents from the Recesses of his Uniform, and, Moistening his Thumb, Read therefrom. Mr. Whitewig Learned in Silent Horror that the Prisoner's Record Included Nine Previous Convictions. When the Prisoner was Asked whether he had Anything to say why Sentence should not be Passed Upon him, he Said some Very Disagreeable Things about the Mug who had Defended him.

Moral.—*Leave Well Alone.*

AMSTERDAM, SEGAL & MILLER, TRIAL MANUAL 3 FOR THE DEFENSE OF CRIMINAL CASES
§§ 370, 371 (1978).*

HANDLING PROSECUTION WITNESSES

Cross-examining prosecution witnesses—generally. Defensive cross-examination should ordinarily be narrowly focused. Most of what the witness is saying is probably true and accurate, and dif-

---
* Copyright 1978 by The American Law Institute. Reprinted with the permission of The American Law Institute–American Bar Association Committee on Continuing Professional Education.

fuse cross-examination will only demonstrate this and bolster the witness. Defense counsel should concentrate on specific weak points and crucial details of the witness's testimony. Except in the relatively rare situation where it is necessary and possible to portray the witness as an outright perjurer—where, for example, the witness's testimony is exceedingly damaging, he could not plausibly be mistaken as to critical details, and substantial motivation for lying can be made to appear—it is probably wise to confine the cross-examiner's attack on the witness's story to the narrowest possible compass. But where a broad and forceful attack on the witness's credibility *is* advised, counsel has the right to pursue it, and should strenuously object to any attempt by the court to " 'protect [the] * * * witness from being discredited,' " * * * by limiting cross examination. Of course, when cross-examining, counsel must keep in mind the elements of the offense and the total state of the prosecutor's record on those elements, so that he can avoid the cardinal sin of helping the prosecution by filling in missing links in its case.

Same—police witnesses. Police testify in almost all criminal cases. Because of their many duties, police officers frequently are not able to do all of the things required or expected of them in any given situation. They will, for instance, omit to file required reports, leave items uncompleted in filling out reports, or fail to follow approved investigative techniques. (For example, it seems virtually impossible to train police not to pick up a gun, found at the scene of a crime, to check whether it is loaded, although the gun may have latent fingerprints on it.) Thus a relatively productive way to impeach the testimony of a policeman is to set him up as an expert in criminal investigation by eliciting his opinion that he is one; then to lead him into agreeing that certain specified methods, described by counsel, are proper (or, better still, required by local police regulations) in gathering evidence to be used at trial or in recording his observations or the progress of his investigation; then to retrace his testimony in detail to demonstrate how negligently he gathered the evidence, how items were omitted, and how much of his testimony was not written into his report at the time of the incident, despite the fact that he handles hundreds of cases and intends to use his notes to refresh his recollection for trial. Counsel will find it helpful to peruse local police instructional manuals, teaching materials used at the local police academy or training center, and standard police texts on criminal investigation to help him identify points of error in police techniques. It is often tempting to try to show that the police have it in for the defendant, or are picking on him, but the effort to do so out of the mouths of the police almost never succeeds. *In no event* should counsel ask a policeman, "What attracted your attention to the defendant?" The reply is guaranteed to put the client's criminal record before the jury (including arrests otherwise inadmissible for any purpose) and may also elicit damaging rumor. If police witnesses volunteer prejudicial prior-crime or prior-arrest evidence—as they will frequently seek some pretext to do—a motion for a mistrial is in order. In general, cross examination of police witnesses should be very specific, calling for short *factual* answers and giving the witness no leeway to stray. Counsel should ask what a policeman *did*, not what he *thought*; "What specifically did you see Mr. Jones do next?" not "What happened next?" If a policeman begins to describe what Mr. Jones did next by saying "he appeared to be * * *," counsel should immediately interrupt and ask the judge to instruct the witness to answer the question, not to state his opinion. And counsel should never ask *why* a policeman did something. He should ask only what the policeman did and the factual circumstances under which he did it. Counsel can argue to the jury in closing argument that the policeman did it for the wrong reasons, if that is a permissible inference from his actions in the circumstances. But trying to elicit a policeman's reasons from him will get counsel nothing except self-serving protestations of angelic good faith, coupled with everything damning to the defendant that the policeman can think of.

KEETON, TRIAL TACTICS AND METHODS
87–90 (1954).*

Cross-examination is that phase of the trial which has potentialities of being the most spectacular. It affords the opportunity for the most successful employment of an aptitude for quick thinking, sharp repartee, and dramatics. To excel in these, one must have native ability. Nearly everyone interested in trial work does have a degree of such ability, however, and it can be developed by practice and experience, just as a talent for music or acting may be so developed. But the talent for cross-examination, in this sense, is the lesser part of the secret of effective cross-examination. Nearly all effective cross-examination is planned, to one degree or another. For one interested in entering trial practice without experience, adequate planning can often produce effective cross-examination from the first. For one who is experienced, greater success in cross-examination is possible as he prepares more diligently and thoroughly for it. This chapter is devoted to consideration of methods customarily used in effective cross-examination, and ways of planning for their use. In this broader sense of "talent," one can enter the courtroom with considerable talent for cross-examination even in his earliest cases.

The potential aims of cross-examination may be classified into four groups: (1) discrediting the testimony of the witness being examined; (2) using testimony of this witness to discredit the unfavorable testimony of other witnesses; (3) using the testimony of this witness to corroborate the favorable testimony of other witnesses; and (4) using the testimony of this witness to contribute independently to the favorable development of your own case.

* Copyright, 1954 by Prentice-Hall, Inc.

Accomplishing one of these aims may require an entirely different method of dealing with the witness from that appropriate for another aim. A method of cross-examination designed to serve one aim may defeat another. In such instances, adequate planning requires an appraisal of the relative advantages associated with each of these aims, as a factor in the choice of methods.

Your selection of methods of cross-examination of the witness will be influenced also by the type of witness before you—for example, whether the witness is an argumentative one, an expert, a woman, or one of a series of witnesses who appear to have a memorized story. The age, education, and mentality of the witness are other important factors. The most ignorant witness is often the hardest to cross-examine because you cannot get him set up to knock over. Also, you must exercise great care to avoid creating jury sympathy for him because you are exposing his ignorance or illiteracy. Your aim is to condemn his testimony as unreliable without condemning the witness for being ignorant. The infliction of personal ridicule upon an ignorant witness, or sarcastic treatment of the witness, may be regarded by jurors as your taking an unfair advantage of the differences in intelligence and education between yourself and the witness.

Some consideration should be given to your general attitude and demeanor toward the witness. Should you let your contempt for the reprobate be obvious for the jury to see, if you feel that way about him? Or should you be the paragon of courtesy? Usually an attitude of courtesy toward the witness should be adopted, for although the jurors expect a lawyer to be an advocate, they very quickly take up sympathy for the witness if they get the idea that the lawyer is badgering the witness unfairly. It is quite possible to be very polite and yet convey to the jury your distrust of the witness' testimony.

Most trial yarns concerning cross-examination are tales of the brilliant cross-examination which won the lawsuit. Others tell of the inept cross-examination which lost the lawsuit. While both types of yarns are usually influenced by a recognized license, like that of the poet and fisherman, they are founded on truths.

These are some of the risks which you incur in cross-examination:

(1) Confronting a witness with a prior written statement inconsistent with his present testimony may result in proof of other facts recorded in the statement and not previously proven, or it may result in incidental disclosure of the existence of liability insurance, where its existence would have been unknown to the jury otherwise.

(2) Confronting the witness with inconsistency between his testimony and that of your own witness may result in impeachment of the testimony of your own witness.

(3) The cross-examination intended to show want of good opportunity for observation of the facts related may serve only to demonstrate that the opportunity was good.

(4) An attempt to prove or even actual proof of bad character of the witness may provoke the sympathy of the jury for the witness and the cases he supports.

(5) The cross-examination intended to reveal indirectly the bias of the witness by committing him to an untenable extreme may result in strengthening the direct examination.

(6) The cross-examination intended to bring out matters about which your adversary failed to inquire, in the belief that the answers will be favorable to your client, may result only in more evidence favorable to the adverse party who called the witness.

(7) Calling on the witness to repeat and elaborate his testimony, as a foundation of proof of prior contradictions or inconsistencies, may emphasize and strengthen the witness' testimony if he has a plausible explanation for the apparent inconsistencies.

(8) Cross-examination intended to show bias from animosity associated with termination of employment may provoke sympathy for the discharged employee.

(9) Asking a "why" question in the belief that the witness can have no reasonable explanation may result in expression of prejudicial arguments which would have been clearly inadmissible in the absence of the invitation by the open question.

(10) Insistence upon a clear answer from an evasive witness may lead to an unexpected and unfavorable disclosure.

(11) Defendant's cross-examination of plaintiff's medical expert regarding fees may emphasize plaintiff's expenses and cause a higher damages finding.

(12) Cross-examination of an expert concerning his qualifications may serve only to bolster less adequate proof of those qualifications during direct examination.

(13) Methods of cross-examination intended to exact disclosures from an unwilling witness may be harmful because of a jury reaction that they are unfair methods.

COLLATERAL READINGS

Cross Examination

McCormick, Handbook of the Law of Evidence §§ 21, 23–27, 29–31 (2d ed. 1972)

Wigmore, Evidence (3rd ed. 1940)

    Vol. 5, §§ 1367, 1390–94

    Vol. 6, §§ 1884–1894

Wellman, The Art of Cross Examination (1936)

Degnan, Non-Rules Evidence Law: Cross-Examination, 6 Utah L. Rev. 323 (1959)

Carlson, Cross-Examination of the Accused, 52 Corn.L.Q. 705 (1967)

Note, Confrontation, Cross-examination, and the Right to Prepare a Defense, 56 Geo.L.J. 939 (1968)

Gair, Cross-examination, 4 Trial 33 (1968)

Sermerjian, Right of Confrontation, 55 ABA J. 152 (1969)

Cotsirilos, Meeting the Prosecution's Case: Tactics and Strategies of Cross-Examination, 62 J.Crim.L.C. & P.S. 142 (1971)

Short, Cross-Examination: A Two-Edged Sword, 24 Okla.L.Rev. 53 (1971)

2. SCOPE OF CROSS-EXAMINATION

CARLSON, CROSS-EXAMINATION OF THE ACCUSED

52 Cornell L.Q. 705–709 (1967).

An important consideration in criminal trials is the extent to which the accused may be cross-examined once he takes the stand. Whether this examination is limited to matters raised in the examination in chief, or whether the scope of cross-examination extends broadly to the entire case can be critically significant in defense counsel's decision to call the accused as a witness.

There are two major views on this problem of cross-examination. The American (or federal) rule limits cross-examination of the defendant to matters stated in the direct examination. Another view, termed the Massachusetts (or English) rule by many writers, allows cross-examination on all relevant phases of the case. Several jurisdictions follow this broad interrogation rule and require an accused to answer cross-examination questions which inquire into matters foreign to the defendant's testimony in chief.

The competing rules have received independent evaluation and rest upon different theories. The Massachusetts rule was brought from England, where it is still in use. In both civil and criminal cases this rule is based on the philosophy that when a witness testifies, he should present all the facts unrestricted by technical rules of evidence. Court and counsel are relieved of the duty of determining when questions are within the proper scope of cross-examination and when they are without. This ease of application was a major factor in winning Wigmore's support for the rule.

An argument often advanced on behalf of the more limited federal rule is that it makes for orderliness of trial. A party may not develop a major portion of his case out of normal order through the vehicle of cross-examination. It has also been suggested that there is an element of basic fairness in preventing the cross-examiner from using a witness called by the opposition to establish his own case through the device of leading questions. The Supreme Court's solicitude for the limited rule is evidenced by its rejection of a proposed provision for the Federal Rules of Civil Procedure which would have permitted cross-examination on every material matter in the case regardless of the scope of direct examination.

The limited federal rule had its genesis in an 1840 decision wherein the Supreme Court indicated "that a party has no right to cross-examine any witness except as to facts and circumstances connected with the matter stated in his direct examination." The rule spread rapidly and was applied fully in federal criminal cases. Significantly, certain decisions treating the rule in criminal prosecutions suggested that its application was not merely appropriate trial procedure, but had a basis in the Constitution. Important judicial language to this effect. * * * indicates that an accused who takes the stand waives his fifth-amendment privilege against self-incrimination only as to matters covered in the direct examination.

RULES OF EVIDENCE FOR UNITED STATES COURTS AND MAGISTRATES

Rule 611

MODE AND ORDER OF INTERROGATION AND PRESENTATION

* * *

(b) **Scope of cross-examination.** Cross-examination should be limited to the subject matter of the direct examination and matters affecting the credibility of the witness. The court may, in the exercise of discretion, permit inquiry into additional matters as if on direct examination.

Comments to Rule 611

Subdivision (b). The tradition in the federal courts and in numerous state courts has been to limit the scope of cross-examination to matters testified to on direct, plus matters bearing upon the credibility of the witness. Various reasons have been advanced to justify the rule of limited cross-examination. (1) A party vouches for his own witness but only to the extent of matters elicited on direct. But the concept of vouching is discredited, and Rule 6–07[607] rejects it. (2) A party cannot ask his own witness leading questions. This is a problem properly solved in terms of what is necessary for a proper development of the testimony rather than by a mechanistic formula similar to the vouching concept. See discussion under subdivision (c). (3) A practice of limited cross-examination promotes orderly presentation of the case. * * * In the opinion of the Advisory Committee this latter reason has merit. It is apparent, however, that the rule of limited cross-examination thus viewed becomes an aspect of the judge's general control over the mode and order of interrogating witnesses and presenting evidence, to be administered as such. The matter is not one in which involvement at the appellant level is likely to prove fruitful. * * * In view of these considerations, the rule is phrased in terms of a suggestion rather than a mandate to the trial judge.

The qualification "as if on direct examination," applicable when inquiry into additional matters is allowed is designed to terminate at that point the asking of leading questions as a matter of right and to bring into operations subdivision (c) of the rule.

The rule does not purport to determine the extent to which an accused who elects to testify thereby waives his privilege against self-incrimination. The question is a constitutional one, rather than a mere matter of administering the trial. Under United States v. Simmons, 390 U.S. 377 (1968), no general waiver occurs when the accused testifies on such preliminary matters as the validity of a search and seizure or the admissibility of a confession. Rule 1–04(d) [104(d)], supra. When he testifies on the merits, however, can he foreclose inquiry into an aspect or element of the crime by avoiding it on direct? The affirmative answer given in Tucker v. United States 5 F.2d 818 (8th Cir. 1925), is inconsistent with the description of the waiver as extending to "all other relevant facts" in Johnson v. United States, 318 U.S. 189, 195 (1943). * * * The situation of an accused who desires to testify on some but not all counts of a multiple-count indictment is one to be approached, in the first instance at least, as a problem of severance under Rule 14 of the Federal Rules of Criminal Procedure. * * * In all events, the extent of the waiver of the privilege against self-incrimination ought not to be determined as a by-product of a rule on scope of cross-examination.

COLLATERAL READINGS

Scope of Cross Examination

McCormick's Handbook of the Law of Evidence, §§ 21, 24–27, 29

Wigmore, Evidence (3rd ed. 1940)

    Vol. 6, §§ 1885–1891, 1896–7

    Vol. 8, §§ 2276, 2278

McCormick, The Scope and Art of Cross-Examination, 47 Nw.U.L. Rev. 177 (1952)

Carlson, Cross-Examination of the Accused, 52 Corn.L.Q. 705 (1967)

Jarowski, Cross-Examination of Witnesses, 19 Ark.L.Rev. 37 (1965)

Redmond, Character Cross-Examinations of Accused Persons, 43 Aust. L.J. 569 (1969)

Note, Confrontation and Cross-Examination in Executive Investigations, 56 Va.L.Rev. 487 (1970)

Margolis. Prosecutorial Cross-Examination: Limitations Upon the Sword of Justice, 65 J.Crim.L. & C. 2 (1974)

Note, Witnesses, 27 Ark.L.Rev. 229 (1973)

C. CROSS–EXAMINATION AND IMPEACHMENT

1. THE CREDIBILITY OF THE WITNESS

a. IN GENERAL

RULES OF EVIDENCE FOR UNITED STATES COURTS AND MAGISTRATES

Rule 607

WHO MAY IMPEACH

The credibility of a witness may be attacked by any party, including the party calling him.

LILLY, AN INTRODUCTION TO THE LAW OF EVIDENCE *

92 (1978).

§ 30. Examining the Witness: The Scope of Cross-Examination

* * *

Note that in all jurisdictions the cross-examiner may ask questions directed to credibility or impeachment. This means that he may propound questions designed to impugn the witness's motive to be truthful or to demonstrate aspects of the witness's prior conduct which cast doubt upon his veracity. For example, the examiner may inquire whether the witness holds a grudge against one of the parties, whether he has a financial stake in the outcome of the case, or whether he has been convicted of a crime that raises doubt about his credibility. Even though inquiry about these facts carries the cross-examiner beyond the scope of direct examination, it is everywhere permissible to elicit testimony pertinent to impeachment. Two reasons justify this practice: first, credibility is always implicitly in issue and, second, a central purpose of cross-examination is to weaken or negate the testimony given during direct examination.

* Reprinted with permission from Lilly's "An Introduction to the Law of Evidence," West Publishing Co. (1978).

McCORMICK'S HANDBOOK ON THE LAW OF EVIDENCE
(97–100 2d ed. 1972).*

Impeachment by "contradiction": Disproving the Facts Testified to by the First Witness.

"Contradiction" may be explained as follows. Statements are elicited from Witness One, who has testified to a material story of an accident, crime, or other matters, to the effect that at the time he witnessed these matters the day was windy and cold and he, the witness, was wearing his green sweater. Let up suppose these latter statements about the day and the sweater to be "disproved." This may happen in several ways. Witness One on direct or cross-examination may acknowledge that he was in error. Or judicial notice may be taken that at the time and place it could not have been cold and windy, e. g., in Tuscon in July. But commonly disproof or "contradiction" is attempted by calling Witness Two to testify to the contrary, i. e., that the day was warm and Witness One was in his shirtsleeves. It is in this latter sense that the term "contradiction" is used in this section.

What impeaching value does the contradiction have in the above situation? It merely tends to show—for Witness One may be right and Witness Two may be mistaken—that Witness One has erred or falsified as to certain particular facts, and therefore is capable of error or lying, and this should be considered negatively in weighing his other statements. But all human beings have this capacity and all testimony should be discounted to some extent for this weakness. It is true that the trial judge in his discretion may permit the cross-examiner to conduct a general test of the power of Witness One to observe, remember and recount facts unrelated to the case, to "test" or "explore" these capacities. To permit a dispute, however, about such extraneous or "collateral" facts as the weather and the clothing of Witness One, that are material only for "testing" the witness, by allowing the attacker to call other witnesses to disprove them, is not practical. Dangers of surprise, of confusion of the jury's attention, and of time-wasting are apparent.

Therefore, the courts maintain the safeguarding rule that a witness may not be impeached by producing extrinsic evidence of "collateral" facts to "contradict" the first witness's assertions about those facts. If the collateral fact sought to be contradicted is elicited on cross-examination, this safeguarding rule is often expressed by saying that the answer is conclusive or that the cross-examiner must "take the answer." By the better view, if the "collateral" fact happens to have been drawn out on direct, the rule against contradiction should still be applied. The danger of surprise is lessened, but waste of time and confusion of issues stand as objections.

* Copyright, 1972 by West Publishing Co.

What is to be regarded here as within this protean word of art, "collateral"? The inquiry is best answered by determining what facts are not within the term, and thus finding the escapes from the prohibition against contradicting upon collateral facts. The classical approach is that facts which would have been independently provable regardless of the contradiction are not "collateral."

Two general kinds of facts meet the test. The first kind are facts that are relevant to the substantive issues in the case. It may seem strained to label this proof of relevant facts with the terms, "contradiction" or "impeachment." But it does have the dual aspect of relevant proof and of reflecting on the credibility of contrary witnesses. Here the "contradiction" theory has at least one practical consequence, namely, it permits contradicting proof, which without the contradiction would be confined to the case in chief, to be brought out in rebuttal.

The second kind of facts meeting the above mentioned test for facts that are not collateral includes facts which would be independently provable by extrinsic evidence, apart from the contradiction, to impeach or disqualify the witness. Among these are facts showing bias, interest, conviction of crime, and want of capacity or opportunity for knowledge. Facts showing misconduct of the witness (for which no conviction has been had) are not within this second kind of facts, but are collateral, and if denied on cross-examination cannot be proved to contradict.

Finally, a third kind of fact must be considered. Suppose a witness has told a story of a transaction crucial to the controversy. To prove him wrong in some trivial detail of time, place or circumstance is "collateral." But to prove untrue some fact recited by the witness that if he were really there and saw what he claims to have to seen, he could not have been mistaken about, is a convincing kind of impeachment that the courts must make place for, although the contradiction evidence is otherwise inadmissible because it is collateral under the tests mentioned above. To disprove such a fact is to pull out the linchpin of the story. So we may recognize this third type of allowable contradiction, namely, the contradiction of any part of the witness's account of the background and circumstances of a material transaction, which as a matter of human experience he would not have been mistaken about if his story were true. This test is of necessity a vague one because it must meet an indefinite variety of situations, and consequently in its application a reasonable latitude of discretionary judgment must be accorded to the trial judge.

Of course, the contradicting witness may simply state the facts as he asserts them, without reference to the prior testimony which is being contradicted. It seems, however, that where appropriate the contradiction may be more direct. Thus it would seem acceptable to recite in the question the pertinent part of the prior testimony of the first witness, and inquire, "What do you say as to the correctness of this statement?"

b. PRIOR BAD ACTS

PEOPLE v. SORGE

Court of Appeals of New York, 1950.
301 N.Y. 198, 93 N.E.2d 637.

FULD, Judge. In this prosecution for the crime of abortion, the evidence given on behalf of the People was more than sufficient to justify the verdict of guilt—for the conflicting testimony of the victim and of the defendant but presented a question of veracity and credibility for the jury. Accordingly, an affirmance is compelled, unless prejudicial error was committed by the district attorney in conducting his cross-examination of defendant. He interrogated her about abortions which she had allegedly performed upon four other women and, after she had answered his questions in the negative, pressed her further as to whether she had not signed a statement admitting that she had aborted one of the women, as to whether that particular operation had not furnished the predicate for her plea of guilty to the crime of practicing medicine without a license, and as to whether she had not been present while a fifth abortion had been performed.

There can, of course, be no doubt as to the propriety of cross-examining a defendant concerning the commission of other specific criminal or immoral acts. A defendant, like any other witness, may be "interrogated upon cross-examination in regard to any vicious or criminal act of his life" that has a bearing on his credibility as a witness. It does not matter that the offenses or the acts inquired about are similar in nature and character to the crime for which the defendant is standing trial. And if the questions have basis in fact and are asked by the district attorney in good faith, they are not rendered improper merely because of their number. Entitled to delve into past misdeeds, the prosecutor may not arbitrarily be shackled by the circumstance that the defendant has pursued a specialized field of crime and has committed many offenses.

Nor is it improper for a district attorney to continue his cross-examination about a specific crime after a defendant has denied committing it. As long as he acts in good faith, in the hope of inducing the witness to abandon his negative answers, the prosecutor may question further. In other words, a negative response will not fob off further interrogation of the witness himself, for, if it did, the witness would have it within his power to render futile most cross-examination. The rule is clear that while a witness' testimony regarding collateral matters may not be refuted by the calling of other witnesses or by the production of extrinsic evidence, there is no prohibition against examining the witness himself further on the chance that he may change his testimony or his answer.

This principle covers not only the questions put to defendant which were based upon her prior statement, but also the questions grounded upon her prior conviction—following her guilty plea—of practicing medicine without a license. Since a witness may be examined properly with respect to criminal acts that have escaped prosecution, there is no reason why indictment followed by conviction should proscribe inquiry as to what those acts were. A knowledge of those acts casts light upon the degree of turpitude involved and assists the jury in evaluating the witness' credibility—all the more so in a case such as the present where conviction of a crime such as practicing medicine without a license gives no inkling whatsoever of the acts upon which the charge and conviction against defendant had been predicated. In point of fact, the matters sought to be elicited by the cross-examination were precisely those matters that could have been established by proof of the official record of defendant's conviction —a course which the People could unquestionably have pursued under section 2444 of the Penal Law, Consol.Laws, c. 40.

While, for the reasons outlined above, we cannot single out any questions and say that they were improper as a matter of law, there still remains the problem of whether the cumulative effect of the sustained cross-examination constituted error, despite the propriety of the individual queries. Basic in this connection is the rule that "The manner and extent of the cross-examination lies largely within the discretion of the trial judge."

Accordingly, although there may be room for a difference of opinion as to the scope and extent of cross examination, the wide latitude and the broad discretion that must be vouchsafed to the trial judge, if he is to administer a trial effectively, precludes this court, in the absence of "plain abuse and injustice", La Beau v. People, 34 N.Y. 223, 230, from substituting its judgment for his and from making that difference of opinion, in the difficult and ineffable realm of discretion, a basis for reversal.

We may not here say that prejudice or "injustice" resulted from the district attorney's interrogation or that permitting the vigorous cross-examination constituted "plain abuse". The evidence against defendant was clear and, since the outcome of the case depended almost entirely upon whether the testimony of the victim or of the defendant was credited by the jury, there was good and ample reason to give both sides a relatively free hand on cross-examination in order to afford the jury full opportunity to weigh and evaluate the credibility of each witness.

The judgment should be affirmed.

LOUGHRAN, C. J., and LEWIS, CONWAY, DESMOND, DYE and FROESSEL, JJ., concur.

Judgment affirmed.

WELLMAN, THE ART OF CROSS-EXAMINATION
56–60 (1903, 1962).*

Henry E. Lazarus, a prominent merchant in this city, was indicted a few years ago by the Federal Grand Jury, charged with the offense of bribing a United States officer and violation of the Sabotage Act, but was honorably acquitted by a jury after a thirty minute deliberation. It was during the height of the war and Mr. Lazarus was a very large manufacturer of rubber coats and had manufactured hundreds of thousands for the Government under contract. The Government for its protection employed large numbers of inspectors, and in the heat and excitement of war times these inspectors occasionally tried to "make good." One of these efforts resulted in the indictment of Lazarus.

The chief witness against Lazarus was Charles L. Fuller, Supervising Inspector attached to the Depot Quartermaster's Office in New York City. Fuller testified that Lazarus gave money to him to influence him in regard to his general duties as an inspector, and to overlook the fact that Lazarus was manufacturing defective coats and thereby violating the Sabotage Act.

Martin W. Littleton acted as chief counsel for the defense and was fully appreciative of Mr. Lazarus's high character and of his conscientious discharge of his duties in the manufacture of material for the Government. He was also well informed as to the general character and history of Fuller. After Fuller testified in chief, he was first questioned closely as to the time when he became an employe of the Government, counsel knowing that he was *required to make and sign and swear to an application as to his prior experience.*

A messenger had been sent to the Government files to get the original of this application, signed by the witness, and came into court with the document in his hand just as counsel was putting the following question:

Q. "Did you sign such an application?"

A. "I did, sir."

Q. "Did you swear to it?"

A. "No, I did not swear to it."

Q. "I show you your name signed on the bottom of this blank, and ask you if you signed that?"

A. "Yes, sir."

Q. "Do you see it is sworn to?"

A. "I had forgotten it."

Q. "You see there is a seal on it?"

A. "I had forgotten that also."

* Copyright, 1962 by Collier.

Q. "This application appears to be subscribed on the 24th of May, 1918, by Charles Lawrence Fuller."

A. "It must be right if I have sworn to it on that date."

Q. "Do you remember in May, 1918, that you signed and swore to this application?"

A. "That is so, I must have sworn to it, sir."

Q. "Do you remember it?"

A. "Let me look at it and I can probably refresh my memory." (Paper handed to witness)

Q. "Look at the signature. Does that help you?

A. "That is my signature."

Q. "You said that. Do you remember in May, 1918, you signed and swore to this?"

A. "Well, the date is there."

Q. "Do you know that?"

A. "Yes, sir, I must have sworn to it. I don't remember the date."

Q. "Don't you remember you signed your name, Charles Lawrence Fuller, there?"

A. "I did, sir."

Q. "And you swore to this paper and signed it?"

A. "That date is correct there, yes, sir."

Q. "Don't you remember you swore to it the date you signed it?"

A. "I swore to it."

Q. "Was your name Fuller?"

A. "Yes, sir."

Q. "Has your name always been Fuller?"

A. "No, sir."

Q. "What was your name?"

The witness protested against any further inquiry along that line, but counsel was permitted to show that his name at one time was Finkler and that he changed his name, back and forth, from Finkler to Fuller.

Counsel then proceeded to bring the witness down to the actual oath he had taken in his application.

Q. "Now, Mr. Fuller, in your application you made to the Government, on which I showed you your signature and affidavit, you attached your picture, did you not?"

A. "Yes, sir."

Q. "And you stated in your application you were born in Atlanta, Georgia, did you not?"

A. "Yes, sir."

Q. "You were asked, when you sought this position, these questions: 'When employed, the years and the months,' and you wrote in, 'February, 1897 to August, 1917, number of years 20; Where employed—Brooklyn; Name of employer—Vulcan Proofing Company; Amount of salary,—$37.50 a week; also superintendent in the rubber and compound room.'"

Q. "You wrote that, didn't you?"

A. "Yes sir."

Q. "And swore to that, didn't you?"

A. "Yes sir."

Q. "Now, were you employed from February 1897, to August, 1917, twenty years, with the Vulcan Proofing Company?"

A. "No, sir."

Q. "That was not true, was it?"

A. "No, sir."

Q. "And had you been assistant superintendent of the rubber and compound room?"

A. "No, sir."

Q. "That was false, wasn't it?"

A. "Yes, sir."

Q. "'And through my experience as chief inspector of the rubber and slicker division,' that was false, wasn't it?"

A. "Yes, sir."

Q. "You knew it was false, didn't you?"

A. "Yes, sir."

Q. "And you knew you were swearing to a falsehood when you swore to it?"

A. "Yes, sir."

Q. "And you swore to it intentionally?"

A. "Yes, sir."

Q. "And you knew you were committing perjury when you swore to it?"

A. "I did not look at it in that light."

Q. "Didn't you know you were committing perjury by swearing and pretending you had been twenty years in this business?"

A. "Yes, sir."

Q. "And you are swearing now, aren't you?"

Ch. 5   IMPEACHMENT AND CROSS–EXAMINATION   257

A. "Yes, sir."

Q. "In a matter in which a man's liberty is involved?"

A. "Yes, sir."

Q. "And you know that the jury is to be called upon to consider whether you are worthy of belief or not, don't you?"

A. "Yes, sir."

Q. "When you swore to this falsehood deliberately, and wrote it in your handwriting, you knew it was false, you swore to it intentionally, and you knew that you were committing prejury, didn't you?"

A. "I did not look at it in that light."

Q. "Well, now, when you know you are possibly swearing away the liberty of a citizen of this community, do you look at it in the same light?"

A. "Yes, sir, I do."

Mr. Littleton then uncovered the fact that the witness, instead of having been twenty years superintendent of a rubber room with the Vulcan Proofing Company, as he had sworn in his own handwriting, was a stag entertainer in questionable houses, was a barker at a Coney Island show, was an advance agent of a cheap road show and had been published in the paper as having drawn checks that were worthless, the witness fully admitting all of the details of his twenty years of questionable transactions. The result was his utter collapse so far as his credibility was concerned, and the Government's case collapsed with him.

The point of the cross-examination and the design of the cross-examiner was to get the witness at the outset of his cross-examination in a position from which he could not possibly extricate himself, by confronting him with this document, written in his own handwriting in which he would be obliged to admit that he had sworn falsely. The witness having been thoroughly subjugated by this process would then, as he actually did, confess to twenty years of gadding about in questionable employment, under different names, and thus completely destroy himself as a reliable witness in the eyes of the jury.

RULES OF EVIDENCE FOR UNITED STATES COURTS AND MAGISTRATES

Rule 608

EVIDENCE OF CHARACTER AND CONDUCT OF WITNESS

* * *

(b) **Specific instances of conduct.** Specific instances of the conduct of a witness, for the purpose of attacking or supporting his credibility, other than conviction of crime as provided in rule 609, may not be proved by extrinsic evidence. They may, however, in the discretion of the court, if probative of truthfulness or untruthfulness, be inquired into on cross-examination of the witness (1) concerning his character for truthfulness or untruthfulness, or (2) concerning the character for truthfulness or untruthfulness of another witness as to which character the witness being cross-examined has testified.

* * *

COLLATERAL READINGS
Prior Bad Acts

McCormick's Handbook of the Law of Evidence §§ 42, 50 (2d ed. 1972)

Wigmore, Evidence (3rd ed. 1940)

    Vol. 3, §§ 891, 980–987, 1002, 1023

    Vol. 8, § 2277

Comment, 1955 Wash.U.L.Q. 209

Ladd, Some Observations on Credibility: Impeachment of Witnesses, 52 Corn.L.Q. 239 (1967)

Paine, Character or Reputation of the Criminal Defendant in Tennessee, 34 Tenn.L.Rev. 351 (1967)

Schulman, Evidence Challenging Credibility, 2 Man.L.J. 287 (1967)

Comment, Criminal Law: Evidence of Prior Misconduct, 51 Marq.L. Rev. 104 (1967)

c. CONVICTION OF A FELONY

UNITED STATES v. JACKSON
United States District Court, E.D. New York, 1975.
405 F.Supp. 938.

WEINSTEIN, District Judge.

[For the facts of this case, see p. 54 above.]

PRIOR CONVICTION

Impeaching witnesses by prior convictions is governed by Rule 609 of the Federal Rules of Evidence. Under Rule 609(a), Jackson's felony conviction for a crime not involving dishonesty or false statement is admissible only if the court determines that its probative value with respect to defendant's credibility outweighs prejudice to him. The Rule provides:

    (a) General rule. For the purpose of attacking the credibility of a witness, evidence that he has been convicted of a crime shall be admitted if elicited from him or established by public record during cross-examination but only if the crime (1) was punishable by death or imprisonment in excess of one year under the law under which he was convicted, and the court determines that the probative value of admitting this evidence outweighs its prejudicial effect to the defendant, or (2) involved dishonesty or false statement, regardless of the punishment."

Legislative History of Rule 609

The Rule, in its present form, constitutes a carefully considered legislative compromise growing out of a series of rigorous debates in committees and on the floor of both Houses of Congress. The legislative history affords important guidelines for the exercise of judicial discretion as contemplated by paragraph (1) of the Rule. * * *

Rule 609(a), as promulgated by the Supreme Court and transmitted to Congress, followed the traditional practice of permitting free use of felony convictions to impeach the credibility of any witness, including a criminal defendant. The Supreme Court's rule provided:

> (a) General rule. For the purpose of attacking the credibility of a witness, evidence that he has been convicted of a crime is admissible but only if the crime (1) was punishable by death or imprisonment in excess of one year under the law under which he was convicted or (2) involved dishonesty or false statement regardless of the punishment."

In hearings before the House Subcommittee considering the proposed Rules of Evidence, this formulation met stiff opposition from members and witnesses who believed that the use of prior convictions tends to deter defendants from testifying and to create unfair prejudice when they do. * * * The Subcommittee amended the Rule to accord a defendant some measure of protection in the trial court's discretion. Its proposal read as follows:

> "For the purpose of attacking the credibility of a witness, evidence that he has been convicted of a crime is admissible only if the crime (1) was punishable by death or imprisonment in excess of one year, unless the court determines that the danger of unfair prejudice outweighs the probative value of the evidence of the conviction, or (2) involved dishonesty or false statement."

Report of Committee on the Judiciary House of Representatives, 93rd Cong., 1st Sess., No. 93–650, p. 11 (1973).

The House Judiciary Committee was not, however, satisfied that the Subcommittee's amendment adequately protected an accused who wished to testify. Consequently, it amended Rule 609(a) to read:

> "(a) General rule.—For the purpose of attacking the credibility of a witness, evidence that he has been convicted of a crime is admissible only if the crime involved dishonesty or false statement."

Report of Committee on the Judiciary, House of Representatives, 93rd Cong., 1st Sess., No. 93–650, p. 11 (1973).

The limitations imposed on the use of prior convictions to impeach by the Judiciary Committee generated an extensive debate on the floor of the House. * * *

Opponents of the Committee's proposed restrictions argued that any past demonstrated willingness to engage in conduct in disregard of accepted legal norms is highly probative with regard to credibility and therefore requisite to a just and accurate assessment by the jury of a witness' testimony; that it was not fair to permit a defense witness who has been comvicted of a felony to appear as an unblemished citizen; and that a rule restricting impeachment to crimes involving dishonesty or false statement was unpredictable and would result in uneven, discriminatory treatment of criminal defendants.

Proponents of the restrictions argued that the conventional free use of convictions conflicts with the generally accepted principle that a defendant not be convicted because he is a person of bad character; that a large proportion of miscarriages of justice occur because a defendant is prejudiced by proof of his prior conviction or deterred from relating his side of the story; and that the use of convictions to impeach necessarily discriminates between defendants who take the stand and those who do not. * * * After considering an amendment which would have substituted the Subcommittee's version, the House voted in favor of the restrictive practice endorsed by the full Judiciary Committee.

* * *

The Senate Committee proposed a compromise for Rule 609(a) limiting impeachment of the defendant to crimes involving false statement or dishonesty, but permitting free use of felonies for all other witnesses. * * * There followed considerable discussion on the floor of the Senate which resulted in the adoption of an amendment which removed the restrictions on impeachment of the accused, thus adopting a formulation equivalent to the one promulgated by the Supreme Court.

The version of Rule 609(a) that was ultimately enacted was worked out by the Committee on Conference as a compromise between the House and Senate formulations. Conference Report, * * *

In its present form, Rule 609(a) codifies a trend of federal cases epitomized by Luck v. United States, 121 U.S.App.D.C. 151, 348 F.2d 763 (1965), which recognized the trial courts' obligation to exercise discretion in excluding evidence of convictions. * * * The *Luck* doctrine also served as the prototype for the early compromise proposals in the House. * * *

Application of the Rule

It is apparent that, in its compromise form, the Rule necessarily embodies both the policy of encouraging defendants to testify by protecting them against unfair prejudice and the policy of protecting the government's case against unfair misrepresentation of an accused's non-criminality. It is incumbent upon the courts, in administering Rule 609(a), to reconcile these competing goals to the extent possible.

In order fully to effectuate the policy of encouraging defendants to testify, trial courts should rule on the admissibility of prior crimes to impeach as soon as possible after the issue has been raised. * * * It is only after the admissibility of a conviction has been ruled on that defense counsel can make an informed decision whether to put his or her client on the stand. In addition, the court's ruling may have a significant impact on opening statements and the questioning of witnesses. It is, therefore, appropriate for the court to rule on defendant's motion now even though it is not possible to make a completely accurate assessment of the probative value of his recent conviction in the absence of an evaluation of the evidence that will be produced at trial.

The general outlines of the proof have emerged in pretrial conferences. There appears to be no doubt that the robbery took place. Surveillance photographs and witnesses apparently will establish that a male closely resembling defendant participated. There will also probably be testimony by at least one co-conspirator that defendant helped obtain one of the vehicles used in the crime. At least one of the possible government witnesses apparently also has a record of assaults. This information affords a sufficient basis for disposition of defendant's motion.

Considered in the abstract, prior assaultive conduct would seem to have little bearing on the likelihood that one will tell the truth. At the same time, the knowledge that the defendant is a recently convicted felon might have an unduly significant impact on the jury's determination of whether the defendant committed an armed bank robbery even though the evidence would not be admissible for that purpose. * * * The availability of surveillance photographs and some identification testimony ensures that the case will not come down to a simple test of the credibility of two witnesses—the co-conspirator and the defendant. The government's case, therefore, will not necessarily hinge on its ability to destroy the defendant's credibility. Accordingly, defendant's motion to exclude his state court conviction is granted.

The court foresees, however, two possible trial developments which will tip the balance in favor of admitting the assault conviction. The first situation would be one in which the defendant, either through direct testimony or by implication, conveys to the jury the false notion that he has never been in trouble with the law. Any such impression would accord the defendant an unfair trial advantage in direct contravention of the spirit of Rule 609(a). It might cause the jury to overestimate the probability that the defendant is telling the truth on the basis of a factually inaccurate assumption. In this context, proof of the recent felony conviction would nullify an erroneous hypothesis and thereby attain a probative significance on the issue of credibility sufficient to outweigh any prejudice to the defendant. Accordingly, it will be a condition of the court's order that the defendant refrain from suggesting a pristine backgound on direct. * * *

A second condition of the order is that defense counsel not present evidence through cross-examination or otherwise of any assault convictions of any of the government's witnesses without specific advance authorization from the court. This condition is designed to prevent the defendant from taking unfair advantage of the protection afforded him by Rule 609(a). Proof that the government's witnesses have criminal records may cause the jury to underestimate their credibility relative to the defendant's, again of the basis of incomplete or distorted information. With the evidence in such a posture, the probative value of defendant's assault conviction would outweigh any resulting prejudice.

This second condition guarantees that the impact of the loss of evidence will be fairly apportioned between the parties. It is not specifically authorized by the rule which is designed to protect defendants rather than the government from unfair prejudice. But it is amply supported by the sense of the legislative history and case law stressing the role of the court in balancing the competing interests. The use of a condition is further supported by Rule 102 of the Federal Rules of Evidence authorizing the court to interpret the Rules creatively so as to promote growth and development in the law of evidence in the interests of justice and reliable fact-finding. The Rule provides:

> These rules shall be construed to secure fairness in administration, elimination of unjustifiable expense and delay, and promotion of growth and development of the law of evidence to the end that the truth may be ascertained and proceedings justly determined."

* * * Finally it should be noted that both conditions are predicated upon the court's pretrial finding that should they be breached the probative value of defendant's assault conviction will then outweigh the risk of prejudice within the meaning of Rule 609(a).

* * *

The motions to exclude under Rules 609 and 403 are granted, subject to the conditions described.

So ordered.

UNITED STATES v. BOYER

United States Court of Appeals, District of Columbia, 1945.
150 F.2d 595.

Before GRONER, Chief Justice, and MILLER and EDGERTON, Associate Justices.

EDGERTON, Associate Justice. Appellee was convicted in the Municipal Court of obtaining money by false pretenses. There was ample evidence that he cashed a check which he knew to be worthless. He was cross-examined about previous convictions on other bad check charges, and was allowed to say in explanation that those charges were all due to a mistake of his secretary. But the court did not allow him to explain the circumstances of a previous conviction of embezzlement. For this reason the Municipal Court of Appeals reversed his present conviction and ordered a new trial. The government appeals from this reversal.

The fact that a witness has been convicted of a crime may be shown, on the theory that it diminishes the value of his testimony. The question is whether he may then explain the circumstances of his conviction in order to mitigate its apparent effect on his credibility. We agree with the Municipal Court of Appeals that it is unfair to the witness to permit no explanation, particularly when he is at the same time a defendant in a criminal case and "the prior conviction, though permitted solely for the purpose of affecting the credibility of the defendant, may have some tendency in the minds of the jury to prove his guilt of the crime for which he is then on trial." It may have such a tendency even when it has no actual bearing on his credibility. Whether the witness is or is not a defendant, if the opposing party introduces his previous convictions we think the witness should be allowed to make such reasonably brief "protestations on his own behalf as he may feel able to make with a due regard to the penalties of perjury." Since not all guilty men are equally guilty and some convicted men are innocent, we think the witness should be allowed either to extenuate his guilt or to assert his innocence of the previous charges.

The government contends that if an explanation or denial is permitted it opens the way to a collateral inquiry which may be long and confusing. Fear of such a result has led some courts to exclude all evidence designed to mitigate or rebut the impeachment which results from proof of a prior conviction. But there is respectable authority to the contrary. It is generally agreed that in order to save time and avoid confusion of issues, inquiry into a previous crime must be stopped before its logical possibilities are exhausted; the witness cannot call other witnesses to corroborate his story and the opposing party cannot call other witnesses to refute it. The disputed question is whether inquiry into a previous crime should stop (1) with proof of the conviction of the witness or (2) with any reasonably brief "protestations on his own behalf" which he may wish to make. The second alternative will seldom be materially more confusing or time-consuming than the first, if the trial judge duly exercises his "considerable discretion in admitting or rejecting evidence." And we think the second alternative is more conducive to the ends of justice. The jury is not likely to give undue weight to an ex-convict's uncorroborated assertion of innocence or of extenuating circumstances. Just where to draw the line, in order to avoid both unfairness to the witness and confusion of issues, is a question which must frequently arise. The correct rule in such cases, we think, is to recognize a wide discretion in the trial judge. He observes the conduct of counsel, the reaction of the witness under examination, and the resulting effect upon the jury. In other words, he is aware as no appellate court can be of the courtroom psychology and can best determine whether particular testimony should or should not be received.

The trial court's refusal in the present case to let appellee offer any explanation whatever of one conviction, while technically wrong, does not justify a reversal. It related to a different kind of offense from the one for which appellee was on trial. There was convincing proof of his guilt of the bad check charge which was the only issue to be tried. The jury knew that he had previously been convicted on similar charges. He was permitted to explain all his convictions but one. In spite of this the jury did not believe his testimony. In view of the number of his offenses, it is scarcely believable that failure to explain only one of them could have affected the verdict. Accordingly the judgment of the trial court should have been affirmed. The judgement of the Municipal Court of Appeals is therefore reversed.

Reversed.

LILLY, AN INTRODUCTION TO THE LAW OF EVIDENCE *

285–292 (1978).

Techniques of Impeachment: Character Traits Reflecting Mendacity

1. *Conviction of a Crime.* As an exception to the general prohibition against the circumstantial use of character, the credibility of a witness may be challenged by showing that he has been convicted of a crime. The desired inference is that a person who commits a criminal offense is likely—or at least more likely than one who has not committed such an act—to give false testimony. Disagreement, however, often occurs over what types of crimes indicate a propensity to falsify. Does a conviction for manslaughter, for example, have proba-

---
* Reprinted with permission from Lilly's "An Introduction to the Law of Evidence," West Publishing Co. (1978).

tive force regarding credibility? Some convictions, such as those for perjury or fraud, yield strong circumstantial inferences relating to truth-telling. Other offenses, however, such as manslaughter or reckless driving, have a tenuous link with credibility. Some courts have tried to solve this problem by resorting to amorphous verbal formulae. The most common are: crimes involving moral turpitude, "crimen falsi," and infamous crimes. A plurality of courts, however, have reached a more practical accommodation: any conviction for a felony may be used to impeach, but a conviction for a misdemeanor may be used only if the illegal act involved dishonesty or a false statement. Some jurisdictions modify this approach by restricting impeachment to felonies; others allow proof of any conviction, no matter what its grade. There also is lack of uniformity regarding the admissibility of juvenile adjudications and the effect of probation or of the passage of a long period of time since the conviction was rendered. It now is settled, however, that the Constitution forbids the use of a prior conviction obtained in violation of the right to counsel.

The Federal Rule governing impeachment by prior conviction permits the use of any conviction—misdemeanor or felony—involving "dishonesty or a false statement." Other convictions, however, may be used only if the underlying offense "was punishable by death or imprisonment in excess of one year * * * and the court determines that the probative value of admitting this evidence outweighs its prejudicial effect to the defendant. * * *" Unfortunately, as noted below, the Rule so far has been read strictly so that the court may only consider the prejudicial effect to the criminal defendant and not to other parties.

There is nearly general agreement concerning the evidentiary means that may be used to prove a conviction: counsel may adduce the evidence during cross-examination by asking the witness to admit the fact of the conviction or he may introduce a certified or exemplified copy of the prior criminal judgment. Neither of these means of proof consumes much time, and the use of evidence of previous convictions usually poses only the problem of assessing probative value and determining if probative worth is outweighed by prejudice. Courts usually disallow detailed descriptions of the previous offense, confining counsel to such essentials as the name of the crime, the time and place of prosecution, and the punishment imposed. Nor will courts allow the impeached witness to give an extended explanation or time-consuming presentation of facts in mitigation of the conviction, although many courts permit a brief ameliorative explanation.

We already have seen that a criminal accused has the privilege of declining to testify. But if he elects to take the stand, he generally is subject to the usual rules governing the examination of witnesses, including the rules that allow the cross-examiner to engage in various kinds of impeachment. In most jurisdictions, an accused-witness may be impeached by evidence that he has been convicted previously of crimes that reflect upon credibility. This evidence is admitted solely to impugn credibility; in theory it may not be used to support the prejudicial inference that an accused-witness who has committed one or more previous crimes is more likely to be guilty of the offense charged. Upon request, the judge will instruct the jury concerning the limited purpose for which the impeaching evidence may be considered. Nonetheless, the risk that such evidence may prejudice the jury has caused some jurisdictions to formulate protective rules when an accused takes the stand.

* * *

Some observers favor a rule that disallows the use of any prior conviction to impeach an accused. An absolute prohibition has not found acceptance, however, because of an unwillingness among courts and legislators to allow the accused to appear as a truthful person when his record of convictions, if made known to the jury, would cast serious doubt on his testimony. Thus, the tension between providing the jury with a full context for determining credibility and the consequent risk of undue prejudice remains the subject of a lively policy debate.

RULES OF EVIDENCE FOR UNITED STATES COURTS AND MAGISTRATES

Rule 609

IMPEACHMENT BY EVIDENCE OF CONVICTION OF CRIME

(a) **General rule.** For the purpose of attacking the credibility of a witness, evidence that he has been convicted of a crime shall be admitted if elicited from him or established by public record during cross-examination but only if the crime (1) was punishable by death or imprisonment in excess of one year under the law under which he was convicted, and the court determines that the probative value of admitting this evidence outweighs its prejudical effect to the defendant, or (2) involved dishonesty or false statement, regardless of the punishment.

(b) **Time limit.** Evidence of a conviction under this rule is not admissible if a period of more than ten years has elapsed since the date of the conviction or of the release of the witness from the confinement imposed for that conviction, whichever is the later date, unless the court determines, in the interests of justice, that the probative value of the conviction supported by specific facts and circumstances substantially outweighs its prejudicial effect. However, evidence of a conviction more than 10 years old as calculated herein, is not admissible unless the proponent gives to the adverse party sufficient advance written notice of intent to use such evidence to provide the adverse party with a fair opportunity to contest the use of such evidence.

(c) **Effect of pardon, annulment, or certificate of rehabilitation.** Evidence of a conviction is not admissible under this rule if (1) the conviction has been the subject of a pardon, annulment, certificate of rehabilitation, or other equivalent procedure based on a finding of the rehabilitation of the person convicted, and that person has not been convicted of a subsequent crime which was punishable by death or imprisonment in excess of one year, or (2) the conviction has been the subject of a pardon, annulment, or other equivalent procedure based on a finding of innocence.

(d) **Juvenile adjudications.** Evidence of juvenile adjudications is generally not admissible under this rule. The court may, however, in a criminal case allow evidence of a juvenile adjudication of a witness other than the accused if conviction of the offense would be admissible to attack the credibility of an adult and the court is satisfied that admission in evidence is necessary for a fair determination of the issue of guilt or innocence.

(e) **Pendency of appeal.** The pendency of an appeal therefrom does not render evidence of a conviction inadmissible. Evidence of the pendency of an appeal is admissible.

COLLATERAL READINGS

Conviction of a Felony

McCormick's Handbook of the Law of Evidence §§ 43, 50 (2d ed. 1972)

Wigmore, Evidence (3rd ed. 1940)

Vol. 1, § 194

Vol. 2, §§ 488, 520

Vol. 3, §§ 924, 980, 985–87

Vol. 4, §§ 1117, 1269, 1270

Weinstein and Berger, Weinstein's Evidence 609–55 to 609–94 (1975)

Note, Prior Criminal Convictions to Impeach Credibility of Testimony, 19 Okla. 430 (1967)

Note, Constitutional Problems Inherent in the Admissibility of Prior Record Conviction Evidence for the Purpose of Impeaching the Credibility of the Defendant Witness, 37 U.Cinc.L.Rev. 168 (1968)

Note, To Take the Stand or Not to Take the Stand: The Dilemma of the Defendant with a Criminal Record, 4 Colum.J.L. & Soc.Prob. 4C (1968)

Note, Evidentiary Use of Constitutionally Defective Prior Conviction, 68 Colum.L.Rev. 1168 (1968)

Cross, Problem of an Accused with a Record, 6 Sydney L.Rev. 173 (1969)

Note, Prior Convictions as Impeaching Evidence, 28 Wash. & Lee L. Rev. 490 (1971)

d. BAD REPUTATION FOR TRUTH AND VERACITY

EVIDENCE OF CHARACTER AND CONDUCT OF WITNESS

(a) Opinion and reputation evidence of character. The credibility of a witness may be attacked or supported by evidence in the form of opinion or reputation, but subject to these limitations: (1) the evidence may refer only to character for truthfulness or untruthfulness, and (2) evidence of truthful character is admissible only after the character of the witness for truthfulness has been attacked by opinion or reputation evidence or otherwise.

LILLY, AN INTRODUCTION TO THE LAW OF EVIDENCE *

295–297 (1978).

Bad Character Regarding Truth and Veracity. Courts usually are reluctant to admit evidence of a party's character to support the inference that on a specific occasion he acted in accordance with the character traits shown. The credibility of witnesses, however, traditionally has been a subject of special concern for the courts; the outcome of many—if not most—trials is determined by which of the conflicting lines of testimony the trier believes. We already have observed that most courts admit evidence of prior conduct that reflects adversely upon a witness's honesty. All courts agree that a witness may be impeached by evidence which speaks even more directly to his present character for truth and veracity: the impeaching party may offer witnesses who assert that based upon their knowledge of the principal witness, derived either from their familiarity with his reputation or (in some jurisdictions) their observations of his conduct, he has a bad character for truth and veracity. Traditionally, the courts have tried to provide the trier with a useful insight into the witness's character for truthfulness, while also attempting to minimize the burdens of delay and distraction caused by the introduction of secondary issues. Thus, the common law usually limits the type of evidence that may be provided by impeaching witnesses. Those who take the stand for the purpose of impugning the character of the principal witness are restricted to giving evidence of the latter's *bad reputation* for truth and veracity. Delay is minimized by limiting the evidence to conclusory statements about the witness's reputation and, concomitantly, by prohibiting proof of the underlying events that may have produced this disrepute. Under this approach, if a witness, W, testifies for the plaintiff, defense counsel can impeach W by calling another witness, X, to testify that W has a bad reputation for truth and veracity. As a predicate for his testimony, X must provide evidence that he is in a position to know about W's bad reputation. Hence, it usually is necessary that X testify he has resided or otherwise been present in the community in which W lives. Presumably, X's knowledge of W's bad reputation for truth and veracity is acquired from

* Reprinted with permission from Lilly's "An Introduction to the Law of Evidence," West Publishing Co. (1978).

others who speak disparagingly about *W*. The intended inferences from this kind of evidence are clear: from *W*'s unfavorable reputation, the trier can infer the existence of a mendacious trait, and then can infer that *W* is giving untruthful testimony.

In a mobile, urban society, the assumptions underlying impeachment by reputation are dubious at best. It may be doubted, for example, whether many persons who live and work in large urban centers have an established community reputation for traits of truth and veracity. Reacting to this problem, some courts have adjusted the traditional restrictions. A minority of jurisdictions allow impeachment by reputation if the impeaching witness has been present in an association or setting (such as a work environment) in which the principal witness may have established a reputation for truthfulness. Other courts permit the impeaching witness, whatever the basis of his familiarity with the principal witness's reputation, to conclude his direct testimony by stating whether, based upon the reputation to which he has testified, he would believe the principal witness under oath.

Increasingly, the mechanical repetition of a set formula by the reputation witness has been seen for what it usually is—a thinly disguised form of personal opinion. Consequently, in recent years there has been a decided shift toward permitting the impeaching witness to give his personal opinion of the veracity of the principal witness. The Federal Rules of Evidence state:

> Opinion and reputation evidence of character—The credibility of a witness may be attacked or supported by evidence in the form of opinion or reputation, but subject to these limitations: (1) the evidence may refer only to character for truthfulness or untruthfulness, and (2) evidence of truthful character is admissible only after the character of the witness for truthfulness has been attacked by opinion or reputation evidence or otherwise.

This provision loosens the traditional restrictions, but does not go so far as to permit the impeaching (opinion) witness to describe, during direct examination, specific instances of conduct that reflect adversely upon the truth and veracity of the principal witness. The cross-examiner, however, may probe the basis of the opinion by inquiring about these specific events.

e. PSYCHIATRIC CONDITION

PEOPLE v. BASTIAN

Supreme Court of Michigan, 1951.
330 Mich. 457, 47 N.W.2d 692.

CARR, Justice. Defendant was tried in circuit court under an information charging statutory rape.

* * *

The information alleged that the offense was committed on February 26, 1948, in the city of Hancock, upon a girl 15 years of age. It was her testimony on the trial that defendant undertook to take her home from the bakery where both parties were employed, that they went for a ride, and that the offense was committed in a part of the city apparently somewhat removed from habitations. She also testified to three or four subsequent occasions when she rode with defendant in a bakery truck. It was her claim that on each occasion he indulged in conduct indicating affectionate feelings toward her. Defendant in his testimony denied his guilt but admitted riding with the girl in question, herein referred to as the prosecutrix, on two or three occasions, including the evening when the prosecution claimed the offense was committed. He testified in substance that prosecutrix made advances to him to the extent of soliciting him to have sexual relations with her, but that he refused to do so and took her to her home. His testimony indicates that he was offended by her conduct, and that she became very angry at him. He further claimed that she told him that she had previously had sexual relations with others.

At the conclusion of the people's case counsel for defendant moved for a directed verdict of not guilty on the ground that the testimony of the prosecutrix, which was not corroborated as to the commission of the specific act in question, was impeached to such extent that the jury ought not to be permitted to pass on the guilt of the defendant. The motion was denied, and it is now claimed in defendant's behalf that the ruling was erroneous. We are unable to agree with this contention. The credibility of the prosecutrix was open to question, but it was for the jury to determine the weight to be given to the impeaching proofs. The jury had the right to believe the testimony of prosecutrix and to base a conviction thereon. There was no error in the denial of the motion.

In the course of the direct examination of the prosecutrix she was asked concerning acts of intercourse with others during the month of June, 1948, and if defendant was the first person with whom she had had intercourse. She answered the latter question in the affirmative, and stated further, in substance, that she had had improper relations with 11 boys during the period referred to in the prosecutor's question. Following a third question along the same line, counsel for defendant moved that the questions and answers be stricken. No reason was assigned in support of the motion. The trial court struck out the last question but permitted the questions and answers above indicated to remain. It is now insisted that this was error. The record shows, however, that the testimony of prosecutrix as to her relations with others was in part at least made the basis of an attempt by defendant to show that prosecutrix was a sexual psychopathic person, and that her testimony should be weighed in the light of that fact. The testimony of a physician who was in the courtroom while prosecutrix was testifying, and who made his observations and conclusions from her statements and general attitude, was introduced in support of this claim. The defendant is scarcely in position now to claim that he was prejudiced by proof as to the misconduct of prosecutrix with others. * * *

Counsel for defendant sought to cross-examine prosecutrix with reference to certain alleged conduct on her part tending to show, as it is claimed, that she was a sexual psychopathic person and indulged in acts of perversion. An objection to such line of questioning was sustained. An attempt was also made to prove such conduct by the testimony of a witness produced by defendant. The proffered testimony was ruled inadmissible. It is the claim of the defendant that the rulings of the trial court were erroneous, and that they were prejudicial to his rights. Emphasis is placed on the fact that the case against defendant rested largely on the testimony of the prosecutrix, that her credibility was questioned, and that for purposes of impeachment defendant was entitled to offer proofs, even though of a revolting nature, tending to show that prosecutrix was a nymphomaniac. While we appreciate the reluctance of the trial judge to permit testimony of the character in question to be placed before the jury, we are constrained to hold that in a case of the character in question such testimony is competent. Commenting on a somewhat analogous situation, this Court said in People v. Cowles, 246 Mich. 429, 224 N.W. 387, 388:

"At the trial defendant called two medical practitioners, who had observed the girl, and in answer to hypothetical questions they expressed opinions that she was a pathological falsifier, a nymphomaniac, and a sexual pervert. Evidence offered to prove acts of the girl showing sexual perversion and lascivious conduct, inclusive of exposure of her person to school boys, was excluded. We think the testimony should have been received, not in extenuation of rape, but for its bearing upon the question of the weight to be accorded the testimony of the girl and the question of whether the mind of the girl was so warped by sexual contemplation and desires as to lead her to accept the imagined as real or to fabricate a claimed sexual experience. The testimony of the medical experts was admitted without objection, and was for the jury to consider. * * *

"The term 'nymphomaniac' is a standard one in medical parlance. If this girl was such, the weight to be given her testimony might or might not have been materially affected thereby, depending, of course, upon the view taken by the jury."

In the case at bar one of the principal questions at issue had reference to the credibility of the prosecutrix. The physician above referred to, called as a witness in defendant's behalf, testified from his observation of prosecutrix that he believed her to be a sexual psychopathic person, and further expressed the opinion that the credibility of an individual of that type is "very poor". The excluded testimony, if of such character as to indicate that prosecutrix was actually a nymphomaniac, would doubtless have furnished a further basis for the opinion of the physician. If believed by the jury it might well have brought about a verdict of acquittal. The rulings excluding the testimony in question require reversal of the conviction. * * *

[Reversed.]

NOTE

Does the technique of impeachment used in *Bastian* remind you of anything you have seen before? See text and statute at pp. 82–86 above.

UNITED STATES v. PUGLIESE

United States Circuit Court of Appeals, Second Circuit, 1945.
153 F.2d 497.

Before L. HAND, SWAN and FRANK, Circuit Judges.

L. HAND, Circuit Judge. Pugliese appeals from a judgement entered upon the verdict of a jury, convicting him of possessing distilled spirits, upon the "containers" of which the required revenue stamps had not been affixed * * * The appellant upon this appeal raises four grounds for reversal. (1) The judge's denial of a mistrial following an episode we shall describe. * * *

The motion for a mistrial was based upon the following circumstance. After Evelyn Esposito had testified on the direct, cross and redirect, the defence again cross-examined her, as appears in the margin.[1] Upon the close of the prosecution's case the defence rested without calling any witnesses, whereupon the prosecution called the attorney for the defence to the stand and examined him, as also ap-

---

1. "Q. Have you been ill within the last eight or nine years? A. Ill?
"Q. Yes. A. No.
"Q. Have you been in any institution or hospitals? A. No.
"Q. Are you certain about that? A. Positive.
"Q. Never in your life, up to today? A. That's right.

"Q. You have never spent any time in any hospital or institution of any kind whatever? A. No, sir.
"Q. And no illness of any kind? A. No.
"Q. Are you sure about that? A. Yes."

pears in the margin.[2] The defence then moved for a mistrial which the judge denied. The recross-examination which we have quoted, whether so designed or not, was certainly calculated to leave in the jury's mind the impression that at some time in the past Evelyn Esposito had been in the hospital for some mental malady; that being the only kind of malady that would have impaired her credibility. After she had once categorically denied that she had been in any hospital at all, the substance of the question was repeated six times, always with the same result. It was indeed permissible to do this, if the defence meant to contradict her; perhaps it was proper to do so, even though it had evidence to contradict her which it did not mean to use. The issue was not one on which it was bound by the witness's answers, for the evidence, if it existed, was competent directly to impeach the witness. Therefore, although the prosecution could not have raised it, once raised, it was entitled to present its own side. It waited to see whether the defence had any basis for the insinuation, and when it appeared that none was to be produced, two courses were open to it. It might rely in summing up upon the failure of the defence to put in any evidence, or it might probe for any that existed, for, if there was any, certainly it was not privileged. This is what the prosecution did; it was quite within its rights, and the judge's ruling was wrong only in not allowing the examination to be pressed so as to disclose whatever evidence the defence might be withholding * * *

[Affirmed.]

1950 ANNUAL SURVEY OF AMERICAN LAW

804–808 (1950) *

EVIDENCE, BY JUDSON FALKNOR

Witnesses: Impeachment by Psychiatric Testimony.—Although similar testimony had been rejected at the first trial of Alger Hiss,[1] Judge Goddard at the second trial held admissible psychiatric testimony designed to impeach the credibility of the Government witness Whittaker Chambers,[2] and in pursuance of this ruling a psychiatrist,

2. "Q. Mr. Singer, have you any documentary proof or any other proof to indicate that the witness, Mrs. Esposito, was in any institution in the last eight years for any mental or physical illness? * * * A. I do.

"Q. Will you kindly produce that evidence. A. I don't have any written evidence, I have oral evidence.

"Q. Will you produce your oral evidence, if you can? * * *. A. And I said I did over objection.

"Q. And I said if you can produce it, kindly produce it.

"The Court: He does not have to produce it.

"Q. You have no documentary proof, is that right? A. I refuse to answer any further on the matter unless the court will instruct me.

"The Court: I won't instruct you. That is enough."

* Copyright, 1951 by New York University School of Law.

1. N.Y. Times, July 1, 1949, p. 1, col. 2.

2. United States v. Hiss, 88 F.Supp. 559 (S.D.N.Y.1950).

Dr. Carl Binger, testified that Chambers was a "psycopath with a tendency toward making false accusations."[3] Dr. Binger testified that his opinion was based on "personal observation of Mr. Chambers at the first trial for five days and on one day at this trial" and that "he had read plays, poems, articles and book reviews written by Mr. Chambers and books he had translated from German." While it has been said that Dr. Binger's diagnosis was "based entirely on courtroom observation"[4] it appears from a trustworthy contemporary newspaper account that Dr. Binger gave his opinion after listening to a 70-minute hypothetical question "that accentuated unpalatable aspects of Mr. Chambers' life."[5] These accounts leave obscure the tenor of the assumptions in the hypothetical question as well as the character and source of evidence in support thereof.

---

3. N.Y. Times, Jan. 6, 1950, p. 1, col. 2. Amplifying this, the psychiatrist testified that Chambers suffered from a condition known as "a psychopathic personality, a disorder of character, the outstanding features of which are amoral and asocial behavior." This condition, said the witness, has "nothing to do with the conventional judgment of sanity"; it is rather a "personality deviation" that would not prevent Chambers from earning the $30,000 a year he got as senior editor of Time magazine up to Dec. 12, 1948. The symptoms of "a psychopathic personality" are variegated, including chronic, persistent and repetitious lying, stealing and deception, abnormal sexuality, alcoholism, panhandling, vagabondage, inability to form regular habits and a tendency to make false accusations. Such a person, the doctor continued, is quite aware of what he is doing but does not always know why he is doing it. He is frequently impulsive and bizarre. The psychopathic holds some kind of middle ground between the psychotic and neurotic. He plays a role: he may be a hero one moment and a gangster the next, but he acts as though the fancied situation were true. He will claim friendships that do not exist and will make false accusations because he is under constant compulsion to make his fancies come true. He is "amazingly isolated and egocentric." Ibid.

The cross-examination of the psychiatrist (N.Y. Times, Jan. 11, 1950, p. 12, col. 4 and Jan. 12, 1950, p. 9, col. 1) appears to have been rather effective. For example: The witness on his direct examination had emphasized and apparently attached importance to Chambers' "untidiness." He agreed on cross-examination that that trait was manifested by such persons as Albert Einstein, Heywood Broun, Will Rogers, Owen D. Young, Bing Crosby and Thomas A. Edison. The expert had testified that Mr. Chambers habitually gazed at the ceiling while testifying and seemed to have no direct relation with his examiner. "We have made a count of the number of times you looked at the ceiling," the prosecutor told Dr. Binger. "During the first ten minutes you looked at the ceiling nineteen times. In the next fifteen minutes you looked up twenty times. For the next fifteen minutes ten times and for the last fifteen minutes ten times more. We counted a total of fifty-nine times that you looked at the ceiling in fifty minutes. Now I was wondering whether that was any symptom of a psychopathic personality?" Shifting in the witness chair, Dr. Binger smiled frostily and said: "Not alone." When the expert insisted that stealing was a psychopathic symptom the prosecutor asked: "Did you ever take a hotel towel or a Pullman towel?" "I can't swear whether I did or not," Dr. Binger replied, "I don't think so." "And if any member of this jury had stolen a towel, would that be evidence of psychopathic personality?" Mr. Murphy asked. "That would have no bearing on it," the psychiatrist said. It should be noted also that Dr. Binger conceded on cross-examination that he "could not form an opinion of a person merely by watching him from the witness stand."

4. 59 Yale L.J. 1324, 1339 (1950).

5. Note 3 supra.

"Since the use of psychiatric testimony to impeach the credibility of a witness is a comparatively modern innovation," said Judge Goddard in his opinion, "there appear to be no Federal cases dealing with this precise question. However, the importance of insanity on the question of credibility of witnesses is often stressed.[6] There are some state cases in which such testimony has been held to be admissible or which indicate that if this question had been presented it would have been admissible."[7] Judge Goddard noted the contrary conclusion of the West Virginia court in State v. Driver,[8] but said, "This was in 1921—before the value of psychiatry had been recognized."

Judge Goddard's instructions relative to the weight to be given the psychiatric testimony are set forth in the margin.[10] * * *

6. Wigmore, Evidence §§ 931, 932 (3d ed. 1940).

7. The cases cited by the Court scarcely support this statement. The cases cited follow: People v. Cowles, 246 Mich. 429, 224 N.W. 387 (1929): In this rape case two physicians who had observed the prosecuting witness expressed the opinion that she was a "pathological falsifier, a nymphomaniac and a sexual pervert." But this testimony was received without objection. It is to be noted, however, that in holding improper the prosecutor's argument deprecating the medical testimony the Court said that "the term 'nymphomaniac' is a standard one in medical parlance * * * the opinion evidence that she was such is entitled to consideration"; State v. Wesler, 1 N.J. 58, 61 A.2d 746 (1948): This was also a rape case and the question on appeal was whether the verdict of guilty was against the weight of the evidence. In determining that it was not, the Court made reference to the testimony of two psychiatrists to the effect that the prosecuting witnesses were "psychopaths and immoral and that psychopaths are prone to be untruthful," but the admissibility of the evidence is not discussed. As far as the opinion discloses it was received without objection.

In any case, the admissibility of the psychiatric testimony was not involved on the appeal; Ellarson v. Ellarson, 198 App.Div. 103, 190 N.Y. Supp. 6 (3d Dep't 1921): This case appears to go no further than to hold that extrinsic evidence of "insanity," in the traditional sense, is admissible for impeachment purposes. The holding is orthodox. Wigmore, Evidence § 932 (3d ed. 1940); Jeffers v. State, 145 Ga. 74, 88 S.E. 571 (1916): In this rape case a physician testified apparently as a State's witness, as to the result of a physical examination of the prosecutrix, a girl of thirteen, and also "relative to her mental condition he testified she was below the average and that he considered her a child." On appeal the convicted defendant questioned the admissibility of this evidence but it was held proper. The case does not seem apposite; Bouldin v. State, 87 Tex.Cr.R. 419, 222 S.W. 555 (1920): In a robbery prosecution defendant proposed to show that a state's witness was, if not insane, an idiot or feeble-minded and also that the mother of the witness was an idiot. On appeal the exclusion of this evidence was held erroneous. This is like the *Ellarson* case, supra.

8. 88 W.Va. 479, 107 S.E. 189 (1921). In this prosecution for rape the trial court excluded the opinions of a neurologist and a psychologist that the prosecuting witness was a moron and as such "untrustworthy of belief." This ruling was affirmed on appeal. The Court said that "we are not convinced that the time-honored and well-settled and defined rule of impeachment of the veracity of a witness [by evidence of bad reputation for truth and veracity] should be thus innovated upon. It is yet to be demonstrated that psychological and medical tests are practical, and will detect the lie on the witness stand."

10. "The defense has called Dr. Binger, a psychiatrist, and Dr. Murray, a psychologist, for the purpose of attacking Mr. Chambers' credibility. Dr. Bin-

STATE v. RENNEBERG

Supreme Court of Washington, En Banc, 1974.
83 Wash.2d 735, 522 P.2d 835.

BRACHTENBACH, Associate Justice. Virginia Sue LaVanway was charged with and convicted of grand larceny. Her codefendant, Milton V. LaVanway, whom she married after they were charged with these crimes, was charged with and convicted of aiding and abetting grand larceny. The Court of Appeals affirmed the convictions and we granted review.

The defendant wife had been employed by a restaurant but had been discharged from that employment. In the early evening of June 24, 1970, the defendants visited the restaurant to obtain her final paycheck. The defendants went to the rest rooms in the rear of the restaurant and then returned to the front where defendant wife used the telephone which was located next to the cash register. Defendant husband stood near the restaurant door where he paced back and forth, looked about and kept moving around, according to the witnesses. The restaurant employee who was the only one operating the cash register that evening heard the register bell, indicating the register was being opened, and went toward the cash register. He saw defendant wife facing the cash register, then the defendants left the restaurant. A witness reported to the employee that his son had seen a young woman at the register with a stack of money bills in her hand. An immediate tally of the register disclosed a shortage of approximately $250.

The first issue arises from the following testimony elicited by the prosecutor:

> Q. Mrs. LaVanway, is it true that in June of this year you were addicted to or were using a narcotic drug? A. Yes. Q. Mrs. LaVanway, is it true that on July 14th, you went onto a methadone program to cure a narcotic addiction or use? A. Yes.

It appears that the question of admissibility of this testimony was discussed in chambers before the trial started. Apparently, although it is not clear from the record, the court indicated that testimony as to drug addiction would be inadmissible in the state's case.

ger, basing his opinion upon certain testimony which for the purpose of a hypothetical question he assumed to be true and on his observations of Mr. Chambers while Mr. Chambers was on the witness stand; and Dr. Murray, basing his opinion upon the same hypothetical situation which he assumed to be true, testified that in their opinion Mr. Chambers was a psychopathic personality and that this tended to reduce his credibility. As is the case with all expert testimony, these opinions are purely advisory. You may reject their opinions entirely if you find the hypothetical situation presented to them in the question to be incomplete or incorrect or if you believe their reasons to be unsound or not convincing. An expert does not pass on the truth of the testimony included in a hypothetical question."

Ch. 5   IMPEACHMENT AND CROSS–EXAMINATION

Only after defendant wife took the stand and testified as to her character, as described later, did the court allow this testimony. Admissibility of evidence of prior drug addiction can be considered on at least two distinctly different grounds. First, that it relates to the witness' credibility and second, that it is an unrelated act of misconduct, admissible to contradict character evidence. It is obvious that there is an immense difference between the practical effect of the two theories of admissibility. If it is admissible to attack credibility, it will come in whenever a defendant testifies while, if it is restricted to countering character evidence, it will only be used against that defendant who chooses to put his or her character into evidence. As to admissibility relating to credibility, there is a division of authority.

We note that we are not confronted with a situation where it is contended that the witness was under the influence of drugs at the time of the events to which he testifies * * * or that the witness is under the influence at the time of testifying * * *.

The Court of Appeals recognized the division in the authorities but felt bound by our decision in Lankford v. Tombari, 35 Wash.2d 412, 213 P.2d 627 (1950), wherein a terse holding concluded that drug use or addiction is relevant to veracity. In view of society's deep concern today with drug usage and its consequent condemnation by many if not most, evidence of drug addiction is necessarily prejudicial in the minds of the average juror. Additionally there is no proof before the court connecting addiction to a lack of veracity. If such medical or scientific proof were made, it might well be admissible as relevant to credibility. Absent such proof its relevance on credibility or veracity is an unknown factor while its prejudice is within common knowledge. The Lankford v. Tombari decision is limited accordingly by our view herein.

However, the alternate and more restrictive ground of character impeachment dictates admissibility here. The defendant wife voluntarily put her character before the jury. She testified to her work experience, that she had attended college, that she had been a candidate in the Miss Yakima pageant, that she had participated in a glee club, drill team, pep club and was the treasurer of a science club. Implicit in such testimony is the painting of a picture of a person most unlikely to commit grand larceny. While the character of defendant husband was not so clearly put into evidence, it was introduced sufficiently to subject the defendant husband to the same questions as recited above which were asked of the wife. There was testimony as to his occupation as a professional photographer, as to his physical dress on the day in question, as to his somewhat lengthy engagement and subsequent marriage to the defendant wife whose character had been so vividly pictured, as to his working in his garden at home and as to the planned attendance at a family barbecue on the day of the alleged crime. The state was entitled to complete the tapestry with his admitted drug addiction.

* * *

[Affirmed.]

[Dissent omitted.]

COLLATERAL READINGS
Psychiatric Condition

McCormick, Handbook of the Law of Evidence § 47 (2d ed. 1972)

Wigmore, Evidence (3rd ed. 1940)
Vol. 3, §§ 931–935, 989–995

Falknor and Steffen, Evidence of Character: From the "Crucible of the Community" to the "Couch of the Psychiatrist," 102 U.Pa.L. Rev. 980 (1954)

Slovenko, Witnesses, Psychiatry and the Credibility of Testimony, 19 U.Fla.L.Rev. 1 (1966)

Kramer, Cross-examination of Defendant's Expert in a Traumatic Neurosis Case, 5 Tr.Law Q. 28 (1969)

O'Regan, Impugning the Credit of the Accused by Psychiatric Evidence, 1975 Crim.L.Rev. 563

Note, Impeachment, 21 Loyola L.Rev. 346 (1975)

2. PRIOR INCONSISTENT STATEMENTS

UNITED STATES v. LONG SOLDIER

United States Court of Appeals, Eighth Circuit, 1977.
562 F.2d 601.

LAY, Circuit Judge.

Charles Long Soldier was convicted on Count I of a three count indictment * * * Count I charged that the defendant used a deadly weapon to assault Victor Provost, a Bureau of Indian Affairs employee.

* * *

We affirm the conviction.

On February 8, 1976 at around 4:30 A.M. near Manderson, South Dakota, on the Pine Ridge Indian Reservation, a number of shots were fired at a Bureau of Indian Affairs patrol car in which Officer Victor Provost was seated. Two of the bullets struck the right rear panel of the vehicle. At the time of the incident, Provost was talking to two off-duty officers, Duane Yellow Hawk and William Jumping Eagle, in a private vehicle parked alongside the patrol car. None of the individuals was injured. All of them agreed that the shots appeared to have been rifle shots.

About two hours after the shooting, Agents Price and Wood of the Federal Bureau of Investigation arrived at the scene and began their investigation. The officers determined that the shots came from the northwest, and approximately 100 yards northwest of the vehicle two empty .30-caliber expended shell casings were discovered. The agents also noticed a number of footprints and car tracks near the area, most of which led in a northerly direction toward the Manderson housing.

As the officers began to conduct a general inspection of the Manderson housing area, Agent Price was informed of the discovery of three one-dollar bills near house number 129. A decision was made to interview the occupants of house 129, Henry and Agnes Black Elk. After approaching the house and identifying themselves, the officers were admitted by Henry Black Elk. They informed the Black Elks that they were looking for a man with a rifle. Henry Black Elk told Agent Price that the defendant was in the back of the house. The two FBI agents then went toward the back of the house where they encountered Charles Long Soldier. Long Soldier, accompanied by Agent Wood, went into the living room and Agent Price asked Agnes Black Elk where the defendant hid the rifle. She pointed to a mattress in the back bedroom, and under the mattress Agent Price found a .30-caliber rifle. Price went to the living room and asked the defendant if he had ever seen the rifle and if he owned a rifle. The defendant answered no to both questions. He was then arrested, advised of his rights, and taken to the tribal jail in Pine Ridge. Agents Price and Wood remained at the Black Elk residence to interview members of the Black Elk family. Statements allegedly given to Agent Price by Henry Black Elk at this time and repeated in Black Elk's testimony before the grand jury are the basis of the defendant's first contention on appeal, that the trial judge erred in allowing improper impeachment of Black Elk as to these statements.

* * *

Out of Court Statements of Black Elk.

Henry Black Elk was called as a witness by the government. He testified as to the events which took place at his home in the early morning hours of February 8, 1976. He recalled with specific clarity that the defendant, whom he did not know at the time, had come to his home at 5:30 A.M. accompanied by Pat White Hawk, a man Black Elk knew. The defendant asked to come in and warm up. Black Elk stated that the defendant had a 30-30 rifle with him and was intoxicated. A short time later Black Elk observed police officers approaching his house. He testified that when they knocked on the door Long Soldier went into a back room with the rifle. Black Elk acknowledged that before the police officers came to the door he and the defendant had a conversation. On direct examination he stated that they talked about Indian history and "stuff" and drank wine. When asked whether Long Soldier had stated "where he had been prior to coming to your house," Black Elk said: "He never mentioned anything; but I did talk with him on that Indian history and stuff." Later in his testimony Black Elk was again asked about this conversation and government counsel said: "[Y]ou talked about some pow wows * * * did you have any other conversation at that time with Long Soldier?" Black Elk responded: "No, we didn't." Thereafter government's counsel asked Black Elk:

> Q. All right, Mr. Black Elk, did you tell Mr. Price the following—or in essence the following: That you sat at the table with Long Soldier—
>
> MR. ARCHULETA: Your Honor—
>
> MR. BULLIS:—and that Long Soldier said in Lakota "I used this gun to shoot into them pigs five times"? Did you make that statement?
>
> THE WITNESS: That I don't remember; but that agent sitting there promised distinctly that he will not take me to court, and I could prove it; but now he's got me in here.
>
> * * *
>
> Q. Did you make that statement to Mr. Price at that time? Did you tell Mr. Price that that's what Mr. Long Soldier had told you?
>
> A. If I did tell him, I don't remember.
>
> Q. All right. Let me ask you: Did you state this to the FBI? Did you tell the FBI agent that Long Soldier showed you a shell from the gun which was a .30-caliber shell? Long Soldier boasted "We're AIMs. Nobody can get us. I'm waiting for the goons."
>
> Did you tell that to Mr. Price?
>
> A. That I don't remember.

Thereafter the following questions were asked:

> Q. (Mr. Bullis continuing) Mr. Black Elk, I'm also going to ask you: Do you recall testifying before a Federal grand jury on March 18th, 1976?
>
> A. Yes.
>
> Q. Your answer was "Yes"?
>
> A. Yes.
>
> Q. Do you remember your testimony at that time?
>
> A. Yes.
>
> * * *
>
> Q. All right. Will you tell us what your testimony was at that grand jury proceedings?

Ch. 5   IMPEACHMENT AND CROSS–EXAMINATION   281

A. My testimony was that Mr. Long Soldier came in my house with a gun and they apprehended him, and I told the grand jury—I said "I'm scared—I'm scared of the AIMs and for my family. Under the Fifth Amendment I cannot testify any more," I said, "because my family will be under what I mean harassment."

Q. All right. Was there anything else that you testified to at that grand jury proceedings?

A. That I don't remember.

Q. You don't remember?

A. Huh-uh. That's been a long time ago.

* * *

Q. Well, Mr. Black Elk, I'm going to ask you whether or not the following question was asked of you and whether you gave the following answer:

Question: "Let me just go back to the time you talked with this man you didn't know and ask you in a conversation if he didn't say to you, 'I used this gun to shoot into them pigs five times?'"

Answer: "At the time he was intoxicated, which he did say."

Did you give—was that question asked and that answer given?

A. That was asked and that's the way I answered. I was intoxicated.

Q. Are you saying, Mr. Black Elk, that you were intoxicated at the time you testified before the grand jury?

A. No. At the time they asked me questions.

Q. Well, I'm asking you if you gave this answer before the grand jury?

A. Yes, I did.

Prior to the examination before the jury the defense had moved to suppress Black Elk's statements to Price and the grand jury on the ground that Black Elk's testimony was not inconsistent with his prior statements. * * * The court ruled * * * that Black Elk could be interrogated concerning his recollection of what Long Soldier had told him and that the grand jury testimony would be admissible.

Rule 801(d)(1)(A) of the Federal Rules of Evidence provides:

(d) Statements which are not hearsay. A statement is not hearsay if—

(1) Prior statement by witness. The declarant testifies at the trial or hearing and is subject to cross-examina-

tion concerning the statement, and the statement is (A) inconsistent with his testimony, and was given under oath subject to the penalty of perjury at a trial, hearing, or other proceeding, or in a deposition.

It is well established that testimony before a grand jury constitutes "other proceedings" within the rule. The question we face is whether proper foundation for the use of the grand jury statement was established by testimony inconsistent with it and harmful to the government's case. The record shows that Black Elk affirmatively denied that Long Soldier had made any statement to him concerning the events in question. We find Black Elk's denial that Long Soldier had admitted culpability inconsistent with his prior statements. * * * There exists a substantive difference between a witness' failure to recall an incriminating statement made by the defendant and an affirmative denial that a defendant made an admission of guilt to him. There is more than a subtle distinction here. In the first instance there is nothing harmful in evidence and any attempt to "impeach" becomes subterfuge. The out of court statement then assumes paramount importance as substantive evidence. * * * However, where a witness affirmatively denies that the defendant made an admission of guilt to him, there is at least an exculpatory inference that something did not take place as alleged and impeachment should be allowed. It should also be noted that Black Elk's testimony as a whole was of vital importance to the government's case. We are not presented with a situation in which the government called this witness solely for the purpose of introducing otherwise inadmissible evidence under the guise of impeachment. * * *

Under the circumstances, the use of Black Elk's alleged statement to Agent Price was likewise proper impeachment of Black Elk's trial testimony. Furthermore, the statement contained substantially the same information which Black Elk told to the grand jury, and therefore the effect was cumulative and could not be considered reversible error.

* * *

The judgment of the trial court is affirmed.

GOLDSTEIN, TRIAL TECHNIQUE

§ 601 (1935)*

§ 601. Former contradictory oral statements

In those instances where the lawyer is in possession of information as to verbal statements made by the witness which are directly contrary to his present testimony, the following procedure is suggested: First—get the witness to repeat upon cross-examination the statements that he has made on direct examination, then put a casual

* Copyright 1935 by Callaghan & Co.

Ch. 5　　IMPEACHMENT AND CROSS–EXAMINATION　　283

and general question as to whether or not he has ever made a statement to the contrary, at any time or place, then identify the person to whom the contradictory statement is purported to have been made, then direct his attention to the time, the place, and the exact language used or in substance, and again ask him whether or not he had made such contradictory statement. Upon his denial he might again be interrogated on the same question for psychological effect and upon a similar denial the witness should be excused.

After opponent's case is in and he rests, the lawyer should then produce the impeaching witness and prove the contradictory statement by him.

RULES OF EVIDENCE FOR UNITED STATES COURTS AND MAGISTRATES

Rule 613

PRIOR STATEMENTS OF WITNESSES

(a) **Examining witness concerning prior statement.** In examining a witness concerning a prior statement made by him, whether written or not, the statement need not be shown nor its contents disclosed to him at that time, but on request the same shall be shown or disclosed to opposing counsel.

(b) **Extrinsic evidence of prior inconsistent statement of witness.** Extrinsic evidence of a prior inconsistent statement by a witness is not admissible unless the witness is afforded an opportunity to explain or deny the same and the opposite party is afforded an opportunity to interrogate him thereon, or the interests of justice otherwise require. This provision does not apply to admissions of a party-opponent as defined in rule 801(d)(2).

RULES OF EVIDENCE FOR UNITED STATES COURTS AND MAGISTRATES

Rule 801

DEFINITIONS

The following definitions apply under this article:

* * *

(d) **Statements which are not hearsay.** A statement is not hearsay if—

(1) *Prior statement by witness.* The declarant testifies at the trial or hearing and is subject to cross-examination concerning the statement, and the statement is (A) inconsistent with his testimony, and was given under oath subject to the penalty of perjury at a trial,

hearing, or other proceeding, or in a deposition, or (B) consistent with his testimony and is offered to rebut an express or implied charge against him of recent fabrication or improper influence or motive, * * *.

* * *

COLLATERAL READINGS
Prior Inconsistent Statements

McCormick's Handbook of the Law of Evidence §§ 34–37 (2d ed. 1972)

Wigmore, Evidence (3rd ed. 1940) Vol. 3, §§ 896–918, 1017–1046, 1051

Ladd, Some Observations on Credibility: Impeachment of Witnesses, 52 Corn.L.Q. 239, 245–256 (1967)

Note, Impeaching the Prosecution Witness: Access to Grand Jury Testimony, 4 Houston L.Rev. 144 (1966)

Thomas, Rehabilitating the Impeached Witness with Consistent Prior Statements, 32 Mo.L.Rev. 472 (1968)

Comment, Evidence—Prior Inconsistent Statements of a Witness as Substantive Evidence [1970] Wis.L.Rev. 202

Comment, Constitutional Law—Evidence—Substantive Use of Witness' Prior Inconsistent Statement Does Not Violate the Confrontation Clause of the Sixth Amendment of the United States Constitution, 2 Loyola L.J. (Chicago) 238 (1971)

Note, Evidence—Impeachment by Prior Inconsistent Opinions, 39 Mo.L.Rev. 614 (1974)

3. BIAS

PEOPLE v. TAYLOR

Supreme Court of Colorado, 1976.
— Colo. —, 545 P.2d 703.

LEE, Justice.

Defendant Donald Taylor was acquitted by a jury of the first-degree assault of a police officer who had attempted to arrest him. The prosecution, * * * appeals certain evidentiary rulings of the trial court. We conclude that the court properly admitted some of the controverted evidence, but that the court erred with respect to the admission of other portions of the evidence.

A brief statement of the facts is necessary in order to make clear the basis of the appeal. On the evening of February 15, 1974, Denver police Officers Malara and Leary approached defendant as he left the "Apex Social Club." Recognizing him as "the party wanted in our daily bulletin," they asked him for identification. Not satisfied with defendant's response, Officer Leary pulled a wallet out of defendant's pocket, opened it, and found a social security card revealing his true identity. Leary then returned the wallet, and was about to frisk defendant when the latter pushed Leary into Malara and fled. The officers testified that as he was running defendant turned and fired several shots, and the officers fired in return. Defendant made good his escape that night, but was apprehended the next day. He denied either having a firearm in his possession or firing any shots at the officers.

At trial, the defense attacked the credibility of Officer Leary by revealing his alleged racial bias toward the defendant. Both officers were white and defendant was black. The impeachment was sought to be accomplished by cross-examining Leary about several arrests of blacks he had made within a few months of defendant's arrest. The prosecution objected on the ground that such cross-examination would inject collateral issues into the proceedings and confuse the jury. The objection was overruled, and the defense attorney was permitted to inquire in considerable detail into these other arrests.

In each instance, the officer firmly disavowed the use of either racial slurs or of excess force. In rebuttal, the defense called several witnesses to testify as to what transpired at these other arrests, and to contradict Leary's version. The prosecutor renewed his objections but these were overruled on the ground that the proffered testimony went to the officer's credibility. The testimony of the rebuttal witnesses again went into great detail concerning each incident, and was to the effect that Leary was sadistic and brutal in the manner in which he effected the arrests.

At the close of the evidence, the prosecution further renewed its objection and moved for a mistrial. The motion was denied.

I.

The trial court properly concluded that the alleged racial biases of Officer Leary might be inquired into for the purpose of impeaching his credibility. Cross-examination should be liberally extended to permit a thorough inquiry into the motives of witnesses. * * * Within broad limits, any evidence tending to show bias or prejudice, or to throw light upon the inclinations of witnesses, may be permitted. * * * The trial court must, however, exercise its sound discretion to preclude inquiries that have no probative force, or are irrelevant * * * or which would have little effect on the witness' credibility but would substantially impugn his moral character. * * *

We hold that the cross-examination was proper insofar as the defense counsel inquired into the officer's asserted racial slurs. Such prejudice, if shown, might have greatly assisted the jury in its weighing of the conflicting testimony.

Once Leary denied that he was racially prejudiced, the defense counsel was entitled to present extrinsic evidence to contradict him.

* * * In other words, a party who on cross-examination inquires into bias is not bound by the denial of the witness, but may contradict him with the evidence of other witnesses.

* * *

We hold that the trial court ruled correctly in admitting the rebuttal testimony about the racial slurs purportedly made by Officer Leary.

II.

We emphasize, however, the dangers of too readily admitting such extrinsic testimony relating to bias.

* * *

Much of the controverted evidence admitted in this case dealt not so much with possible racial bias as with details of the arrests made on other occasions by Officer Leary. We believe that the trial judge erred in permitting inquiry into the details of those arrests, both on cross-examination and on rebuttal. Such questions were aimed not merely at impeaching the credibility of the officer, but at maligning his character and official conduct generally. To routinely allow this sort of questioning could greatly delay the trial and in effect make the officer the defendant in a series of mini-trials dealing with the manner in which he arrested countless other persons at other times. The potential for harm would become especially great if the defense could introduce witnesses to testify as to such other arrest; for, if the defense witnesses could give their view of the officer's conduct on these occasions, surely the officer himself should have the right to present witnesses to tell his side of the story. The sideshow could indeed "take over the circus."

* * *

In this area, what may not be asked of the witness himself may not thereafter be proven by the testimony of defense witnesses. Defendant could, of course, have called witnesses to testify as to Officer Leary's reputation in the community for truth and veracity. But even then specific instances of alleged misconduct could not have been detailed. * * *

The evidentiary rulings of the trial court permitting detailed examination into the collateral arrests are therefore disapproved, except that evidence relating directly to racial slurs in connection with collateral arrests was admissible.

[Affirmed.]

Ch. 5   IMPEACHMENT AND CROSS–EXAMINATION   287

PEOPLE v. TORRES

Supreme Court of New York, Appellate Division, 1976.
51 A.D.2d 225, 380 N.Y.S.2d 654.

STEVENS, Presiding Justice. Defendant was charged with the fatal shooting of Gabriel Sanchez on February 17, 1973, at approximately 10:00 P.M. in front of 801 East Tremont Avenue. The People produced two eyewitnesses to the crime, Santiago Oriol, who was double parked in a car driven by defendant, and Mabel Saladini, who was looking through her kitchen window on the second floor of the building.

The proof adduced by the People afforded ample basis to support the verdict and if that were the only question before us, reversal would not be indicated. However, on this appeal, defendant alleges serious error which he claims deprived him of his right to a fair trial.
* * *

Oriol, a key prosecution witness, testified in substance that defendant was driving a Pontiac G.T.O. and picked him up shortly before the crime occurred. They stopped in front of 801 East Tremont Avenue, and defendant, who left the motor running, approached Sanchez with gun in hand, made a few remarks and shot him. As he stepped away defendant, observing movement by Sanchez, returned and fired additional shots into his body.

Oriol testified that defendant threatened to shoot him if he didn't keep quiet and that he accompanied defendant to a Newark, New Jersey restaurant, then later to defendant's apartment in the Bronx, before returning to New Jersey, where they remained for several weeks. Oriol worked briefly as an electrician. Following an argument with and beating by defendant, Oriol went to the Newark police who then took both men into custody. New York City Detective Lugo testified that on March 8, 1973, he obtained a statement from Oriol in the Newark police station where, according to Lugo, Oriol was detained as a material witness in connection with defendant's assault upon him.

A felony complaint * * * charged defendant and Oriol, while acting in concert, with the murder of Sanchez and possession of a weapon. Defendant and Oriol were returned to New York on March 14, 1973.

At trial, Oriol testified that he was brought back to New York as a material witness. On cross-examination, the court refused to allow defense counsel to ask Oriol if he had been charged with the murder of Sanchez. The defense then made an offer of proof that Oriol was brought back on the Criminal Court complaint; that a "DD–5" report indicated a possible indictment of Oriol on the charge of murder; that Oriol, after the homicide, had been indicted for the crime of arson; and, that Oriol's subsequent plea to hindering prosecution also covered the arson indictment. The court was shown the Criminal Court complaint and the "DD–5" report but rejected the offer of proof and also refused to permit defense counsel to ask Oriol if he had recently had a fight with Sanchez and was looking for him on the night of the murder. This was clearly error since the offer of proof was designed to show bias or prejudice on the part of the witness and thus to affect his credibility.

While the general rule is that a witness may not be asked if he has been indicted or arrested for a crime, since an indictment is merely an accusation, there are recognized exceptions to the rule. "The witness' bias in favor of the party calling him, or his hostility to the party against whom he testifies, may be shown to affect his credibility". In light of the lenient plea afforded Oriol, a plea "to hindering prosecution", which covered that indictment as well as the indictment for arson, reasonable latitude should have been afforded defense counsel in making inquiry into the circumstances affecting or leading to the plea. Such inquiry is relevant to show the witness' interest in testifying favorably for the People. This was not done. Since the felony complaint charged Oriol with murder, the later comparatively minor charge and plea, coupled with his becoming a witness for the People, warranted giving the defense an opportunity for reasonable exploration. Bias in favor of the prosecution or hostility toward the defendant may be shown by any competent evidence and could have been shown by cross-examination of the witness. Moreover, the crime occurred on February 17, 1973, and Oriol did not go to the police until March 8, 1973. It appears from the record, despite Oriol's professed fear of the defendant, that there were previous opportunities for him to seek police protection had he so desired.

Defense counsel should have been allowed to explore the question of whether Oriol earlier had a fight with Sanchez and was looking for him on the night of the crime, since there then could have been a motive for Oriol to participate in the crime and his role then would not have been merely that of an innocent bystander. Had he been permitted to do so and if it were shown that Oriol was an accomplice, then the court's failure to charge, as requested by the defense, with respect to the law on accomplice testimony would have been serious error.

Where one seeks to interrogate for the purpose of impeachment, the discretion of the trial court permits it to limit the quantity of such evidence but does not encompass a refusal to admit such evidence.

* * *

[Reversed.]

WALTZ, CRIMINAL EVIDENCE

127–8 (1975).*

* * *

Proof of bias and the like is always relevant to credibility and can be inquired into thoroughly. This can run the gamut from showing that the accused's solitary alibi witness is his devoted wife to demonstrating that the witness on the stand has been bribed by the side whose cause his testimony favors.

Thus it can be brought out that an accomplice who has turned "State's evidence" was granted immunity from prosecution or promised a reduced sentence as a *quid pro quo* for testimony advantageous to the prosecution. Less dramatic circumstances can be revealed. Perhaps the defendant's witnesses can all be shown to be his relatives or close friends. Or perhaps—and this will be more difficult for the criminal investigator to develop—the defendant's witnesses, such as alibi witnesses, are persons over whom the defendant has some sort of hold. He has threatened them, or gotten others to threaten them, with bodily harm unless they testify in his favor. Threats to the witness's loved ones can be shown, as can threats to destroy the witness's business or reputation. Promises of a monetary or other type of reward for favorable testimony can be brought out.

Sometimes defense counsel, lacking anything more solid, will bear down on the fact that the prosecution's key witness has been housed in a good hotel, wined and dined, and supported financially pending and during the trial.

Example:

BY THE PROSECUTING ATTORNEY: Let's get this straight, Miss Adams. You state, as I understand it, that the accused was with you during all of the night in question?

A: That's correct.

Q: It is a fact, is it not, that you have been living with the accused, although not married to him, for the past five years?

A: That's true. But we're going to get married sometime. He's promised me.

Q: That is your hope, is it?

A: Yes.

Q: You won't be able to get married if he goes to jail on this charge, will you?

A: No. Maybe I could wait for him.

Q: And the fact also is that the accused has been and is now your sole source of financial support, isn't that so?

A: Yes.

* Copyright, 1975 by Jon R. Waltz.

Q: And he could not continue to support you if he goes to prison, could he?

A: I guess not. They don't earn much in there.

Q: You have everything to gain if Charlie is acquitted and everything to lose if he is convicted, is that not correct?

A: Yes, but I'm not lying.

Q: Can you give the court and jury the name of any person who saw you and Charlie together on the night in question?

A: No.

It is proper to ask expert witnesses, such as a psychiatrist who has supported an insanity defense, whether he is being paid a fee for his testimony, although a carefully coached expert will usually sidestep this sort of cross-examination fairly artfully.

RULES OF EVIDENCE FOR UNITED STATES COURTS AND MAGISTRATES

Rule 806

ATTACKING AND SUPPORTING CREDIBILITY OF DECLARANT

When a hearsay statement, or a statement defined in Rule 801(d)(2), (C), (D), or (E),* has been admitted in evidence, the credibility of the declarant may be attacked, and if attacked may be supported, by any evidence which would be admissible for those purposes if declarant had testified as a witness. Evidence of a statement or conduct by the declarant at any time, inconsistent with his hearsay statement, is not subject to any requirement that he may have been afforded an opportunity to deny or explain. If the party against whom a hearsay statement has been admitted calls the declarant as a witness, the party is entitled to examine him on the statement as if under cross-examination.

COLLATERAL READINGS

Bias

McCormick, Handbook of the Law of Evidence § 40 (2d ed. 1972)
Wigmore, Evidence (3rd ed. 1940)
   Vol. 3, §§ 943–969
Schmertz and Czapanskiy, Bias Impeachment and the Proposed Federal Rules of Evidence, 61 Geo.L.J. 257 (1972)

* See p. 148.

4. REHABILITATION OF THE IMPEACHED WITNESS

PEOPLE v. SINGER

Court of Appeals of New York, 1949.
300 N.Y. 120, 89 N.E.2d 710.

DESMOND, Judge.

Defendant, convicted of manslaughter in the first degree, * * * and abortion, * * * argues in this court: first, that his guilt was not established beyond a reasonable doubt; second, that there was neither sufficient corroboration of the accomplice testimony nor a proper charge by the court on the subject; third, that it was error to allow the exhibition before the jury of mangled parts of a fetus and parts of the organs of the aborted woman; and fourth, that it was error to receive into evidence proof of a prior extra-judicial "consistent statement" made by the accomplice-witness Schneidewind. We reject each of those contentions, but find it necessary to comment on the fourth point, only.

Schneidewind, at the trial, gave testimony most damaging to defendant. When cross-examined, he admitted that when he (Schneidewind) had first appeared before the grand jury as a witness, on November 12, 1947, four weeks after the abortion, he had made statements utterly at variance with his trial testimony, and not inculpating defendant at all. Previously when giving his evidence in chief at the trial, he had told the jury that he, with defendant and another accomplice had, just after the abortion, gotten together and concocted the false story. Later, during Schneidewind's cross-examination, it was brought out that after his first (November 12, 1947) grand jury appearance, he was taken into custody and that he then went again before the grand jury on November 14, 1947, and that on that second occasion he recanted, and gave the grand jury the same version of the occurrence that he related in his direct testimony on this trial During this cross-examination of Schneidewind, defense counsel brought out the fact that Schneidewind, although guilty on his own story, had not been indicted. By those and other questions, the defense at least suggested to the jury that Schneidewind hoped for clemency for himself, and that his trial testimony was a fabrication, as a reward for which he hoped to go unwhipped of justice.

The prosecutor then called as a rebuttal witness the father of the victim of the abortion. Over objection, the father was permitted to tell the jury that, on the day following the abortion (thirteen months before the trial), Schneidewind had told the father the same things that he told the jury on this trial, as to his (Schneidewind's) and defendant's complicity in the abortion.

Defendant argues to us that this rebuttal testimony of the father was an illegal buttressing of Schneidewind's sworn trial testimony by a showing of previous extrajudicial, unsworn statements of like import. The contention is that this rebuttal did not come within the exception to the hearsay rule, stated by this court * * * as follows: "where the testimony of a witness is assailed as a recent fabrication, it may be confirmed by proof of declarations of the same tenor before the motive to falsify existed." Defendant says that two essential bases for the application of that exception are missing here: first, in that Schneidewind's trial testimony was not claimed by the defense to have been a *recent* fabrication, since it was the same story he had told before the grand jury a year earlier, and also at an earlier trial of this very case; and, second, in that, according to defendant, there was no sufficient accusation or showing here of any motive to falsify, arising after the disclosure to the father and before the first telling of Schneidewind's present version of the facts. We think both conditions necessary for the use of the exception, were fairly present here.

Of course, if the word "recent" in this court's formulation of the exception, in the cases above cited, means that the witness' statements at the trial must have been assailed as having been fabricated at some point just before the trial, this was no case for applying the exception. But we think that "recent" as so used, has a relative, not an absolute meaning. It means, we think, that the defense is charging the witness not with mistake or confusion, but with making up a false story well after the event. * * * "Recently fabricated" means the same thing as fabricated to meet the exigencies of the case. * * * Judge Hand, in Di Carlo v. United States, 2 Cir., 6 F.2d 364, 366, after careful examination of authorities and reasons, stated the exception thus: "That, when the veracity of a witness is subject to challenge because of motive to fabricate, it is competent to put in evidence statements made by him consistent with what he says on the stand, made before the motive arose." We think that well describes the situation in this case, and that the father's evidence was properly received, to refute the inference urged by the defense, that Schneidewind was testifying at the trial under the influence of a motive which prompted him to falsify. Defense counsel was obviously trying to get the jury to conclude that Schneidewind was motivated by a hope, still strong at the time of trial, that he would be favorably treated because of his co-operation with the prosecutor. Of course, in this instance, Schneidewind, before the girl's father was called to the witness stand, had told the exculpating story at least twice and the damaging story at least three times, but nonetheless, it was the defense's position that he had made up the latter to save his own skin, and so the exception came into play, and it was for the jury to choose between the two versions, after a full disclosure of all the times and occasions on which each had been put forward by Schneidewind. All this accords with the view anciently expressed in Evans' Pothier on Contracts (Vol. II, 1826, pp. 251–252) that the idea of fabrication may be rebutted "by circumstances shewing that the motive upon which it is supposed to have been founded, could not have had existence at the time when the previous relation was made, and which therefore repel the supposition of the fact related being an afterthought or fabrication". * * *

The testimony of the girl's father, when received, illustrated the justice and soundness of the exception, since the father told the jury that Schneidewind, at the hospital, when the girl was near death, disclosed his own and defendant's guilt, in urging the father to dismiss defendant as his daughter's physician.

The judgment should be affirmed

LOUGHRAN, C. J., and LEWIS, CONWAY, DYE, FULD and BROMLEY, JJ., concur.

Judgment affirmed.

Chapter VI

PRIVILEGE AND CONFIDENTIALITY

A. THE ATTORNEY–CLIENT RELATIONSHIP

1. INTRODUCTION

HAZARD, ETHICS IN THE PRACTICE OF LAW
20–21, 127–135 (1978).*

[The American Bar Association Code of Professional Responsibility] deals with essentially three problems:

—Confidentiality: What matters learned by a lawyer should he treat as secret, and from whom, and under what conditions may the secrecy be lifted?
—Conflict of Interest: When and to what extent is a lawyer prohibited from acting because there is a conflict of interest between his clients or between himself and a client?
—Prohibited assistance: What kinds of things is a lawyer prohibited from doing for a client?

These are all tough problems, and not only for lawyers. What is perhaps not fully appreciated, by lawyers and laymen alike, is that similar problems arise in everyday life. If this fact were appreciated by lawyers, they might be able to perceive and to discuss the problems free of the introverted assumption that lawyers alone can appreciate their complex and stressful nature. If laymen recognized the similarity, they might regard the lawyers' ethical dilemmas with greater comprehension and perhaps even greater sympathy.

Many illustrations might be suggested from other walks of life, at work and at home, of problems involving confidentiality, conflict of interest, and prohibited assistance. A few will suffice to make the point. Thus, regarding confidentiality: What should a parent do who knows that his child has stolen something from a store? A pediatrician who discovers physical abuse of a child by its parents? A teacher who finds out that a student has been using drugs? An accountant who knows that his client is understating income for tax purposes? Regarding conflict of interest: Does a parent send a healthy child to college rather than send a sick one to the Mayo Clinic? A plant manager trim on safety systems to keep his company financially afloat? A doctor order hospitalization because medical insurance will not otherwise cover the patient? A supervisor commend

---
* Copyright, 1978 by Yale University Press.

a subordinate who may become a rival? Regarding prohibited assistance: Do you help a friend by lying to the police? Omit adverse information when asked to evaluate a former student or employee? Help sell stock that may be overvalued? Maintain the "character of a neighborhood" by not renting to a black?

If there is any peculiarity about these problems as they are confronted by lawyers, it is that a lawyer confronts them every day and is supposed to resolve them in a fashion that is compatible with a conception of his professional role. The Code of Professional Responsibility undertakes to tell him how he should do so.

* * *

No question of legal ethics is more difficult than the question whether an advocate can help suppress the truth in order to protect his client. In so far as litigation is concerned, the effect is to immobilize the law's enforcement. A lawyer can, within the limits of the law, obstruct its enforcement by advising his client to refuse to testify. At the borderland of the law, and without much risk to himself, he can go a considerable way in helping his client build a coverup. For example, he can advise the client about the consequences of preserving records or indicate to him the legal consequences of a certain line of testimony that the client might give. To the extent that such advice is given and acted upon, the effect is much the same as putting a client on the stand when it is known that his testimony will be false: The truth of the matter, which might have been discovered if the lawyer had not been involved, will less likely be discovered because he is involved. The problem is whether the benefits are worth that cost.

Paradoxically, the primary benefit of the system is often said to be the promotion of truth. For every instance in which truth is suppressed or distorted by the adversary system, it is thought there are more instances in which the system uncovers truth that otherwise would not have been uncovered. There is no practicable way to test this claim. It is worth considering, however, whether the situation would really be much better if we gave up the adversary system in favor of the interrogative system. But even if the claim were false we might want to keep the rule as it is. Under the present system, using ostensibly open competition for discovery of the truth, the law has troubles with suppression and distortion; what sort of troubles would it have if we depended on *ex officio* procedures for getting the evidence? If the truth suffers from our use of the adversary system, we ought to consider how it might suffer if we used some other system. In our political culture, the interrogative system of trial could well turn out to resemble Congressional hearings.

The real value of the adversary system thus may not be its contribution to truth but its contribution to the ideal of individual autonomy. This is the rationale underlying many rules that obscure the truth, such as the privilege against self-incrimination and the rule that private premises may not be searched without a warrant. The proposition, as applied to the adversary system, is that there is good in being able to say what one wants to say, even if it involves the commission of perjury. Stated baldly, the proposition is shocking. The norms of our society condemn lying, although it is perhaps worth noting that the biblical rule is the much narrower proposition that one should not bear false witness against a neighbor. At any rate, conventional morality does not openly recognize the value of being able to lie. Still, our commitment to truthfulness may actually go no further than homily; when it comes to serious business such as negotiation and diplomacy, most people accept the utility, the inevitability, and perhaps even the desirability of dissimulation in various forms.

Why should dissimulation not be acceptable in court? There are many cultures in which it is assumed that parties to legal conflict lie on their own behalf; no pretense is made that they should be expected to do otherwise. The common law formerly exhibited the same attitude, for it did not allow testimony from a criminal defendant or any "party in interest" in civil litigation. The present ethical dilemma in the adversary system may therefore be ultimately traceable to the abolition of the common law rules of witness disqualification.

The reform of the common law rules occurred in the nineteenth century. It was based on the proposition that few injustices would result if interested persons were allowed to testify. It was believed that with cross-examination and the good sense of the jury, the truth will out most of the time. Perhaps it is time that this premise was reexamined, for it seems evident that if the stakes involved in a lawsuit are substantial, if the outcome depends on the truth, and if the parties are authorized to give evidence as to what the truth is, the parties will distort their submissions to the maximum extent possible. The artistry and self-consciousness of the distortion will of course vary. In many cases it may be supposed that at least one party will tell the unvarnished truth, hoping if not trusting that it will be seen as such. But to require a party to choose between imprisonment or financial self-destruction on the one hand, and complete truthfulness on the other, is to impose a moral burden that may simply be too heavy. And, directly to the point of the present discussion, it imposes nearly as difficult a burden on the advocate who must advise the party in making the choice.

There is much ambivalence concerning the advocate's responsibility in this respect. The rules clearly say that, even in the defense of criminal cases, the advocate may not assist his client in committing perjury or in otherwise fabricating or suppressing evidence. In practice, lawyers often wind up violating these rules, some of them quite frequently. But they seek escapes from moral responsibility for having done so.

There are several escapes. It is said that no client is guilty until found so by a court; therefore, one cannot know what the truth is until then; therefore, one cannot conclude that a client's testimony will constitute perjury. This is pure casuistry. Of course there are doubtful situations, but there are also ones that are not doubtful. A thing is not made true or not by a court's pronouncing on it, and a lawyer can reach conclusions about an issue without having a judge tell him what to think.

Another escape is for the advocate to indicate to the client how inconvenient it would be if the evidence were such and so, and leave it to the client to do the dirty work—well illustrated in "the lecture" in *Anatomy of a Murder*.[3] Another is for the advocate to pretend that the rules governing his responsibility are different from what they are—to pretend that duty to client requires aiding him in whatever the client feels he must do to vindicate himself in court. The advocate is then absolved because he is merely an instrument.

As the situation stands, the advocate is supposed to be both the champion of his client and a gatekeeper having a duty to prevent his client from contaminating the courtroom. In principle, these responsibilities are compatible. The duty to the court simply limits the ways in which a lawyer can champion his client's cause. In practice, however, the duties have come to be in perhaps uncontrollable conflict.

* * *

If the adversary system is to be changed, it will not be a simple undertaking. The system as it exists expresses a number of strongly held beliefs and ideals. One is that justice should be free. It is this proposition that supports the rule that the loser in litigation does not have to pay the winner's expenses. From this in turn follows the contingent fee system and the lack of inhibitions on running up an opposing party's costs, with the corresponding impairment of the advocate's gatekeeper function. Another belief is that entry into the legal profession should be relatively democratic. From this proposition it follows that admission is relatively easy, levels of training uneven, and professional esprit de corps weak. From this it follows that the images of professional lawyers are fuzzy and the potential for self-policing correspondingly low. Another is that litigation should secure not only justice under law but natural and popular justice. From this it follows that litigation often has inherently political, redistributive, and sometimes subversive characteristics, which infuse not only the merits of the controversies but the way they are prosecuted or defended. The "Chicago Seven" trial is an illustration. Still another belief is the notion that militant advocacy is an especially genuine and efficacious expression of social conscience. Exemplars of this style are the relentless prosecutor, the fearless vindicator of the oppressed, the wiley strategist for the establishment. It would be better if there were a larger constituency that understood,

---

3. Traver, Anatomy of a Murder (1958).

with Judge Learned Hand, that being in litigation, whatever its outcome, can justly be compared with sickness and death.

Perhaps the problem is this: We can have a system that does not charge user fees, lets everyone play, seeks both law and common justice, and is subject to few inhibitions in style. We can also have a system in which a trial is a serious search for the truth or at least a ceremony whose essential virtue is solemnity. But we probably cannot have both. So long as the advocate in the American system is supposed to be at once a champion in forensic roughhouse and a guardian of the temple of justice, he can fulfill his responsibilities only if he combines extraordinary technical skill with an ususually disciplined sense of probity. That seems to be asking too much of any profession.

MITCHELL, THE ETHICS OF DEFENDING THE GUILTY AND DANGEROUS—NEW ANSWERS TO OLD QUESTIONS 3–5

(Unpublished manuscript of paper delivered to University of California School of Law, Berkeley, Cal., March, 1978).

By providing a rigorous defense for the factually guilty, an attorney fulfills two significant functions. First, the attorney insures that the guilty defendant (to whom our society has promised the absolute right to the full benefit of our legal process, regardless of guilt or innocence) will be treated with fairness, equanimity and human decency while in that legal process. * * * The second function is one which protects every one of us in this society. I will call this function making the "screens" work.

Our criminal justice system should be more appropriately defined as a screening system, rather than a truth-seeking one. The principal function of the criminal justice system is to actively engage in a screening process throughout our entire society. (The system also deters crime through use and threat of its sanction and teaches lessons in justice). This screening process is directed at accurately sorting out those members of the society whose deviancy has gone beyond what is considered tolerable and has passed into the area which substantive law labels as criminal. * * * The ultimate objective of this screening is to determine who is a proper subject of the criminal sanction. This screening process goes on continually at every level of the society. We all make constant judgments about, e. g., someone's unusual behavior, a window that looks pryed open, a suspicious looking stranger. Neighbor talks to neighbor and information is filtered to the police. The police in turn comb the streets night and day gathering information to help them determine whose behavior warrants being selected out from the rest. Finally, prosecutors, courts and juries are constantly sifting through those the police have selected to make final determinations regarding the most serious question of who is to be subject to the criminal sanction, including decisions regarding who is to be forcibly removed from our society or even executed.

In carrying out this screening process, however, the criminal justice system does not operate as a truth-seeking process in the scientific sense. It is weighted at trial in favor of protecting the innocent at the cost of acquitting the guilty. It is weighted on the streets in favor of protecting the individual from intrusion by the state at the cost of the more efficient method of crime control which would result if police could stop, question and search anyone they desired. In so doing, our process protects two interrelated and overlapping values (or perhaps, more accurately, two aspects of the same value, i. e., human freedom)—dignity and autonomy.

The "weighting" of the system to avoid conviction of the innocent reflects the paramount value this society places upon the dignity of the individual, as well as our concern for the value of human autonomy, a concern which makes us reluctant to allow government to enter our daily lives, either to restrict our freedom or to intrude into our privacy. The "weighting" against police intrusion similarly reflects these two interrelated values.

Despite the screening system discussed [above] most defendants never get near a trial court.

It is common wisdom that in most instances (at least in the metropolitan-urban areas of state court systems) our legal system operates as an administrative system, processing 90% of its dispositions through an "assembly-line" like plea bargaining system. The prosecutor assumes the position of the central figure in the system, while the judge assumes more of a figure-head role, rubber-stamping consummated plea bargains through the hollow incantation of the "cop out" litany. Of most significance, I believe, is that, for the most part, there are no true advocates for the defendant. In short, for most criminal defendants, our legal system has ceased in practice to be the traditional accusatorial-adversarial-judicial.

* * *

Those who are brought into the process * * * arrive there as the result of the probable cause determination of the arresting police officer and the prosecutors' discretionary decision to file charges, both of these determinations falling well below "beyond a reasonable doubt." Thus if the tendency of the institution to deny trials to all who enter it is left unchecked, many whose guilt has not been established beyond a reasonable doubt will be coerced by the institution into pleading guilty. Among these will be innocent people.

In theory, several different sources could serve as a check on this tendency and insure that the innocent are still protected. The legal system is a political institution. The general public thus could serve as a check on hasty convictions. * * * But fear of violent crime has made the public far more concerned about the conviction of the guilty than the protection of the innocent and has thus, if anything, encouraged, rather than checked the tendency of the legal institution to coerce guilty pleas. * * *

* * *

The last possible restraint on the court could come from an independent advocate who would insure that the innocent were protected by reasonable doubt and jury trials if necessary. * * *

The relationship between the defense of the guilty and the protection of the innocent in our plea bargaining system thus becomes a complex one * * *. No doubt, regardless of the dedication of the defense attorney, most defendants will still plead guilty due to strong evidence of guilt and good "deals." Yet in order to convince innocent defendants that if they refuse such "deals", there are competent attorneys who are willing to fight their cases at trial, attorneys must go to trial as much as possible. This means representing guilty as well as innocent defendants. * * *

[The author goes on to make the point that the only time the screening system is realistically tested is when the accused, who is probably himself guilty, goes to trial. As a result, the lawyer who defends the guilty is also making sure the screening system works on behalf of the great majority of defendants who are taken into the system and induced into pleading guilty.]

2. THE ATTORNEY–CLIENT PRIVILEGE

a. THE STATUTORY FRAMEWORK

RULES OF EVIDENCE FOR UNITED STATES COURTS AND MAGISTRATES

Rule 501

GENERAL RULE

Except as otherwise required by the Constitution of the United States or provided by Act of Congress or in rules prescribed by the Supreme Court pursuant to statutory authority, the privilege of a witness, person, government, State, or political subdivision thereof shall be governed by the principles of the common law as they may be interpreted by the courts of the United States in the light of reason and experience. However, in civil actions and proceedings, with respect to an element of a claim or defense as to which State law supplies the rule of decision, the privilege of a witness, person, government, State, or political subdivision thereof shall be determined in accordance with State law.

WEST'S ANNOTATED CALIFORNIA EVIDENCE CODE

CHAPTER 3. GENERAL PROVISIONS RELATING TO PRIVILEGES

§ 911. General rule as to privileges

Except as otherwise provided by statute:

(a) No person has a privilege to refuse to be a witness.

(b) No person has a privilege to refuse to disclose any matter or to refuse to produce any writing, object, or other thing.

(c) No person has a privilege that another shall not be a witness or shall not disclose any matter or shall not produce any writing, object, or other thing.

Comment. This section codifies the existing law that privileges are not recognized in the absence of statute. * * *

This is one of the few instances where the Evidence Code precludes the courts from elaborating upon the statutory scheme. Even with respect to privileges, however, the courts to a limited extent are permitted to develop the details of declared principles. * * *

§ 912. Waiver of privilege

(a) Except as otherwise provided in this section, the right of any person to claim a privilege provided by Section 954 (lawyer-client privilege), 980 (privilege for confidential marital communications), 994 (physician-patient privilege), 1014 (psychotherapist-patient privilege), 1033 (privilege of penitent), or 1034 (privilege of clergyman) is waived with respect to a communication protected by such privilege if any holder of the privilege, without coercion, has disclosed a significant part of the communication or has consented to such disclosure made by anyone. Consent to disclosure is manifested by any statement or other conduct of the holder of the privilege indicating his consent to the disclosure, including his failure to claim the privilege in any proceeding in which he has the legal standing and opportunity to claim the privilege.

(b) Where two or more persons are joint holders of a privilege provided by Section 954 (lawyer-client privilege), 994 (physician-patient privilege), or 1014 (psychotherapist-patient privilege), a waiver of the right of a particular joint holder of the privilege to claim the privilege does not affect the right of another joint holder to claim the privilege. In the case of the privilege provided by Section 980 (privilege for confidential marital communications), a waiver of the right of one spouse to claim the privilege does not affect the right of the other spouse to claim the privilege.

(c) A disclosure that is itself privileged is not a waiver of any privilege.

(d) A disclosure in confidence of a communication that is protected by a privilege provided by Section 954 (lawyer-client privilege), 994 (physician-patient privilege), or 1014 (psychotherapist-patient privilege), when such disclosure is reasonably necessary for the accomplishment of the purpose for which the lawyer, physician, or psychotherapist was consulted, is not a waiver of the privilege.

§ 913. Comment on, and inferences from, exercise of privilege

(a) If in the instant proceeding or on a prior occasion a privilege is or was exercised not to testify with respect to any matter, or to refuse to disclose or to prevent another from disclosing any matter, neither the presiding officer nor counsel may comment thereon, no presumption shall arise because of the exercise of the privilege, and the trier of fact may not draw any inference therefrom as to the credibility of the witness or as to any matter at issue in the proceeding.

(b) The court, at the request of a party who may be adversely affected because an unfavorable inference may be drawn by the jury because a privilege has been exercised, shall instruct the jury that no presumption arises because of the exercise of the privilege and that the jury may not draw any inference therefrom as to the credibility of the witness or as to any matter at issue in the proceeding.

§ 915. Disclosure of privileged information in ruling on claim of privilege

(a) Subject to subdivision (b), the presiding officer may not require disclosure of information claimed to be privileged under this division in order to rule on the claim of privilege.

(b) When a court is ruling on a claim of privilege under Article 9 (commencing with Section 1040) of Chapter 4 (official information and identity of informer) or under Section 1060 (trade secret) and is unable to do so without requiring disclosure of the information claimed to be privileged, the court may require the person from whom disclosure is sought or the person authorized to claim the privilege, or both, to disclose the information in chambers out of the presence and hearing of all persons except the person authorized to claim the privilege and such other persons as the person authorized to claim the privilege is willing to have present. If the judge determines that the information is privileged, neither he nor any other person may ever disclose, without the consent of a person authorized to permit disclosure, what was disclosed in the course of the proceedings in chambers.

§ 916. Exclusion of privileged information where persons authorized to claim privilege are not present

(a) The presiding officer, on his own motion or on the motion of any party, shall exclude information that is subject to a claim of privilege under this division if:

(1) The person from whom the information is sought is not a person authorized to claim the privilege; and

(2) There is no party to the proceeding who is a person authorized to claim the privilege.

(b) The presiding officer may not exclude information under this section if:

(1) He is otherwise instructed by a person authorized to permit disclosure; or

(2) The proponent of the evidence establishes that there is no person authorized to claim the privilege in existence.

§ 917. Presumption that certain communications are confidential

Whenever a privilege is claimed on the ground that the matter sought to be disclosed is a communication made in confidence in the course of the lawyer-client, physician-patient, psychotherapist-patient, clergyman-penitent, or husband-wife relationship, the communication is presumed to have been made in confidence and the opponent of the claim of privilege has the burden of proof to establish that the communication was not confidential.

§ 918. Effect of error in overruling claim of privilege

A party may predicate error on a ruling disallowing a claim of privilege only if he is the holder of the privilege, except that a party may predicate error on a ruling disallowing a claim of privilege by his spouse under Section 970 or 971.

§ 919. Admissibility where disclosure erroneously compelled

(a) Evidence of a statement or other disclosure of privileged information is inadmissible against a holder of the privilege if:

(1) A person authorized to claim the privilege claimed it but nevertheless disclosure erroneously was required to be made; or

(2) The presiding officer did not exclude the privileged information as required by Section 916.

(b) If a person authorized to claim the privilege claimed it, whether in the same or a prior proceeding, but nevertheless disclosure erroneously was required by the presiding officer to be made, neither the failure to refuse to disclose nor the failure to seek review of the order of the presiding officer requiring disclosure indicates consent to the disclosure or constitutes a waiver and, under these circumstances, the disclosure is one made under coercion.

ARTICLE 3. LAWYER–CLIENT PRIVILEGE

§ 950. "Lawyer"

As used in this article, "lawyer" means a person authorized, or reasonably believed by the client to be authorized, to practice law in any state or nation.

Comment. "Lawyer" is defined to include a person "reasonably believed by the client to be authorized" to practice law. Since the privilege is intended to encourage full disclosure, the client's reasonable belief that the person he is consulting is an attorney is sufficient to justify application of the privilege. * * *

There is no requirement that the lawyer be licensed to practice in a jurisdiction that recognizes the lawyer-client privilege. Legal transactions frequently cross state and national boundaries and require consultation with attorneys from many different jurisdictions. When a California resident travels outside the State and has occasion to consult a lawyer during such travel, or when a lawyer from another state or nation participates in a transaction involving a California client, the client should be entitled to assume that his communications will be given as much protection as they would be if he consulted a California lawyer in California. A client should not be forced to inquire about the jurisdictions where the lawyer is authorized to practice and whether such jurisdictions recognize the lawyer-client privilege before he may safely communicate with the lawyer.

§ 951. "Client"

As used in this article, "client" means a person who, directly or through an authorized representative, consults a lawyer for the purpose of retaining the lawyer or securing legal service or advice from him in his professional capacity, and includes an incompetent (a) who himself so consults the lawyer or (b) whose guardian or conservator so consults the lawyer in behalf of the incompetent.

§ 952. "Confidential communication between client and lawyer"

As used in this article, "confidential communication between client and lawyer" means information transmitted between a client and his lawyer in the course of that relationship and in confidence by a means which, so far as the client is aware, discloses the information to no third persons other than those who are present to further the interest of the client in the consultation or those to whom disclosure is reasonably necessary for the transmission of the information or the accomplishment of the purpose for which the lawyer is consulted, and includes a legal opinion formed and the advice given by the lawyer in the course of that relationship.

Comment. The requirement that the communication be made in the course of the lawyer-client relationship and be confidential is in accord with existing law. * * *

Confidential communications also include those made to third parties—such as the lawyer's secretary, a physician, or similar expert—for the purpose of transmitting such information to the lawyer because they are "reasonably necessary for the transmission of the information." This codifies existing law. * * *

A lawyer at times may desire to have a client reveal information to an expert consultant in order that the lawyer may adequately advise his client. The inclusion of the words "or the accomplishment of the purpose for which the lawyer is consulted" assures that these communications, too, are within the scope of the privilege. This part of the definition may change existing law. Himmelfarb v. United States, 175 F.2d 924, 938–939 (9th Cir. 1949), applying California law, held that the presence of an accountant during a lawyer-client consultation destroyed the privilege, but no California case directly in point has been found. Of course, if the expert consultant is acting merely as a conduit for communications from the client to the attorney, the doctrine of City & County of San Francisco v. Superior Court, applies and the communication would be privileged under existing law as well as under this section. * * *

The words "other than those who are present to further the interest of the client in the consultation" indicate that a communication to a lawyer is nonetheless confidential even though it is made in the presence of another person—such as a spouse, parent, business associate, or joint client—who is present to further the interest of the client in the consultation. These words refer, too, to another person and his attorney who may meet with the client and his attorney in regard to a matter of joint concern. This may change existing law, for the presence of a third person sometimes has been held to destroy the confidential character of the consultation, even where the third person was present because of his concern for the welfare of the client.

§ 954. Lawyer-client privilege

Subject to Section 912 and except as otherwise provided in this article, the client, whether or not a party, has a privilege to refuse to disclose, and to prevent another from disclosing, a confidential communication between client and lawyer if the privilege is claimed by:

(a) The holder of the privilege;

(b) A person who is authorized to claim the privilege by the holder of the privilege; or

(c) The person who was the lawyer at the time of the confidential communication, but such person may not claim the privilege if there is no holder of the privilege in existence or if he is otherwise instructed by a person authorized to permit disclosure.

* * *

Comment. Section 954 is the basic statement of the lawyer-client privilege. Exceptions to this privilege are stated in Sections 956–962.

Persons entitled to claim the privilege. The persons entitled to claim the privilege are specified in subdivisions (a), (b), and (c). See Evidence Code § 953 for the definition of "holder of the privilege."

Eavesdroppers. Under Section 954, the lawyer-client privilege can be asserted to prevent *anyone* from testifying to a confidential communication. Thus, clients are protected against the risk of disclosure by eavesdroppers and other wrongful interceptors of confidential communications between lawyer and client. * * *

Penal Code Section 653j makes evidence obtained by *electronic* eavesdropping or recording in violation of the section inadmissible in "any judicial, administrative, legislative, or other proceeding." The section also provides a criminal penalty and contains definitions and exceptions. Penal Code Section 653i makes it a felony to eavesdrop by an electronic or other device upon a conversation between a person in custody of a public officer or on public property and that person's lawyer, religious advisor, or physician.

Section 954 is consistent with Penal Code Sections 653i and 653j but provides broader protection, for it protects against disclosure of confidential communications by anyone who obtained knowledge of the communication without the client's consent. See also Evidence Code § 912 (when disclosure with client's consent constitutes a waiver of the privilege). The use of the privilege to prevent testimony by eavesdroppers and those to whom the communication was wrongfully disclosed does not, however, affect the rule that the making of the communication under circumstances where others could easily overhear it is evidence that the client did not intend the communication to be confidential. * * *

Termination of privilege. The privilege may be claimed by a person listed in Section 954, or the privileged information excluded by the presiding officer under Section 916, only if there is a holder of the privilege in existence. Hence, the privilege ceases to exist when the client's estate is finally distributed and his personal representative is discharged.

* * * Although there is good reason for maintaining the privilege while the estate is being administered—particularly if the estate is involved in litigation—there is little reason to preserve secrecy at the expense of excluding relevant evidence after the estate is wound up and the representative is discharged.

§ 955. When lawyer required to claim privilege

The lawyer who received or made a communication subject to the privilege under this article shall claim the privilege whenever he is present when the communication is sought to be disclosed and is authorized to claim the privilege under subdivision (c) of Section 954.

Comment. The obligation of the lawyer to claim the privilege on behalf of the client, unless otherwise instructed by a person authorized to permit disclosure, is consistent with Section 6068(e) of the Business and Professions Code.

§ 956. Exception: Crime or fraud

There is no privilege under this article if the services of the lawyer were sought or obtained to enable or aid anyone to commit or plan to commit a crime or a fraud.

WEST'S ANNOTATED CALIFORNIA PENAL CODE

§ 636. Eavesdropping or recording conversation between prisoner and his attorney, clergyman or physician; offense; exception

Every person, who, without permission from all parties to the conversation, eavesdrops on or records by means of an electronic or other device, a conversation, or any portion thereof, between a person who is in the physical custody of a law enforcement officer or other public officer, or who is on the property of a law enforcement agency or other public agency, and such person's attorney, religious advisor, or licensed physician, is guilty of a felony; provided, however, the provisions of this section shall not apply to any employee of a public utility engaged in the business of providing service and facilities for telephone or telegraph communications while engaged in the construction, maintenance, conduct or operation of the service or facilities of such public utility who listens in to such conversation for the limited purpose of testing or servicing such equipment.

b. CONFIDENTIALITY IN ACTION

AMSTERDAM, SEGAL & MILLER, TRIAL MANUAL 3 FOR THE DEFENSE OF CRIMINAL CASES § 80 *

Same—explaining the attorney-client privilege. It is not easy for a lawyer to convince a client to trust him when the client has never seen the lawyer before, and particularly when the lawyer is of a different race and social background from the client's. As far as the client is concerned, the lawyer is "the law," along with the cops and the judge; he has no reason to believe that the lawyer is on *his* side. His distrust will likely be greater if he is indigent and the lawyer is court-appointed, since, in his experience, things one gets for nothing are ordinarily worth nothing; and the only sure way to obtain loyalty is to buy it. In order to overcome these attitudes, it is seldom sufficient to promise the client that counsel is going to do something for him; counsel must actually *do* something for the client. This is why it is so important in building the attorney-client relationship that, when possible, counsel take early effective action that visi-

---

* Copyright 1978 by The American Law Institute. Reprinted with the permission of The American Law Institute–American Bar Association Committee on Continuing Professional Education.

bly benefits the client, such as stopping police mistreatment, getting the client released from jail, or standing up firmly for the client in front of an impatient or overbearing magistrate at preliminary arraignment. But at the preliminary interview, there is often little of immediate practical consequence that counsel can do for the client to win his confidence. Counsel can, and should, assure him that counsel's only job is to represent him. He should state clearly and forcefully, "I am *your* lawyer; my job is to represent *you*, to go to bat for *you*; and I intend to do everything that can possibly be done to help you from now on in this case." However, abstract protestations of this sort cannot be developed or repeated too much without their beginning to sound hollow; and a useful way to emphasize counsel's fidelity to the client, without sounding like counsel is trying to sell himself to the client in the manner of a used car salesman, is to find some obviously relevant, operational reason for describing counsel's role. Often the best occasion comes in connection with an explanation of the attorney-client privilege—an explanation that is independently desirable, in any event, in order to assure the client that he can tell counsel his story in complete confidence. Counsel may say something like this, for example: "Now, I am going to ask you to tell me some things about yourself, and also about this charge they have against you. Before I do, I want you to know that everything you tell me is strictly private, just between you and me. Nothing you tell me goes to the police, or to the District Attorney, or to the judge, or to anybody else. Nobody can make me tell them what you said to me, and I won't. You've probably heard about this thing that they call the attorney-client privilege. The law says that, when a person is consulting with his lawyer, what he tells his lawyer is confidential and secret between the two of them. This is because the law recognizes that the lawyer's obligation is to his client and to nobody else; that he is supposed to be one hundred per cent on his client's side; and that he is only supposed to help his client, and never do anything —or disclose any information—that might hurt the client in any way. The District Attorney is the one who is supposed to represent the government in prosecuting cases; and the judge's job is to judge the cases. But the law wants to make sure that—even if everybody else is lined up against a defendant—there is one person who is not obliged to look out for the government, but to be completely for the defendant. That is his lawyer. As your lawyer, I am completely for you. And I couldn't be completely for you if I were required to tell anybody else the things that you say to me in private. So you can trust me and tell me anything you want without worrying that I will ever pass it along to anyone else, because I won't. I can't be subpoenaed or questioned or made to talk because I am 100 per cent on your side, and my job is to work for you and only for you; and everything we talk about stays just between us. Okay?"

PEOPLE v. BELGE

Onondaga County Court, 1975.
83 Misc.2d 186, 372 N.Y.S.2d 798.

GALE, J. In the summer of 1973 Robert F. Garrow, Jr., stood charged in Hamilton County with the crime of murder. The defendant was assigned two attorneys, Frank H. Armani and Francis R. Belge. A defense of insanity had been interposed by counsel for Mr. Garrow. During the course of the discussions between Garrow and his two counsel, three other murders were admitted by Garrow, one being in Onondaga County. On or about September of 1973 Mr. Belge conducted his own investigation based upon what his client had told him and with the assistance of a friend the location of the body of Alicia Hauck was found in Oakwood Cemetery in Syracuse. Mr. Belge personally inspected the body and was satisfied, presumably, that this was the Alicia Hauck that his client had told him that he murdered.

This discovery was not disclosed to the authorities, but became public during the trial of Mr. Garrow in June of 1974, when to affirmatively establish the defense of insanity, these three other murders were brought before the jury by the defense in the Hamilton County trial. Public indignation reached the fever pitch, statements were made by the District Attorney of Onondaga County relative to the situation and he caused the Grand Jury of Onondaga County, then sitting, to conduct a thorough investigation. * * * [Attorney Belge was subsequently indicted for violation of a public health law requiring persons to report the existence of a dead body.] Defense counsel moves for a dismissal of the indictment on the grounds that a confidential, privileged communication existed between him and Mr. Garrow, which should excuse the attorney from making full disclosure to the authorities.

The National Association of Criminal Defense Lawyers, * * * succinctly state the issue in the following language: If this indictment stands, "The attorney-client privilege will be effectively destroyed. No defendant will be able to freely discuss the facts of his case with his attorney. No attorney will be able to listen to those facts without being faced with the Hobson's choice of violating the law or violating his professional code of Ethics."

Initially in England the practice of law was not recognized as a profession, and certainly some people are skeptics today. However, the practice of learned and capable men appearing before the court on behalf of a friend or an acquaintance became more and more demanding. Consequently, the King granted a privilege to certain of these men to engage in such practice. There had to be rules governing their duties. These came to be known as "Canons". The King has, in this country been substituted by a democracy, but the "Canons" are with us today, having been honed and refined over the years to meet the changes of time. Most are constantly being studied and revamped by the American Bar Association and by the bar associations of the various States. While they are, for the most part, general by definition, they can be brought to bear in a particular situation. Among those is the following, cited in United States v. Funk (84 F. Supp. 967, 968): "Confidential communications between an attorney and his client are privileged from disclosure * * * as a rule of necessity in the administration of justice."

* * *

Our system of criminal justice is an adversary system and the interests of the State are not absolute, or even paramount. "The dignity of the individual is respected to the point that even when the citizen is known by the state to have committed a heinous offense, the individual is nevertheless accorded such rights as counsel, trial by jury, due process, and the privilege against self incrimination."

* * *

The concept of the right to counsel has again been with us for a long time, but since the decision of Gideon v. Wainwright (372 U.S. 335), it has been extended more and more * * *.

The effectiveness of counsel is only as great as the confidentiality of its client-attorney relationship. If the lawyer cannot get all the facts about the case, he can only give his client half of a defense. This, of necessity, involves the client telling his attorney everything remotely connected with the crime.

Apparently, in the instant case, after analyzing all the evidence, and after hearing of the bizarre episodes in the life of their client, they decided that the only possibility of salvation was in a defense of insanity. For the client to disclose not only everything about this particular crime but also everything about other crimes which might have a bearing upon his defense, requires the strictest confidence in, and on the part of, the attorney.

When the facts of the other homicides became public, as a result of the defendant's testimony to substantiate his claim of insanity, "Members of the public were shocked at the apparent callousness of these lawyers, whose conduct was seen as typifying the unhealthy lack of concern of most lawyers with the public interest and with simple decency." A hue and cry went up from the press and other news media suggesting that the attorneys should be found guilty of such crimes as obstruction of justice or becoming an accomplice after the fact. From a layman's standpoint, this certainly was a logical conclusion. However, the Constitution of the United States of America attempts to preserve the dignity of the individual and to do that guarantees him the services of an attorney who will bring to the Bar and to the Bench every conceivable protection from the inroads of the State against such rights as are vested in the Constitution for one accused of crime * * *

* * *

* * * In the case at bar we must weigh the importance of the general privilege of confidentiality in the performance of the defendant's duties as an attorney, against the inroads of such a privilege on the fair administration of criminal justice as well as the heart tearing that went on in the victim's family by reason of their uncertainty as to the whereabouts of Alicia Hauck. In this type situation the court must balance the rights of the individual against the rights of society as a whole. There is no question but Attorney Belge's failure to bring to the attention of the authorities the whereabouts of Alicia Hauck when he first verified it, prevented bringing Garrow to the immediate bar of justice for this particular murder. This was in a sense, obstruction of justice. * * *

* * *

It is the decision of this court that Francis R. Belge conducted himself as an officer of the court with all the zeal at his command to protect the constitutional rights of his client. Both on the grounds of a privileged communication and in the interests of justice the indictment is dismissed.

CLARK v. STATE

Court of Criminal Appeals, Texas 1953.
159 Tex.Cr.R. 187, 261 S.W.2d 339.
Cert. denied 346 U.S. 855, 905, 74 S.Ct. 69(3), 217(2), 98 L.Ed. 360, 404.

MORRISON, Judge. The offense is murder; the punishment, death.

The deceased secured a divorce from appellant on March 25, 1952. That night she was killed, as she lay at home in her bed, as the result of a gunshot wound. From the mattress on her bed, as well as from the bed of her daughter, were recovered bullets which were shown by a firearms expert to have been fired by a .38 special revolver having Colt characteristics. Appellant was shown to have purchased a Colt .38 Detective Special some ten months prior to the homicide.

* * *

Marjorie Bartz, a telephone operator in the City of San Angelo, testified that at 2:49 in the morning of March 26, 1952, while on duty, she received a call from the Golden Spur Hotel; that at first she thought the person placing the call was a Mr. Cox and so made out the slip; but that she then recognized appellant's voice, scratched out the word "Cox" and wrote "Clark." She stated that appellant told her he wanted to speak to his lawyer, Jimmy Martin in Dallas, and that she placed the call to him at telephone number Victor 1942 in that city and made a record thereof, which record was admitted in evidence. Miss Bartz testified that, contrary to company rules, she listened to the entire conversation that ensued, and that it went as follows:

> The appellant: "Hello, Jimmy, I went to the extremes."
> The voice in Dallas: "What did you do?"
> The appellant: "I just went to the extremes."
> The voice in Dallas: "You got to tell me what you did before I can help."
> The appellant: "Well, I killed her."
> The voice in Dallas: "Who did you kill; the driver?"
> The appellant: "No, I killed her."
> The voice in Dallas: "Did you get rid of the weapon?"
> The appellant: "No, I still got the weapon."
> The voice in Dallas: "Get rid of the weapon and sit tight and don't talk to anyone, and I will fly down in the morning."

It was stipulated that the Dallas telephone number of appellant's attorney was Victor 1942.

* * *

We now discuss the contentions raised by appellant's able counsel in their carefully prepared brief.

* * *

Proposition (1b) is predicated upon the contention that the court erred in admitting the testimony of the telephone operator, because the conversation related was a privileged communication between appellant and his attorney.

As a predicate to a discussion of this question, we note that the telephone operator heard this conversation through an act of eavesdropping.

In 20 Am.Jur., p. 361, we find the following:

> "Evidence procured by eavesdropping, if otherwise relevant to the issue, is not to be excluded because of the manner in which it was obtained or procured * * *."

This Court has recently, in Schwartz v. State, supra, affirmed by the Supreme Court of the United States on December 15, 1952, 73 S. Ct. 232, authorized the introduction of evidence secured by means of a mechanical interception of a telephone conversation.

We now discuss the question of the privileged nature of the conversation. Wigmore on Evidence (Third Edition), Section 2326, reads as follows:

> "The law provides subjective freedom for the client by assuring him of exemption from its processes of disclosure against himself or the attorney or their agents of communication. This much, but not a whit more, is necessary for the maintenance of the privilege. Since the means of pre-

serving secrecy of communication are entirely in the client's hands, and since the privilege is a derogation from the general testimonial duty and should be strictly construed, it would be improper to extend its prohibition to third persons who obtain knowledge of the communications."

The precise question here presented does not appear to have been passed upon in this or other jurisdictions.

In Hoy v. Morris, 13 Gray 519, 79 Mass. 519, a conversation between a client and his attorney was overheard by Aldrich, who was in the adjoining room. The Court therein said:

"Aldrich was not an attorney, not in any way connected with Mr. Todd; and certainly in no situation where he was either necessary or useful to the parties to enable them to understand each other. On the contrary, he was a mere bystander, and casually overheard conversation not addressed to him nor intended for his ear, but which the client and attorney meant to have respected as private and confidential. Mr. Todd could not lawfully have revealed it. But, in consequence of a want of proper precaution, the communications between him and his client were overheard by a mere stranger. As the latter stood in no relation of confidence to either of the parties, he was clearly not within the rule of exemption from giving testimony; and he might therefore, when summoned as a witness, be compelled to testify as to what he overheard, so far as it was pertinent to the subject matter of inquiry upon the trial * * *."

In Walker v. State, 19 Tex.App. 176, we find the following:

"Mrs. Bridges was not incompetent or disqualified because she was present and heard the confessions made by defendant, even assuming that the relation of attorney and client subsisted in fact between him and Culberson."

The above holding is in conformity with our statute, Article 713, Code Cr.Proc.

"All other persons, except those enumerated in articles 708 and 714, whatever may be the relationship between the defendant and witness, are competent to testify, except that an attorney at law shall not disclose a communication made to him by his client during the existence of that relationship, nor disclose any other fact which came to the knowledge of such attorney by reason of such relationship."

Attention is also called to Russell v. State, 38 Tex.Cr.R. 590, 44 S.W. 159.

Appellant relies upon Gross v. State, 61 Tex.Cr.R. 176, 135 S.W. 373, 376, 33 L.R.A.,N.S., 477, wherein we held that a letter written by the accused to his wife remained privileged even though it had fallen into the hands of a third party. We think that such opinion is not authority herein, because therein we said:

> "There is a broad distinction between the introduction of conversations overheard by third parties occurring between husband and wife and the introduction of letters written by one to the other, as shown by practically, if not all, the authorities. It is unnecessary to take up or discuss the question as to conversations going on between husband and wife which are overheard by other parties. That question is not in the case, and it is unnecessary to discuss it. We hold that the introduction of the contents of the letter through the witness Mrs. Maud Coleman was inadmissible. It was a privileged communication under the statute, and therefore interdicted. Article 774, Code of Criminal Procedure."

And, further on the opinion, we find the following:

> "Not minimizing the same relation of client and attorney, but we do say that the relation between husband and wife is far more sacred, and to be the more strongly guarded, than that of relation between attorney and client."

We hold that the trial court properly admitted the evidence of the telephone operator.

* * *

Finding no reversible error, the judgment of the trial court is affirmed.

On Appellant's Motion for Rehearing

WOODLEY, Judge. We are favored with masterful briefs and arguments in support of appellant's motion for rehearing including amicus curiae brief by an eminent and able Texas lawyer addressed to the question of privileged communications between attorney and client.

* * *

As to the testimony of the telephone operator regarding the conversation between appellant and Mr. Martin, the conversation is set forth in full in our original opinion. Our holding as to the admissibility of the testimony of the operator is not to be considered as authority except in comparable fact situations.

For the purpose of this opinion we assume that the Dallas voice was that of Mr. Martin, appellant's attorney. If it was not appellant's attorney the conversation was not privileged.

It is in the interest of public justice that the client be able to make a full disclosure to his attorney of all facts that are material to his defense or that go to substantiate his claim. The purpose of the privilege is to encourage such disclosure of the facts. But the interests of public justice further require that no shield such as the protection afforded to communications between attorney and client shall be interposed to protect a person who takes counsel on how he can safely commit a crime.

We think this latter rule must extend to one who, having committed a crime, seeks or takes counsel as to how he shall escape arrest and punishment, such as advice regarding the destruction or disposition of the murder weapon or of the body following a murder.

One who knowing that an offense has been committed conceals the offender or aids him to evade arrest or trial becomes an accessory. The fact that the aider may be a member of the bar and the attorney for the offender will not prevent his becoming an accessory.

Art. 77, P.C. defining an accessory contains the exception "One who aids an offender in making or preparing his defense at law" is not an accessory.

The conversation as testified to by the telephone operator is not within the exception found in Art. 77, P.C. When the Dallas voice advised appellant to "get rid of the weapon" (which advice the evidence shows was followed) such aid cannot be said to constitute aid "in making or preparing his defense at law". It was aid to the perpetrator of the crime "in order that he may evade an arrest or trial."

Is such a conversation privileged as a communication between attorney and client?

If the adviser had been called to testify as to the conversation, would it not have been more appropriate for him to claim his privilege against self-incrimination rather than that the communication was privileged because it was between attorney and client?

Appellant, when he conversed with Mr. Martin, was not under arrest nor was he charged with a crime. He had just inflicted mortal wounds on his former wife and apparently had shot her daughter. Mr. Martin had acted as his attorney in the divorce suit which had been tried that day and had secured a satisfactory property settlement. Appellant called him and told him that he had gone to extremes and had killed "her", not "the driver". Mr. Martin appeared to understand these references and told appellant to get rid of "the weapon".

We are unwilling to subscribe to the theory that such counsel and advice should be privileged because of the attorney-client relationship which existed between the parties in the divorce suit. We think, on the other hand, that the conversation was admissible as not within the realm of legitimate professional counsel and employment.

The rule of public policy which calls for the privileged character of the communication between attorney and client, we think, demands that the rule be confined to the legitimate course of professional employment. It cannot consistent with the high purpose and policy supporting the rule be here applied.

The murder weapon was not found. The evidence indicates that appellant disposed of it as advised in the telephone conversation. Such advice or counsel was not such as merits protection because given by an attorney. It was not in the legitimate course of professional employment in making or preparing a defense at law.

Nothing is found in the record to indicate that appellant sought any advice from Mr. Martin other than that given in the conversation testified to by the telephone operator. We are not therefore dealing with a situation where the accused sought legitimate advice from his attorney in preparing his legal defense.

Some of the citations and quotations have been deleted from our original opinion.

We remain convinced that the appeal was properly disposed of on original submission.

Appellant's motion for rehearing is overruled.

3. THE ATTORNEY'S DUTY OF LOYALTY TO THE CLIENT

IN RE RYDER

United States District Court, E.D. Virginia, 1967.
263 F.Supp. 360.

MEMORANDUM

PER CURIAM. This proceeding was instituted to determine whether Richard R. Ryder should be removed from the roll of attorneys qualified to practice before this court. Ryder was admitted to this bar in 1953. He formerly served five years as an Assistant United States Attorney. He has an active trial practice, including both civil and criminal cases.

In proceedings of this kind the charges must be sustained by clear and convincing proof, the misconduct must be fraudulent, intentional, and the result of improper motives. * * * We conclude that these strict requirements have been satisfied. Ryder took possession of stolen money and a sawed-off shotgun, knowing that the money had been stolen and that the gun had been used in an armed robbery. He intended to retain this property pending his client's trial unless the government discovered it. He intended by his possession to destroy the chain of evidence that linked the contraband to his client and to prevent its use to establish his client's guilt.

On August 24, 1966 a man armed with a sawed-off shotgun robbed the Varina Branch of the Bank of Virginia of $7,583. Included in the currency taken were $10 bills known as "bait money," the serial numbers of which had been recorded.

On August 26, 1966, Charles Richard Cook rented safety deposit box 14 at a branch of the Richmond National Bank. Later in the day

Cook was interviewed at his home by agents of the Federal Bureau of Investigation, who obtained $348 from him. Cook telephoned Ryder, who had represented him in civil litigation. Ryder came to the house and advised the agents that he represented Cook. He said that if Cook were not to be placed under arrest, he intended to take him to his office for an interview. The agents left. Cook insisted to Ryder that he had not robbed the bank. He told Ryder that he had won the money, which the agents had taken from him, in a crap game. At this time Ryder believed Cook.

Later that afternoon Ryder telephoned one of the agents and asked whether any of the bills obtained from Cook had been identified as a part of the money taken in the bank robbery. The agent told him that some bills had been identified. Ryder made inquiries about the number of bills taken and their denominations. The agent declined to give him specific information but indicated that several of the bills were recorded as bait money.

The next morning, Saturday, August 27, 1966, Ryder conferred with Cook again. He urged Cook to tell the truth, and Cook answered that a man, whose name he would not divulge, offered him $500 on the day of the robbery to put a package in a bank lockbox. Ryder did not believe this story. Ryder told Cook that if the government could trace the money in the box to him, it would be almost conclusive evidence of his guilt. He knew that Cook was under surveillance and he suspected that Cook might try to dispose of the money.

That afternoon Ryder telephoned a former officer of the Richmond Bar Association to discuss his course of action. He had known this attorney for many years and respected his judgment. The lawyer was at home and had no library available to him when Ryder telephoned. In their casual conversation Ryder told what he knew about the case, omitting names. He explained that he thought he would take the money from Cook's safety deposit box and place it in a box in his own name. This, he believed, would prevent Cook from attempting to dispose of the money. The lawyers thought that eventually F.B.I. agents would locate the money and that since it was in Ryder's possession, he could claim a privilege and thus effectively exclude it from evidence. This would prevent the government from linking Ryder's client with the bait money and would also destroy any presumption of guilt that might exist arising out of the client's exclusive possession of the evidence.

Ryder testified:

"I had sense enough to know, one, at that time that apparently the F.B.I. did have the serial numbers on the bills. I had sense enough to know, from many, many years of experience in this court and in working with the F.B.I. and, in fact, in directing the F.B.I. on some occasions, to know that eventually the bank—that the F.B.I. would find that money if I left that money in the bank. There was no doubt in my mind that eventually they would find it. The only thing I could think of to do was to get the money out of Mr. Cook's possession. * * * [T]he idea was that I assumed that if anybody tried to go into a safety deposit box in my name, the bank officials would notify me and that I would get an opportunity to come in this court and argue a question of whether or not they could use that money as evidence."

The lawyers discussed and rejected alternatives, including having a third party get the money. At the conclusion of the conversation Ryder was advised, "Don't do it surreptitiously and to be sure that you let your client know that it is going back to the rightful owners."

On Monday morning Ryder asked Cook to come by his office. He prepared a power of attorney, which Cook signed:

"KNOW YOU ALL MEN BY THESE PRESENTS, that I, CHARLES RICHARD COOK do hereby make, constitute and appoint, R. R. RYDER as my Attorney at Law and in fact and do authorize my said Attorney to enter a safety deposit box rented by me at the Richmond National Bank and Trust Company, 2604 Hull Street, Richmond, Virginia, said box requiring Mosler Key Number 30 to open the same and I further authorize the said Attorney to remove the contents of the said box and so dispose of the said contents as he sees fit and I direct the officials of the said bank to cooperate with my said attorney towards the accomplishment of this my stated purpose."

Ryder did not follow the advice he had received on Saturday. He did not let his client know the money was going back to the rightful owners. He testified about his omission:

"I prepared it myself and told Mr. Cook to sign it. In the power of attorney, I did not specifically say that Mr. Cook authorized me to deliver that money to the appropriate authorities at any time because for a number of reasons. One, in representing a man under these circumstances, you've got to keep the man's confidence, but I also put in that power of attorney that Mr. Cook authorized me to dispose of that money as I saw fit, and the reason for that being that I was going to turn the money over to the proper authorities at whatever time I deemed that it wouldn't hurt Mr. Cook."

Ryder took the power of attorney which Cook had signed to the Richmond National Bank. He rented box 13 in his name with his office address, presented the power of attorney, entered Cook's box, took both boxes into a booth, where he found a bag of money and a sawed-off shotgun in Cook's box. The box also contained miscellaneous items which are not pertinent to this proceeding. He transferred the contents of Cook's box to his own and returned the boxes to the vault. He left the bank, and neither he nor Cook returned.

Ryder testified that he had some slight hesitation about the propriety of what he was doing. Within a half-hour after he left the bank, he talked to a retired judge and distinguished professor of law. He told this person that he wanted to discuss something in confidence. Ryder then stated that he represented a man suspected of bank robbery. The judge recalled the main part of the conversation:

> " * * * And that he had received from this client, under a power of attorney, a sum [of] money which he, Mr. Ryder, suspected was proceeds of the robbery, although he didn't know it, but he had a suspicion that it was; that he had placed this money in a safety deposit vault at a bank; that he had received it with the intention of returning it to the rightful owner after the case against his client had been finally disposed of one way or the other; that he considered that he had received it under the privilege of attorney and client and that he wanted responsible people in the community to know of that fact and that he was telling me in confidence of that as one of these people that he wanted to know of it.
>
> "Q. Did he say anything to you about a sawed-off shotgun?
> A. I don't recall. If Mr. Ryder says he did, I would not deny it, but I do not recall it, because the—my main attention in what he was saying was certainly drawn to the fact that the money was involved, but I just cannot answer the question emphatically, but if Mr. Ryder says he told me, why, I certainly wouldn't deny it."

Ryder testified that he told about the shotgun. The judge also testified that Ryder certainly would not have been under the impression that he—the judge—thought that he was guilty of unethical conduct.

The same day Ryder also talked with other prominent persons in Richmond—a judge of a court of record and an attorney for the Commonwealth. Again, he stated that what he intended to say was confidential. He related the circumstances and was advised that a lawyer could not receive the property and if he had received it he could not retain possession of it.

On September 7, 1966 Cook was indicted for robbing the Varina Branch of the Bank of Virginia. A bench warrant was issued and the next day Ryder represented Cook at a bond hearing. Cook was identified as the robber by employees of the bank. He was released on bond. Cook was arraigned on a plea of not guilty on September 9, 1966.

On September 12, 1966 F.B.I. agents procured search warrants for Cook's and Ryder's safety deposit boxes in the Richmond National Bank. They found Cook's box empty. In Ryder's box they discovered $5,920 of the $7,583 taken in the bank robbery and the sawed-off shotgun used in the robbery.

On September 23, 1966 Ryder filed a motion to suppress the money obtained from Cook by the agents on August 26, 1966. The motion did not involve items taken from Ryder's safety deposit box. The motion came on to be heard October 6, 1966. Ryder called Cook as a witness for examination on matters limited to the motion to suppress. The court called to Ryder's attention papers pertaining to the search of the safety deposit boxes. Ryder moved for a continuance, stating that he intended to file a motion with respect to the seizure of the contents of the lockbox.

On October 14, 1966 the three judges of this court removed Ryder as an attorney for Cook; suspended him from practice before the court until further order; referred the matter to the United States Attorney, who was requested to file charges within five days; set the matter for hearing November 11, 1966; and granted Ryder leave to move for vacation or modification of its order pending hearing.

The United States Attorney charged Ryder with violations of Canons 15 and 32 of the Canons of Professional Ethics of the Virginia State Bar. Ryder did not move for vacation or modification of the order, and the case was heard as scheduled by the court en banc. After the transcript was prepared and the case briefed, the court heard the argument of counsel on December 27, 1966.

At the outset, we reject the suggestion that Ryder did not know the money which he transferred from Cook's box to his was stolen. We find that on August 29 when Ryder opened Cook's box and saw a bag of money and a sawed-off shotgun, he then knew Cook was involved in the bank robbery and that the money was stolen. The evidence clearly establishes this. Ryder knew that the man who had robbed the bank used a sawed-off shotgun. He disbelieved Cook's story about the source of the money in the lockbox. He knew that some of the bills in Cook's possession were bait money.

* * *

We also find that Ryder was not motivated solely by certain expectation the government would discover the contents of his lockbox. He believed discovery was probable. In this event he intended to argue to the court that the contents of his box could not be revealed, and even if the contents were identified, his possession made the stolen money and the shotgun inadmissible against his client. He also recognized that discovery was not inevitable. His intention in this event, we find, was to assist Cook by keeping the stolen money and the shotgun concealed in his lockbox until after the trial. His conversations, and the secrecy he enjoined, immediately after he put the money and the gun in his box, show that he realized the government might not find the property.

We accept his statement that he intended eventually to return the money to its rightful owner, but we pause to say that no attorney should ever place himself in such a position. Matters involving the possible termination of an attorney-client relationship, or possible subsequent proceedings in the event of an acquittal, are too delicate to permit such a practice.

We reject the argument that Ryder's conduct was no more than the exercise of the attorney-client privilege. The fact that Cook had not been arrested or indicted at the time Ryder took possession of the gun and money is immaterial. Cook was Ryder's client and was entitled to the protection of the lawyer-client privilege. Continental Oil Co. v. United States, 330 F.2d 347 (9th Cir. 1964).

Regardless of Cook's status, however, Ryder's conduct was not encompassed by the attorney-client privilege. * * *

It was Ryder, not his client, who took the initiative in transferring the incriminating possession of the stolen money and the shotgun from Cook. Ryder's conduct went far beyond the receipt and retention of a confidential communication from his client. Counsel for Ryder conceded, at the time of argument, that the acts of Ryder were not within the attorney-client privilege.

* * *

Ryder, an experienced criminal attorney, recognized and acted upon the fact that the gun and money were subject to seizure while in the possession of Cook.

In Clark v. United States, * * * Mr. Justice Cardozo expressed a dictum, which is apt to the aid Ryder gave Cook:

> "We turn to the precedents in the search for an analogy, and the search is not in vain. There is a privilege protecting communications between attorney and client. The privilege takes flight if the relation is abused. A client who consults an attorney for advice that will serve him in the commission of a fraud will have no help from the law. He must let the truth be told."

* * *

We conclude that Ryder violated Canons 15 and 32. His conduct is not sanctioned by Canons 5 or 37 [of the American Bar Association Canons of Professional Ethics].

* * *

> "5. *The Defense or Prosecution of Those Accused of Crime.* It is the right of the lawyer to undertake the defense of a person accused of crime, regardless of his personal opinion as to the guilt of the accused; otherwise innocent persons, victims only of suspicious circumstances, might be

denied proper defense. Having undertaken such defense, the lawyer is bound by all fair and honorable means, to present every defense that the law of the land permits, to the end that no person may be deprived of life or liberty, but by due process of law.

"The primary duty of a lawyer engaged in public prosecution is not to convict, but to see that justice is done. The suppression of facts or the secreting of witnesses capable of establishing the innocence of the accused is highly reprehensible.

* * *

"15. *How Far a Lawyer May Go in Supporting a Client's Cause.* Nothing operates more certainly to create or to foster popular prejudice against lawyers as a class and to deprive the profession of that full measure of public esteem and confidence which belongs to the proper discharge of its duties than does the false claim, often set up the unscrupulous in defense of questionable transactions, that it is the duty of the lawyer to do whatever may enable him to succeed in winning his client's cause.

"It is improper for a lawyer to assert in argument his personal belief in his client's innocence or in the justice of his cause.

* * *

"32. *The Lawyer's Duty In Its Last Analysis.* No client, corporate or individual, however powerful, nor any cause, civil or political, however important, is entitled to receive, nor should any lawyer render any service or advice involving disloyalty to the law whose ministers we are, or disrespect of the judicial office, which we are bound to uphold, or corruption of any person or persons exercising a public office or private trust, or deception or betrayal of the public. When rendering any such improper service or advice, the lawyer invites and merits stern and just condemnation. Correspondingly, he advances the honor of his profession and the best interests of his client when he renders service or gives advice tending to impress upon the client and his undertaking exact compliance with the strictest principles of moral law. He must also observe and advise his client to observe the statute law, though until a statute shall have been construed and interpreted by competent adjudication, he is free and is entitled to advise as to its validity and as to what he conscientiously believes to be its just meaning and extent. But above all a lawyer will find his highest honor in a deserved reputation for fidelity to private trust and to public duty, as an honest man and as a patriotic and loyal citizen.

* * *

"37. *Confidence of a Client.* It is the duty of a lawyer to preserve his client's confidences. This duty outlasts the lawyer's employment, and extends as well to his employees; and neither of them should accept employment which involves or may involve the disclosure or use of these confidences, either for the private advantage of the lawyer or his employees or to the disadvantage of the client, without his knowledge and consent, and even though there are other available sources of such information. A lawyer should not continue employment when he discovers that this obligation prevents the performance of his full duty to his former or to his new client.

The money in Cook's box belonged to the Bank of Virginia. The law did not authorize Cook to conceal this money or withhold it from the bank. His larceny was a continuing offense. Cook had no title or property interest in the money that he lawfully could pass to Ryder. * * * No canon of ethics or law permitted Ryder to conceal from the Bank of Virginia its money to gain his client's acquittal.

Cook's possession of the sawed-off shotgun was illegal. 26 U.S.C. § 5851. Ryder could not lawfully receive the gun from Cook to assist Cook to avoid conviction of robbery. Cook had never mentioned the shotgun to Ryder. When Ryder discovered it in Cook's box, he took possession of it to hinder the government in the prosecution of its case, and he intended not to reveal it pending trial unless the government discovered it and a court compelled its production. No statute or canon of ethics authorized Ryder to take possession of the gun for this purpose.

Canon 15 states in part:

"* * * [T]he great trust of the lawyer is to be performed within and not without the bounds of law. The office of attorney does not permit, much less does it demand of him for any client, violation of law or any manner of fraud or chicane. He must obey his own conscience and not that of his client."

In helping Cook to conceal the shotgun and stolen money, Ryder acted without the bounds of law. He allowed the office of attorney to be used in violation of law. The scheme which he devised was a deceptive, legalistic subterfuge—rightfully denounced by the canon as chicane.

Ryder also violated Canon 32. He rendered Cook a service involving deception and disloyalty to the law. He intended that his actions should remove from Cook exclusive possession of stolen money, and thus destroy an evidentiary presumption. His service in taking possession of the shotgun and money, with the intention of retaining them until after the trial, unless discovered by the government merits the "stern and just condemnation" the canon prescribes.

* * *

Ryder's testimony that he intended to have the court rule on the admissibility of the evidence and the extent of the lawyer-client privilege does not afford justification for his action. He intended to do this only if the government discovered the shotgun and stolen money in his lockbox. If the government did not discover it, he had no intention of submitting any legal question about it to the court. If there were no discovery, he would continue to conceal the shotgun and money for Cook's benefit pending trial.

Ryder's action is not justified because he thought he was acting in the best interests of his client. To allow the individual lawyer's belief to determine the standards of professional conduct will in time reduce the ethics of the profession to the practices of the most unscrupulous. * * *

There is much to be said, however, for mitigation of the discipline to be imposed. Ryder intended to return the bank's money after his client was tried. He consulted reputable persons before and after he placed the property in his lockbox, although he did not precisely follow their advice. Were it not for these facts, we would deem proper his permanent exclusion from practice before this court. In view of the mitigating circumstances, he will be suspended from practice in this court for eighteen months effective October 14, 1966.

* * *

So ordered.

AN EXCHANGE OF LETTERS

The following correspondence is printed with the permission of the authors.

Charles Flynn
825 W. 8th
Anchorage, Alaska 99501

Dear Charles:

After conferring most recently on conference call with * * * , I have decided I would like to take them and you up on your offer to get an informal consensus from two members of the Ethics Committee. I understand you and * * * agree to send up your thoughts if I would submit the problem in the form of a hypothetical. So, here it is:

> Defendant is arrested, charged with robbing a bank. The teller was held at gun point, bound with tape to a red bandana, while the safe was blown with plastic explosives.

Defendant tells me he is innocent—wasn't there. He can't get out of jail because of high bail. While defendant is in jail a friend comes to town and with defendant's consent occupies his trailer.

About a month after he is bound over by the grand jury and while he is still in jail, Defendant authorizes his friend to "clean out" the car in his driveway.

In the car, friend finds the following:

(1) a set of roller skates

(2) a detailed floor plan of the bank robbed

(3) a list of "things to take with me", including roller skates, plastic explosives, and "tape and red bandana to tie teller"

(4) receipt for purchase of plastic explosives dated two days before robbery took place

Friend, without asking defendant's permission or disclosing to him his intentions, calls me, and turns over the above. I take possession of the writings.

All of the above were documents in handwriting of defendant. I approached defendant and asked him if he wrote them, he admitted it, however explained they were written "after I read of the bank robbery—I was fantasizing how I *would* have done it, if it were me". I, as his attorney cannot, in good faith, say I believe him.

QUESTIONS:

(1) Do I have an ethical obligation to turn over the material—or part of it, to the District Attorney or police? (If so, should I withdraw from the case?)

(2) If I keep the material, should I keep it in my personal possession or return it to the car where it was found?

(a) see A.S. 11.30.315

(b) also note; car could be repossessed soon

Thanks for your work on this. I know you have a considerable time investment already Charles. If you and * * * could get your opinion off to me as soon as possible, I would appreciate it—especially if you determine I'll have to get off the case, and if he must get a new attorney he'll need all the time he can get.

Very truly yours,

STEPHEN R. CLINE
Ass't Public Defender

See also ABA Opinion 1057.

July 23, 1975

Stephen R. Cline
Assistant Public Defender
State of Alaska
Public Defender Agency
950 Cowles Street, Room 120
Fairbanks, Alaska 99701

Re: Ethics Committee
    Our File A–1945

Dear Mr. Cline:

The Committee has considered the question posed in your letter of July 11, 1975, and has formulated an opinion as to your present ethically-required course of conduct.

I wish to stress, at the beginning, that this letter represents the opinion of the Ethics Committee solely, and has not been approved by the Board of Governors of the Alaska Bar Association, as is normally the case with our opinions. Likewise, our consideration and opinion is based solely upon the ethical requirements which may be imposed upon you as an attorney. You are also, of course, a citizen, and subject to the law in the same manner and to the same extent as other citizens. As you suggest in your letter, AS 11.30.315 may arguably impose upon you some duty with respect to the physical evidence in your possession. The Committee has taken the statute into consideration, but obviously can render no definitive opinion as to its applicability, or the applicability of other civil and criminal law of the State of Alaska. The course of conduct outlined in this letter is based upon ethical considerations, but if a different course of action is required by the statute, your observance of the statutory requirement would also be ethically proper. See DR4–101(c)(2).

It is your duty under Canon 4 of the Code of Professional Responsibility to preserve the confidences and secrets of a client. As DR4–101(c) points out, you may ethically reveal confidences or secrets of a client when required by law, but otherwise, such revelation of confidences or secrets is prohibited. As EC4–4 properly points out, this duty to safeguard the confidences and secrets of a client is broader than the attorney/client evidentiary privilege, and "* * * exists without regard to the nature or source of information or the fact that others share the knowledge." Thus, it seems clear to us that you are ethically obligated not to reveal the existence of the physical evidence which has come into your possession, unless required to do so by statute.

We have also considered informal opinion # 1057 of the American Bar Association Committee on Ethics, and find the analysis therein persuasive. The American Bar Association has advised that when a client, or one acting on behalf of a client, presents evidence of the type you have described to us to the attorney, the attorney should decline to take possession of it and should advise the client with respect to his obligations regarding the evidence under relevant state law. If the client then declines to follow the course that he is legally obligated to follow, the attorney should either decline employment or withdraw from employment previously accepted. In our opinion, this is the correct balancing of the interests of society, the attorney's duty to preserve the confidences and secrets of a client.

Therefore, in the situation you have posed, it is our opinion that you are ethically required to contact the "friend" who tendered the evidence to you, return it to his possession, and advise him in the clearest possible terms as to his obligations and potential liabilities with respect to that physical evidence. This is done to re-create, as nearly as possible, the status quo ante.

If, after returning the physical evidence to the friend, you know, or it becomes obvious, that the physical evidence has been destroyed or concealed, we believe it is your ethical obligation, pursuant to DR7–102 and DR2–110, to withdraw from representation of the accused.

Finally, the Committee is concerned that the situation posed in your letter of July 11, 1975, or situations substantially similar and raising substantially the same issues, may arise with some frequency in the defense of those accused of crime. It is the Committee's view that attorneys should not be used, even temporarily, as a repository for the physical evidence of a crime. We therefore believe that it would be highly desirable, from an ethical standpoint, if yourself, Mr. Shortell, and the agency in general, were to formulate an office policy with respect to physical evidence such as that you have described in your letter, consistent with the Code of Professional Responsibility and the opinions of the various committees interpreting it.

Very truly yours,

ETHICS COMMITTEE OF THE
ALASKA BAR ASSOCIATION

By Charles P. Flynn, Chairman

NOTE

In Morrell v. State, 575 P.2d 1200 (Alaska, 1978), the Alaska Supreme Court found an affirmative duty requiring lawyers to turn over incriminating physical evidence in their possession, especially where the evidence comes from third parties. The case seems to be the culmination of the actual case involving public defender Stephen Cline discussed in the above exchange of letters. Mr. Cline, however, seems to have changed the facts in his letters sufficiently to disguise the identity of his client, in accordance with his duty of loyalty.

B. MISCELLANEOUS PRIVILEGES

1. THE MARITAL PRIVILEGES

a. THE "SPOUSAL INCAPACITY"

WEST'S ANNOTATED CALIFORNIA EVIDENCE CODE

§ 970. Privilege not to testify against spouse

Except as otherwise provided by statute, a married person has a privilege not to testify against his spouse in any proceeding.

Comment. Under this article, a married person has two privileges: (1) a privilege not to testify against his spouse in any proceeding (Section 970) and (2) a privilege not to be called as a witness in any proceeding to which his spouse is a party (Section 971).

The privileges under this article are not as broad as the privilege provided by existing law. Under existing law, a married person has a privilege to prevent his spouse from testifying against him, but only the witness spouse has a privilege under this article. Under the existing law, a married person may refuse to testify *for* the other spouse, but no such privilege exists under this article. * * *

The rationale of the privilege provided by Section 970 not to testify against one's spouse is that such testimony would seriously disturb or disrupt the marital relationship. Society stands to lose more from such disruption than it stands to gain from the testimony which would be available if the privilege did not exist. * * *

§ 971. Privilege not to be called as a witness against spouse

Except as otherwise provided by statute, a married person whose spouse is a party to a proceeding has a privilege not to be called as a witness by an adverse party to that proceeding without the prior express consent of the spouse having the privilege under this section unless the party calling the spouse does so in good faith without knowledge of the marital relationship.

Comment. The privilege of a married person not to be called as a witness against his spouse is somewhat similar to the privilege given the defendant in a criminal case not to be called as a witness (Section 930). This privilege is necessary to avoid the prejudicial effect, for example, of the prosecution's calling the defendant's wife as a witness, thus forcing her to object before the jury. The privilege not to be called as a witness does not apply, however, in a proceeding where the other spouse is not a party. Thus, a married person may be called as a witness in a grand jury proceeding because his spouse is not a party to that proceeding, but the witness in the grand jury proceeding may claim the privilege under Section 970 to refuse to answer a question that would compel him to testify *against* his spouse.

§ 972. When privilege not applicable

A married person does not have a privilege under this article in:

(a) A proceeding brought by or on behalf of one spouse against the other spouse.

(b) A proceeding to commit or otherwise place his spouse or his spouse's property, or both, under the control of another because of the spouse's alleged mental or physical condition.

(c) A proceeding brought by or on behalf of a spouse to establish his competence.

(d) A proceeding under the Juvenile Court Law, Chapter 2 (commencing with Section 500) of Part 1 of Division 2 of the Welfare and Institutions Code.

(e) A criminal proceeding in which one spouse is charged with:

(1) A crime against the person or property of the other spouse or of a child of either, whether committed before or during marriage.

(2) A crime against the person or property of a third person committed in the course of committing a crime against the person or property of the other spouse, whether committed before or during marriage.

(3) Bigamy.

(4) A crime defined by Section 270 or 270a of the Penal Code.

§ 973. Waiver of privilege

(a) Unless erroneously compelled to do so, a married person who testifies in a proceeding to which his spouse is a party, or who testifies against his spouse in any proceeding, does not have a privilege under this article in the proceeding in which such testimony is given.

* * *

Comment. Section 973 contains special waiver provisions for the privileges provided by this article.

Subdivision (a). Under subdivision (a), a married person who testifies in a proceeding to which his spouse is *a party* waives both privileges provided for in this article. Thus, for example, a married person cannot call his spouse as a witness to give favorable testimony and have that spouse invoke the privilege provided in Section 970 to keep from testifying on cross-examination to unfavorable matters; nor can a married person testify for an adverse party as to particular matters and then invoke the privilege not to testify against his spouse as to other matters.

In any proceeding where a married person's spouse is *not a party*, the privilege not to be called as a witness is not available, and a married person may testify like any other witness without waiving the privilege provided under Section 970 so long as he does not *testify against* his spouse. However, under subdivision (a), the privilege not to testify against his spouse in that proceeding is waived as to all matters if he *testifies against* his spouse as to any matter.

The word "proceeding" is defined in Section 901 to include any action, civil or criminal. Hence, the privilege is waived for all purposes in an action if the spouse entitled to claim the privilege testifies at any time during the action. For example, if a civil action involves issues being separately tried, a wife whose husband is a party to the litigation may not testify for her husband at one trial and invoke the privilege in order to avoid testifying against him at a separate trial of a different issue. Nor may a wife testify against her husband at a preliminary hearing of a criminal action and refuse to testify against him at the trial.

WYATT v. UNITED STATES

Supreme Court of the United States, 1960.
362 U.S. 525, 80 S.Ct. 901, 4 L.Ed.2d 931.

Mr. Justice HARLAN delivered the opinion of the Court.

Petitioner was tried and convicted of knowingly transporting a woman in interstate commerce for the purpose of prostitution, in violation of the White Slave Traffic Act * * *. At the trial, the woman, who had since the date of the offense married the petitioner, was ordered, over her objection and that of the petitioner, to testify on behalf of the prosecution. The Court of Appeals, on appeal from a judgment of conviction, affirmed the ruling of the District Court. As the case presented significant issues concerning the scope and nature of the privilege against adverse spousal testimony, treated last Term in Hawkins v. United States, we granted certiorari. We affirm the judgment.

First. Our decision in Hawkins established, for the federal courts, the continued validity of the common-law rule of evidence ordinarily permitting a party to exclude the adverse testimony of his or her spouse. However, as that case expressly acknowledged, the common law has long recognized an exception in the case of certain kinds of offenses committed by the party against his spouse. * * * Exploration of the precise breadth of this exception, a matter of some uncertainty, * * * can await a case where it is necessary. For present purposes it is enough to note that every Court of Appeals which has considered the specific question now holds that the exception, and not the rule, applies to a Mann Act prosecution, where the defendant's wife was the victim of the offense. Such unanimity with respect to a rule of evidence lends weighty credentials to that view.

While this Court has never before decided the question, we now unhesitatingly approve the rule followed in five different Circuits. We need not embark upon an extended consideration of the asserted bases for the spousal privilege * * * and an appraisal of the applicability of each here, id., § 2239, for it cannot be seriously argued that one who has committed this "shameless offense against wifehood," should be permitted to prevent his wife from testifying to the crime by invoking an interest founded on the marital relation or the desire of the law to protect it. Petitioner's attempt to prevent his wife from testifying, by invoking an asserted privilege of his own, was properly rejected.

Second. The witness-wife, however, did not testify willingly, but objected to being questioned by the prosecution, and gave evidence only upon the ruling of the District Court denying her claimed privilege not to testify. We therefore consider the correctness of that ruling.

The United States argues that, once having held, as we do, that in such a case as this the petitioner's wife could not be prevented from testifying voluntarily, Hawkins establishes that she may be compelled to testify. For, it is said, that case specifically rejected any distinction between voluntary and compelled testimony. * * * This argument fails to take account of the setting of our decision in Hawkins. To say that a witness-spouse may be prevented from testifying voluntarily simply means that the *party* has a privilege to exclude the testimony; when, on the other hand, the spouse may not be compelled to testify against her will, it is the *witness* who is accorded a privilege. In Hawkins, the Government took the position that the spousal privilege should be that of the witness, and not that of the party, so that while the wife could decline to testify, she could not be prevented from giving evidence if she elected not to claim a privilege which, it was said, belonged to her alone. * * * In declining to hold that the party had no privilege, we manifestly did not thereby repudiate the privilege of the witness.

While the question has not often arisen, it has apparently been generally assumed that the privilege resided in the witness as well as in the party. Hawkins referred to "a rule which bars the testimony of one spouse against the other unless *both* consent," * * *. In its Hawkins brief, the Government, while calling for the abolition of the party's privilege, urged that the common-law development could be explained, and its policies fully vindicated, by recognition of the privilege of the witness. * * * At least some of the bases of the party's privilege are in reason applicable to that of the witness. As Wigmore puts it, op. cit., supra, at p. 264: "[W]hile the defendant-husband is entitled to be protected against condemnation through the wife's testimony, the witness-wife is also entitled to be protected against becoming the instrument of that condemnation,—the sentiment in each case being equal in degree and yet different in quality." In light of these considerations, we decline to accept the view that the privilege is that of the party alone.

Third. Neither can we hold that, whenever the privilege is unavailable to the party, it is *ipso facto* lost to the witness as well. It is a question in each case, or in each category of cases, whether, in light of the reason which has led to a refusal to recognize the party's privilege, the witness should be held compellable. Certainly, we would not be justified in laying down a general rule that both privileges stand or fall together. We turn instead to the particular situation at bar.

Where a man has prostituted his own wife, he has committed an offense against both her and the marital relation, and we have today affirmed the exception disabling him from excluding her testimony against him. It is suggested, however, that this exception has no application to the witness-wife when she chooses to remain silent. The exception to the party's privilege, it is said, rests on the necessity of preventing the defendant from sealing his wife's lips by his own unlawful act, * * * and it is argued that where the wife has chosen not to "become the instrument" of her husband's downfall, it is her own privilege which is in question, and the reasons for according it to her in the first place are fully applicable.

We must view this position in light of the congressional judgment and policy embodied in the Mann Act. "A primary purpose of the Mann Act was to protect women who were weak from men who were bad." * * * It was in response to shocking revelations of subjugation of women too weak to resist that Congress acted. As the legislative history discloses, the Act reflects the supposition that the women with whom it sought to deal often had no independent will of their own, and embodies, in effect, the view that they must be protected against themselves. * * * It is not for us to re-examine the basis of that supposition.

Applying the legislative judgment underlying the Act, we are led to hold it not an allowable choice for a prostituted witness-wife "voluntarily" to decide to protect her husband by declining to testify against him. For if a defendant can induce a woman, against her "will," to enter a life of prostitution for his benefit—and the Act rests on the view that he can—by the same token it should be considered that he can, at least as easily, persuade one who has already fallen victim to his influence that she must also protect him. To make matters turn upon *ad hoc* inquiries into the actual state of mind of particular women, thereby encumbering Mann Act trials with a collateral issue of the greatest subtlety, is hardly an acceptable solution.

Fourth. What we have already said likewise governs the disposition of the petitioner's reliance on the fact that his marriage took place after the commission of the offense. Again, we deal here only with a Mann Act prosecution, and intimate no view on the applicability of the privilege of either a party or a witness similarly circumstanced in other situations. The legislative assumption of lack of independent will applies as fully here. As the petitioner by his power over the witness could, as we have considered should be assumed, have secured her promise not to testify, so, it should be assumed, could he have induced her to go through a marriage ceremony with him, perhaps "in contemplation of evading justice by reason of the very rule which is now sought to be invoked." United States v. Williams, D.C., 55 F.Supp. 375, 380.

The ruling of the District Court was correctly upheld by the Court of Appeals.

Affirmed.

[Dissents omitted.]

b. THE PRIVILEGE FOR CONFIDENTIAL MARITAL COMMUNICATIONS

WEST'S ANNOTATED CALIFORNIA EVIDENCE CODE

§ 980. Privilege for confidential marital communications

Subject to Section 912 and except as otherwise provided in this article, a spouse (or his guardian or conservator when he has a guardian or conservator), whether or not a party, has a privilege during the marital relationship and afterwards to refuse to disclose, and to prevent another from disclosing, a communication if he claims the privilege and the communication was made in confidence between him and the other spouse while they were husband and wife.

Comment. Section 980 is the basic statement of the privilege for confidential marital communications. Exceptions to this privilege are stated in Sections 981–987.

Who can claim the privilege. Under Section 980, both spouses are the holders of the privilege and either spouse may claim it. Under existing law, the privilege *may* belong only to the nontestifying spouse inasmuch as Code of Civil Procedure Section 1881(1), superseded by the Evidence Code, provides: "[N]or can either * * * be, *without the consent of the other*, examined as to any communication made by one to the other during the marriage." (Emphasis added.) It is likely, however, that Section 1881(1) would be construed to grant the privilege to both spouses.

A guardian of an incompetent spouse may claim the privilege on behalf of that spouse. However, when a spouse is dead, no one can claim the privilege for him; the privilege, if it is to be claimed at all, can be claimed only by or on behalf of the surviving spouse.

Termination of marriage. The privilege may be claimed as to confidential communications made during a marriage even though the marriage has been terminated at the time the privilege is claimed. This states existing law. * * * Free and open communication between spouses would be unduly inhibited if one of the spouses could be compelled to testify as to the nature of such communications after the termination of the marriage.

Eavesdroppers. The privilege may be asserted to prevent testimony by anyone, including eavesdroppers. To a limited extent, this constitutes a change in California law. See the *Comment* to Evidence Code § 954. Section 980 also changes the existing law which permits a third party, to whom one of the spouses had revealed a confidential communication, to testify concerning it. Under Section 912, such conduct would constitute a waiver of the privilege only as to the spouse who makes the disclosure.

§ 981. Exception: Crime or fraud

There is no privilege under this article if the communication was made, in whole or in part, to enable or aid anyone to commit or plan to commit a crime or a fraud.

Comment. California recognizes this as an exception to the lawyer-client privilege, but it does not appear to have been recognized in the California cases dealing with the confidential marital communications privilege. Nonetheless, the exception does not seem so broad that it would impair the values that the privilege is intended to preserve; in many cases, the evidence which would be admissible under this exception will be vital in order to do justice between the parties to a lawsuit. This exception would not, of course, infringe on the privileges accorded to a married person under Sections 970 and 971.

It is important to note that the exception provided by Section 981 is quite limited. It does not permit disclosure of communications that merely reveal a plan to commit a crime or fraud; it permits disclosure only of communications made to *enable* or *aid* anyone to commit or plan to commit a crime or fraud. Thus, unless the communication is for the purpose of obtaining assistance in the commission of the crime or fraud or in furtherance thereof, it is not made admissible by the exception provided in this section. * * * (husband and wife who conspire only between themselves against others cannot claim immunity from prosecution for conspiracy on the basis of their marital status).

§ 985. Exception: Certain criminal proceedings

There is no privilege under this article in a criminal proceeding in which one spouse is charged with:

> (a) A crime committed at any time against the person or property of the other spouse or of a child of either.

(b) A crime committed at any time against the person or property of a third person committed in the course of committing a crime against the person or property of the other spouse.

(c) Bigamy.

(d) A crime defined by Section 270 or 270a of the Penal Code.

§ 986. Exception: Juvenile court proceeding

There is no privilege under this article in a proceeding under the Juvenile Court Law, Chapter 2 (commencing with Section 500) of Part 1 of Division 2 of the Welfare and Institutions Code.

§ 987. Exception: Communication offered by spouse who is criminal defendant

There is no privilege under this article in a criminal proceeding in which the communication is offered in evidence by a defendant who is one of the spouses between whom the communication was made.

Comment. This exception does not appear to have been recognized in any California case. Nonetheless, it is a desirable exception. When a married person is the defendant in a criminal proceeding and seeks to introduce evidence which is material to his defense, his spouse (or his former spouse) should not be privileged to withhold the information.

LILLY, AN INTRODUCTION TO THE LAW OF EVIDENCE *

320–325 (1978).

§ 87. Spousal Privilege for Confidential Communications

This privilege protects confidential communications between spouses. It most often is justified on the ground that it promotes marital harmony. The theory usually invoked by courts is that the privilege encourages marital partners to share their most closely-guarded secrets and thoughts, thus adding an additional measure of intimacy and mutual support to the marriage. Serious doubt can be raised as to whether the evidentiary protection produces the supposed effect. To begin with, it may be safe to assume that many marital partners are unaware of the existence of the privilege. Generally, when a privilege is conferred a professional advisor (such as an attorney, doctor, or clergyman) is a party to the protected relationship. Such a person, of course, is likely to be aware of any privileges available to himself or the person with whom he is conferring and can advise his confidant accordingly. But no professional or other person knowledgeable about privileged communications is a party to the protected husband-wife relationship. Furthermore, even assuming the

---

* Reprinted with permission from Lilly's "An Introduction to the Law of Evidence," West Publishing Co. (1978).

marriage partners know about the privilege, one may ask whether its existence materially affects the flow of information between husband and wife. If there were no privilege and if the communicating spouses were aware of the absense of such protection, would marital communications be inhibited? Perhaps only in unusual circumstances, such as where a courtroom appearance was anticipated, would any chilling effect be found.

Justification of the privilege, however, may be put on a different footing. There is much to be said for the notion that certain aspects of one's private life should be free from public disclosure. This especially is true in light of recent history, which has witnessed both diminished privacy in general and increased use of sophisticated electronic devices to collect and store information. The invasion of private marital communications is an indelicate and distasteful undertaking; it should not be sanctioned unless society's interest in disclosure is compelling.

McCormick argues that the marital privilege for confidential communications should "yield if the trial judge finds that the evidence of the communication is required in the due administration of justice." Although this may accommodate fairly the competing interests involved, most legislatures and courts—perhaps doubting that such discretion would be wisely and evenly exercised—have made the privilege absolute.

The privilege for marital communications extends to any *confidential* statement made *between spouses* during the existence of a legal marriage. In some jurisdictions, a broader construction of the privilege gives protection to the actions of one spouse in the presence of the other, at least where it reasonably can be inferred that the actor-spouse did not want his activity revealed. Finally, there is some authority that the privilege attaches to facts or information that one spouse discovers, if it reasonably can be said that the discovery would not have been made except for the marital relationship. The application of the privilege in this latter instance can not be justified on the theory that the privilege encourages communication, except in the unusual circumstance where the actor-spouse intended that the discovery be made. Whether the privilege nevertheless should apply because of society's distaste for public disclosure of private marital affairs is a question that is difficult to answer in the abstract. In an area such as this, a trial judge should be permitted to exercise discretion concerning the applicability of the privilege. He can take into account such matters as the importance of the testimony and the relationship of the spouses at the time of trial.

Although legislatures and courts differ somewhat on the scope of the privilege—that is, as to whether it extends beyond written or verbal communications—most authorities hold that the known presence of a third party when the spousal communication is made renders the privilege inapplicable for lack of confidentiality. This limiting principle recognizes the cost of conferring a privilege (namely, the suppression of relevant evidence) and indicates an unwillingness to extend protection beyond the private husband-wife relationship. Thus, even where the third party is a family member or is brought intentionally into the confidences of the spouses, the privilege generally does not apply. It also should be emphasized that the privilege does not attach unless the court finds from all of the surrounding circumstances that the statements were intended to be imparted in confidence. While courts probably tend to resolve doubts in favor of confidentiality, at least where the subject matter of the conversation is not apt to be widely shared outside the marriage, this inclination usually does not extend to statements relating to business or other matters likely to be openly discussed. Furthermore, subsequent revelations by one of the spouses may be influential in causing the judge to find that no confidentiality was ever intended. If, however, the court concludes that the statements were intended to be confidential, a wrongful disclosure amounting to a betrayal or breach of faith (as opposed to confirmation that no confidence ever existed) does not destroy the privilege. Whether the privilege exists is a question for the judge.

Several aspects of the privilege have disquieted the commentators. Most jurisdictions hold that the privilege survives the termination of the marriage either by death or divorce. This extended protection appears to go beyond the fulfillment of any reasonable policy underlying the privilege and represents an unwarranted obstacle to reliable factfinding. In contrast, there is co-existing authority that when a communication intended to be private is overheard or intercepted by a third person, that person can give testimony revealing what was said by the marital partners. Although seemingly prompted by a desire to minimize the suppression of relevant evidence, this latter result is questionable—at least in those instances in which spouses have taken reasonable precautions to preserve confidentiality. Indeed, recent authority suggests that placing the full burden of maintaining secrecy on the spouses is too great a demand, especially in light of modern communication devices (often involving other parties in the process of transmission) and technological advances in eavesdropping. If the privilege is worth maintaining, it should not fail where the spouses have taken reasonable steps to ensure privacy. In the near future, there is likely to be a legislative and judicial shift to a position compatible with this proposition.

The question often arises whether only the communicating spouse is the holder of the privilege. Wigmore felt that because the privilege was designed to foster marital communication, only the communicating spouse need be the holder. This is the law in some jurisdictions. In others, however, a statute or judicial decision makes both spouses holders. This means that the party seeking to introduce a privileged statement must secure a waiver from both spouses or, in the case of a holder's death, from the successor in interest (usually the executor or administrator) of the deceased. In some situations the law will intercede and terminate the privilege; this occurs, for example, when one spouse is prosecuted for an offense against the other (or the children of either) or in certain civil actions, such as divorce, where the marital partners have assumed an antagonistic posture.

PEOPLE v. MELSKI

Court of Appeals of New York, 1961.
10 N.Y.2d 78, 217 N.Y.S.2d 65, 176 N.E.2d 81.

BURKE, Judge. The threshold question is whether a wife can testify in an action against her husband as to the presence in her home of visitors in the company of the husband. We believe that she may since the "communication" was neither induced by the marital relation nor made in confidence. This is made apparent by the facts that it was made in the presence of the third parties, and that it was voluntarily disclosed by the husband to a State trooper prior to the trial.

In a statement given to the police, defendant related how he drove a few friends to Batavia where they proceeded, allegedly without his knowledge, to illegally appropriate some guns from a local shop. Upon their return to Buffalo they stopped at his house. He stated that when his wife came into the kitchen and saw the guns she told them to leave.

The wife was permitted to testify, over objection, that she arose at approximately 6:00 a. m. on the morning in question in order to get some milk for the baby. She stated that as she entered the kitchen she saw her husband and a few of his friends. When she testified that she was not sure if there were any guns, she was reminded that she told the Grand Jury that she had seen the guns. She further testified that she and her husband as well as the others later went on a previously planned picnic.

The friends testified that the defendant was their accomplice in the crime, and that the guns were taken to his house because he was to dispose of them. They further testified that when defendant's wife entered the kitchen, defendant put a gun to her head. Defendant's wife denied this.

It is urged upon these facts that defendant, in confidence, communicated to his wife the incriminating fact that accomplices were present in the home completing the crime. Appellant argues, citing People v. Daghita, 299 N.Y. 194, 86 N.E.2d 172, 10 A.L.R.2d 1385, that their presence was the "disclosive act" observed by the wife. We do not agree that this disclosure was privileged.

In Daghita (supra) this court held, and rightfully so, that acts as well as words may be the subject of communications. However, we by no means intended by that decision to circumvent the limitation of our statute (Penal Law, Consol.Laws, c. 40, § 2445) that the communications must be *confidential* in order to be privileged, as distinguished from the common-law rule which *completely disqualified* one spouse from testifying against the other. * * *

Most jurisdictions, as in New York, have by legislative enactments substituted a privilege based upon communications sometimes characterized as *confidential.* * * * As is obvious, these statutes were designed to protect not all the daily and ordinary exchanges between the spouses, but merely those which would not have been made but for the absolute confidence in, and induced by, the marital relationship. * * * This standard must be preliminarily applied by the Trial Judge to the challenged communication so that he may ascertain whether the witness can properly be compelled to relate it to the jury. Of course, since each case contains peculiar circumstances it is, as a practical matter, "impossible to formulate an all-embracing definition or an infallible guide", Poppe v. Poppe, 3 N.Y.2d 312, 315, 165 N.Y.S.2d 99, 102, 144 N.E.2d 72, 73. There are, however, some principles and illustrations at hand. For example, where the communication involved ordinary business matters * * * or unfounded accusations of adultery or other abusive language * * * the privilege was not held to attach. On the other hand, where there has been an admission or confession of adultery, as distinguished from an abusive disclosure * * *, we have allowed the privilege to be invoked, stating: "It cannot be supposed that both husband and wife would have been willing to discuss such a subject in the presence of other persons, or would have consented to a repetition of the conversation by either party to it. Its nature, and the relation of the parties, forbade the thought of its being told to others, and the law stamped it with that seal of confidence which the parties in such a situation would feel no occasion to exact." Warner v. Press Pub. Co., 132 N.Y. 181, 186, 30 N.E. 393, 395.

The application of these decisions to the present case reveals at once the common character of the communication deemed confidential. Not only was it originally made in the presence of the friends and voluntarily repeated prior to the trial, but it seems to have been made under circumstances which would indicate that it was not originally intended to be communicated to the wife. Although we hesitate to believe that the defendant put a revolver to his wife's head, it is our opinion that defendant and the others were surprised by the wife's untimely entrance. The attempt by the District Attorney to impeach the witness or refresh her recollection in regard to her testimony before the Grand Jury was merely reference to matter already disclosed by the husband. Although this prior disclosure may not be deemed a waiver, it, along with other circumstances, certainly confirms the fact that the communication was never intended to be confidential.

Moreover, the oft-stated *presumption* (not rebutted in this record) relied on by a majority of jurisdictions is that communications originally made in the presence of third parties are not confidential. * * * "[L]itigants have often sought to have a spouse's testimony as to transactions of the witness' husband or wife excluded on the ground that its revelation would be a violation of marital confidence. Such attempts have been generally unsuccessful, the testimony being admitted on the ground that the acts did not constitute communications to the spouse, or that knowledge of the acts was not obtained as a result of the marital relation." * * * Those few States, which prohibit such disclosures, base this exclusion either upon statutes or common-law rules * * * neither of which are applicable in New York.

In the Wolfle decision (supra) there is a suggestion that a communication may at times be made in confidence although in the presence of a third person. However, the court in that case concluded that the written communication by a husband to his wife was not privileged because of the voluntary disclosure by him to his stenographer who prepared the letter. This conclusion based upon the accepted rule in regard to communications in the presence of third parties was expressed in the following language: "The uniform ruling that communications between husband and wife, voluntarily made in the presence of their children, old enough to comprehend them, or other members of the family within the intimacy of the family circle, are not privileged * * * is persuasive that communications like the present, *even though made in confidence*, are not to be protected. The privilege suppresses relevant testimony, and should be allowed only when it is plain that marital confidence can not otherwise reasonably be preserved" (emphasis supplied).

The admission of this communication is no threat to the preservation of marital confidences and certainly no more sacrosanct than a confidence communicated in the presence of "other members of the family within the intimacy of the family circle" (Wolfle v. United States, supra).

If there were no other facts evidencing an absence of confidence, *and* if we could sever the "disclosive act" from the presence of the third parties, we might be inclined to agree that the communication was confidential. For example, defendant might have told his wife, while alone, that his accomplices and the stolen goods were in the house. However, when the communication is made in their presence, we prefer to rely on the presumption that it was not deemed a confidence between *husband and wife*, regardless of the fact that all present may have expressly sworn themselves to secrecy. While the acts and statements of the visitors may be deemed confidences between accomplices, they by no means come within the husband-wife privilege.

The implications of a reversal would be far reaching and clearly not allied with the legislative design to abolish the common-law incompetency which found it generally distasteful to incriminate one spouse by any knowledge obtained by the other, *confidential or otherwise*. The instant privilege, although characterized by some as an "extremely effective * * * stumbling block * * * to obstruct the attainment of justice" * * * is founded on a sound public policy to promote confidence between husband and wife. Its application to the circumstances here under consideration is certainly not supported by this policy.

Accordingly, the judgment must be affirmed.

DESMOND, Chief Judge, dissenting.

This conviction should be reversed because of the error committed at the trial in admitting against defendant, despite objection, the testimony of defendant's wife as to what she saw in their home a few hours after the alleged burglary. It is not possible to affirm here without overruling People v. Daghita, 299 N.Y. 194, 86 N.E.2d 172, 10 A.L.R.2d 1385, and New York's public policy as expressed in section 2445 of the Penal Law and explained in Daghita forbids such a change.

Defendant was convicted of grand larceny, second degree, on an indictment which charged that on August 9, 1959 he and three other men broke into a sporting goods store in Batavia, New York, and carried away several guns and some ammunition. It was part of the theory of the prosecution that during the early morning hours after the alleged crime the stolen goods were taken in defendant's automobile to defendant's home in Buffalo and that two (or three) other members of the robbery gang met with defendant in the kitchen of his home where the stolen guns were laid out on a table. Obviously, this was a secret meeting. Communication to defendant's wife of the fact of the meeting and of its purpose and significance was essentially confidential. Allowing the wife to testify as to the fact so discovered by her in her own home was a violation of law so fundamental and so damaging to her husband's defense that it cannot be excused without a major change in our construction of section 2445.

The prosecution put in testimony that defendant had furnished the car in which the stolen goods were transported and had acted as a lookout and that the guns and ammunition were taken to his home where they were placed on a kitchen table and where the culprits had a meeting. Two of the participants called as prosecution witnesses swore that during the kitchen conference defendant's wife came into the room to get milk for her baby and, seeing the men and the guns, told the men to get the guns out of her house. Then the wife herself was called to the stand as a prosecution witness. The court overruled the defense's objections based on section 2445. She testified that about six o'clock that morning she came into the dark kitchen to get milk for her child and saw two of the alleged robbers there with her husband. She ordered them from the house.

In Daghita's case, 299 N.Y. 194, 86 N.E.2d 172, 10 A.L.R.2d 1385, supra, this court unanimously rejected the same two arguments made by the People here: first, that actions of one spouse in the presence of another do not constitute confidential communications; and, second, that absence of an intent to make defendant's actions confidential was shown by the fact that a coculprit was present when the disclosure took place. Daghita was a policeman who stole merchandise from a store he was supposed to protect. He was observed by his wife bringing the goods into his home during the night and hiding them there. On one occasion, so the wife testified, she went with her husband and his accomplice to the store and sat in an automobile while the two men brought out stolen articles. In reversing the Daghita conviction, we held (299 N.Y. at page 199, 86 N.E.2d at page 173) that the term "communication" includes "knowledge derived from the observance of disclosive acts done in the presence or view of one spouse by the other because of the confidence existing between them by reason of the marital relation and which would not have been performed except for the confidence so existing". Thus we turned into an express holding the dictum found in People v. Woltering, 275 N.Y. 51, 57, 61, 9 N.E.2d 774, 775, 777. As we pointed out in Daghita, there is no essential difference between testimony as to what a husband told his wife and testimony as to what he allowed her to learn for herself from observing his conduct.

As to defendant's associates being in the kitchen with him when the wife made her observations, it is true that communications made in the presence of a third party are usually regarded as not privileged because not made in confidence. But confidentiality sometimes exists even in such instances (Wolfle v. United States, 291 U.S. 7, 14, 17, 54 S.Ct. 279, 280, 281, 78 L.Ed. 617). When the presence of the third person or persons is, as in Daghita (supra) and as in this case, part of the very fact confidentially communicated, the presence of those others cannot destroy confidentiality.

The opinion for affirmance in this court suggests that the husband's privilege under the statute was in some way removed or waived because the wife testified before the Grand Jury * * * and because the husband made pretrial admissions including the statement: "My wife got up and saw that there were guns laying on the kitchen table. She told them to get out and get the guns out which they did." There is nothing to show that the husband consented to his wife's giving the Grand Jury testimony or that she then knew anything about the law of husband-wife privilege. The husband's statement to a State trooper before trial said nothing about waiver. A waiver to be effective would have to be made at the trial and at the trial defendant strongly objected to any testimony by his wife.

Proof of the defendant's guilt is strong but much stronger is our public policy as announced in People v. Daghita, 299 N.Y. 194, 86 N. E.2d 172, 10 A.L.R.2d 1385, supra. Founded on "the sanctities of the marriage relation", the rule as to nondisclosure is to be "strictly construed" and an error in relation to it is not technical but affects "the substantial rights of the defendant".

The judgment should be reversed and a new trial ordered.

FULD, FROESSEL and FOSTER, JJ., concur with BURKE, J.

DESMOND, C. J., dissents in an opinion in which DYE and VAN VOORHIS, JJ., concur.

Judgment affirmed.

2. PHYSICIAN–PATIENT PRIVILEGE; PSYCHOTHERAPIST–PATIENT PRIVILEGE

LILLY, AN INTRODUCTION TO THE LAW OF EVIDENCE *

357–358 (1978).

Physician-Patient Privilege. There are additional evidentiary privileges not treated in this chapter. Jurisdictional variations in the recognition and scope of these privileges make it essential that the practitioner avoid the assumption that a privilege long recognized in his state similarly applies in a sister state. The statutes must be carefully researched. Many jurisdictions, for example, have passed statutes protecting communications between patient and physician if the statements were reasonably necessary to enable the physician to render treatment. But this privilege does not receive universal recognition, and among jurisdictions according the privilege there are substantial variations in applicability and waiver. Typically, the privilege is confined to civil proceedings where public interest in full disclosure is not as great as in criminal trials. But even in the civil context, the privilege often is inapplicable where a court or public officer engages a doctor to conduct an examination; nor does it usually apply where the patient, who is the holder, puts his own physical condition in issue—as, for example, where he claims personal injuries. Under some of the statutes, a judge may negate the privilege when, in his judgment, the interest of justice so requires. See Va.Code Ann. § 8.01–399. For a thorough and thoughtful discussion of the physician-patient privilege, see McCormick §§ 98–105.

Should there be a separate privilege applicable to communications between psychotherapist and patient? The same rationale that supports the physician-patient privilege, the encouragement of the

* Reprinted with permission from Lilly's "An Introduction to the Law of Evidence," West Publishing Co. (1978).

patient to reveal his condition, also serves as a justification for the psychotherapist-patient privilege. In the case of the psychotherapist, effective treatment in most cases largely depends upon the patient's willingness to talk freely. Thus, the need to ensure confidentiality is even more important. * * * Accordingly, while some jurisdictions simply extend the physician-patient privilege to include psychotherapists, others have special provisions for the psychotherapist-patient privilege. See, e. g., Conn.Gen.Stat. § 52–146a (1966 Supp.). Note that the proposed Federal Rules would have granted a privilege for psychotherapist-patient communications but not for physicians. Prop.Fed.R.Evid. 504. The drafters felt that most states that have the latter privilege have so riddled it with exceptions as to leave little, if any, basis for it. Suppose in the course of treatment the therapist learns that the patient has committed criminal offenses and is likely to repeat this conduct. What is the appropriate course of action? See generally Tarasoff v. Regents of University of California, 13 Cal.3d 177, 529 P.2d 553 (1974).

Priest-Penitent Privilege. A vast majority of the states recognize a clergyman-penitent privilege that shields statements made to a clergyman in his religious office. VIII Wigmore § 2395 (McNaughton). Again, however, care must be exercised in defining the limits of the privilege. Note that this privilege has no constitutional support. See In Re Moren, 564 F.2d 567 (D.C.C., 1977). Some statutes follow the pattern of Rule 29 of the 1953 Uniform Rules of Evidence and limit the privilege to statements that are the outgrowth of "enjoined religious discipline." McCormick notes, however, that more recent enactments protect against any disclosure that "would violate a sacred or moral trust." McCormick, § 77, at 158. See Unif.R.Evid. 505 (1974); Prop.Fed.R.Evid. 506.

Journalist-Source Privilege. A number of state legislatures have decided that confidential relationships between a journalist and his source should be protected. The result has been the passage of "shield laws" that vary from jurisdiction to jurisdiction but, basically, provide the newsman with immunity from forced disclosure of the identity of his source. See, e. g., West's Ann.Calif.Evid.Code § 1070. See generally Branzburg v. Hayes, 408 U.S. 665 (1972). The student might ask whether these statutes also should protect unpublished information obtained in confidence. Should the privilege belong to the reporter or to his informant, or both? Typically the journalist is the holder and thus can waive the privilege. Does the public interest in being informed by the press require that a reporter be prohibited from waiving his privilege without the consent of the informant?

Chapter VII

THE PRIVILEGE AGAINST COMPULSORY SELF–INCRIMINATION

A. INTRODUCTION

CONSTITUTION OF THE UNITED STATES, AMENDMENT V

No person * * * shall be compelled in any criminal case to be a witness against himself * * *.

HISTORICAL BACKGROUND

The privilege against self-incrimination can only be understood against the background of English history which produced it. In very brief and simplified form, this is what happened:

Early in the reign of Henry VIII, about 450 years ago, England was a Roman Catholic state. Protestants were vigorously persecuted. Then, when Henry broke with the Roman Catholic Church and Parliament established the Church of England, the Protestants reversed the situation and began to persecute the Catholics, until Queen Mary once again persecuted the Protestants. This situation was reversed after the death of Mary, when Elizabeth took the throne. From the 1560's Elizabeth's Church began persecuting (in addition to the Catholics) dissident Protestants called Puritans. This continued under James I and Charles I and helped provoke the Revolution in which Puritans and their allies were victorious.

After the Puritan victory, the authorities continued to persecute Catholics, while also persecuting both the Anglican clergy, less reform-minded than themselves, and the "left wing" dissenters who broke away from the main body of Puritans. Then, after the accession to power of Oliver Cromwell, the center of the Puritan establishment moved left and began its own campaigns against the "ungodly," persecuting the Catholics, the High Anglicans and the right-wing Puritans. By the time of the Restoration of the monarchy under Charles II, all England was sick of religious persecution and for the most part it ceased.

This history is quite remarkable. In the course of about 150 years, members of every major religious group in England had been both the initiators and the victims of persecution—and the roles had changed with bewildering rapidity.

Of course, these persecutions were only partly religious. They were also political. The divorce of religion from politics is, in historical terms, a relatively recent phenomenon. It is obvious that the break of Henry VIII with Rome (not to mention the later excommunication of Elizabeth) had political as well as religious significance.

In any event, a major method of these persecutions was the oath. During the persecution of the Puritans by the Church of England under Elizabeth and James, for example, Puritan ministers were called before the High Commission and asked questions under oath about their beliefs. Being men of God, they could not lie—and, if they admitted to their deviant and nonconformist views, they could be very seriously punished. As a result, increasingly, they claimed the right not to answer and the existence or non-existence of such a right gradually became a major issue in 17th century England. One of the most celebrated cases involving the right was that of John Lilburne: *

> "In 1637, Lilburne, A Puritan dissenter, was brought before the Star Chamber. Having just returned from Holland, he was charged with sending "factitious and scandalous books" from there to England. Lilburne repeatedly contended that he was entitled to notice, indictment, and court trial under the known laws of England; that he had a right to have witnesses summoned in his behalf and be confronted by witnesses against him; and that he could not be compelled to testify against himself.
>
> "For refusing to respond to the questions, Lilburne was fined, was tied to a cart and, his body bared, was whipped through the streets of London. At Westminster he was placed in a pillory—his body bent down, his neck in the hole, and his lacerated back bared to the midday sun; there he stood for two hours and exhorted all who would listen to resist the tyranny of the bishops. Refusing to be quiet, he was gagged so cruelly that his mouth bled. After all this, he was kept in solitary confinement in the Fleet Prison with irons on his hands and legs and without anything to eat for ten days. After Lilburne's release, his cruel treatment and bold resistance had two consequences. The first was the vote of the Long Parliament that his sentence was illegal and that he be paid reparations. The second was the abolition of both the Star Chamber and the Court of the High Commission by the same Parliament. * * *"

The development of the privilege was by no means complete at this point. As has been pointed out,

> "[The] objections to compulsory self-incrimination were not, however, aimed at the practice in the regular

---

* *The Bill of Rights, A Source Book for Teachers,* California State Department of Education (1967, pp. 79–81).

criminal courts but, rather, at the practice as it was carried out by the Star Chamber and the High Commission. After the abolition of the Courts of the Star Chamber and of the High Commission, [q]uestioning of the accused at his trial continued unaltered for nearly two decades; the examination of the prisoner by the committing magistrate continued for as long as two centuries. Nevertheless, a gradual repugnance to compulsory self-incrimination developed. By the end of the reign of Charles II, the privilege was recognized in all courts when claimed by defendant or witness.

MALLOY v. HOGAN

Supreme Court of the United States, 1964.
378 U.S. 1, 84 S.Ct. 1489, 12 L.Ed.2d 653.

Mr. Justice BRENNAN delivered the opinion of the Court.

In this case we are asked to reconsider prior decisions holding that the privilege against self-incrimination is not safe-guarded against state action by the Fourteenth Amendment. Twining v. New Jersey, 211 U.S. 78 * * *.

The petitioner was arrested during a gambling raid in 1959 by Hartford, Connecticut, police. He pleaded guilty to the crime of pool selling, a misdemeanor, and was sentenced to one year in jail and fined $500. The sentence was ordered to be suspended after 90 days, at which time he was to be placed on probation for two years. About 16 months after his guilty plea, petitioner was ordered to testify before a referee appointed by the Superior Court of Hartford County to conduct an inquiry into alleged gambling and other criminal activities in the county. The petitioner was asked a number of questions related to events surrounding his arrest and conviction. He refused to answer any question "on the grounds it may tend to incriminate me." The Superior Court adjudged him in contempt, and committed him to prison until he was willing to answer the questions. Petitioner's application for a writ of habeas corpus was denied by the Superior Court, and the Connecticut Supreme Court of Errors affirmed. * * * We reverse. We hold that the Fourteenth Amendment guaranteed the petitioner the protection of the Fifth Amendment's privilege against self-incrimination, and that under the applicable federal standard, the Connecticut Supreme Court of Errors erred in holding that the privilege was not properly invoked.

* * *

The marked shift to the federal standard in state cases began with Lisenba v. California, 314 U.S. 219, 62 S.Ct. 280, 86 L.Ed. 166, where the Court spoke of the accused's "free choice to admit, to deny, or to refuse to answer."

* * *

The shift reflects recognition that the American system of criminal prosecution is accusatorial, not inquisitorial, and that the Fifth Amendment privilege is its essential mainstay. * * * Governments, state and federal, are thus constitutionally compelled to establish guilt by evidence independently and freely secured, and may not by coercion prove a charge against an accused out of his own mouth. Since the Fourteenth Amendment prohibits the States from inducing a person to confess through "sympathy falsely aroused," * * * or other like inducement far short of "compulsion by torture," * * * it follows *a fortiori* that it also forbids the States to resort to imprisonment, as here, to compel him to answer questions that might incriminate him. The Fourteenth Amendment secures against state invasion the same privilege that the Fifth Amendment guarantees against federal infringement—the right of a person to remain silent unless he chooses to speak in the unfettered exercise of his own will, and to suffer no penalty, as held in Twining, for such silence. * * *

We turn to the petitioner's claim that the State of Connecticut denied him the protection of his federal privilege. It must be considered irrelevant that the petitioner was a witness in a statutory inquiry and not a defendant in a criminal prosecution, for it has long been settled that the privilege protects witnesses in similar federal inquiries. * * * Hoffman v. United States, 341 U.S. 479, 71 S.Ct. 814, 95 L.Ed. 1118. We recently elaborated the content of the federal standard in Hoffman:

> "The privilege afforded not only extends to answers that would in themselves support a conviction * * * but likewise embraces those which would furnish a link in the chain of evidence needed to prosecute. * * * [I]f the witness, upon interposing his claim, were required to prove the hazard * * * he would be compelled to surrender the very protection which the privilege is designed to guarantee. To sustain the privilege, it need only be evident from the implications of the question, in the setting in which it is asked, that a responsive answer to the question or an explanation of why it cannot be answered might be dangerous because injurious disclosure could result." 341 U.S., at 486–487, 71 S.Ct. at 818.

We also said that, in applying that test, the judge must be

> "*'perfectly clear*, from a careful consideration of all the circumstances in the case, that the witness is mistaken, and that the answer[s] *cannot possibly* have such tendency' to incriminate." 341 U.S., at 488, 71 S.Ct., at 819.

The State of Connecticut argues that the Connecticut courts properly applied the federal standards to the facts of this case. We disagree.

The investigation in the course of which petitioner was questioned began when the Superior Court in Hartford County appointed the Honorable Ernest A. Inglis, formerly Chief Justice of Connecticut, to conduct an inquiry into whether there was reasonable cause to believe that crimes, including gambling, were being committed in Hartford County. Petitioner appeared on January 16 and 25, 1961, and in both instances he was asked substantially the same questions about the circumstances surrounding his arrest and conviction for pool selling in late 1959. The questions which petitioner refused to answer may be summarized as follows: (1) for whom did he work on September 11, 1959; (2) who selected and paid his counsel in connection with his arrest on that date and subsequent conviction; (3) who selected and paid his bondsman; (4) who paid his fine; (5) what was the name of the tenant of the apartment in which he was arrested; and (6) did he know John Bergoti. The Connecticut Supreme Court of Errors ruled that the answers to these questions could not tend to incriminate him because the defenses of double jeopardy and the running of the one-year statute of limitations on misdemeanors would defeat any prosecution growing out of his answers to the first five questions. As for the sixth question, the court held that petitioner's failure to explain how a revelation of his relationship with Bergoti would incriminate him vitiated his claim to the protection of the privilege afforded by state law.

The conclusions of the Court of Errors, tested by the federal standard, fail to take sufficient account of the setting in which the questions were asked. The interrogation was part of a wide-ranging inquiry into crime, including gambling, in Hartford. It was admitted on behalf of the State at oral argument—and indeed it is obvious from the questions themselves—that the State desired to elicit from the petitioner the identity of the person who ran the pool-selling operation in connection with which he had been arrested in 1959. It was apparent that petitioner might apprehend that if this person were still engaged in unlawful activity, disclosure of his name might furnish a link in a chain of evidence sufficient to connect the petitioner with a more recent crime for which he might still be prosecuted.

Analysis of the sixth question, concerning whether petitioner knew John Bergoti, yields a similar conclusion. In the context of the inquiry, it should have been apparent to the referee that Bergoti was suspected by the State to be involved in some way in the subject matter of the investigation. An affirmative answer to the question might well have either connected petitioner with a more recent crime, or at least have operated as a waiver of his privilege with reference to his relationship with a possible criminal. * * * We conclude, therefore, that as to each of the questions, it was "evident from the implications of the question, in the setting in which it [was] asked, that a responsive answer to the question or an explanation of why it [could not] be answered might be dangerous because injurious disclosure could result," Hoffman v. United States, 341 U.S., at 486–487, 71 S.Ct. 818 * * *.

Reversed.

(The dissenting opinion of Mr. Justice HARLAN joined by Mr. Justice CLARK and the dissenting opinion of Mr. Justice WHITE, with whom Mr. Justice STEWART joins, are omitted.)

B. IN THE COURTS

GRIFFIN v. CALIFORNIA

Supreme Court of the United States, 1965.
380 U.S. 609, 85 S.Ct. 1229, 14 L.Ed.2d 106.

Mr. Justice DOUGLAS delivered the opinion of the Court.

Petitioner was convicted of murder in the first degree after a jury trial in a California court. He did not testify at the trial on the issue of guilt, though he did testify at the separate trial on the issue of penalty. The trial court instructed the jury on the issue of guilt, stating that a defendant has a constitutional right not to testify. But it told the jury:[2]

> "As to any evidence or facts against him which the defendant can reasonably be expected to deny or explain because of facts within his knowledge, if he does not testify or if, though he does testify, he fails to deny or explain such evidence, the jury may take that failure into consideration as tending to indicate the truth of such evidence and as indicating that among the inferences that may be reasonably drawn therefrom those unfavorable to the defendant are the more probable."

It added, however, that no such inference could be drawn as to evidence respecting which he had no knowledge. It stated that failure of a defendant to deny or explain the evidence of which he had knowledge does not create a presumption of guilt nor by itself warrant an inference of guilt nor relieve the prosecution of any of its burden of proof.

Petitioner had been seen with the deceased the evening of her death, the evidence placing him with her in the alley where her body

---

2. Article I, § 13, of the California Constitution provides in part:
"* * * in any criminal case, whether the defendant testifies or not, his failure to explain or to deny by his testimony any evidence or facts in the case against him may be commented upon by the court and by counsel, and may be considered by the court or the jury."

was found. The prosecutor made much of the failure of petitioner to testify:

"The defendant certainly knows whether Essie Mae had this beat up appearance at the time he left her apartment and went down the alley with her.

"What kind of a man is it that would want to have sex with a woman that beat up if she was beat up at the time he left?

"He would know that. He would know how she got down the alley. He would know how the blood got on the bottom of the concrete steps. He would know how long he was with her in that box. He would know how her wig got off. He would know whether he beat her or mistreated her. He would know whether he walked away from that place cool as a cucumber when he saw Mr. Villasenor because he was conscious of his own guilt and wanted to get away from that damaged or injured woman.

"These things he has not seen fit to take the stand and deny or explain.

"And in the whole world, if anybody would know, this defendant would know.

"Essie Mae is dead, she can't tell you her side of the story. The defendant won't."

The death penalty was imposed and the California Supreme Court affirmed. * * * The case is here on a writ of certiorari which we granted, to consider whether comment on the failure to testify violated the Self-Incrimination Clause of the Fifth Amendment which we made applicable to the States by the Fourteenth in Malloy v. Hogan, * * *, decided after the Supreme Court of California had affirmed the present conviction.

If this were a federal trial, reversible error would have been committed. * * * It is said, however, that the Wilson decision rested not on the Fifth Amendment, but on an Act of Congress, now 18 U.S.C. § 3481.[3] That indeed is the fact, as the opinion of the Court in the Wilson case states. But that is the beginning, not the end, of our inquiry. The question remains whether, statute or not, the comment rule, approved by California, violates the Fifth Amendment. We think it does. It is in substance a rule of evidence that allows the State the privilege of tendering to the jury for its considera-

---

3. Section 3481 reads as follows:
"In trial of all persons charged with the commission of offenses against the United States and in all proceedings in courts martial and courts of inquiry in any State, District, Possession or Territory, the person charged shall, at his own request, be a competent witness. His failure to make such request shall not create any presumption against him." June 25, 1948, c. 645, 62 Stat. 833.

tion the failure of the accused to testify. No formal offer of proof is made as in other situations; but the prosecutor's comment and the court's acquiescence are the equivalent of an offer of evidence and its acceptance.

* * *

If the words "Fifth Amendment" are substituted for "act" and for "statute" the spirit of the Self-Incrimination Clause is reflected. For comment on the refusal to testify is a remnant of the "inquisitorial system of criminal justice," Murphy v. Waterfront Comm., 378 U.S. 52, 55, * * * which the Fifth Amendment outlaws. It is a penalty imposed by courts for exercising a constitutional privilege. It cuts down on the privilege by making its assertion costly. It is said, however, that the inference of guilt for failure to testify as to facts peculiarly within the accused's knowledge is in any event natural and irresistible, and that comment on the failure does not magnify that inference into a penalty for asserting a constitutional privilege. * * * What the jury may infer, given no help from the court, is one thing. What it may infer when the court solemnizes the silence of the accused into evidence against him is quite another. That the inference of guilt is not always so natural or irresistible is brought out in the Modesto opinion itself:

> "Defendant contends that the reason a defendant refuses to testify is that his prior convictions will be introduced in evidence to impeach him * * * and not that he is unable to deny the accusations. It is true that the defendant might fear that his prior convictions will prejudice the jury, and therefore another possible inference can be drawn from his refusal to take the stand." * * *

We said in Malloy v. Hogan, * * *, that "the same standards must determine whether an accused's silence in either a federal or state proceeding is justified." We take that in its literal sense and hold that the Fifth Amendment, in its direct application to the Federal Government and in its bearing on the States by reason of the Fourteenth Amendment, forbids either comment by the prosecution on the accused's silence or instructions by the court that such silence is evidence of guilt.

Reversed.

The Chief Justice took no part in the decision of this case.

[The concurring opinion of Mr. Justice HARLAN is omitted.]

Mr. Justice STEWART, with whom Mr. Justice WHITE joins, dissenting.

* * *

We must determine whether the petitioner has been "compelled * * * to be a witness against himself." Compulsion is the focus of the inquiry. Certainly, if any compulsion be detected in the California procedure, it is of a dramatically different and less palpable nature than that involved in the procedures which historically gave rise to the Fifth Amendment guarantee. When a suspect was brought before the Court of High Commission or the Star Chamber, he was commanded to answer whatever was asked of him, and subjected to a far-reaching and deeply probing inquiry in an effort to ferret out some unknown and frequently unsuspected crime. He declined to answer on pain of incarceration, banishment, or mutilation. And if he spoke falsely, he was subject to further punishment. Faced with this formidable array of alternatives, his decision to speak was unquestionably coerced.

Those were the lurid realities which lay behind enactment of the Fifth Amendment, a far cry from the subject matter of the case before us. I think that the Court in this case stretches the concept of compulsion beyond all reasonable bounds, and that whatever compulsion may exist derives from the defendant's choice not to testify, not from any comment by court or counsel. In support of its conclusion that the California procedure does compel the accused to testify, the Court has only this to say: "It is a penalty imposed by courts for exercising a constitutional privilege. It cuts down on the privilege by making its assertion costly." Exactly what the penalty imposed consists of is not clear. It is not, as I understand the problem, that the jury becomes aware that the defendant has chosen not to testify in his own defense, for the jury will, of course, realize this quite evident fact, even though the choice goes unmentioned. Since comment by counsel and the court does not compel testimony by creating such an awareness, the Court must be saying that the California constitutional provision places some other compulsion upon the defendant to incriminate himself, some compulsion which the Court does not describe and which I cannot readily perceive.

It is not at all apparent to me, on any realistic view of the trial process, that a defendant will be at more of a disadvantage under the California practice than he would be in a court which permitted no comment at all on his failure to take the witness stand. How can it be said that the inferences drawn by a jury will be more detrimental to a defendant under the limiting and carefully controlling language of the instruction here involved than would result if the jury were left to roam at large with only its untutored instincts to guide it, to draw from the defendant's silence broad inferences of guilt? The instructions in this case expressly cautioned the jury that the defendant's failure to testify "does not create a presumption of guilt or by itself warrant an inference of guilt"; it was further admonished that such failure does not "relieve the prosecution of its burden of proving every essential element of the crime," and finally the trial judge warned that the prosecution's burden remained that of proof "beyond a reasonable doubt." Whether the same limitations would be observed by a jury without the benefit of protective instructions shielding the defendant is certainly open to real doubt.

* * *

The formulation of procedural rules to govern the administration of criminal justice in the various States is properly a matter of local concern. We are charged with no general supervisory power over such matters; our only legitimate function is to prevent violations of the Constitution's commands. California has honored the constitutional command that no person shall "be compelled in any criminal case to be a witness against himself." The petitioner was not compelled to testify, and he did not do so. But whenever in a jury trial a defendant exercises this constitutional right, the members of the jury are bound to draw inferences from his silence. No constitution can prevent the operation of the human mind. Without limiting instructions, the danger exists that the inferences drawn by the jury may be unfairly broad. Some States have permitted this danger to go unchecked, by forbidding any comment at all upon the defendant's failure to take the witness stand. Other States have dealt with this danger in a variety of ways, as the Court's opinion indicates. * * * Some might differ, as a matter of policy, with the way California has chosen to deal with the problem, or even disapprove of the judge's specific instructions in this case. But, so long as the constitutional command is obeyed, such matters of state policy are not for this Court to decide.

I would affirm the judgment.

TRAVER, ANATOMY OF A MURDER

Part One, Chapter 24, pp. 155–57 (1958) *

"That's one of the things I've been mulling over, Paul," Parnell said. "You know, of course, that under the statute we must serve timely notice on the prosecution of our intention to claim the defense of insanity and at least four days before the trial. When do you propose to serve that notice, boy? Time's a-flyin'."

"That problem's been bothering me most all night, Parn—ever since I read that damned letter. Up to now I've been putting off serving the notice for several reasons: till I saw we could actually get a psychiatrist; then with the vague idea of not tipping our hand to the other side any sooner than we had to; and also to possibly prevent or delay the People from sicking their own rebuttal psychiatrists on our man." I paused. "I'm glad you raised the subject because I've just about made up my mind that we should serve the notice now —today—and let the chips fall where they may. What do you think?"

"But won't that do just what you're trying to avoid?" Parnell said thoughtfully. "Tip off our defense and give the other side a

* Copyright, 1958 by Robert Traver.

longer psychiatric crack at him, as it were? Mind, now, I'm not objectin', boy; I'm merely tryin' to test your thinkin'—our little game, you know. I'm listenin'."

So Parnell and I were away again, endlessly debating the pros and cons of our strategy for the fast approaching trial. I pointed out that if we delayed the serving of our notice this might in itself give the People their grounds for a continuance since Mitch could then argue that he needed additional time in which to obtain a decent rebuttal psychiatric examination. Parnell agreed and then raised the question of whether the People could ever get to examine our man.

"It's a little brainstorm I had during the night," he added.

"What do you mean?" I said. "Surely you're familiar with the procedure that permits a prosecutor in felony cases to file a petition with the Court suggesting insanity and asking for a psychiatric examination and sanity hearing? The moment we file our notice of insanity Mitch can petition the court—on the sole ground that we've thereby furnished him—that the defendant *may* have been insane (he needn't admit it), and hence get to paw over our man."

Parnell grinned evilly. "I'm aware of that procedure, boy," he said. "I have it fully in mind. If and when such a petition is filed we'll simply tell our man to clam up and tell the People's psychiatrist to go fly a kite. He simply won't play."

I fidgeted uneasily. "You mean, Parn, we'd tell Lieutenant Manion not to let the People's psychiatrist have at him?"

"Not only tell him not to let them examine him—but not even talk with them," he said. "I mean our man will tell 'em all to go plumb to hell."

"But how can you expect to get away with it, Parn? That procedure's on the law books, man, and has been for years. Won't I risk being jailed for contempt or something?"

"We'll chance it," Parnell replied. "There are a lot of rusty old things in the law and on the law books, boy, that couldn't stand up for five minutes if their constitutionality were seriously challenged. Nearly every new supreme court report that comes out has at least one shining example. The Legislature's forever getting some unconstitutional bug in its britches, and I think this old law is one of them. I've had my droopy eye on this statute for years and in my opinion it isn't worth the paper it's written on. Constitutionally, I mean."

"I'm beginning to see," I murmured. "I'm beginning to see * * *"

"Don't you see," Parnell went on, warming to his subject, "one of the basic provisions of both the State and Federal constitutions is that no man shall be compelled to testify against himself in any criminal case. That's of course the Fifth Amendment—the very one that's getting to be such a dirty word these days in certain sturdy flag-waving quarters. * * * "

"Let's not get on that now, Parn," I said, rolling up my eyes.

Parnell had awakened during the night with the whole argument laid out cold. "I must have put a nickel in me subconscious." If any statute or procedure purported to *force* a person charged with crime to submit to a hostile psychiatric examination, wasn't it thereby unconstitutional and bad?

"Hm," I mused, over the bold soundness of the old man's vision. "But supposing the good judge overrules all our fine constitutional arguments? Either we appeal—which is tantamount to a People's continuance—or the other side still gets its examination."

Parnell grinned and shook his head. "No, boy. No such thing. If the judge rules against us our man still tells 'em all to go to hell. And if he tells them that what're they going to do? The Judge, Mitch, the Doctor, anyone? If our man simply won't talk *who's* going to make him talk? They can't threaten to jail *him* for contempt, the poor bastard's already there. And you're in the clear, Polly. You co-operated. And what kind of a psychiatric examination would they have if he wouldn't play ball? The whole procedure of psychoanalysis, to be effective, presumes ardent co-operation from the subject; hence the overstuffed couch."

WALTZ, CRIMINAL EVIDENCE

147–150 (1975).

The Impact of the Privilege of Pretrial Discovery of Evidence in Criminal Cases. A party to a civil case is entitled to learn virtually everything there is to know about his adversary's case. The term *pretrial discovery* is applied to this process. It refers to formal investigatory methods, authorized by enforceable procedural rules and available to the parties only after a lawsuit has been commenced. In the civil practice, as distinguished from the field of criminal litigation, the following pretrial discovery devices are typical:

1. *Written Interrogatories to Parties.* A party to a civil suit can require any adverse party to answer, in writing and under oath, relevant written questions served on him. Written interrogatories are usually used to get detailed information which the answering party must obtain from records in his procession or control.

2. *Oral Depositions.* Parties and nonparty witnesses alike can be required, by means of a subpoena, to come to legal counsel's office for deposition purposes in a civil case. Counsel will ask questions orally, much as he would at trial, and the questions and answers, given under oath, will be taken down and transcribed by a court reporter. In this way counsel gets desired information from the witness.

Furthermore, the transcription of the witness's deposition testimony will rise to haunt him at trial if he then tries to shift his story in any significant way.

3. *Motions for the Production of Documents and the Like.* A party to a civil case can obtain a court order requiring an opposing party to produce relevant documents and objects for inspection, copying, or photographing.

4. *Physical and Mental Examinations.* In any civil lawsuit in which the mental or physical condition of a party is in dispute, the court can order him (or her) to submit to a mental or physical examination by a qualified physician.

5. *Requests for Admissions of Facts.* A party to a civil lawsuit can serve a request on his opponent for a formal admission of relevant facts set forth in the request, including such matters as the genuineness of writings. If the opposing party refuses the requested admission and the side requesting it later establishes the truth of the disputed matter, the adverse party can be required to pay the expenses involved in proving the matter.

From this brief outline of available procedures it can be sensed that there is almost no limit to the ability of parties to civil litigation to smoke out the facts of a case. No such liberality in pretrial discovery procedures exists on the criminal side of American courthouses. Some jurisdictions will permit the prosecution and the defense to obtain a court order requiring the other side to produce the names, addresses, and the gist of the expected testimony of its witnesses. A large number of jurisdictions will order the production of witnesses' prior written statements for impeachment purposes. But the most important criminal discovery development came in a 1966 amendment to Rule 16 of the Federal Rules of Criminal Procedure.

Under this amendment to the rules governing federal prosecutions, a trial judge can give the accused discovery of confessions or statements which he himself made, including his testimony before a grand jury. A judge can also permit an accused to obtain the results of tests and examinations made by the prosecution. After a demonstration of need and reasonableness, the accused may also be granted discovery with respect to "books, papers, documents, tangible objects, buildings or places." An order of this sort can be conditioned upon the accused's letting the prosecution have discovery of "scientific or medical reports, books, papers, documents, [and] tangible objects" which are in the accused's possession and which he plans to use at trial.

Criminal discovery rules generally favor the accused. They are not a two-way street. The reason for this is plain enough. The giving of discovery rights to the prosecution in criminal cases raises serious Fifth Amendment questions. It has been argued that forcing the defendant to cooperate in any fashion with the making of the case against him would conflict with his Fifth Amendment privilege. By and large, however, this argument has not impressed the courts, which hold that the privilege does not come into play unless the conduct compelled is of a testimonial nature.

The leading judicial decision in this somewhat confused area is Jones v. Superior Court of Nevada County, 372 P.2d 919 (S.Ct.Calif. 1962). Jones was charged with rape. He asked the trial court for a continuance, saying that he needed more time to produce medical evidence in support of his claim that he had been rendered impotent by injuries suffered in 1953 and 1954. The State, alerted to Jones's defense, then demanded production of the names and addresses of any physicians who would be called by the defense to testify about the defendant's injuries, the names and addresses of any physicians who had treated the defendant prior to trial, any reports pertaining to the defendant's injuries and his asserted impotence, and any relevant X-rays.

The State's discovery effort in *Jones* would have given rise to an implied representation by the defendant that the materials he produced were the materials that the State had demanded. To this extent the compelled conduct would be testimonial in nature. It is as though the prosecution were to demand that defense counsel produce for inspection "the murder weapon used by the defendant in this case." Were the defense to produce a knife in response to this request, an inference of a distinctly testimonial and incriminating nature would arise. In *Jones* the State sought even more. It sought not merely the production of described materials of which the prosecution was already aware. It also attempted to use the defendant's knowledge to discover whether other suspected evidence was in existence. This would have significantly increased the testimonial aspect of the compelled production.

In *Jones* the California Supreme Court ruled that discovery could properly be allowed only as to (1) the names and addresses of witnesses the defendant intended to call to the witness stand at trial and (2) reports and X-rays that he planned to offer in support of his impotence defense. This, the court said, would not require Jones to reveal anything that he was not already planning to reveal. Anything more would force the accused to disclose his knowledge of possible evidence. The court held that this would be violative of the accused's Fifth Amendment privilege.

Whether discovery procedures in criminal cases will ever closely parallel those presently available in civil suits, and whether discovery in criminal cases will ever become a two-way street, depends on the degree to which courts are willing to erode interests usually thought to be shielded by the Fifth Amendment. If the erosion is counterbalanced by an increase in the amount of pretrial discovery available to criminal defendants, courts can be expected to move toward more nearly parallel discovery procedures since they make for more accurate fact-finding in trials.

C. IN THE STATIONHOUSE

YALE KAMISAR—EQUAL JUSTICE IN THE GATEHOUSES AND MANSIONS OF AMERICAN CRIMINAL PROCEDURE

Kamisar, Inbau & Arnold, Criminal Justice in Our Time 19–36
(Howard ed. 1965)

THE SHOW IN THE "GATEHOUSE" VS. THE SHOW IN THE "MANSION"

The courtroom is a splendid place where defense attorney bellow and strut and prosecuting attorneys are hemmed in at many turns. But what happens before an accused reaches the safety and enjoys the comfort of this veritable mansion? Ah, there's the rub. Typically he must first pass through a much less pretentious edifice, a police station with bare back rooms and locked doors.

In this "gatehouse" of American criminal procedure—through which most defendants journey and beyond which many never get—the enemy of the state is a depersonalized "subject" to be "sized up" and subjected to "interrogation tactics and techniques most appropriate for the occasion"; he is "game" to be stalked and cornered. Here, ideals are checked at the door, "realities" faced, and the prestige of law enforcement vindicated. Once he leaves the "gatehouse" and enters the "mansion"—if he ever gets there—the enemy of the state is repersonalized, even dignified, the public invited, and a stirring ceremony in honor of individual freedom from law enforcement celebrated.

I suspect it is not so much that society knows and approves of the show in the gatehouse, but that society does not know or care. "[S]ociety, by its insouciance, has divested itself of a moral responsibility and unloaded it on to the police. Society doesn't want to know about criminals, but it does want them put away, and it is incurious how this can be done provided it is done. Thus society, in giving the policeman power and wishing to ignore what his techniques must be, has made over to him part of its own conscience."

True, the man in the street would have considerable difficulty explaining why the Constitution requires so much in the courtroom and means so little in the police station, but that is not his affair. "The task of keeping the two shows going at the same time without losing the patronage or the support of the Constitution for either," as Thurman Arnold once observed, is "left to the legal scholar." Perhaps this is only fitting and proper, for as Thomas Reed Powell used to say, if you can think about something that is related to something else without thinking about the thing to which it is related, then you have the legal mind.

* * *

Evidently, so long as neither the proceedings nor the presiding officer is "judicial," basic traditions are honored and self-incrimination problems avoided. * * *

IS THE PRIVILEGE CHECKED AT THE "GATEHOUSE" DOOR?

* * *

[O]ne who would apply the privilege to the police station may select from the vast conglomerate of determinants which form its history the fact that the maxim "no man shall be compelled to accuse himself" first meant (and until the seventeenth century probably only meant) that no man shall be compelled to make the *first charge* against himself, to submit to a "fishing" interrogation about his crimes, to furnish his own indictment from his own lips. Until the 1600's all parties concerned seemed to have operated on the premise that *after* pleading to the indictment, the accused could be compelled to incriminate himself. * * * When we apply the privilege to "arrests for investigation" or "routine pickups," do we disguise a revolutionary idea in the garb of the past or do we restore the privilege to its primordial state?

Nor should it be forgotten that for many centuries there were simply no "police interrogators" to whom the privilege could be applied. Although what Dean Wigmore calls "the first part" of the history of the privilege, the opposition to the ex officio oath of the ecclesiastical courts, began in the 1200's "criminal investigation by the police, with its concomitant of police interrogation, is a product of the late nineteenth century"; in eighteenth-century America as in eighteenth-century England "there were no police [in the modern sense] and, though some states seem to have had prosecutors, private prosecution was the rule rather than the exception." In fact as well as in theory, observes Professor Edmond M. Morgan, "there can be little question that the modern American police have taken over the functions performed originally by the English committing magistrates [and at least by some colonial magistrates]; they are in a real sense administrative officers and their questioning of the person under arrest is an investigative proceeding in which testimony is taken." If modern police are permitted to interrogate under the coercive influence of arrest and secret detention, then, insists Professor Albert R. Beisel, "they are doing the very same acts which historically the judiciary was doing in the seventeenth century but which the privilege against self-incrimination abolished."

I do not contend that "the implications of a tangled and obscure history" dictate that the privilege apply to the police station, only that they permit it. I do not claim that this long and involved history displaces judgment, only that it liberates it. I do not say that the distinct origins of the confession and self-incrimination rules are irrelevant, only that it is more important (if we share Dean Charles T. McCormick's views) that "the kinship of the two rules is too apparent for denial" and that "such policy as modern writers are able to discover as a basis for the self-incrimination privilege * * * pales to a flicker beside the flaming demands of justice and humanity for protection against extorted confessions."

Those who applaud the show in the mansion without hissing the show in the gatehouse may also:

Find refuge in the notion that compulsion to testify means *legal* compulsion. Since he is threatened neither with perjury for testifying falsely nor contempt for refusing to testify at all, it cannot be said, runs the argument, that the man in the back room of the police station is being "compelled" to be a "witness against himself" within the meaning of the privilege. Since the police have no legal right to make him answer, "there is no legal obligation to which a privilege in the technical sense can apply."

Can we accept this analysis without forgetting as lawyers and judges what we know as men? Without permitting logic to triumph over life? So long as "what on their face are merely words of request take on color from the officer's badge, gun and demeanor"; so long as his interrogators neither advise him of his rights nor permit him to consult with a lawyer who will; can there be any doubt that many a "subject" will *assume* that the police have a legal right to an answer? That many an incriminating statement will be extracted under "color" of law? So long as the interrogator is instructed to "get the idea across * * * that [he] has 'all the time in the world' "; so long as "the power [legal or otherwise] to extract answers begets a forgetfulness of the just limitations of the power" and "the simple and peaceful process of questioning breeds a readiness to resort to bullying and to physical force"; can there be any doubt that many a subject will assume that there is an *illegal* sanction for contumacy?

If these inferences are unfair, if very few "subjects" are misled to believe that there is either a legal obligation to talk or unlimited time and illegal means available to make them do so—if, in short, they know they can "shut up"—why are the police so bent on preventing counsel from telling them what they already know? Why, at least, don't the officers themselves tell their "subjects" plainly and emphatically that they need not and cannot be made to answer? That they will be permitted to consult with counsel, or be brought before a magistrate in short order? And why is the "subject" questioned in *secret?* Why does the modest proposal that a suspect be interrogated by or before an impartial functionary immediately after arrest "meet with scant favor in police circles, even from the most high-minded and highly respected elements in those circles"?

Finally, those who have learned to live with the widespread practices in the gatehouse may take the "waiver" tack. They may:

Concede that the privilege against self-incrimination exists in the police station, but maintain that when (instead of exercising his right to remain silent or to make only self-serving remarks) a suspect "volunteers" damaging statements he has *waived* his rights. This is not much of a concession for "if the privilege is easily waived, there is really no privilege at all." However, if "when the state is putting questions, the answers to which will disclose criminal activities by the witness, there is likely to be an especially high insistence checked by an especially high reluctance," then there is likely to be an especially low incidence of valid waiving of the privilege.

So long as "the classic definition of waiver enumerated in Johnson v. Zerbst—'an intelligent relinquishment or abandonment of a known right or privilege'—furnishes the controlling standard," so long as the courts "indulge every reasonable presumption against [such] waiver," it is difficult to see how the contention that an unadvised suspect waives the privilege simply by talking even presents a substantial question. "The Fourteenth Amendment," announced the Supreme Court only a year ago, "secures against state invasion the same privilege that the Fifth Amendment guarantees against federal infringement—the right of a person to remain silent unless he chooses to speak in the unfettered exercise of his own will." Can it seriously be said of the routine police interrogation that the suspect so speaks? Again, only a year ago, the Court pointed out that "no system of criminal justice can, or should, survive if it comes to depend for its continued effectiveness on the citizens' abdication through unawareness of their constitutional rights." On what else does the existing system depend? * * *

The trouble with both the "waiver" and "no legal compulsion" rationalizations of the existing *de facto* inquisitorial system is this: when we expect the police dutifully to notify a suspect of the very means he may utilize to frustrate them—when we rely on them to advise a suspect unbegrudgingly and unequivocally of the very rights he is being counted on *not* to assert—we demand too much of even our best officers. As Dean Edward L. Barrett has asked: "[I]s it the duty of the police to persuade the suspect to talk or persuade him not to talk? They cannot be expected to do both."

Suspects there are who feel in a "pleading guilty" mood, for some of the many reasons most defendants do plead guilty. Suspects there are who would intentionally relinquish their rights for some hoped-for favor from the state. I do not deny this. I do deny that such suspects do not need a lawyer.

Surely the man who, in effect, is pleading guilty in the gatehouse needs a lawyer no less than one who arrives at the same decision only after surviving the perilous journey through that structure.

* * *

SUTHERLAND, CRIME AND CONFESSION
79 Harvard L.Rev. 21 (1965) 36–37.

When men in authority are convinced that some governmental practice such as compulsory self-incrimination is convenient or essential, but the practice conflicts with an established constitutional principle, the unconstitutional practice may be given a euphemistic name suggestive of conformity with all the ancient freedoms. In the confession business this is accomplished by reciting the evident freedom of a man to admit his guilt if he wants to, and by then solemnly calling an extorted confession "voluntary." To be sure, as exemplified in a dreary series of records on appeal, criminal suspects frequently, under somewhat extraordinary circumstances, exercise their right thus to confess of their own volition. Their choice to forego constitutional immunities is often made during secret interrogations in which information as to constitutional rights is kept from the accused, or is hastily mentioned for the record and then avoided with persistent ingenuity. The man who under these circumstances "voluntarily" surrenders his right to remain silent, who gives away his constitutional shield, designed alike for the guilty and the innocent, surrenders it under circumstances in which no other legal act would be sustained as "voluntary" by any court anywhere.

Suppose a well-to-do testatrix says she intends to will her property to Elizabeth. John and James want her to bequeath it to them instead. They capture the testatrix, put her in a carefully designed room, out of touch with everyone but themselves and their convenient "witnesses," keep her secluded there for hours while they make insistent demands, weary her with contradictions of her assertions that she wants to leave her money to Elizabeth, and finally induce her to execute the will in their favor. Assume that John and James are deeply and correctly convinced that Elizabeth is unworthy and will make base use of the property if she gets her hands on it, whereas John and James have the noblest and most righteous intentions. Would any judge of probate accept the will so procured as the "voluntary" act of the testatrix?

At once one will hear the response that the testatrix is not a criminal; that obtaining a surrender of rights from a criminal is different; that the interest of the state demands that criminals be not coddled. That is to say we are told that a man with his life at stake should be able to surrender an ancient constitutional right to remain silent, under compulsions which in a surrender of a little property would obviously make the transaction void. No consensual dealing in any other field of the law—no signature of a deed, no execution of a contract, none whatever—would stand in any court when made under the circumstances of the confession in Cicenia v. Lagay in 1958 in New Jersey when police barricaded a suspect from his lawyer; or when obtained by the fraud practiced on the accused in Spano v. New York in 1959; or when procured by a police doctor posing as the prisoner's physician, the device used in Leyra v. Denno in 1954. The sorry catalogue could be extended indefinitely. The underlying vice in the confession cases is the involuntary "voluntariness" which until recently we have somehow come to think adequate to justify depriving a man of a deep-rooted constitutional privilege. We have been ready to let a man sign away his life under circumstances in which we would not recognize his conveyance of a subdivided lot. Sooner or later this was bound to end.

MIRANDA v. ARIZONA

Supreme Court of the United States, 1966.
384 U.S. 436, 86 S.Ct. 1602, 1609–1618, 1655–1659, 16 L.Ed.2d 694.

Mr. Chief Justice WARREN delivered the opinion of the Court.

The cases before us raise questions which go to the roots of our concepts of American criminal jurisprudence: the restraints society must observe consistent with the Federal Constitution in prosecuting individuals for crime. More specifically, we deal with the admissibility of statements obtained from an individual who is subjected to custodial police interrogation and the necessity for procedures which assure that the individual is accorded his privilege under the Fifth Amendment to the Constitution not to be compelled to incriminate himself.

* * *

Our holding will be spelled out with some specificity in the pages which follow but briefly stated it is this: the prosecution may not use statements, whether exculpatory or inculpatory, stemming from custodial interrogation of the defendant unless it demonstrates the use of procedural safeguards effective to secure the privilege against self-incrimination. By custodial interrogation, we mean questioning initiated by law enforcement officers after a person has been taken into custody or otherwise deprived of his freedom of action in any significant way. As for the procedural safeguards to be employed, unless other fully effective means are devised to inform accused persons of their right of silence and to assure a continuous opportunity to exercise it, the following measures are required. Prior to any questioning, the person must be warned that he has a right to remain silent, that any statement he does make may be used as evidence against him, and that he has a right to the presence of an attorney, either retained or appointed. The defendant may waive effectuation of these rights, provided the waiver is made voluntarily, knowingly and intelligently. If, however, he indicates in any manner and at any stage of the process that he wishes to consult with an attorney before speaking there can be no questioning. Likewise, if the individual is alone and indicates in any manner that he does not wish to be interrogated, the police may not question him. The mere fact that he may have answered some questions or volunteered some statements on his own does not deprive him of the right to refrain from answering any further inquiries until he has consulted with an attorney and thereafter consents to be questioned.

I.

The constitutional issue we decide in each of these cases is the admissibility of statements obtained from a defendant questioned while in custody or otherwise deprived of his freedom of action in any significant way. In each, the defendant was questioned by police officers, detectives, or a prosecuting attorney in a room in which he was cut off from the outside world. In none of these cases was the defendant given a full and effective warning of his rights at the outset of the interrogation process. In all the cases, the questioning elicited oral admissions, and in three of them, signed statements as well which were admitted at their trials. They all thus share salient features—incommunicado interrogation of individuals in a police-dominated atmosphere, resulting in self-incriminating statements without full warnings of constitutional rights.

An understanding of the nature and setting of this in-custody interrogation is essential to our decisions today. The difficulty in depicting what transpires at such interrogations stems from the fact that in this country they have largely taken place incommunicado. From extensive factual studies undertaken in the early 1930's, including the famous Wickersham Report to Congress by a Presidential Commission, it is clear that police violence and the "third degree" flourished at that time. In a series of cases decided by this Court long after these studies, the police resorted to physical brutality— beatings, hanging, whipping—and to sustained and protracted questioning incommunicado in order to extort confessions. The Commission on Civil Rights in 1961 found much evidence to indicate that "some policemen still resort to physical force to obtain confessions," 1961 Comm'n on Civil Rights Rep., Justice, pt. 5, 17. The use of physical brutality and violence is not, unfortunately, relegated to the past or to any part of the country. Only recently in Kings County, New York, the police brutally beat, kicked and placed lighted cigarette butts on the back of a potential witness under interrogation for the purpose of securing a statement incriminating a third party. People v. Portelli, 15 N.Y.2d 235, 257 N.Y.S.2d 931, 205 N.E.2d 857 (1965).[7]

---

7. In addition, see People v. Wakat, 415 Ill. 610, 114 N.E.2d 706 (1953); Wakat v. Harlib, 253 F.2d 59 (C.A.7th Cir. 1958) (defendant suffering from broken bones, multiple bruises and injuries sufficiently serious to require eight months' medical treatment after being manhandled by five policemen); Kier v. State, 213 Md. 556, 132 A.2d 494 (1957) (police doctor told accused, who was strapped to a chair completely nude, that he proposed to take hair and skin scrapings from anything that looked like blood or sperm from various parts of his body); Bruner v. People, 113 Colo. 194, 156 P.2d 111 (1945) (defendant held in custody over two months, deprived of food for 15

The examples given above are undoubtedly the exception now, but they are sufficiently widespread to be the object of concern. Unless a proper limitation upon custodial interrogation is achieved—such as these decisions will advance—there can be no assurance that practices of this nature will be eradicated in the foreseeable future. The conclusion of the Wickersham Commission Report, made over 30 years ago, is still pertinent:

> "To the contention that the third degree is necessary to get the facts, the reporters aptly reply in the language of the present Lord Chancellor of England (Lord Sankey): 'It is not admissible to do a great right by doing a little wrong. * * * It is not sufficient to do justice by obtaining a proper result by irregular or improper means.' Not only does the use of the third degree involve a flagrant violation of law by the officers of the law, but it involves also the dangers of false confessions, and it tends to make police and prosecutors less zealous in the search for objective evidence. As the New York prosecutor quoted in the report said, 'It is a short cut and makes the police lazy and unenterprising.' Or, as another official quoted remarked: 'If you use your fists, you are not so likely to use your wits.' We agree with the conclusion expressed in the report, that 'The third degree brutalizes the police, hardens the prisoner against society, and lowers the esteem in which the administration of justice is held by the public.'" IV National Commission on Law Observance and Enforcement, Report on Lawlessness in Law Enforcement 5 (1931).

Again we stress that the modern practice of in-custody interrogation is psychologically rather than physically oriented. As we have stated before, "Since Chambers v. State of Florida, 309 U.S. 227, 60 S.Ct. 472, 84 L.Ed. 716, this Court has recognized that coercion can be mental as well as physical, and that the blood of the accused is not the only hallmark of an unconstitutional inquisition." * * * Interrogation still takes place in privacy. Privacy results in secrecy and this in turn results in a gap in our knowledge as to what in fact goes on in the interrogation rooms. A valuable source of information about present police practices, however, may be found in various police manuals and texts which document procedures employed with success in the past, and which recommend various other effective tactics. These texts are used by law enforcement agencies

---

hours, forced to submit to a lie detector test when he wanted to go to the toilet); People v. Matlock, 51 Cal.2d 682, 336 P.2d 505, 71 A.L.R.2d 605 (1959) (defendant questioned incessantly over an evening's time, made to lie on cold board and to answer questions whenever it appeared he was getting sleepy). Other cases are documented in American Civil Liberties Union, Illinois Division, Secret Detention by the Chicago Police (1959); Potts, The Preliminary Examination and "The Third Degree," 2 Baylor L.Rev. 131 (1950); Sterling, Police Interrogation and the Psychology of Confession, 14 J.Pub.L. 25 (1965).

themselves as guides. It should be noted that these texts professedly present the most enlightened and effective means presently used to obtain statements through custodial interrogation. By considering these texts and other data, it is possible to describe procedures observed and noted around the country.

The officers are told by the manuals that the "principal psychological factor contributing to a successful interrogation is privacy—being alone with the person under interrogation." The efficacy of this tactic has been explained as follows:

> "If at all practicable, the interrogation should take place in the investigator's office or at least in a room of his own choice. The subject should be deprived of every psychological advantage. In his own home he may be confident, indignant, or recalcitrant. He is more keenly aware of his rights and more reluctant to tell of his indiscretions or criminal behavior within the walls of his home. Moreover his family and other friends are nearby, their presence lending moral support. In his office, the investigator possesses all the advantages. The atmosphere suggests the invincibility of the forces of the law."

To highlight the isolation and unfamiliar surroundings, the manuals instruct the police to display an air of confidence in the suspect's guilt and from outward appearance to maintain only an interest in confirming certain details. The guilt of the subject is to be posited as a fact. The interrogator should direct his comments toward the reasons why the subject committed the act, rather than court failure by asking the subject whether he did it. Like other men, perhaps the subject has had a bad family life, had an unhappy childhood, had too much to drink, had an unrequited desire for women. The officers are instructed to minimize the moral seriousness of the offense, to cast blame on the victim or on society. These tactics are designed to put the subject in a psychological state where his story is but an elaboration of what the police purport to know already—that he is guilty. Explanations to the contrary are dismissed and discouraged.

The texts thus stress that the major qualities an interrogator should possess are patience and perseverance. One writer describes the efficacy of these characteristics in this manner:

> "In the preceding paragraphs emphasis has been placed on kindness and stratagems. The investigator will, however, encounter many situations where the sheer weight of his personality will be the deciding factor. Where emotional appeals and tricks are employed to no avail, he must rely on an oppressive atmosphere of dogged persistence. He must interrogate steadily and without relent, leaving the subject no prospect of surcease. He must dominate his subject and overwhelm him with his inexorable will to obtain the truth.

He should interrogate for a spell of several hours pausing only for the subject's necessities in acknowledgement of the need to avoid a charge of duress that can be technically substantiated. In a serious case, the interrogation may continue for days, with the required intervals for food and sleep, but with no respite from the atmosphere of domination. It is possible in this way to induce the subject to talk without resorting to duress or coercion. The method should be used only when the guilt of the subject appears highly probable."

The manuals suggest that the suspect be offered legal excuses for his actions in order to obtain an initial admission of guilt. Where there is a suspected revenge-killing, for example, the interrogator may say:

"Joe, you probably didn't go out looking for this fellow with the purpose of shooting him. My guess is, however, that you expected something from him and that's why you carried a gun—for your own protection. You knew him for what he was, no good. Then when you met him he probably started using foul, abusive language and he gave some indication that he was about to pull a gun on you, and that's when you had to act to save your own life. That's about it, isn't it, Joe?"

Having then obtained the admission of shooting, the interrogator is advised to refer to circumstantial evidence which negates the self-defense explanation. This should enable him to secure the entire story. One text notes that "Even if he fails to do so, the inconsistency between the subject's original denial of the shooting and his present admission of at least doing the shooting will serve to deprive him of a self-defense 'out' at the time of trial."

When the techniques described above prove unavailing, the texts recommend they be alternated with a show of some hostility. One ploy often used has been termed the "friendly-unfriendly" or the "Mutt and Jeff" act:

"* * * In this technique, two agents are employed. Mutt, the relentless investigator, who knows the subject is guilty and is not going to waste any time. He's sent a dozen men away for this crime and he's going to send the subject away for the full term. Jeff, on the other hand, is obviously a kindhearted man. He has a family himself. He has a brother who was involved in a little scrape like this. He disapproves of Mutt and his tactics and will arrange to get him off the case if the subject will cooperate. He can't hold Mutt off for very long. The subject would be wise to make a quick decision. The technique is applied by having both investigators present while Mutt acts out his role. Jeff may stand by quietly and demur at some of Mutt's tactics. When Jeff makes his plea for cooperation, Mutt is not present in the room." [17]

The interrogators sometimes are instructed to induce a confession out of trickery. The technique here is quite effective in crimes which require identification or which run in series. In the identification situation, the interrogator may take a break in his questioning to place the subject among a group of men in a line-up. "The witness or complainant (previously coached, if necessary) studies the line-up and confidently points out the subject as the guilty party." Then the questioning resumes "as though there were now no doubt about the guilt of the subject." A variation on this technique is called the "reverse line-up":

> "The accused is placed in a line-up, but this time he is identified by several fictitious witnesses or victims who associated him with different offenses. It is expected that the subject will become desperate and confess to the offense under investigation in order to escape from the false accusations."

The manuals also contain instructions for police on how to handle the individual who refuses to discuss the matter entirely, or who asks for an attorney or relatives. The examiner is to concede him the right to remain silent. "This usually has a very undermining effect. First of all, he is disappointed in his expectation of an unfavorable reaction on the part of the interrogator. Secondly, a concession of this right to remain silent impresses the subject with the apparent fairness of his interrogator." After this psychological conditioning, however, the officer is told to point out the incriminating significance of the suspect's refusal to talk:

> "Joe, you have a right to remain silent. That's your privilege and I'm the last person in the world who'll try to take it away from you. If that's the way you want to leave this, O.K. But let me ask you this. Suppose you were in my shoes and I were in yours and you called me in to ask me about this and I told you, 'I don't want to answer any of your questions.' You'd think I had something to hide, and you'd probably be right in thinking that. That's exactly

---

17. O'Hara, supra, at 104, Inbau & Reid, supra, at 58–59. See Spano v. People of State of New York, 360 U.S. 315, 79 S.Ct. 1202, 3 L.Ed.2d 1265 (1959). A variant on the technique of creating hostility is one of engendering fear. This is perhaps best described by the prosecuting attorney in Malinski v. People of State of New York, 324 U.S. 401, 407, 65 S.Ct. 781, 784, 89 L.Ed. 1029 (1945): "Why this talk about being undressed? Of course, they had a right to undress him to look for bullet scars, and keep the clothes off him. That was quite proper police procedure. That is some more psychology—let him sit around with a blanket on him, humiliate him there for a while; let him sit in the corner, let him think he is going to get a shellacking."

what I'll have to think about you, and so will everybody else. So let's sit here and talk this whole thing over."

Few will persist in their initial refusal to talk, it is said, if this monologue is employed correctly.

In the event that the subject wishes to speak to a relative or an attorney, the following advice is tendered:

"[T]he interrogator should respond by suggesting that the subject first tell the truth to the interrogator himself rather than get anyone else involved in the matter. If the request is for an attorney, the interrogator may suggest that the subject save himself or his family the expense of any such professional service, particularly if he is innocent of the offense under investigation. The interrogator may also add, 'Joe, I'm only looking for the truth, and if you're telling the truth, that's it. You can handle this by yourself.'"
* * *

[Reversed.]

[The dissenting opinions of Justices HARLAN, CLARK, STEWART, and WHITE are omitted.]

REPRINTED FROM HALL AND KAMISAR, MODERN CRIMINAL PROCEDURE

119–120 (1965) *

ANONYMOUS—AN HONEST CONFESSION MAY BE GOOD FOR THE SOUL, BUT NOT FOR THE F.B.I.

Scene: Office of F.B.I.

A few straight chairs, a desk, at which is seated an investigator for the F.B.I., reading the recent decision of McNabb v. the United States * * *

Enter: A hill billy backwoodsman.

Hill Billy: Is this the F.B.I.?
Investigator: Yes. Is there anything I can do for you?
H. B.: Yes, sir. I've killed a revenooer and I want to confess.
F.B.I.: Wait a minute. I'll have to hunt you an upholstered and plush-covered chair. A man can't confess unless he is comfortable. It's been so held by the court.
H. B.: But I'm only uncomfortable in mind. I don't keer to set.

* Copyright, 1965 by West Publishing Co.

F.B.I.:	You surely must not have read the ruling of Judge Frankfurter in which he held that you could not have a man uncomfortable who is about to confess a murder.
H. B.:	Shore nuff?
F.B.I.:	Were are your kin folks?
H. B.:	I ain't got none lessen you think my mother-in-law's kin.
F.B.I.:	You can't confess unless you brought your relatives along.
H. B.:	Well, me and her ain't a speakin' and she won't help me none.
F.B.I.:	Did you graduate from college?
H. B.:	Did I what?
F.B.I.:	How far did you get in school?
H. B.:	To the 4th grade.
F.B.I.:	I'm afraid you can't qualify. The Supreme Court has held that confessions by men who had not passed the 4th grade were no good. You've got to be educated to confess.
H. B.:	But that's agin the Preacher and the Good Book. They say confess yer sins, and they don't say nothin' about schoolin' and kin folks.
F.B.I.:	But it's the law, brother. Furthermore, I haven't seen your lawyer. Where's he?
H. B.:	Mister, you don't seem to understand. I want to tell the truth—not to git around it. I don't have to hire a lawyer before I can tell the truth, do I?
F.B.I.:	I'm sorry, but your notions are old fashioned. It used to be the law that a criminal could confess, provided he was advised and warned of his rights, and provided no force or violence was used, and provided no promise or reward was made to him, and provided he was not put in fear or duress. Lots of them used to confess when they found we had the proof on them, but that was horse and buggy law. Now a criminal must have his kin folks with him, must be comfortable, must have a lawyer, whether he asks for one or not, must have been educated past the 4th grade, and must have traveled at least further than Jasper. By the way, how far have you traveled away from home?

H. B.:	I ain't ever been out of the state in my life. I never run away. I jes' decided I'd stay and take my medicine.
F.B.I.:	Hell, that lets you out. You haven't got a single characteristic of a qualified confessor.
H. B.:	But mister, I killed a man—
F.B.I.:	Stop! I've been talking to you now nearly an hour, and that alone would disqualify you.
H. B.:	But the parson says that an honest confession is good for the soul.
F.B.I.:	I sympathize with you, brother, but there are only two courses left open to you: One is to bear your troubles in silence; the other is to go back to school, then travel abroad, marry you some kin folks, hire you a lawyer, and bring them down here with you. In the meantime, I'll try to get this office air-conditioned, and also have a nice overstuffed chair for you. Then I will hear your confession. But remember, you will have to make it short and snappy.
H. B.:	(Departing perplexedly) Well, I'll be damned.

HARRIS v. NEW YORK

Supreme Court of the United States, 1971.
401 U.S. 222, 91 S.Ct. 643, 28 L.Ed.2d 1.

Mr. Chief Justice BURGER delivered the opinion of the Court.

We granted the writ in this case to consider petitioner's claim that a statement made by him to police under circumstances rendering it inadmissible to establish the prosecution's case in chief under Miranda v. Arizona, * * * may not be used to impeach his credibility.

The State of New York charged petitioner in a two-count indictment with twice selling heroin to an undercover police officer. At a subsequent jury trial the officer was the State's chief witness, and he testified as to details of the two sales. A second officer verified collateral details of the sales, and a third offered testimony about the chemical analysis of the heroin.

Petitioner took the stand in his own defense. He admitted knowing the undercover police officer but denied a sale on January 4, 1966. He admitted making a sale of contents of a glassine bag to the officer on January 6 but claimed it was baking powder and part of a scheme to defraud the purchaser.

On cross-examination petitioner was asked seriatim whether he had made specified statements to the police immediately following his arrest on January 7—statements that partially contradicted petitioner's direct testimony at trial. In response to the cross-examination, petitioner testified that he could not remember virtually any of the questions or answers recited by the prosecutor. At the request of petitioner's counsel the written statement from which the prosecutor had read questions and answers in his impeaching process was placed in the record for possible use on appeal; the statement was not shown to the jury.

The trial judge instructed the jury that the statements attributed to petitioner by the prosecution could be considered only in passing on petitioner's credibility and not as evidence of guilt. In closing summations both counsel argued the substance of the impeaching statements. The jury then found petitioner guilty on the second count of the indictment. The New York Court of Appeals affirmed in a *per curiam* opinion, * * *.

At trial the prosecution made no effort in its case in chief to use the statements allegedly made by petitioner, conceding that they were inadmissible under Miranda v. Arizona, * * *. The transcript of the interrogation used in the impeachment, but not given to the jury, shows that no warning of a right to appointed counsel was given before questions were put to petitioner when he was taken into custody. Petitioner makes no claim that the statements made to the police were coerced or involuntary.

Some comments in the *Miranda* opinion can indeed be read as indicating a bar to use of an uncounseled statement for any purpose, but discussion of that issue was not at all necessary to the Court's holding and cannot be regarded as controlling. *Miranda* barred the prosecution from making its case with statements of an accused made while in custody prior to having or effectively waiving counsel. It does not follow from *Miranda* that evidence inadmissible against an accused in the prosecution's case in chief is barred for all purposes, provided of course that the trustworthiness of the evidence satisfies legal standards.

In Walder v. United States, 347 U.S. 62, * * * the Court permitted physical evidence, inadmissible in the case in chief, to be used for impeachment purposes.

> "It is one thing to say that the Government cannot make an affirmative use of evidence unlawfully obtained. It is quite another to say that the defendant can turn the illegal method by which evidence in the Government's possession was obtained to his own advantage, and provide himself with a shield against contradiction of his untruths. Such an extension of the *Weeks* doctrine would be a perversion of the Fourth Amendment.
>
> "[T]here is hardly justification for letting the defendant affirmatively resort to perjurious testimony in reliance

on the Government's disability to challenge his credibility." 347 U.S., at 65, 74 S.Ct., at 356.

It is true that Walder was impeached as to collateral matters included in his direct examination, whereas petitioner here was impeached as to testimony bearing more directly on the crimes charged. We are not persuaded that there is a difference in principle that warrants a result different from that reached by the Court in *Walder*. Petitioner's testimony in his own behalf concerning the events of January 7 contrasted sharply with what he told the police shortly after his arrest. The impeachment process here undoubtedly provided valuable aid to the jury in assessing petitioner's credibility, and the benefits of this process should not be lost, in our view, because of the speculative possibility that impermissible police conduct will be encouraged thereby. Assuming that the exclusionary rule has a deterrent effect on proscribed police conduct, sufficient deterrence flows when the evidence in question is made unavailable to the prosecution in its case in chief.

Every criminal defendant is privileged to testify in his own defense, or to refuse to do so. But that privilege cannot be construed to include the right to commit perjury. * * * Having voluntarily taken the stand, petitioner was under an obligation to speak truthfully and accurately, and the prosecution here did no more than utilize the traditional truth-testing devices of the adversary process.[2] Had inconsistent statements been made by the accused to some third person, it could hardly be contended that the conflict could not be laid before the jury by way of cross-examination and impeachment.

The shield provided by *Miranda* cannot be perverted into a license to use perjury by way of a defense, free from the risk of confrontation with prior inconsistent utterances. We hold, therefore, that petitioner's credibility was appropriately impeached by use of his earlier conflicting statements.

Affirmed.

[Dissent omitted.]

---

2. If, for example, an accused confessed fully to a homicide and led the police to the body of the victim under circumstances making his confession inadmissible, the petitioner would have us allow that accused to take the stand and blandly deny every fact disclosed to the police or discovered as a "fruit" of his confession, free from confrontation with his prior statements and acts. The voluntariness of the confession would, on this thesis, be totally irrelevant. We reject such an extravagant extension of the Constitution. * * *

D. NON–TESTIMONIAL EVIDENCE

SCHMERBER v. CALIFORNIA

Supreme Court of the United States, 1966.
384 U.S. 757, 86 S.Ct. 1826, 16 L.Ed.2d 908.

Mr. Justice BRENNAN delivered the opinion of the Court.

Petitioner was convicted in Los Angeles Municipal Court of the criminal offense of driving an automobile while under the influence of intoxicating liquor. He had been arrested at a hospital while receiving treatment for injuries suffered in an accident involving the automobile that he had apparently been driving. At the direction of a police officer, a blood sample was then withdrawn from petitioner's body by a physician at the hospital. The chemical analysis of this sample revealed a percent by weight of alcohol in his blood at the time of the offense which indicated intoxication, and the report of this analysis was admitted in evidence at the trial. Petitioner objected to receipt of this evidence of the analysis on the ground that the blood had been withdrawn despite his refusal, on the advice of his counsel, to consent to the test. He contended that in that circumstance the withdrawal of the blood and the admission of the analysis in evidence denied him due process of law under the Fourteenth Amendment, as well as specific guarantees of the Bill of Rights secured against the States by that Amendment: his privilege against self-incrimination under the Fifth Amendment; his right to counsel under the Sixth Amendment; and his right not to be subjected to unreasonable searches and seizures in violation of the Fourth Amendment. The Appellate Department of the California Superior Court rejected these contentions and affirmed the conviction. * * * We affirm.

* * *

II.

THE PRIVILEGE AGAINST SELF–INCRIMINATION CLAIM

Breithaupt summarily rejected an argument that the withdrawal of blood and the admission of the analysis report involved in that state case violated the Fifth Amendment privilege of any person not to "be compelled in any criminal case to be a witness against himself," citing Twining v. State of New Jersey * * *. But that case, holding that the protections of the Fourteenth Amendment do not embrace this Fifth Amendment privilege, has been succeeded by Malloy v. Hogan * * *. We there held that "[t]he Fourteenth Amendment secures against state invasion the same privilege that the Fifth Amendment guarantees against federal infringement—the right of a person to remain silent unless he chooses to speak in the unfettered exercise of his own will, and to suffer no penalty * * * for such silence." We therefore must now decide whether the withdrawal of the blood and admission in evidence of the analysis involved in this case violated petitioner's privilege. We hold that the privilege protects an accused only from being compelled to testify against himself, or otherwise provide the State with evidence of a testimonial or communicative nature,[5] and that the withdrawal of blood and use of the analysis in question in this case did not involve compulsion to these ends.

It could not be denied that in requiring petitioner to submit to the withdrawal and chemical analysis of his blood the State compelled him to submit to an attempt to discover evidence that might be used to prosecute him for a criminal offense. He submitted only after the police officer rejected his objection and directed the physician to proceed. The officer's direction to the physician to administer the test over petitioner's objection constituted compulsion for the purposes of the privilege. The critical question, then, is whether petitioner was thus compelled "to be a witness against himself." [6]

If the scope of the privilege coincided with the complex of values it helps to protect, we might be obliged to conclude that the privilege was violated. In Miranda v. Arizona, * * * the Court said of the interests, protected by the privilege: "All these policies point to one overriding thought: the constitutional foundation underlying the privilege is the respect a government—state or federal—must accord to the dignity and integrity of its citizens. To maintain a 'fair state-individual balance,' to require the government 'to shoulder the entire load,' * * * to respect the inviolability of the human personality, our accusatory system of criminal justice demands that the government seeking to punish an individual produce the evidence

---

5. A dissent suggests that the report of the blood test was "testimonial" or "communicative," because the test was performed in order to obtain the testimony of others, communicating to the jury facts about petitioner's condition. Of course, all evidence received in court is "testimonial" or "communicative" if these words are thus used. But the Fifth Amendment relates only to acts on the part of the person to whom the privilege applies, and we use these words subject to the same limitations. A nod or head-shake is as much a "testimonial" or "communicative" act in this sense as are spoken words. But the terms as we use them do not apply to evidence of acts non-communicative in nature as to the person asserting the privilege, even though, as here, such acts are compelled to obtain the testimony of others.

6. Many state constitutions, including those of most of the original Colonies, phrase the privilege in terms of compelling a person to give "evidence" against himself. But our decision cannot turn on the Fifth Amendment's use of the word "witness." "[A]s the manifest purpose of the constitutional provisions, both of the states and of the United States, is to prohibit the compelling of testimony of a self-incriminating kind from a party or a witness, the liberal construction which must be placed upon constitutional provisions for the protection of personal rights would seem to require that the constitutional guaranties, however differently worded, should have as far as possible the same interpretation * * *." Counselman v. Hitchcock, 142 U.S. 547, 584–585, 12 S.Ct. 195, 206, 35 L.Ed. 1110. 8 Wigmore, Evidence § 2252 (McNaughton rev. 1961).

against him by its own independent labors, rather than by the cruel, simple expedient of compelling it from his own mouth." The withdrawal of blood necessarily involves puncturing the skin for extraction, and the percent by weight of alcohol in that blood, as established by chemical analysis, is evidence of criminal guilt. Compelled submission fails on one view to respect the "inviolability of the human personality." Moreover, since it enables the State to rely on evidence forced from the accused, the compulsion violates at least one meaning of the requirement that the State procure the evidence against an accused "by its own independent labors."

As the passage in Miranda implicitly recognizes, however, the privilege has never been given the full scope which the values it helps to protect suggest. History and a long line of authorities in lower courts have consistently limited its protection to situations in which the State seeks to submerge those values by obtaining the evidence against an accused through "the cruel, simple expedient of compelling it from his own mouth. * * * In sum, the privilege is fulfilled only when the person is guaranteed the right 'to remain silent unless he chooses to speak in the unfettered exercise of his own will.'" The leading case in this Court is Holt v. United States, 218 U.S. 245 * * *. There the question was whether evidence was admissible that the accused, prior to trial and over his protest, put on a blouse that fitted him. It was contended that compelling the accused to submit to the demand that he model the blouse violated the privilege. Mr. Justice Holmes, speaking for the Court, rejected the argument as "based upon an extravagant extension of the 5th Amendment," and went on to say: "[T]he prohibition of compelling a man in a criminal court to be witness against himself is a prohibition of the use of physical or moral compulsion to extort communications from him, not an exclusion of his body as evidence when it may be material. The objection in principle would forbid a jury to look at a prisoner and compare his features with a photograph in proof." 218 U.S., at 252–253, 31 S.Ct., at 6.

It is clear that the protection of the privilege reaches an accused's communications, whatever form they might take, and the compulsion of responses which are also communications, for example, compliance with a subpoena to produce one's papers. * * * On the other hand, both federal and state courts have usually held that it offers no protection against compulsion to submit to fingerprinting, photographing, or measurements, to write or speak for identification, to appear in court, to stand, to assume a stance, to walk, or to make a particular gesture. The distinction which has emerged, often expressed in different ways, is that the privilege is a bar against compelling "communications" or "testimony," but that compulsion which makes a suspect or accused the source of "real or physical evidence" does not violate it.

Although we agree that this distinction is a helpful framework for analysis, we are not to be understood to agree with past applications in all instances. There will be many cases in which such a distinction is not readily drawn. Some tests seemingly directed to obtain "physical evidence," for example, lie detector tests measuring changes in body function during interrogation, may actually be directed to eliciting responses which are essentially testimonial. To compel a person to submit to testing in which an effort will be made to determine his guilt or innocence on the basis of physiological responses, whether willed or not, is to evoke the spirit and history of the Fifth Amendment. Such situations call to mind the principle that the protection of the privilege "is as broad as the mischief against which it seeks to guard." Counselman v. Hitchcock, 142 U.S. 547, 562, 12 S.Ct. 195, 198.

In the present case, however, no such problem of application is presented. Not even a shadow of testimonial compulsion upon or enforced communication by the accused was involved either in the extraction or in the chemical analysis. Petitioner's testimonial capacities were in no way implicated; indeed his participation, except as a donor, was irrelevant to the results of the test, which depend on chemical analysis and on that alone.[7] Since the blood test evidence, although an incriminating product of compulsion, was neither petitioner's testimony nor evidence relating to some communicative act or writing by the petitioner, it was not inadmissible on privilege grounds. * * *

Affirmed.

[The separate concurring opinion of Mr. Justice HARLAN, who was joined by Mr. Justice STEWART, is omitted, as are the dissent-

---

7. This conclusion would not necessarily govern had the State tried to show that the accused had incriminated himself when told that he would have to be tested. Such incriminating evidence may be an unavoidable by-product of the compulsion to take the test, especially for an individual who fears the extraction or opposes it on religious grounds. If it wishes to compel persons to submit to such attempts to discover evidence, the State may have to forgo the advantage of any *testimonial* products of administering the test —products which would fall within the privilege. Indeed, there may be circumstances in which the pain, danger, or severity of an operation would almost inevitably cause a person to prefer confession to undergoing the "search," and nothing we say today should be taken as establishing the permissibility of compulsion in that case. But no such situation is presented in this case. See text at n. 13 infra.

Petitioner has raised a similar issue in this case, in connection with a police request that he submit to a "breathalyzer" test of air expelled from his lungs for alcohol content. He refused the request, and evidence of his refusal was admitted in evidence without objection. He argues that the introduction of this evidence and a comment by the prosecutor in closing argument upon his refusal is ground for reversal under Griffin v. State of California, 380 U.S. 609, 85 S.Ct. 1229, 14 L.Ed.2d 106. We think general Fifth Amendment principles, rather than the particular holding of *Griffin* would be applicable in these circumstances, see Miranda v. Arizona, 384 U.S. at p. 468, n. 37, 86 S.Ct. 1624.

ing opinions of Mr. Chief Justice WARREN, and Justices BLACK, DOUGLAS, and FORTAS.]

NOTE

See also People v. Sudduth, 65 Cal.2d 543, 55 Cal.Rptr. 393, 421 P.2d 401 (1966) (privilege against self-incrimination of a defendant in a drunk driving prosecution not violated by the admission of evidence of, and comment on his refusal to take a Breathalyzer test); People v. Ellis, 65 Cal.2d 529, 55 Cal.Rptr. 385, 421 P.2d 393 (1966) (voice identification tests are not within the privilege against self-incrimination, following *Schmerber*). See Weintraub, Voice Identification, Writing Exemplars and the Privilege Against Self-Incrimination, 10 Vander.L.Rev. 485 (1957).

COLLATERAL READINGS

The Privilege Against Compulsory Self-Incrimination

McCormick's Handbook of the Law of Evidence §§ 114–143, 145, 151–154, 163 (2d ed. 1972)

Wigmore, Evidence (3rd ed. 1940)

    Vol. 3, § 823

    Vol. 8, §§ 2250–2284 (McNaughton rev. 1961)

Griswold, The Fifth Amendment Today (1955)

Hook, Common Sense and the Fifth Amendment (1957)

Mayers, Shall We Amend The Fifth Amendment? (1959)

Levy, Origins of the Fifth Amendment (1968)

Waltz, Criminal Evidence, Ch. 8 (1975)

Eli, Confessions: The Problem and a Practical Solution—The Case for an Absolute Fifth Amendment, 7 Linc.L.Rev. 225 (1972)

Note, Extension of the Fifth Amendment Right Against Self-Incrimination, 52 Bost.U.L.Rev. 149 (1972)

Comment, Kastigar v. United States (92 Sup.Ct. 1653): The Required Scope of Immunity, 58 Va.L.Rev. 1099 (1972)

Aronson, Should the Privilege Against Self-Incrimination Apply to Compelled Psychiatric Examinations?, 26 Stan.L.Rev. 55 (1973)

Note, Constitutional Law—Privilege Against Self-Incrimination, 25 Baylor L.Rev. 181 (1973)

Comment, Protection of Privacy by the Privilege Against Self-Incrimination: A Doctrine Laid to Rest? 59 Iowa L.Rev. 1336 (1974)

Gorecki, Miranda and Beyond—The Fifth Amendment Reconsidered, 1975 U.Ill.L.F. 295

Morgan, The Privilege Against Self-Incrimination, 34 Minn.L.Rev. 1 (1949)

Falknor, Self-Crimination Privilege: "Links in the Chain," 5 Vand. L.Rev. 479 (1952).

Ratner, Consequences of Exercising the Privilege against Self-Incrimination, 24 U.Chi.L.Rev. 472 (1957)

McNaughton, The Privilege Against Self-Incrimination, Its Constitutional Affectation, Raison d'Etre and Miscellaneous Implications, 51 J.Crim.L., C. & P.S. 138 (1960)

Louisell, Criminal Discovery and Self-Incrimination: Roger Traynor Confronts the Dilemma, 53 Calif.L.Rev. 89 (1965)

Duke, Prosecutions for Attempts to Evade Income Tax: A Discordant View of a Procedural Hybrid, 76 Yale L.J. 1 (1966)

Mansfield, Albertson Case: Conflict between the Privilege against Self-Incrimination and the Government's Need for Information, 1966 Supreme Court Rev. 103

Note, Federalism and the Fifth: Configurations of the Grant of Immunity, 12 U.C.L.A.L.Rev. 561 (1965)

McKay, Self-Incrimination and the New Privacy, 1967 Supreme Court Rev. 193

Schwartz and Bator, Criminal Justice in the Mid-Sixties: Escobedo Revisited, 42 F.R.D. 463 (1967)

Carlson, Cross-Examination of the Accused, 52 Corn.L.Q. 705 (1967)

Note, Interrogations in New Haven: The Impact of Miranda, 76 Yale L.J. 1519 (1967)

Comment, Criminal Law: Self-Incrimination: Right to Counsel, 51 Marq.L.Rev. 191 (1967)

Comment, Criminal Law—Self-Incrimination—Compulsory Mental Examinations, 19 Case W.Res.L.Rev. 382 (1968)

Note, Constitutionally Privileged False Statements, 22 Stan.L.Rev. 783 (1970)

Comment, Constitutional Law—Self-Incrimination—Use of Confessions for Impeachment Purposes—The United States Supreme Court Has Held that the Voluntary Confessions of Criminally Accused, Made in the Absence of Full Miranda Warnings, May Be Used to Impeach His Credibility, 10 Duquesne L.Rev. 128 (1971)

Comment, Criminal Law—Statements Obtained in Violation of Miranda May Be Used for Impeachment, 25 Ark.L.Rev. 190 (1971)

Comment, Evidence—Criminal Law—"Trustworthy" Self-Incriminating Evidence Not Otherwise Admissible to Impeach an Accused's Trial Testimony, 49 Tex.L.Rev. 1119 (1971)

Comment, Evidence-Statements Obtained in Violation of Miranda Guidelines May Be Used to Impeach Testifying Defendant's Credibility, 24 Vand.L.Rev. 843 (1971)

Dershowitz and Ely, Harris v. New York: [401 U.S. 222] Some Anxious Observations on the Candor and Logic of the Emerging Nixon Majority, 80 Yale L.J. 1198 (1971)

Chapter VIII

GOVERNMENTAL PRIVILEGES

A. STATE SECRETS

WEST'S ANNOTATED CALIFORNIA EVIDENCE CODE

§ 1040. Privilege for official information

(a) As used in this section, "official information" means information acquired in confidence by a public employee in the course of his duty and not open, or officially disclosed, to the public prior to the time the claim of privilege is made.

(b) A public entity has a privilege to refuse to disclose official information, and to prevent another from disclosing such information, if the privilege is claimed by a person authorized by the public entity to do so and:

(1) Disclosure is forbidden by an act of the Congress of the United States or a statute of this state; or

(2) Disclosure of the information is against the public interest because there is a necessity for preserving the confidentiality of the information that outweighs the necessity for disclosure in the interest of justice; but no privilege may be claimed under this paragraph if any person authorized to do so has consented that the information be disclosed in the proceeding. In determining whether disclosure of the information is against the public interest, the interest of the public entity as a party in the outcome of the proceeding may not be considered.

UNITED STATES v. NIXON

Supreme Court of the United States, 1974.
418 U.S. 683, 94 S.Ct. 3090, 41 L.Ed.2d 1039.

Mr. Chief Justice BURGER delivered the opinion of the Court.

* * *

On March 1, 1974, a grand jury of the United States District Court for the District of Columbia returned an indictment charging seven named individuals [3] with various offenses, including conspiracy

---

3. The seven defendants were John N. Mitchell, H. R. Haldeman, John D. Ehrlichman, Charles W. Colson, Robert C. Mardian, Kenneth W. Parkinson, and Gordon Strachan. Each had occupied either a position of responsibility on the White House staff or the Committee for the Re-election of the President. Colson entered a guilty plea on another charge and is no longer a defendant.

to defraud the United States and to obstruct justice. Although he was not designated as such in the indictment, the grand jury named the President, among others, as an unindicted coconspirator. On April 18, 1974, upon motion of the Special Prosecutor, see n. 8, infra, a subpoena *duces tecum* was issued pursuant to Rule 17(c) to the President by the United States District Court and made returnable on May 2, 1974. This subpoena required the production, in advance of the September 9 trial date, of certain tapes, memoranda, papers, transcripts or other writings relating to certain precisely identified meetings between the President and others. The Special Prosecutor was able to fix the time, place, and persons present at these discussions because the White House daily logs and appointment records had been delivered to him. On April 30, the President publicly released edited transcripts of 43 conversations; portions of 20 conversations subject to subpoena in the present case were included. On May 1, 1974, the President's counsel, filed a "special appearance" and a motion to quash the subpoena under Rule 17(c). This motion was accompanied by a formal claim of privilege. * * *

On May 20, 1974, the District Court denied the motion to quash and the motions to expunge and for protective orders. * * * It further ordered "the President or any subordinate officer, official, or employee with custody or control of the documents or objects subpoenaed," * * * to deliver to the District Court, on or before May 31, 1974, the originals of all subpoenaed items, as well as an index and analysis of those items, together with tape copies of those portions of the subpoenaed recordings for which transcripts had been released to the public by the President on April 30. * * *

THE CLAIM OF PRIVILEGE

A

* * * [W]e turn to the claim that the subpoena should be quashed because it demands "confidential conversations between a President and his close advisors that it would be inconsistent with the public interest to produce." The first contention is a broad claim that the separation of powers doctrine precludes judicial review of a President's claim of privilege. The second contention is that if he does not prevail on the claim of absolute privilege, the court should hold as a matter of constitutional law that the privilege prevails over the subpoena *duces tecum*.

In the performance of assigned constitutional duties each branch of the Government must initially interpret the Constitution, and the interpretation of its powers by any branch is due great respect from the others. The President's counsel, as we have noted, reads the Constitution as providing an absolute privilege of confidentiality for all Presidential communications. Many decisions of this Court, however, have unequivocally reaffirmed the holding of Marbury v. Madison, 1

Cranch. 137, 2 L.Ed. 60 (1803), that "[i]t is emphatically the province and duty of the judicial department to say what the law is." Id., at 177, 2 L.Ed. 60.

* * *

* * * Notwithstanding the deference each branch must accord the others, the "judicial Power of the United States" vested in the federal courts by Art. III, § 1, of the Constitution can no more be shared with the Executive Branch than the Chief Executive, for example, can share with the Judiciary the veto power, or the Congress share with the Judiciary the power to override a Presidential veto. Any other conclusion would be contrary to the basic concept of separation of powers and the checks and balances that flow from the scheme of a tripartite government. * * *

B

In support of his claim of absolute privilege, the President's counsel urges two grounds, one of which is common to all governments and one of which is peculiar to our system of separation of powers. The first ground is the valid need for protection of communications between high Government officials and those who advise and assist them in the performance of their manifold duties; the importance of this confidentiality is too plain to require further discussion. Human experience teaches that those who expect public dissemination of their remarks may well temper candor with a concern for appearances and for their own interests to the detriment of the decisionmaking process. Whatever the nature of the privilege of confidentiality of Presidential communications in the exercise of Art. II powers, the privilege can be said to derive from the supremacy of each branch within its own assigned area of constitutional duties. Certain powers and privileges flow from the nature of enumerated powers; the protection of the confidentiality of Presidential communications has similar constitutional underpinnings.

The second ground asserted by the President's counsel in support of the claim of absolute privilege rests on the doctrine of separation of powers. Here it is argued that the independence of the Executive Branch within its own sphere, insulates a President from a judicial subpoena in an ongoing criminal prosecution, and thereby protects confidential Presidential communications.

However, neither the doctrine of separation of powers, nor the need for confidentiality of high-level communications, without more, can sustain an absolute, unqualified Presidential privilege of immunity from judicial process under all circumstances. The President's need for complete candor and objectivity from advisers calls for great deference from the courts. However, when the privilege depends solely on the broad, undifferentiated claim of public interest in the confidentiality of such conversations, a confrontation with other values arises. Absent a claim of need to protect military, diplomatic, or sensitive national security secrets, we find it difficult to accept the argument that even the very important interest in confidentiality of Presidential communications is significantly diminished by production of such material for *in camera* inspection with all the protection that a district court will be obliged to provide.

The impediment that an absolute, unqualified privilege would place in the way of the primary constitutional duty of the Judicial Branch to do justice in criminal prosecutions would plainly conflict with the function of the courts under Art. III. In designing the structure of our Government and dividing and allocating the sovereign power among three co-equal branches, the Framers of the Constitution sought to provide a comprehensive system, but the separate powers were not intended to operate with absolute independence.

> "While the Constitution diffuses power the better to secure liberty, it also contemplates that practice will integrate the dispersed powers into a workable government. It enjoins upon its branches separateness but interdependence, autonomy but reciprocity." Youngstown Sheet & Tube Co. v. Sawyer, 343 U.S., at 635, * * * (Jackson, J., concurring).

To read the Art. II powers of the President as providing an absolute privilege as against a subpoena essential to enforcement of criminal statutes on no more than a generalized claim of the public interest in confidentiality of nonmilitary and nondiplomatic discussions would upset the constitutional balance of "a workable government" and gravely impair the role of the courts under Art. III.

C

Since we conclude that the legitimate needs of the judicial process may outweigh Presidential privilege, it is necessary to resolve those competing interests in a manner that preserves the essential functions of each branch. The right and indeed the duty to resolve that question does not free the Judiciary from according high respect to the representations made on behalf of the President.

The expectation of a President to the confidentiality of his conversations and correspondence, like the claim of confidentiality of judicial deliberations, for example, has all the values to which we accord deference for the privacy of all citizens and, added to those values, is the necessity for protection of the public interest in candid, objective, and even blunt or harsh opinions in Presidential decisionmaking. A President and those who assist him must be free to explore alternatives in the process of shaping policies and making decisions and to do so in a way many would be unwilling to express except privately. These are the considerations justifying a presumptive privilege for Presidential communications. The privilege is fundamental to the operation of Government and inextricably rooted in the separation of powers under the Constitution. In Nixon v. Sirica,

159 U.S.App.D.C. 58, 487 F.2d 700 (1973), the Court of Appeals held that such Presidential communications are "presumptively privileged," * * * and this position is accepted by both parties in the present litigation. We agree with Mr. Chief Justice Marshall's observation, therefore, that "[i]n no case of this kind would a court be required to proceed against the president as against an ordinary individual." Unites States v. Burr * * *.

But this presumptive privilege must be considered in light of our historic commitment to the rule of law. This is nowhere more profoundly manifest than in our view that "the twofold aim [of criminal justice] is that guilt shall not escape or innocence suffer." Berger v. United States, 295 U.S., at 88, * * *. We have elected to employ an adversary system of criminal justice in which the parties contest all issues before a court of law. The need to develop all relevant facts in the adversary system is both fundamental and comprehensive. The ends of criminal justice would be defeated if judgments were to be founded on a partial or speculative presentation of the facts. The very integrity of the judicial system and public confidence in the system depend on full disclosure of all the facts, within the framework of the rules of evidence. To ensure that justice is done, it is imperative to the function of courts that compulsory process be available for the production of evidence needed either by the prosecution or by the defense.

* * *

In United States v. Reynolds, 345 U.S. 1, 73 S.Ct. 528, 97 L.Ed. 727 (1953), dealing with a claimant's demand for evidence in a Tort Claims Act case against the Government, the Court said:

> "It may be possible to satisfy the court, from all the circumstances of the case, that there is a reasonable danger that compulsion of the evidence will expose military matters which, in the interest of national security, should not be divulged. When this is the case, the occasion for the privilege is appropriate, and the court should not jeopardize the security which the privilege is meant to protect by insisting upon an examination of the evidence, even by the judge alone, in chambers." Id., at 10.

No case of the Court, however, has extended this high degree of deference to a President's generalized interest in confidentiality. Nowhere in the Constitution, as we have noted earlier, is there any explicit reference to a privilege of confidentiality, yet to the extent this interest relates to the effective discharge of a President's powers, it is constitutionally based.

The right to the production of all evidence at a criminal trial similarly has constitutional dimensions. The Sixth Amendment explicitly confers upon every defendant in a criminal trial the right "to be confronted with the witnesses against him" and "to have compulsory process for obtaining witnesses in his favor." Moreover, the Fifth Amendment also guarantees that no person shall be deprived of liberty without due process of law. It is the manifest duty of the courts to vindicate those guarantees, and to accomplish that it is essential that all relevant and admissible evidence be produced.

In this case we must weigh the importance of the general privilege of confidentiality of Presidential communications in performance of the President's responsibilities against the inroads of such a privilege on the fair administration of criminal justice. The interest in preserving confidentiality is weighty indeed and entitled to great respect. However, we cannot conclude that advisers will be moved to temper the candor of their remarks by the infrequent occasions of disclosure because of the possibility that such conversations will be called for in the context of a criminal prosecution.

On the other hand, the allowance of the privilege to withhold evidence that is demonstrably relevant in a criminal trial would cut deeply into the guarantee of due process of law and gravely impair the basic function of the courts. A President's acknowledged need for confidentiality in the communications of his office is general in nature, whereas the constitutional need for production of relevant evidence in a criminal proceeding is specific and central to the fair adjudication of a particular criminal case in the administration of justice. Without access to specific facts a criminal prosecution may be totally frustrated. The President's broad interest in confidentiality of communications will not be vitiated by disclosure of a limited number of conversations preliminarily shown to have some bearing on the pending criminal cases.

We conclude that when the ground for asserting privilege as to subpoenaed materials sought for use in a criminal trial is based only on the generalized interest in confidentiality, it cannot prevail over the fundamental demands of due process of law in the fair administration of criminal justice. The generalized assertion of privilege must yield to the demonstrated, specific need for evidence in a pending criminal trial.

* * *

It is therefore necessary in the public interest to afford Presidential confidentiality the greatest protection consistent with the fair administration of justice. The need for confidentiality even as to idle conversations with associates in which casual reference might be made concerning political leaders within the country or foreign statesmen is too obvious to call for further treatment. We have no doubt that the District Judge will at all times accord to Presidential records that high degree of deference suggested in United States v. Burr, supra and will discharge his responsibility to see to it that until released to the Special Prosecutor no *in camera* material is revealed to anyone. This burden applies with even greater force to excised material; once the decision is made to excise, the material is restored to its privileged status and should be returned under seal to its lawful custodian.

* * *

Affirmed.

Mr. Justice REHNQUIST took no part in the consideration or decision of these cases.

B. THE INFORMER PRIVILEGE

ROVIARO v. UNITED STATES

Supreme Court of the United States, 1957.
353 U.S. 53, 77 S.Ct. 623, 1 L.Ed.2d 639.

Mr. Justice BURTON delivered the opinion of the Court.

This case concerns a conviction for violation of the Narcotic Drugs Import and Export Act, as amended. The principal issue is whether the United States District Court committed reversible error when it allowed the Government to refuse to disclose the identity of an undercover employee who had taken a material part in bringing about the possession of certain drugs by the accused, had been present with the accused at the occurrence of the alleged crime, and might be a material witness as to whether the accused knowingly transported the drugs as charged. For the reasons hereafter stated, we hold that, under the circumstances here present, this was reversible error.

In 1955, in the Northern District of Illinois, petitioner, Albert Roviaro, was indicted on two counts by a federal grand jury. The first count charged that on August 12, 1954, at Chicago, Illinois, he sold heroin to one "John Doe" * * *. The second charged that on the same date and in the same city he "did then and there fraudulently and knowingly receive, conceal, buy and facilitate the transportation and concealment after importation of * * * heroin, knowing the same to be imported into the United States contrary to law; * * *."

Before trial, petitioner moved for a bill of particulars requesting, among other things, the name, address and occupation of "John Doe." The Government objected on the ground that John Doe was an informer and that his identity was privileged. The motion was denied.

Petitioner, who was represented by counsel, waived a jury and was tried by the District Court. During the trial John Doe's part in the charged transaction was described by government witnesses, and counsel for petitioner, in cross-examining them, sought repeatedly to learn John Doe's identity. The court declined to permit this cross-examination and John Doe was not produced, identified, or otherwise made available. Petitioner was found guilty on both counts and was sentenced to two years' imprisonment and a fine of $5 on each count, the sentences to run concurrently. The Court of Appeals sustained the conviction, holding that the concurrent sentence was supported by the conviction on Count 2 and that the trial court had not abused its discretion in denying petitioner's requests for disclosure of Doe's identity. * * * We granted certiorari, * * *, in order to pass upon the propriety of the nondisclosure of the informer's identity * * *.

At the trial, the Government relied on the testimony of two federal narcotics agents, Durham and Fields, and two Chicago police officers, Bryson and Sims, each of whom knew petitioner by sight. On the night of August 12, 1954, these four officers met at 75th Street and Prairie Avenue in Chicago with an informer described only as John Doe. Doe and his Cadillac car were searched and no narcotics were found. Bryson secreted himself in the trunk of Doe's Cadillac, taking with him a device with which to raise the trunk lid from the inside. Doe then drove the Cadillac to 70th Place and St. Lawrence Avenue, followed by Durham in one government car and Field and Sims in another. After an hour's wait, at about 11 o'clock, petitioner arrived in a Pontiac, accompanied by an unidentified man. Petitioner immediately entered Doe's Cadillac, taking a front seat beside Doe. They then proceeded by a circuitous route to 74th Street near Champlain Avenue. Both government cars trailed the Cadillac but only the one driven by Durham managed to follow it to 74th Street. When the Cadillac came to a stop on 74th Street, Durham stepped out of his car onto the sidewalk and saw petitioner alight from the Cadillac about 100 feet away. Durham saw petitioner walk a few feet to a nearby tree, pick up a small package, return to the open right front door of the Cadillac, make a motion as if depositing the package in the car, and then wave to Doe and walk away. Durham went immediately to the Cadillac and recovered a package from the floor. He signaled to Bryson to come out of the trunk and then walked down the street in time to see petitioner re-enter the Pontiac, parked nearby, and ride away.

Meanwhile, Bryson, concealed in the trunk of the Cadillac, had heard a conversation between John Doe and petitioner after the latter had entered the car. He heard petitioner greet John Doe and direct him where to drive. At one point, petitioner admonished him to pull over to the curb, cut the motor, and turn out the lights so as to lose a "tail." He then told him to continue "further down." Petitioner asked about money Doe owed him. He advised Doe that he had brought him "three pieces this time." When Bryson heard Doe being ordered to stop the car, he raised the lid of the trunk slightly. After the car stopped, he saw petitioner walk to a tree, pick up a package, and return toward the car. He heard petitioner say, "Here it is," and "I'll call you in a couple of days." Shortly thereafter he heard Durham's signal to come out and emerged from the trunk to find

Durham holding a small package found to contain three glassine envelopes containing a white powder.

A field test of the powder having indicated that it contained an opium derivative, the officers, at about 12:30 a. m., arrested petitioner at his home and took him, along with Doe, to Chicago police headquarters. There petitioner was confronted with Doe, who denied that he knew or had ever seen petitioner. Subsequent chemical analysis revealed that the powder contained heroin.

I.

Petitioner contends that the trial court erred in upholding the right of the Government to withhold the identity of John Doe. He argues that Doe was an active participant in the illegal activity charged and that, therefore, the Government could not withhold his identity, his whereabouts, and whether he was alive or dead at the time of trial. The Government does not defend the nondisclosure of Doe's identity with respect to Count 1, which charged a sale of heroin to John Doe, but it attempts to sustain the judgment on the basis of the conviction on Count 2, charging illegal transportation of narcotics. It argues that the conviction on Count 2 may properly be upheld since the identity of the informer, in the circumstances of this case, has no real bearing on that charge and is therefore privileged.

What is usually referred to as the informer's privilege is in reality the Government's privilege to withhold from disclosure the identity of persons who furnish information of violations of law to officers charged with enforcement of that law. * * * The purpose of the privilege is the furtherance and protection of the public interest in effective law enforcement. The privilege recognizes the obligation of citizens to communicate their knowledge of the commission of crimes to law-enforcement officials and, by preserving their anonymity, encourages them to perform that obligation.

The scope of the privilege is limited by its underlying purpose. Thus, where the disclosure of the contents of a communication will not tend to reveal the identity of an informer, the contents are not privileged. Likewise, once the identity of the informer has been disclosed to those who would have cause to resent the communication, the privilege is no longer applicable.

A further limitation on the applicability of the privilege arises from the fundamental requirements of fairness. Where the disclosure of an informer's identity, or of the contents of his communication, is relevant and helpful to the defense of an accused, or is essential to a fair determination of a cause, the privilege must give way. In these situations the trial court may require disclosure and, if the Government withholds the information, dismiss the action. Most of the federal cases involving this limitation on the scope of the informer's privilege have arisen where the legality of a search without a warrant is in issue and the communications of an informer are claimed to establish probable cause. In these cases the Government has been required to disclose the identity of the informant unless there was sufficient evidence apart from his confidential communication.

Three recent cases in the Courts of Appeals have involved the identical problem raised here—the Government's right to withhold the identity of an informer who helped to set up the commission of the crime and who was present at its occurrence. * * * In each case it was stated that the identity of such an informer must be disclosed whenever the informer's testimony may be relevant and helpful to the accused's defense.

We believe that no fixed rule with respect to disclosure is justifiable. The problem is one that calls for balancing the public interest in protecting the flow of information against the individual's right to prepare his defense. Whether a proper balance renders nondisclosure erroneous must depend on the particular circumstances of each case, taking into consideration the crime charged, the possible defenses, the possible significance of the informer's testimony, and other relevant factors.

II.

* * *

The circumstances of this case demonstrate that John Doe's possible testimony was highly relevant and might have been helpful to the defense. So far as petitioner knew, he and John Doe were alone and unobserved during the crucial occurrence for which he was indicted. Unless petitioner waived his constitutional right not to take the stand in his own defense, John Doe was his one material witness. Petitioner's opportunity to cross-examine Police Officer Bryson and Federal Narcotics Agent Durham was hardly a substitute for an opportunity to examine the man who had been nearest to him and took part in the transaction. Doe had helped to set up the criminal occurrence and had played a prominent part in it. His testimony might have disclosed an entrapment. He might have thrown doubt upon petitioner's identity or on the identity of the package. He was the only witness who might have testified to petitioner's possible lack of knowledge of the contents of the package that he "transported" from the tree to John Doe's car. The desirability of calling John Doe as a witness, or at least interviewing him in preparation for trial, was a matter for the accused rather than the Government to decide.

Finally, the Government's use against petitioner of his conversation with John Doe while riding in Doe's car particularly emphasizes the unfairness of the nondisclosure in this case. The only person, other than petitioner himself, who could controvert, explain or amplify Bryson's report of this important conversation was John Doe. Contradiction or amplification might have borne upon petitioner's knowledge of the contents of the package or might have tended to show an entrapment.

This is a case where the Government's informer was the sole participant, other than the accused, in the transaction charged. The informer was the only witness in a position to amplify or contradict the testimony of government witnesses. Moreover, a government witness testified that Doe denied knowing petitioner or ever having seen him before. We conclude that, under these circumstances, the trial court committed prejudicial error in permitting the Government to withhold the identity of its undercover employee in the face of repeated demands by the accused for his disclosure. * * *

Reversed and remanded.

Mr. Justice BLACK and Mr. Justice WHITTAKER took no part in the consideration or decision of this case.

Mr. Justice CLARK, dissenting.

It is with regret that I dissent from the opinion of the Court, not because I am alone, but for the reason that I have been unable to convince the majority of the unsoundness of its conclusion on the facts here and the destructive effect which that conclusion will have on the enforcement of the narcotic laws. The short of it is that the conviction of a self-confessed dope peddler is reversed because the Government refused to furnish the name of its informant whose identity the undisputed evidence indicated was well known to the peddler. Yet the Court reverses on the ground of "unfairness" because of the Government's failure to perform this fruitless gesture. In my view this does violence to the common understanding of what is fair and just.
* * *

WEST'S ANNOTATED CALIFORNIA EVIDENCE CODE

§ 1041. Privilege for identity of informer

(a) Except as provided in this section, a public entity has a privilege to refuse to disclose the identity of a person who has furnished information as provided in subdivision (b) purporting to disclose a violation of a law of the United States or of this state or a public entity in this state, and to prevent another from disclosing such identity, if the privilege is claimed by a person authorized by the public entity to do so and:

(1) Disclosure is forbidden by an act of the Congress of the United States or a statute of this state; or

(2) Disclosure of the identity of the informer is against the public interest because there is a necessity for preserving the confidentiality of his identity that outweighs the necessity for disclosure in the interest of justice; but no privilege may be claimed under this paragraph if any person authorized to do so has consented that the

identity of the informer be disclosed in the proceeding. In determining whether disclosure of the identity of the informer is against the public interest, the interest of the public entity as a party in the outcome of the proceeding may not be considered.

(b) This section applies only if the information is furnished in confidence by the informer to:

(1) A law enforcement officer;

(2) A representative of an administrative agency charged with the administration or enforcement of the law alleged to be violated; or

(3) Any person for the purpose of transmittal to a person listed in paragraph (1) or (2).

(c) There is no privilege under this section to prevent the informer from disclosing his identity.

§ 1042. Adverse order or finding in certain cases

(a) Except where disclosure is forbidden by an act of the Congress of the United States, if a claim of privilege under this article by the state or a public entity in this state is sustained in a criminal proceeding, the presiding officer shall make such order or finding of fact adverse to the public entity bringing the proceeding as is required by law upon any issue in the proceeding to which the privileged information is material.

(b) Notwithstanding subdivision (a), where a search is made pursuant to a warrant valid on its face, the public entity bringing a criminal proceeding is not required to reveal to the defendant official information or the identity of an informer in order to establish the legality of the search or the admissibility of any evidence obtained as a result of it.

(c) Notwithstanding subdivision (a), in any preliminary hearing, criminal trial, or other criminal proceeding, any otherwise admissible evidence of information communicated to a peace officer by a confidential informant, who is not a material witness to the guilt or innocence of the accused of the offense charged, is admissible on the issue of reasonable cause to make an arrest or search without requiring that the name or identity of the informant be disclosed if the judge or magistrate is satisfied, based upon evidence produced in open court, out of the presence of the jury, that such information was received from a reliable informant and in his discretion does not require such disclosure.

(d) When, in any such criminal proceeding, a party demands disclosure of the identity of the informant on the ground the informant is a material witness on the issue of guilt, the court shall conduct a hearing at which all parties may present evidence on the issue of disclosure. Such hearing shall be conducted outside the presence of the jury, if any. During the hearing, if the privilege provided for in Section 1041 is claimed by a person authorized to do so or if a person who is authorized to claim such privilege refuses to answer any question on the ground that the answer would tend to disclose the identity of the informant, the prosecuting attorney may request that the court hold an in camera hearing. If such a request is made, the court shall hold such a hearing outside the presence of the defendant and his counsel. At the in camera hearing, the prosecution may offer evidence which would tend to disclose or which discloses the identity of the informant to aid the court in its determination whether there is a reasonable possibility that nondisclosure might deprive the defendant of a fair trial. A reporter shall be present at the in camera hearing. Any transcription of the proceedings at the in camera hearing, as well as any physical evidence presented at the hearing, shall be ordered sealed by the court, and only a court may have access to its contents. The court shall not order disclosure, nor strike the testimony of the witness who invokes the privilege, nor dismiss the criminal proceeding, if the party offering the witness refuses to disclose the identity of the informant, unless, based upon the evidence presented at the hearing held in the presence of the defendant and his counsel and the evidence presented at the in camera hearing, the court concludes that there is a reasonable possibility that nondisclosure might deprive the defendant of a fair trial.

McCRAY v. ILLINOIS

Supreme Court of the United States, 1967.
386 U.S. 300, 87 S.Ct. 1056, 18 L.Ed.2d 62.

Mr. Justice STEWART delivered the opinion of the Court.

The petitioner was arrested in Chicago, Illinois, on the morning of January 16, 1964, for possession of narcotics. The Chicago police officers who made the arrest found a package containing heroin on his person and he was indicted for its unlawful possession. Prior to trial he filed a motion to suppress the heroin as evidence against him, claiming that the police had acquired it in an unlawful search and seizure in violatiom of the Fourth and Fourteenth Amendments. * * * After a hearing, the court denied the motion, and the petitioner was subsequently convicted upon the evidence of the heroin the arresting officers had found in his possession. The judgment of conviction was affirmed by the Supreme Court of Illinois, and we granted certiorari to consider the petitioner's claim that the hearing on his motion to suppress was constitutionally defective.

The petitioner's arrest occurred near the intersection of 49th Street and Calumet Avenue at about seven in the morning. At the hearing on the motion to suppress, he testified that up until a half hour before he was arrested he had been at "a friend's house" about a block away, that after leaving the friend's house he had "walked with a lady from 48th to 48th and South Park," and that, as he approached 49th Street and Calumet Avenue, "[t]he Officers stopped me going through the alley." "The officers," he said, "did not show me a search warrant for my person or an arrest warrant for my arrest." He said the officers then searched him and found the narcotics in question. The petitioner did not identify the "friend" nor the "lady," and neither of them appeared as a witness.

The arresting officers then testified. Officer Jackson stated that he and two fellow officers had had a conversation with an informant on the morning of January 16 in their unmarked police car. The officer said that the informant had told them that the petitioner, with whom Jackson was acquainted, "was selling narcotics and had narcotics on his person and that he could be found in the vicinity of 47th and Calumet at this particular time." Jackson said that he and his fellow officers drove to that vicinity in the police car and that when they spotted the petitioner, the informant pointed him out and then departed on foot. Jackson stated that the officers observed the petitioner walking with a woman, then separating from her and meeting briefly with a man, then proceeding alone, and finally, after seeing the police car, "hurriedly walk[ing] between two buildings." "At this point," Jackson testified, "my partner and myself got out of the car and informed him we had information he had narcotics on his person, placed him in the police vehicle at this point." Jackson stated that the officers then searched the petitioner and found the heroin in a cigarette package.

Jackson testified that he had been acquainted with the informant for approximately a year, that during this period the informant had supplied him with information about narcotics activities "fifteen, sixteen times at least," that the information had proved to be accurate and had resulted in numerous arrests and convictions. On cross-examination, Jackson was even more specific as to the informant's previous reliability, giving the names of people who had been convicted of narcotics violations as the result of information the informant had supplied. When Jackson was asked for the informant's name and address counsel for the State objected, and the objection was sustained by the court.

Officer Arnold gave substantially the same account of the circumstances of the petitioner's arrest and search, stating that the informant had told the officers that the petitioner "was selling narcotics and had narcotics on his person now in the vicinity of 47th and Calumet." The informant, Arnold testified, "said he had observed [the petitioner] selling narcotics to various people, meaning various addicts, in the area of 47th and Calumet." Arnold testified that he had known the informant "roughly two years," that the informant had given him information concerning narcotics "20 or 25 times," and that the information had resulted in convictions. Arnold too was asked on cross-examination for the informant's name and address, and objections to these questions were sustained by the court. * * * It is the petitioner's claim, however, that even though the officers' sworn testimony fully supported a finding a probable cause for the arrest and search, the state court nonetheless violated the Constitution when it sustained objections to the petitioner's questions as to the identity of the informant. We cannot agree.

In permitting the officers to withhold the informant's identity, the court was following well-settled Illinois law. When the issue is not guilt or innocence, but, as here, the question of probable cause for an arrest or search, the Illinois Supreme Court has held that police officers need not invariably be required to disclose an informant's identity if the trial judge is convinced, by evidence submitted in open court and subject to cross-examination, that the officers did rely in good faith upon credible information supplied by a reliable informant. This Illinois evidentiary rule is consistent with the law of many other States. * * *

The reasoning of the Supreme Court of New Jersey in judicially adopting the same basic evidentiary rule was instructively expressed by Chief Justice Weintraub in State v. Burnett, 42 N.J. 377, 201 A.2d 39:

> "If a defendant may insist upon disclosure of the informant in order to test the truth of the officer's statement that there is an informant or as to what the informant related or as to the informant's reliability, we can be sure that every defendant will demand disclosure. He has nothing to lose and the prize may be the suppression of damaging evidence if the State cannot afford to reveal its source, as is so often the case. And since there is no way to test the good faith of a defendant who presses the demand, we must assume the routine demand would have to be routinely granted. The result would be that the State could use the informant's information only as a lead and could search only if it could gather adequate evidence of probable cause apart from the informant's data. Perhaps that approach would sharpen investigatorial techniques, but we doubt that there would be enough talent and time to cope with crime upon that basis. Rather we accept the premise that the informer is a vital part of society's defensive arsenal. The basic rule protecting his identity rests upon that belief.
>
> * * *
>
> "We must remember also that we are not dealing with the trial of the criminal charge itself. There the need for a truthful verdict outweighs society's need for the informer privilege. Here, however, the accused seeks to avoid the truth. The very purpose of a motion to suppress is to escape the inculpatory thrust of evidence in hand, not because

its probative force is diluted in the least by the mode of seizure, but rather as a sanction to compel enforcement officers to respect the constitutional security of all of us under the Fourth Amendment. * * * If the motion to suppress is denied, defendant will still be judged upon the untarnished truth.

* * *

"The Fourth Amendment is served if a judicial mind passes upon the existence of probable cause. Where the issue is submitted upon an application for a warrant, the magistrate is trusted to evaluate the credibility of the affiant in an *ex parte* proceeding. As we have said the magistrate is concerned, not with whether the informant lied, but with whether the affiant is truthful in his recitation of what he was told. If the magistrate doubts the credibility of the affiant, he may require that the informant be identified or even produced. It seems to us that the same approach is equally sufficient where the search was without a warrant, that is to say, that it should rest entirely with the judge who hears the motion to suppress to decide whether he needs such disclosure as to the informant in order to decide whether the officer is a believable witness." * * *

What Illinois and her sister States have done is no more than recognize a well-established testimonial privilege, long familiar to the law of evidence. Professor Wigmore, not known as an enthusiastic advocate of testimonial privileges generally, has described that privilege in these words:

"A genuine privilege, on * * * fundamental principle * * *, must be recognized for the *identity of persons supplying the government with information concerning the commission of crimes.* Communications of this kind ought to receive encouragement. They are discouraged if the informer's identity is disclosed. Whether an informer is motivated by good citizenship, promise of leniency or prospect of pecuniary reward, he will usually condition his cooperation on an assurance of anonymity—to protect himself and his family from harm, to preclude adverse social reactions and to avoid the risk of defamation or malicious prosecution actions against him. The government also has an interest in nondisclosure of the identity of its informers. Law enforcement officers often depend upon professional informers to furnish them with a flow of information about criminal activities. Revelation of the dual role played by such persons ends their usefulness to the government and discourages others from entering into a like relationship.

"That the government has this privilege is well established and its soundness cannot be questioned." * * *

In the federal courts the rules of evidence in criminal trials are governed "by the principles of the common law as they may be interpreted by the courts of the United States in the light of reason and experience." This Court, therefore, has the ultimate task of defining the scope to be accorded to the various common law evidentiary privileges in the trial of federal criminal cases. * * * This is a task which is quite different, of course, from the responsibility of constitutional adjudication. In the exercise of this supervisory jurisdiction the Court had occasion 10 years ago, in Roviaro v. United States, 353 U.S. 53, 77 S.Ct. 623, to give thorough consideration to one aspect of the informer's privilege, the privilege itself having long been recognized in the federal judicial system.

The *Roviaro* case involved the informer's privilege, not at a preliminary hearing to determine probable cause for an arrest or search, but at the trial itself where the issue was the fundamental one of innocence or guilt. * * *

What *Roviaro* thus makes clear is that this Court was unwilling to impose any absolute rule requiring disclosure of an informer's identity even in formulating evidentiary rules for federal criminal trials.

* * * Yet we are now asked to hold that the Constitution somehow compels Illinois to abolish the informer's privilege from its law of evidence, and to require disclosure of the informer's identity in every such preliminary hearing where it appears that the officers made the arrest or search in reliance upon facts supplied by an informer they had reason to trust. The argument is based upon the Due Process Clause of the Fourteenth Amendment, and upon the Sixth Amendment right of confrontation, applicable to the State through the Fourteenth Amendment. * * * We find no support for the petitioner's position in either of those constitutional provisions.

The arresting officers in this case testified, in open court, fully and in precise detail as to what the informer told them and as to why they had reason to believe his information was trustworthy. Each officer was under oath. Each was subjected to searching cross-examination. The judge was obviously satisfied that each was telling the truth, and for that reason he exercised the discretion conferred upon him by the established law of Illinois to respect the informer's privilege.

Nothing in the Due Process Clause of the Fourteenth Amendment requires a state court judge in every such hearing to assume the arresting officers are committing perjury. "To take such a step would be quite beyond the pale of this Court's proper function in our federal system. It would be a wholly unjustifiable encroachment by this Court upon the constitutional power of States to promulgate their own rules of evidence * * * in their own state courts. * * *" * * *

The petitioner does not explain precisely how he thinks his Sixth Amendment right to confrontation and cross-examination was violated by Illinois' recognition of the informer's privilege in this case. If the claim is that the State violated the Sixth Amendment by not producing the informer to testify against the petitioner, then we need no more than repeat the Court's answer to that claim a few weeks ago in Cooper v. California:

> "Petitioner also presents the contention here that he was unconstitutionally deprived of the right to confront a witness against him, because the State did not produce the informant to testify against him. This contention we consider absolutely devoid of merit." * * *

On the other hand, the claim may be that the petitioner was deprived of his Sixth Amendment right to cross-examine the arresting officers themselves, because their refusal to reveal the informer's identity was upheld. But it would follow from this argument that no witness on cross-examination could ever constitutionally assert a testimonial privilege, including the privilege against compulsory self-incrimination guaranteed by the Constitution itself. We have never given the Sixth Amendment such a construction, and we decline to do so now.

Affirmed.

[The opinion of Mr. Justice DOUGLAS, with whom The Chief Justice, Mr. Justice BRENNAN and Mr. Justice FORTAS concur, dissenting, is omitted.]

WALTZ, CRIMINAL EVIDENCE

258–260 (1975).*

Identity of an Informer

The Rule of Privilege. The federal government or a state or a subdivision of a state, such as a city, has a privilege to refuse to disclose the identity of a person who has supplied to a law enforcement agent information purporting to reveal a violation of law. This privilege reflects a recognition that anonymity is essential to the effective use of informants in law enforcement. As the Supreme Court said in Roviaro v. United States, 353 U.S. 53 (1957), the privilege is one that is "well established at common law." It applies to the concerned citizen who comes forward with information and it applies to police undercover agents, such as narcotics agents.

Who May Claim the Privilege. In times past it has been said that this privilege could be invoked by the prosecution, by the trial judge, or by the informer. Today, however, the tendency is to hold that the privilege belongs exclusively to the government, since it is the flow of information to law enforcement agencies that is sought to be protected.

* Copyright, 1975 by Jon R. Waltz.

The privilege can be invoked by an appropriate representative of the government, regardless of whether the information was supplied to an officer of the government. Usually the appropriate representative of the government will be legal counsel in the case, but this will not invariably be true since the United States, a state, or a subdivision may not be a party to the litigation.

Example:

Bocchicchio v. Curtis Publishing Co., 203 F.Supp. 403 (E.D.Pa. 1962), was a civil libel action. A police officer, who was not represented by counsel, successfully invoked the privilege to conceal the identity of an informant.

Exceptions. Three fundamental exceptions to the rule of privilege pertaining to the identity of a police informant are emerging in the law. One of them involves voluntary disclosure of the informant's identity; another involves the situation in which the informant probably could give testimony helpful to the accused were his identity made known; a third involves situations in which an informer's statements were relied on to provide probable cause for an arrest.

1. *Voluntary Disclosure.* No privilege exists if an informer's identity or his interest in the subject matter of his communication has been disclosed to those who would have cause to resent the communication, or if the informant actually appears in court as a witness on behalf of the prosecution.

Obviously, if the informant's identity is revealed, nothing further is to be gained by efforts to suppress it. Disclosure of his identity can be direct or it can result from actions plainly revealing the informant's interest in the subject matter of the prosecution or civil suit.

If the informant becomes a witness in the case, the interests of justice favor disclosing his status since it might be a source of bias upon which the opposing side could impeach his veracity. The interests of justice are thought to outweigh any interest in nondisclosure that might remain after the informant has taken the stand.

It is usually held that waiver of the privilege does not occur unless the informer's identity, or his interest in the subject matter, is revealed to those whose interests are adversely affected by his communication.

2. *Testimony Helpful to an Accused.* The informer privilege cannot be employed where society's interest in the flow of information to law enforcement agents is outweighed by the right of the accused to prepare his defense. Sometimes, as the saying goes, the prosecution must "fish or cut bait." If it appears from the evidence in the case that an informant might be able to give testimony necessary to a fair determination of guilt or innocence (or, for that matter, of a material issue in a civil case), and the government asserts

the privilege, the trial judge will accord the government an opportunity to show facts, in a hearing that is usually closed to all but the trial judge, the government's representative, and a court reporter, that are relevant to deciding whether the informant can give such testimony. This showing is usually made by means of sworn statements (affidavits), but the trial judge may direct that witnesses be called and testimony taken if he determines that the matter cannot be resolved satisfactorily on the basis of written statements alone.

If the judge decides that there is a reasonable probability that the informant can give testimony helpful to the defendant and the prosecution elects not to disclose his identity, the judge on motion of the accused in a criminal case will dismiss any charges to which the informant's testimony would relate. A judge can also dismiss the case, or parts of it, on his *own* motion. (In civil cases, the trial court can enter any order that the best interests of justice dictate. For example, he might enter a finding against the government on an issue to which the informer's testimony would be relevant).

Evidence submitted to the trial judge at a hearing of the sort just described is sealed and carefully preserved so that it will be available to reviewing courts in the event of an appeal. The contents of the evidence will not be disclosed to anyone else without the prosecution's consent.

3. *Legality of Securing Evidence.* Occasionally information from a police informant is relied upon to establish the legality of the means by which evidence was obtained. If a judge is not satisfied that this sort of information was received from an informant whom the police reasonably believed to be reliable or credible, he can direct that the identity of the informer be disclosed to him. If the prosecution requests it, this disclosure can be made in a hearing at which no legal counsel or party will be allowed to be present. In the absence of such a request by the prosecution, all counsel and any parties concerned with the issue of legality will be permitted to be present at the hearing. If disclosure of the informant's identity is made at a closed session, the record of the hearing will be sealed and preserved for possible use by reviewing courts and the contents, again, will not in any other way be revealed without the prosecution's approval.

JEFFERSON, CALIFORNIA EVIDENCE BENCHBOOK (1975) AND SUPPLEMENT (1978) *

Illustrations:

(1) (*Failure of prosecution to disclose informer's identity after trial judge's ruling against the claim of privilege results in dismissal of the action*) D is charged with possession of heroin. At D's preliminary hearing, PO, a police officer, testifies that an untested informer told him he had pur-

* Copyright, 1975, 1978 by Regents of the University of California.

chased heroin from a "Mr. X" at a particular apartment; that PO gave the informer $25 and watched him go to an apartment and return with a *red* balloon containing heroin; that PO then forced entry into the apartment and found D in the bathroom flushing the toilet; that PO reached into the bowl and retrieved a *green* balloon containing heroin. The prosecution introduces the green-balloon heroin into evidence but does not produce the red-balloon heroin. D moves for disclosure of the informer's identity and the prosecutor claims the privilege for nondisclosure. D calls S, his sister, who testifies that she was in D's apartment when PO entered and that when PO emerged from the bathroom, he was holding an empty plastic bag and exclaimed: "The son of a bitch, the son of a bitch, he downed it." The trial judge then overrules the prosecutor's claim of privilege and orders disclosure of the informer's identity. The prosecutor refuses to disclose. The trial judge should then order dismissal of the action. (See *Borunda,* 11 C3d 523.)

In Illustration (1), does D make a showing of reasonable possibility that PO's informer could give evidence on the issue of D's guilt that might result in D's exoneration? *Yes.* In view of S's testimony, if the informer were to testify that the balloon of heroin which he delivered to PO after visiting D's apartment was *green*, rather than *red* as PO claimed, the jury might be led to conclude that PO had in fact recovered no heroin in the apartment as D's sister, S, testified, and that PO had offered in evidence against D the heroin which the informer had provided him.

* * *

* * * This was the holding of *Borunda*.

In *Borunda,* the prosecution argued that the informant could not have been a material witness on the issue of guilt because he was not present in D's apartment when the arrest was made. In rejecting this argument, the court points out that even though PO's testimony were to be believed that he was alone with D in the bathroom when D was apprehended while flushing the toilet, D could be found guilty of the offense charged only if the substance he was flushing down the toilet was in fact heroin, and if the informer were to testify that the balloon which he delivered to PO was *green* in color, the jury could reasonably believe the testimony of D's sister rather than that of the officer, and accordingly acquit D of the offense charged.

The *Borunda* decision is significant because it illustrates the principle that there can be a great variety of circumstances in which a defendant may show how an informer's testimony could possibly exonerate him. In Illustration (1), the defendant's theory involves the crucial question of S's credibility as against the credibility of PO. The circumstances presented by D are such that the informer's testimony might favor the credibility of D's sister, S, over that of PO, the police officer.

Similar to Illustration (1) is the *Goliday* case. In *Goliday*, defendant was charged with selling dangerous drugs. An undercover officer testified to making a purchase from defendant at defendant's home in the presence of two confidential informers who had accompanied the officer. In moving for disclosure of the identity of the two informers, defendant testified that he declined to make a sale to the officer on the date in question. The prosecution asserted the privilege for nondisclosure of the identity of the two informers. The court held that defendant was entitled to disclosure because the two informers were material witnesses since they might have supported defendant's defense by testifying that defendant did refuse to sell the officer any drugs. In *Goliday*, as in Illustration (1), the issue of defendant's guilt or innocence revolves around the question of the defendant's *credibility* as a witness as compared to the credibility of a prosecution witness. Since the two informers were present at the alleged transaction, they *could* testify contrary to the officer's version of the incident and in support of defendant's version.

> (2) *(Claim of privilege for nondisclosure of informer's identity valid because defendant unable to make a showing that informer might give exonerating testimony for defendant)* D and CD are charged with possession of heroin for sale. PO, a police officer, obtains a premises search warrant based on an informer's statement that at a certain house he had purchased heroin from CD in the presence of D. PO makes a search of the house, finds D present, finds heroin in the house, and also finds heroin in D's pants pocket. At D's preliminary hearing, the prosecutor offers against D only the heroin found in his pants pocket. D moves for disclosure of the informer's identity. The prosecutor claims the privilege for nondisclosure of the informer's identity. The prosecutor's claim of privilege should be sustained. (See *Acuna*, 35 CA3d 987.)

In Illustration (2), there is no way for D to validly contend that there is a reasonable possibility that the informer could give exonerating evidence in D's favor. Here, the prosecution is based solely on the heroin found on D's person. The informer cannot possibly help D since the informer was not present at the search of the house and the arrest of D. Since the balloons were found in D's pocket, it was not a reasonable possibility that the informant might have planted the heroin. Had the prosecutor offered against D the heroin found in the house, D might have been able to present a theory for disclosure of the informer's identity because of the information about CD making a sale to the informer.

* * *

(3) *(Claim of privilege for nondisclosure of informer's identity sustained—informer held not to be a material witness)* D is charged with possession of a machine gun and, as an ex-felon, with possession of a concealable firearm. At D's preliminary hearing, PO, a police officer, testifies that a reliable informer gave him information that he had seen D in possession of heroin at D's home and that PO then obtained a search warrant to search for narcotics, that PO than searched D's house and found the weapon in a hidden compartment behind a bedroom wall panel. D makes a pretrial motion for disclosure of the informer's identity. The prosecutor asserts the privilege for nondisclosure. The claim of privilege should be sustained. (See *Kilpatrick*, 31 CA3d 431.)

In Illustration (3), can D sustain his burden to show that there is a reasonable *possibility* that the informer *might* be able to give exonerating testimony for D? *No.* In *Kilpatrick*, from which Illustration (3) is taken, the court held that the informer supplied PO with information about narcotics only, and nothing about any secret compartment holding forbidden weapons. Hence, D makes no showing of how the informer could testify to any facts that would exonerate D. As in [Illustration (2)], the *Kilpatrick* court points out that there is no showing that the informer might have "planted" the weapons since the informer provided PO with no information concerning the weapons.

Illustration (3) is similar to Illustration (1) * * * because the elements of the crime of *possession* by D of a forbidden weapon are established without reference to anything the informer might have witnessed on his prior visits to defendant's premises, and the suggestion that the informer could have "planted" the contraband is sheer and rank speculation.

(4) *(Informer considered a material witness because of the possibility that he could give testimony that would support defendant's defense of mistaken identification in a narcotics sale)* D is charged with sale of heroin to PO, an undercover police officer, on January 24, 1974, at D's home. At a pretrial hearing on a motion for disclosure of identity of an informant, PO testifies that in November, 1973, he went to an address with an informer who introduced him to "Fat Robert," a man whom PO believed to be D; that the informer left and PO then made a purchase of heroin from this individual. PO testifies that in January, 1974, he and the informer went back to the same address and PO made a heroin purchase from the same individual but doesn't know whether the informer witnessed the transaction; that a number of persons were in the room at the time of the

transaction. PO testifies that on January 24, 1974, the date of the charged offense, he went back to the same address alone and purchased heroin from "Fat Robert," whom he identified as D. On cross-examination, PO testifies that from September, 1973, to March, 1974, he purchased heroin on over 100 occasions from about 50 different persons, including three or four purchases from other persons at the same address as that of D. D indicates that his defense is that he was not the person who sold heroin to PO on any of the three occasions testified to by PO. The trial judge sustains the prosecution's claim of privilege for nondisclosure of the informer's identity. Is this ruling correct? No! (See *Bowens*, 47 CA3d 127.)

The *Bowens* court held that there was a reasonable possibility that the informer could give testimony that might exonerate D. The evidence adduced at the hearing indicated the possibility of a mistake in identification. Thus, the informer might testify that "Fat Robert," to whom the informer introduced PO, was not D on the occasion of the first sale or on the occasion of the second sale when the informer was present. If so, it would be reasonable to conclude that D was not the "Fat Robert" from whom PO made the third purchase, the subject of the charged offense. This reasoning is sound; D is entitled to disclosure of the informer's identity under Rule (7) of this section.

COLLATERAL READINGS

Governmental Privileges

Wigmore, Evidence (3rd ed. 1940)
   Vol. 8, §§ 2360–2363, 2367, 2368–2379 (McNaughton rev. 1961)

McCormick's Handbook of the Law of Evidence §§ 106–113 (2d ed. 1972)

Calkins, Grand Jury Secrecy, 63 Mich.L.Rev. 455 (1965)

Louisell, Criminal Discovery: Dilemma Real or Apparent? 49 Calif. L.Rev. 56, 68–71 (grand jury) (1961)

Sherry, Grand Jury Minutes: The Unreasonable Rule of Secrecy, 48 Va.L.Rev. 668 (1962)

Note, Disclosure of Informers' Identities, 17 Hastings L.J. 99 (1966)

Comment, Constitutional Law: Even When Arrest is Made Without a Warrant, Officers Not Required to Disclose Source of Information Used to Establish Probable Cause, 1967 Duke L.J. 888 (1967)

Comment, Criminal Law—Prosecution's Privilege to Withhold the Identity of an Informer, 7 Washburn L.J. 115 (1967)

Note, Informer's Privilege in Criminal Cases, 1967 U.Ill.L.F. 665
    Quinn, McCray v. Illinois (87 Sup.Ct. 1056): Probable Cause and the Informer Privilege, 45 Denver L.J. 399 (1968)

Note, Governmental Privileges: Roadblock to Effective Discovery, 7 U.San Fran.L.Rev. 282 (1973)

Berger, The President, Congress, and the Courts, 83 Yale L.J. 1111 (1974)

Cox, Executive Privilege, 122 U.Pa.L.Rev. 1383 (1974)

United States v. Nixon (94 Sup.Ct. 3090): A Symposium, 22 U.C.L.A. L.Rev. 4 (1974)

Chapter IX

REAL EVIDENCE

A. AUTHENTICATION OF REAL EVIDENCE

1. DOCUMENTS

McCORMICK, EVIDENCE

395–96 (1954).*

One who seeks to introduce evidence of a particular fact, or item of proof, must generally give evidence (or offer assurance that he will do so) of those circumstances which make this fact or item relevant to some issue in the case. In respect to writings one of the commonest and most obvious of these circumstances on which relevancy may depend is the *authorship* of the writing. By whom was it written, signed, or adopted? Certainly any intelligible system of procedure must require that if the legal significance of the writing depends upon its authorship by a particular person, some showing must be made that he was the author, if the writing is to be accepted for consideration. The question is, what showing? In the everyday affairs of business and social life, the practice is to look first to the writing itself and if it bears the purported signature of X, or recites that it was made by him, we assume if no question of authenticity is raised that the writing is what it purports to be, that is, the writing of X.

It is just here that the common law trial procedure departs sharply from men's customs in ordinary affairs, and adopts the opposite attitude, namely, that the purported signature or the recitation of authorship on the face of the writing will not be accepted as sufficient preliminary proof of authenticity to secure the admission of the writing in evidence. * * *

The term authentication is here used in the limited sense of proof of authorship. It is sometimes employed in a wider meaning, embracing all proof which may be required as a preliminary to the admission of a writing, chattel, photograph or the like. Thus in the case of business records not only is proof of authorship required for admission, but at common law various other facts such as that they were made in the course of the business must also be proved as part of the "foundation." Similarly the identity of a bullet offered in a murder case as the fatal bullet, or the correctness of a photograph would be part of the necessary foundation-proof for admission. * * *

* Copyright, 1954 by West Publishing Co.

RULES OF EVIDENCE FOR UNITED STATES COURTS AND MAGISTRATES

Rule 901

REQUIREMENT OF AUTHENTICATION OR IDENTIFICATION

* * *

(b) **Illustrations.** By way of illustration only, and not by way of limitation, the following are examples of authentication or identification conforming with the requirements of this rule:

(1) *Testimony of witness with knowledge.* Testimony that a matter is what it is claimed to be.

(2) *Nonexpert opinion on handwriting.* Nonexpert opinion as to the genuineness of handwriting, based upon familiarity not acquired for purposes of the litigation.

(3) *Comparison by trier or expert witness.* Comparison by the trier of fact or by expert witnesses with specimens which have been authenticated.

(4) *Distinctive characteristics and the like.* Appearance, contents, substance, internal patterns, or other distinctive characteristics, taken in conjunction with circumstances.

(5) *Voice identification.* Identification of a voice, whether heard firsthand or through mechanical or electronic transmission or recording, by opinion based upon hearing the voice at any time under circumstances connecting it with the alleged speaker.

(6) *Telephone conversations.* Telephone conversations, by evidence that a call was made to the number assigned at the time by the telephone company to a particular person or business, if (A) in the case of a person, circumstances, including self-identification, show the person answering to be the one called, or (B) in the case of a business, the call was made to a place of business and the conversation related to business reasonably transacted over the telephone.

(7) *Public records or reports.* Evidence that a writing authorized by law to be recorded or filed and in fact recorded or filed in a public office, or in a purported public record, report, statement, or data compilation, in any form, is from the public office where items of this nature are kept.

(8) *Ancient documents or data compilation.* Evidence that a document or data compilation, in any form, (A) is in such condition as to create no suspicion concerning its authenticity, (B) was in a place where it, if authentic, would likely be, and (C) has been in existence 20 years or more at the time it is offered.

(9) *Process or system.* Evidence describing a process or system used to produce a result and showing that the process or system produces an accurate result.

(10) *Methods provided by statute or rule.* Any method of authentication or identification provided by Act of Congress or by other rules prescribed by the Supreme Court pursuant to statutory authority.

Rule 902

SELF-AUTHENTICATION

Extrinsic evidence of authenticity as a condition precedent to admissibility is not required with respect to the following:

(1) **Domestic public documents under seal.** A document bearing a seal purporting to be that of the United States, or of any State, district, Commonwealth, territory, or insular possession thereof, or the Panama Canal Zone, or the Trust Territory of the Pacific Islands, or of a political subdivision, department, officer, or agency thereof, and a signature purporting to be an attestation or execution.

(2) **Domestic public documents not under seal.** A document purporting to bear the signature in his official capacity of an officer or employee of any entity included in paragraph (1) hereof, having no seal, if a public officer having a seal and having official duties in the district or political subdivision of the officer or employee certifies under seal that the signer has the official capacity and that the signature is genuine.

(3) **Foreign public documents.** A document purporting to be executed or attested in his official capacity by a person authorized by the laws of a foreign country to make the execution or attestation, and accompanied by a final certification as to the genuineness of the signature and official position (A) of the executing or attesting person, or (B) of any foreign official whose certificate of genuineness of signature and official position relates to the execution or attestation or is in a chain of certificates of genuineness of signature and official position relating to the execution or attestation. A final certification may be made by a secretary of embassy or legation, consul general, consul, vice consul, or consular agent of the United States, or a diplomatic or consular official of the foreign country assigned or accredited to the United States. If reasonable opportunity has been given to all parties to investigate the authenticity and accuracy of official documents, the court may, for good cause shown, order that they be treated as presumptively authentic without final certification or permit them to be evidenced by an attested summary with or without final certification.

(4) **Certified copies of public records.** A copy of an official record or report or entry therein, or of a document authorized by law to be recorded or filed and actually recorded or filed in a public office, including data compilations in any form, certified as correct by the custodian or other person authorized to make the certification, by certificate complying with paragraph (1), (2), or (3) of this rule or complying with any Act of Congress or rule prescribed by the Supreme Court pursuant to statutory authority.

(5) **Official publications.** Books, pamphlets, or other publications purporting to be issued by public authority.

(6) **Newspapers and periodicals.** Printed materials purporting to be newspapers or periodicals.

(7) **Trade inscriptions and the like.** Inscriptions, signs, tags, or labels purporting to have been affixed in the course of business and indicating ownership, control, or origin.

(8) **Acknowledged documents.** Documents accompanied by a certificate of acknowledgment executed in the manner provided by law by a notary public or other officer authorized by law to take acknowledgments.

(9) **Commercial paper and related documents.** Commercial paper, signatures thereon, and documents relating thereto to the extent provided by general commercial law.

(10) **Presumptions under Acts of Congress.** Any signature, document, or other matter declared by Act of Congress to be presumptively or prima facie genuine or authentic.

Rule 903

SUBSCRIBING WITNESS' TESTIMONY UNNECESSARY

The testimony of a subscribing witness is not necessary to authenticate a writing unless required by the laws of the jurisdiction whose laws govern the validity of the writing.

2. OTHER REAL EVIDENCE

LILLY, AN INTRODUCTION TO THE LAW OF EVIDENCE *

414–416 (1978).

§ 108. Real and Demonstrative Evidence: In General

The term "real evidence" generally refers to animate or inanimate physical things exhibited to the jury. Often, however, the term is used narrowly to refer only to tangible items (such as a weapon or a damaged mechanical part) originally involved in the litigated occur-

---

* Reprinted with permission from Lilly's "An Introduction to the Law of Evidence," West Publishing Co. (1978).

rence. The term "demonstrative evidence" often is employed to indicate those tangible items (such as maps, diagrams, or models) not directly involved in the litigated occurrence, but subsequently constructed or obtained by the parties to illustrate (demonstrate) their factual contentions or to help the jury understand the case. It has been suggested that although most real evidence itself has probative value, demonstrative evidence has none, being a mere visual or artificial aid designed to assist the trier in understanding the probative testimony or contentions of the parties. The validity of this distinction is doubtful, at least if the term "probative value" denotes the tendency of evidence to make the existence of a fact more probable than it would be in the absence of the evidence. In any event, this distinction often is ignored by the appellate opinions and, as we shall see, the use of both real and demonstrative evidence is conditioned upon criteria that reduce the risk of improperly influencing the trier.

In the following discussion, the term "real evidence," unless otherwise indicated, is used in its broadest sense to include any tangible thing ("res") exhibited to the jury. However, there is a distinction that should be grasped regarding the proper evidentiary foundation: When the exhibited item allegedly was involved in the occurrence or controversy in question (*original* real evidence), its admission is conditioned upon a showing by the proponent that the thing displayed is the *same* tangible that originally was involved. But where the real evidence is used only demonstratively—that is to illustrate or clarify—its origin is not important: what matters is whether the properties or characteristics of the item (map, model, or so forth) are sufficiently clear and accurate to assist, without misleading, the trier in understanding some aspect of the case.

When a party presents real evidence, its perceptible qualities can be ascertained by the trier without reliance on the testimonial capacities (observation, memory, and sincerity) of others. Nonetheless, the use of real evidence also involves some reliance upon the foundation testimony establishing the origin or nature of the evidence. If the proponent fails to persuade the jury of the authenticity or accuracy of his real evidence, they may disregard it. In any event, the jury has the function of assessing the credibility of testimony relating to the imperceptible aspects of real evidence.

Finally, real evidence, like other forms of proof, can be used directly or circumstantially. If an ultimate issue in a case rests on whether a certain antique is chipped and discolored, display of the item provides direct evidence of the defects. But if the issue is the cause of the damage, the item is mere circumstantial proof generating an inference as to the cause of the defect. Likewise, the perceptible characteristics of a child (color of eyes, skin, or hair, for example) are direct evidence of their nature, but circumstantial evidence that X is the father.

§ 109. Real and Demonstrative Evidence: Conditions of Admissibility and Required Foundation

In order to be admissible, tangible evidence must provide the trier of fact with some knowledge or understanding it lacked before viewing the thing presented. Further, the insights gained must be material to the controversy being tried. This is a familiar theme. Relevant evidence makes the consequential proposition to which it is directed more likely than it would be without the evidence; often, however, courts relax even this undemanding standard when dealing with real evidence. Although real evidence sometimes can have very high probative force—as, for example, where it is used as direct proof of an ultimate issue—it also may serve only to illustrate or explain testimony directed to the background or setting of the litigated transaction. In this latter circumstance the probative force of the real evidence is marginal at best, but courts nonetheless admit it unless it has a potential for causing confusion or delay. Perhaps it may be generalized that courts consider real evidence "relevant" if it either increases the probability of consequential proposition *or* assists the trier in understanding the case.

All evidence, of course, is subject to the objection that its probative weight is outweighed by prejudice, distraction, confusion, or undue delay. With real evidence this balancing test most often is required when the proffered item likely will inspire a sharp emotional response such as pity, repugnance, or resentment. Nonetheless, when the evidence displays a condition that is in issue the courts almost always will admit it. And even where probative force is comparatively weak, the tendency still is toward admission: such things as a plaintiff's preserved knee cap, decedent's blood-stained clothing, and pictures of a deceased victim of a crime all have been admitted. Because the trial judge has considerable discretion in balancing the worth of real evidence against its negative aspects, reversals of his rulings are relatively rare.

The proponent of real evidence must provide a proper foundation, a process variously referred to as identification or authentication. This generally consists of having one or more witnesses describe the item, supply information about its origin, and, if needed, provide such additional testimony as is required to show that the item is relevant. Where the evidence is "original" in the sense that it played a part in the controversy, identification entails a showing that the thing offered is the *same item* involved in the litigated transaction—for example that the proffered rifle is the weapon used by the defendant or the proffered ring is the one that was falsely claimed to be a diamond. It will be seen immediately that this logical condition requiring that the origin of the thing be shown is a function of the principle of relevance—more specifically of conditional relevance. The weapon or the ring is not helpful unless it is the one involved in the parties' conduct. Observe, however, that where the evidence only is demonstrative, authentication involves having a witness identify the proffered item—for example, as the map of a certain region or a model of the human skeleton—or provide such brief additional explanation as is necessary for the trier to understand what is exhibited. The origin of the res is not important.

There is an additional requirement—again based upon relevance—that must be satisfied during identification, and it too varies with whether or not the real evidence is original. With original evidence, the proponent should elicit testimony that the relevant quality or condition of the proffered thing *has not changed substantially* since the time of its involvement in the controversy. The basic principle of relevance, which demands probative force but weighs this against countervailing practical considerations, requires this showing. If the item has been substantially altered, its probative value is reduced or negated and it may mislead or confuse the jury. On the other hand, if the proffered thing is not original but rather is demonstrative, the proponent need show only that the proffered item is a fair representation of what it purports to be. For example, if a map or a model is used it should be sufficiently accurate in all pertinent respects so as not to mislead the trier of fact.

There is some uncertainty about the proper role of the judge in determinations of identification. In most instances he performs only a screening function: if a reasonable jury could find that the object is what its proponent claims, the real evidence will be admitted. But real evidence, which appeals directly to the visual sense, can sometimes have a telling probative impact upon the jury. Thus in certain instances where there is a danger that the jury might be misled, the judge may himself determine if authentication is satisfactory. In such cases, he is treating the real evidence as raising an issue of competence and not as simply raising an issue of conditional relevance. Although the governing rules are not always clear, the judge sometimes—at least in common-law jurisdictions—assumes a fact-finding role where scientific evidence is offered or, as we shall see shortly, where there is a question involving a chain of custody. In these instances he is demanding more than simply a prima facie evidentiary foundation that, *if believed by the jury*, would entitle it reasonably to find the elements of identification.

In any event, when the foundation is complete, the proffered thing should be formally introduced into evidence. This invariably is the practice with original evidence, but some jurisdictions do not require that demonstrative evidence be introduced into the record. This relaxation of the usual requirement of having a complete trial record seems ill-advised because it leads to uncertainty at the appellate review stage.

As the foregoing suggests, the general principles governing the introduction of real evidence are relatively simple. Practical complications, however, often arise in the case of original real evidence when the proffered res has no distinguishing characteristic, or when, even though such a characteristic exists, the witness is unable to recall having observed this characteristic. The practical problem posed is this: How shall the proponent fulfill that requirement of identification which demands that there be foundation evidence that the proffered item is the same one involved in the controversy? The difficulty can arise with any kind of original evidence—for example, a weapon, a bottle, or a piece of rope; its resolution is found in establishing a *chain of custody*, through the testimony of successive custodians, that substantially eliminates the possibility the proffered item is not the original res. Identification through a chain of custody usually is necessary where a sample (such as blood, semen, or clothing particles) is collected and subjected to scientific tests. Typically, the specimen passes through the custody of several persons: the police, for example, give the sample to a technician, who delivers it to an expert who, after conducting tests, places the sample in the prosecutor's safekeeping. The evidentiary foundation must show that the original item was the thing tested, that it is the same as the thing now offered, and that the test results reported in court were derived from analysis of the sample. Again, the solution lies in the testimony of the various custodians, perhaps supplemented by business entries that help to substantiate authenticity.

There is some variation in the degree of certainty required when a chain of custody is used to fulfill the requirement of identification. If tracing an item by its chain of custody is tested by the principle of conditional relevance, the chain adequately should be forged if the evidence accounting for the item is *sufficient* to allow a reasonable jury to conclude that the offered res is the original. Presumably, if the trier concluded that an item other than the original had been introduced, it would ignore the evidence because it readily would see that a false or substituted thing had no probative force. Yet some cases, most commonly criminal, appear to require that the evidence of custody render it *reasonably certain* that the original evidence has been traced accurately. This more rigorous requirement arguably is justified by the seriousness of a criminal proceeding and by the obligation of the government to adopt standard, trustworthy procedures for safeguarding evidence. An added safeguard—now employed by many courts—is to require that the judge determine preliminarily that this standard has been satisfied before admitting the real evidence. In this regard, he departs from his usual role of screening the foundation for sufficiency.

GALLEGO v. UNITED STATES

United States Court of Appeals, Ninth Circuit, 1960.
276 F.2d 914.

Before MATHEWS, HAMLEY, and MERRILL, Circuit Judges.

HAMLEY, Circuit Judge. Albert Lopez Gallego appeals from his conviction and sentence on a charge of unlawful importation of marijuana, * * *. Two questions are presented here. The first is whether, because of an asserted missing link in the chain of evidence relating to the custody of a can and a sack containing marijuana, it was error to admit these articles into evidence as exhibits. The second is whether the sentence imposed * * * constitutes cruel and unusual punishment within the meaning of the Eighth Amendment.

Concerning the question as to the admissibility of evidence, the relevant facts are as follows: Appellant entered the United States from Mexico on April 3, 1959, and was stopped at the border by an immigration inspector and a customs inspector. In the trunk of appellant's car the immigration inspector found a paper sack which contained a substance which appeared to be marijuana. He handed the sack to the customs inspector who, in turn, gave it to Fred Valenzuela, Deputy Collector of Customs, at the latter's nearby home. Valenzuela then took the sack to his office in the Customs House at Naco and put it in his desk.

Immediately afterwards he searched appellant at the Customs House and found upon the latter's person a Prince Albert tobacco can containing what appeared to be marijuana cigarettes. As soon as the can was found it was placed in Valenzuela's desk.

The sack and can were kept in the desk for approximately one hour, during which Valenzuela was at all times in the vicinity of the desk. That night Valenzuela placed the sack and can in a safe in the Customs House. The next day he personally took these two articles to the Commissioner's hearing, after which he returned them to the safe. Valenzuela took the can and sack from the safe about ten days later and sent them by registered mail to the customs laboratory in Los Angeles. They were returned by registered mail and replaced in the safe, where they remained until the morning of the trial.

At the trial the immigration inspector who had found the paper sack in the trunk of appellant's car examined a paper sack which was handed to him, and its contents, and identified the sack as that which he had found. His initials appeared thereon. He similarly examined a can which was handed to him, on which his initials appeared, and identified the can as the one which had been taken from appellant's person. He testified that the contents of the can appeared to be the same as when the can was first found, but was unable to testify that the contents actually were the same.

Valenzuela similarly examined the same paper sack and can which were produced at the trial. He identified the sack as the one which had been turned over to him at his home. He identified the can as the one which he had found on appellant's person and testified that its contents appeared to be "very much" the same as when the can was discovered. A customs inspector who had been present when the automobile was searched examined the paper sack which was produced at the trial, and its contents, and identified the sack as the article found in the trunk of appellant's car.

A chemist for the United States Customs Service identified these two containers as the ones which had reached him by registered mail. On the basis of his analysis of their contents he testified that the sack and can each contained marijuana.

The safe at the customs office in Naco, where the sack and can were placed for a period of time, had a combination lock. The combination was known only by Valenzuela and by the acting deputy collector of customs who takes Valenzuela's place when the latter is away. The acting deputy collector was not called as a witness.

After all of the evidence reviewed above had been received the government offered the paper sack and its contents in evidence as exhibit 1–A, and the can and its contents as exhibit 1–B. Appellant objected on the ground that the government had failed to show that it had exclusive control and possession of the articles during the ten days they were in the safe before being sent to the Los Angeles laboratory. The objection was overruled and the articles were admitted in evidence.

It is this objection which appellant renews here in contending that it was error to receive exhibits 1–A and 1–B in evidence. Specifically, appellant argues that the "claim of custody" must be complete and exclusive and that it was incumbent upon the government to prove that the articles could not have been tampered with during this ten-day period. In permitting the introduction of the exhibits, appellant contends, the court drew the impermissible conclusion that the acting deputy collector, who knew the combination of the safe but was not called as a witness, did not change or tamper with the evidence.

Before a physical object connected with the commission of a crime may properly be admitted in evidence there must be a showing that such object is in substantially the same condition as when the crime was committed. This determination is to be made by the trial judge. Factors to be considered in making this determination include the nature of the article, the circumstances surrounding the preservation and custody of it, and the likelihood of intermeddlers tampering with it. If upon the consideration of such factors the trial judge is satisfied that in reasonable probability the article has not been changed in important respects, he may permit its introduction in evidence.
* * *

The jury, of course, is free to disregard such evidence upon its finding that the article was not properly identified, or that there had been a change in its nature.

The trial judge's determination that the showing as to identification and nature of contents is sufficient to warrant reception of an article in evidence may not be overturned except for a clear abuse of discretion. No abuse of discretion was shown here.

The only other person who knew the combination of the safe was the acting deputy collector of customs. In the absence of any evidence to the contrary, the trial judge was entitled to assume that this official would not tamper with the sack and can or their contents. Where no evidence indicating otherwise is produced, the presumption of regularity supports the official acts of public officers, and courts presume that they have properly discharged their official duties. Pasadena Research Laboratories v. United States, 9 Cir., 169 F.2d 375, 381–382.

There is no rule requiring the prosecution to produce as witnesses all persons who were in a position to come into contact with the article sought to be introduced in evidence. * * *

Accordingly, the failure of the government to produce the acting deputy collector of customs as a witness did not require the trial court to reject exhibits 1–A and 1–B.

The trial court did not err in admitting these exhibits in evidence

* * *

Affirmed.

WALTZ, CRIMINAL EVIDENCE

(1975).

Chain of Custody; Time Lapse. Tracing an unbroken chain of custody can be crucial to the effective use of firearms identification evidence. This does not mean, however, that changes in the condition of firearms evidence or the passage of a substantial period of time between the shooting and the recovery of the firearms evidence will foreclose admissibility at trial. Such considerations usually go only to the amount of weight the factfinder will give to the evidence.

Example a.:

Ignacio v. People of the Territory of Guam, 413 F.2d 513 (9th Cir. 1969), cert. denied, 397 U.S. 943 (1970) (bullet recovered two days after discovery of victim; held admissible).

Example b.:

State v. Lane, 233 P.2d 437 (S.Ct.Ariz.1951) (cartridges had been dropped in river months before recovery; held admissible).

Of course, it is important that, to the extent possible, all law enforcement agencies provide for the safe storage of vital evidence prior to trial. Police departments are well advised to maintain a locked evidence room manned by an officer who keeps detailed records not only of its contents but of the disposition of items of evidence and the names of persons entering the room for any purpose.

COLLATERAL READINGS

Documents and Real Evidence

Wigmore, Evidence (3rd ed. 1940)
    Vol. 4, §§ 1173–75, 1177–1282

McCormick's Handbook of the Law of Evidence §§ 229–243 (2d ed. 1972)

Rogers, The Best Evidence Rule, 1945 Wis.L.Rev. 278

Conrad, Magnetic Recordings in the Court, 40 Va.L.Rev. 23 (1954)

Comment, Critical Appraisal of the Application of the Best Evidence Rule, 21 Rutgers L.Rev. 526 (1967)

Note, Photostatic Copies and the Best Evidence Rule: Time for a Change, 40 Tenn.L.Rev. 709 (1973)

Note, Best Evidence and Authentication of Documents, 21 Loyola L. Rev. 450 (1975)

Wigmore, Evidence (3rd ed. 1940)
    Vol. 5, §§ 1679–1684
    Vol. 7, §§ 2128–2169

McCormick's Handbook of the Law of Evidence §§ 218–228 (2d ed. 1972)

Strong, Liberalizing the Authentication of Private Writings, 52 Corn.L.Q. 284 (1967)

Brown, Authentication and Contents of Writing, 1969 Law & Soc. Order 611 (1969)

L. Alexander and E. Alexander, Authentication of Documents Requirement: Barrier to Falsehood or to Truth, 10 San Diego L. Rev. 266 (1973)

Note, Authentication and Identification, 27 Ark.L.Rev. 332 (1973)

Note, Best Evidence and Authentication of Documents, 21 Loyola L. Rev. 450 (1975)

B. THE BEST EVIDENCE RULE

McCORMICK, EVIDENCE

409, 411–12 (1954).*

The specific tenor of [the best evidence rule] needs to be definitely stated and its limits clearly understood. The rule is this: in

---

* Copyright, 1954 by West Publishing Co.

proving the terms of a writing, where such terms are material, the original writing must be produced, unless it is shown to be unavailable for some reason other than the serious fault of the proponent.

* * *

A rule which permitted the judge to insist that all evidence must pass his scrutiny as the "best" or most reliable means of proving the fact would be a sore incumbrance upon the parties, who in our system have the responsibility of proof. In fact, * * * no such general scrutiny is sanctioned, but only as to "writings" is a demand for the "best," the original, made. Accordingly, as to objects bearing no writing, the judge (unless in some exceptional cases when the exact features of the object have become as essential to the issue, as the precise words of a writing usually are) may not exclude oral testimony describing the object and demand that the object itself be produced. * * * If, however, the object, such as a policeman's badge, a revolver, an engagement ring, or a tombstone, bears a number or inscription the terms of which are relevant, we face the question, shall we treat it as a chattel or as a "writing"? Probably most modern cases would support the view advocated by Wigmore, that the judge shall have discretion, to follow the one analogy or the other in the light of such factors as the need for precise information as to the exact inscription, the ease or difficulty of production, and the simplicity or complexity of the inscription.

LILLY, AN INTRODUCTION TO THE LAW OF EVIDENCE *

(1978).

§ 116. The Best Evidence Rule

We have noted that the rule requiring the production of the original document applies only when the proponent is attempting to prove the contents or terms of a writing. The original is preferred because its use eliminates the risk of mistranscriptions or testimonial misstatements of what the document said; inspection of the original also reduces somewhat the chance of undetected tampering. Note that sometimes a writing recites or records a perceivable event or condition such as a marriage (marriage certificate), payment of money (receipt), or the utterance of certain words (transcript). Here, the proponent wishing to prove the underlying event may proceed in either of two ways: he may (1) offer the testimony of an observer, or (2) offer the writing that records or recites the event. The first approach does not involve the best evidence rule because the proponent is not attempting to prove the terms of a writing, but merely is presenting evidence of an event perceived by a witness. It makes no difference that the occurrence of the event is recited in a writing that was made subsequent to its occurrence, for the writing does not, so far as legal rules of proof are concerned, "erase" or supplant the preceding event. Of course, if the proponent chooses to make his proof

* Reprinted with permission from Lilly's "An Introduction to the Law of Evidence," West Publishing Co. (1978).

by use of a writing, the best evidence rule must be satisfied. There are, moreover, some instances where the law prescribes that a writing has the effect of subsuming, so to speak, any prior events. In these situations, illustrated by a deed, a written contract, or a judgment, the law regards the transaction as "essentially written" and the proponent must make his proof by the writing if it is available.

The courts are in general accord with the foregoing analysis, although there has been some tendency in criminal cases to prefer a written, signed confession over the testimony of a person claiming to have heard an oral confession. Perhaps this preference can be justified as a protective measure, but analytically the proponent does not seek to prove the terms of a writing; therefore his choice should affect only the weight of his evidence.

Where there are several writings, application of the best evidence rule requires a determination of which one (or ones) constitutes an original. Preliminarily, it should be noted that parties can create *multiple* originals: if copies (such as carbons or photostatic reproductions) of a contract, will, or other agreement are duly executed (signed), the parties have manifested their intention to accord equal status to all of the identical writings regardless of their mechanical characteristics. Beyond this, reference to the substantive law is often necessary to determine what constitutes an "original" for purposes of the best evidence rule. Suppose, for example, a defendant types an original of a libelous document; he then makes a photostatic copy, but he publishes only the latter. The copy is the operative document under the substantive law and, as such, constitutes the original with respect to the best evidence rule. A similar analysis should be employed with regard to telegrams. If D writes out a contractual offer at the telegraph office and the terms of the offer then are embodied in a telegram, the telegram is the original—assuming the telegraph company is acting as D's agent. This result turns not upon which writing was created first, but rather upon which document has an operative legal effect. In addition to the problems created by certain substantive legal doctrines, modern technology often blurs the line between an original and a copy. For instance, data can be entered and stored in a computer or similar device and then, upon command, returned in printed form. All such printouts should be considered originals, and this characterization appears to have been accepted by the courts. The term "duplicate or multiple original" often is used to describe these documents of equal evidentiary status.

Once an original has been identified, it should be produced if feasible, assuming the proponent seeks to prove its terms. Unexecuted photographic copies of the original are considered secondary evidence and, quite obviously, oral testimony purporting to give the terms of the original falls into the same category. Unexecuted carbon copies probably should stand on the same footing as photographic copies, but some authorities treat a carbon as a duplicate original.

It might be asked whether there is any longer a need for the best evidence rule, given the reliability of modern means of reproduction. Because of technological accuracy, it is difficult to base one's choice between the original and a copy (as opposed to one's choice between the original and verbal testimony) on the ground that the copy lacks reliability because it more likely contains accidental inaccuracies or omissions. Perhaps the rule preferring the original can be justified on the ground that as between the original and a copy, the former is more likely to yield clues to tampering or fraud.

The Federal Rules of Evidence strike a balance which preserves a preference for the original and at the same time gives due recognition to the accuracy of copies produced by modern means. Rule 1002 provides that "To prove the content of a writing, recording, or photograph, the original * * * is required, except as otherwise provided. * * *" Rule 1003, however, states that "A duplicate is admissible to the same extent as an original unless (1) a genuine question is raised as to the authenticity of the original or (2) in the circumstances it would be unfair to admit the duplicate in lieu of the original." Thus, the federal draftsmen adopted a middle ground between rejection of the best evidence principle and adherence to its traditional formulation. Another feature of the Federal Rules is noteworthy: the application of the best evidence rule extends beyond writings to include sound recordings and photographs. This enlargement of the rule can be traced to similar extensions in several of the states, and it should not be viewed as a far-reaching change.

The original of a sound recording usually is the initial recording, and the original of a photograph is the "negative or any print therefrom." In most cases the proponent would offer these "originals" even without the force of a rule. With regard to still and moving pictures, proof of the photographic contents is not necessary very often. Commonly, photographic evidence is admitted as a graphic representation of a scene or subject that a testifying witness has observed. This illustrative use of photographic evidence does not involve proving the contents of the picture but rather is an attempt to establish the scene itself by testimony. But if no witness has observed the pictured scene or event (as in the case of an x-ray or where an automatic camera photographs a litigated event), or a photograph is alleged to be libelous, obscene, violative of a copyright or of one's privacy, the photographic contents are in issue and the best evidence rule applies.

Federal or state statutory provisions sometimes modify the usual application of the best evidence rule. Congress, for example, has enacted a statute allowing photographic reproduction of tax returns and certain Treasury documents. State and federal statutes permitting copies of public records are common, as are provisions that apply to regularly kept business records. If no exception to the best evidence rule can be discovered, then care should be taken to determine what circumstances will excuse production of the original.

If the original is lost or destroyed (excepting bad faith destruction by the proponent himself) production is excused. The same result occurs where the original is difficult or impossible to obtain, or where the original is in the hands of the opponent and, after due notice, he fails to produce it.

Finally, the careful practitioner should ascertain if the jurisdiction in question prefers a particular kind of *secondary* evidence. Many courts extend the principle of the best evidence rule and thus give it an operative effect even after production of the original has been excused. The most common extension to secondary evidence is to require a copy (when available) in lieu of oral testimony purporting to give the terms of the original. But the Federal Rules of Evidence contain no provision for "classes" of secondary evidence. Usually, the self-interest of the proponent will operate to place before the trier the most reliable secondary evidence.

CHANDLER v. UNITED STATES

United States Court of Appeals, Tenth Circuit, 1963.
318 F.2d 356.

Before BREITENSTEIN, HILL and SETH, Circuit Judges.

SETH, Circuit Judge. Appellant was indicted in two counts of unlawfully removing and transporting twenty-six and one-half gallons of non-tax-paid distilled spirits in violation of Title 26 U.S.C. §§ 5601(a)(12) and 5604(a)(1). A non-jury trial was had and appellant was found guilty on both counts.

Appellant urges that it was error for the trial court to admit testimony of the government's agents that the containers of whiskey seized did not bear revenue stamps, and asserts instead that the containers themselves or some of them should have been produced at the trial. On this point the appellant argues that the "best evidence" rule requires the production of the original containers.

In his argument appellant cites and relies upon Watson v. United States, 224 F.2d 910, a decision in 1955 by the Fifth Circuit. However, even should this cited case be followed, it nevertheless held that the use of secondary evidence would be justified in the event evidence showed that the containers were destroyed "without any fraudulent purpose or any intent to create an excuse for its non-production." There was no evidence or testimony whatever in the case at bar that there was any fraudulent purpose involved in the destruction of the whiskey containers. The agents who appeared testified that the containers were not produced for the reason that they were destroyed under Internal Revenue Service regulations. This testimony, given by one of the agents who examined the seized contents of the car trunk, described the containers as half-gallon fruit jars. On cross-examination when asked where the containers were at the time of trial, the agent stated they had been destroyed for the reason that it was "in our regulations that we only maintain a sample." It would appear that the witness was referring to Title 26 U.S.C. § 5609(a), which applies to the destruction of seized distilled spirits. The court overruled a motion to exclude this testimony with reference to the containers.

As indicated above there is nothing in the evidence to indicate any fraudulent purpose in the destruction of the containers, although it would appear to have been somewhat hasty and such action should not be encouraged. The "best evidence" rule as it is generally applied does not relate to situations such as this, but is ordinarily limited to cases or situations where the question relates to the contents of written documents. [citations omitted.] In the case at bar, we have instead the witness giving a description of the half-gallon glass jars in which the whiskey was contained, and in so doing, he was describing a physical thing in testifying as to the absence of revenue stamps on such containers. This testimony was adequate proof. Atkins v. United States, 240 F.2d 849 (5th Cir.).

* * *

We find no error, and the case is affirmed.

PEOPLE v. ENSKAT

Appellate Department, Superior Court, Los Angeles County, California.
20 Cal.App.3d Supp. 1, 98 Cal.Rptr. 646 (1971).

ZACK, Judge. The complaint charges appellant with two counts of [exhibiting obscene motion pictures].

* * *

The motion picture involved was not seized under a warrant, or otherwise offered or placed in evidence by the prosecution. The officers entered the theater and then took pictures of portions of the film. Such pictures, including pictures of the theater exterior, are People's 1 through 9, 11, and 12. The balance of the film, audio and visual, was the subject of testimony. A best evidence objection was overruled on the ground that the rule does not apply. Such ruling was error.

Evidence Code section 1500 states that "* * * no evidence other than the writing itself is admissible to prove the content of a writing." There is no question but that the contents of the material must be considered in an obscenity case. * * * Motion pictures are accorded the same constitutional protection as books and other forms of expression. * * * As the content of a film is always an issue in an obscenity case, the best evidence rule will apply if a film is a writing under the Evidence Code.

Evidence Code section 250 defines a "writing" as including " * * * photographing, and every other means of recording upon any tangible thing any form of communication or representation, including letters, words, pictures, sounds, or symbols." A photographic transparency, e. g., a "slide," is a writing under this definition, because it is a picture recorded upon a tangible thing, the celluloid.[1] A motion picture film is a series of such pictures recorded upon a celluloid film strip. * * * Each picture in each frame is slightly different from the preceding one, so that when the film is moved through a projector, these individual pictures appear to merge into a continuous "moving" picture. This movement is only an optical illusion, for in actuality each separate picture is projected onto the screen for a split second, rapidly followed by the next one. That there *appears* to be a "motion picture" does not alter the fact that a series of single pictures on the filmstrip, each one a "writing," is casting an image on a screen.

Respondent argues, however, that it is not the film, but these light images on the screen, that constitute the offense of exhibiting an obscene motion picture. Respondent argues that as this moving image is unrecorded, it cannot be a writing, and therefore is not subject to the best evidence rule. This argument ignores the essential fact that the moving image is merely the consequence of passing a writing (the film) through a machine. Without the projector and the filmstrip, no moving image is cast at all. The content of the moving image, "evanescent" or not, is totally dependent upon the content of the filmstrip. Just as it is better for the trier of fact to read a document than have it described, it is better for the trier of fact to see a movie than have it described. The policy considerations upholding the rule for written documents apply with full force to movies as well. It is to be noted that the instant prosecution under Penal Code section 311.2 is for exhibiting *obscene matter*. The latter is defined in section 311, subdivisions (a)(2), (b) to include a "motion picture." It is the character of the contents of the motion picture exhibited which, strictly speaking is in issue, not the character of the images on the screen resulting from its exhibition.

Our ruling herein does not mean that obscenity cases may not, under any circumstances, be prosecuted by means of secondary evidence of the obscene material. It means that in this case, the prosecution, in presenting such secondary evidence, did not comply with the Evidence Code. An example of how the prosecution may proceed is contained in Evidence Code section 1503, subdivision (a): If (1) a defendant is in possession or control of the material at the time he is

---

1. A photograph printed from a negative is still considered secondary evidence. (Hopkins v. Hopkins (1958) 157 Cal.App.2d 313, 320 P.2d 918.)

expressly or impliedly notified of the existence of a criminal action against him involving such alleged obscene material, and (2) if a request that he produce it is made at the trial (out of the presence of the jury), secondary evidence can be used.

But the prosecution has, as does the proponent of secondary evidence in any civil or criminal case, the burden of making a prima facie showing as to both (1) and (2). * * * Here, the proponent of the secondary evidence made no factual showing as to (1) nor did it do (2). Nor did the proponent attempt to make any other showing which might be construed as a foundation for use of secondary evidence other than the example we have mentioned. * * *

The judgment is reversed, and the cause remanded for a new trial.

WHYTE, P. J., and KATZ, J., concur.

RULES OF EVIDENCE FOR UNITED STATES COURTS AND MAGISTRATES

Rule 1001

DEFINITIONS

For purposes of this article the following definitions are applicable:

(1) Writings and recordings. "Writings" and "recordings" consist of letters, words, or numbers, or other equivalent, set down by handwriting, typewriting, printing, photostating, photographing, magnetic impulse, mechanical or electronic recording, or other form of data compilation.

(2) Photographs. "Photographs" include still photographs, X-ray films, video tapes, and motion pictures.

(3) Original. An "original" of a writing or recording is the writing or recording itself or any counterpart intended to have the same effect by a person executing or issuing it. An "original" of a photograph includes the negative or any print therefrom. If data are stored in a computer or similar device, any printout or other output readable by sight, shown to reflect the data accurately, is an "original".

(4) Duplicate. A "duplicate" is a counterpart produced by the same impression as the original, or from the same matrix, or by means of photography, including enlargements and miniatures, or by mechanical or electronic re-recording, or by chemical reproduction, or by other equivalent techniques which accurately reproduces the original.

Rule 1002

REQUIREMENT OF ORIGINAL

To prove the content of a writing, recording, or photograph, the original writing, recording, or photograph is required, except as otherwise provided in these rules or by Act of Congress.

Rule 1003

ADMISSIBILITY OF DUPLICATES

A duplicate is admissible to the same extent as an original unless (1) a genuine question is raised as to the authenticity of the original or (2) in the circumstances it would be unfair to admit the duplicate in lieu of the original.

Rule 1004

ADMISSIBILITY OF OTHER EVIDENCE OF CONTENTS

The original is not required, and other evidence of the contents of a writing, recording, or photograph is admissible if—

(1) **Originals lost or destroyed.** All originals are lost or have been destroyed, unless the proponent lost or destroyed them in bad faith; or

(2) **Original not obtainable.** No original can be obtained by any available judicial process or procedure; or

(3) **Original in possession of opponent.** At a time when an original was under the control of the party against whom offered, he was put on notice, by the pleadings or otherwise, that the contents would be a subject of proof at the hearing, and he does not produce the original at the hearing; or

(4) **Collateral matters.** The writing, recording, or photograph is not closely related to a controlling issue.

Rule 1005

PUBLIC RECORDS

The contents of an official record, or of a document authorized to be recorded or filed and actually recorded or filed, including data compilations in any form, if otherwise admissible, may be proved by copy, certified as correct in accordance with rule 902 or testified to be correct by a witness who has compared it with the original. If a copy which complies with the foregoing cannot be obtained by the exercise of reasonable diligence, then other evidence of the contents may be given.

Rule 1006

SUMMARIES

The contents of voluminous writings, recordings, or photographs which cannot conveniently be examined in court may be presented in the form of a chart, summary, or calculation. The originals, or duplicates, shall be made available for examination or copying, or both, by other parties at reasonable time and place. The court may order that they be produced in court.

Rule 1007

TESTIMONY OR WRITTEN ADMISSION OF PARTY

Contents of writings, recordings, or photographs may be proved by the testimony or deposition of the party against whom offered or by his written admission, without accounting for the nonproduction of the original.

Chapter X

OPINION, EXPERTS AND EXPERTISE; SCIENTIFIC AND DEMONSTRATIVE EVIDENCE

A. OPINION TESTIMONY

1. LAY WITNESSES

STATE v. GARVER

Supreme Court of Oregon, 1950.
190 Or. 291, 225 P.2d 771.

LUSK, Chief Justice. The defendant, Robert Edgar Garver, has appealed from a conviction of first degree murder. The jury, by its verdict, did not recommend life imprisonment, and the death penalty followed as a matter of course.

* * *

The actual substantial controversy arises out of the defense of insanity.

* * *

As to the testimony of Mrs. Mitchell, if there was error in striking her statement that the defendant was mentally ill, it was cured when later she was permitted to give her opinion that he was insane.

Apparently, the court struck the phrases used by her, "such a terrible shape" and "physically ill", on the theory that they were the opinions or conclusions of the witness. The general rule, of course, is that a lay witness may testify only to facts and not to opinions or conclusions. But lay witnesses are frequently permitted to use so-called "short hand" descriptions, in reality opinions, in presenting to the court their impression of the general physical condition of a person. * * * This court has held it proper in a personal injury case to permit laymen, who were intimately acquainted with the plaintiff prior to her injury and observed her condition thereafter, to testify that her health and general physical condition had materially changed for the worse. * * * This seems to us to be a common sense view of the matter. It leaves the witness free to speak his ordinary language, unbewildered by admonitions from the judge to testify to facts, when all the while the witness is sure in his own mind that he *is* testifying to facts. The jury understands what the witness means, and the right of cross-examination removes the likelihood of harm to the other side. Too strict an adherence to the "opinion" rule is undesirable. * * * When a witness of less than ordinary education and powers of expression is on the stand, technical rulings not infrequently result in bickerings between counsel and vain attempts of the court to make the witness comply with its rulings; while in the end the opinion of the witness usually comes out anyway, and nothing whatever is gained.

Mrs. Mitchell was a fairly intelligent witness, but she became so confused by the objections and rulings that at one time she said to counsel for the defendant: "Mr. Johns, I don't know what you mean by—when you ask me a question and I answer it to the best of my ability; I don't know what you mean for me to answer. I just try to tell what you ask me." A little later, after another of her answers was stricken, she said: " * * * I don't know how to express it; when I say what was in my heart then it is stricken from the records."

Mrs. Mitchell related to the jury the history of her son from infancy to the day of the alleged crime—including his illnesses, both mental and physical; his hospitalizations; his moral delinquencies; and his crimes—whatever might throw light on his mental condition. She used the expression "in such a terrible shape" when trying to explain why she had not taken the defendant back to the State Hospital as she had intended to do, and immediately afterwards said: "He asked me if he could get built up a little bit before he went back up there." She testified that "he was mentally and physically ill" in answer to a question as to why the defendant did nothing when he was at home with her in December, 1948. Presumably, she knew as much about his condition of health as any lay person could. Before giving the testimony which was stricken, she had described his former physical appearance to the jury, told of his robust health, and how he had lost sixty pounds during a certain period. The ruling complained of may not have been reversible error; but the same reasons which led the court in the cases cited to approve the admission of testimony of lay witnesses that a person injured in an accident was in a worse condition of health after the accident, than before, impel us to hold that the court should have let the stricken testimony stand.

* * *

[Reversed.]

COMMONWEALTH v. HOLDEN

Supreme Court of Pennsylvania, 1957.
390 Pa. 221, 134 A.2d 868.

[Prosecution for first degree murder. The court affirmed the judgment of conviction, holding the evidence sufficient. The court gave no attention to the point discussed in the following dissenting opinion—Ed.]

* * *

MUSMANNO, Justice (dissenting). The Majority Opinion fails to discuss a very important matter raised by the defendant Charles Holden in his appeal to this Court for a new trial.

On December 31, 1955, between 5:15 and 6:40 a. m., Cora Smith was killed in her home as the result of being struck over the head. The defendant, Charles Holden, was accused, tried, and convicted of her murder. He maintained in his defense that he was innocent since he was not in the victim's home at the time of the brutal attack.

At the time of Holden's arrest, he was taken by the police to the home of a Ralph Jones who had been with Holden for several hours prior to the killing. In Holden's presence, Jones was questioned by the police. The matter of this questioning became a subject for inquiry at the later trial. The assistant district attorney representing the Commonwealth asked Jones if, at the time he was being quizzed by the police in Holden's presence, Holden did anything that was unusual. Jones replied:

> "Well, during the period of time that the detectives were questioning me in his presence, I believe one of them noticed him to sort of wink or something."

The assistant district attorney then asked Jones what Holden meant, and Jones replied:

> "I didn't rightfully know whether it was a wink or something that was in his eye."

The prosecuting attorney's question was a flagrant violation of the rules of evidence and should not have been permitted. What Jones may have thought that Holden meant by the wink, if it was a wink, was entirely speculative. The prosecuting attorney might just as well have asked: "What was Holden thinking of at the time?" In fact, the question imported that very type of query because obviously the eye, no matter how eloquent it is supposed to be in the minds of poets, novelists, and dreamers, is still not capable, by a blink, to telegraph complicated messages, unless, of course, the blinker and the blinkee have previously agreed upon a code.

When Jones replied that he did not know whether Holden had actually winked or had been troubled by a foreign substance in his eye, the Commonwealth's attorney asked him about a statement he had made to the police some time following the winking incident. On January 11th, a few days after the blinking affair, Captain Flynn of the City Detective Bureau asked Jones: "What did you take this wink to be?" and Jones replied:

> "I think he was trying to get me to make an alibi for him to cover up some of his actions and I don't know nothing about any of his actions."

Commonwealth's counsel sought to introduce this statement at the trial and defense counsel properly objected, explaining:

> "We object to that. Whatever it was, it wasn't made in the presence of the defendant, Charles Holden."

The objection was overruled and the jury was thus informed that the defendant endeavored to have Jones frame an alibi for him. On what evidence was this information based? On a wink.

And what did the wink say? I repeat:

> "I think he was trying to get me to make an alibi for him to cover up some of his actions and I don't know nothing about any of his actions."

It will be noted that the stupendous and compendious wink not only solicited the fabrication of a spurious alibi but specified that it was "to cover up some of his actions." One movement of the eyelid conveyed a message of 21 words. Not even the most abbreviated Morse code could say so much with such little expenditure of muscular and mechanical power.

Although the statement of the interpretation of the wink is preposterous on its face, I can see how it could be made to seem very informative and convincing to the jury, since it was given to the jury with the Court's approval. If Holden had actually spoken to Jones the words which Jones related in his interpretation of the wink, no more effective admission of guilty knowledge could be imagined. Jones and Holden had been together prior to the killing. Holden tells Jones to make up an alibi so that Jones can extend their companionship of the evening to an hour including and beyond the time of the killing. And then Jones not only refuses to do what Holden asks him to do, but relates the criminal attempt on the part of Holden to suborn perjury.

But the fact of the matter is that Holden did not ask Jones to fabricate an alibi. He did not ask him to "cover up some of his actions." All that Holden did was to wink. No one knows whether he was trying to convey a message, whether he was attempting to shut out a strong ray of light, or whether a bit of dust troubled him at the moment. The Court, however, allowed the jury to believe that the wink was a semaphoric signal to Jones to commit perjury.

Was ever more ridiculous evidence presented in a murder trial? What is to happen to our rules of evidence in criminal trials if they can be breached so glaringly, without reproof or criticism by this Court? Holden was convicted and sentenced to life imprisonment. He might have been sentenced to death. On a wink.

And the Majority does not consider the matter of sufficient importance even to mention it.

If a witness is to be allowed to state what he believes a wink said, why should he not be allowed to interpret a cough? Or a sneeze? Or a grunt? Or a hiccough? Why should he indeed not be empowered to testify as to what is passing through an accused's brain? Why not permit mind readers to read a defendant's mind, and thus eliminate the jury system completely because who knows better than the defendant himself whether or not he committed the crime of which he stands accused?

The refusal of this Court to grant a new trial, with so momentous a violation of the defendant's rights, duly noted and excepted to on the record, would suggest that here the law has not only winked but closed both eyes.

LILLY, AN INTRODUCTION TO THE LAW OF EVIDENCE *

84–88 (1978).

§ 29. Examining the Witness: The Opinion Rule

In deciding the historical facts, the factfinder (often a jury) frequently must rely upon circumstantial evidence. When direct proof is unavailable, the trier finds the historical facts by a process of inference: from the evidence supporting one fact, the trier infers the existence of a related fact. Since the jury has the principal responsibility of deciding the facts through the inference-drawing process, it is generally deemed inappropriate for a lay witness to incorporate in his testimony his own inferences in the form of an "opinion" or "conclusion." This prohibition applies generally to any testimonial statement or description in which the lay witness's opinion is *unnecessary* —that is, the rule forbidding opinions is applicable in circumstances where the witness could, if requested, describe his observations in "factual" terms. If the witness can adequately reveal the facts, the jury is then in a position to draw the necessary inferences.

The rule against opinion stems in part from the apprehension that testimonial opinion might unduly influence the jury and, in larger part, from the conviction that the allocation of function between witness and jury makes lay opinion unnecessary. Perhaps there is some risk that the trier's factual determinations will be unduly influenced by a witness who, refusing to confine himself to an objective statement of what he has seen or heard, goes further and gives an interpretation or opinion. The fundamental and more persuasive rationale for excluding lay opinion, however, rests upon the assumption that if the jury is in a position to draw the inferences, opinion offered by a lay witness is superfluous. Many courts now accept this rationale, and recent cases display a tendency to justify the admission of a witness's opinion on the straightforward ground that, in the circumstances, its reception appears helpful to the trier. This preferred ratiocination also explains the long-standing practice of courts to ad-

---

* Reprinted with permission from Lilly's "An Introduction to the Law of Evidence," West Publishing Co. (1978).

mit expert opinion (which is usually helpful) while prohibiting most, but not all, lay opinion.

The traditional formulation of the rule against opinion holds that a lay witness should recite the observed "facts," but should not offer his "opinion." The difficulty of administering this rule is that there is no precise method of classifying a testimonial statement as either fact or opinion. Almost every statement contains some degree of inference. As McCormick indicates, the difference between fact and opinion is one of degree. When a witness describes a tree as "gnarled and decaying" he is, in the strict sense, giving an opinion, although, as we shall see, the courts would deem this statement one of fact. The same is true when a witness states that the voice he heard was that of X. Brief reflection about routine social and business conversation demonstrates that it is saturated with inferences. What, then, is the judicial dividing line between fact and opinion?

The more general and conclusory a statement, the more likely it will be classified an opinion. Conversely, the closer a statement comes to describing the separate components of an observation, the more likely it will be deemed a statement of fact. The statement "X is drunk" is a statement of opinion (although, perhaps, admissible anyway); the statement "X had poor muscular control, and the odor of alcohol on his breath" is a statement of fact, as that term is used by the courts. Obviously, these two statements are not diametrically opposed. The difference between them is found in the degree to which the separate bases of a conclusion are individually identified and described. The opinion rule poses no barrier to any testimony that is deemed factual. However, the rule bans most, but not all, lay testimony that is cast in the form of an opinion.

A guiding principle of general application in common-law jurisdictions is one founded on practicality: lay opinion is usually inadmissible if it is reasonably practical and efficient for the witness to express the separate factual components underlying it. If it is feasible to break an opinion into its rudimentary factual parts, then, presumably, the trier will be in as favorable a position as the witness to draw inferences. The opinion, thus unnecessary, is inadmissible. Conversely, when it is impractical to place the trier in a position of equal competence to draw inferences, the witness may give his opinion. Suppose, for instance, the witness testifies that "*X became angry* when his appointment was cancelled" or that "*Y looked fatigued and worried* when he reported to work." These statements are, under the usual judicial classification, opinions. Nonetheless, they are admissible opinions because of the impracticality of reducing them into their component parts. It will thus be observed that all statements of fact and some statements of opinion are admissible.

Although most generalizations in this area can be challenged by some of the many disparate court rulings, it is possible to further characterize that class of statements regarded as permissible lay opinion. Where the observer-witness forms an impression immediately upon perceiving an event—that is, where he would naturally gain an impression or opinion without time for reflection and deductive reasoning—he can usually convey his perception to the trier in a conclusory statement. This situation normally occurs where perception is not sequential, but rather the witness perceives a thing or an event at once, as a unified whole. Thus, when a witness testifies that a car "passed at high speed," or that "Y looked youthful," an objection based upon the opinion rule should fail. The same may be said of the statement "X was drunk", although one could argue that it is feasible to dissect this statement into such components as impaired speech, telltale breath, poor physical coordination, and so forth. Often, however, observers do not isolate these separate manifestations; rather they perceive drunkenness as an integrated whole. Even where separate observations can be detailed, the witness's account may not adequately convey the total impression, and thus his opinion is still helpful. Accordingly, many recent decisions have approved lay opinion that the actor in question was intoxicated.

A number of cases express the principle that lay opinion on the ultimate issue is improper. It appears, however, that this should be true only in certain circumstances. A witness's opinion should be rejected if it contains conclusions or expressions of opinion that are superflous and unhelpful (e. g., testimony that a party was negligent). The same is true where his opinion contains a legal component which has not been adequately explained, and consequently might be misunderstood by the witness or jurors. An example of this latter circumstance is found in testimony that "X had the capacity to make a valid will." Standing alone, this is objectionable opinion. Most jurisdictions explicitly define testamentary capacity in a rather technical manner as including a capacity to know the nature and extent of one's property, to identify the objects of one's bounty, and to understand the nature and effect of a will. During the evidence-taking stage of trial, neither the witness nor the jury may be aware of these legal requirements; thus a witness's opinion concerning X's capacity may be subject to ambiguity and misunderstanding. However, in situations where an opinion involving a legal criterion would be helpful to the trier, there is recent authority supporting admissibility if the legal concept is adequately explained to the witness and the jury.

At an early date, a distinguished English jurist remarked that an opinion does not constitute evidence. This assertion, which may have referred only to situations where the witness had no personal knowlege of the event in question, can not be given a literal meaning in the light of modern developments. A lack of any personal knowledge about the subject of one's testimony is one thing; rendering testimony in a general or conclusory mode is quite another. We have already seen that certain opinions are freely admitted for jury consideration and that the true basis of the opinion rule is the lack of necessity for the witness's opinion. An opinion which is correctly permitted over objection or even one which comes in without objection may be considered as evidence by the factfinder. The only time an opinion does not constitute evidence is when a judge, on motion or objection, rules that the opinion is improper and orders it stricken from the record or instructs the jury to disregard it.

RULES OF EVIDENCE FOR UNITED STATES COURTS AND MAGISTRATES

Rule 701

OPINION TESTIMONY BY LAY WITNESSES

If the witness is not testifying as an expert, his testimony in the form of opinions or inferences is limited to those opinions and inferences which are (a) rationally based on the perception of the witness and (b) helpful to a clear understanding of his testimony or the determination of the fact in issue.

2. EXPERT WITNESSES

WALTZ, CRIMINAL EVIDENCE
300–319 (1975).*

Experts and Expertise

An Exception to the Opinion Rule. Opinion testimony by expert witnesses comes in through an important exception to the general rule against opinion testimony.

The Definition of "Expert." There are those who have the mistaken notion that the title of "expert" can properly be bestowed only on a few members of professional groups who have a cluster of postgraduate degrees after their names. Some people think that only a scientist of one sort or another and perhaps a few engineers can rightly be called experts. But the term "expert," at least in the law and in common sense, is far broader in meaning than this. Anyone who has ever tried to repair his own automobile or television set knows that some people are experts at these kinds of work and some are not. The proficient garage mechanic is an expert in his field even though a Ph.D. may be the last thing he ever hoped to acquire; the trained and experienced television repairman is just as surely an expert as is the most renowned neurosurgeon. The same sort of thing can be said of the brick mason, the sheet metal worker, the plumber, the carpenter, and the electrician, just to name a few more genuine experts.

* Copyright, 1975 by Jon R. Waltz.

Getting closer to the immediate point, the label "expert" applies to the firearms identification technician and those who are proficient at fingerprint or handwriting comparison. And it applies to the policeman who knows how to use, interpret, and explain special equipment, such as radar vehicular speed measuring devices and equipment for measuring blood-alcohol ratios. Thus a basic law dictionary, Black's, sweepingly defines experts as "men of science educated in the art, or persons possessing special or peculiar knowledge *acquired from practical experience*" (italics added).

The Four Basic Conditions of Expert Testimony. An expert witness, such as a pathologist or ballistics technician, can testify to an opinion, inference, or conclusion if four basic conditions are met:

(1) The opinions, inferences, or conclusions depend on special knowledge, skill, or training not within the ordinary experience of lay jurors;

(2) The witness must be shown to be qualified as a true expert in the particular field of expertise;

(3) The witness must testify to a reasonable degree of certainty (probability) regarding his opinion, inference or conclusion; and

(4) Although this fourth condition is currently in the process of modification, at least in times past it has generally been true that an expert witness must first describe the data (facts) on which his opinion, inference, or conclusion is based or, in the alternative, he must testify in response to a hypothetical question that sets forth the underlying data.

Rationale Behind the Expert Witness Exception to the Rule Against Opinion Testimony. The reasoning behind letting expert witnesses give testimony in the form of opinions or conclusions is that experts have special training, knowledge, and skill in drawing conclusions from certain sorts of data that lay jurors do not have. Expert witnesses and their opinions are permissible only in areas in which lay jurors cannot draw conclusions unassisted.

* * *

Qualifying the Witness as an Expert. From what has been said thus far it follows that the exception for expert testimony is available only when the witness is shown to be a true expert in the field that is involved. Before a witness can testify to an expert opinion, examining counsel must lay the necessary foundation by bringing out the witness's training, experience, and special skills. Trial lawyers call this process "qualifying the witness."

At the conclusion of the direct questions aimed at qualifying the witness as an expert, and before examining counsel gets into the meat of the witness's testimony, opposing counsel is entitled to interrupt and engage in cross-examination as to the witness's expertise. This

Ch. 10 OPINION, EXPERTS AND EXPERTISE 437

examination will be limited strictly to probing the witness's credentials as an expert.

Example a.:

BY THE PROSECUTING ATTORNEY: Give your full name if you would, please.

A: Fred Stitz.

Q: Where do you live, Mr. Stitz?

A: In Chicago, Illinois. 373 West Pavon Street.

Q: What is your occupation or profession?

A: I'm an examiner of questioned documents.

Q: What does your work consist of?

A: I examine disputed documents and make reports as to their genuineness. I examine typewriting and matters of disputed interlineations, erasures, and deal with matters of papers, pens, and inks.

Q: How long have you had this profession?

A: I have been doing this work since 1940.

Q: Do you devote all of your time to this work?

A: Yes, I do.

Q: Have you ever testified before in a court regarding questioned documents?

A: I have testified in forty-two of the states and in Canada.

Q: Have you had any special study to prepare yourself to be an examiner of questioned documents?

A: Oh, yes. I have read all of the texts on the subject of questioned documents and on the related subjects that I mentioned. I have studied microscopy, inks and their manufacture, paper and paper manufacturing, and photography. I have all the necessary equipment. I have an office and a laboratory for my work and I exchange ideas constantly with other experts in this field.

Q: Where is your office and lab?

A: 662 North Pennell Street, Chicago.

Q: You are able, I take it, to compare handwriting of known origin with handwriting of unknown origin and form a conclusion or opinion as to whether they were written by the same person?

A: That's right.

Q: Then I will show you what has been marked Prosecution Exhibit Number 3 for Identification.

BY DEFENSE COUNSEL: Just a moment, if you please. May I ask this witness a few questions, Your Honor?

THE COURT: With respect to his qualifications?

BY DEFENSE COUNSEL: Yes.

THE COURT: You may proceed.

BY DEFENSE COUNSEL: Mr. Stitz, have you attended any special schools that teach one how to become a handwriting expert?

A: No, I don't think there are any.

Q: So you have no special degrees or certificates that reflect special study in a college or university?

A: No, I do not.

Q: Your supposed expertise is simply based on your own experience in examining documents, is that it?

A: That's right, and my reading and so on.

BY DEFENSE COUNSEL: Well, we have no strong objection to this witness testifying, Your Honor.

THE COURT: If that it supposed to be some kind of objection, counsel, it is overruled.

* * *

Stipulating to the Witness's Expertise. Sometimes counsel, realizing that the opposing side's witness has impressive credentials that will probably awe the jurors, will try to prevent the jury from hearing them described. Counsel does this by offering to stipulate (agree) that the witness is qualified to testify as an expert, thereby magnanimously saving opposing counsel from having to elicit the witness's full catalogue of credentials through the questioning process. This gambit is not usually successful. Opposing counsel is not obligated to accept an offered stipulation unless it gives him everything that he would be entitled to prove with evidence. And counsel is entitled to prove his expert witness's qualifications in some detail; a mere stipulation that he is qualified to testify does not give the side offering him everything to which it is entitled. Experienced counsel will know that it is important to show the details of his expert's training and experience in any case in which there is to be a battle of experts. This is so because the jurors must decide what weight to attach to the testimony of each side's experts. They can rationally apportion evidentiary weight only if they are in a position to compare the witnesses' relative qualifications.

Example:

Q: Doctor, will you give the jury your full name?

A: Jeffrey Eddy.

Q: Where do you reside?

A: 820 West Addison Street, Chicago, Illinois.

Q: What is your profession?

A: Physician and surgeon.

Q: Are you duly licensed to practice as a physician and surgeon in Illinois?

A: Yes, I am.

Q: What specialty, if any, have you made in your medical practice?

A: I specialize in neurosurgery.

Q: We'll come back to that, Doctor Eddy. How long have you practiced medicine?

A: Thirteen years this coming April.

Q: Of what medical school are you a graduate?

A: Northwestern University Medical School in Chicago.

Q: Have you done any postgraduate work?

BY OPPOSING COUNSEL: Pardon me just a moment. We would be willing to stipulate that Doctor Eddy is a qualified neurosurgeon and can testify here.

BY EXAMINING COUNSEL: We would rather make our proof on this, Your Honor. The jurors are entitled to hear his training and his experience in medicine and neurosurgery. They have to decide what weight to give his testimony, possibly in comparison with the testimony of an expert called by the other side, and they can't very well make that decision without hearing his qualifications.

THE COURT: It might speed things up a little if you accepted the stipulation, counsel, but I can't force you to do so. You may proceed to establish the witness's qualifications. Just don't get into the most minute details.

BY EXAMINING COUNSEL: Very well, Your Honor. We'll limit ourselves to the most important things. Doctor Eddy, have you had some postgraduate training?

BY OPPOSING COUNSEL: In view of our offer to stipulate, we object to counsel's going into this, Your Honor.

THE COURT: Overruled.

Sources of the Expert Witness's Data. Three sources of information are open to the expert witness in the formation of his opinions.

(1) The expert witness can express an opinion or conclusion based on facts personally observed by him, as occurs in the case of a medical examiner who renders a conclusion concerning cause of death on the basis of data clinically observed. (Such an expert can take into account facts communicated to him by another expert. For example, the medical examiner can base his opinion in part on the report of an X-ray technician. If the data upon which the expert bases his opinion or inference are of a type reasonably relied on by experts in the field when forming opinions or inferences on the subject in question, the data need not themselves be independently admissible in evidence.)

(2) An expert witness who has been present in the courtroom can base an opinion on the evidence adduced if that evidence is not in conflict. (An expert will not be permitted to weigh conflicting evidence since, unbeknownst to anyone, he might accord it a weight different from that given it by the jurors.)

(3) An expert witness can base an opinion on data conveyed to him by means of a hypothetical question that is drawn from the evidence introduced during the trial.

Efforts to Eliminate the Hypothetical Question. Obviously, the hypothetical question is often awkward and hypertechnical. It is fraught with possibilities of reversible error. Hypothetical questions can be extremely time-consuming and they are frequently confusing to jurors. More often than not they are used by counsel to make an extra summation in the middle of the case. Although counsel may think there is some advantage in getting this opportunity to summarize the evidence far in advance of closing arguments, it is more likely that he is putting the jurors to sleep. Still, there are lawyers who believe that the hypothetical question represents the best method yet devised for extracting helpful opinions from an expert witness who is not directly familiar with the facts of the case.

Efforts are occasionally made to do away with the necessity for using hypothetical questions. For example, Rule 705 of the Proposed Federal Rules of Evidence would provide that an expert can testify in terms of opinion "without prior disclosure of the underlying facts or data." The major change intended to be accomplished by this language is the elimination of the necessity for the hypothetical question in eliciting expert testimony. Under Rule 705 examining counsel does not have to disclose underlying facts to his expert witness by means of a hypothetical question posed to him in open court as a preliminary to his opinion. The necessary data can be conveyed to the expert prior to his direct examination and it need not be disclosed during that examination. Of course, opposing counsel can cross-examine the expert about the data on which his opinion testimony is based.

* * *

Court-Appointed Experts. Ever since 1946 there has been a comprehensive procedure for court-appointed experts in Rule 28 of the Federal Rules of Criminal Procedure and many states have similar procedures. Under Rule 28 a trial judge can order the accused or the Government, or both, to show cause why expert witnesses should not be appointed and can request the parties to submit the names of possible witnesses. The judge can either appoint experts agreed upon by the parties or he can appoint experts of his own selection. A court-appointed expert is informed of his duties by the judge, either in writing or at a conference at which the parties have an opportunity to take part. A court-appointed expert will inform the parties of his findings and can thereafter be called to the stand by the trial judge or any party to give testimony. Court-appointed experts are subject to full cross-examination by all parties.

Experts appointed by the trial court are most commonly encountered in cases in which it is suggested either that the accused was legally insane at the time of the offense charged or that the accused is presently incompetent to stand trial because of his inability to comprehend the proceedings and cooperate with his defense counsel. In such situations the trial court may appoint one or more psychiatrists to examine the accused and report.

The use of court-appointed experts occasionally avoids the frustrating phenomenon known as the battle of experts. Both sides in criminal and civil cases alike will shop for experts who are receptive to the position being taken by the side retaining them. Furthermore, some experts are in fact venal; one often hears remarks about "the best expert witness money can buy." And many reputable experts are unwilling to involve themselves in litigation. So, although the suggestion is occasionally made that court-appointed experts take on an aura of infallibility which they may not deserve, the trend is increasingly to provide for their use. The very availability of this appointment procedure reduces the need for resorting to it. This is because the mere possibility that the trial judge *might* appoint an objective, disinterested expert in a given case exerts a sobering influence on a party's expert and on the lawyer who is making use of his services.

Impeachment of Expert Witnesses. Aside from attacking his qualifications and disinterestedness or the thoroughness and competence of his investigation, there are two commonly encountered methods of attacking or impeaching an expert witness's opinion. They involve (1) contradictory material in authoritative publications in the field and (2) alteration of the facts of a hypothetical question put to the witness during his direct examination.

1. An expert witness can be confronted, on cross-examination, with contradictory material from authoritative published works in the pertinent field of expertise. In most jurisdictions it is not essential that the witness have relied on the particular treatise or other items of literature in forming the conclusions given in his direct examination, although this was once a common requirement and can still be found in § 721(b) of the California Evidence Code.

Example:

BY THE PROSECUTING ATTORNEY: Dr. Faust, you insisted in your direct testimony earlier this afternoon that a person who is a manic depressive may have a propensity for committing murder or assault to murder, didn't you?

A: Well, "insist" is a pretty strong word but that's what I said.

Q: And you believe your statement to be correct? You think it is medically and psychiatrically sound?

A: Certainly I do.

Q: Dr. Faust, at any given time a manic depressive can be in either the manic or exhilarated phase or the depressive, the subdued or depressed phase of the psychosis, can he not?

A: That's true.

Q: Would your statement about a propensity to commit violent acts be as true of a person in the depressive state as it would be of a person who was in a manic state?

A: I think so, yes.

Q: Do other psychiatrists agree with your position in this respect?

A: I don't know specifically but I would presume so. My position is the correct one.

Q: I see. Do you know Dr. Carl S. Milcher's work entitled *The Murderer's Mind?*

A: I know of it. Everyone does.

Q: Is Dr. Milcher a recognized authority on the psychotic condition of persons who have committed murder?

A: I would say so. He is a distinguished psychiatrist.

Q: And has done a great deal of work in this area?

A: Yes.

Q: Did you in any way rely on Dr. Milcher's work in forming your opinions regarding the accused in this case? [This question, although not required in a number of jurisdictions, is usually asked anyway.]

A: I may have unconsciously. His work is a part of the fund of knowledge that I carry around in my head.

Q: Dr. Faust, I hand you a copy of Dr. Milcher's book, *The Murderer's Mind*, published in 1973, which I have opened to page 492. On that page Dr. Milcher is discussing the manic depressive state, is he not? Take your time and look at it, Dr. Faust, and then you can answer.

A: Yes, he describes the state here.

Q: He mentions there that a person in the manic phase may have a propensity for murder or assault to murder, doesn't he?

A: Yes, he does.

Q: And Dr. Milcher is a widely recognized expert, is he not?

A: I said so.

Q: Yes, you did. Now look at the last full sentence on page 492 of Dr. Milcher's book. I want you to read that sentence to the court and jury. You can read it over to yourself first, if you want to, but then read it to the members of the jury, loud and clear.

A: [Reading.] "The depressive aspect of the illness manifests itself more commonly in suicide."

BY THE PROSECUTING ATTORNEY: Thank you, sir. That will be all.

2. Examining counsel will frequently omit certain facts from a hypothetical question put to his expert witness on direct examination.

It is entirely permissible for opposing counsel to inquire whether consideration of the omitted facts would have an impact on the witness's opinion.

Example:

BY THE PROSECUTING ATTORNEY: Doctor Faust, if you were requested to assume these additional facts, which were not mentioned by defense counsel in his hypothetical question to you, namely [the omitted facts are recounted], would your opinion remain the same?

A: No, it wouldn't.

Q: What would your opinion be if we include those facts, Doctor?

A: [The witness gives his revised opinion.]

Sometimes facts included in a hypothetical question are later disproved by the evidence. In this situation the expert witness will be asked on cross-examination whether his conclusion would remain the same if those facts were eliminated from the hypothetical question.

Example:

BY THE PROSECUTING ATTORNEY: Doctor Faust, would your response to the hypothetical question have been different if in putting the question to you defense counsel had left out of consideration the statement that the blood found under the left shoulder was clotted?

A: My answer would have been different, yes.

* * *

PEOPLE v. CROOKS

Court of Appeals of California, 1967.
250 Cal.App.2d 788, 59 Cal.Rptr. 39.

KAUS, Presiding Justice. Defendant, a prostitute, was convicted of grand theft. The alleged victim was a client whom we shall call Norton. Trial was to the court.

The only question of substance involved in this appeal is the propriety of the admission of certain expert testimony. These are the facts: In the afternoon of January 11, 1965, Norton drove down Western Avenue, alone in his automobile. He saw defendant at a street corner. She motioned him to stop and asked him whether he would like to have a good time. A price of $10.00 was agreed on. She got into the car and directed him to a house which was in the back of another house. The route which she made Norton take was circuitous. At one point he asked her whether she was "being safe" so that no one would follow them and she said: "Yes." When they arrived at the house defendant made Norton remove his clothes, which included a money belt. It contained about $420.00. He put the money belt in his pants pocket.

444 OPINION, EXPERTS AND EXPERTISE Ch. 10

At that point someone knocked on the door, defendant went to the door, opened it a crack to stick her head out and said something, which Norton could not hear, to the person who was outside.

Defendant removed her clothes except her bra and panties and told Norton to come into the bathroom. There she washed his penis for what appeared to him as an unreasonably long time. They then returned to the other room where * * *. After the sex act, she went to the window and said "there is people outside" and ran out the door. That is the last he saw of her that day. He could not run after her, since he had no clothes on. He started to get dressed and noticed that the money belt was empty. He later identified defendant at a police lineup.

The People called Officer Putnam, who had served about ten years on the vice squad. Over objection he testified that he was familiar with a modus operandi used by prostitutes in Los Angeles County known as "the creeper." "A creeper" is worked by two people: "They work on the corner. Two girls walking the streets. And after the man makes his selection as to which one he wants she will direct him to a certain address or residence or location. They usually follow a roundabout route to get there in order to give the accomplice time to get to the room and either conceal themselves in the closet or somewhere in the building.

"Following this the female that he has selected will engage him in either an act of sexual intercourse or they will go to the bathroom and enable the accomplice to come in and go through the man's clothes. Or wallet. Take whatever is there." He was then asked whether there was a method to get the victim out of the room in a hurry. His answer: "Well, if he—if he finds that the money is missing or something of that nature they will create enough confusion between the two of them, or to direct that there is probably police outside; that she hears somebody outside; it's probably the cops. And she'll run or cause enough confusion that the man is left there not knowing what's happening."

Defendant took the stand. The relevant portions of her testimony were as follows: When she was picked up by Norton she was standing at the corner of Western and 52nd Street with Barbara, a fellow prostitute. When she and Norton arrived at the place where she had her "trick bed," they got undressed, she washed him and while she was copulating Norton he told her that there was someone at the door. She went to the window and saw that it was Barbara with a date. She opened the door a little and told her that she would have to wait. She then completed the act, Norton offered her a lift to her corner, she declined and he departed.

Whether or not the People had a prima facie case without the expert testimony need not be decided. Officer Putnam's testimony, from which it could be clearly inferred that defendant kept Norton in the bathroom to facilitate the theft, was obviously very telling.

To sustain the admission of the expert testimony, the People rely on People v. Clay, 227 Cal.App.2d 87, 38 Cal.Rptr. 431, 100 A.L.R.2d 1421. It is necessary to analyze the facts of *Clay* in detail.

Clay and one Davis were jointly charged and convicted of second degree burglary. Clay only appealed. The People's evidence was that Clay and Davis entered a market together. Earl Giacolini, one of the owners of the store, saw Clay at the check out stand and went there to wait on him. Clay had a bag of potato chips for which he handed Giacolini a one dollar bill. Giacolini rang up the sale, put the bill in the till and gave Clay his change. Clay then asked for various items of merchandise. His requests made it necessary for Giacolini to turn and take his eyes off the cash register. While this went on, Clay was standing three to four feet from the cash register. Giacolini never saw anyone else around the check stand. Another witness, however, saw Davis' hand come out of the till "balled in a fist." He could not see whether Davis had anything in his hand. Both Clay and Davis left the store. The witness followed them and accused Davis of having taken something from the store. Clay intervened saying that Davis had not been in the store. Later that day both Clay and Davis were arrested together. No money was found on either one, although $380.00 was missing from the cash register.

As part of its case the People called a police inspector who for several years had "handled all the till taps and store boosts in the City of Oakland." A hypothetical question was asked which included the fact that Clay and Davis entered the store together and described their activities at the check out stand. After overruling an objection the court said: "* * * the question concerning your opinion as to that set of facts and what, if any, crime it involved maybe answered." The witness replied: "That is the usual procedure of till tappers."

Applying the classic test of People v. Cole, 47 Cal.2d 99, 103, 301 P.2d 854, the court held the expert testimony to be admissible since the subject of inquiry was a matter "sufficiently beyond common experience that the opinion of an expert would assist the trier of fact." * * * Specifically the court held that the testimony of the inspector on the modus operandi of till tapping "threw a spotlight on the episode as a whole and thus enabled the jury to see the possibility of a relationship between the acts of the two men. This gave meaning to the evidence and permitted the jury to appreciate that defendant's activities while in themselves seemingly harmless, when considered with those of Davis, might well have been part of a cleverly planned and precisely executed scheme * * *." (Ibid., p. 95, 38 Cal.Rptr. p. 436.)

We think that People v. Clay is indistinguishable from the present case. The only difference is that in *Clay* there was eyewitness testimony that the confederate of the defendant had his hand in the till, while in the present case the entry into the room where the money belt was and the taking of the money by someone had to be inferred from the presence of such a person just before defendant and Norton went to the bathroom. Such an inference was of course permissible and had the prosecutor asked a hypothetical question—as was done in *Clay*—it would have been entirely proper to ask the witness to assume that someone entered the room while defendant and Norton were in the bathroom.

We reach our conclusion that this case is governed by People v. Clay with some reluctance. While we do not doubt the correctness of the holding on the facts of that case, if it is interpreted too broadly, the use of expert testimony would convict defendants not of what they have done, but of what others are doing. The court, in *Clay*, relied on the test for admissibility announced by Professor Wigmore: "On *this subject* can a jury from *this person* receive appreciable help?" * * * We mean no disparagement when we say that in almost every criminal case expert policemen can be and undoubtedly are only more than willing to be of appreciable help to the jury, yet it is easy to imagine hypothetical situations in which the help derived from the expert is too appreciable to permit a conviction to stand. Simply because something a defendant does is "consistent with" the modus operandi of some underworld caper, does not make him guilty of an offense.

The limitation to the admissibility of such expert testimony is perhaps the very sentence in *Clay* which holds that there it was properly admitted: "Here the expert witness * * * merely described the *modus operandi* of a certain class of criminals. His expert testimony was * * * directed * * * towards assisting the jury in determining a factual issue, namely that of defendant's *intent* at the time he diverted Giacolini's attention." * * *

Neither in *Clay*, nor in the case before us, was the expert testimony necessary to fill a factual gap in the People's case. The witnesses' expertise merely gave the respective triers of facts background from which they could infer that the somewhat unusual acts on the part of the respective defendants were motivated by an intent to enable a confederate to tap the till or empty the money belt, as the case may be. * * *

[Affirmed.]

Ch. 10 OPINION, EXPERTS AND EXPERTISE 447

RULES OF EVIDENCE FOR UNITED STATES COURTS AND MAGISTRATES

Rule 602

LACK OF PERSONAL KNOWLEDGE

A witness may not testify to a matter unless evidence is introduced sufficient to support a finding that he has personal knowledge of the matter. Evidence to prove personal knowledge may, but need not, consist of the testimony of the witness himself. This rule is subject to the provisions of Rule 703, relating to opinion testimony by expert witnesses.

Rule 702

TESTIMONY BY EXPERTS

If scientific, technical, or other specialized knowledge will assist the trier of fact to understand the evidence or to determine a fact in issue, a witness qualified as an expert by knowledge, skill, experience, training, or education, may testify thereto in the form of an opinion or otherwise.

Rule 703

BASES OF OPINION TESTIMONY BY EXPERTS

The facts or data in the particular case upon which an expert bases an opinion or inference may be those perceived by or made known to him at or before the hearing. If of a type reasonably relied upon by experts in the particular field in forming opinions or inferences upon the subject, the facts or data need not be admissible in evidence.

Rule 704

OPINION ON ULTIMATE ISSUE

Testimony in the form of an opinion or inference otherwise admissible is not objectionable because it embraces an ultimate issue to be decided by the trier of fact.

Rule 705

DISCLOSURE OF FACTS OR DATA UNDERLYING EXPERT OPINION

The expert may testify in terms of opinion or inference and give his reasons therefor without prior disclosure of the underlying facts or data, unless the court requires otherwise. The expert may in any event be required to disclose the underlying facts or data on cross-examination.

Rule 706

COURT APPOINTED EXPERTS

(a) **Appointment.** The court may on its own motion or on the motion of any party enter an order to show cause why expert witnesses should not be appointed, and may request the parties to submit nominations. The court may appoint any expert witnesses agreed upon by the parties, and may appoint expert witnesses of its own selection. An expert witness shall not be appointed by the court unless he consents to act. A witness so appointed shall be informed of his duties by the court in writing, a copy of which shall be filed with the clerk, or at a conference in which the parties shall have opportunity to participate. A witness so appointed shall advise the parties of his findings, if any; his deposition may be taken by any party; and he may be called to testify by the court or any party. He shall be subject to cross-examination by each party, including a party calling him as a witness.

(b) **Compensation.** Expert witnesses so appointed are entitled to reasonable compensation in whatever sum the court may allow. The compensation thus fixed is payable from funds which may be provided by law in criminal cases and civil actions and proceedings involving just compensation under the fifth amendment. In other civil actions and proceedings the compensation shall be paid by the parties in such proportion and at such time as the court directs, and thereafter charged in like manner as other costs.

(c) **Disclosure of Appointment.** In the exercise of its discretion, the court may authorize disclosure to the jury of the fact that the court appointed the expert witness.

(d) **Parties' Experts of Own Selection.** Nothing in this rule limits the parties in calling expert witnesses of their own selection.

WALTZ, THE NEW FEDERAL RULES OF EVIDENCE: AN ANALYSIS

112–113 (2d ed. 1975).*

Rule 705 is important and, rightly or wrongly, somewhat controversial. It provides that an expert can testify in terms of opinion "without prior disclosure of the underlying facts or data."

* * *

Rule 705 does not do away with the hypothetical question absolutely; it simply does away with any absolute requirement that a hypothetical be used by counsel. The use of the hypothetical question sometimes has its advantages and it remains to be seen whether trial lawyers will accept with any frequency this Rule's invitation to forego its use.

In any event, Rule 705 probably forecloses successful assignments of error based on a claim that opposing counsel's hypothetical question was incomplete, *i. e.*, did not include all of the "underlying facts or data." In effect, the new rule places on the cross-examiner the burden of eliciting any missing data. Thus Rule 705 should serve to make examining counsel less nervous about the use of hypotheticals; no longer will it be essential to include each and every scrap of arguably pertinent data on pain of a successful objection or reversal.

COLLATERAL READINGS

Opinion, Expertise and Experts

McCormick's Handbook of the Law of Evidence §§ 11–18 (2d ed. 1972)

Wigmore Evidence (3rd ed. 1940)
- Vol. 2, §§ 555–571, 650–670, 672–686
- Vol. 3, §§ 687–8
- Vol. 7, §§ 1917–2028

Maguire and Hahesy, Requisite Proof of Basis for Expert Opinion, 5 Vand.L.Rev. 42 (1952)

Beuscher, The Use of Experts by the Courts, 54 Harv.L.Rev. 1105 (1941)

Louisell, The Psychologist in Today's Legal World: Part I, The Psychologist as an Expert Witness, 39 Minn.L.Rev. 235 (1955)

Rose, The Social Scientist as an Expert Witness, 40 Minn.L.Rev. 205 (1956)

Morgan, Suggested Remedy for Obstructions to Expert Testimony by Rules of Evidence, 10 U.Chi.L.Rev. 284 (1943)

---

* Copyright, 1975 by Multi-State Media, Inc.

Diamond, The Fallacy of the Impartial Expert, 3 Archives of Criminal Psychodynamics 221 (1959)

Louisell, Book Review, Report of the Special Committee, Association of the Bar of the City of New York, Impartial Medical Testimony, 45 Cal.L.Rev. 572 (1957)

Foreman, Accident Reconstruction and the Use of Experts, 36 J.Air.L. 489 (1970)

Weihofen, An Alternative to the Battle of Experts: Hospital Examination of Criminal Defendants Before Trial, 2 Law & Contemp. Problems 419 (1935)

Frank, Obscenity: Some Problems of Values and the Use of Experts, 41 Wash.L.Rev. 631 (1966)

Clendenning, Expert Testimony, 9 Crim.L.Q. 415 (1967)

Schuck, Techniques for Proof of Complicated Scientific and Economic Facts, 40 F.R.D. 33 (1966)

Weihofen, Detruding the Experts, 1973 Wash.U.L.Q. 38 (1972)

Kornblum, The Expert as Witness and Consultant, 20 Prac.Law. 13 (1974)

Note, Expert Testimony in Aviation Accident Litigation: The Common Law and Proposed Federal Rules of Evidence, 40 J.Air.L. 509 (1974)

Note, Evidence: The Hypothetical Question in the Examination of Expert Witnesses, 28 Okla.L.Rev. 650 (1975)

B. SCIENTIFIC AND DEMONSTRATIVE EVIDENCE

1. SELECTED ISSUES IN SCIENTIFIC EVIDENCE

a. THE "LIE DETECTOR"

STATE v. VALDEZ

Supreme Court of Arizona, 1962.
91 Ariz. 274, 371 P.2d 894.

[Some footnotes omitted.]

UDALL, Vice Chief Justice. Defendant was tried for and convicted of possession of narcotics. Pursuant to a written stipulation entered into by defendant, his counsel and the county attorney before trial defendant submitted to a polygraph (lie-detector) examination. The stipulation also provided that the results of such examination would be admissible at the trial. Accordingly, the polygraph operator was permitted, over objection by defendant to testify to the results of the examination (unfavorable to defendant) at defendant's jury trial. After the jury returned a verdict of guilty and before sentence was entered, the trial court, * * * certified the following question to this court:

> "In a criminal case, if prior to trial the defense attorney, on behalf of his client and with his client's consent, and the deputy county attorney agree in a written stipulation that the results of a polygraph test, to be taken by the defendant, will be admissible as evidence at the trial, on behalf of either the State of Arizona or the accused, may the trial court admit the results of the test over the objection of defense counsel?"

Because *any* case involving admissibility of lie-detector evidence would be one of first impression in Arizona and also because of the particular disposition herein of the question certified the following observations and review of the authorities are set forth for the guidance of the Bar.

The polygraph or lie-detector is a pneumatically operated device which simultaneously records changes in a subject's blood pressure, pulse, respiration rate and depth, psychogalvanic skin reflex (skin resistance to electrical current) and, in some cases, muscular activity. "The basis for the use of the so-called lie-detector * * * is the hypothesis that conscious deception can be deduced from certain involuntary physiological responses in the same manner as physicians diagnose various diseases. The thesis is that lying engenders emotional disturbances which are transmuted into tangible bodily manifestations." The machine itself reflects and records only the subject's physiological responses to the questions propounded by the operator. He then interprets the poly*graph* (meaning, literally, "many pictures") and determines whether the subject is lying.

I. *Admissibility in General*

The first reported American case involving admissibility of lie-detector evidence was Frye v. United States, 54 App.D.C. 46, 293 F. 1013 (1923). Frye, convicted of murder in the second degree, appealed alleging as his sole assignment of error the trial court's refusal to allow an expert to testify as to the results of a systolic blood pressure test to which Frye had submitted. In affirming the conviction and in upholding the trial court's refusal of the proffered testimony the Circuit Court observed:

> "Just when a scientific principle or discovery crosses the line between the experimental and demonstrable stages is difficult to define. Somewhere in this twilight zone the evidential force of the principle must be recognized, and while courts will go a long way in admitting expert testimony deduced from a well-recognized scientific principle or discovery, the thing from which the deduction is made must

be sufficiently established to have gained general acceptance in the particular field in which it belongs.

"We think the systolic blood pressure deception test has not yet gained such standing and scientific recognition among physiological and psychological authorities as would justify the courts in admitting expert testimony deduced from the discovery, development, and experiments thus far made."

* * *

Further, it is uniformly held that a defendant is not permitted to introduce evidence of his willingness to take a lie-detector test. * * * Nor can a defendant's refusal to submit to polygraphic interrogation be shown by the state directly * * *.

But judicial reluctance to recognize generally the worth of lie-detector evidence in the court room has not been due to mere inertia. For, in affirming a first degree rape conviction, the Oklahoma Criminal Court of Appeals quoted from two leading authorities the following " ' * * * factors which occasion the chief difficulties in the diagnosis of deception by the lie-detector technique * * *.' "

" ' (1) Emotional tension—, "nervousness"—experienced by a subject who is innocent and telling the truth regarding the offense in question, but who is nevertheless affected by

" ' (a) fear induced by the mere fact that suspicion or accusation has been directed against him, and particularly so in instances where the subject has been extensively interrogated or perhaps physically abused by investigators prior to the time of the interview and testing by the lie-detector examiner; and

" ' (b) a guilt complex involving another offense of which he is guilty.

" ' (2) Physiological abnormalities, such as

" ' (a) excessively high or excessively low blood pressure;

" ' (b) diseases of the heart;

" ' (c) respiratory disorders, etc.

" ' (3) Mental abnormalities, such as

" ' (a) feeblemindedness, as in idiots, imbeciles, and morons;

" ' (b) psychoses or insanities, as in manic depressives, paranoids, schizphrenics, paretics, etc.;

" ' (c) psychoneuroses, and psychopathia, as among so-called "peculiar" or "emotionally unstable" persons—those who are neither psychotic nor normal, and who form the borderline between these two groups.

" ' (4) Unresponsiveness in a lying or guilty subject, because of

" ' (a) lack of fear of detection;

" ' (b) apparent ability to consciously control responses by means of certain mental sets or attitudes;

" '(c) a condition of "sub-shock" or "adrenal exhaustion" at the time of the test;

" ' (d) rationalization of the crime in advance of the test to such an extent that lying about the offense arouses little or no emotional disturbance;

" ' (e) extensive interrogation prior to the test.

" ' (5) Unobserved muscular movements which produce ambiguities or misleading indications in the blood pressure tracing.' "

* * * And in addition to the above enumerated scientific shortcomings of the polygraph technique the following objections to the unrestricted use of its results in the court room have been registered:

(1) The supposed tendency of judges and juries to treat lie-detector evidence as conclusive on the issue of defendants' guilt. * * *

(2) Lack of standardization of test procedure, * * *.

(3) Difficulty for jury evaluation of examiners' opinions.

Finally, it appears " * * * that at the present time the technique is not an 'accepted' one among the scientists whose approval is a prerequisite to judicial recognition." Inbau and Reid, Lie Detection and Criminal Interrogation, (3rd ed. 1953) at 130. * * * Of course absolute infallibility is not the standard for admissibility of scientific evidence. But at this time it seems wise to demand greater standardization of the instrument, technique and examiner qualifications and the endorsement by a larger segment of the psychology and physiology branches of science before permitting general use of lie-detector evidence in court. Accordingly, in the absence of a stipulation lie-detector evidence should not be received in an Arizona court for the present.

II *Admissibility Upon Stipulation*

The first reported decision involving stipulated admissibility of lie-detector results was LeFevre v. State, 242 Wis. 416, 8 N.W.2d 288 (1943). Before the trial defendant submitted to a lie-detector (Keeler polygraph) test the results of which were favorable to him. At trial, however, on objection by the district attorney to defendant's proffer of the test results, the trial judge excluded them. This ruling was upheld on appeal although the conviction was reversed on the grounds of insufficient evidence. Without mentioning the stipulation the Wisconsin Supreme Court simply cited the Bohner case, supra, and said "They were properly excluded." Oddly enough the court then referred to testimony of the district attorney to the effect that the test results indicated defendant was not lying, and remarked that:

> "We have the word of the district attorney that those tests were favorable to the defendant. While the findings of these experts were properly excluded from the jury, the district attorney's testimony came in without objection and we regard it as very significant." 242 Wis. at 427, 8 N.W. 2d at 293.

* * *

In 1960 the Iowa Supreme Court held that there was sufficient evidence to affirm a woman's second-degree murder conviction and then disposed of her contention that lie-detector evidence was improperly admitted notwithstanding a stipulation by announcing that:

> "We hold the lie-detector evidence was admissible by reason of her agreement."

State v. McNamara, 252 Iowa 19, 104 N.W.2d 568, 574 (1960). Significantly, "at the trial defendant [McNamara] strenuously objected to any evidence regarding the tests on the ground that they were unreliable and prejudicial." 252 Iowa at 28, 104 N.W.2d at 573.

* * *

Generally speaking, even those experts who warn against admissibility in the absence of a stipulation favor admission of lie-detector evidence upon a proper stipulation. And although polygraphic interrogation has not attained that degree of scientific acceptance in the fields to which it belongs to be admissible at the instance of either the state or defendant (supra, section I of this opinion), it has been considerably improved since Frye v. Unites States, supra, was decided in 1923. A conservative estimate of the accuracy of such tests is as follows:

(1) In 75–80 per cent of the cases the examination correctly indicates the guilt or innocence of the accused;

(2) in 15–20 per cent of the cases the results are too indefinite to warrant a conclusion by the examiner one way or the other; and

(3) 5 per cent or less is the margin of proven error.

With improvement in and standardization of instrumentation, technique and examiner qualifications the margin of proven error is certain to shrink. "Modern court procedure must embrace recognized modern conditions of mechanics, psychology, sociology, medicine, or other sciences, philosophy, and history. The failure to do so will only serve to question the ability of courts to efficiently administer justice." * * * Although much remains to be done to perfect the lie-detector as a means of determining credibility we think it has been developed to a state in which its results are probative enough to warrant admissibility upon stipulation. * * *

Accordingly, and subject to the qualifications announced herein, we hold that polygraphs and expert testimony relating thereto are admissible upon stipulation in Arizona criminal cases. And in such cases the lie-detector evidence is admissible to corroborate other evidence of a defendant's participation in the crime charged. If he takes the stand such evidence is admissible to corroborate or impeach his own testimony.

The "qualifications" are as follows:

(1) That the county attorney, defendant and his counsel all sign a written stipulation providing for defendant's submission to the test and for the subsequent admission at trial of the graphs and the examiner's opinion thereon on behalf of either defendant or the state.

(2) That notwithstanding the stipulation the admissibility of the test results is subject to the discretion of the trial judge, i. e. if the trial judge is not convinced that the examiner is qualified or that the test was conducted under proper conditions he may refuse to accept such evidence.

(3) That if the graphs and examiner's opinion are offered in evidence the opposing party shall have the right to cross-examine the examiner respecting:

    a. the examiner's qualifications and training;

    b. the conditions under which the test was administered;

    c. the limitations of and possibilities for error in the technique of polygraphic interrogation; and

    d. at the discretion of the trial judge, any other matter deemed pertinent to the inquiry.

(4) That if such evidence is admitted the trial judge should instruct the jury that the examiner's testimony does not tend to prove or disprove any element of the crime with which a defendant is charged but at most tends only to indicate that at the time of the examination defendant was not telling the truth. Further, the jury members should be instructed that it is for them to determine what corroborative weight and effect such testimony should be given.

The case as certified is remanded for action consistent with this opinion.

BERNSTEIN, C. J., and STRUCKMEYER, JENNINGS and LOCKWOOD, JJ., concur.

NOTE

The Michigan Supreme Court has ruled that polygraph evidence may be admissible (at the judge's discretion) in a hearing on a motion for a new trial. People v. Barbara, 400 Mich. 352, 255 N.W.2d 171 (1977). Certain enumerated conditions must be filled before such evidence may be considered (machine, operator and procedure must be approved; data can only be offered for a limited purpose). Under no circumstances may the evidence be introduced at trial (absent proper stipulation) if a new trial is indeed granted.

One or two courts have allowed admission of a favorable lie detector test of the accused on the sole issue of illegal search and seizure to support his testimony that the police had acted illegally. Should this be permitted?

WALTZ, CRIMINAL EVIDENCE
400–405 (1975).*

Polygraph Testing

The Polygraph Technique; Equipment and Examiner. Polygraph ("lie detector") testing is a diagnostic procedure that requires both specialized equipment and a qualified examiner. The premise underlying Polygraph testing is that the natural human tendency is to tell the truth and that the telling of a falsehood causes psychological conflict which in turn produces involuntary physiological responses measurable as indicia of the anxiety caused by lying.

The most commonly used Polygraph equipment consists of two basic components: (1) a recorder of changes in *blood pressure* and *pulse*, and (2) a recorder of changes in *respiration*. (There is also a type of unit that records *electrodermal response*—galvanic skin reflex—which is said to be the result of alterations in the activity of the sweat pores in the subject's hands. Another type of unit records *muscular pressures and movements*.)

Body attachments are employed to record blood pressure, pulse, and respiration: (1) a flexible pneumograph tube is fastened around the chest or abdomen of the test subject and (2) a blood pressure cuff, of the sort commonly used by physicians, is wrapped around the subject's upper arm. For recording electrodermal response, electrodes are fastened to the fingers or hand. No body attachments are used to record muscle pressure and movement; this is accomplished by means of inflated bladders fastened to the chair in which the test subject sits.

Training to be a Polygraph examiner is gained through individualized training and internship. It has been said by such experts in the field as Professor Fred E. Inbau that a Polygraph examiner should be a college graduate who has studied both psychology and physiology. The examiner must also have certain personality traits that permit him to work easily with test subjects. Internship training involves individualized training given by a competent and thoroughly experienced examiner who has enough cases to afford the

* Copyright, 1975 by Jon R. Waltz.

trainee an opportunity to observe a substantial number of actual Polygraph examinations.

Polygraph Test Procedure. A competent Polygraph examiner will conduct a pretest interview with the subject, during which the nature and purpose of the examination will be explained. The examiner will often impress upon the subject, in a scrupulously objective way, the effectiveness of the technique since this serves to precondition both the honest and the lying subject.

Three types of questions are used in a Polygraph test: (1) relevant questions, (2) control questions, and (3) irrelevant questions.

Relevant questions, quite obviously, are those relating to the very matter under investigation. *Control questions* are questions that are not directly related to the matter under investigation but which are of a similar, though less serious, nature. For example, the robbery suspect will be asked, "Have you ever robbed anyone?" The recorded physiological response (or lack of one) to this question will then be compared with the responses obtained to relevant questions. *Irrelevant questions* are used in order to determine the subject's norm under test conditions. For example, he may be asked, "Are you twenty-one years of age?"

The following is a run of Polygraph test questions in a moderately complicated case:

(1) Are you called Charlie? [The examiner learned during the pretest interview that the subject is generally called "Charlie."]

(2) Are you over twenty-one years of age?

(3) Did you rob Clyde Bushmat last Saturday night?

(4) Are you in Chicago now?

(5) Did you knife Clyde Bushmat last Saturday night?

(6) Have you ever stolen anything?

(7) Did you ever go to high school?

(8) Do you know who knifed Clyde Bushmat?

(9) Were those your footprints next to Bushmat's body?

(10) Have you ever stolen anything from an employer?

One such run of questions does not constitute a complete Polygraph examination, however; at least three more runs of similar makeup—usually more—will be conducted before a diagnosis is attempted. The time interval between the questions is fifteen or twenty seconds and the entire examination will last about an hour. Surprise has nothing to do with the Polygraph technique. The subject is told, ahead of the examination, precisely what the questions will be.

It is an oversimplification, but it is nonetheless generally true that a subject is considered to be telling the truth if his Polygraph responses are greater in connection with the control questions. If the subject's reactions to the relevant questions are greater, deception is suggested.

Even the Polygraph's stoutest defenders recognize that it is not invariably a conclusive diagnostic tool. It has been said that truthfulness or deception will be sharply indicated in about 25 percent of all Polygraph examinations. In about 65 percent of the examinations, the indications will be much more subtle, making it difficult for the examiner to explain them adequately to a fact-finder. In the remaining 10 percent of examinations, diagnosis will be completely impossible because of the subject's peculiar psychological or physiological attributes or other special factors beyond the examiner's control.

Despite increasing reliance upon the Polygraph test over the last decades on the part of businesses and employers as well as police investigators, there remain substantial judicial hurdles to the admissibility of such evidence in courts of law, to be discussed below.

The Frye Case and the General Rule of Inadmissibility. The first judicial consideration of the Polygraph technique came in Frye v. United States, 293 F. 1013 (D.C.Cir. 1923). In 1923 the Polygraph test was referred to by the *Frye* court as "the systolic blood pressure deception test." In *Frye* the trial court was affirmed in its refusal of both the offer of the defendant's expert testimony as to the results of the test and the defense's offer to conduct a test in the presence of the jury. The court said that the test had "not yet gained such standing and scientific recognition among physiological and psychological authorities as would justify the courts in admitting expert testimony deduced from the discovery, development, and experiments thus far made."

Another oft-quoted excerpt from the *Frye* opinion stated a more general rule: "Just when a scientific principle or discovery crosses the line between the experimental and demonstrable stages is difficult to define. Somewhere in this twilight zone the evidential force of the principle must be recognized, and while courts will go a long way in admitting expert testimony deduced from a well-recognized scientific principle or discovery, the thing from which the deduction is made must be sufficiently established to have gained general acceptance in the particular field in which it belongs."

The *Frye* standard was interpreted as requiring acceptance within the relevant scientific field and the rule has continued to be that results of Polygraph testing are inadmissible in courts of law. There are some exceptions to this general rule, however.

Evidence of "Willingness." Polygraph evidence being inadmissible, courts generally hold it to be error for either side in a criminal case to make reference to the willingness or unwillingness of a party or witness to subject himself to testing. The reasoning is that if Polygraph evidence is incompetent, willingness or unwillingness to undergo such testing must also be considered inadmissible; on the one hand it would encourage the jury to draw the same inferences that would be drawn if the actual test results were presented to it, while on the other hand it avoids the normal requirement of laying of a proper foundation for scientific evidence and expert testimony, all the while effectively foreclosing opposing counsel from vital cross-examination.

Courts have rejected the argument that "unwillingness" evidence should be received as evidence of consciousness of guilt, and consider it reversible error in some instances.

(But a number of courts have considered the error harmless, curable by appropriate instruction to the jury, or simply not prejudicial where the defendant did not object or where a motion for a mistrial was untimely.)

Confessions During Polygraph Testing. As for confessions obtained as an incident to Polygraph testing, the rule generally is that the testing does not itself render a confession inadmissible. It is, however, a factor that is considered by many courts in their determination of the voluntariness of the confessions. In addition, at least one author has contested the general rule on the grounds that the examinee's bodily responses are by definition involuntary and therefore barred by the Fifth Amendment privilege against self-incrimination. The argument is that no matter how anxious a party is to take the test, his responses cannot be said to have been freely given and so confessions given as a result of the Polygraph testing should be barred in later trial proceedings. * * *

NOTE, THE PSYCHOLOGICAL STRESS EVALUATOR: YESTERDAY'S DREAM—TOMORROW'S NIGHTMARE

24 Cleve.St.L.Rev. 299–304 (1975).[*]

From time immemorial man has sought a failsafe method of truth verification. The techniques have run the gamut from the ancients' trial by ordeal to modern man's lie detectors. Since the turn of the century, this search has focused on the development of a device which would detect deception by measuring the "cause and effect of psychological stimuli and physiological response" during the interrogation of a suspect. Beginning with Cesare Lombroso's primitive attempts in the 1890's through Reid's sophisticated polygraph of today, the desire for a reliable lie detector has continued unabated. In the 1960's, in response to a burgeoning desire for further refinement, the quest began for a "wireless" lie detector which would dispense with the need for physical attachment to the subject.

Interest by the federal government in a "wireless" lie detector added impetus to the quest; and shortly thereafter the Psychological Stress Evaluator (PSE) was invented by Alan Bell and Colonel

[*] Copyright, 1975 by Cleveland State University.

Charles McQuiston and placed on the market by Dektor Counterintelligence and Security, Inc. (Dektor) of Springfield, Virginia. This latest development in lie detection is premised on the thesis that psychological stress is detectable through identification and measurement of physiological changes in the human voice.

Claims made by the manufacturer suggest a multiplicity of uses for the PSE, including employment applicant screening, periodic testing of employees as a check on theft, and investigation of criminal suspects by both private and public employers as well as law enforcement agencies. Dektor itself has suggested that the PSE can aid both the psychiatrist, in distinguishing "fact from fancy" in patient statements; and the physician, in diagnosing brain damage in newborns. More importantly, unlike the polygraph, the PSE is operative in both overt and covert testing situations, since it need not be physically attached to the subject. As a corollary to this, Dektor has stated in its literature that a test could be administered over the telephone. And if this be the case, it is quite possible that stress level determinations could be made of voices originating on either television or radio.

Although Dektor has emphasized the fact that a rigid test procedure is mandatory in effectively evaluating veracity, an analysis of the variety of uses for which the PSE is propounded evinces the likelihood of its use for truth evaluation by an assortment of individuals too inadequately trained to adhere to such rigid procedures. Moreover, the major institutional value of the PSE is not so much its potential for use in detecting whether a subject is telling the truth in the context of a dialogue, but rather the relative ease with which the device can be employed for this purpose. The foregoing, coupled with the fact that the PSE may be used without the knowledge of the subject, suggests frightening possibilities for its abuse.

With this in mind, this note will examine the manner in which the PSE functions and explore the legal implications stemming from its use as a lie detector. More specifically, three issues which arise in connection with the use of the PSE will be discussed: first, the validity and reliability of the PSE; second, the admissibility of PSE test results in evidence; and third, the potential remedies for subjects of PSE tests who have occasion to object.

Background

The PSE itself merely indicates levels of stress in the voice, while the examiner interprets this data and so derives a conclusion concerning the truthfulness of the subject. Because of this dichotomy, PSE advocates argue that the term "lie detector" is a misnomer, preferring instead to emphasize the concept of "stress analysis." The fact remains, however, that the PSE is not marketed as a device which measures the stress of the subject merely for the sake of curiosity. Rather, PSE customers are interested in using the machine solely for the purpose of detecting false statements. Consequently, the term "lie detector" is hardly misleading.

While the polygraph utilizes responses stimulated by the autonomic nervous system, the functional indicators of the PSE originate in the central nervous system. In order to more fully understand the technology underlying the PSE, some explanation of the functioning of the human voice is necessary.

Two types of sound are produced by the voice. The first of these is audible sound (AM), which is produced by both the vibration of the vocal cords (vocal cord sounds) and the resonance of the cavities of the head (formant sounds). The second type of sound is inaudible sound, which is superimposed on the audible voice frequency. The latter is an infrasonic frequency modulation (FM) which is present in both the vocal cord and formant sounds. This infrasonic frequency is produced by a muscle micro-tremor which occurs in the muscles controlling exhalation during the vocalization response.

The operation of the PSE rests on the theory that this tremor is affected by stress. Muscular tension decreases or eliminates the muscular undulations which produce the frequency modulation, thus dampening the inaudible frequency modulation (FM) in the voice. Hence, "[t]he strength and pattern of the * * * [FM in the voice] relate inversely to the degree of stress in the speaker at the moment of the utterance."

The PSE applies this theory by identifying changes in the frequency modulation of the voice and emitting data reflecting these changes. To utilize this operation in a lie detector context, a four-part system is employed: the examiner; a tape recorder; the test subject; and the PSE instrument itself. This instrument produces a strip chart, not unlike that provided by a polygraph. The PSE, however, uses a single stylus instead of the three found on a polygraph, and while there is but one stylus, the electronic mode combinations allow thirty-two individual charts to be made from every recorded statement.

The procedure in a PSE examination necessarily varies with the purpose for which the system is used, but a procedural model has been developed by PSE expert, Morton Sinks, which aptly illustrates the usual deception testing situation:

(1) The pre-test interview: basic information about the subject is elicited, preliminary interview questions are formulated and the statement the subject will make during the test is structured;

(2) Input: the questions are asked;

(3) Data retrieval: a tape recording is made of the subject's answers;

(4) Charting: the subject's oral answers are electronically converted by the PSE into mechanical motion producing measurable differences on a chart;

(5) Interpretation of the charts: the charts are analyzed for indications of stress, relative values are assigned to the responses, and conclusions as to deception are made;

(6) Follow-up: consists of either the elimination of suspicion or further investigation, interviewing or interrogation.

Because of the system's dependence upon the examiner for accurate test results, the training of a PSE examiner is of great importance. Dektor requires that all prospective purchasers undergo training, and in fact has reportedly refused to sell to customers who would not take the training course. The Orientation Course is the basic course in the operation of the instrument and instruction in interpretation of strip charts. It lasts three days, with out-of-classroom work for the intervening two nights. Also available to the customer is a continuous consultation service, and if necessary, retraining. Further, there is a two-week course available, in which the particular type of interrogation and interviewing techniques necessary for the valid operation of the PSE are taught.

With this digest of general information about the PSE as a backdrop, the remainder of this note will focus on the legal issues which arise from the use of the PSE as a technique of truth verification.

Validity and Reliability of the PSE

If the PSE is to have any value within the context of the legal system, it must be demonstrated that it is possible to detect deception both consistently and correctly by examination of the strip chart results of the PSE. To make such a determination, the concepts of "validity" and "reliability" must be addressed. Although these terms are often used interchangeably by laymen, each is a distinct concept. Validity is the determination of how well the instrument does what it purports to do, or in this case, "the extent to which a deceptive * * * person will be identified * * * as a result of the examination."

* * *

Summary

The Psychological Stress Evaluator is in its nascent stage of influence in both the private and public sectors of American society. This device operates on the theory that differential stress in the voice produced by vibrations of the vocal cords can be measured so as to detect deception. This note has sought to explain the functioning of the PSE and to denominate the issues which its use will thrust upon the American legal system.

Empirical studies reveal vast discrepancies in reported validity, suggesting that the resolution of this issue must await further independent study. Moreover, the issue of reliability has yet to be addressed. Insofar as acceptability by the scientific community is dependent on the positive resolution of these two issues, PSE examination results will not be readily admitted as scientific evidence by either state or federal courts. Beyond the mere question of its efficacy as scientific evidence, the courts will be forced to confront other evidentiary issues which will jeopardize the quest for admission of PSE results.

Implicit in the utilization of the PSE for detection of deception is its extraordinary potential for abuse. Unfortunately, traditional tort remedies will prove ineffective in combating such abuse due to the limitations imposed by the legal system itself.

But the major question which the PSE presents to the legal system is neither its validity, its admissibility nor the lack of actionable remedies. Rather, further inquiry must be made into the basic question of whether the use of even the most valid and scientifically accepted PSE has any place in American society. While all Americans deplore the increase in industrial crime, at the same time the American worker cannot be said to have "surrendered his basic rights and liberties as a citizen by entering the job market." Clearly the public is entitled to protection from the PSE before its use becomes so commonplace that it prevades the American way of life; for, by then, it will be virtually impossible to either control or eradicate its pernicious influence on the individual in society.

b. "VOICE PRINTS"

WALTZ, CRIMINAL EVIDENCE
390–392 (1975).*

Voiceprints

The Need for Scientific Voice Identification. Courts have long permitted the identification of one person by another on the basis of the former's voice. The identifying witness can be termed an "earwitness," as distinguished from an eyewitness who identifies another individual on the basis of observed physical characteristics. Unfortunately, this sort of voice identification is probably even less reliable than eyewitness identification testimony. It is therefore natural that law enforcement authorities have hoped for the development of scientific instrumentation for the identification of persons by their voices. Such instrumentation would be of substantial assistance in cases involving recorded telephone threats (e. g., bomb threats), ransom demands, extortion attempts, and the like.

Development of the Sound Spectrograph. The sound spectrograph, an electromagnetic instrument which can produce a graphic picture of human speech, was developed in the early 1940s by the Bell Telephone Laboratories. It could "read" the frequencies of a speech sample recorded on a loop of magnetic tape. A Bell employee, Lawrence G. Kersta, adapted the sound spectrograph for voice identifica-

* Copyright, 1975 by Jon R. Waltz.

tion purposes by means of the so-called voiceprint method. Kersta's idea was that a person's voice, like his fingerprints, has unique characteristics. If these characteristics could be demonstrated by spectrographic analysis, an important new identification technique could be made available to law enforcement agencies.

Voiceprint Identification. Spectrographic devices adapted for voiceprint analysis make use of (1) a recording of the questioned voice, and (2) a comparison voice recording of known origin. The parallel between questioned voice identification techniques and questioned documents analysis is superficially obvious. Kersta's theory of voice uniqueness has two sources: (1) the processes by which a person learns to talk, and (2) the physiological manner in which persons produce speech. In other words, the uniqueness of a voice is based on the *mechanism* of speech. This involves an understanding of those aspects of the vocal tract that make for the individuality of one's voice: the vocal cavities and the articulators.

The vocal cavities (nasal, oral, and pharyngeal) act as resonators. The contribution of the vocal cavities to voice individuality comes from their size and relationship to each other. It is said to be unlikely that any two people will have vocal cavities of identical size and relationship.

The manipulation of the articulators to vary the vocal cavities is of even greater significance in Kersta's theory of voice identification. The articulators are the tongue, teeth, lips, soft palate, and jaw muscles. By manipulating these articulators we produce understandable speech. Implicit in Kersta's theory is the notion that no two people are likely to use their articulators in precisely the same way, producing identical use patterns. Different people learn to talk in different ways. The improbability of identical articulator use patterns, taken together with the improbability of identical vocal cavity structure, makes for positive and accurate voice identification, according to Kersta.

Kersta originally made use of two different types of voice spectrograms. There was the *bar spectrogram* and the *contour spectrogram*. The bar spectrogram showed the resonance bars of a human voice in terms of loudness, frequency, and time dimensions. Contour spectrograms measure levels of loudness, frequency, and time as shapes which look much like a topographical map or the whorls of a fingerprint (thus the designation, *voiceprint*). Contour spectrograms are employed in the computerized classification of voiceprints; bar spectrograms are used in the comparison (matching) of known and unknown voice samples.

The Kersta voiceprint technique requires the comparison of questioned speech with a known speech sample recorded from a suspect. The spectrographic impressions of ten frequently used cue words found in the questioned speech are compared with the spectrographic impressions of the same ten cue words in the known speech specimen. The cue words are *a, and, I, is, it, the, to,* and *you.* If the spectrographic impressions of these word-sounds substantially match, Kersta would conclude that the samples had each been produced by the same speaker.

From time to time, Kersta, on the basis of experiments conducted by him, has claimed a high degree of accuracy for his voiceprint technique. In 1962 he stated that more than fifty thousand tests produced an accuracy record greater than 99 percent. Some years later Dr. Oscar Tosi of Michigan State University's Audiology Department conducted tests that failed to produce the level of accuracy which Kersta had announced. Kersta, Tosi, and other experts are carrying on continuing experimentation, and increasing scientific acceptance of the voiceprint technique is to be expected.

Two Legal Hurdles to the Use of Voiceprints. In dealing with voiceprints, courts have confronted two major legal hurdles. First, they have had to assess the reliability of the voiceprint technique from a scientific vantagepoint. Second, the courts have had to address such important constitutional issues as the privilege against self-incrimination, the right to legal counsel, and unlawful search and seizure.

UNITED STATES v. FRANKS

United States Court of Appeals, Sixth Circuit, 1975.
511 F.2d 25, cert. denied 422 U.S. 1042, 95 S.Ct. 2654, 45 L.Ed.2d 693.

PECK, Circuit Judge.

Defendants-appellants Franks and Britton were convicted, after a sixteen-day (16-day) jury trial in district court, of causing others on or about June 2, 1971, to commit physical violence to Jett Hair Care Center ("Jett Hair") and Tri-State Beauty Supply ("Tri-State"), two Memphis, Tennessee, businesses whose operation affected commerce, in furtherance of a plan and purpose to obstruct commerce * * *. Franks and Britton also were convicted of aiding and abetting the malicious damaging and attempt to destroy on or about June 2, 1971, by means of an explosive, Jett Hair and Tri-State * * *. Defendant-appellant Mitchell, tried together with Franks and Britton, was convicted of knowingly causing on or about June 1, 1971, certain explosives (blasting caps) to be transported in interstate commerce without being licensed to do so * * *.

Together, appellants have asserted no fewer than twenty-five claims on appeal. We have found, however, no reversible error.

* * *

Britton and Mitchell also complain that voiceprint ("spectographic") analysis is too inaccurate to be admitted into evidence. Though the only circuit ruling on the admissibility of voiceprints has found them inadmissible, United States v. Addison, 498 F.2d 741 (D. C.Cir. 1974), aff'g 337 F.Supp. 641 (D.C.C.1972), other courts are somewhat divided over, but the trend favors, the admissibility of voiceprints. Although we, of course, are aware of the differences of judicial and scientific opinion concerning the use of voiceprints, we also are mindful of "a considerable area of discretion on the part of the trial judge in admitting or refusing to admit" evidence based on scientific processes. * * *

> "[N]either newness nor lack of absolute certainty in a test suffices to render it inadmissible in court. Every useful new development must have its first day in court. And court records are full of the conflicting opinions of doctors, engineers and accountants * * *." 433 F.2d at 438.

Moreover, *Stifel* recognized that those opposing the admissibility of scientific tests can direct their criticisms toward the weight of such evidence.[11] Applying *Stifel*, which admitted expert testimony concerning neutron activation analysis, we find that the district court was within its discretion in admitting voiceprint analysis. The district court qualified the expert voiceprint witness only after an extensive 25-page inquiry into his qualifications and the reliability of the scientific process; defense counsel were permitted to cross-examine the witness concerning his purported role as an advocate of the process and some other courts' refusals to admit voiceprint evidence. Moreover, neither Britton nor Mitchell produced a witness rebutting the government's claim that voiceprint analysis is sufficiently accurate to be admissible.[12]

We also reject Britton's claim that the expert improperly testified to what he heard on the tapes as well as to identifying voices. After all, the district judge cautioned that "it [was] for the jury to weigh the expert's testimony [as to what was said]." Trial Transcript at 109. Moreover, the jury listened to the tapes. Even transcripts of taped conversations have been admitted.

[Affirmed.]

---

11. [a]ppellants aired their criticism of voiceprints in cross-examining the voice exemplar test." Trial Tranmoreover, specifically instructed the jury that Mitchell's refusal to submit voice exemplars may stem from a "lack of trust in the validity of the **voice exemplar test."** Trial Transcript at 3683.

12. * * * Though United States v. Stifel, 433 F.2d 431, 438, 441 (6th Cir. 1970), cert. denied, 401 U.S. 994, 91 S. Ct. 1232 (1971), applied the Frye v. United States, 54 App.D.C. 46, 293 F. 1013 (1923), standard governing admissibility of scientific evidence as whether the scientific process has gained "general acceptance in the particular field in which it belongs," we deem general acceptance as being nearly synonymous with reliability. If a scientific process is reliable, or sufficiently accurate, courts may also deem it "generally accepted."

LISKO, ARE THE COURTS LISTENING TO VOICEPRINTS?

12 Creighton L.Rev. 517 (1978).

The issue of whether or not to admit voiceprints cannot be resolved by aligning the cases into two columns. There is no well-defined controlling authority in the case law. However, several common concerns are manifested in the decisions and require scrutiny in any discussion on voiceprint admissibility. Three major points of analysis often recur: (1) the impact of the evidence upon the jury; (2) establishing voiceprint evidence as generally accepted within the scientific community; and (3) qualifying the expert.

The impact of a voiceprint upon a jury is an issue that has caused considerable discussion in both jurisdictions that accept voiceprints and in those that reject them. In jurisdictions which admit voiceprints courts have guarded their admission with the use of carefully worded jury instructions. In this manner the jury remains free to exercise its traditional role of weighing the evidence and assessing the credibility of the expert. This view also reflects a general attitude of appellate courts to refrain from emasculating the trial judges' power to admit evidence at their discretion.

Of critical importance in any case involving scientific evidence is the problem of deciding whether the particular scientific principle underlying the technique has been generally accepted by scientists who are qualified in that area or specialization. In numerous cases where the courts rejected the voiceprint evidence, there are indications that general acceptance could have been proved. The major weakness in the cases analyzed throughout this article has been the prosecution's reliance upon one or two well-known experts to speak for the scientific community. In all but isolated cases, the experts have been Professor Tosi and Lieutenant Nash. Although these two men are unquestionably experts in spectrographic analysis of the human voice, they are also advocates of the technique and their opinion is justifiably subjected to careful cross-examination.

A final thread of concern that runs through many of the voiceprint cases is the problem of establishing the offering party's witness as an expert. As with other forensic science witnesses, the trial court must be convinced that the witness has attained the requisite knowledge, through formal training or experience, to satisfy the title of expert. Notwithstanding People v. Kelly, which appeared to require of experts a college degree, most courts and rules of evidence are satisfied if the witness is able to demonstrate specific skill, knowledge, or training in his field of expertise. With the aid of cross-examination it is the jury's function to determine the weight and credibility to be given to the expert's testimony.

The final resolution of the admissibility problems presented by voiceprints may depend upon the judiciary's balancing the evidentiary worth of the scientific principle against these three recurring fears. Whether the voiceprint analysis will ever gain general acceptance as a tool for identification or elimination of suspects remains to be seen. For the present, it would appear that admissibility of voiceprint evidence will be handled on a case by case analysis; in the words of Mr. Justice Holmes: "Any solution in general terms seems * * * to mark a want of analytic power."

c. TESTS FOR INTOXICATION AND DRUGS

WALTZ, CRIMINAL EVIDENCE

(1975).

Toxicology and the Chemical Sciences

Their Role in Criminalistics. Toxicology and the chemical sciences loom larger and larger in modern-day efforts to detect and combat crime. Chemical tests for intoxication identify the drunk driver, separating him from the innocent person whose symptoms stem from a diabetic condition, carbon monoxide poisoning, or head injuries. The forensic serologist can use blood found at a crime scene as a source of proof linking a suspect to the offense. Other biochemical procedures are available to identify saliva, semen, fecal matter, vomitus, even perspiration. The forensic toxicologist can identify poisonous (toxic) substances and describe their effects. Other toxicological experts can analyze seized substances to determine whether they are illegal drugs.

The Need for Expertise. Except in connection with intoxication tests, criminal investigators are rarely qualified as experts in clinical toxicological-chemical testing, where practical experience must ordinarily be combined with fairly formal training in such fields as chemistry, biochemistry, and hematology.

Example:

In Scott v. State, 37 So. 357 (S.Ct.Ala.1904), the witness who was held qualified to testify that death was caused by morphine in the stomach was a university professor of chemistry who also had for many years been a state chemist and toxicologist. (It made no difference that he was neither a pathologist nor a pharmacist.)

Of course, law enforcement agents can occasionally give an opinion that is based not on clinical testing of a type requiring special expertise but on their own eyewitness observation of physical phenomena. Thus some courts would permit a police officer to testify to his opinion that a person was under the influence of drugs, based on his experience in dealing with persons later established to have been narcotics addicts. Even a lay citizen is sometimes allowed to give this sort of testimony.

Example:

In Pointer v. State, 467 S.W.2d 426 (Tex.Crim.App.1971), a layman who had been robbed was allowed to give his opinion that the accused was under the influence of narcotics at the time of the offense. The witness's opinion was based on his observations of the physical condition of narcotics addicts while he was in the Air Force.

It has sometimes been said that a narcotics addict is a qualified expert on the addictive properties of substances.

Example:

In Howard v. State, 496 P.2d 657 (S.Ct. Alaska 1972), it was held that a drug addict could testify to the narcotic quality of the substance in question, and in State v. Johnson, 196 N.W.2d 717 (S.Ct.Wis.1972), a user of LSD was permitted to express an opinion that a substance was LSD.

While holding it in mind that toxicological-chemical procedures are used by trained experts in the investigation of blood and a wide range of other biological matter, we will focus this discussion on intoxication tests since law enforcement officers are frequently directly involved in this type of testing. Identification of narcotic substances is also discussed briefly.

Chemical Intoxication Testing. The scientific validity of chemical intoxication tests is now so firmly established that most states make the results of them admissible under express statutory provisions. Thus in 1967 McIntyre and Chabraja could report in their article *The Intensive Search of a Suspect's Body and Clothing* in 58 Journal of Criminal Law, Criminology & Police Science 18, that forty states then had chemical test laws which provided that 0.15 percent of alcohol in a suspect's blood, as determined by chemical testing, is *prima facie* evidence of intoxication.

Because, among other things, tolerance for alcohol varies from person to person, it is not possible accurately to measure the degree to which a person is intoxicated on the basis of the *amount* of alcohol he has consumed. Intoxication can, however, be reliably demonstrated by scientific measurement of the amount of alcohol that has reached the subject's brain, since the brain's alcohol content is the cause of most of the effects of alcohol.

The alcohol in liquor is ethyl alcohol. It has a low boiling point, is volatile, almost odorless (the "odor" of liquor comes from flavoring matter), colorless, and toxic in that an overdose can be fatal. Ethyl alcohol is produced by the enzymatic breakdown of sugar, the process known as fermentation.

Alcohol is not digested when it goes into the stomach. Approximately 10 to 20 percent of any alcohol in the stomach is absorbed through the stomach's membranes into the bloodstream, the remainder being absorbed in the small intestine. A number of factors control the speed and amount of absorption of alcohol from the stomach into the bloodstream, such as (1) the amount of alcohol the person has consumed, (2) the nature and amount of coating in the stomach, and (3) the concentration of alcohol in the beverage consumed.

Other conditions being equal, alcohol consumed after a substantial meal has a slower absorption rate than alcohol drunk on an empty stomach. It has been reported that straight whiskey taken on an empty stomach attains maximum concentration in the bloodstream within half an hour. In contrast, alcohol consumed along with or after the ingestion of food may reach maximum concentration as much as an hour and a half after consumption. Sugar, fatty foods, and milk retard alcohol absorption somewhat.

Alcohol absorbed into the bloodstream does not undergo significant transformation; it is still alcohol. After it has been absorbed into the bloodstream, it is distributed throughout the body in a constant proportional relationship to the water content of the various body tissues. It is eliminated from the tissues by being oxidized to energy, water and carbon dioxide. A great deal of alcohol's metabolism (assimilation) takes place in the liver. A smaller percentage is excreted unchanged in the urine, breath, and perspiration. Needless to say, the higher the concentration of alcohol in the bloodstream, the higher will be the relative proportion of alcohol that is excreted. The percentage of alcohol excreted in the breath or as urine varies proportionately with the concentration of alcohol in the blood. While blood-alcohol concentration is decreasing, the urine-alcohol concentration may be as much as one and one-half that of blood alcohol. Blood alcohol concentration is about twenty-one hundred times that of the same unit volume in the deep alveolar breath. While varying somewhat from person to person, the rate of elimination is fairly constant in relation to body size. The average person weighing 150 pounds can eliminate one-third of an ounce of pure alcohol per hour. This equals two-thirds of an ounce of 100-proof whiskey per hour.

The quantity of alcohol ingested does not dictate the degree of mental and physical impairment; the level of impairment is governed by the quantity of alcohol that has been absorbed into the bloodstream and carried to the central nervous system. Alcohol is not a stimulant; it depresses the central nervous system's responses (brain, spinal cord, spinal nerves). Alcohol-laden blood entering the brain through the vascular system has a depressing effect until the alcohol is eliminated. Its main depressant effect occurs in the brain's cerebral areas, which control the human body's higher functions. It is in this way that the ingestion of alcohol causes diminution of judgment, self-restraint, and responses to stimuli. At elevated concentrations, blood-alcohol ratio produces loss of muscular control, lengthened reaction time, diminished sensitivity to pain, disturbances of sensory perception (vision, hearing), confusion, thick or slurred speech and unsteady gait. If the blood alcohol concentration is even higher, a state of stupor approaching paralysis results. If the concentration is sublethal, the person will pass from stupor into unconsciousness.

Many jurisdictions have enacted statutory standards describing the smallest percentage of blood alcohol necessary to create a rebuttable presumption of intoxication. Since no presumption in a criminal case is ever absolutely conclusive, test results can be weighed and accepted or rejected by the fact-finder.

In the absence of a statute, the prosecution must place its reliance entirely on the testimony of expert witnesses.

1. *Chemical Testing; Blood Analysis.* There are a number of chemical tests for intoxication. The most reliable of them involves direct analysis of brain tissue. This method is not used on a large scale since it is confined to corpses, just as is spinal fluid analysis. The tests most commonly used on living persons involve analysis of the blood, urine, and breath. Direct analysis of the blood is thought to be the most reliable of these three methods, but there is a practical problem in that direct analysis of the blood requires that a physician or qualified medical technician secure a blood sample under proper conditions. It also generates chain-of-custody requirements. For these reasons, blood analysis is not used as widely as breath testing.

2. *Breath Tests.* Breath testing for intoxication operates on the assumption that a breath sample is saturated with alcoholic vapor at normal respiratory tract temperature. In other words, alcohol breath testing is an indirect means of detecting blood-alcohol levels. As was suggested earlier, the validity of this type of testing is based on the circumstance that blood will contain about twenty-one hundred times as much alcohol as alveolar air.

The first device for breath analysis of blood-alcohol ratio was graphically named the Drunkometer by its inventor, Dr. R. N. Harger of the University of Indiana Medical School. The Drunkometer, perfected in 1931, was rapidly followed by the Intoximeter, D.P.C. Intoximeter, Photo-Electric Intoximeter, Alcometer, Infrared Intoxograph, the Kitagawa-Wright device, and the Breathalyzer, and this is not a complete list of such equipment. Today the Drunkometer, Breathalyzer, and the Intoximeter are the most commonly used. All three of them function in accordance with the principles worked out by Harger.

Harger's Drunkometer operates on the principle that the alcohol present in breath will cause discoloration of permanganate, a salt of permanganic acid. The alcohol concentration is determined from the amount of breath that is necessary to cause the chemical reaction, which is evidenced by the discoloration of a measured amount of permanganate. The last step is a mathematical conversion from the reading on the Drunkometer to blood-alcohol ratio. Any police officer can operate a Drunkometer and provide essential courtroom testimony about test results after a short period of training.

The Intoximeter lacks certain of the Drunkometer's advantages. It uses magnesium perchlorate rather than permanganate, and foundation testimony regarding the pretest condition of the device and any changes caused by the breathtesting process is essential. Police officers do not ordinarily develop the level of expertise required by the Intoximeter process.

The Breathalyzer was perfected by a member of the Indiana State Police, Captain R. F. Borkenstein. The theory behind it is that the normal yellow color of a solution of potassium dichromate and liquid sulphuric acid will turn green if alcohol is present in breath that passes through the solution. When a person suspected of being intoxicated blows his breath forcefully through a mouthpiece into a heated plastic tube in the Breathalyzer, it raises a piston in a metal cylinder. The suspect's breath fills the cylinder and the pistol then drops down to seal it. When a valve is rotated, a measured quantity of the breath is forced through 3 milliliters of 50 percent (by volume) sulphuric acid in water, which contains 0.25 milligrams of potassium dichromate per milliliter, and a catalytic agent. The breath bubbles through this test solution in approximately thirty seconds. Before the Breathalyzer test is commenced the solution in the test ampul (a glass vessel) is photometrically balanced against a reference ampul until a meter marked "Null" centers. This indicates that each of two photocells is receiving the same amount of light through the two ampuls. After the suspect has blown his breath into the mouthpiece, the photometric reading light is again turned on. More light will be received by the righthand photo cell and the "Null" meter will no longer be centered if some of the potassium dichromate in the test ampul has been consumed by alcohol. By means of a thumb wheel the light is moved until the "Null" meter is again centered. The distance which the light has to be moved is directly related to the quantity of alcohol in the suspect's breath. The light scale is calibrated to show blood-alcohol percent or ratio.

A new device known as an Intoxilyzer has recently been developed. It relies on infrared absorption of energy by ethyl alcohol vapors in breath samples. It provides a direct and rapid means of measuring breath alcohol quantitatively. The Intoxilyzer is easy to operate because it uses no chemicals; it may eventually supplant the older equipment described in the preceding paragraph. A more detailed description of the Intoxilyzer can be found in Harte, *An Instrument for the Determination of Ethanol in Breath*, 16 Journal of Forensic Science 493 (1971).

Breath testing will lack accuracy if the chemical reagents are not fresh (e. g., permanganate is unstable and will decompose quickly, producing a falsely high breath alcohol reading). Improper operator conduct can lead to error—so can a failure to employ the equilibration and standardization tests recommended by the manufacturers of the equipment. Essential test procedures, aimed at assuring accuracy, are described in Hall, *The Equilibrator—An Answer for Improving Breathalyzer Techniques and Field Testing Suspect Alcohol Solutions,* 1 Police Law Quarterly 11 (1971).

A breath test will not produce an accurate picture if more than fifteen minutes have passed between the ingestion of the alcohol and the taking of the breath sample. Recent use of breath fresheners and mouthwashes that have an alcoholic content can throw off the results of breath testing. Alcohol remaining in the subject's throat and the mouth can produce a falsely high reading; this can happen when the subject has regurgitated.

Evidentiary Aspects. Not surprisingly, the results of blood-alcohol tests are not considered conclusive of intoxication in the eyes of the law. This means that juries can accept or reject test results when considering the evidence of intoxication in totality. State chemical test statutes usually call for some corroboration of test results.

Example:

The Wisconsin Statute, Wis.Stats.Ann. § 325.235(1), reads: "The fact that the analysis shows that there was fifteen-hundredths of one per cent or more by weight of alcohol in the person's blood is prima facie evidence that he was under the influence of an intoxicant, but shall not, without corroborating physical evidence thereof, be sufficient upon which to find the person guilty of being under the influence of intoxicants."

The corroborating physical evidence referred to in statutes of the sort quoted above usually consists of the testimony of police officers who administered or observed coordination tests in which the subject engaged in nose-touching, name-writing, line-walking, and the like. (Actually, coordination test results alone are enough to sustain a driving-while-intoxicated conviction: there is no absolute requirement that the prosecution produce scientific evidence in intoxication cases.)

If scientific tests are to be relied upon, the prosecution must lay a preliminary foundation. Usually this foundation has three principal components: (1) testimony that there was periodic inspection of the test equipment and supervision of the operator by a person having a clear understanding of the scientific principles on which the test method is based; (2) testimony that the chemicals utilized in the test procedure were fresh and properly compounded; and (3) proof that the witness who will testify to the test results is qualified to do so. The third foundation requirement dictates the use of a witness who possesses enough knowledge of his own to convert the breath-analysis reading to blood alcohol without exclusive reliance on a chart provided by the manufacturer of the testing equipment, since this would inject a hearsay element.

Whenever chemical testing of body fluids, such as blood or urine, or other substances, such as compounds thought to be illegal drugs, is conducted, special care must be taken to preserve a provable chain of custody.

STATE v. BAKER

Supreme Court of Washington, 1960.
56 Wash.2d 846, 355 P.2d 806.

DONWORTH, Judge. Appellant was charged by information with the crime of negligent homicide * * *. The charging portion of the information reads as follows:

> "That the said Charles E. Baker in the County of Pierce, in the State of Washington, on or about the 13th day of September, Nineteen Hundred and Fifty-eight did then and there unlawfully and feloniously operate a motor vehicle in a reckless manner with disregard for the safety of others, and while under the influence of or affected by the use of intoxicating liquor, and while so operating said vehicle and being in physical control thereof, did, as a result of such negligent operation strike and injure Ernest E. Eichhorn, a human being, from which said injuries the said Ernest E. Eichhorn, did on the 16th day of September, 1958, die, contrary to the form of the statute in such cases made and provided, and against the peace and dignity of the State of Washington."

The facts giving rise to the above charge may be briefly summarized as follows:

On Saturday evening, September 13, 1958 the opening night of the western Washington fair in Puyallup, Washington, Ernest E. Eichhorn, an officer of the Washington state patrol, was directing traffic at the intersection of Seventh avenue southeast and Meridian avenue, which is located approximately one block north of the fair grounds. The intersection was lighted by a single mercury vapor light, and Officer Eichhorn was wearing a light blue state patrol jacket with white threading in the material, which would reflect light.

Appellant was driving his automobile south along Meridian avenue on his way to the fair grounds to pick up his wife who was employed at the fair. As he approached the intersection, Officer Eichhorn had just stopped the east-west traffic, and the north-south traffic had commenced to move. There is a conflict in the evidence as to the precise manner in which the accident occurred. However, as appellant passed through the intersection, his car struck Officer Eichhorn, whose body was flung through the air. It came to rest in front of a Ford automobile which was traveling north on Meridian avenue and stopped with its front wheel touching Officer Eichhorn's body. Although it had been raining shortly prior to the accident, the evidence was conflicting as to whether or not it was raining at the time of the accident. The accident occurred a few minutes before eleven o'clock p. m.

Appellant admitted that he had consumed one stubby and four eight-ounce glasses of beer between six o'clock p. m. and the time of the accident. He denied that he was then under the influence of, or affected by, intoxicating liquor.

Shortly after the accident, appellant was taken in a patrol car by Officer Alfred F. Stewart of the state patrol to the police station of the neighboring city of Sumner, Washington. Officer Richard E. Mefferd of the Sumner police department put appellant through various physical observation tests for intoxication, and also administered a breathalyzer test, which appellant took of his own volition.

Neither Officer Stewart nor Officer Mefferd was able to form an opinion as to appellant's sobriety from their physical observations of him. However, the result of the breathalyzer test indicated that appellant had .185 per cent alcohol by weight in his blood (185 milligrams in 100 cc. of blood).

Appellant entered a plea of not guilty. The case was tried to the court sitting with a jury. At the close of the state's case, appellant moved to dismiss the case on the ground that the state had failed to produce sufficient legally admissible evidence to support a conviction. The motion was denied. Appellant renewed his motion at the close of all the evidence and it was again denied. The case was then submitted to the jury, which returned a verdict of guilty. Appellant's motion in arrest of judgment or, in the alternative, for a new trial was denied, and judgment and sentence was entered upon the verdict. This appeal followed.

The case, in so far as it relates to the breathalyzer test, is one of first impression in this state. Since the few cases that have been cited to us from other jurisdictions pertaining to breath-testing devices do not cover the precise issues that have been raised here, we make no reference to them.

There are twenty-one assignments of error, nine of which relate to the admissibility in evidence of the breathalyzer test result. We shall first consider these nine assignments. In order to understand the problems presented thereby, it is necessary to describe in some detail the nature of the breathalyzer and its method of operation as shown by the state's evidence.

The breathalyzer is a machine designed to measure the amount of alcohol in the alveolar breath and is based upon the principle that the ratio between the amount of alcohol in the blood and the amount in the alveolar breath from the lungs is a constant 2100 to 1. In other words, the machine analyzes a sample of breath to determine the alcoholic content of the boood. At the time of the trial of this case, there were twenty-three such machines in operation in the state of Washington.

To operate the machine, the subject blows into the machine through a mouthpiece until he has emptied his lungs in one breath. The machine is so designed that it traps only the last 52½ cubic centimeters of air that has been blown into it. This air is then forced, by weight of a piston, through a test ampoule containing a solution of sulphuric acid and potassium dichromate. This test solution has a yellow hue to it. As the breath sample bubbles through the test solution, the sulphuric acid extracts the alcohol, if any, therefrom, and the potassium dichromate then changes the alcohol to acetic acid, thereby causing the solution to lose some of its original yellow color. The greater the alcoholic content of the breath sample, the greater will be the loss in color of the test solution. By causing a light to pass through the test ampoule and through a standard ampoule containing the same chemical solution as the test ampoule (but through which no breath sample has passed), the amount of the change in color can be measured by photoelectric cells which are connected to a galvanometer. By balancing the galvanometer, a reading can be obtained from a gauge which has been calibrated in terms of percentage of alcohol in the blood.

It should be made clear at the outset that appellant does not contend that results of breathalyzer tests, in general, are not admissible in evidence. He does contend that four basic requirements must be shown by the state before the results of such tests may be admitted in evidence, to wit: (1) That the machine was properly checked and in proper working order at the time of conducting the test; (2) that the chemicals employed were of the correct kind and compounded in the proper proportions; (3) that the subject had nothing in his mouth at the time of the test and that he had taken no food or drink within fifteen minutes prior to taking the test; (4) that the test be given by a qualified operator and in the proper manner.

The expert testimony introduced by the state in this case pertaining to the breathalyzer and its operation shows that unless the above four requirements are satisfied, the result of the test is wholly unreliable. We therefore hold that before the result of a breathalyzer test can be admitted into evidence, the state must produce *prima facie* evidence that each of the four requirements listed above have been complied with.

Appellant takes the position that the first three requirements were not met in the instant case. As to the first requirement, it is contended that the machine was not properly checked, in that Lt. DeWitt Whitman of the Washington state patrol did not use a test thermometer to check the temperature of the breath chamber of the machine during his periodic maintenance checks. Along this same line, it is further contended that Lt. Whitman failed to properly test the machine because he did not use a *test* thermometer to check the temperature of the test ampoule.

Neither contention has any merit. The breath chamber is heated to a temperature between forty-five to fifty degrees centigrade to prevent condensation. If condensation is present in the breath chamber, there is a danger that the piston which compresses the air through the test ampoule will stick and not operate properly. The test ampoule is heated about sixty-five degrees centigrade so that it can rapidly oxidize the alcohol in the breath sample.

Lt. Whitman testified that he was in charge of the chemical testing program for the state patrol, and that he had studied and worked in that field since 1944. He said that the breathalyzer came into existence in 1955, and that he has been familiar with its operation since that time. He performed maintenance checks on the machine involved herein on July 1, 1958, and on November 14, 1958, and that on both occasions he checked the chamber and ampoule heat with the thermometer which is located in the machine itself, and that the temperatures were accurately recorded in each instance.

Appellant argues that the temperature checks should have been made with a thermometer other than the one used in the machine itself, as the machine thermometer could be faulty.

Lt. Whitman testified that that machine thermometer was checked against a calibrated thermometer at the time the machine was first obtained. In the absence of any indication that the machine thermometer was defective, we think the initial check was sufficient to establish its probable accuracy.

The evidence also discloses that both the ampoule and the chamber heat may vary somewhat without affecting the results of the test. The chamber heat (45–50 degrees centigrade) is marked on the thermometer by a green area, and the ampoule heat (65 degrees centigrade) is designated by a red mark. Lt. Whitman testified that if the temperature of either were substantially higher or lower, the only *possible* result would be a lower reading on the alcoholic content gauge. Thus, appellant could not be prejudiced even if the machine thermometer were inaccurate as any error in temperature would only result in his favor.

Lt. Whitman was cross-examined on the *voir dire* and, in the absence of the jury, appellant's counsel argued his objection to the witness' testifying as to whether in his opinion the machine had been properly checked and, also, argued a motion to strike all evidence as to the breathalyzer. The trial court gave careful consideration to these motions and, after stating his reasons, denied them.

It is next contended that the state failed to satisfy the second basic requirement for the admissibility of the breathalyzer test in that the test ampoule used in the test given appellant was never checked to insure that the chemicals therein were of the correct kind and compounded in the proper proportions.

The ampoules are sealed glass containers which are made and compounded by the same company which makes the breathalyzer machine. The ampoule cannot be tested as to chemical content without being broken, and once it is broken it can no longer be used. Thus, it was impossible to check the particular test ampoule that was used in the test on appellant. However, the state's evidence shows that the ampoules are shipped from the manufacturer in batches and each batch has a control number, which is stamped on each and every ampoule in that particular batch. Every time a new batch is received, Lt. Whitman spot checks at least six ampoules from that particular batch. During the course of his work, Lt. Whitman has tested hundreds of ampoules and has never found one which did not contain what it was certified to contain.

The fact that the *sealed* ampoules are delivered by the manufacturer of the breathalyzer machine for exclusive use in such machine plus the additional fact of regular spot checking of the ampoules is, in our opinion, sufficient *prima facie* proof that the chemicals in any one ampoule are of the proper kind and mixed to the proper proportion.

Appellant argues further that Lt. Whitman was not qualified to conduct spot checks to determine the chemical contents of the ampoules as he was not a chemist.

Lt. Whitman described the method of spot checking as follows:

"I run, first, a check using known alcohol samples. By using an equilibrating device, I can then check this ampoule against a known alcohol solution and find out if the answer arrived at is the proper answer. If you arrive at the proper answer, then there has to be the proper solution in this ampoule. I then use, by another method, by titration, I titrate against the potassium dichromate in this solution with a solution which will reduce the potassium dichromate."

It is not contended that the methods of testing employed by Lt. Whitman are improper. Appellant did not produce a chemist or other qualified expert witness at the trial to challenge the methods of testing used by Lt. Whitman. The qualifications which Lt. Whitman possessed, according to his testimony, are that he is in charge of the chemical testing program of the state patrol; that he took a course in chemical testing at Northwestern University Traffic Institute; that since 1944 he has received extensive training in the field of chemical testing from leading pathologists and toxicologists; and that he has done considerable independent study of his own.

Although Lt. Whitman is not a chemist, he has had sufficient experience in the field of chemical testing of the type involved in this case to warrant the trial court's allowing him to testify concerning his spot checking of the ampoules.

Appellant contends the state failed to meet the third basic requirement in two respects, to wit, (1) Officer Mefferd failed to examine appellant's mouth for the presence of any foreign matter prior to giving him the test; and (2) the police did not have appellant under observation for fifteen minutes prior to giving him the test.

From our examination of the record, we think that this contention is well taken. The testimony of both Lt. Whitman and Dr. Charles P. Larson, the state's two experts on the operation of the breathalyzer machine, makes it clear that unless a subject's mouth is free of all alcohol the test result will be unreliable. Their testimony further establishes that the subject must be kept under observation for at least fifteen minutes to insure that he has not taken anything alcoholic to drink during that period and to allow any alcohol present in the mouth to be absorbed by the skin.

Officer Mefferd candidly admitted that he did not examine appellant's mouth before giving him the test. There is evidence tending to show that appellant may have had an absorbent poultice and a packing impregnated with a medicine (toothache drops) containing alcohol in a cavity in his tooth at the time he took the test. Furthermore, there is evidence tending to show that appellant may have taken some cough medicine containing forty-five to forty-six per cent alcohol by volume within fifteen minutes of the test.

Appellant testified that he took a drink of cough medicine just before being brought to the Sumner police station. Officer Stewart testfied that the trip to Sumner took six to ten minutes. Officer Mefferd testified that appellant was in his presence at the police station for eight to ten minutes. Thus, under the state's own evidence appellant may have been given the test after having been under observation for only fourteen minutes. Although this is only one minute less than the required fifteen-minute minimum, the state is bound by its own evidence to the effect that the minimum period of delay must be *fifteen* minutes.

This rule is recognized by Robert L. Donigan, general counsel for the Traffic Institute of Northwestern University, in his work entitled "Chemical Tests and the Law," at page 173, where the author states:

> "A breath test will only give an accurate measure of the concentration of alcohol in the circulating blood, if there has been a lapse of *at least* 15 minutes between the taking of the last drink and the taking of the breath for analysis. During this 15-minute interval, any alcoholic liquor remaining in the mouth and throat or under a dental plate will have been washed down by saliva. Thereafter, the alcohol concentra-

tion of the *breathed* air (alveolar breath) will reflect the alcohol concentration of the blood circulating through the lungs." (First italics ours.)

Both Lt. Whitman and Dr. Larson testified at some length as to the reliability and accuracy of breath-testing machines in general. In addition, Dr. Larson, a physician specializing in forensic pathology and a leading authority on the subject of breath tests, described in great detail what various percentages of alcohol by weight in the blood meant in terms of intoxication. His testimony, if believed by the jury, could leave no doubt that a reading of .185 on the breathalyzer would indicate that the subject was very intoxicated.

We have no way of knowing whether the verdict of guilty stemmed from the jury's finding that, at the time of the accident, appellant was driving in a reckless manner, or that he was then under the influence of, or affected by, intoxicating liquor, or that both of these facts were proven beyond a reasonable doubt. Since the state failed to satisfy the third requirement for the admissibility of the breathalyzer test, the admission of such test was error. In view of the evidence in this case concerning the reliability of breathalyzer tests and the significance of a .185 reading, we are further of the opinion that the error was prejudicial. Appellant is therefore entitled to a new trial. * * *

Because of the trial court's error in admitting in evidence the result of the breathalyzer test, the judgment and sentence are reversed and the case is remanded with directions to grant appellant a new trial.

WEAVER, C. J., and FINLEY, OTT, ROSELLINI, FOSTER and HUNTER, JJ., concur.

MALLERY and HILL, JJ., dissent.

PEOPLE v. WILLIAMS

Appellate Department, Superior Court, Alameda County, California, 1958.
164 Cal.App.2d Supp. 858, 331 P.2d 251.

WAGLER, Presiding Judge. The defendants were convicted of a violation of Section 11721 of the Health and Safety Code of the State of California. Each has appealed from the judgment of conviction and the order denying him a new trial.

Section 11721 makes it unlawful for any one to use, be under the influence of, or to be addicted to the use of narcotics except when administered by or under the direction of a licensed person.

It is the contention of each defendant that the admission in evidence of the result of a Nalline test administered shortly following his arrest constituted prejudicial error. Each defendant also contends that proper venue was not shown and that the evidence was insufficient to sustain his conviction.

Following their arrest defendants were taken to the Oakland City Prison. They were there interviewed by police officers attached to the Special Service Detail who testified that each defendant admitted the prior use of narcotics but denied any recent use, and that each had old as well as fresh needle marks on the inside of the left forearm. Each officer also testified without objection that in his opinion, based upon his experience and observations, each defendant was addicted to the use of narcotics and had recently used the same.

A written release and authorization for the administration of a Nalline test signed by each defendant was received in evidence. It is conceded that this consent was freely and voluntarily given.

The Nalline test was administered by Dr. James G. Terry, Medical Officer of Santa Rita Rehabilitation Center. The method used was summarized by him substantially as follows: After a cursory physical examination the suspect is seated in a specially designed barber type chair with a fixed lamp on one side and a steel hand rest on the other. By means of a card containing a series of dots known as a "pupillometer" the doctor then measures and records the size of the pupil. This is done by using the hand rest to steady the hand and by matching the pupil size with the size of one of the dots on the pupillometer. Thereafter three milligrams of Nalline (N-allylnormorphine, a synthetic opiate antinarcotic in action) is injected under the skin, and the suspect is placed in another room for a period of at least 30 minutes. After the lapse of 30 minutes or longer the suspect is again placed in the chair and his pupils are again measured in the manner above described.

When tested in the above manner, the pupils of each defendant dilated. This according to Dr. Terry indicated a positive reaction, i. e., the recent use of narcotics.

Based upon defendants' history of prior use, the needle marks which were observed and the results of his Nalline tests, Dr. Terry expressed the opinion that each defendant was at the time of his examination mildly under the influence of a narcotic. It is the admission of this testimony of which defendants complain.

If the above testimony was based upon adequate data it would, of course, fall within a well-recognized exception to the rule which excludes opinion evidence. * * *

However, the results of tests of the type here under attack, as well as opinions based thereon, are admissible only if the tests have gained acceptance in the field of learning in which they are in use. [Citations omitted.]

Wigmore states the rule as follows: "When the testimony thus appearing to the ordinary layman to lack a rational basis is founded on observations made with esoteric methods or apparatus * * * the method should be explained by the witness, and if it be vouched for as accepted in his branch of learning, it suffices to admit his testimony." * * *

Dr. Terry testified that during the past three years he had carried on experimental work with Nalline at the Santa Rita Rehabilitation Center (Alameda County Jail); that his experimentation had been done by means of controlled tests with approximately 2,300 persons, that some of said tests dealt with non-users, others with moderate users, and still others with addicts; that during this experimental work he had conferred personally with Dr. Victor Vogel, former head of the U. S. Public Health Hospital, at Lexington, Kentucky, a pioneer in the use of the Nalline test, and that Dr. Vogel had participated in the tests with him at Oakland, California; that his experiments had resulted in findings that in small dosage Nalline produced a pupillary reaction; that under controlled conditions, after an injection of three milligrams of Nalline, a non-user's pupils will contract, a mild or moderate user's pupils will remain about the same size, and that the pupils of a person who is using a substantial amount of narcotics tending toward addiction will dilate.

In addition to Dr. Terry, the People called as experts Dr. Joseph Lamberti, a specialist in psychiatry, and Dr. William D. Perry, a specialist in internal medicine.

Each of the experts, including Dr. Terry, testified in substance that he had spent some time in making studies of and inquiries concerning the methods used for the detection of narcotic addiction, and more particularly the use of the drug N-allylnormorphine (Nalline) in this connection. Each had read numerous articles on the subject in medical periodicals and had discussed the test with many other physicians. None had ever read or heard anything critical or derogatory concerning the Nalline test. Each was familiar with the writings of Doctors Harris Isbell, Victor Vogel, A. W. Wikler, and H. F. Frazer, and other recognized authorities in the field of narcotic addiction. Each testified that in his opinion the medical profession generally had accepted the use of Nalline as a reliable means of detecting the presence of an opiate in a person's system and that he personally accepted it as such.

No experts were called by the defendants and the expert testimony as above summarized stands uncontradicted in the record with this exception: Each of the People's experts did admit on cross-examination that the medical profession generally is unfamiliar with the use of Nalline and therefore it cannot be truthfully said that the Nalline test has met with general acceptance by the medical profession as a whole, general acceptance being at present limited to those few in a specialized field who deal with the narcotic problem.

Should this fact render the testimony inadmissible? We believe not. All of the medical testimony points to the reliability of the test. It has been generally accepted by those who would be expected to be familiar with its use. In this age of specialization more should not be required.

The medical testimony, however, is not the only evidence in the record of reliability. In 1957 the Legislature of this State enacted Section 11722 of the Health and Safety Code. This section reads in part as follows:

> "Whenever any court in this State grants probation to a person who the court has reason to believe is or has been a user of narcotics, the court may require as a condition to probation that the probationer submit to a periodic tests by a city or county health officer, or by a physician and surgeon appointed by the city or county health officer with the approval of the State Division of Narcotic Enforcement, to determine, by means of the use of *synthetic opiate antinarcotic in action* whether the probationer is a narcotic addict." (Emphasis added.)

There being uncontradicted evidence in the record before us that the Legislature had the Nalline test in mind when it enacted Section 11722, this enactment must be accepted as a legislative mandate that the Nalline test has probative value. * * *

The order denying motion for a new trial is in each case affirmed. The judgment of conviction is in each case affirmed.

LEDWICH and HOYT, JJ., concur.

2. DEMONSTRATIVE EVIDENCE

WALTZ, CRIMINAL EVIDENCE

416–424 (1975).*

DEMONSTRATIVE EVIDENCE

A.

Historical Background

It is pointed out in [an earlier chapter] that demonstrative evidence is to be distinguished from real evidence in that demonstrative evidence consists of tangible materials that are used for illustrative or explanatory purposes only and do not purport to be "the real thing"—the murder weapon, the burglary tools actually used by the accused, the heroin seized by the narcotics agents when they arrested the defendant. It was also mentioned in [an earlier chapter] that there are two basic types of demonstrative evidence: (1) *selected* demonstrative evidence, such as handwriting exemplars, and (2) *prepared* or *reproduced* demonstrative evidence, such as a sketch or diagram * * *. In this chapter we go into somewhat greater depth

---

* Copyright, 1975 by Jon R. Waltz.

in describing types of demonstrative evidence and the range of possible objections to its use.

There has been a resurgence of interest in the imaginative use of demonstrative evidence, after a lengthy period during which trial lawyers were reluctant to rely on it for fear of causing an adverse reaction by jurors who might draw the implication that an essentially weak case was being overproved by means of unsubstantial gimmickry. Unquestionably, the use of demonstrative evidence has had its ups and downs, as the following commentary—made almost a hundred years ago—attests:

> In the early and rude ages there was a strong leaning toward the adoption of demonstrative and practical tests upon disputed questions. Doubting Thomases demanded the satisfaction of their senses. * * * As society grew civilized and refined, it seemed disposed to despise these demonstrative methods, and inclined more to the preference of a narration, at second-hand, by eye and ear witnesses. But in this busy century there seems to have been a relapse toward the earlier experimental spirit, and a disposition to make assurance doubly sure by any practical method addressed to the senses. (Browne, *Practical Tests in Evidence*, 4 Green Bag 510 (1892).)

Of course, there is nothing inherently wrong with evidence which is addressed to some sense other than that of hearing. One character in the musical *My Fair Lady* may have unwittingly summed up the attitude of many jury members when she said, "Words, words, words—I'm sick of words. Is that all you lawyers can do? *Show me!*" (Italics added.)

For a number of years now, trial lawyers have paid increasing attention to demonstrative evidence as a means of *showing* the elements of a case to the fact-finder.

Perhaps the earliest reported use of demonstrative evidence was in the *Case of James Watson, the elder, Surgeon, on an Indictment charging him with High Treason*, 32 Howard State Trials 1 (1817). There was offered into evidence in that case a sketch of a flag that allegedly had been used to whip up a "treasonous assemblage" in England. Defense counsel objected, arguing that the flag "was a matter of verbal description not of description by drawing." The trial judge sneered and overruled the objection: "Can there be any objection to the production of a drawing, or a model, as illustrative of evidence? Surely there is nothing in the objection."

Another leading case, this time arising in America but not many years after the Watson trial, is Commonwealth v. Webster, 5 Cush. 295 (Sup.Jud.Ct.Mass.1850). Professor Webster had been charged with murdering Doctor Parkman and burning his body in a furnace.

A mold of Doctor Parkman's jaw, made several years previously when he had been fitted for dentures, taken together with some teeth that had survived the furnace fire, was credited with securing Webster's conviction.

Today the propriety, in fact the wisdom, of using demonstrative evidence to help jurors follow the trial evidence goes pretty much without question in many cases, both criminal and civil. Objections to demonstrative evidence are frequently voiced, however.

B.

Bases for Objection to Demonstrative Evidence

Misguided Objections. Some objections to demonstrative evidence are misguided and will be swiftly overruled. Occasionally a lawyer will become confused about the proper application of the best evidence rule, discussed in [an earlier chapter], and contend that the "original," and not "a mere example," must be produced in court. Thus one hears about the Texas judge who prohibited the use of a skeletal model because it did not consist of the very bones of the complaining witness (who was not dead). This judge had forgotten, if he ever knew, that the best evidence rule applies only to written documents.

Then, too, one sometimes encounters a misguided hearsay objection to demonstrative evidence. Defense counsel leaps up to object to the prosecution's offer of a witness's freehand sketch of a crime scene, asking, "How can we cross-examine a sketch, Your Honor?" What this objection misses, of course, is the fact that the sketch is being offered as a part of the testimony of a witness on the stand who is fully subject to confrontation and cross-examination.

Objections Grounded on Lack of Verity or Accuracy. As was suggested in [an earlier chapter] * dealing with the perfecting of the trial record, a proper foundation or predicate must be laid before an item of demonstrative evidence can successfully be offered. The witness who is in a position to "sponsor" (authenticate) the exhibit must identify it and verify the verity, the accuracy of whatever it portrays. This does not mean that the sponsoring witness must be the person who took the photograph or prepared the drawing, chart, or map.

Example:

BY THE PROSECUTING ATTORNEY: Officer Ham, you have testified that you were present, in your investigative capacity, at the scene of the murders, isn't that correct?

A: That's right, I was in the room for maybe three hours.

Q: And you have testified to its general layout and appearance, have you not?

---
* See Chapter I, Evidence in Criminal Trials, supra.

A: I have.

Q: To your knowledge, were photographs of the room taken while you were there?

A: Yes, our photographer took a number of shots of the place.

Q: Officer Ham, I now hand you what previously has been marked Prosecution Exhibit 12 for Identification, being a photographic print, and ask you whether or not it is a fair and accurate representation of the room at 421 Melrose Street on the day in question?

A: Yes, sir, it is. That's exactly the way it looked.

BY THE PROSECUTING ATTORNEY: Your Honor, we offer prosecution's 12 into evidence.

BY DEFENSE COUNSEL: We have no objection.

THE COURT: The exhibit will be received.

There can be no stronger an objection to demonstrative evidence than that it is not a fair representation of what it supposedly depicts. If, for example, a photograph or map significantly distorts relevant aspects of the scene depicted, it will be subject to successful objection, or at least to an instruction that the jury is to disregard the distorted parts.

Occasionally photographs can be obtained only after autopsy procedures have in a sense distorted the picture of a deceased: the head has been shaved; large incisions have been made; sutures may be visible. Still, the tendency is to admit such photographs if they add to the case anything of real probative value. Thus in Young v. State, 299 P. 682 (S.Ct.Ariz.1931), the court, commenting on the receipt in evidence of post-autopsy photographs, said, "[T]he fact [of] the ghastly appearance of the wounds, even though such appearance was heightened by the shaving of the head and the use of mercurochrome * * * did not make [the photographs] inadmissible."

So long as the color has not been artificially and misleadingly heightened, there is a trend toward preferring natural color to black-and-white photographs. Some years ago Professor Conrad, an authority on photographic evidence, wrote, "[W]e have used black and white photographs for so long that we accept them as the real thing. Actually, black and white photography is considered an abstract medium and does not represent reality as such. * * * The inherent realism of color photography has been urged [as preferable to black and white]. * * *" (Conrad, *Evidential Aspects of Color Photography*, 4 Jour. of Forensic Science 176, 178 (1959).)

The fact that a photograph or other item of demonstrative evidence has been retouched or marked will not, in and of itself, result in inadmissibility. For example, in State v. Weston, 64 P.2d 536 (S. Ct.Ore.1937), plaster casts of a body containing gunshot wounds had been prepared prior to autopsy. Many small blue dots had been placed on the casts by a witness who compared the casts with the body in order to distinguish the bullet wounds from air bubbles in the plaster casts. When the casts were offered in evidence to exemplify the location of the bullet wounds, defense counsel objected that "after the blue dots which indicate the wounds had been placed upon the cast it was no longer * * * a true representation of deceased's forearm and hand." The Oregon Supreme Court laid down the applicable principles:

> The jury was amply informed that the sole purpose of the blue dots was to indicate the presence of the wounds. Since the jurors could rightfully look at the indications of the wounds, we cannot understand how the help which these small dots gave them in locating the wounds would have prejudiced any interest properly claimed by the defendant.
> * * *
>
> [W]e deduce the rule that maps, photographs et cetera, containing markings, are not inadmissible if they are otherwise relevant and if the individual who made the mark or wrote the legend was familiar with the facts and so testifies, or if some other witness, familiar with the facts, adopts the mark or legend as his own. (See also Busch, *Photographic Evidence*, 4 DePaul Law Rev. 195 (1955).)

Models are sometimes rejected by trial courts because they may be misleading or confusing due to difference in scale.

Example a.:

San Mateo County v. Christian, 71 P.2d 88 (Cal.App.1937) ("While models may frequently be of great assistance to a court and jury, it is common knowledge that, even when constructed to scale, they may frequently, because of the great disparity in size between the model and the original, also be very misleading. * * *").

Example b.:

Martindale v. City of Mountain View, 25 Cal.Rptr. 148 (Cal. App.1962) (in assault and battery case, testimony was that victim had been beaten with 2' stick; offer in evidence of axe handle 3' long rejected).

Courts are suspicious of filmed reenactments and posed photographs, lest they be misleading. A leading case, Richardson v. Missouri-K. T. R. Co. of Texas, 205 S.W.2d 819 (Tex.Civ.App.1947), arose on the civil side. To establish that the plaintiff himself had been negligent, the defendant introduced a color film showing plaintiff's shop foreman demonstrating how plaintiff's hand "*could* be caught and run through the blades" of a shaping machine (italics added). The foreman testified that "he did not know how the fingers of [plaintiff] were caught in the machine and therefore his experiments did not undertake to show how [plaintiff] was operating it at the time."

The Texas court brushed aside the plaintiff's objections to this filmed reenactment. "In the final analysis," the court said, "the increased danger of fraud peculiar to posed photographs must be weighed against their communicative value. Only the additional danger of fraud or suggestion separates this question from that of the admissibility of ordinary photographs."

In line with the *Richardson* decision, posed and photographed reenactments of a crime are sometimes admitted in evidence after a careful foundation, which manifests the accuracy of the reenactment, has been laid by the prosecuting attorney.

Gruesome Films and Photographs. Another prime basis of objections to demonstrative evidence is that the motion picture or still photograph is gruesome and inflammatory; in other words, that its potential for prejudice to the accused's right to a fair trial outweighs whatever probative worth it may have. An objection of this sort is directed to the trial judge's discretion.

A photograph or motion picture is not inadmissible simply because it is gruesome. That has been understood ever since the opinion in Franklin v. State, 69 Ga. 36 (S.Ct.Ga.1882), involving some gruesome photographs:

> The throat of the deceased was cut; the character of the wound was important * * * ; the man was killed and buried * * * ; we cannot conceive of a more impartial and truthful witness than the sun, as its light stamps and seals the similitude of the wound on the photograph put before the jury; it would be more accurate than the memory of witnesses, and as the object of all evidence is to show the truth, why should not this dumb [in the sense of mute] witness show it?

Ever since *Franklin* it has been the rule that photographs and films are not rendered inadmissible simply because they depict in a graphic way the details of a shocking or revolting crime. They will be deemed inadmissible only if they are irrelevant to the issues in the case or where their probative worth is outweighed by their potential for unfair prejudice.

Example a.:
    Johnson v. Commonwealth, 445 S.W.2d 704 (S.Ct.Ky.1970) (hideous photographs showing mangled body in morgue, *held*, admissible to support autopsy surgeon's explanatory testimony).

Example b.:
    Henninger v. State, 251 So.2d 862 (S.Ct.Fla.1971) (three gruesome photographs showing knife wounds in back, partially

severed head, and pantyhose wrapped around neck, *held*, admissible to establish identity of accused, cause of death, and to rebut claim of self-defense).

Appellate courts will conclude that it was an abuse of judicial discretion to receive gruesome photographs only when they were unnecessary, cumulative to the narrative testimony of witnesses, or where, although of minimal evidentiary value, they have been overemphasized to the jury. Thus it may be error to admit gruesome photographs when the testimony of an available pathologist would do just as well (see, e. g., State v. Bischert, 308 P.2d 969 (S.Ct.Mont. 1957)). In an early California case, Thrall v. Smiley, 9 Cal.Rep. 529 (S.Ct.Cal.1858), the court rejected drawings of the defendant's damaged teeth, noting that the sketches were not "necessary to illustrate the fact asserted [since] the extent of the injury could be as well understood from the statement of the dentist who repaired them." And projecting color slides of the deceased's wounds for a full half day during a four and one-half day trial has led to reversal. (Commonwealth v. Johnson, 167 A.2d 511 (S.Ct.Pa.1961).) Some additional examples are given below:

Example a.:
>Commonwealth v. Dankel, 301 A.2d 365 (S.Ct.Pa.1973) (where only factual dispute was whether accused aided in burglary during which a homicide occurred, introduction by prosecution of four gruesome photographs of victim, showing face eroded by ammonia burns, was reversible error).

Example b.:
>Terry v. State, 491 S.W.2d 161 (Tex.Crim.App.1973) (where bruises and other injuries sustained by infant homicide victim had already been shown with pre-autopsy photographs, it was prejudicial error to receive four post-autopsy photographs depicting massive mutilation to child caused by autopsy procedures).

Example c.:
>Beagles v. State, 273 So.2d 796 (Fla.App.1973) (where defense in first degree murder case admitted victim's death, the cause of death, and her identity, the admission of numerous gruesome color photographs of the victim was error: "Photographs should be received in evidence with great caution and photographs which show nothing more than a gory or gruesome portrayal should not be admitted.").

Trial judges will protect an accused against the use of demonstrative evidence the primary purpose of which is to whip jurors into a vindictive mood. But demonstrative evidence has a firmly settled place in criminal litigation. If it is used sparingly, with scrupulous accuracy, and only when it holds out genuine promise of making the case more readily understandable by judge and jurors, courts can be expected to be liberal in their rulings on the admissibility question.

COLLATERAL READINGS

Scientific and Demonstrative Evidence

Wigmore, Evidence (3rd ed. 1940)

    Vol. 2, §§ 410–418, 445–460

    Vol. 3, §§ 790–798(a), 997–999a

    Vol. 7, §§ 1991–2028

McCormick's Handbook of the Law of Evidence §§ 202–217 (2d 1972)

Houts, From Evidence to Proof (1956)

Louisell and Williams, Medical Malpractice ¶¶ 7.10–7.13 (1973)

Belli, Modern Trials, Vols. 2 & 3 (1954)

Scott, Photographic Evidence (1942)

Peckinpaugh & Beckham, Proper Role of Demonstrative Evidence, 1965 A.B.A.Sect.Ins.N. & C.L. 316

Lanhan, The Propriety of Demonstrative Evidence When Exploited by Trial Lawyers, 18 Ala.L.Rev. 447 (1966)

Cady, Objections to Demonstrative Evidence, 32 Mo.L.Rev. 333 (1967)

Field, Uses and Limitations of X-Ray Pictures as Evidence, 2 Forum 219 (1967)

Comment, Evolving Methods of Scientific Proof, 13 N.Y.L.F. 679 (1967)

Comment, The Evidentiary Uses of Neutron Activation Analysis, 59 Cal.L.Rev. 997 (1971)

Courtney, Effective Use of the Evidence Photographer, 17 Prac.Law 33 (1971)

Note, Evidence—Admissibility of the Neutron Activation Analysis Test, 18 St. Louis U.L.J. 235 (1973)

Coleman and Walls, Evaluation of Scientific Evidence, 1974 Crim. Law.Rev. 276 (1974)

Note, Beyond the Prima Facie Case in Employment Discrimination Law: Statistical Proof and Rebuttal, 89 Harv.L.Rev. 387 (1975)

Note, Voiceprint Dilemma: Should Voices Be Seen and Not Heard?, 35 Md.L.Rev. 267 (1975)

Chapter XI

THE EXCLUSIONARY RULE

MAPP v. OHIO

Supreme Court of the United States.
367 U.S. 643, 81 S.Ct. 1684, 6 L.Ed.2d 1081 (1961).

Mr. Justice CLARK delivered the opinion of the Court. * * *

On May 23, 1957, three Cleveland police officers arrived at appellant's residence in that city pursuant to information that "a person [was] hiding out in the home, who was wanted for questioning in connection with a recent bombing, and that there was a large amount of policy paraphernalia being hidden in the home." * * * Upon their arrival at that house, the officers knocked on the door and demanded entrance but appellant, after telephoning her attorney refused to admit them without a search warrant. They advised their headquarters of the situation and undertook a surveillance of the house.

The officers again sought entrance some three hours later when four or more additional officers arrived on the scene. When Miss Mapp did not come to the door immediately, at least one of the several doors to the house was forcibly opened and the policemen gained admittance. Meanwhile Miss Mapp's attorney arrived, but the officers, having secured their own entry, and continuing in their defiance of the law, would permit him neither to see Miss Mapp nor to enter the house. It appears that Miss Mapp was halfway down the stairs from the upper floor to the front door when the officers, in this high-handed manner, broke into the hall. She demanded to see the search warrant. A paper, claimed to be a warrant, was held up by one of the officers. She grabbed the "warrant" and placed it in her bosom. A struggle ensued in which the officers recovered the piece of paper and as a result of which they handcuffed appellant because she had been "belligerent" in resisting their official rescue of the "warrant" from her person. Running roughshod over appellant, a policeman "grabbed" her, "twisted [her] hand," and she "yelled [and] pleaded with him" because "it was hurting." Appellant, in handcuffs, was then forcibly taken upstairs to her bedroom where the officers searched a dresser, a chest of drawers, a closet and some suitcases. They also looked into a photo album and through personal papers belonging to the appellant. The search spread to the rest of the second floor including the child's bedroom, the living room, the kitchen and a dinette. The basement of the building and a trunk found therein were also searched. The obscene materials for possession of which she was ultimately convicted were discovered in the course of that widespread search.

At the trial no search warrant was produced by the prosecution, nor was the failure to produce one explained or accounted for. At best, "There is, in the record, considerable doubt as to whether there ever was any warrant for the search of defendant's home." * * *

* * * [T]his Court in Weeks v. United States, 232 U.S. 383, 34 S.Ct. 341, 58 L.Ed. 652 (1914), stated that

"the Fourth Amendment * * * put the courts of the United States and Federal officials, in the exercise of their power and authority, under limitations and restraints [and] * * * forever secure[d] the people, their persons, houses, papers and effects against all unreasonable searches and seizures under the guise of law * * * and the duty of giving to it force and effect is obligatory upon all entrusted under our Federal system with the enforcement of the laws." At pp. 391–392.

Specifically dealing with the use of the evidence unconstitutionally seized, the Court concluded:

"If letters and private documents can thus be seized and held and used in evidence against a citizen accused of an offense, the protection of the Fourth Amendment declaring his right to be secure against such searches and seizures is of no value, and, so far as those thus placed are concerned, might as well be stricken from the Constitution. The efforts of the courts and their officials to bring the guilty to punishment, praiseworthy as they are, are not to be aided by the sacrifice of those great principles established by years of endeavor and suffering which have resulted in their embodiment in the fundamental law of the land." At p. 393.
* * *

"The striking outcome of the *Weeks* case and those which followed it was the sweeping declaration that the Fourth Amendment, although not referring to or limiting the use of evidence in courts, really forbade its introduction if obtained by government officers through a violation of the Amendment." * * *

In 1949, 35 years after *Weeks* was announced, this Court, in Wolf v. Colorado, supra, again for the first time, discussed the effect of the Fourth Amendment upon the States through the operation of the Due Process Clause of the Fourteenth Amendment. It said:

"[W]e have no hesitation in saying that were a State affirmatively to sanction such police incursion into privacy it would run counter to the guaranty of the Fourteenth Amendment." * * *

Nevertheless, * * * the Court decided that the *Weeks* exclusionary rule would not then be imposed upon the States as "an essential ingredient of the right." * * * While in 1949, prior to the *Wolf* case, almost two-thirds of the States were opposed to the use of the exclusionary rule, now despite the *Wolf* case, more than half of those since passing upon it, by their own legislative or judicial decision, have wholly or partly adopted or adhered to the *Weeks* rule. * * * Significantly, among those now following the rule is California, which, according to its highest court, was "compelled to reach that conclusion because other remedies have completely failed to secure compliance with the constitutional provisions * * *."

* * *

Today we once again examine *Wolf's* constitutional documentation of the right to privacy free from unreasonable state intrusion, and, after its dozen years on our books, are led by it to close the only courtroom door remaining open to evidence secured by official lawlessness in flagrant abuse of that basic right, reserved to all persons as a specific guarantee against that very same unlawful conduct. We hold that all evidence obtained by searches and seizures in violation of the Constitution is, by that same authority, inadmissible in a state court.

Since the Fourth Amendment's right of privacy has been declared enforceable against the States through the Due Process Clause of the Fourteenth Amendment, it is enforceable against them by the same sanction of exclusion as is used against the Federal Government. Were it otherwise, then just as without the *Weeks* rule the assurance against unreasonable federal searches and seizures would be "a form of words," valueless and undeserving of mention in a perpetual charter of inestimable human liberties, so too, without that rule the freedom from state invasions of privacy would be so ephemeral and so neatly severed from its conceptual nexus with the freedom from all brutish means of coercing evidence as not to merit this Court's high regard as a freedom "implicit in the concept of ordered liberty." * * * In short, the admission of the new constitutional right by *Wolf* could not consistently tolerate denial of its most important constitutional privilege, namely, the exclusion of the evidence which an accused had been forced to give by reason of the unlawful seizure. To hold otherwise is to grant the right but in reality to withhold its privilege and enjoyment. Only last year the Court itself recognized that the purpose of the exclusionary rule "is to deter—to compel respect for the constitutional guaranty in the only effectively available way—by removing the incentive to disregard it."

* * *

There are those who say, as did Justice (then Judge) Cardozo, that under our constitutional exclusionary doctrine "[t]he criminal is to go free because the constable has blundered." * * * In some cases this will undoubtedly be the result. But, as was said, in *Elkins*, "there is another consideration—the imperative of judicial integrity." 364 U.S., at 222. The criminal goes free, if he must, but it is the law that sets him free. Nothing can destroy a government more quickly than its failure to observe its own laws, or worse, its disregard of the charter of its own existence. As Mr. Justice Brandeis, dissenting, said in Olmstead v. United States, 277 U.S. 438, 485, (1928): "Our Government is the potent, the omnipresent teacher. For good or for ill, it teaches the whole people by its example. * * * If the Government becomes a lawbreaker, it breeds contempt for law; it invites every man to become a law unto himself; it invites anarchy." Nor can it lightly be assumed that, as a practical matter, adoption of the exclusionary rule fetters law enforcement. * * *

The ignoble shortcut to conviction left open to the State tends to destroy the entire system of constitutional restraints on which the liberties of the people rest. Having once recognized that the right to privacy embodied in the Fourth Amendment is enforceable against the States, and that the right to be secure against rude invasions of privacy by state officers is, therefore, constitutional in origin, we can no longer permit that right to remain an empty promise. Because it is enforceable in the same manner and to like effect as other basic rights secured by the Due Process Clause, we can no longer permit it to be revocable at the whim of any police officer who, in the name of law enforcement itself, chooses to suspend its enjoyment. Our decision, founded on reason and truth, gives to the individual no more than that which the Constitution guarantees him, to the police officer no less than that to which honest law enforcement is entitled, and, to the courts, that judicial integrity so necessary in the true administration of justice.

The judgment of the Supreme Court of Ohio is reversed and the cause remanded for further proceedings not inconsistent with this opinion.

Reversed and remanded.

STONE v. POWELL

Supreme Court of the United States, 1976.
428 U.S. 465, 96 S.Ct. 3037, 49 L.Ed.2d 1067.

[The Supreme Court held that a state prisoner could not bring suit for habeas corpus relief in federal court on the ground that evidence used against him was obtained through illegal search and seizure if the state had provided a full and fair hearing on the fourth Amendment claim. The Court reasoned that the exclusionary rule was only one policy among many which the courts must consider in the administration of criminal justice.]

Mr. Justice POWELL delivered the opinion of the Court.

* * *

The exclusionary rule was a judically created means of effectuating the rights secured by the Fourth Amendment.

* * *

Decisions prior to *Mapp* advanced two principal reasons for application of the rule in federal trials. The Court in *Elkins,* for example, in the context of its special supervisory role over the lower federal courts, referred to the "imperative of judicial integrity," suggesting that exclusion of illegally seized evidence prevents contamination of the judicial process. * * * But even in that context a more pragmatic ground was emphasized:

> "The rule is calculated to prevent, not to repair. Its purpose is to deter—to compel respect for the constitutional guaranty in the only effectively available way—by removing the incentive to disregard it."

The *Mapp* majority justified the application of the rule to the States on several grounds, but relied principally upon the belief that exclusion would deter future unlawful police conduct. 367 U.S., at 658, 81 S.Ct. at 1693.

Although our decisions often have alluded to the "imperative of judicial integrity," * * * they demonstrate the limited role of this justification in the determination whether to apply the rule in a particular context. Logically extended this justification would require that courts exclude unconstitutionally seized evidence despite lack of objection by the defendant, or even over his assent. * * * It also would require abandonment of the standing limitations on who may object to the introduction of unconstitutionally seized evidence, * * * and retreat from the proposition that judicial proceedings need not abate when the defendant's person is unconstitutionally seized * * *. Similarly, the interest in promoting judicial integrity does not prevent the use of illegally seized evidence in grand jury proceedings. * * * Nor does it require that the trial court exclude such evidence from use for impeachment of a defendant, even though its introduction is certain to result in conviction in some cases. * * * The teaching of these cases is clear. While courts, of course, must ever be concerned with preserving the integrity of the judicial process, this concern has limited force as a justification for the exclusion of highly probative evidence. The force of this justification becomes minimal where federal habeas corpus relief is sought by a prisoner who previously has been afforded the opportunity for full and fair consideration of his search-and-seizure claim at trial and on direct review.

The primary justification for the exclusionary rule then is the deterrence of police conduct that violates Fourth Amendment rights. Post-*Mapp* decisions have established that the rule is not a personal constitutional right. It is not calculated to redress the injury to the privacy of the victim of the search or seizure, for any "[r]eparation comes too late." * * * Instead, "the rule is a judicially created remedy designed to safeguard Fourth Amendment rights generally through its deterrent effect * * *." * * *

* * *

Mapp involved the enforcement of the exclusionary rule at state trials and on direct review. The decision in *Kaufman,* as noted above, is premised on the view that implementation of the Fourth Amendment also requires the consideration of search-and-seizure claims upon collateral review of state convictions. But despite the broad deterrent purpose of the exclusionary rule, it has never been interpreted to proscribe the introduction of illegally seized evidence in all proceedings or against all persons. As in the case of any remedial device, "the application of the rule has been restricted to those areas where its remedial objectives are thought most efficaciously served." * * * Thus, our refusal to extend the exclusionary rule to grand jury proceedings was based on a balancing of the potential injury to the historic role and function of the grand jury by such extension against the potential contribution to the effectuation of the Fourth Amendment through deterrence of police misconduct:

"Any incremental deterrent effect which might be achieved by extending the rule to grand jury proceedings is uncertain at best. Whatever deterrence of police misconduct may result from the exclusion of illegally seized evidence from criminal trials, it is unrealistic to assume that application of the rule to grand jury proceedings would significantly further that goal. Such an extension would deter only police investigation consciously directed toward the discovery of evidence solely for use in a grand jury investigation. * * * We therefore decline to embrace a view that would achieve a speculative and undoubtedly minimal advance in the deterrence of police misconduct at the expense of substantially impeding the role of the grand jury."
* * *

The same pragmatic analysis of the exclusionary rule's usefulness in a particular context was evident earlier in *Walder* * * * where the Court permitted the Government to use unlawfully seized evidence to impeach the credibility of a defendant who had testified broadly in his own defense. The Court held, in effect, that the interests safeguarded by the exclusionary rule in that context were outweighed by the need to prevent perjury and to assure the integrity of the trial process. The judgment in *Walder* revealed most clearly that the policies behind the exclusionary rule are not absolute. Rather, they must be evaluated in light of competing policies. In that case, the public interest in determination of truth at trial was deemed to outweigh the incremental contribution that might have been made to the protection of Fourth Amendment values by application of the rule.

The balancing process at work in these cases also finds expression in the standing requirement. Standing to invoke the exclusionary rule has been found to exist only when the Government attempts to use illegally obtained evidence to incriminate the victim of the illegal search. * * * The standing requirement is premised on the view that the "additional benefits of extending the * * * rule" to defendants other than the victim of the search or seizure are outweighed by the "further encroachment upon the public interest in prosecuting those accused of crime and having them acquitted or convicted on the basis of all the evidence which exposes the truth."
* * *

* * *

In sum, we conclude that where the State has provided an opportunity for full and fair litigation of a Fourth Amendment claim, a state prisoner may not be granted federal habeas corpus relief on the ground that evidence obtained in an unconstitutional search or seizure was introduced at his trial. In this context the contribution of the exclusionary rule, if any, to the effectuation of the Fourth Amendment is minimal, and the substantial societal costs of application of the rule persist with special force.

Accordingly, the judgments of the Courts of Appeals are

Reversed.

Mr. Chief Justice BURGER, concurring.
* * *

I [previously] suggested that, despite its grave shortcomings, the rule need not be totally abandoned until some meaningful alternative could be developed to protect innocent persons aggrieved by police misconduct. With the passage of time, it now appears that the continued existence of the rule, as presently implemented, inhibits the development of rational alternatives. The reason is quite simple: incentives for developing new procedures or remedies will remain minimal or nonexistent so long as the exclusionary rule is retained in its present form.

It can no longer be assumed that other branches of government will act while judges cling to this Draconian, discredited device in its present absolutist form. Legislatures are unlikely to create statutory alternatives, or impose direct sanctions on errant police officers or on the public treasury by way of tort actions so long as persons who commit serious crimes continue to reap the enormous and undeserved benefits of the exclusionary rule. And of course, by definition the direct beneficiaries of this rule can be none but persons guilty of crimes. With this extraordinary "remedy" for Fourth Amendment violations, however slight, inadvertent or technical, legislatures might assume that nothing more should be done, even though a grave defect of the exclusionary rule is that it offers no relief whatever to victims of overzealous police work who never appear in court. And even if legislatures were inclined to experiment with alternative remedies, they have no assurance that the judicially created rule will be abolished or even modified in response to such legislative innovations. The unhappy result, as I see it, is that alternatives will inevitably be stymied by rigid adherence on our part to the exclusionary rule. I venture to predict that overruling this judicially contrived doctrine —or limiting its scope to egregious, bad-faith conduct—would inspire a surge of activity toward providing some kind of statutory remedy for persons injured by police mistakes or misconduct.

SILBERMAN, CRIMINAL VIOLENCE, CRIMINAL JUSTICE

Random House 262–264 (1978).*

By itself, the fact that proportionately more offenders are punished now than in the 1920s, or that fewer cases drop out of court, does not demonstrate that the courts are fulfilling their crime-control function in an adequate way. To assess the courts' performance, we need to know a lot more about the reasons for judges and prosecutors taking the actions they do. Why do prosecutors and judges dismiss all charges against one arrested felon in three? Why do prosecutors and judges permit another third to plead guilty to a misdemeanor, instead of being tried on the felony charges on which they were arrested? And why do judges sentence only about half of those who are convicted to time in jail or prison?

The most popular (and most enduring) explanation puts the blame on archaic procedures and excessive concern for the rights of defendants. "Our dangers do not lie in too little tenderness to the accused," Judge Learned Hand wrote in 1923. "Our procedure has been always haunted by the ghost of the innocent man convicted. It is an unreal dream. What we need to fear is the archaic formalism and watery sentiment that obstructs, delays, and defeats the prosecution of crime." More than a half-century later, President Gerald Ford echoed this sentiment. "For too long, law has centered its attention more on the rights of the criminal defendant than on the victim of crime," Ford told the Congress in 1975. "It is time for law to concern itself more with the rights of the people it exists to protect."

Arguments of this sort are rooted in ideological preferences rather than in empirical research. When the data are assembled and analyzed, it becomes clear that the pendulum has not swung too far. Only a handful of criminals go free or escape punishment because of exclusionary rules, search-and-seizure laws, collateral attacks or appeals, and other "technicalities" designed to protect defendants' rights. As part of their study of robbery in California, Floyd Feeney and Adrianne Weir analyzed what happened to a sample of 260 Oakland and Los Angeles robbery arrests. Not a single case was lost on

* Copyright 1978 by Charles E. Silberman.

"search-and-seizure" grounds; not a single case involved any serious legal issue involving interrogation; no evidence was excluded as a result of the Miranda rule, which requires policemen to inform suspects of their rights before questioning them; and not a single identification of a suspect was lost to the prosecution because of violation of the Supreme Court's rules governing identification of suspects in line-ups.

Nor are the Oakland data atypical in any way. "Many believe that offenders escape punishment because of 'technicalities' induced by Supreme Court rulings or because of unwarranted leniency of judges," Brian Forst and his colleagues at the Institute for Law and Social Research have written. After analyzing what happened to everyone arrested for a street crime, and why, over a six-year period, the INSLAW researchers found both beliefs to be untrue, concluding that "the public needs to discard its myths and begin to ask 'Why?'"

In New York City, the Vera Institute analyzed a sample of felony cases to determine why arrests did not stand up in court. The researchers found that exclusionary rules played no discernible role at all in the dismissal or reduction of charges in six of the seven offense categories—assault, rape, murder and attempted murder, robbery, burglary, and grand larceny—that were analyzed in depth.** And a Rand Corporation study of the prosecution of adult felony defendants in Los Angeles County, the largest prosecutor's office in the United States, found that only 3 percent of the burglary arrests were dismissed because of an illegal search and seizure, unlawful arrest, or other violation of defendants' rights; none of the burglary arrests were reduced to misdemeanors for those reasons.

The exclusionary rule seems unimportant in the Midwest as well. Of the 248 cases on the docket of the criminal court serving an Illinois county of 120,000 residents, 114 involved defendants who had made an oral or written admission to the police; yet only seven confessions were challenged, and only one challenge was sustained. (Two searches were also challenged, one of them successfully.)

** In addition to its "wide" sample of 1,888 cases selected to develop statistics on case mortality and disposition, the Vera researchers selected an additional probability sample of 369 cases that reached disposition in 1973. Researchers studied the files and interviewed the principal officials involved —policemen, prosecutors, defense attorneys, and judges—to determine the reasons for the decisions that were made in each of the cases in this "deep" sample. Because the cases in the deep sample were not weighted in the same way as those in the wide sample, the former is not a statistically valid subsample of the latter. From a substantive standpoint, however, the differences are so slight that the deep sample cases can be used with confidence to illustrate the reasons for the disposition patterns of the entire caseload. Moreover, a later sampling of 1976 court data indicated that the mix of cases and the way they were handled had not changed in the intervening years.

It is only in cases of so-called "victimless crimes" that any significant number of seemingly guilty offenders go free because tainted evidence—evidence acquired as a result of an illegal search, seizure, or arrest—is excluded from court; and even here, the number is considerably smaller than critics assume. In the Vera Institute sample, a number of gun possession cases *were* dismissed—but not because of search-and-seizure problems; the dismissals occurred because there was no evidence to connect the defendants with the guns (or, in one case, because there was no gun at all). Search-and-seizure problems did affect the outcome of some of the cases that remained, almost all of them involving defendants with minor records or none at all. Because the prosecutors themselves had doubts about the legality of the searches or arrests that uncovered the guns, they accepted guilty pleas to a misdemeanor count, preferring the certainty of a misdemeanor conviction to the possibility that the case would be dismissed altogether if it went to trial.

Search-and-seizure problems play a larger role in drug cases, especially those where the defendant is charged with possession of a drug. Large numbers of drug arrests are made; in the Rand Corporation study of the prosecution of adult felons in Los Angeles, more than a third of the felony arrests were on drug charges, most of them for possession of marijuana, heroin, and other narcotics, and dangerous drugs ("uppers" and "downers"). The prosecutor rejected over 40 percent of the arrests, either through outright dismissal or reduction to a misdemeanor. In the case of arrests for possession of dangerous drugs, most of the rejections were due to insufficient evidence (32 percent) or trivial or insufficient quantity of contraband (40 percent). Search-and-seizure problems, illegal arrests, and other violations of defendants' rights accounted for only 17.5 percent of the overall rejections, and 25 percent of the outright dismissals.

KAPLAN, THE LIMITS OF THE EXCLUSIONARY RULE

26 Stanford Law Review 1027, 1050–1052 (1974).

For those who are wedded to the present rule, and even more for those who would expand it, any restriction would be a retreat in the face of the enemy, a cutting back when it is most necessary to hold firm. A cutting back of the exclusionary rule, however, can also be regarded as a pruning, a method of making it more acceptable and hence more lasting; it is indeed a method of giving more, not less, protection to fourth amendment values.

The modification I would suggest in the exclusionary rule is related to the controversy over police department behavior. There is no doubt that a major defect in the exclusionary rule is its neglect of the basic sociological principle that organizations mediate individual action. The exclusionary rule, which appears to be focused upon the misbehavior of the individual policeman, does not take into account the fact that the policeman approaches his job with departmental expectations, with his own departmental training, either official or unofficial, and with the fear of departmental discipline for improper conduct. These departmental rewards and sanctions are far more important to him than the threat of exclusion of any evidence he might illegally seize. Before the introduction of the exclusionary rule, one might have predicted that a police department angered by the exclusion of evidence in a particular case would move against the offending officer, or at least take seriously training him to make certain that the illegality did not occur again. Apparently, this a priori assumption has been falsified by experience under the rule. Instead of disciplining their employees, police departments generally have adopted the attitude that the courts cannot be satisfied, that the rules are hopelessly complicated and subject to change, and that the suppression of evidence is the courts' problem and not the departments'.

The focus of the exclusionary rule, therefore, should be changed so that its application is directed against the police department itself, as well as against the misbehavior of the individual police officer. The police hierarchies, more than the courts, have the initial responsibility for protecting fourth amendment values. The exclusionary rule is a step of last resort, an attempt by the courts to enforce the fourth amendment when the police departments have proven unwilling to do the job.

The proposed modification, therefore, is to hold the exclusionary rule inapplicable to cases where the police department in question has taken seriously its responsibility to adhere to the fourth amendment. Specifically, departmental compliance would require a set of published regulations giving guidance to police officers as to proper behavior in situations such as the one under litigation, a training program calculated to make violations of fourth amendment rights isolated occurrences, and, perhaps most importantly, a history of taking disciplinary action where such violations are brought to its attention.

Such a modification of the rule would require a somewhat more elaborate procedure at the suppression hearing. First, the judge would make a finding whether the defendant's fourth amendment rights had been violated. If the judge decided that no violation had occurred, the evidence would be admitted, subject only to appeal. On the other hand, if the judge found a search and seizure unconstitutional, he would not automatically exclude the evidence obtained. Rather, he would announce his decision and give the prosecutor an opportunity to make the next move. At this point the prosecutor would be permitted, and would have every incentive, to ask the judge for a further hearing on the police department's regulations, training programs, and disciplinary history. Presumably, the hearing on such a motion need not be very lengthy, for generally the records of the police department would settle all the factual issues.

The burden of proof would be placed on the prosecution to show that the police complied with its standards. This allocation does not force the defendant to discover police records. It also makes the task of appellate review easier. A trial judge cannot hold a police department in compliance simply because he does not believe a defendant. Rather, he must check to see whether the department's evidence proves its case. Indeed, the major difficulty in such hearings would not be factfinding but rather drawing standards defining sufficient departmental behavior. Yet one of the major advantages of this suggested procedure is its flexibility. At first, relatively modest beginnings might be accepted. After all, at present police departments need not do anything to protect fourth amendment rights. And, in fact, they generally have not done so. Gradually, judges could require greater showings: more particular regulations; discipline not only where a suppression hearing had determined that a citizen's rights had been violated, but also where successful civil rights actions had been brought against the offending policeman; and finally, perhaps, the establishment of some fair method of processing citizen complaints which had not been the subject of any litigation. One significant aspect of such a progression would be that for the first time the exclusionary rule could be used to protect the rights of the law-abiding citizen rather than those of the criminal.

If such a rule were to be adopted today, probably no police department could meet even modest standards. As a result, judges would continue applying the current exclusionary rule. Gradually, at least some departments, perhaps under pressure from district attorneys, newspapers, and the public, would begin to investigate and discipline offending police officers. Very soon prosecutors and defense attorneys would begin to keep files of results of suppression hearings involving various police departments, and both parties would have strong incentives to investigate whether the departments had altered their practices in an attempt to make unnecessary the sanctions of the exclusionary rule. In cases involving those departments which developed more effective systems of self-regulation, prosecutors would begin making, and courts begin granting, motions to exempt particular illegal searches and seizures from the exclusionary rule. Some police departments would be held to have measured up to the appropriate standards and hence have their occasional illegal searches not subject to the exclusionary rule, while others would still be subject to it. The difference could hardly fail to be noticed, and would act as a spur to the laggards. When some departments have reached an accommodation with the courts it will be hard for others to claim that the courts' demands are unreasonable. And the complaint that the courts are turning loose criminals becomes much less impressive when it is obvious that a well-run department can prevent this result.

Chapter XII

EYEWITNESS IDENTIFICATION

PEOPLE v. HORODECKI

Supreme Court of Illinois, 1958.
15 Ill.2d 130, 154 N.E.2d 67.

HOUSE, Justice. The defendant, Albert Horodecki, was tried before a jury in the criminal court of Cook County on an indictment charging him and two others with armed robbery in a tavern on West Sixty-third Street in the city of Chicago on May 13, 1947. The court entered judgment on the jury's verdict of guilty and sentenced him to a term of not less than 25 nor more than 40 years in the penitentiary. A writ of error was issued to review this judgment and sentence.

Defendant's principal contention for reversal is that the evidence was insufficient to prove him guilty beyond a reasonable doubt in that there was no unimpeachable identification of him as one of the three men who perpetrated the crime. He argues that the witnesses identified him only after seeing him in court as the person charged with the crime; that he was never picked out of a line-up of other persons; that the proprietor was influenced by seeing his picture in the newspaper and being told by the police that he had committed the robbery; and that the other witnesses had not recognized the newspaper picture nor given a description of him to the police. There is no dispute as to what took place at the time of the robbery since the defendant's defense was that of an alibi. The facts surrounding the robbery are important only to the extent that they add credence to the witnesses' identification of the defendant.

About 10:00 P.M. three men entered the tavern, ordered beers and were served by the proprietor. About 10:30 P.M., after four card players left the tavern, one of the trio drew a gun and announced the robbery. A second man vaulted over the bar, led the proprietor to the cash register made him place his hands on the bar and began taking the money from the cash register. The third man, who was later identified as the defendant, took his position at one end of the bar, leaning on the counter on his left elbow and keeping his right hand in his jacket pocket. He wore a grey hat and an army field jacket with slash pockets, and maintained his station at the bar during the entire time the robbery was taking place, 20 to 30 minutes.

One of the men went through the wallets and handbags of the seven patrons sitting at the bar. The proprietor's wife, who had come into the bar to bid the patrons goodnight, fainted when she learned that the three men were engaged in a robbery. One of the lady patrons was given permission by the man standing at the end of the bar to assist her. When the proprietor's wife recovered she asked the same man if she could go into the back rooms to see about her children, and she and the lady giving first aid were granted permission to do so.

In the meantime, the man who remained at the bar was asked by one of the patrons to leave them enough money for a drink whereupon he graciously ordered "beers for everybody." When the men left they admonished their victims, "Don't nobody call the police or come out right away."

The trio was in the tavern about one hour with the robbery taking approximately twenty to thirty minutes of that time. The tavern was lighted by a 24-inch fluorescent light in the ceiling, another light about six feet from the entrance door, two window lights and a clock light. The man who remained at the bar was face to face with the proprietor, the proprietor's wife and one of the lady patrons, and there was nothing to prevent his being observed by the other patrons.

During the trial the proprietor, his wife and three of the patrons identified the defendant as being the man who stood at the end of the bar. A sixth witness testified that the defendant resembled the man but she could not be sure. The other witness was unable to identify the defendant. On cross-examination the proprietor admitted that he had seen a picture of the defendant in the newspaper and was later told by the police that this was one of the men who robbed his tavern. All the witnesses admitted that they had not been called upon to pick the defendant out of a line-up of other persons, and the first time they were called upon to identify him was in the court room at the time of the first trial of the case. One of the identifying witnesses also admitted that at the first trial he had pointed out one of the jurors as the robber rather than the defendant. Defendant's identification argument is not persuasive when considered in the light of the positive identification of the defendant by five eyewitnesses. The testimony of these witnesses coincides on nearly every detail comprising the *res gesta* of the crime. Each of them had ample opportunity to observe the defendant during a robbery lasting from 20 to 30 minutes, conducted in a calm business-like manner, in a lighted public tavern, by a trio who not only made no attempt to disguise their identity but issued orders, conversed with the patrons, and ordered drinks "on the house."

This court is cognizant of the power of suggestion which may be exercised by police officials over witnesses when they present a person they have arrested as the perpetrator of the crime charged. Our courts must remain ever alert to detect such methods and protect those accused of crimes from becoming victims of mistaken identity. We are aware, also, that an opportunity for a witness to view a suspect within a group of other people, if conducted under proper safeguards, would considerably strengthen the proof of identity offered at the trial of the cause. However, the failure to do so does not render the identification incompetent, * * * nor detract from the essential requirement that a person charged with a crime must ultimately be identified in a court of proper jurisdiction by competent evidence beyond a reasonable doubt pursuant to constitutional safeguards. It was for the jury to weigh the testimony and determine the credibility of the several witnesses. * * *

There was ample evidence from which the jury could conclude that the defendant was one of the participants in the robbery.

The defendant testified in his own behalf, denying that he had committed any crime, stating that he was at home with his wife and children on the night of the robbery. Four character witnesses testified to his good character and reputation during the time they had known him. There are corroborating circumstances which militate against his alibi. He left the State soon after the crime. The defendant testified that he went to Los Angeles, California, eight days after the robbery, but stated that it was for the purpose of making his home there. However, during the eighteen months he lived in California he went under the name of Albert Kasbruk and his wife and two children remained in Chicago. Moreover a prior murder conviction record was introduced to impeach his credibility. We are of the opinion that there was sufficient competent evidence presented to the jury to support their verdict of guilty. * * *

Defendant next contends that the trial court erred in failing to grant the defendant a new trial because an instruction relating to identification, which had been marked "given" by the court, was not read to the jury. The instruction stated, in substance, that in determining whether or not the identifying witnesses were mistaken the jury had a right to consider the lapse of time between the date of the crime and the occasion when the witnesses first saw the defendant, together with the circumstances existing during both occasions and from all the circumstances in evidence it was for the jury to determine whether or not the witnesses were mistaken. He argues that the failure to give this instruction denied him the opportunity to have the jury charged as to his theory of the case.

Identification of the defendant was one of the material issues of fact presented to the jury. The refusal to give any instruction on the issue of identification would have constituted reversible error, * * * but it is not error if the instructions, considered as a series, fully and fairly announce the law applicable to the theory of the respective parties and do not ignore or nullify the defendant's theory that the jury should consider the circumstances of the identification to determine if the witnesses were mistaken. * * *

A review of the instructions shows the jury was instructed on the credibility of the witnesses; on the opportunities of the witnesses for knowing the things about which they testified; on their interest, if any, in the result of the trial; on the probability or improbability of the truth of the testimony; on the extent to which any witness was contradicted or corroborated by other credible evidence; that they should not be influenced by anything other than the law and the evidence in the case; that the surrounding circumstances might influence witnesses seeking to identify a person charged with a crime; that if the jury had a reasonable doubt of the defendant's presence when and where the crime was committed they should should give him the benefit of the doubt; and that the identification of the person under arrest brought alone before the identifying witnesses is not to be given the same weight and credibility as where the witnesses picked out the accused person from among other persons unknown to the witness. From this resumé of the instructions given, it appears that the jury was adequately instructed concerning defendant's theory of the case, and in the light of all the evidence he could not have been prejudiced by the failure of the trial court to give his instruction.

* * * We find that the trial was fairly conducted, that the defendant was ably represented, and that there was sufficient evidence to support the jury's verdict of guilty.

The judgment of the criminal court of Cook County is affirmed.

Judgment affirmed.

AMSTERDAM, SEGAL AND MILLER, TRIAL MANUAL 3 FOR THE DEFENSE OF CRIMINAL CASES § 36

(1977).[*]

[36]. **Same—protection against lineups and showups.** (A) A defendant in police custody is in danger not only of being interrogated but also of being exhibited to possible eyewitnesses for the purpose of identification as the perpetrator of the crime for which he was arrested or of other crimes. Counsel who reaches an in-custody client by telephone must therefore advise him how to respond to lineup or other identification procedures. It is presently unclear to what extent the police can lawfully compel an unwilling accused to submit to identification confrontations in the absence of counsel. * * * The client should accordingly be advised to object to any lineup, showup, or confrontation for identification unless his lawyer is present; to tell the police that he refuses to appear in a lineup or showup or to be viewed by any witness without his lawyer being there; and, if any sort of confrontation is going to be held, to ask permission to telephone his lawyer first. The client should also be told to say to the police that he refuses to speak in any lineup or showup, and then to say nothing if he is forced into a lineup or showup and told to speak or is asked questions, even his name. He should be told, however, not

---

[*] Copyright 1978 by The American Law Institute. Reprinted with the permission of The American Law Institute-American Bar Association Committee on Continuing Professional Education.

to resist physically if the police should order him into a lineup or identification situation; not to disobey police instructions to go up on a lineup stage, or to step forward or walk about on the stage, or refuse any other police orders to move about in the presence of identifying witnesses; and not to cover his face or make faces. These latter tactics will only direct attention to the client and enhance the likelihood of a positive identification; they may also be used against him as evidence of guilt; and physical resistance to the officers may result in a beating or the lodging of additional charges. If the client learns that he is being taken to a lineup room, he should orally object to the absence of counsel, but he should not do a sitdown or physically refuse to go, since such action will often result in the witnesses' being brought back to him for a cellblock showup—a far more suggestive form of confrontation that the lineup itself. If he is told that he is being taken for a showup, he should insist, *first*, that his lawyer be present, and *second*, that a lineup with other persons resembling himself be held. Once in a lineup or identification confrontation, he should be told to observe and remember everything about it that he can, particularly (a) how many other men were in the lineup, how they were dressed, and what they looked like (getting their names, before the lineup if possible without attracting attention to himself, or afterwards if he later sees the men around the cell area); (b) how many witnesses were asked for identifications, what they said, what the officers said to them, who they were or what they looked like; (c) how many police officers were present, and their names, numbers and descriptions; and (d) the time and place of the lineup. * * * The client should not, of course, attempt to take notes during the lineup or in any place where he may be observed by the witnesses to the lineup; but he should write down everything that he can remember as soon as he returns to his cell.

(B) Counsel should also specifically demand, when speaking to the investigating officer, that his client not be shown in a lineup or exposed for identification in his absence and should ask the officers (a) whether there is any plan to hold a lineup or identification with the client; (b) if so, when and where; and (c) if not, to telephone counsel if the police later decide to hold a lineup or identification of any sort. Should the police indicate that they may proceed to conduct an identification confrontation in counsel's absence, counsel should insist, *first*, that the client not be displayed except in a lineup of persons resembling him, and, *second*, that the names of all subjects in the lineup, all witnesses brought to observe it, and all officers present at the lineup or who bring witnesses or subjects to it be recorded and preserved, together with sufficient information to enable these people to be located.

(C) The most effective protection against station house identifications, of course, is for counsel to arrange the defendant's release, as rapidly as possible, by *habeas corpus* or on bail. * * * If *habeas* is unavailable and bail cannot be set or posted quickly, counsel is well advised to go to the police station and to stay there with the defendant so that counsel can be present at any attempts to identify his client. He can in this way obtain firsthand knowledge of both the fairness of the police procedures and the circumstances of alleged identifications. * * *

FISHMAN AND LOFTUS, EXPERT PSYCHOLOGICAL TESTIMONY ON EYEWITNESS IDENTIFICATION *

I. *Introduction*

Eyewitness identification in criminal cases has long been recognized by social scientists and legal practitioners as having a high potential for error. The legal and psychological literature is replete with accounts of the factors which affect the reliability of an eyewitness account. Numerous examples of mistaken identification have been documented. In a startling depiction of the seriousness of the situation, Professor Borchard describes the criminal prosecutions and convictions of sixty-five persons:

> These cases illustrate the fact that the emotional balance of the victim or eyewitness is so disturbed by his extraordinary experience that his powers of perception become distorted and his identification is frequently most untrustworthy. Into the identification enter other motives, not necessarily stimulated originally by the accused personally—the desire to requite a crime, to exact vengeance upon the person believed guilty, to find a scapegoat, to support, consciously or unconsciously, an identification already made by another. Thus doubts are resolved against the accused. How valueless are these identifications by the victim of a crime is indicated by the fact that in eight of these cases the wrongfully accused person and the really guilty criminal bore not the slightest resemblance to each other, whereas in twelve other cases, the resemblance, while fair, was still not at all close.

The problems inherent in eyewitness testimony have been confronted squarely by the judicial establishment of Great Britain. Astonished by the recent pardons of two individuals who had been independently convicted on the basis of erroneous identifications, the Home Secretary appointed a committee to investigate this area of criminal law and police procedure. The committee, chaired by Lord Devlin, made the following recommendations:

> The trial judge should be required by statute
>
> a. to direct the jury that it is not safe to convict upon eyewitness evidence unless the circumstances of the identifi-

* Copyright 1978 by Elizabeth Loftus.

cation are exceptional or the eyewitness evidence is supported by substantial evidence of another sort; and

    b. to indicate to the jury the circumstances, if any, which they might regard as exceptional and the evidence, if any, which they might regard as supporting the identification; and

    c. if he is unable to indicate either such circumstances or such evidence, to direct the jury to return a verdict of not guilty.

The English experience suggests that members of the legal profession are beginning not only to understand the hazards involved with eyewitness testimony, but they are also beginning to respond to those hazards. Laypersons, however, have given every indication that they do not have this understanding. Most people continue to place great faith in an eyewitness account, even one that is weak. Nowhere has this point been made more dramatically than in the report of a recent psychological experiment on the impact a single eyewitness can have in the courtroom. One hundred and fifty subjects acted as jurors in a criminal trial. They received a written description of a grocery store robbery in which the owner and his granddaughter were killed. In addition, they received a summary of the evidence and arguments presented at the defendant's trial. Their task was to arrive at a verdict. Fifty of the jurors were informed that a few pieces of circumstantial evidence were presented against the defendant. Only 18% of these found the defendant guilty. Fifty different jurors were given the same set of facts with one additional piece of evidence: a store clerk's eyewitness identification. Of these, 72% judged the defendant to be guilty. A third group of jurors was given the additional item of information that the eyewitness had vision poorer than 20/400 and had not been wearing his glasses on the day of the robbery. Still, 68% of the jurors who heard about the discredited witness voted for conviction. The case law reveals that not only jurors, but many judges, lawyers and police personnel continue to view an eyewitness identification as the most concrete and convincing form of evidence.

Experts in the field of psychology are currently being asked to offer testimony in court on the factors which affect the accuracy of the eyewitness account. This testimony is designed to educate juries on the problems inherent in eyewitness identification. Courts holding against the admissibility of such testimony do not properly take into account a substantial body of psychological research. This article will suggest a manner in which the courts might better analyze the question of admissibility of such psychological testimony by using a more rational application of standards of admissibility and review. Although California cases and statutes are discussed, the ideas and principles in the article are applicable in all jurisdictions.

II. The Nature of Human Perception and Memory

Psychological research indicates that when we experience an event we do not simply record that event in memory as would a videotape recorder. Rather, we store bits and pieces of information gleaned from the original perception depending on our particular abilities, background, attitudes, and motives. Our recollection is based upon information from many different sources. These include the original perception of the event, knowledge acquired prior to the event, and inferences drawn *after* the event. In the time between an event and our recollection of it, information from these sources becomes integrated so that we are unable to identify the source of knowledge of any particular detail. Rather, we experience a single "memory." Recent experiments have demonstrated that both individual visual experiences and individual verbal experiences can become integrated to form a new memory representation that corresponds to something different from that which was actually experienced.

III. Factors Affecting the Reliability of Identification

Psychological research has isolated a number of factors which influence the accuracy and completeness of an eyewitness account of a particular event. The determinants can be divided into two groups: (1) those inherent in the event and (2) those inherent in the witness.

(A) Factors Inherent in the Event

An analysis of the "retention interval" factor serves to illuminate the process by which psychologists study eyewitness identification. The retention interval is the time interval between an experience and a subsequent test for recollection of that experience. It is well established that recollections are less accurate and less complete after a long retention interval than after a short one. Ebbinghaus' classic experiment on remembering nonsense syllables is perhaps the most often cited study which documents the loss of retention with the lapse of time. In his experiment, Ebbinghaus learned lists of nonsense syllables, neglected them for a certain period of time, and then relearned them. He recorded the savings in numbers of readings necessary for relearning. A typical "curve of forgetting," which plots performance against the retention interval, is negatively accelerated downward. This means one forgets very rapidly immediately after an event, but subsequently the forgetting becomes more and more gradual.

The phenomenon represented by Ebbinghaus' forgetting curve has been confirmed in subsequent research with different types of subjects and different materials remembered. In 1913, for example, Dallenbach reached the same result with pictorial materials. In his study, male students were asked to look at a picture and, after a certain interval of time, answer a set of sixty questions about the picture. After answering each question, the students indicated whether they would be prepared to take an oath as to its accuracy or whether they were only moderately certain about the answer. Dallenbach found that the length of the retention interval affected both the average number of wrong answers as well as the average number of wrong answers that were sworn to.

These data are shown in the following table:

Number of days since experience	0	5	15	45
Average number of wrong answers	8	10	12	13
Average number of wrong answers sworn to	3	4	6	7

More recently, Shepard tested thirty-four clerical workers for recognition of pictures after intervals of two hours, three days, one week, and four months. Shepard found that retention of the pictorial material dropped from 100% correct recognition after a two-hour delay to only 57% correct recognition after four months. (Note that if the subject simply guessed he would have been correct 50% of the time by chance.)

Finally, in a study conducted by Buckhout, 141 students witnessed a staged assault on a professor. Seven weeks later they were asked to pick out the assailant from a group of six photographs. Although the episode had been a dramatic one, only 40% of the witnesses chose the right man. While this was not strictly a "retention interval" experiment (only one interval was used), it was significant because it resembled the more common process of photographic identification.

Other factors inherent in the identification situation affect the reliability of the eyewitness account. For example, significant events appear to be remembered better than insignificant ones. This phenomenon is important since, in placing someone at or near the scene of a crime, witnesses are often asked to recall seeing the accused at a time when they were not attaching any particular significance to the event. Another determinant of reliability is length of observation time. The longer a witness has to look at something, the better he will remember it. Fleeting glimpses are common in eyewitness accounts, particularly in fast-moving, threatening situations. Events that occur between an incident and a witness' statement about that incident can affect memory. Subjects exposed to misleading details frequently report that they have witnessed those details when questioned later. Once a witness has made a statement, he tends to adhere to it, and the more often he repeats it, the less likely he is to change it. Relatively unexplored factors which are thought to influence the reliability of the eyewitness report include the atmopshere of the interview and the authority of the interviewer.

(B) Factors Inherent in the Witness

One recurring factor in criminal identification is stress. Psychological research has shown that, in general extreme stress in an identification situation results in less reliable testimony. Others have found that not only is the witness more susceptible to suggestion under stressful circumstances, but the tendency for an individual to isolate himself from the occurrence leads to a narrowing in the range of incoming information such that one's attention is directed at the source of the stress to the exclusion of the surrounding stimuli. Thus, a witness accosted by a man with a gun may remember every detail of the gun but little of the man's face.

Another recurring circumstance in criminal identification is that of cross-racial identification. The psychological literature clearly indicates the lack of reliability of such testimony compared with identification of persons of the same race. Related to the variable of expectancy are those studies which reveal the effect of biases or prejudices on the accuracy of the eyewitness report. In a classic study of this phenomenon, subjects looked briefly at a drawing of several people on a subway train, among whom were depicted a white man standing with a razor in his hand and a black man. Fifty percent of the subjects later reported that the razor was in the hand of the black man. Findings with respect to other factors inherent in the witness are more controversial. Among those are the age and sex of the witness as well as his relative state of self-confidence.

IV. *The Phenomenon of Unconscious Transference*

Unconscious transference is the term used to describe the phenomenon by which an otherwise insignificant event, occurring immediately before or after a significant event may, upon recall, become merged with the more significant event. One consequence is that, upon recollection, one could confuse the face of a person seen in an insignificant event with that of a person involved in a subsequent significant event. Wall provides an excellent demonstrative example: A ticket agent in a railroad station was held up at gun point. Subsequently, the agent recognized a sailor in a line-up as the guilty party. The sailor had a good alibi, however, and was eventually released from custody. When later interviewed in an attempt to determine why he had misidentified the sailor, the ticket agent said that when he saw the sailor in the line-up his face looked familiar. As it happened, the sailor's base was near the railroad station and on three occasions prior to the robbery he had purchased tickets from the agent. Apparently, the ticket agent mistakenly assumed that the familiarity was based on the robbery when it was actually based on the three times the sailor bought train tickets.

Unconscious transference may have occurred in an experiment in which students witnessed a staged assault on a professor, and seven weeks later, were asked to identify the assailant from a group of six photographs. Forty percent of the subjects chose the actual assailant; the other 60% either failed to make any identification or chose the wrong man. Of the five photographs that did not depict the assailant, one was a photograph of an individual who had been at the scene of the crime, but who was an innocent bystander. If the tendency to identify the bystander was no greater than the tendency to identify one of the other non-assailants, then 20% of those who made a misidentification should have identified the bystander. In fact, 41% identified the innocent bystander. This result may be the consequence of a type of unconscious transference in which a person who is at the scene of the crime is confused with the person who committed the crime. However, it is also possible that when the witness made a mistake, the bystander was identified most often because he looked most like the assailant. The design of the study, unfortunately, does not permit the elimination of this possibility.

Another experiment indicates that people tend to misidentify a face seen in another context as that of a criminal. In this experiment, fifty subjects were presented, via tape recorder, a story concerning six fictitious college students. The introduction of each character was accompanied by a photograph of that character, which was shown for approximately two seconds. Only pictures of white males with medium length brown hair were used. After three days the subjects attempted to identify the criminal in the story from a set of five photographs presented to them. For one-half of the subjects, the criminal's face was included in the set of photographs. For the remaining subjects, the criminal's face was not among the photographs, but the face of an incidental character was included. The experiment was designed so that a particular photograph was the criminal for some subjects, and an incidental character was the criminal for other subjects. Still another group of subjects were tested with an identification set that did not include the face of the criminal. If the tendency to choose the incidental character was no greater than the tendency to choose one of the other non-criminals, then 20% of those who made a selection should have chosen the incidental character. In fact, 79% of those making a selection chose the incidental character.

The problem with unconscious transference is that in any given case it is nearly impossible to tell whether it has occurred or not. A witness says the defendant committed the crime. The defendant says he did not, but admits he was at the scene of the crime, either at the time of the crime or on a prior occasion. Without other information, one cannot prove whether or not unconscious transference has taken place. All that can be done is to distinguish between the conditions under which unconscious transference could and could not have taken place.

V. *The Role of the Psychologist*

Although one can often determine whether or not a particular factor was operating at the time of the crucial incident, he cannot be certain whether the factor actually distorted the original memory in a way that rendered the testimony erroneous. For example, it can be shown that a cross-racial identification took place, that the witness was particularly fearful, and that these factors affect memory, but it cannot be said that because these factors were present, the eyewitness testimony was necessarily erroneous.

Herein lies the role of the psychologist. His testimony is designed to give the jury additional information to use when assessing the credibility of a particular witness. His testimony does not indicate whether or not any particular witness is telling the truth. It is limited to describing the aforementioned scientific phenomena by way of citing literature and experiments in the field of psychology and to indicating the extent to which such phenomena might have affected an eyewitness identification in the case.

VI. *The Judicial Response*

Three recent California appellate decisions are representative of the cases holding that testimony of psychologists regarding the credibility of particular witnesses is inadmissible. In each case, the court dismissed defendants' contention that the trial judge had abused his discretion in refusing to allow psychological testimony on the effects of certain factors on the reliability of the identification. Unfortunately, these decisions focused on the possible usurpation of the jury's function of determining the weight and credibility of the witness's testimony and not on any standard of admissibility under applicable law.

Viewing this area of law through the prism of these few appellate reports is not completely satisfactory, for two reasons. First, it may be a bit misleading. There are many cases in which such testimony has been admitted by the trial court. Many of these cases did not reach the appellate level, since acquittals cannot be appealed. Second, none of these decisions offers any meaningful guidelines for the trial judge whose task is to weigh the factors involved in each case in determining whether or not such testimony should be admitted.

In People v. Johnson, defendants were convicted of first degree murder, robbery, and assault with a deadly weapon arising out of a liquor store hold-up. One defendant was identified by a customer in the store and the other by the store clerk. At the trial the prosecution produced no physical evidence identifying defendants as the robbers. Not only were two other suspects taken into custody and identified by a passerby as having been seen running from the store, but one of these suspects was also identified by the customer as one of the robbers. Defendants' offer of expert testimony by a psychologist on the effects of excitement and fear on the ability of witnesses to accurately perceive, recall and relate was rejected by the trial court, which declared in part:

> The evidence should be examined with a view to preserving the integrity of the jury as the finder of facts: expert opinion is admitted in this area in order to inform the jury of the effect of a certain medical condition upon the ability of the witness to tell the truth—not in order to decide for the jury whether the witness was or was not telling the truth on a particular occasion.

The Court ruled that the trial court's determination that such testimony would usurp the jury's task of determining the weight and credibility of the witness's testimony was well within the permissible range of discretion.

People v. Guzman also involved robbery and murder. Again defendant was identified as the robber by a store clerk. Defendant attempted to present the expert testimony of a psychologist concerning certain factors involved in the identification situation, specifically, the effects of the emotional state of the witness and the exposure time of the incident on the reliability of the identification. The expert was also to have testified on the phenomenon of unconscious transference. The trial court's refusal to admit such testimony was upheld by the appellate court.

> The good judgment of the trial judge as to whether the particular case contains such unusual factors as to make the "expert testimony" a help to jury determination or whether the case is one where the effect of such testimony threatens to take over the jury's function must control in the absence of a clear abuse of discretion.

In People v. Brooks, defendant was identified as having shot and killed a waitress during the course of an attempted robbery of a restaurant. Again, defendant's offer of psychological testimony tending to indicate the unreliability of the identification was refused by the trial court. The appellate court affirmed the trial court's ruling, quoting language in *Johnson* to the effect that such practice "would take over the jury's task of determining the weight and credibility of the witness's testimony."

VII. *Standard of Admissibility and Review Under California Evidence Law*

Although most cases do not clearly articulate the principles by which a determination should be made on the admissibility of expert testimony, the law under the California Evidence Code is fairly clear and representative of the general view. Under the Code, the opinion testimony of experts is subject to two restrictions: (1) The testimony must be "related to a subject that is sufficiently beyond common experience for the opinion of an expert to be of assistance to the trier of fact" and (2) must be "based on matter * * * that is of a type that reasonably may be relied upon by an expert in forming an opinion upon the subject to which his testimony relates. * * *"

In the cases mentioned above, the courts never reached the second consideration. These decisions indicate a belief that the subject matter of the testimony is within the range of common experience of the trier of fact. The *Johnson* court quotes with approval the suggestion of the court in People v. Russell that "the expert witness may be in no better position to evaluate credibility than the jurors." Likewise, the *Guzman* court quotes the trial judge to the effect that "it is not a matter that the jury needs expert testimony regarding. It is something that everyone knows about, the problems of identification." Although it has been held that, in determining whether or not expert testimony should be admitted, much must be left to the discretion of the trial judge, a court on appeal may review certain questions raised by the trial court's exercise of discretion. In reviewing the respective lower court decisions, the appellate court decisions under consideration here are arguably deficient in that: (1) they fail to take into account the trend in California towards acceptance of psychological testimony, (2) they fail to realize the special impact of their rulings on criminal defendants with no other grounds of defense, (3) they appear to be based on a standard which does not conform with applicable evidence law, and, as already mentioned, (4) they offer no guidelines for the trial judge's exercise of discretion in the matter.

* * *

Conclusion

In light of the substantial body of psychological research which has established the unreliability of eyewitness identification under certain circumstances, and in view of the gravity of the situation in which an innocent person is convicted of a crime, there appears to be no reasonable justification for excluding expert psychological testimony relating to the reliability of eyewitness identification. As long as juries are kept unaware of the dangers inherent in eyewitness identification, the burden of blame for the resulting miscarriages of justice will weigh heavily on those who have the power to expose and thus minimize those dangers.

MANSON v. BRAITHWAITE

Supreme Court of the United States, 1977.
432 U.S. 98, 97 S.Ct. 2243, 53 L.Ed.2d 140.

Mr. Justice BLACKMUN delivered the opinion of the Court.

[After purchasing heroin in an apartment, Glover, an undercover state police officer, left the building and reported to a back-up officer outside (Detective D'Onofrio), giving him a general description of the seller: "a colored man, approximately five feet eleven inches tall, dark complexion, black hair, short Afro style, and having high cheekbones, and of heavy build. * * *" On the basis of this description, D'Onofrio thought that respondent might be the seller. He obtained a single photograph of respondent from the police records division and left it at Glover's office. Two days after the sale occurred, Glover, while alone, viewed the photograph of respondent and identified it as a photograph of the seller. Respondent was not arrested until almost three months later. At the trial, Glover testified to the photographic identification and also made an in-court identification of respondent, who was sitting at the defense counsel table. The prosecution conceded that the exhibition of the single photograph was "suggestive" and "unnecessarily so" because no exigent circumstances prevented D'Onofrio from assembling a suitable array of photographs from the many fitting Glover's description of the seller that were available in police files. On federal habeas corpus, the * * * lower court held because the showing of the single photograph was unnecessarily suggestive evidence pertaining to it should have been excluded, regardless of reliability, and that the identification was unreliable in any event.]

* * * [R]espondent, in agreement with the Court of Appeals, proposes a *per se* rule of exclusion that he claims is dictated by the demands of the Fourteenth Amendment's guarantee of due process. He rightly observes that this is the first case in which this Court has had occasion to rule upon strictly post-*Stovall* out-of-court identification evidence of the challenged kind.

Since the decision in *Biggers*, the courts of appeals appear to have developed at least two approaches to such evidence. The first, or *per se* approach, employed by the Second Circuit in the present case, focuses on the procedures employed and requires exclusion of the out-of-court identification evidence, without regard to reliability, whenever it has been obtained through unnecessarily suggested confrontation procedures. The justifications advanced are the elimination of evidence of uncertain reliability, deterrence of the police and prosecutors, and the stated "fair assurance against the awful risks of mis-identification."

The second, or more lenient, approach is one that continues to rely on the totality of the circumstances. It permits the admission of the confrontation evidence if, despite the suggestive aspect, the out-of-court identification possesses certain features of reliability. Its adherents feel that the *per se* approach is not mandated by [the Constitution]. This second approach, in contrast to the other, is *ad hoc* and serves to limit the societal costs imposed by a sanction that excludes relevant evidence from consideration and evaluation by the trier of fact. * * *

The respondent here stresses [the] need for deterrence of improper identification practice, a factor he regards as preeminent. Photographic identification, it is said, continues to be needlessly employed. * * * He argues that a totality rule cannot be expected to have a significant deterrent impact; only a strict rule of exclusion will have direct and immediate impact on law enforcement agents. Identification evidence is so convincing to the jury that sweeping exclusionary rules are required. Fairness of the trial is threatened by suggestive confrontation evidence, and thus, it is said, an exclusionary rule has an established constitutional predicate.

There are, of course, several interests to be considered and taken into account. * * * *Wade* and its companion cases reflect the concern that the jury not hear eyewitness testimony unless that evidence has aspects of reliability. It must be observed that both approaches before us are responsive to this concern. The *per se* rule, however, goes too far since its application automatically and peremptorily, and without consideration of alleviating factors, keeps evidence from the jury that is reliable and relevant.

The second factor is deterrence. Although the *per se* approach has the more significant deterrent effect, the totality approach also has an influence on police behavior. The police will guard against unnecessarily suggestive procedures under the totality rule, as well as the *per se* one, for fear that their actions will lead to the exclusion of identifications as unreliable.

The third factor is the effect on the administration of justice. Here the *per se* approach suffers serious drawbacks. Since it denies the trier reliable evidence, it may result, on occasion, in the guilty going free. Also, because of its rigidity, the *per se* approach may make error by the trial judge more likely than the totality approach. And in those cases in which the admission of identification evidence is error under the *per se* approach but not under the totality approach—cases in which the identification is reliable despite an unnecessarily suggestive identification procedure—reversal is a draconian sanction. Certainly, inflexible rules of exclusion, that may frustrate rather than promote justice, have not been viewed recently by this Court with unlimited enthusiasm. * * *

We therefore conclude that reliability is the linchpin in determining the admissibility of identification testimony for both pre- and post-*Stovall* confrontations. The factors to be considered are set out in *Biggers*. These include the opportunity of the witness to view the criminal at the time of the crime, the witness' degree of attention, the accuracy of his prior description of the criminal, the level of certainty demonstrated at the confrontation, and the time between the crime and the confrontation. Against these factors is to be weighed the corrupting effect of the suggestive identification itself.

We turn, then, to the facts of this case and apply the analysis:

1. The opportunity to view. Glover testified that for two to three minutes he stood at the apartment door, within two feet of the respondent. The door opened twice, and each time the man stood at the door. The moments passed, the conversation took place, and payment was made. Glover looked directly at his vendor. It was near sunset, to be sure, but the sun had not yet set, so it was not dark or even dusk or twilight. Natural light from outside entered the hallway through a window. There was natural light, as well, from inside the apartment.

2. The degree of attention. Glover was not a casual or passing observer, as is so often the case with eyewitness identification. Trooper Glover was a trained police officer on duty—and specialized and dangerous duty—when he called at the [apartment where he purchased the heroin]. Glover himself was a Negro and unlikely to perceive only general features of "hundreds of Hartford black males," as the Court of Appeals stated. It is true that Glover's duty was that of ferreting out narcotics offenders and that he would be expected in his work to produce results. But it is also true that, as a specially trained, assigned, and experienced officer, he could be expected to pay scrupulous attention to detail, for he knew that subsequently he would have to find and arrest his vendor. In addition, he knew that his claimed observations would be subject later to close scrutiny and examination at any trial.

3. The accuracy of the description. Glover's description was given to D'Onofrio within minutes after the transaction. It included the vendor's race, his height, his build, the color and style of his hair, and the high cheekbone facial feature. * * * No claim has been made that respondent did not possess the physical characteristics so described. D'Onofrio reacted positively at once. Two days later, when Glover was alone, he viewed the photograph D'Onofrio produced and identified its subject as the narcotics seller.

4. The witness' level of certainty. There is no dispute that the photograph in question was that of respondent. Glover, in response to a question whether the photograph was that of the person from whom he made the purchase, testified: "There is no question whatsoever." This positive assurance was repeated.

5. The time between the crime and the confrontation. Glover's description of his vendor was given to D'Onofrio within minutes of the crime. The photographic identification took place only two days

later. We do not have here the passage of weeks or months between the crime and the viewing of the photograph.

These indicators of Glover's ability to make an accurate identification are hardly outweighed by the corrupting effect of the challenged identification itself. Although identifications arising from single-photograph displays may be viewed in general with suspicion, we find in the instant case little pressure on the witness to acquiesce in the suggestion that such a display entails. D'Onofrio had left the photograph at Glover's office and was not present when Glover first viewed it two days after the event. There thus was little urgency and Glover could view the photograph at his leisure. And since Glover examined the photograph alone, there was no coercive pressure to make an identification arising from the presence of another. The identification was made in circumstances allowing care and reflection.

Although it plays no part in our analysis, all this assurance as to the reliability of the identification is hardly undermined by the facts that respondent was arrested in the very apartment where the sale had taken place, and that he acknowledged his frequent visits to that apartment.

Surely, we cannot say that under all the circumstances of this case there is "a very substantial likelihood of irreparable misidentification." * * * Short of that point, such evidence is for the jury to weigh. We are content to rely upon the good sense and judgment of American juries, for evidence with some element of untrustworthiness is customary grist for the jury mill. Juries are not so susceptible that they cannot measure intelligently the weight of identification testimony that has some questionable feature.

Of course, it would have been better had D'Onofrio presented Glover with a photographic array including "so far as practicable * * * a reasonable number of persons similar to any person then suspected whose likeness is included in the array." Model Code of Pre-Arraignment Procedure § 160.2(2) (1975). The use of that procedure would have enhanced the force of the identification at trial and would have avoided the risk that the evidence would be excluded as unreliable. But we are not disposed to view D'Onofrio's failure as one of constitutional dimension to be enforced by a rigorous and unbending exclusionary rule. The defect, if there be one, goes to weight and not to substance.

We conclude that the criteria laid down in *Biggers* are to be applied in determining the admissibility of evidence offered by the prosecution concerning a post-*Stovall* identification, and that those criteria are satisfactorily met and complied with here.

The judgment of the Court of Appeals is reversed.

* * *

Mr. Justice STEVENS, concurring.

While I join the Court's opinion, I would emphasize two points.

First, as I indicated in my opinion in United States ex rel. Kirby v. Sturges the arguments in favor of fashioning new rules to minimize the danger of convicting the innocent on the basis of unreliable eyewitness testimony carry substantial force. Nevertheless, for the reasons stated in that opinion, as well as those stated by the Court today, I am persuaded that this rulemaking function can be performed "more effectively by the legislative process than by a somewhat clumsy judicial fiat," and that the Federal Constitution does not foreclose experimentation by the States in the development of such rules.

Second, in evaluating the admissibility of particular identification testimony it is sometimes difficult to put other evidence of guilt entirely to one side. Mr. Justice Blackmun's opinion for the Court carefully avoids this pitfall and correctly relies only on appropriate indicia of the reliability of the identification itself. Although I consider the factual question in this case extremely close, I am persuaded that the Court has resolved it properly.

DEPARTMENTAL GENERAL ORDER 67–9 OAKLAND POLICE DEPARTMENT

PRISONER SHOW-UPS

The purpose of this order is to state Departmental policy and procedures for conducting prisoner show-ups in order to promote fairness, eliminate witness suggestion, and document the proceedings for use in court.

I. *Planning a Show-up*
   A. Whenever a police investigator desires to conduct a show-up, he shall:
      1. Contact complainants and witnesses by telephone and determine mutually convenient date and time for the show-up. Inform each person contacted that they are to view a show-up but do not advise them that a person in the show-up is believed responsible for the crime.
      2. Determine if the subject has an attorney by asking him or by inquiring at the Jail Division.
      3. If the subject does not have an attorney, conduct the show-up at the scheduled date and time.
      4. If the subject has an attorney, notify the attorney that a show-up will be held. Give him the scheduled date and time, and request him to attend.

       a. If the attorney is unable to attend at the scheduled date and time, request that he ask substitute counsel to attend.
       b. If subsitute counsel cannot attend or none is available, determine if a more convenient time can be arranged.
       c. If the attorney cannot attend and a more convenient time cannot be arranged, advise him that the show-up will be conducted as originally scheduled and that it will be held in accordance with this Department's policy and procedures which are based upon existing law.

   5. Inform all persons contacted and requested to attend the show-up that it will be conducted at the Police Administration Building, Room 239, Second Floor, 455 Seventh Street, Oakland.

II. *Conducting a Show-up*
   A. The investigator shall conduct all show-ups as follows:
      1. Notify the Jail Division watch supervisor at least two hours before the scheduled time of the show-up whenever it is practical to do so.
      2. Furnish the Jail Division watch supervisor with the name of the subject or subjects under investigation and ascertain (if previously not known) whether the subject has secured legal counsel. If the subject has secured legal counsel, notify the attorney as stated in Part I, A, 4.
      3. Go to the Jail Division 15 minutes prior to the scheduled show-up time and obtain the key to the outer security door leading to the show-up room. Return the key immediately upon completion of the show-up.
      4. Establish security at the main entrance to the show-up room to insure that unauthorized persons are not permitted to enter. There shall always be not less than two police officers present at all show-ups and adequate security shall be maintained at all times. If the investigator believes that there is a possibility that any of the subjects in the show-up may attempt flight, the investigator shall inform his immediate supervisor who in turn shall assign additional officers to maintain maximum security during the show-up.

5. The investigator conducting the show-up shall show a copy of this order to any defense attorney immediately upon his arrival at the show-up room. Attorneys shall be requested to refrain from asking questions during the show-up proceedings; should they have any questions, the investigator will answer them after the subjects have left the show-up room.

6. If an attorney has any objections regarding the proceedings, he shall be referred to the investigator's superior officer. If the investigator's superior officers are not on duty at the time, the attorney shall be referred to the Patrol Division watch commander.

7. Upon their arrival at the show-up room, witnesses and complainants shall be separated and given the following directions before the show-up begins. The directions shall be given in the presence of any attorney in attendance if he so requests:

   a. The witnesses and complainants are not to point at a subject if they identify him or her as the responsible person.

   b. They shall not speak to anyone in the room except when the investigator asks questions of them.

   c. They shall not nod their heads or make other body motions indicating that a particular subject is identified.

   d. All subjects in the show-up line will be referred to by number, with number 1 being on the left of the show-up line, as viewed by the audience.

8. After all witnesses and complainants have been seated and instructed, unlock the outer security door leading to the show-up corridor and determine that the subjects are present.

9. Advise the participants of the show-up that if they are directed to speak for voice identification, make some physical motion, or wear articles of clothing or glasses and they refuse to comply, the right to remain silent under the 5th Amendment (as per Miranda vs. Arizona) does not include the right to refuse to participate in such a test, that refusal to speak or wear such articles may be considered as evidence of consciousness of guilt and may be ad-

mitted into evidence should they become a defendant in a subsequent trial.

10. Return to the show-up room. Turn off the main lights and turn on the stage lights.

11. Instruct the subjects of the show-up to walk onto the stage in the pre-arranged order and form a rank facing the audience. Point to the first subject (the first on the left) and state in a loud voice so that all witnesses and complainants can hear, "You are standing in position #1." Continue orally numbering each position until all subjects have been numbered.

12. Instruct all of the subjects to face the left wall first, then the right wall, then the rear wall, then the audience.

13. Instruct each subject, in numerical sequence, to step from his place in the show-up, walk the full length of the stage and then return to his position in the line.

14. If words were used by the suspect in a crime, direct each subject, in numerical sequence, to step forward and repeat the same words.

15. Whenever articles of clothing or glasses were worn during the commission of the offense, direct each subject in turn to wear such articles.

16. Upon completion of the show-up, direct all subjects into the corridor between the Jail and the show-up room, having them maintain their predetermined positions in line.

17. Ask each viewer if he wants the show-up subjects to perform any other actions, such as speaking other words or making other physical motions.

   a. If there are such requests, return the show-up line to the stage in the same predetermined order and have them perform the requested action.

18. Upon completion of the above procedures, direct the assigned Jailer to take photographs of the show-up line.

19. Return all subjects to the custody of the Jailer, who shall wait in the corridor for the completed Identification Line-Up Form.

20. Interview each witness and complainant separately and in the presence of the subject's attorney in attendance, if he so requests.

a. Record any information relating to identification on the Identification Line-Up Form (536–425), indicating the name of the witness or complainant giving such information. Do not allow the viewers themselves to make notes of their observations regarding identification and do not take a formal statement from them.

21. Sign the Identification Line-Up Form (536–425) that was furnished by the assigned Jailer. In the "Remarks" section, enter any special requests by viewers for the show-up subjects to perform, such as additional movements, other physical actions or words. Distribute copies of this form as follows:

   a. 1st copy: file in case jacket.

   b. 2nd copy: give to the Jailer assigned to take photographs.

   c. 3rd copy: return to the assigned Jailer accompanying the inmates.

III. *Jail Division Responsibilities*

   A. Upon notification by an investigator that a show-up is to be conducted, the Jail Division watch supervisor shall:

   1. Cause the Security Section watch jailer to assemble the person or persons named as the subject under investigation and provide additional inmates for the show-up.

      a. There shall be a minimum of five other inmates selected to participate in the show-up. Therefore, if there is one subject, the show-up shall consist of six persons. If there are two subjects, the show-up shall consist of seven persons, etc.

      b. The other inmates provided for the show-up shall be closely similar in type, particularly in age, height, weight, race, complexion, physical peculiarities and dress.

   2. Notify the investigator who ordered the show-up whenever there are not enough inmates of similar appearance available. The investigator shall then contact the Patrol Division or other Departmental units to obtain police officers to stand in the show-up line.

   3. Detail a Jailer to accompany the inmates to the show-up room.

4. Detail another Jailer to be present at the show-up for the purpose of taking a minimum of two photographs of the show-up.
5. Insure that the second copy of the Identification Line-Up Form (536–425) accompanied the exposed negatives to the Identification Section for processing and for filing in the identification jacket of the subject under investigation.
6. Insure that the copy of the Identification Line-Up Form (536–425) is returned by the assigned Jailer at the completion of the show-up and filed in the Jail Division main office.

B. Upon assignment by the Jail Division watch supervisor to accompany inmates to the show-up, the assigned Jailer shall:

1. Prepare three copies of the Identification Line-Up Form as a record of the show-up.
2. Arrange the order of appearance of the inmates. Positioning shall be by random selection. Each inmate, beginning with the subject or subjects under investigation, shall draw a 3 x 5 card with a number which corresponds to their order of appearance from the position assignment box.
3. Remain in the show-up room while the show-up is in progress to provide additional security.
4. Return all inmates to their respective cells and dormitories after the show-up is completed.
5. Return one copy of the completed Identification Line-Up Form to the Jail Division watch supervisor.

C. Upon assignment by the Jail Division watch supervisor to take photographs of the show-up, the assigned Jailer shall:

1. Remain in the show-up room during the show-up for security purposes.
2. Take a minimum of two photographs of the show-up, as they appeared to the viewers, when directed to do so by the investigator.
3. Attach the second copy of the Identification Line-Up Form (536–425) to the exposed negatives and forward to the Identification Section for processing.

INDEX

References are to Pages

ADMISSIBILITY OF EVIDENCE
Admissibility, defined, 5
Competency, 9
Criminal defendant's statements,
    Impeachment purposes only, 373–374
    Privilege against self-incrimination, 364–370
Exclusionary rule, 491–502
    Balancing, 496–497
    Habeas corpus, 494–497
    Proposed modification, 500–502
    Shortcomings, discussion of, 497–500
    Standing, 497
Eyewitness identification,
    Approaches to exclusion,
        Totality of circumstances, 517–521
        Unnecessarily suggestive confrontation procedures, 517–521
Federal Rules of Evidence,
    Limited admissibility, 53
Limited admissibility, 53
Materiality, 8
Probativeness, 8–9
Problems with,
    Jury-protection argument, 5
    Wasting of time, 5
Weight of, 9–10

ADMISSIONS
    Generally, 146–157
Co-conspirators, by, 154–156
Conduct, by, 152–154
Elements, 147
False exculpatory statements, 154
Federal Rules of Evidence, 148
Flight, 153
Important exception, 146–147
Silence, by, 149–152

ADVERSARY TRIAL SYSTEM
Characteristics, 2–3
Evidence and, 1–5
Fact, questions of, 4
Judge's role, 3
Law, propositions of, 4
Lawyer's role, 3–4
Unscientific, 2

ALCOHOL
See Scientific Evidence, Intoxication and drugs, tests for

ATTORNEY
See Adversary Trial System, Lawyer's role; Privileges, Attorney-client

ATTORNEY-CLIENT PRIVILEGE
See Privileges

AUTHENTICATION
See Real Evidence

BEST EVIDENCE RULE
See Real Evidence

BLOOD TESTS
See Scientific Evidence, Intoxication and drugs, tests for

BREATH TESTS
See Scientific Evidence, Intoxication and drugs, tests for

BURDEN OF PROOF
    See also Presumptions
    Generally, 15–26
Beyond a reasonable doubt,
    Defined, 20
    Discussed, 15–19
    Juvenile proceeding, 15–18
    Quantitative terms, not expressed in, 18–19
Preponderance of the evidence,
    Arguments against, 17–18

BUSINESS AND PUBLIC RECORDS
    See also Hearsay, Exceptions
    Generally, 202–212
Federal Rules of Evidence, 211–212
Police reports, 203–211

CANONS OF ETHICS
Confidentiality, 310
    See Privileges, Attorney-client
Helping client to commit or conceal crime, 321–327
History, 309–310

CHARACTER EVIDENCE
See also Relevancy, Crimes, evidence of other
Generally, 57–99
Cross-examination of defendant's character witness, 73–77
Defendant's character,
    Bad character, inadmissibility of, 57–61
      See also Relevancy, Crimes, evidence of other
    Cross-examination of defendant's character witness, 73–77
    Good character, 61–72
      Community reputation, 63, 68
      Relevance requirement, 62
      Types of evidence 62–63, 69–72
Defendant's right to use, 61–86
Federal Rules of Evidence, 72, 81, 82–83
Methods of proving character,
    Past conduct, specific instances of, 63, '69–70
    Reputation vs. opinion, 63, 68, 70–72
Rape cases, 80–81, 82–86
Victim's character, 77–86

CIRCUMSTANTIAL EVIDENCE
See also Character Evidence
Corpus delicti, 33–37
Direct, compared, 5–7
False exculpatory statements, 154
Flight, 153

CO-CONSPIRATORS
See Admissions

COMPROMISE
See Relevancy

CONFRONTATION CLAUSE OF SIXTH AMENDMENT
See Hearsay

CORPUS DELICTI
Circumstantial evidence, proof by, 33–37

CREDIBILITY OF WITNESS
See Witnesses, Impeachment

CRIMES, EVIDENCE OF OTHER
See Relevancy

CRIMINAL DISCOVERY
See Self-Incrimination, Privilege Against

CROSS-EXAMINATION
See Witnesses

DECLARATIONS AGAINST INTEREST
Generally, 172–176
Federal Rules of Evidence, 172–176
Penal interest, 173–174
Trustworthiness, 174–176

DEMONSTRATIVE EVIDENCE
See Real Evidence

DIRECT EXAMINATION
See Witnesses

DOCTORS
See Privileges, Physician-patient

DRUGS
See Scientific Evidence; Witnesses, Impeachment

DYING DECLARATIONS
Generally, 163–166
Federal Rules of Evidence, 163

ETHICS
See Canons of Ethics

EVIDENCE
Adversary system and, 1–5
Forms of,
    Judicially noticed, 7–8
    Tangible, 7
    Tangible-testimonial, 7
    Testimonial, 7
Probability,
    See Relevancy, "Mathematical" relevance
Proper use of admitted evidence, 4–5
Sources of the law of,
    Case law, 1–2
    Codes, 1–2
Statistics,
    See Relevancy, "Mathemetical" relevance
Types of,
    Direct, 5–6
    Indirect or circumstantial, 6–7

EVIDENCE RULES
See Federal Rules of Evidence

EXCITED UTTERANCE
See also Spontaneous and Contemporaneous Declarations
Federal Rules of Evidence, 167, 171

EXCLUSIONARY RULE
See Admissibility of Evidence

EXECUTIVE PRIVILEGE
See Governmental Privileges, State secrets

INDEX

References are to Pages

EXPERT WITNESSES
See Opinion Testimony

EYEWITNESS IDENTIFICATION
Generally, 503–526
Exclusion, approaches to,
  Totality of circumstances, 517–521
  Unnecessarily suggestive confrontation procedures, 517–521
Expert psychological testimony on, 508–516
Lineup,
  Failure to conduct, 503–506
  Protection against, 506–508
  Suggested procedures, 521–526
Photographs,
  Exhibition of single photograph, 517–521

FEDERAL RULES OF CRIMINAL PROCEDURE
Pleas, offers of pleas, and related statements, 102–105

FEDERAL RULES OF EVIDENCE
Admissibility,
  Limited, 53
Authentication or identification, 408–410
Best evidence (requirement of original), 425–427
Business and public records, 211–212
Character,
  Admissibility of character evidence, 81
  Methods of proving, 72
  Rape cases, 82–83
Cross-examination, scope of, 247–248
Excited utterance, 171
Experts,
  Bases of opinion testimony, 447
  Court appointed, 448
  Disclosure of underlying facts or data. 448, 449
  Testimony by, 447
Hearsay,
  Admission by party-opponent, 148
  Defined, 120
  Dying declarations, 163
  Exclusions, 113
  Existing mental, emotional or physical condition, 176
  Former testimony, 157
  General rule, 121
  Hearsay within hearsay, 206
  Judgment of previous conviction, 214
  Other exceptions, 216, 219
  Present sense impression, 171
  Prior identification, 188–193

FEDERAL RULES OF EVIDENCE—Cont'd
Hearsay—Cont'd
  Prior statement by witness, 281–282, 283–284
  Recorded recollection, 201
  Statement, defined, 129
  Statement against interest, 172–176
Impeachment,
  Conviction of a crime, 258–262, 266–267
  Prior inconsistent statement of witness, 283
  Specific instances of conduct, 257–258
Interrogation and presentation, mode and order of, 238–239, 247–248
Judicial notice of adjudicative facts, 12, 15
Lack of personal knowledge, 447
Leading questions, 239
Opinion on ultimate issue, 447
Pleas, plea discussions and related statements, 100
Presumptions in criminal cases, 22–23
Relevancy, 31, 52–53, 55, 56
Source of law of evidence, as, 1
Writing used to refresh memory, 201

FORMER TESTIMONY
Generally, 157–163
Federal Rules of Evidence, 157
Unavailability, 159–161
Video tape, 161–163

GOVERNMENTAL PRIVILEGES
Generally, 382–406
Informers, disclosure of identity, 388–405
  California Evidence Code, 392–394
  Dismissal of action for failure to disclose, 401–403
  Legality of securing evidence, 401
  Material witness, 404–405
  Testimony helpful to an accused, 400–401, 403
  Voluntary disclosure, 400
  Who may claim the privilege, 399–400
State secrets, 382–388
  California Evidence Code, 382

HEARSAY
See also Admissions; Declarations Against Interest; Dying Declarations; Federal Rules of Evidence; Former Testimony; Past Recollection Recorded; Prior Identification; Spontaneous and Contemporaneous Declarations; State of Mind
Generally, 109–234

References are to Pages

HEARSAY—Cont'd
Admission,
    Not Hearsay under Federal Rules of Evidence, 148
Assertive documentary evidence, 124
Belief, as, 114–115
Bloodhounds, 131–136
Conduct,
    Assertive, 137
    Non-assertive, 137–141
Confession of third party, 110–113
Confrontation clause of 6th Amendment, 221–223
Declarant's knowledge, evidence limited to issue of, 123, 124
Defendant's right to present evidence, 223–231
Definitions, 113, 120
Effect of statement upon another person, purpose to show, 122–123, 124, 125–126
Exceptions, 146–214
    See also specific exceptions detailed in separate topics
    Admissions, 146–157
    "Ancient" documents, 213
    Business and public records, 202–212
    Commercial and scientific publications, 213
    Declarations against interest, 172–176
    Dying declarations, 163–166
    Family history, reputation regarding, 213–214
    Family records, 213
    Former testimony, 157–163
    Marriage certificates, 213
    Past recollection recorded, 197–201
    Prior convictions, 212–213
    Prior identification, 188–196
    Reputation as to character, 214
    Spontaneous and contemporaneous declarations, 166–171
    State of mind, 176–187
    Vital statistics, 213
Federal Rules of Evidence,
    Business and public records, 211–212
    Definitions,
        Declarant, 120
        Hearsay, 120
        Statement, 129
    Dying declarations, 163
    Exclusions, 113
    Existing mental, emotional or physical condition, 176
    Former testimony, 157
    General rule, 121

HEARSAY—Cont'd
Federal Rules of Evidence—Cont'd
    Hearsay within hearsay, 206
    Judgment of previous conviction, 214
    Other exceptions, 216, 219
    Prior identification, 188–193
    Recorded recollection, 201
    Statement against interest, 172–176
Future of, 215–231
Hearsay within hearsay, 206
History, 109–110, 116
Independent legal significance, 121, 124
Law school examination, 142–145, 232–234
Lessening the restrictions on admissibility, 215–221
Non-hearsay out-of-court statements, 121–129
Non-human evidence, 129–136
Radar, 129–130
Rationale and meaning, 109–146
Statement, 129–141
Testimonial triangle, 117–120
Three-part process, 114
Truth of statement, purpose to show, 122, 125
Types, 114

HYPOTHETICAL QUESTION
See Opinion Testimony, Expert witnesses

IDENTIFICATION
See Eyewitness Identification

IMPEACHMENT
See Witnesses

INCOMPETENT
See Admissibility of Evidence, Competency

INFERENCE
See Presumptions

INFORMERS
See Governmental Privileges

INTERROGATION PRIOR TO TRIAL
See Self-Incrimination, Privilege Against

JOURNALISTS
See Privileges

JUDICIAL NOTICE
    Generally, 7–8, 11–15
    Adjudicative facts, 15
    Conclusiveness, 11–12
    Defined, 11
    Value, of, 12–14

INDEX

References are to Pages

JUVENILE PROCEEDING
See Burden of Proof, Beyond a reasonable doubt

LAW SCHOOL EXAMINATION
Hearsay, on, 142–145, 232–234

LAY WITNESSES
See Opinion Testimony

LEADING QUESTIONS
See Witnesses

LIE DETECTOR TESTS
See Scientific Evidence

LINEUP
See Eyewitness Identification

MANN ACT
See Privileges, Marital

MATERIALITY
See Admissibility of Evidence

NALLINE TEST
See Scientific Evidence, Intoxication and drugs, tests for

NOLO CONTENDERE PLEA
See Relevancy

OPINION TESTIMONY
Generally, 428–450
Expert witnesses, 435–449
  Conditions for admission, 436
  Court-appointed experts, 440–441, 448
  Expert, defined, 435–436
  Federal Rules of Evidence, 447–448
  Hypothetical question,
    Efforts to eliminate, 440, 449
  Impeachment of, 441–443
  Police testimony on modus operandi, 443–446
  Qualifying the witness, 436–438
    Stipulating to witness's expertise, 438–439
  Sources of expert's data, 439–440
    Disclosure of, 448
Lay witnesses, 428–435
  Fact vs. opinion, 433–434
  Federal Rules of Evidence, 435
  Ordinary language, use of, 428–429
  Ultimate issue, 434, 447
  Wink, opinion about, 430–432
Personal knowledge, lack of, 447

PAST RECOLLECTION RECORDED
Generally, 197–201
Federal Rules of Evidence, 201

PAST RECOLLECTION RECORDED—Cont'd
Refreshing witness's present recollection, compared, 200–201

PHOTOGRAPHS
See Eyewitness Identification

PHYSICIANS
See Privileges

POLYGRAPH TESTS
See Scientific Evidence, Lie detector tests

PRESIDENTIAL PRIVILEGE
See Governmental Privileges, State secrets

PRESUMPTIONS
Generally, 20–26
Beyond a reasonable doubt requirement, 22, 25
"Conclusive presumption", 21
Inference, distinguished, 21
Mandatory effect, unconstitutionality of, 21–22
Prima facie evidence, 23–26
Rebuttal, 21–22

PRIESTS
See Privileges

PRIOR IDENTIFICATION
Generally, 188–196
Federal Rules of Evidence, 188–193
Photographic identification, 193
Reliability of, 195–196

PRIVILEGES
  See also Governmental Privileges; Self-Incrimination, Privilege Against
Generally, 294–344
Attorney-client,
  In general, 294–327
  Confidentiality, 294 et seq., 307–316
    Balancing, 311
    Explaining attorney's role to client, 307–308
  Conflict of interest, 294 et seq.
  Dissimulation, 296–297
  Duty of loyalty to client, 316–327
  Eavesdropping, 306, 307, 311–314
  Helping client to commit or conceal crime, 307, 311–327
  Prohibited assistance, 294 et seq.
  Screening process, 298–300
  Statutory framework, 300–307
    California Evidence Code, 301–307

References are to Pages

PRIVILEGES—Cont'd
Attorney-client—Cont'd
  Statutory framework—Cont'd
    California Penal Code, 307
    Federal Rules of Evidence, 300
Executive,
  See Governmental Privileges, State secrets
Husband-wife,
  See Marital, this topic
Informers,
  See Governmental Privileges
Journalist-source, 344
Marital,
  In general, 328–343
  Confidential marital communications, 333–343
    California Evidence Code, 333–335
    Eavesdroppers, 334
    Presence of third party, 336–337, 338–343
    Termination of marriage, 334, 337
    When not applicable, 334–335
    Who can claim the privilege, 333, 337–338
  "Incapacity", 328–333
    California Evidence Code, 328–330
    Mann Act prosecution, 330–333
    Waiver, 329–330
    When not applicable, 329, 330–331
    Who can claim the privilege, 328, 330–333
Physician-patient, 343
Priest-penitent, 344
Psychotherapist-patient, 343–344
Spouses,
  See Marital, this topic

PROBABILITY
See Relevancy, "Mathematical" relevance

PSYCHOLOGICAL STRESS EVALUATOR
See Scientific Evidence, Lie detector tests

PSYCHOTHERAPISTS
See Privileges

RADAR
See Hearsay

RAPE
  See also Character Evidence
"Rape shield" laws, 83–86

REAL EVIDENCE
Generally, 407–427

REAL EVIDENCE—Cont'd
Authentication, 407–418
  Chain of custody, 414, 416, 417–418
  Defined, 407
  Documents, 407–410
  Federal Rules of Evidence, 408–410
  Not changed substantially, 413, 416, 417
  Same item, 412–413, 416
  Self-authentification, 409–410
  Subscribing witness's testimony unnecessary, 410
  Time lapse, 417–418
Best evidence rule, 418–427
  Duplicate, admissibility of, 421, 426
  Federal Rules of Evidence, 425–427
  Movies, 423–425
  Original,
    Determination of, 420–421, 425
    Lost or destroyed, 422
  Physical items vs. contents of written documents, 422–423
  Rule stated, 418–419
  Secondary evidence, 422
  Statutory modifications, 421
Conditions of admissibility and required foundation, 412–414
Defined, 410–411
Demonstrative, 483–489
  Historical background, 483–485
  Objections,
    Gruesome films and photographs, 488–489
    Lack of verity or accuracy, 485–488
    Misguided, 485
  Real evidence, compared, 411, 483
Use of, 411

RELEVANCY
  See also Character Evidence
  Generally, 28–108
Circumstantial evidence and, 29
Compromise, 100–105
Content vs. form, 29
Crimes, evidence of other, 56, 89–99
  Acquittal, effect of, 98
  Balancing approach, 96
  Conviction, necessity for, 99
  Exceptions to rule of absolute exclusion, 87, 90–94
  Narrow rule of absolute exclusion, 87–88
Defined, 55
Definitions, 29–31, 32
Elements of, 8–9, 29
Federal Rules of Evidence, 31, 52–53, 55, 56

INDEX

References are to Pages

RELEVANCY—Cont'd
Flight, 55–56
Gruesome pictures,
    Use of to influence jury, 53–54
Materiality, 8, 29
"Mathematical" relevance, 37–50
Nolo contendere plea, 107–108
Pleas, plea discussions and related statements,
    Inadmissibility of under federal rules,
        Rules of Criminal Procedure, 102–105
        Rules of Evidence, 100
    Withdrawn pleas of guilty, 105–107
Prejudicial effect balanced against probative value, 52–57
Probability,
    See "Mathematical" relevance, this topic
Probative value balanced against prejudicial effect, 52–57
Probativeness, 8–9, 29
State of mankind's knowledge, 30
Statistics,
    See "Mathematical" relevance, this topic
Tests of, 28–30

RULES
See Federal Rules of Evidence

SCIENTIFIC EVIDENCE
Generally, 450–483
Intoxication and drugs, tests for, 468–483
    Alcohol, 469–480
        Types of tests, 471
    Blood analysis, 375–378, 471
    Breath tests, 379, 471–473, 474–480
    Corroborating physical evidence, 473
    Criminalistics, role in, 468
    Expertise, need for, 468–469
    Foundation for admission, 473
    Nalline test, 480–483
Lie detector tests, 450–463
    Admissibility,
        In general, 451–453, 458
            Qualifications, 455
                Upon motion for new trial, 455–456
            Upon stipulation, 453–455
    Confessions during, 459
    Equipment and examiner, 456–457
    Evidence of willingness to take, 458–459
    Psychological stress evaluator, 459
    Test procedure, 457

SCIENTIFIC EVIDENCE—Cont'd
Polygraph tests,
    See Lie detector tests, this topic
Radar, 129–130
Voiceprint analysis, 379, 463–468
    Acceptance by scientific community, 467
    Impact on jury, 467
    Qualification of expert, 467

SECRETS
See Governmental Privileges, State secrets

SELF-INCRIMINATION, PRIVILEGE AGAINST
Generally, 345–381
Comment on accused's failure to testify, 350–354
Discovery procedures in criminal cases, 356–358
Fifth Amendment, 345
Historical background, 345–347
Interrogation prior to trial, 359–374
    Admissibility of statements, 364–370
        Impeachment purposes only, 372–374
    Techniques, 365–372
Non-testimonial evidence, 375–379
    Blood sample, 375–378
    Breathalyzer test, 379
    Voice identification test, 379
State action, 347–350

SEPARATION OF POWERS
Presidential privilege, 384–385

SOURCES
See Evidence

SPONTANEOUS AND CONTEMPORANEOUS DECLARATIONS
Generally, 166–171
Federal Rules of Evidence, 167, 171

SPOUSES
See Privileges, Marital

STATE ACTION
See Self-Incrimination, Privilege Against

STATE OF MIND
Generally, 176–187
Federal Rules of Evidence, 176
Hillmon doctrine, 183–186
Issue, must be in, 180, 184
Letters, 177–179

STATE SECRETS
See Governmental Privileges

INDEX

References are to Pages

STATISTICS
See Relevancy, "Mathematical" relevance

TRIAL PROCEDURE
See also Witnesses
Direct examination, 235–239
Federal Rules of Evidence, 238–239

TRIAL SYSTEM
See Adversary Trial System

VIDEO TAPE
See Former Testimony

VOICEPRINT ANALYSIS
See Scientific Evidence

WITNESSES
See also Trial Procedure
Cross-examination, 239–248
  "Bound by" witness' testimony, not, 236
  Impeachment and,
    See Impeachment, this topic
  Leading questions, 236
  Leave well enough alone, 241
  Police witnesses, 242–243
  Prosecution witnesses, 241–242
  Risks, 244–245
  Scope, 246–248
    Federal Rules of Evidence, 247–248
  Tactics and methods, 243–245
Direct examination, 235–239
  "Bound by" witness' testimony, 236
  Defendant, of, 236–238
  Leading questions, 235

WITNESSES—Cont'd
Impeachment, 249–293
  Admissibility of criminal defendant's statements for impeachment purposes only, 372–374
  Bad reputation for truth and veracity, 268–269
  Bias, 284–290
  Contradiction, 250–252
    "Collateral facts" rule, 250–251
  Conviction of a crime,
    Dishonesty or false statement, involving, 265
    Federal Rules of Evidence, 258–262, 266–267
  Credibility, 249–278
    Federal Rules of Evidence,
      Attacking and supporting, 290
      Who may impeach, 249
  Drug addiction, 276–278
  Expert witnesses, of, 441–443
  Prior bad acts, 252–258
    Federal Rules of Evidence, 257–258
  Prior inconsistent statements, 278–284
  Psychiatric condition, 270–278
  Rehabilitation of impeached witness, 291–293
Leading questions,
  Cross-examination, 236
  Direct examination, 235, 239
  Federal Rules of Evidence, 239

WOMEN
See Rape

WRITING USED TO REFRESH MEMORY
Federal Rules of Evidence, 201